Modern Comparative Politics Series
edited by
Peter H. Merkl
University of California,
Santa Barbara

FRANCE
The politics of continuity
in change

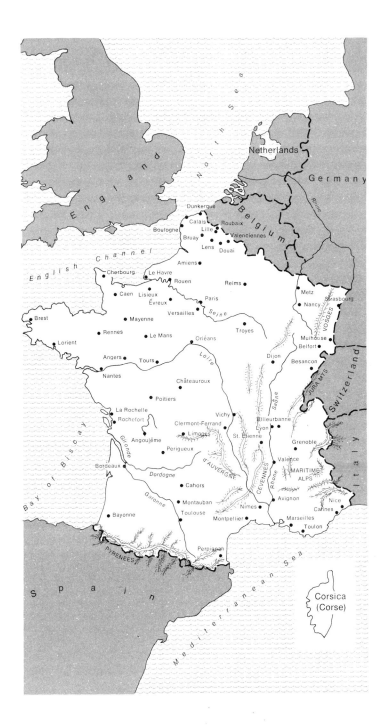

FRANCE

The politics of continuity in change

Lowell G. Noonan
San Fernando Valley
State College

HOLT, RINEHART AND WINSTON, INC.
New York Chicago San Francisco Atlanta
Dallas Montreal Toronto London Sydney

To Claire and Louise

FOREWORD
TO THE SERIES

This new series in comparative politics was undertaken in response to the special needs of students, teachers, and scholars that have arisen in the last few years, needs that are no longer being satisfied by most of the materials now available. In an age when our students seem to be getting brighter and more politically aware, the teaching of comparative politics should present a greater challenge than ever before. We have seen the field come of age with numerous comparative monographs and case studies breaking new ground, and the Committee on Comparative Politics of the Social Science Research Council can look back proudly on nearly a decade of important spade work. But teaching materials have lagged behind these changing approaches to the field. Most comparative government series are either too little coordinated to make systematic use of any common methodology or too conventional in approach. Others are so restricted in scope and space as to make little more than a programmatic statement about what should be studied, thus suggesting a new scholasticism of systems theory that omits the idiosyncratic richness of the material available and tends to ignore important elements of a system for fear of being regarded too traditional in approach.

In contrast to these two extremes, the Modern Comparative Politics Series attempts to find a happy combination of rigorous, systematic methodology and the rich sources of data available to area and country specialists. The series consists of a core volume, *Modern Comparative Politics,* by Peter H. Merkl, country volumes covering one or more nations, and comparative topical volumes.

Rather than narrowing the approach to only one "right" method, the core volume leaves it to the teacher to choose any of several approaches he may prefer. The authors of the country volumes are partly bound by a framework common to these volumes and the core volume, and are partly free to tailor their approaches to the idiosyncrasies of their respective countries. The emphasis in the common framework is on achieving a balance between such elements as theory and application, as well as among developmental perspectives, sociocultural aspects, the group processes, and the decision-making processes of government. It is hoped that the resulting tension between comparative approaches and politicocultural realities will enrich the teaching of comparative politics and provoke discussion at all levels from undergraduate to graduate.

The group of country volumes is supplemented by a group of analytical comparative studies. Each of the comparative volumes takes an important topic and explores it cross-nationally. Some of these topics are covered in a more limited way in the country volumes, but many find their first expanded treatment in the comparative volumes—and all can be expected to break new scholarly ground.

The ideas embodied in the series owe much to the many persons whose names are cited in the footnotes of the core volume. Although they are far too numerous to mention here, a special debt of spiritual paternity is acknowledged to Harry Eckstein, Gabriel A. Almond, Carl J. Friedrich, Sidney Verba, Lucian W. Pye, Erik H. Erikson, Eric C. Bellquist, R. Taylor Cole, Otto Kirchheimer, Seymour M. Lipset, Joseph La Palombara, Samuel P. Huntington, Cyril E. Black, and many others, most of whom are probably quite unaware of their contribution.

P. H. M.

Santa Barbara, California

PREFACE

This study is primarily an inquiry into government and politics in contemporary France. As a *bilan,* or account sheet, it inventories affairs and weighs important aspects of the enterprise. France is portrayed both in terms of what it is and what it is engaged in becoming. Throughout the work attention is directed to issues and questions that France will have to deal with in this new era after de Gaulle. Although the work is concerned only in a minor way with governments and politics of regimes that preceded the Fifth Republic, it discusses phenomena that originated in earlier times and that continue to give to French government and politics a definite configuration. If General de Gaulle touches numerous pages in this work, it is because the Fifth Republic was his creation and because he left so great an imprint on its structure and performance. It should be noted, however, that General de Gaulle is not the central figure in this work; that position is occupied by the citizen himself, the matrix by which any republic is made and sustained—as General de Gaulle discovered in 1968 and 1969.

The organization of the book is coordinated with the other country volumes in the series and with the core volume, but it is equally adaptable for use on its own. The text contains data for presidential, legislative, and municipal elections, as well as for national referenda. Included in an appendix are maps of the presidential elections of 1965 and 1969, the legislative elections of 1958, 1962, 1967, and 1968, and the referendum of April 27, 1969. A copy of the Constitution of the Fifth Republic is included in another appendix.

The author wishes to express his thanks for the cooperation and aid given him by Professor Peter H. Merkl, editor of this series, and by members of the editorial staff of Holt, Rinehart and Winston, Inc. His thanks go also to members of the faculty and staff of the Institut d'études politiques of the University of Paris, who made available to him various of its facilities in 1957–1958, and again in 1967. A special debt of gratitude is expressed to Professors Eric C. Bellquist and C. Dwight Waldo for many years of assistance that helped make it possible for the author to pursue his interest in French government and politics. The author also wishes to express his appreciation to those people in France who have done so much to educate him in the meaning of the French way of life, people who by their amity and generosity have made his stays in their country both pleasant and rewarding.

All errors of fact, omission, and interpretation are, of course, the author's responsibility.

L. G. N.

Canoga Park, California
November 1969

CONTENTS

INTRODUCTION

One of the most brilliant observers of French politics remarked in 1955 that "A personality incapable of changing and developing and following unforeseen paths is a dead personality. This is the danger for France today. In spite of all the convulsions to which she has been and still is subject, the great question against the future is whether she is capable of such change and development." [1] These sentences were written when France was caught in the political paralysis of the Fourth Republic, three years before the Gaullist revolution of 1958. After 1958 the Gaullist state reshaped some aspects of French existence and virtually ignored others. In 1968, however, the Gaullist state entered a new era in which it was confronted by circumstances and problems different from those it faced previously. General de Gaulle presided over the political system, but he could not be expected to serve too much longer. His France no longer was a "monocracy," for new expressions of public opinion had been developed during the massive strikes of May 1968, and the public—in a display of "collective bargaining" unprecedented

[1] Herbert Luethy. *France against Herself* (New York: Meridian Books, 1957), p. 4.

1

in French history—succeeded in extracting from the Gaullist regime promised concessions which foresee great economic and social transformation. It was up to the Gaullist state to implement these changes. The victory won by the Gaullists in the legislative elections of June 1968 was great, but that triumph failed to obscure from the viewer the continuing crisis in Gaullism. The results of those elections invested Gaullism with a "security" that was primarily "arithmetical." The General—"safe" until his presidential mandate expired in 1972—now wielded a greatly reduced authority. No longer could he brush aside as unimportant those considerations held paramount by the populace. No longer could he downgrade public opinion as drastically as he did before the massive demonstrations of 1968. No longer could he exercise a personal power so unheedful of counsel or criticism. The shield of "republican monocracy" had been penetrated. President de Gaulle's political future now came to depend in large part on his ability to deliver realistically to the populace some of the things promised them by "his" regime in 1968.

In April 1969 General de Gaulle asked the populace to vote a single *oui* or *non* in a referendum on proposed constitutional change that totaled sixty-eight articles and approximately 8000 words. Various proposals of the referendum clearly were at odds with popular demands. Many had nothing to do with pressing exigencies and the promises of 1968. Nevertheless, de Gaulle threatened to leave the presidency if the referendum failed. The referendum was defeated, and de Gaulle retired to private life. The era of de Gaulle had ended; however, he left behind him a Gaullist premier and a large Gaullist majority in the National Assembly. Approximately a month and a half later France elected Gaullist Georges Pompidou president of the Republic, verifying at least temporarily, that Gaullism had survived the departure of de Gaulle and that the system bequeathed by de Gaulle to the Fifth Republic had outlasted him.

Georges Pompidou's election suggests that the system is destined subsequently for some important transformations, for a Gaullism without de Gaulle is bound to differ from a Gaullism with de Gaulle. One Gaullism has now been replaced by another. What kind of Gaullism is it? What does it promise to become? How broadly and effectively will it implement the promises made to the populace by the Gaullists during the great social upheavals of 1968? Will it be capable of taking France on newly developed paths?

In exploring the answers to these questions, this book follows the organization of the other country volumes in the Modern Comparative Politics Series and is coordinated with the core volume. Chapter One examines demographic and economic considerations, the rise of France as a nation-state, social stratification and mobility, and some consequences of the technological revolution presently in progress in French society. Chapter Two describes the Frenchman's socialization, or how he interacts with the organs of his society, giving particular attention to the relationship of socialization to housing, education, recruiting, and the acquisition of political partisanships. Chapter Three investigates themes of French culture, inquiring into the meaning and significance of diverse doctrines, the nature of the different "political families," relationships among Catholics, the state, and society, and the role of violence. Attention also is extended to communications media, with discussion of the roles played by the press, radio, and television. Chapter Four briefly traces national-local relationships along administrative and political lines, with emphasis on how problems of local existence relate to the national power and on the ways in which national power attempts to address itself to these problems. Chapter Five examines the party system in detail, focusing on the important divisions in the party Left, the consequences of that disunity, and possibilities of future Left unity. The Center is assessed in terms of its own peculiar qualities, its decline and future orientation. Detailed attention is given to the Gaullist party and its significance and prospects for the future. The party Right (long in "hiding," as it bided its time and awaited the era after de Gaulle) is also discussed. The first part of Chapter Five deals with the party system itself, whereas the latter part examines the parties individually, thereby introducing the reader to both the system and its components. Chapter Six describes the electoral process, inquiring into practices and trends and examining individual elections and referenda so as to clarify further these perplexing phenomena. Chapter Seven deals with interest groups, Chapter Eight with policy-making roles and structures. Chapter Nine describes the policy-making process itself, giving examples of policy making by governmental and nongovernmental instrumentalities. Chapter Ten discusses law and the judiciary, giving close attention to both theoretical and practical distinctions between Roman and American law. Chapter Eleven inquires into foreign policy, examining its premises and positions; the latter part of this chapter considers the French record of decolonization and tells how the Fourth Republic gave way to the Fifth Republic. Chapter Twelve investigates issues of primary significance in the new era after de Gaulle and poses questions relative to it. Finally, a Postscript explains in detail the presidential election of June 1969.

ONE
SOCIAL TRANSFORMATION AND IMMOBILISM
A brief developmental history

In 1958 Pierre Emmanuel, a well-known Frenchman, wrote:

> The French are the most conservative people on earth.
> . . . The French believe, rightly enough, that they have
> reached a level of civilization, an intellectual refinement, whose
> influence has pervaded even their daily lives; to lose it would
> be like losing one's identity. They feel also—though refusing
> to confess it—that they must change or perish. The survival
> of France is conditioned by external forces, especially in the
> economic field, but pride and prejudice make it hard for us to
> adopt a way of life foreign to our traditional tempo. We are,
> if I may say so, the Southerners of the West. . . . The para-
> dox in France is that we are both slow to move and rapidly
> moving. We have the fastest trains in the world, the best in-
> ternational railway and plane connections, one of the highest
> percentages of cars, a remarkable birth rate, a surprisingly
> promising economy; but these new energies have come after
> half a century of relative standstill, if we compare our own
> development with England's or Germany's. We are now com-
> pelled to adjust ourselves, as quickly as possible, to new forces
> and an expanding nation. . . .[1]

[1] Pierre Emmanuel, "Is France Being Americanized?" *The Atlantic Monthly,* Vol. 201, No. 6 (June 1958), 36–37.

Emmanuel goes on to explain that the French owe their stability to their long tradition of cosmopolitan culture, their desire to preserve fundamental values, and their provincialism (Paris and Mantes, although only thirty miles apart, are farther removed from each other than New York and San Francisco). Emmanuel argues that these phenomena are not contradictory but "interwoven," and that their common result is the consequence of a "slow but serious" assimilation "which adds to our cultural treasure without upsetting it." [2] Emmanuel concedes that Frenchmen may not make the world but maintains that they will give it, nonetheless, a human shape and that they will refuse to take it for granted until it "fulfills some universal and basic human demands." [3] The Frenchman, states Emmanuel, continues to live by one of man's great attributes, *la raison*. This may save the Frenchman, he says, from falling prey to diverse "heresies of progress" and "make progress itself a firm ground for further human achievements of a spiritual nature." [4]

PROFILE OF A FRENCHMAN

A Frenchman is a person who satisfies all legal requirements for citizenship and claims it within a part of Europe bounded by the Atlantic, Belgium, Germany, Italy, Switzerland, Luxembourg, Monaco, Andorra, Spain, and the Mediterranean. Confronted by other nation-states on three sides, and on the fourth side by the English mainland, only twenty-three miles across the "English" channel, the Frenchman has suffered periodically from a sense of geographical insecurity. Yet, in this era he exhibits hardly any fear of his neighbors and would prefer to share with them some form of European confederation or federation. What ever his feelings relative to nationalism, he acknowledges the futility of isolationism. He believes that the great European wars finally have been terminated and that it is unlikely that they will occur again.

[2] Emmanuel, 37.
[3] Emmanuel, 38.
[4] Emmanuel, 38.

Approximately 80 percent of France's 50 million people live in a *commune,* or juridical unit, which may be a tiny area or an urban complex as large as Paris. Almost 38,000 *communes* are distributed throughout the whole of his nation, but among them only 300 exceed 2000 inhabitants each; therefore, the Frenchman's place of residence is likely to be of limited size. His *commune* generally contains an assortment of unpainted stone buildings, small business enterprises, cafés, and frequently a monument to the dead of two wars. His life in the *commune* usually is less than dynamic, and events there seldom lead to broad changes in his communal behavior. His communal mayor continues to record births, marriages, and deaths, and each day the Frenchman goes about his business much as he did the day before. His life there is different from life in Paris, which is a center for most things, whether French or foreign, and which comprises more than 8 million people (including its suburbs). Paris' world is big, and in the eyes of its citizens Paris and the nation are identical. Paris represents the France with which Americans are most familiar. However, the "real France" is found in the small *commune* inhabited by a Frenchman whose identification with his immediate locale usually is greater than his identification with the nation itself.[5] The *commune* is where he works, lives, and dies, and his world hardly is larger than it. Most of his notions about politics and political behavior are molded by it. His preoccupation—both morally and materially —is with the things closest to his daily existence, and not with abstractions removed from his immediate physical whereabouts. For him, *la patrie* refers more to the locale in which he resides than to the nation itself. And beyond his *commune*—in the "outside world"—exist Paris, the "political class," foreigners,

[5] Nonetheless, each year the Paris region is a magnet for approximately 100,000 people who descend on it from other parts of the nation. Within the past century the Paris region has accumulated 6 million inhabitants, and now comprises approximately 8.5 million (as against 2.5 million in 1861). The Paris region represented in 1965 almost 19 percent of the total population, having gained between the censuses of 1954 and 1962 some 1.2 million people. The Paris basin contains approximately 25 percent of all civil servants, and 60 percent of all industrial societies.

and others who "bear watching." [6] Only a decade ago the late Jean Cocteau commented,

> People amuse me who are afraid that France is turning into a village. She has always been one. She was one under Louis XV. A village with its *café du commerce,* the newspaper kiosk, and its *bureau de tabac,* where everyone discusses and argues. From this endless argument is born the flow of that soft, intense light which Guillaume Apollinaire used to say the eye could gaze into tirelessly. [7]

The Frenchman's income, high by European standards, is substantially less than the American's annual earnings. The Frenchman must manage and allocate his income carefully. [8] The prices he pays for food and clothing are similar to those paid by Americans, and if he owns an automobile gasoline costs him at least 75 cents a gallon (most of that amount reverting in the form of taxes to the French nation). He pays little for his housing—if the dwelling he occupies has been in his ownership or rental for a long time (benefiting in the latter case from the rent-control laws of the regime). If, however, he is without housing and searching for it, he must pay a stiff price for whatever he can find (and more than likely it will be worth less). If he dwells in Paris, Marseilles, or Bordeaux, or in one of the other urban centers which comprise more than 100,000 inhabitants each, he spends much of his time rushing to and from work surrounded by the din of traffic and polluted air. If, however, he lives in

---

[6] So broad a person as the late Albert Camus, for example, once commented that Parisians are interested only in two things, ideas and fornication. This is not to say that Camus did not belong to the "outside world." He of course did—although his outlook did have a Mediterranean coloration.

[7] Jean Cocteau, "France," *The Atlantic Monthly,* Vol. 201, No. 6 (June 1958), 27.

[8] Jean-Marcel Jeanneney, *Économie politique* (Paris: Presses universitaires, 1962), p. 235. Professor Jeanneney, now deputy from Grenoble, states that it is allocated in the following manner: 43 percent —food; 12 percent—clothing; 17 percent—housing; 8 percent—hygiene and needs; 7 percent—transport and communications; 7 percent—culture and leisure; and 6 percent—hotels, cafés, restaurants.

a small *commune*—and chances are that he does—the pace is much less hectic and he is inclined to complain about the monotony of life there.

More than 90 percent of France is Catholic, but religion does not mean very much to the Frenchman. In his eyes churches are primarily cultural artifacts. In fact, he may be tempted to jest that his real religion is cuisine, and when traveling in neighboring countries he is legendary for refusing to tolerate what they describe as edible fare. Wine is a regular part of his diet, not because of the alcoholic "kick" that may be derived from it, but because it complements his cuisine and offers that "afterbite" that goes with any good *cru*. Like the American, he refers frequently to his mode of existence, or the "French way of life"; unlike the American, he is apt to be critical of it. Nonetheless, he is not inclined to emigrate elsewhere, and whenever he responds to a public opinion poll, he usually submits that only in France can he find "true happiness." If he is other than the son of a bourgeois, that is, if he is the son of a worker or peasant, it is unlikely that he attended school beyond his fourteenth year. If this contributes to his feeling of having been "disprivileged," he also believes that it will be a long time before real educational opportunity and equality are made available to all social categories. If he is about thirty or more, he knows that the French demographic situation has changed greatly since he was a child. He probably is unaware of many of the details of this change, but the general transformation is there before his eyes. His father was unfamiliar with Monoprix, Uniprix, and other supermarket services, but already he is inclined to take such conveniences for granted. However, his household is not yet a collecting place for innumerable time-saving gadgets (nor are American dwellings yet like the mechanized cinema fantasies of Jacques Tati). New, modern dwellings exist but generally they are beyond his financial reach, most being upper-middle-class luxuries. Finally, the Frenchman's life has its anxieties too, but he is not likely to complain of suffering from that favorite American malady, the "tummy upset." He is usually much more specific when he "hurts"—it is due invariably to malfunctioning of his *foie,* or liver, and he generally attributes this to rich food or excessive wine consumption, and seldom to tension.[9]

The Frenchman lives in a society in which verbalization plays an important role—so much so that observers sometimes wonder whether the French language encourages articulation of what is expressed in some other cultures in a physical and more primitive fashion. One soon notices the way in which almost everything in French society seemingly manages to get put into language (French traffic jams, for example, often are productive of exaggerated verbal interaction, but seldom of physical violence; admittedly, legal fines for violence are heavy, but it would be difficult to contend that they alone act as a principal deterrent). However, extensive verbalization is associated more commonly with adult rather than juvenile behavior. Recesses serve frequently in lower levels of the primary schools as occasions for physical interaction (often taking the form of kicks on the shin).[10] As the child grows older, his verbalization increases and serves more and more as a substitute for physical expression.[11]

The Frenchman lives in a society in which politics are all around him; nevertheless, he feels that only infrequently can he influence those politics that "really count." He is aware of the great gap between himself and those who exercise the power of decision making, and he suspects that over the years this gap will increase rather than diminish. Politics of importance are reserved for the manipulators and the "political class," who are far away from him; he knows that his political destiny generally will be controlled by those in the "outside world." However, he has other and more important consolations, for he knows that

---

[9] Liver pills are one of the biggest advertisers in the *métropole*. One of France's great bottled waters presents itself as the best for the *foie*.

[10] Lawrence Wylie, *Village in the Vaucluse* (Cambridge, Mass.: Harvard University Press, 1957). In this classic study the author noticed in the lower school system of the *commune* of Peyrane absence of physical interaction. This author noticed in the communal primary school in Bourg-la-Reine (Seine) physical interaction of this type.

[11] Even during the grave days immediately after May 13, 1958, when civil war was thought to be a possibility, one heard frequently in the Paris region, "We're French. We don't act—we just talk and talk."

certain aspects of his personal behavior never will be controlled by anybody except himself—and these are the things that are for him truly important and with whose sanctification and preservation he remains very much concerned. His government may govern, or fail to govern—however, it is its own responsibility as to how well it discharges its functions. Whatever it does, it does in that "outside world." When, however, it governs so that its directives adversely affect the Frenchman's personal behavior and relationships, then it becomes part of his world and his reaction to it is likely to be great. Government policies that refer to the individual, the family, and relationships among individuals and families are tolerated by him as long as they remain sufficiently detached from those areas of his life that "really matter."

The Frenchman lives in an old society in which people have been manipulated for centuries—where, in earlier eras, human exploitation was more than incidental, being a way of life. The France in which he lives today is different from what it was a century ago (or thirty years ago, during the Occupation and Vichy period, when one had to be crafty and resort to all kinds of behavior simply in order to survive). Nonetheless, social perspectives and practices which originated in earlier eras frequently outlast the conditions that produced them. Suspicion continues to be common in French society. A Frenchman is apt to be suspicious when presented with an offered service, and somewhat apprehensive of what will be asked of him in return. If some service is rendered by him, he very likely will expect one in return. Finally, whatever his close personal relationships, it takes some time before the Frenchman feels that he can be completely "open" with friends.

The Frenchman lives in a society of considerable stratification and low professional mobility. Studies by the National Bureau of Statistics reveal that, among members of the male population working since 1959, approximately 42 percent of those who are farmers are sons of farmers.[12] Approximately 35 percent of those who are sons of salaried agricultural workers

---

[12] *Le Monde,* November 17, 1966, p. 7.

are agricultural workers themselves.[13] Approximately 74 percent of those who are sons of workers are workers too.[14] The structure of French society is rigid, and the tendency is for sons to follow their fathers occupationally, and thus socially. Moreover, evidence clearly shows that origins in certain social categories make it infinitely easier to acquire an education, and that birth in a modest social category impedes greatly one's chances for undertaking intensive educational studies. Fifty-five percent of those children whose fathers came from the liberal professions undertake and complete higher education, whereas only 0.1 percent of the sons of salaried agricultural workers manage it.[15] As *Le Monde* comments:

> There are some very strong differences in access to instruction and in the training received by children according to their social *milieu* origins. Access to extended studies, very frequent among the young originating from well-to-do *milieux*, is very rare among those who come from the most disprivileged categories.[16]

And the French Institute of Public Opinion comments, "Passage from one social category to another . . . is relatively rare. Social rigidity . . . remains great." [17] Thus, birth in a well-to-do social *milieu* permits the child not only more easily to gain advanced studies, but it also adds to his chances of remaining in the same *milieu;* whereas birth in a modest *milieu* constitutes a handicap for the following of advanced studies, and consequently the changing of social categories becomes even more difficult.

---

[13] *Le Monde,* November 17, 1966, p. 7. The study of the French Institute of Public Opinion written by Jacques Duquesne, *Les 16–24 ans* (Paris: Le Centurion, 1963), reveals different figures. Covering 1500 people in 127 different localities of France, among their respondents two of every three sons of agricultural workers also are agricultural workers.

[14] *Le Monde,* November 17, 1966, p. 7; Duquesne, *Les 16–24 ans.*

[15] *Le Monde,* November 17, 1966, p. 7.

[16] *Le Monde,* March 10, 1967, p. 7.

[17] Duquesne, p. 38; see also Henri Bastide and Alain Girard, "Les tendances démographiques en France et les attitudes de la population," *Population,* 1 (January–February 1966), 29. This inquiry, which covered 2541 people in 198 *communes,* concludes that the population would be more mobile if given the opportunity.

As for professional mobility, it, too, is restricted. Between 1959 and 1964, 29 percent of the males and 24 percent of the females changed employment.[18] Approximately 56 percent of the men in the twenty to twenty-four-year age category changed employment at least once in five years.[19] Professional mobility between 1959 and 1964 was more restricted at older ages: of those between fifty-five and fifty-nine years of age, approximately 18 percent changed employment.[20] Among every 100 men changing *manual* professions during these five years, approximately 55 percent acquired comparable positions, 23 percent acquired better ones, and 23 percent acquired less favorable ones.[21] Approximately 50 percent of those who secured inferior positions came from sectors of the economy where employment had been diminishing—principally the clothing, mining, and textile industries.[22]

Finally, the Frenchman lives in a society characterized by noticeable disparities in distribution of family incomes. The French Republic published in 1961 for the first time in French history a precise description of these disparities.[23] It was revealed that approximately 713,000 families then earned fewer than 125 francs per month (1 franc = approximately 20 cents American), and that within this group a number of aged had a monthly revenue not in excess of 60 francs. The study also showed two thirds of all families having incomes of fewer than 870 francs per month, and one third as disposing of fewer than 500 francs. At the apex of the pyramid, however, 14,000 families received incomes of more than 6250 francs per month (some 3000 families among this group averaged 3000 francs per month, and slightly more than 500 families earned in excess of 6000 francs per month). Later figures—released by the government in 1965—show the earnings of nonagrarian families to be as follows

[18] *Le Monde,* November 17, 1966, p. 7.
[19] *Le Monde,* November 17, 1966, p. 7.
[20] *Le Monde,* November 17, 1966, p. 7.
[21] *Le Monde,* November 17, 1966, p. 7.
[22] *Le Monde,* November 17, 1966, p. 7.
[23] See *Le Monde,* August 20–21, 1961, p. 7, for detailed description of report.

(earnings of agrarian families which are considerably lower were not released):

11 percent earn below 432 francs per month
13 percent earn between 432 and 864 francs per month
17 percent earn between 864 and 1296 francs per month
20 percent earn between 1296 and 1728 francs per month
21 percent earn between 1728 and 2592 francs per month
13 percent earn between 2592 and 4320 francs per month
 5 percent earn more than 4320 francs per month

Data published in 1967 by the National Institute of Statistics show that one in every four salaried persons in industry and commerce then earned fewer than 565 francs per month.[24] The average salary in industry and commerce was described as approximately 950 francs per month. However, this average can be deceiving, for there are disparities in earnings in regions and sex; in the Paris region, salaried employees earn more than those situated in less-favored departments; moreover, female income is less than male.[25]

THE RISE OF THE FRENCH NATION

French political and social structures owe a large debt to diverse cultural origins and the country's exposed geographical position. Celts were predominant in the country before the second century A.D. Subsequently the Roman invasion and occupation converted the country into a province into which was introduced Roman law, language, and political organization. Later, Rome's collapse

---

[24] *Le Monde,* August 21–22, 1967, p. 8.

[25] The National Institute of Statistics published in 1965 data on salaries in industry and commerce (after inquiring into the salaries paid in 1963 and declared in 1964 by employers in industry and commerce). Some 11,415,000 remunerations were photocopied. The Institute discovered that about a quarter of these employees received fewer than 562 francs per month, and that the majority earned fewer than 750 francs per month. *Le Monde* (June 4, 1965, p. 20) commented, "These figures surprise some people accustomed to believing that salaries are higher than they are in reality . . . it would be better to recognize the facts than to imagine them."

was followed by frequent invasions from the east, and by further cultural absorption, from the Gauls, Franks, Burgundians, and Normans, for example. Invasion and cultural intermixture culminated by the year 1000 A.D., and consequently there emerged early in the country both a state and a consciousness of French nationality. The subsequent story of national unification and development, as Carl Friedrich states, is a turbulent one subject to the "law of the pendulum"; nonetheless, it is one that "progressed steadily toward greater consolidation of the nation" without the forces of disintegration being able to gain ascendancy.[26]

For almost a thousand years subsequent to the collapse of the Roman Empire French history was characterized by reductions in central political power, or what André Philip calls "the decomposition of public authority." [27] The economy lacked developed monetary and commercial systems, and the basis of work was not money but personal fidelity within the framework of a social hierarchy. French peasants lived in multiple closed economies, each under the protection of a château. The system was known as feudalism. A small and limited artisan industry existed, but after the seventh century commerce was relatively insignificant. This system, which attained its peak at the beginning of the tenth century, remained closed until the end of the twelfth century, when the approach of the Crusades heralded the coming of commercial capitalism.

Feudalism acted as a barrier against the rise of national power, for the great landed barons operated outside royal authority, the church claimed special rights and exemptions, and local municipalities developed their own corporate existence. Consolidation of national power was the result of years of monarchical effort, beginning first at the central government level and extending subsequently to the provinces. The barons were brought under royal control by the twelfth and thirteenth centuries and their lands added to those of the monarchy. Other

---

[26] Carl J. Friedrich, *Constitutional Government and Democracy* (Boston: Little, Brown, 1941), p. 9.

[27] André Philip, *Histoire des faits économiques et sociaux*, Vol. I (Paris: Aubier, 1963), p. 8.

royal controls, particularly over the nobility, were achieved in the seventeenth and eighteenth centuries through creation of central government institutions and the efforts of such famous ministers as Mazarin, Colbert, and Richelieu. Government was transformed in the provinces; there it had been based on a feudal conception, being anchored in a system of provincial governorships, many of them hereditary. These posts were reduced in importance, and *intendants* took over the duties once performed by provincial governors. Few offices had as much to do with strengthening royal authority as that of the *intendant,* for he was the precursor of the modern departmental prefect, keeping the central government informed, arbitrating conflicts, directing the economy of his area by issuance of regulations, regulating the military stationed in his district, overseeing the local police, controlling taxes, and supervising municipalities. The municipalities, which conducted their own administration, some by magistrates, and others by mayors, consuls, or aldermen who were elected generally by local elites who dominated local offices, had been subject only to as much authority as the central government had been able to inflict on them. They were brought under central government supervision when Colbert undershored the authority of the *intendants.*[28]

By 1660 France had reached the peak of royal absolutism. As Godechot states, absolute monarchy combined three elements of diverse origins. One, borrowed from Rome, was the principle of the sovereignty of the king; another, a heritage from Christianity, made the sovereign the representative of God on earth; the third, a legacy of feudalism, represented the king as universal and paramount.[29] State and king were not distinguished from each other as far as the royal power was concerned (although groups such as the Monarchomachs argued to the contrary), and the king's authority was limited only by its own interest or obligations to God. No practical limitations could be imposed on

[28] See the chapter on administration in Geoffrey Treasure, *Seventeenth Century France: A Study of Absolutism* (New York: Doubleday, 1967), pp. 40–55.

[29] Jacques Godechot, *Les institutions de la France sous la révolution et l'empire* (Paris: Presses universitaires, 1951), p. 4.

royal power, for as Louis XV said in his address in Paris on March 3, 1766:

> It is in my person that the sovereign power resides; to me alone belongs the legislative power, without dependence and unshared, it is by my authority alone that the officers of my courts proceed not in the formation but in the registration of my law. . . . The entire public order emanates from me, I am the supreme guardian; my people is nothing without me, and the rights and interest of the nation . . . reside not other than in my hands.[30]

France, by 1760, "had almost attained its modern territorial limits."[31] As Gordon Wright states:

> The duchy of Lorraine was still a border enclave, but its absorption was only a matter of time; it was quietly annexed six years later. The island of Corsica, under Genoese rule, was to be purchased in 1768; while along the Alpine frontier, the province of Savoy and the city of Nice were not to come under the French flag for another century. If France had a territorial destiny, it was largely fulfilled two hundred years ago, much in advance of most European nations.[32]

The monarchy based itself on a given territory, a common literary language, and a national culture of whose existence there was definite consciousness. "The elements of a rich nationality were present," as Sir Lewis Namier says, but "the welding force of an active civic development was wanting."[33] Within the territory any number of regional diversities stubbornly survived. The north had its system of common law, the south had its Roman law, and within the country over 400 interpretations of law existed.

Society under the *ancien régime* was highly stratified. Just

---

[30] Godechot, p. 4.

[31] Gordon Wright, *France in Modern Times* (Skokie, Ill.: Rand McNally, 1960), p. 3.

[32] Wright, p. 3.

[33] Sir Lewis Namier, *Vanished Supremacies: Essays on European History, 1812–1918* (New York: Harper & Row, 1963), p. 35.

prior to 1789 the nobility comprised about 1 percent of a population totaling some 20 million people. Some were enormously wealthy, others were impoverished. Consequently, their cohesiveness as a group was detracted from by great gaps among their individual incomes. The clergy approximated 2 percent of the population. Its total income was great, being derived from landed holdings, but there existed among this group, also, great discrepancies in wealth. The high clergy generally was well off, whereas the low clergy was frequently impoverished. The middle class was distributed among business and the professions; some held state offices. Artisans generally were restricted by a system of arbitrary assignment to masters for purposes of work and could not leave their positions without permission. The peasantry, working plots so small that it had difficulty getting a living, did, however, often own its land, almost 50 percent of it in the east and south.

Royal absolutism professed to be "absolute" but practically it finally came to rest on a grotesque coalition of nobility, clergy, and some elements of the bourgeoisie. As Schumpeter says, the "centerpiece" of the system remained the king, and although the root of his position was feudal, he took advantage of capitalist economic possibilities.[34] Numerous state offices were staffed on the basis of feudal arrangements permitting their sale, which was legitimized in 1522. More than 50,000 such offices were created during the first half of the seventeenth century, and many were purchased by the bourgeoisie. Such transactions were "strictly business," producing money for the monarchy and, for the purchaser, security and a future. The monarchy was interested in money and it experienced few qualms as to how it came by it. It would sell almost anything—even pieces of the state itself—in order to secure it. If bad government was its business, it also was big business. As somebody once remarked, the monarchy developed a huge interest in misgovernment.

The French Revolution introduced a new principle of unity, finding it in a community of people whom it declared to be free

---

[34] Joseph A. Schumpeter, *Capitalism, Socialism, and Democracy* (New York: Harper & Row, 1950), p. 136.

and equal, recognizing their individuality but integrating them completely into a sovereign nation. Awareness of the nation as the major force itself, which under the *ancien régime* had not fully arrived on the scene, now was in the making. In feudal society allegiance had been emphasized on a contractual and personal basis. Under royal absolutism the king presented himself to his people as "the head of his family," but in the "absence of any visible organic unity, only the person of the king truly unified France." [35] Now, however, the Revolution claimed power not only in behalf of the nation but also its people.

Did the Revolution produce real change for society? The answer to this question need not be ambiguous. It did produce in some areas some very great changes, while in others it fell short of its goals or simply failed to extend priorities. The Revolution prescribed for French society a form of political organization different from any that the nation had known previously, extending political liberty to commoners and favoring rationalism rather than Catholicism as a means of solving human problems. It struck at the organization of political society along traditional lines, asking instead that men vest sovereignty in themselves and that they collaborate *consciously* in planning their future. Special privileges for nobility and clergy were condemned, and property was declared to be subordinate to the general welfare. The Revolution was sympathetic to science, and it urged that it be enlisted in behalf of human development. Transportation was altered, provincialism was reduced, and for the first time in the history of the country national unification became a reality. The old political jurisdictions were abolished and replaced by new administrative divisions known as departments, *arrondissements,* and *communes.* Guilds were abolished. Feudalism was destroyed. At the same time, some changes wrought by the Revolution created profound problems. The "solution" to the religious issue divided the nation for decades to come. Problems resulted from the creation of a highly centralized administration modeled along the lines of a military organization. Business became easier to transact, but under bourgeois domination there evolved a liberalism that often was excessive and

[35] Treasure, p. 41.

exploitive. Small independent peasant proprietors became commonplace; in fact they got so strong a toehold in the economy that they later seriously retarded France's transition from an agricultural to an industrial economy. Small-scale industry got a hold on the state too, and for years the latter's favors to it precluded the emergence of a real large-scale industrialism.

In short, the Revolution had certain achievements to its credit; but many of its ideals remained detached from the realities of the postrevolutionary social order. Many of the cleavages of the *ancien régime* were maintained through the era of the Revolution and on into those that followed. Those cleavages were augmented by others when, in the nineteenth century, industrial revolution created an industrial working class that barely managed to survive and to whom the revolutionary slogan "Liberty, Equality, and Fraternity" had little meaning.

After 1789 the chronology of French history (Table 1–1) goes on to rule by the Convention, and then by the Directory—which lasted from 1795 until Napoleon's seizure of power in 1799. His Consulate terminated in 1804, when he named himself Emperor and created the First Empire. His regime fell in 1815 and was followed by restoration of the Bourbon monarchs (Louis XVIII, Charles X, and Louis Philippe, France's last king). The Second Republic, which began in 1848 with the

Table 1–1   Regimes in France

Before 1789	*Ancien Régime*
1789–1792	Constituent Assembly and Legislative Assembly
1792–1795	The Convention
1795–1799	The Directory
1799–1804	The Consulate
1804–1815	First Empire
1815–1830	Monarchical Restoration: Louis XVIII and Charles X
1830–1848	Louis Philippe's Monarchy
1848–1852	Second Republic
1852–1870	Second Empire
1875–1940	Third Republic
1940–1944	Vichy Regime
1944–1946	Provisional Republic
1946–1958	Fourth Republic
1958——	Fifth Republic

election of Louis Napoleon Bonaparte as president, was converted by him in 1851 into a dictatorial regime that lasted until 1870. After France's defeat in 1870 by Prussia, and suppression in 1871 of the bloody uprising known as the Paris Commune, the Third Republic was created in 1875. That regime lasted until France's defeat by Germany in 1940. The Vichy regime, which ruled France until its liberation in 1944, was followed by the Provisional Republic, and then by the Fourth Republic, which lasted from 1946 to 1958. The Fifth Republic dates from 1958, after the Gaullist *coup* of that year.

Certain patterns exist in the French historical chronology. First, there are many different forms of political organization—absolute monarchy, constitutional monarchy, dictatorship, parliamentary government, and presidential government among them. Second, a fondness of antirepublicans for the seizure of power is matched by an early association of republican forces with revolutionary action—the revolutions of 1830, and 1848, and 1871 having all been, in fact, at one time or another republican. After 1875 the relationship between republicans and revolution declined, for by then the republicans were predominant in the cities and strong in the east and south and revolutionary action by them was then no longer necessary. Third, a giant step toward creation of a democratic system was taken in 1875, with the establishment of the Third Republic. Universal manhood suffrage finally became a reality (female suffrage was not granted until 1946), and state political offices then became accessible, through election, to qualified males. Only restricted versions of manhood suffrage had existed previously under the Constitution of 1791, the Directory, the Consulate, and the Charters of 1814 and 1830. Although universal male suffrage had been introduced in 1848, it became insignificant after 1852 in the regime of Louis Napoleon Bonaparte. The Third Republic's legitimatization of popular access to elected offices encouraged the movement closer to the established political order of groups considered subversive by previous regimes. Part of the socialist movement became less theoretical and more practical; in moving in the direction of the parliamentary tradition, it acquired a new "respectability" among elements of the populace. Fourth, the reader should note the closeness historically of the French Revolution and the Industrial Revolution, and the fact that many of the collectivist ideas that we associate with modern times crashed forcefully on the scene when technology was realtering French society and when the legitimacy of the political regime still was very much in question. The French Revolution produced republicanism; however, it also set the stage for the emergence of diverse social movements that produced different and conflicting versions of republicanism. As Middleton states, these conflicts repeatedly *diverted the course of French political evolution.* "A tolerable order could be evolved only when the two main tendencies, the political and the social, were brought on to a sufficient area of common ground. Each had to yield something to the other. Republicanism and anti-republicanism had to incorporate in their principles a certain amount of social doctrine." [36] That compromise eventually did arrive. When it did, it was fundamental not only to the creation of the Third Republic but also to its survival. Stanley Hoffmann analyzes that "republican synthesis" in his stimulating essay in *In Search of France;* [37] he notes that it followed years of political instability and pronounced social structure cleavage. Hoffmann states that the Third Republic's "staying power" had much to do with its limited goals, with the fact that it sought stabilization of and not transformation of society, and that the regime undoubtedly represented what so many people sought in it—namely, resistance to change.[38] It was by intent not too "social." What resulted was a "stalemate society." The Third Republic maintained traditional values and a certain way of life. Its political system was dominated by a "political class" (elites at the local and national levels, numbering fewer than 25,000 people), whose separation from the populace was great. Its weak political parties never functioned as effective intermediaries between the nation and the people.

After examining the "liberal-democratic compromise," or

---

[36] W. L. Middleton, *The French Political System* (New York: Dutton, 1933), p. 21.

[37] Stanley Hoffmann (ed.), *In Search of France* (Cambridge, Mass.: Harvard University Press, 1963). See pp. 15, 30, 36, 42, 60.

[38] Hoffmann, pp. 15, 30, 36, 42, 60.

"the adjustment of the forces released by the French Revolution in the society and civilization of France," J. B. Wolf concludes that the history of France before and after 1919 must be told in different terms.[39] He states that the men who led France between 1879 and 1914 headed a nation of villages and small towns, with agriculture as its major resource and urban centers concerned with commerce and small manufactures. The "liberal-democratic solution," says Wolf, satisfied the needs of the politically conscious majority until World War I. After 1919, however, a new industrial system was created, after a war that had turned most aspects of French life upside down. However, France's industrial reorganization lagged behind that of her neighbors. Traditional political policies and traditional economic forms, and raw material shortages, precluded the emergence of a modern industrial technology. The gap "between the French economy and that of the other technologically advanced countries became tragically apparent."[40] The war, which so greatly stimulated technology elsewhere, failed to achieve that in France. French leaders looked aside as France moved into this new era, one that marked the "end of the period when the French nation could hope to control its own destiny as well as of the period when the political life of the nation was primarily concerned with adjustment of the several political traditions in its own national history."[41] Wolf states that it was then that the liberal-democratic system, that complex of laws, institutions, customs, ideas, and practices, many of them not fully formulated but pieced together by a century of compromises, came under attack.[42]

World War II terminated the "stalemate" society. Once it was ended, economic planning arrived and production, distribution, and technology grew. The economy became highly industrialized and expansionist. The agrarian population began to shrink at the fastest pace recorded in French history, and the movement of peoples from the country to urban areas became

---

[39] John B. Wolf, *France 1814–1919: The Rise of a Liberal Democratic Society* (New York: Harper & Row, 1963), p. ix.

[40] Wolf, p. ix.

[41] Wolf, p. ix.

[42] Wolf, p. ix.

pronounced. The worker, considered a beast of burden by some earlier regimes, succeeded in bettering his material condition considerably and became better integrated within society. The stigma of "pauperization" passed from him to some elements of the agrarian society. The technocrat, or specialized manager, came to the fore, both in the public and private sectors of the economy and at the highest levels of government. France eventually became a member of the European Economic Community; her economy became more competitive than it had been previously; it also became more dependent upon the economies of the other participant states. Many of these changes occurred not because France wanted them, but because France's survival depends upon her ability to adapt to great transformations in the world economy. French political forms changed greatly too— after the end of the Fourth Republic and the creation of the Fifth —and some of the new ones, such as presidentialism, appear to be more than just transitory. Yet, at the same time there is growing and justified apprehension about France's inability to develop intermediate political bodies strong enough to function effectively as "transmission belts" between populace and government, for in the era of "after de Gaulle" their existence as viable instrumentalities may prove to be the difference between a democratic and dictatorial regime. The regime of de Gaulle, which lay somewhere in between both, was tenable only as long as he remained on the scene.

RECENT DEMOGRAPHIC TRANSFORMATION

High population growth, population redistribution, increased urbanization, growth of the work force, and an increase in the size of the youth category have all altered the configuration of French society since the end of World War II.

Average annual population increases of 1 percent now constitute the norm. The census of 1962 counted the population of metropolitan France as approximately 46.53 million; by the following year that population had increased to approximately 48 million, or almost double the population of the year 1800. By 1965 the population exceeded 49 million persons. That year the increase of approximately 470,000 people constituted a figure equivalent to the population of Bordeaux.[43] This great population growth is in contrast to the low rate of expansion maintained between the world wars. Between the censuses of 1954 and 1962 the total population increase was 8.2 percent. There was during that period a 5.5 percent excess of births over deaths, which accounted for approximately 2,350,000 persons, and an increase of 2.7 percent in immigration, which accounted for approximately another 1,150,000 people—150,000 Algerian workers, 450,000 Europeans repatriated from Morocco and Tunisia, and about 550,000 foreigners. Approximately one third of the total population increase between 1954 and 1962 was absorbed by the Paris region, the Seine-et-Oise department receiving 593,000 and the Seine 420,000. Elsewhere, Bouches-du-Rhône received 193,000, Nord 175,000, Moselle 153,000, Rhône 143,000, Isère 100,000, and Alpes-Maritimes 98,000.[44] The high birthrate—averaging 810,000 to 830,000 persons after World War II—displays a regional nature, being, with the exception of the Paris area, elevated in the north, northwest, and west, and low in central France, the Pyrenees, the Mediterranean coast, and the southern Alps.

An increasing trend toward uneven regional distribution of population has been characteristic of France since the end of World War II. As of 1963 each of the populations of three of France's departments exceeded 2 million inhabitants—Seine 5,646,000, Seine-et-Oise 2,298,000, and Nord 2,293,000. Each of the populations of five other departments ranged from 1 to 2 million; seventy-nine other departments each comprised populations of 100,000 to 500,000; three departments each contained fewer than 100,000 inhabitants—Lozère, Hautes-Alpes, Basses-Alpes. Between 1954 and 1962, fifteen departments underwent depopulation, primarily in the west, the Pyrenees, and the Massif Central. Losses were registered in Creuse (−5.3 percent), Cantal (−3.5 percent), and Gers (−3 percent). During these same years the total population increase was, nevertheless, 3,630,000, of which almost 80 percent was registered in the Paris region,

[43] *Le Monde*, February 4, 1966, p. 21.
[44] "Les résultats généraux du recensement démographique," *Le Monde*, November 1, 1962, p. 8.

Alsace, Lorraine, the Nord, the Riviera, and the Rhône Alps.[45]

The census of 1962 confirmed the trend of peoples to urban areas. The trend itself is not new but the rate of acceleration is novel. Between 1936 and 1942 a population increase of approximately 4,330,000 went primarily to cities averaging 100,000 inhabitants each, representing a gain of 29 percent. Between 1936 and 1962 villages of fewer than 1500 inhabitants each underwent depopulation of approximately 1,300,000 persons, a loss of about 20 percent. By 1963 the exodus from the country to the city was elevated in 41 departments, average in 15, less than average in 12, and insignificant in 18.[46] Between 1954 and 1962 Grenoble led the nation with an increase of 43,000 inhabitants, a growth rate of 37 percent.[47] Even those departments undergoing depopulation registered population increases in some of their cities. Rennes gained, for example, 22,000 inhabitants and yet the department in which it is situated, Ille-et-Vilaine, diminished by 7200 people.[48] During these years only Paris and Bordeaux accounted for fewer inhabitants than in 1954, 100,000 and 9000 respectively. The Paris population loss was due primarily to the push to the suburbs, and during this period the Paris region itself accumulated more than a million additional inhabitants.[49] In the "old days" of more restricted incomes and limited transportation, people generally lived closer to their places of work; now many ex-Parisians think little of commuting daily between the Chevreuse Valley (once known as "little Switzerland" but now often smog-bound) and Paris, a round trip of approximately fifty miles.

Another important phenomenon of French demography is the increase that soon will take place in the size of its work force. The active population now is in excess of 20 million people. Somewhat in excess of 12.5 million are wage earners. This work force, which is now relatively small for the size of the total popu-

[45] "Les résultats généraux. . . ."
[46] By the calculations of *Le Monde*, August 13, 1963, p. 9.
[47] "Les résultats généraux. . . ."
[48] "Les résultats généraux. . . ."
[49] "Les résultats généraux. . . ."

lation, owes its limited size to years of war and consequent human destruction, and to a birthrate that was previously very low. However, the new high birthrate, introduction of more liberal family allowances, and increases in life expectancy will bring to the work force in future years additional thousands of people. This transformation will place heavier demands on French employment, and contribute possibly to an increase in the number of unemployed.[50]

Finally, attention is called to two other areas of French society presently in transformation. One is the growth in the size of the age category comprising people under twenty years old; the other is the growing numerical superiority of females over males. In 1965 more than 50 percent of the whole of French society was between twenty and sixty-four years of age; almost 34 percent was below the age of twenty, and almost 17 percent exceeded sixty years. The category comprising those between twenty and sixty-four years of age was undergoing decline, however, whereas the category including those under twenty was increasing rapidly.[51] By 1966 women outnumbered men in French society by approximately 52 to 48 percent, although that ratio is dependent upon region too (the more urban the area, the greater the numerical superiority of females).[52] Life expectancy now averages seventy-three years for women and sixty-seven for men. Women comprise today three fifths of the age category of over sixty-five.

[50] Unemployment in 1967 was approximately 1.5 percent of the work force. Considering that output had risen in 1966 by 5 percent, showing that workers had become more productive, one cannot ignore the fact that there was not a corresponding increase in jobs. One area productive of unemployment is high-cost dwelling construction. Approximately four of every five unemployed skilled workers are from the construction trades. Other areas of unemployment are the long-depressed textile mills of the north and ship-building yards in the west. Le Monde (March 18, 1967, p. 7) notes that reductions between 1962 and 1966 in the number of textile enterprises reduced the number of textile workers by approximately 14,000; recent increases in unemployment show no signs, however, of endangering the French economy.

[51] Le Monde, February 4, 1966, p. 21.
[52] Le Monde, February 4, 1966, p. 21.

ECONOMIC POLICY

The French economy is more regimented by the state than the American economy, due to a tradition of mercantilism. Mercantilism, which was at its peak under Colbert, from 1661 to 1683, was a system which involved royal licensing of virtually all enterprise. Pre-Revolutionary regimes supported certain industries, controlling through their large administrative apparatus parts of the economy both in production and distribution. Policy making, which originated with the monarch, was aided by advisers and enforced throughout the country by a network of central government representatives.[53] The outcome was a system of intranational tariffs calculated to discourage the passage of commodities from region to region. Taxes were levied on transit and roads, as well as on transport itself. Tariffs and taxes both had the effect of reducing trade among regions, restricting their sizes, and increasing trade interdependencies within each region itself. This system bequeathed to subsequent and more modern eras a tendency for the diverse areas to develop at disproportionate rates of growth.

Today the French nation is trying to make up for the past, being engaged in efforts to introduce into the economy changes that will result in an industrialization suited to the needs of a modern society. This program of modernization requires extensive state planning, and the expending of state energies to the rational determination of the societal environment for the acquisition of various human ends. Emphasis is given to an advanced technology, elevation of the role of science, increased production and distribution, and an allocation of the national income that is more equitable than the one that presently exists. This program—if it is to be successful—requires psychological, social, behavioral, and political changes in society.

State economic planning is practiced in the private sector on a voluntary rather than an arbitrary basis. The *Commissariat général du Plan,* which is charged with the execution of planning, creates each year committees composed of civil servants, representatives of unions and employers, and experts selected by

---

[53] Primarily by *intendants,* whose many duties included collection of taxes and whose practices did much to encourage evasion.

the state for their competence. Once formulated, the "Plan" then is scrutinized by the Economic and Social Council and subjected subsequently to a vote by Parliament (the First and Third Plans were not). Recommendations of the Plan are not legally binding upon the populace, requiring of it, theoretically, no particular compliance. Outside the private sector, state enterprises and administrations carry out in the public sector of the economy recommendations of the Plan only if the necessary funds are made available to them by the annual finance law.

The First Plan (introduced in 1945) was designed to develop key resources, giving to certain sectors of the economy definite priorities and targets. Later, after postwar shortages had disappeared, the Second Plan (1954–1957) sought guidelines for the economy and a framework for investments. Attention was given to improvement and modernization of agriculture, processing industries, housing, and overseas production, to upgrading underdeveloped parts of the economy, and to retraining and readapting manpower and research for production. Second Plan guidelines were carried over to both the Third and Fourth Plans. Upon termination of the Second Plan, production had risen, but increased imports, decreased exports, and inflation led to a financial crisis. The Third Plan (1958–1961) sought and finally achieved financial stability.[54] The Fourth Plan (1962–1965) was a plan of economic and social development which dealt only with essential branches of production (numerous enterprises were not included within its recommendations), seeking to increase the gross national product by 24 percent in four

---

[54] The Pinay-Rueff plan was introduced to deal with the crisis of the franc. A devaluation was resorted to, followed by creation of a new heavy franc, and currency convertibility for nonresidents. Customs duties were reduced 10 percent in keeping with the Treaty of Rome, the Charter of the European Economic Community. According to Pierre Viansson-Ponté in *Le Monde* ("Bilan du septennat. I. L'indépendance et ses conditions," November 23, 1965, p. 3), gold reserves, down to 19 millions in dollars when de Gaulle came to power, had increased by the end of 1960 to 2068 millions. Short-term debts also disappeared almost entirely by the end of 1960; after the events of May 1968, and the slowdown of the economy, France sold back to the United States more than $200 million in gold. As of November 1968, estimated losses were approximately a third of all gold reserves.

years (requiring during that period an increase of 23 percent in consumption). Of particular importance in the Fourth Plan was the question of how much of the gross national product was to be devoted to public and private investments, how much of it was to be reserved for consumption and which kinds were to be encouraged, which underdeveloped social categories and regions were to receive priorities, what levels of production were to be maintained, and ways in which the levels of production of the different branches of the economy could be interrelated effectively. The approach adopted required maintaining full employment by the creation of 1 million nonagricultural jobs, development of foreign trade so as to achieve a surplus in the balance of payments, and further development in public and private investments. The Fifth Plan (1966–1970) constitutes an attempt at a national "new look," seeking the development of public facilities, fairer distribution of the benefits of expansion, and elimination of social inequities.[55] It seeks broader expansion at an annual 5 percent increase in the gross national product, approximately a 25 percent increase in private consumption, and increases in foreign aid, defense, and social progress (particularly schools, hospitals, research, communications, housing, social allowances, and farm incomes). It foresees the evolution of industry, business, and agriculture into larger and more competitive units, more scientific and technical research, town and country planning (involving farm modernization, reforestation, industrialization of the west, and creation there of new universities and research centers), reorganization of the Paris region, water conservation and air pollution plans, and limiting of speculation in real estate.

The "Plan," although "nonmandatory" for private enterprise, exercises a marked influence on both the decision making

[55] Ambassade de France, Service de presse et d'information (Speeches and Press Conferences), "Complete Text of the Interview of French Premier Georges Pompidou over French Radio and Television on July 27, 1965," No. 226A. Pompidou stated that the top guidelines of the Fifth Plan give top priority to productive investments—that is, "to everything connected with modernizing agriculture and industry." With reference to equipment, preference will be given to things that directly promote economic development—particularly communications channels and scientific research. He alluded also to the necessity of reducing consumption for the sake of going farther in international competition.

of enterprisers and the volume and direction of their investments. Professor Jeanneney explains that the Plan influences private enterprisers to follow state recommendations because "they are fearful lest they be unable to make requests of the State or of the organisms dependent upon it for credit or budgetary subsidies not clearly prescribed by law." [56] Therefore, it is understandable that private decisions frequently refer to the Plan as a justification.[57] Pierre Mendès-France states that the Plan tends to focus for a given period of time on certain prospects, and that its decisions are anticipated by private enterprise with clear effect on its own plans and decisions. Some enterprisers, knowing that the Plan will make and sustain their own markets, undertake investments that might not have been considered otherwise, whereas other enterprisers, knowing that the Plan is not receptive to risks and innovations to which previously they had given serious consideration, sometimes are inclined to abandon them.

At the state's disposal are methods which it can bring to bear on private enterprise so as to secure its orientation to the Plan. These include government regulation of currency, lower interest rates on loans, subsidies, government orders and contracts, tax reductions and exemptions, undershoring of exports, and the like. The state's most effective weapon, however, is credit, which it can bring to bear on the investment programs of private firms in order to divert them in the direction of the Plan. If it wishes to do so, the state can stimulate the expansion of truly productive enterprises. Finally, the state acknowledges that its planning would be fruitless were it to allocate its credit so as to enable enterprises to undertake developmental activities contrary to or unheedful of the Plan.[58]

The state is responsible for economic modernization and development, and so it seeks to take the lead in this effort. Construction and implementation of the Plan is the responsibility of the administration. The state holds the "directing hand" over private enterprise. However, that hand sometimes wavers. In exercising its role as repository of and potential allocator of

[56] Jeanneney, p. 284.

[57] Jeanneney, p. 284.

[58] Pierre Mendès-France, *A Modern French Republic* (New York: Hill & Wang, 1963), p. 93.

resources, the state is constantly pursued by private groups who seek to manipulate decision making in order to orient it in the direction of their own interests. These groups are primarily in the realm of business; lesser pressure is exerted by groups drawn from labor and agriculture.[59]

Pierre Mendès-France, a persistent critic of Gaullist economic policy, has argued for years that some of the most favorable aspects of the economy are outweighed by the Gaullist's policy of *déplanification,* which is characterized by a reduction in the role of the state in economic life and a drift toward some aspects of a partial "free market." [60] He argues that this policy is

[59] As far as the unorganized general populace is concerned, its knowledge of the Plan is limited, as is its comprehension of economic phenomena. Mendès-France states, "Of all the great industrial nations France is, perhaps, the one where public opinion is least well informed about economic problems . . . . Schools and colleges allow young people to grow up in complete ignorance of these problems. Later on, having had little preparation for their role as citizens of a modern industrial country, they are subject to the influence of the major channels of communication which disseminate official opinion at one moment and the opinion of private interests the next. As a result of this carefully fostered ignorance . . . Frenchmen have reached the point of convincing themselves that matters of this kind are for experts only and much too complicated for the common run of mortals." See Mendès-France, pp. 93–94.

[60] *Le Monde,* November 12, 1966, p. 22. Mendès-France states, "In fact there is no more today a true plan nor even a coherent economic policy, but some operational efforts which appear particularly unwelcome when we see so many organized private groups gravitating around the seat of power." See also his *A Modern French Republic,* p. 121. He calls attention to the fact that governments have not always recognized the precedence of the Plan "or been determined to insure its success. Time and time again in the last fifteen years, a particular service or department, a minister, or Parliament itself, has taken decisions which upset the emphasis and priorities of the Plan." He also states that some large firms do resist the Plan, this being the basis of the recommendation by the Club Jean Moulin that any monopoly or industry which seeks to block state economic policy should be nationalized. See also Jacques Malterre, "La démocratie à construire," *France-Observateur* (December 20, 1962), pp. 10–11, for recapitulation of the criticisms of Mendès-France. Finally, see *Le Monde,* November 12, 1966, p. 22, for the address by Mendès-France to the luncheon of the Association of Economic and Financial Journalists and his severe criticisms of *déplanification* and comments on underemployment.

injurious to construction, and conducive to inflation, underemployment, stagnation of some geographical zones, and underproduction in some factories. This condition, Mendès-France states, will persist as long as the state invests so much money in "totally unproductive expenses," as, for example, atomic power for the military. "The policy followed by the government," he contends, "deprives the nation of a part of its national revenue. . . . In 1965, for example, we calculated the reduction in growth lost the country 12 million new francs." [61]

What has the Plan done for the economy? In 1966 the gross national product increased by approximately 5 percent,[62] and between 1958 and 1966 industrialization increased by 52 percent.[63] (During 1966 price increases were not particularly large, amounting only to 2.75 percent,[64] but for the period 1958–1966, however, prices increased by 36 percent).[65] The increase in 1967 in the gross national product was less than that foreseen by the Plan, but revenue increased per inhabitant by approximately 3.5 percent, consumption rose by about 4 percent, and investments rose by about 6 percent over those of 1966. Foreign trade difficulties underwent some accentuation. As of 1967 imports increased by approximately 11 percent, whereas exports increased by only 6.5 percent, introducing a deficit in the commercial balance and creating some anxieties about its future. Six countries—the United Kingdom, Germany, Holland, the United States, Switzerland and Belgium—absorb approximately 60 percent of all French exports, and the slowing down of various of these economies could retard French trade in a very seri-

[61] Mendès-France, p. 89.

[62] *Le Monde,* March 5–6, 1967, p. 2. During the same year the increase in the United States was 5.5 percent, Italy 5.3 percent, Germany 2.5–3 percent, United Kingdom 0.5 percent.

[63] *Le Monde,* March 5–6, 1967, p. 2. During the same period Italy increased 110 percent, Holland 81 percent, United States 70 percent, Germany 65 percent, Belgium 53 percent, United Kingdom 34 percent.

[64] *Le Monde,* March 5–6, 1967, p. 2. During the same year Germany increased 3.4 percent, United States 3 percent, United Kingdom 4 percent, Belgium 4.3 percent, Holland 5.9 percent.

[65] *Le Monde,* March 5–6, 1967, p. 2. For the same period Holland increased 33.5 percent, Italy 32.5 percent, United Kingdom 26 percent, Germany 22 percent, Belgium 20 percent, United States 12 percent.

ous way. Consequently, France is watching them carefully, particularly the economy of her large neighbor and customer Germany, for decreases in German imports from France could inflict heavy injury on the French economy.

The Plan's program of industrial decentralization has fallen short of its target.[66] The Fourth Plan made the industrialization of the west one of its objectives. Factories were created in Brittany, special consideration was given to the development of the Nord, Pas-de-Calais, and the Massif Central, and financial aid went to ten regional programs in the southwest and west.[67] In 1963 decrees delegated authority to a commission for the management of territory and regional action, in order to create for the France of 1985 *métropoles d'équilibre* (consisting of Lille, Roubaix, Tourcoing; Metz, Nancy, Thionville; Strasbourg; Lyon, Saint-Étienne; Aix-Marseilles; Toulouse; Bordeaux; Nantes) to act as counterbalances to the already congested and overdeveloped Paris region. Statistics available for the period between 1960 and 1962 illustrate the stagnation of industrial decentralization—1359 units in 1960, 1545 in 1961, and 1534 in 1962.[68] Of these units "decentralized" in 1962, only 451 could be classified as "real factories," the others representing a workshop here and a small tool unit there.[69] Investments in the provinces also have declined, despite the state's attempt to make them the object of its direct and indirect financial aid.[70]

What has the Plan achieved for the citizen? Has it successfully eliminated gross social inequalities? *Le Monde* comments that the "first seven years of de Gaulle" constituted an era in which "social inequalities in France have been sensibly aggravated." [71] Between 1958 and 1965 prices increased by approximately 30 percent, while the purchasing power of workers paid by the hour rose approximately 25 percent. However, during that same period of time the incomes of minimum wage workers increased by only approximately 3 percent. Incomes of workers

[66] Viansson-Ponté, "Bilan du septennat."
[67] Viansson-Ponté, "Bilan du septennat."
[68] *Le Monde,* August 11–12, 1963, p. 5.
[69] *Le Monde,* August 11–12, 1963, p. 5.
[70] *Le Monde,* March 9, 1967, p. 22.
[71] Viansson-Ponté, "Bilan du septennat."

in the private sector forged ahead, while those of civil servants and people on salary lagged behind. The incomes of people engaged in agriculture increased during that seven-year span perhaps 3 percent per year. And despite increases in the incomes of those attempting to live on state pensions, many of the aged were forced to manage on fewer than 5 francs per day.[72] Disparities in incomes, pronounced under the Fourth Republic, have been intensified by the Fifth.

Gaullist modifications in fiscal structure have not ameliorated significantly long-standing tax inequities. State monetary receipts increased more than 100 percent in the period between 1958 and 1966. During the same period receipts derived from the progressive income tax increased by more than 270 percent. Only 4.9 million families paid the tax in 1958, a figure that increased subsequently to 8 million. Nonetheless, the progressive income tax presently is the source only of approximately 15 percent of state resources (instead of 8 percent, as was the case in 1958).[73] Consumption taxes—which hit hardest those least able to pay—continue to provide the state with the largest single source of its income, approximating at least 54 percent of its receipts (some claim that the figure is in excess of this).[74] Great progressive strides in the direction of tax modernization—imperative if the state is interested in concerning itself seriously with remedying inequities—have not been taken by the Gaullists.

There was no indication prior to the great strikes and disorder of May 1968 that the populace viewed the Gaullists as capable of substantially improving its material condition. The National Institute of Demographic Studies in 1965 questioned 2541 people in 198 *communes* (the inquiry was concerned primarily with changes in thought and behavior in recent years). The results revealed certain apprehensions on the part of re-

[72] *Le Monde,* August 11–12, 1963, p. 5. Minimum resources for the aged passed from 848 francs in 1958 to 1800 francs per year in July 1965.

[73] *Le Monde,* March 5–6, 1967, p. 2. According to studies of the European Economic Community, the French pay each year more taxes per capita ($437, or 2343 francs) than Germans ($432), Luxembourgers ($419), Belgians ($340), Dutchmen ($319), or Italians ($203).

[74] *Le Monde,* September 11–12, 1966, p. 9.

spondents. A majority felt their resources insufficient for their needs, wishing for a 25 to 45 percent increase in incomes. When asked the question, "Do you think your level of existence is superior, inferior or equal to what it was ten years ago?," 35 percent responded superior, 35 percent said equivalent, and 27 percent declared inferior.[75] The institute classified their views of the future as 19 percent optimistic, 10 percent pessimistic, and approximately 70 percent as being rather "uncertain." [76] Fear of an important crisis existed among the respondents (six of every ten looked forward to an unemployment crisis).[77] Evident also were fears of overproduction, automation, and population increases.[78] Among less privileged social categories, fear was expressed that France has too high a birthrate, and more than 80 percent of those interrogated declared in favor of birth control dispensaries.[79]

Inquiries conducted by the French Institute of Public Opinion between May 1966 and December 1967 reveal among respondents important reservations relative to economic and social phenomena in France. These people were less optimistic about prospects for the future than they were the previous year.[80] This decline in morale was due primarily to the economic situation, and 60 percent feared unemployment, higher prices, and social conflicts.[81] Such concerns were not new, however, having been manifested earlier, in 1966.[82] Yet, in 1967, the number of respondents who foresaw a decrease rather than an increase in their standard of living doubled (workers, peasants, and retired persons were troubled most).[83] Respondents estimated that the state gave excessive financial attention to the military, underdeveloped countries, and the nationalized sector, and not enough

[75] Bastide and Girard, p. 27.

[76] Bastide and Girard, p. 27.

[77] Bastide and Girard, p. 27.

[78] Bastide and Girard, p. 35.

[79] Bastide and Girard, p. 35.

[80] Institut français d'opinion publique, "La vie politique de mai 1966 à décembre 1967," *Sondages,* 1 (1968), 5.

[81] "La vie politique de mai 1966. . . ," 5.

[82] "La vie politique de mai 1967. . . ," 15.

[83] "La vie politique de mai 1967. . . ," 17.

money to housing, education, professional training, agriculture, and scientific research.[84] A majority thought that strikes in the private sector were justified, and in the majority also were those who favored lowering retirement ages and limiting the entry of foreign workers into France.[85]

Many of the people interrogated maintained lively interest in the plan for "association of management and labor" calling for participation by workers in enterprise (the Vallon amendment), announced by General de Gaulle in his press conference of October 1966.[86] Many were workers (even members of the Communist party showed attention); despite some opposition by industrialists and businessmen, a strong majority declared in its support. Finally, among those interrogated, two out of every three expressed the conviction that economic development which increases the richness of the country will not result in equitable distribution of wealth among the different social categories.[87] They attributed this phenomenon to ineffectiveness of the unions, the power of great private interests, and the policy of the Pompidou government.[88] Two of every three persons felt that they belong to a social class (although not all conceded the existence of "class struggle"; on this question responses were divided almost equally, with a very slight edge belonging to those who believe that it exists. Belief in its existence was more elevated among workers, salaried employees, and foremen).[89]

Despite growing social discontent, few people foresaw the great strikes of May 1968 and the many weeks of true national economic paralysis. Those strikes were ended only by the government's coaxing millions of strikers back to work with promises

[84] "La vie politique de mai. . . ," 17.
[85] "La vie politique de mai. . . ," 28.
[86] "La vie politique de mai. . . ," 33.
[87] "La vie politique de mai. . . ," 43.
[88] "La vie politique de mai 1966. . . ," 43.
[89] "La vie politique de mai 1966. . . ," 44. The institute concludes, "But if the majority of electors of the Federation of the Left and of the Communist party believe in the reality of the struggle of classes today, one-third do not share this view, respectively 35 percent and 30 percent."

of future broad economic and social reforms (embodied in the "Agreements of Grenelle").[90] Implementation of the Agreements of Grenelle will make future revisions of the Fifth Plan imperative. The Agreements seek social improvement on a national scale, effective integration of workers in enterprise by a new, larger distribution of responsibilities, a "new deal" for the youth of France, increases in pay both in the public and private sectors, and extension of union rights. The Gaullists have agreed to reductions in working hours, increases in minimum pensions for the aged, and increases in social security benefits; increases in civil service salaries, budgeted earlier for 5 percent, now are scheduled for an average raise of 13 percent. Also foreseen is the creation of 16,000 new teaching posts, the opening of centers of professional training for unemployed youths, and more aid for agriculture. Of particular importance is the regime's plan for worker's participation in enterprise, although no set version of it has yet been adopted (the conception offered by Left Gaullist René Capitant foresees creation of a directory [the government of the enterprise], which would be accountable to a supervisory council [a representative organ of salaried personnel, or cooperative]. Sharing by workers in profits as they increase in the enterprise is foreseen).[91]

Workers appear to be receptive to the Gaullist's generalized version of participation in enterprise, but as of now the unions do not regard the scheme with optimism. The CGT described it in July 1968 as a capitalistic venture, stating that "They change the words, but it's always the same old product." [92] Georges Seguy (CGT) described the project as "closer to alienation than

[90] For description of the Agreements and benefits granted, see *Le Monde, Sélection hebdomadaire,* June 13–19, 1968, p. 6. It is not possible to generalize here figures that vary from branch to branch of the economy and from the public to the private sector; as for the effects of the strikes of May on the gross national product, differences in duration and sectors of the economy make assessment difficult. Some say that the loss represents 2 to 4 percent of the national product. Others describe it as being in excess of 4 percent.

[91] For description see "La participation: Bouleversement ou évolution," *Le Figaro,* July 2, 1968, p. 7.

[92] *L'Express,* 886 (July 1–7, 1968), 6.

emancipation." [93] The CFDT is suspicious too, and the FO wants "contracts" for workers, not "association." [94] Finally, private enterprise also shows some reservations, one of its units stating that "Participation should not be confused with the disorder of hierarchical structures. . ." [95]

Implementation of the "Agreements of Grenelle" will involve great costs both in the public and private sectors of the economy, and the adoption of state measures calculated to prevent inflation and devaluation. Some initial dislocations are inevitable—particularly among some small and average size enterprises who will choose to close rather than support wage increases, and among agricultural owners who probably will reduce the number of people in their employ. One consequence of the Agreements will be greater dependence upon the state by practically all of its elements. Finally, the future of the Gaullist regime will depend upon its ability to translate the Agreements from promises to realities.

AGRICULTURE

A variety of types of farming exist in France, chiefly direct ownership, tenant farming, and sharecropping (Table 1–2). Owner-operated enterprises account for more than 50 percent of all French territory, and about half of all the farms. Tenant farming, or the working of rented lands, accounts for more than a third of the territory and less than a fifth of the farms. The type of farming called sharecropping involves equal division of the harvest with responsibility for management falling on the owner. The small farm predominates in France. By 1955 almost 1.8 million farms—or 80 percent of the total number—covered about 40 percent of French territory, and comprised fewer than fifty acres each. Some 800,000 comprised fewer than twelve

[93] *L'Express*, 886 (July 1–7, 1968), 6. The CGT is the General Confederation of Labor, the CFDT the Christian Federation of Trade Unions, the FO the Worker's Force.

[94] *L'Express*, 886 (July 1–7, 1968), 6.

[95] *L'Express*, 886 (July 1–7, 1968), 6; see also *Le Monde,* June 23–24, 1968, p. 21, for statements of business associations that oppose worker participation in enterprise.

Table 1–2 Breakdown of farms and land according to system of tenure

Tenure	Number of farms	Percent-age	Acreage	Percent-age
Direct tenure	1,196,000	52.9	49,817,430	55.3
Tenant farming	389,000	17.2	34,244,080	38.0
Sharecropping	72,000	3.2	5,720,520	.3
Undeclared	39,000	1.3	405,080	0.4
Mixed tenures [a]				
Farmers owning buildings	458,000	20.3		
Farmers not owning buildings	114,000	5.1		
Total	2,268,000	100.0	90,187,110	100.0

[a] By mixed tenure is meant an enterprise in which the farmer owns some land, with or without farm buildings, and leases other lands. This is characteristic of more than 20 percent of all farms.

acres each, covered less than 5 percent of the territory, and furnished a living for more than two million people.

France's 124 million acres of farmland constitute approximately 50 percent of all farmland in the European Economic Community.[96] Almost 92 percent of all of France is devoted to cultivation and pasture land.[97] In some parts of the country the climate is predominantly marine, in other parts it is Mediterranean; water supplies are great, soils are good, and agricultural diversification comes easy.

[96] Ambassade de France (Service de presse et d'information), "France and Agriculture," December 1963, p. 6.

[97] Leading crops are grains, including wheat, barley, corn, oats, rye, and rice. Fruits are abundant; more than 50 percent of those marketed come from the Vaucluse and Roussillon areas in the south, the Saint-Pol-de-Léon and Nantes regions in the west, and from the Paris area. Vineyards account for 3 percent of the entire territory. Root crops are common, consisting primarily of sugar beets (north), potatoes (north, east, Brittany). Other crops are olives (south), flax, oilseeds, hemp and chicory (north), as well as hops (north and west), tobacco (Alsace and southwest), and mushrooms. Oak, beech and pine forests cover approximately 20 percent of the territory. France ranks fourth in the world in beef and pork production, and eighth in mutton and lamb. Numerous sheep and goats are raised. Poultry ranks third among France's agricultural occupations.

Originally an agricultural nation, France was transformed in the nineteenth century into an industrial one. Agriculture, which produced some 60 percent of the national income in 1870, was by the twentieth century responsible for less than 20 percent of it. Farming declined, rural populations began to migrate to the cities, and the small peasant found it increasingly difficult to arrange for himself the relatively autonomous productive activities to which he was accustomed. He became an anachronism, as the type of France that had made his existence possible, and about which Alain wrote so eloquently—that is, the France characterized by smallness—became an anachronism too. The peasantry, an important force in the beginnings of the Third Republic, having shaped with considerable success the political institutions of that regime, witnessed political control fall more and more under middle class influence.

The old French agriculture was characterized by the presence of numerous handworkers who were badly fed and housed, and who received for their efforts low salaries. Farms often were organized as primitive autarkies, living in isolation and having but remote ties with the rest of the economy.[98] This arrested development was aided by the lack of concern of the Third Republic to push French agriculture into the modern world—protecting it, instead, in order to gain its good will, and generalizing about the peasant's attractive qualities and his "religion of the soil." By 1936 the peasantry still formed 36 percent of the population, and slight attention was given to its efficiency and modernization. Its static and subsidized condition paralleled that of French industry (which lived also under protectionism, being relatively unconcerned with exports, imports, and state investments). The condition of French agriculture was but part of a complex of general retardation.

The aftermath of World War II forced change on the French economy. After the Liberation a new, modern economy had to be created, one that could keep pace with post-Liberation demands. Foreign exchange achieved a new prominence in which agriculture had to play an important role. Efforts at modernization were undertaken by the state, but agriculture continued to

---

[98] Numerous farms raised only enough pigs for their own annual consumption and none for the commercial market.

suffer, nonetheless, from the existence of a chronic state of imbalance. During the 1950s, 8 percent of the farms were responsible for more than 30 percent of the production of agriculture, and 56 percent produced less than 20 percent. Areas in the west remained overpopulated and not greatly productive, while the center and southwest suffered from underproduction and underpopulation. The state, seriously concerned with problems of underproduction and high farm prices and costs, abandoned farm subsidies in 1958 in order to open the domestic market to competition from home and abroad. When France entered the European Economic Community (which meant accepting the Community's common agricultural policy), the nation agreed to market stabilization through price alignment, regulation of internal and external supply and demand for the purpose of achieving balance, and planning in order to deal with agricultural surpluses. By 1961 the European Economic Community received 32 percent of French food and agricultural exports, and by then France imported from the Community only small amounts of foodstuffs. By 1961 French agricultural production *exceeded* the needs of the European Economic Community. The Fourth Plan, in seeking between 1959 and 1965 a 30 percent increase in agrarian production, laid the groundwork for overproduction by refusing to put restraints on agricultural expansion (probably in order to avoid the stagnation of individual family plots).[99] By the census of 1962 the active agrarian

[99] Suzanne Quiers-Valette, "Les causes économiques du mécontentement des agriculteurs français en 1961," *Revue française de science politique*, Vol. XII, No. 3 (September 1962), 553–592. See also Yves Tavernier, "Le syndicalisme paysan et la cinquième république," *Revue française de science politique*, Vol. XVI, No. 5 (October 1966), 869–912. Those forces defined as traditional in French agriculture defend "the old rural civilization," the individual family unit, a large agricultural population, and the old parliamentary system, which they regard as that which best accommodates the pressures they are able to generate. Stifled by presidentialism and the peripheral status of the National Assembly, they lack the methods of pressure once theirs but, politically, they cannot be ignored by any government; the agrarian budget also is an "electoral budget," as was pointed out by Minister of Agriculture Edgar Faure when introducing it to the National Assembly in one of the most brilliant orations of 1967.

population had declined to 19.7 percent of the total population, as each year approximately 120,000 to 160,000 people moved off the land, and yet agriculture still was producing only 10 percent of the national income.

Today French governments are confronted with an agriculture that languished too long in a chronic state of inefficiency and overprotection. Within the nation different agricultural zones reside in conditions of development that range from good to bad —and in some cases interests vary considerably from zone to zone. Moreover, now French governments are confronted with a peasant who was more restrained previously, who does not refuse to violate the public order to express his dissatisfaction (the 1950s ushered in many peasant demonstrations, beginning in 1953 with those in the Aude, Gard, Pyrénées-Orientales, and Hérault, and continuing throughout the decade. The trend has been sustained into the 1960s. In 1963 a peasant demonstration took place in Perpignan, and in 1967 disturbances occurred in the west and southwest).[100] Governments realize that total modernization of agriculture is imperative, but the alterations they wish to effect are made more difficult by centuries of neglect and inactivity. They know that they must take the lead in standardizing and concentrating production, mechanizing the industry, reorganizing the various agricultural networks, and encouraging more people to leave the land (for a ratio of one farmer for every five nonfarmers is not characteristic of a modern state).

In 1966 the French Institute of Public Opinion published the results of its survey of 3000 peasants (agricultural workers were excluded);[101] its findings go a long way toward revealing what the peasant believes and what he seeks. The great majority of those interrogated feel that their problems are greater than those of other social categories, and among them professional preoccupations rank first. Practically all of their criticisms relate

[100] See Henri Mendras and Yves Tavernier, "Les manifestations du juin 1961," *Revue française de science politique,* Vol. 12, No. 3 (September 1962), 647–691; and in the same issue, Jean Meynaud, "Les groupes de pression sous la Ve République," 672–697.

[101] Institut français d'opinion publique, "Les agriculteurs français," *Sondages,* 3 and 4 (1966).

to the low prices they receive for their products. In emphasizing those pecuniary difficulties that result for them, they are far less concerned with problems such as housing, profession, and "life in the country" (these, in fact, are not a source of particular difficulty for them). What would they like to earn? When asked this question, 53 percent said that they would like an income equal to or around 12,000 francs per year ($2400). Fifty-three percent report that they earn 7200 or fewer francs per year ($1450). Six of every ten feel that their lives have not improved during the previous five years, and 54 percent think that those who already have left the land enjoy lives that are much easier than theirs.[102]

The peasants interrogated by the French institute express a clear consciousness of class—that is to say, they feel as a social group that their standard of living is low, and that "society excludes them from its system of values and its economic and social development." Their outlook is not very optimistic; 49 percent believe that an increase in prosperity will not result in improvement of their standard of living. They show no love for the agricultural policy of the government; 55 percent have a bad opinion of it, and 33 percent are "circumspect." Approximately 53 percent report no interest in politics (only 6 percent say that they genuinely are interested.)[103]

The French Institute of Public Opinion's report on the peasantry recognizes that the magnitude of peasant discontent is related to region, age, sex, the type of agrarian activity undertaken, and also to other variables, as well; nonetheless, the institute states that there exists an "exceptional intensity of lack of satisfaction, and even discontent among certain categories of farmers in different regions." [104] The report is in line with other studies of the plight of the peasant. In 1965 the BAC (Bureau agricole commun pour l'étude de la conjoncture économique), created by five large national peasant associations, described 1965 as a "bad year," and estimated that peasant incomes had declined 4 percent in relation to those of the previous year.[105] Although

[102] "Les agriculteurs français," p. 68.
[103] "Les agriculteurs français," p. 82.
[104] "Les agriculteurs français," p. 131.
[105] Le Monde, December 9, 1965, p. 21.

the National Institute of Statistics disagreed (describing peasant income in 1965 as stationary in relation to 1964), the institute estimates peasant income as having declined in 1964 approximately 6 percent in relation to 1963.[106] Whatever the discrepancies existing among various estimates, there is broad agreement that the average decline in agrarian revenue was at least 3 percent in 1964 and 1965.[107]

The 1962 census reflects the magnitude of peasant dissatisfaction. Between the censuses of 1954 and 1962 approximately 1.5 million people left the land, representing a loss of one person in every four. Those who left most frequently were farmer's children; 50 percent of the children censused among the agrarian population in 1954 had left it by 1962. Salaried agricultural workers departed almost as frequently from the land, 25 percent of the men and 43 percent of the women changing professions between 1954 and 1962. Only 830,000 salaried workers remained on the farms by 1962.

Historians like to point out that the great exodus of 1954–1962 is not without precedent in French history, and that approximately one out of every four persons also quit the land between 1862 and 1896. It must be observed, however, that this earlier exodus was achieved over a period of thirty-five years, not just in eight. Previously, between 1946 and 1954, approximately 680,000 men left agriculture. In the period between 1954 and 1962 they were followed by another 750,000. There is a precedent for the trend—there is, however, no precedent for its rate of acceleration.

The authors of *Une France sans paysans* show that departures from the land are relatively numerous south of the Caen-Nîmes line, but that losses north of it were greatest in the years between 1954 and 1962—that is to say, from within the regions where the peasantry was not as numerous.[108] Many of these people were taken off by industry, particularly in areas where newly created enterprises offer the opportunity for individuals to change positions without altering residence. In regions gener-

---

[106] *Le Monde,* December 9, 1965, p. 21.

[107] *Le Monde,* December 9, 1965, p. 21.

[108] See Michel Gervais, Claude Servolin, and Jean Weil, *Une France sans paysans* (Bourges: Éditions du Seuil, 1965).

ally described as underindustrialized, changes from agriculture as a profession also are increasing. The Caen-Nîmes line separates modern France from the France that is not so modern, or from the France of the nineteenth century. North of it fewer individuals depend upon agriculture for a living. The decline of French agriculture in the north is a phenomenon of the greater industrialization of French society.

The technical revolution in which French agriculture presently is involved—consisting of the application of new scientific techniques, mechanization, and better selection of seeds and fertilizers—is commendable; nevertheless, it is no panacea for the overstimulation of production and the inability of national consumption to increase to the point where it can accommodate it. Agricultural prices continue to decrease, leading to decreased agrarian incomes. It is true that the technical revolution has stimulated in some instances the emergence in agriculture of a "new breed"—that is, a type of young peasant determined not to operate occupationally as did his father and grandfather, who is not interested in purchasing land for the sake only of ownership when he can rent and exploit it, who is inclined to rent out his land when he can, who is attracted greatly to participation in cooperative enterprises, and who is attempting to address himself to the creation of his own institutions while gravitating away from what once was his almost complete dependence upon the state. Unfortunately, this desirable transformation seems to be running far ahead of the young peasant's technical competence, for—as the French Institute of Public Opinion observes—he appears "the least impregnated by technical civilization," even if "he does manifest a lively desire to modernize the methods of cultivation." [109] The institute describes his efforts as not too significant, and less supportable all the time.

INDUSTRY AND LABOR

French industry is also engaged in a technical transformation. The small, individual entrepreneur so characteristic of France of the Third Republic is now less frequent a phenomenon. Individuals who cannot be classified as entrepreneurs, but act as

[109] Jacques Duquesne, p. 232.

directors of teams of specialized technicians, have become commonplace in large industry. Seldom, however, are they immersed in the technical activities of their enterprises. They act primarily as coordinators of teams which handle most of the technicalities. Their view of capital seldom is like the conception of it entertained by their fathers—it is something that is to be employed for reinvestment, for expansive purposes, and for stimulation of greater production. Consequently, the perspectives of these people are shaped by certain societal considerations. Many have been trained in the *grandes écoles,* having left the high civil service in order to participate in large industry.[110] Higher salaries undoubtedly are a great attraction for them; perhaps greater "power" also is a consideration. Challenges simply are greater for them in large private industry than in state enterprise, and some men make such a change in order to exercise a leeway they seldom could enjoy in the *grands corps.* The process is very different from that employed in American society where government continually seeks to attract to it men from high industry. In France it often is the other way around, with high industry seeking to capture from the state high administrators.

These managerial technocrats, or "super-technocrats," offer a decided advantage over the "old type" of French entrepreneur who had profit on the brain and who often let capital reinvestment go down the drain. These men belong to the future, not to the past, as was often the case with so many of their predecessors. Nonetheless, these men often are a source of definite anxiety for those Frenchmen who see in them the coming of a technocratic authoritarianism which will be to the detriment of French society. Some of these men worry lest new developments and combinations of capital get a tight hold over the economy, one from which it will be impossible to pry lose these technocratic managers. Frenchmen fearful of such a possibility concede that technocracy is inevitable, in both the public and private realms, but they hold that it is possible to mitigate its authoritarian aspects by resorting to industrial democratization—that is, by

---

[110] Some top civil servants go into politics, winning first a parliamentary seat and then going on to a ministership (in which case they frequently have a tie to the corps to which they belonged previously).

recruiting these directors and submitting them to public controls. Their argument is that a technocrat can be technocratic and still be checked by certain restraints. Other advocates of reform of enterprise argue for the adoption of steps that go in a different direction. One group contends that—as a result of the concentration of great enterprise—average-size enterprises are drawing near to the point where their survival on today's market is dependent upon their ability to develop a specialization in products which they can carry through to the final stage of consumption. New automated industries must be created, they say, to create new products capable of creating new demands. Others feel that the economy must be planned so that industrial workers no longer undergo temporary displacements, with the state guaranteeing them immediate access to new employment and further professional training. All such pleas are for a general planning and adoption of institutional safeguards which would bring between the state and major enterprises a close relationship, so as to prepare rationally for coming industrial and technical revolutions. If some of these pleas have a Saint-Simonian flavor, most seek to counterbalance it so as to avoid for society the disadvantages of an authoritarian capitalism presided over by a hierarchical order. Consequently, some of these presentations add here and there a dash of Proudhon.[111]

[111] Claude Henri de Saint-Simon (1760–1825) supported creation on a scientific basis of a new society—led by a scientific elite ruling in behalf of society's most numerous category, the industrial class. He believed that his elite could develop science into a perfected body of beliefs. His society would have operated according to the principle, "To each according to his capacity; to each capacity according to its works." Pierre Joseph Proudhon (1809–1865) was an opponent of the State. Not opposed to the principle of property, he was opposed to its exploitive usage. He believed that labor should control credit instruments and avoid working for others, emancipating itself by creating its own productive units. Society, he believed, should be founded on local producer cooperatives based on local administration. If Proudhon is portrayed sometimes as a fascist, this erroneous interpretation probably derives more from his intense ethnic and religious biases than from his "system." For a good description of Saint-Simon and Proudhon, see the very helpful book by Philip Taft, *Movements for Economic Reform* (New York: Holt, Rinehart and Winston, Inc., 1950), pp. 38–45, 103–109.

French labor currently is involved in its own transformation, and it is now difficult to apply the term "working class" without encountering certain ambiguities. No longer is the unskilled worker in the majority in French labor, and that position now is occupied by specialists who show few secessionist tendencies toward society. The integration of the working class in society is proceeding at a rapid pace (although class analysts like François Sellier believe it to be greater in the worker's technical class than in society itself).[112] A sentiment of inevitable pauperization continues to linger on among workers (as is affirmed by Roger Quilliot)[113] which is exploited tirelessly by the Communist party, and yet it clearly is demonstrable that great improvements in material conditions have taken place among workers during the past two decades. Andrée Andrieux and Jean Lignon after numerous interrogations conclude in their work *L'ouvrier d'aujourd'hui* that the French worker seeks personal betterment rather than improvement of his class, and that his classical attitude of searching for social solutions in the destruction of capitalism has undergone transformation and now is dated.[114] A much older study, conducted in 1956 by the French Institute of Public Opinion, shows that what the French worker then wanted was more from the economy than he was able to derive from it—namely, higher wages, a status in society not less than that enjoyed by the bourgeois, better housing, protection of his wages and savings from inflationary losses, and equality of opportunity for him and his children (particularly in education).[115] His wants were suggestive of a desire to exercise vertical mobility in the very society he felt was exploiting him. Finally, French worker support for Marxist political parties is declining.

---

[112] François Sellier, *Stratégie de la lutte sociale* (Paris: Les éditions ouvrières, 1961).

[113] Roger Quilliot, *La société de 1960 et l'avenir politique de France* (Paris: Gallimard, 1960).

[114] Andrée Andrieux and Jean Lignon, *L'ouvrier d'aujourd'hui* (Paris: Marcel Rivière, 1961).

[115] French Institute of Public Opinion, *French Workers: Their Problems, Their Morale, Their Hopes,* English edition (Paris: 1956). This is a study of 1039 factory manual workers, 396 white-collar workers, and 221 middle-rank industry staff workers.

According to the studies of Mattei Dogan, the Communist and Socialist parties both receive about 55 percent of worker votes (36 percent for the Communist party and 19 percent for the SFIO),[116] but worker support for the Communist party has declined during the last decade and a half. In the elections of 1951, the Communist party alone had accounted for 49 percent of the worker vote.[117]

THE CONSTITUTION OF THE FIFTH REPUBLIC

France has had many constitutions since the Revolution of 1789. A few have lasted some number of years, while others were not implemented at all. Many were preceded by violence and seizure of the state by revolutionary forces, as was the case in 1958 with the Gaullists.

The Constitution of the Fifth Republic was not dictated to the French people by de Gaulle in the manner of a Bonaparte, but presented to them in September 1958 in the form of a referendum on a "take it or leave it" basis. The Constitution, which is almost entirely the result of the thought of the General, shows, however, curiously few streaks of presidential domination. It calls for creation of a government which determines and directs the policy of the nation. The government stands responsible before the National Assembly—that is, "When the National Assembly adopts a motion of censure or when it disapproves the program or a declaration of general policy of the Government, the Premier must submit the resignation of the Government to the President of the Republic." The executive and legislative powers are separated legally. Therefore, membership in the government is incompatible with membership in Parliament. The Constitution seeks an equilibrium between the government and National Assembly. The president is described as an "arbiter" between both, and in the event of conflict between them he may dissolve the National Assembly after consultation with the premier and presidents of the National Assembly and Senate.

---

[116] In Léo Hamon (ed.), *Les nouveaux comportements politiques de la classe ouvrière* (Paris: Presses universitaires, 1965).

[117] Leo Hamon (ed.), *Les nouveaux comportements politiques. . . .*"

Running throughout the constitutional document is what Professor Georges Vedel describes as a *syncrétisme,* or a system which introduces multiple doctrines.[118] The document reflects conservative tendencies, it offers a "rationalized parliamentarism," it exudes a scent of "historic mission" and dependence on "popular consensus," it allows for arbitration—to be exercised by an incumbent president who rejects the very notion of party itself—and it enables the president to "confiscate the ball" whenever the players in the game prove themselves too divided or inept.[119] In allowing the president to dissolve the National Assembly, it ensures "a method for the Chief of State to appeal to the people in order to disavow a parliamentary majority which no longer serves him." Also present is the referendum, which may be invoked only at the discretion of the president, and to which the people may respond only when interrogated. If this Constitution creates a "parliamentarism," it is very different from the classical type. As Lidderdale states, under the latter system "the three powers are neither completely separated, nor concentrated. They are associated in a balanced collaboration. The characteristic of this collaboration is that, under a titular head of the State (whether constitutional monarch or president), the real executive power lies with a cabinet of ministers, who are, however, responsible to the Legislature (of which they are members) for their individual and collective actions—the system known in England as cabinet government." [120] As Professor Duverger states, in creating a "partial parliamentarism," this Constitution creates consequently a totally different regime.[121]

The Constitution gives the president of the republic special powers, ones which are held in reserve for him in times of emergency and embodied in Article 16; they enable him to

[118] Georges Vedel, "Les sources idéologiques de la Constitution de 1958," in *Commentaires de la Constitution de la Ve République, Études juridiques et économiques,* 23 (November 1959), 5.

[119] Georges Vedel, 5.

[120] David W. S. Lidderdale, *The Parliament of France* (New York: Praeger, 1952), p. 33.

[121] Maurice Duverger, "Les rapports entre le parlement et l'exécutif," in *Commentaires de la Constitution de la Ve République, Études juridiques et économiques,* 23 (November 1959), 5.

address himself to threats to the republic, its institutions and territorial integrity "whenever the regular functioning of the constitutional public authorities has been interrupted." The Constitution creates two legislative houses, the National Assembly and Senate, which are almost of coequal powers, which vote all laws of the regime, but whose powers in lawmaking are severely restricted. A Constitutional Council is required to see to it that the legally separated powers remain within the bounds of their authority, and it may determine only whether the government may modify laws by decree. An amending procedure belongs "both to the President of the Republic on the proposal of the Premier, and to members of Parliament," and all bills for constitutional amendment require passage by identical motions by both assemblies, becoming law only after public approval is registered in a referendum. An alternative route for constitutional amendment also is provided: submission to Parliament convened in a Congress and voted by them by three fifths of the total votes cast. Finally, the Constitution provides for an independent judiciary divided into ordinary and administrative court systems.

The foregoing description of the Constitution offers only a brief glimpse at some of the document's more important features, and a reading of the work is indispensable. When examining it, readers should remain aware of frequent discrepancies between what it orders and actual practices within the French political system. In the France of de Gaulle, the incumbent President often was unrestrained by constitutional provisions, and at times he did not hesitate to act outside the legal framework he created in 1958.[122] Whenever constitutional requirements and political practices diverged, this paradox derived not from juridical inadequacies of brevity and ambiguity—purportedly demanded by Napoleon III in his constitutions—but from the relative nonconcern of the former president of the republic with the primacy of the fundamental law. His Constitution served him well

[122] The final text of the Constitution was adopted September 3, 1958, by the Council of Ministers headed by de Gaulle and including Pinay, Mollet, Soustelle, Debré, Pflimlin, Jacquinot, and others. The following day it was described to the people by de Gaulle in a speech at the *Place de la République,* and on September 28 submitted to the populace and approved by it in a referendum.

whenever it could be employed to command what he felt should exist; and when it proved incompatible with the means he essayed to gain a solution to a problem, occasionally he disregarded it. If the regard of President de Gaulle for the primacy of the Constitution was, however, not of the highest it should be observed that constitutions have not carried under the Fourth and Fifth Republics the significance they have attained in some other countries. Under the Fourth Republic good democrats in the National Assembly often were heedless of constitutional transgressions except when they were perpetrated by the Opposition. Their arguments in behalf of constitutional conformity often were invoked for polemical reasons. In fact, the constitutional debate received from the deputies during the Fourth Republic less attention than many other phenomena that came before that body, being described by some as an everlasting nuisance.[123] President de Gaulle's contempt for constitutional regularity was legendary, and yet can any other leader of France lay claim to receiving from the populace as much support as he received from it? In a referendum, that populace even overwhelmingly endorsed perhaps the most flagrant of his unconstitutional acts, namely, that one in October 1962 when the mode of election of the president of the republic was altered by the most obvious of unconstitutional means.

CONCLUSION

The French presently are involved in broad transformation. Many of the pressures inflicted on them are of external origin. France came late to the modern technological world, and now it must make quick adjustments if it would participate effectively and realistically in the game of "catching up." That effort is subjecting a very conservative people to any number of internal dislocations.

French political and social structures owe a great deal to

---

[123] After May 13, 1958, hours before the National Assembly invested de Gaulle, whose express purpose was to abolish the Fourth Republic and to create a new one in its stead, the Assembly in dispensing with some of its unfinished business turned its attention to an old bill for constitutional reform!

diverse social origins, France's exposed geographical position, centuries of feudalism, royal absolutism, and the French Revolution. The Revolution, which brought national unity to France, found that unity in a community of people, which it declared free and equal, integrating them in a sovereign nation. Some of the changes promoted by the Revolution were vast, introducing a form of political organization different from any that the nation had known previously, prescribing for commoners political liberty and various rights. Yet, some of the Revolution's "solutions" divided the nation for years to come. Certain patterns established themselves in France's post-1789 historical development; among these were the seizure of power, revolutionary action, and diverse forms of political organization ranging from dictatorship to parliamentarism. In 1875 a democratic system arrived with the creation of the "compromise" Third Republic. Along with it came—in Hoffman's words—a "stalemate society" dedicated to the maintenance of traditional values and retention of a certain way of life. However, after 1919 that arrangement was no longer adequate for France's survival in a world in transition. The "stalemate society" terminated with the end of World War II, and a new economic order was adopted. Social changes were accelerated, and unprecedented transformations occurred in French demography. Efforts were undertaken by the state to introduce into the economy changes that will result in the acquisition of a modern industrialization suited to the needs of a modern society. Some societal groups have adjusted to these changes, and others have adopted attitudes apprehensive of transformation. There is, however, no objective indication that state efforts have succeeded in eliminating gross social inequalities, social stratification, low mobility, limited distribution of income, or relieved the plight of those engaged in agriculture. The latter, having languished too long in a chronic state of inefficiency and overprotection, pose a particular problem for the nation. Many of its people—not the workers—are the ones who are endangered by "pauperization."

Finally, the Constitution of the Fifth Republic introduces a rationalized parliamentarism, dependence upon popular consensus and arbitration, and a political system that is entirely different from those of previous regimes.

TWO
FRENCHMEN
IN POLITICS
Political socialization, participation, and recruitment

SOCIALIZATION

Socialization is the term used to describe those processes by
which the child learns to adjust to his society, evolving eventually
into adult membership in it.[1] That evolution involves individual
acquisition of the knack of responding to the demands of society,
and adoption of mechanisms which realize social behavior and
moral norms.

American sociology (which is inclined to start with the
individual) seeks ways in which the individual can be adjusted
to his society; French sociology (which is inclined to regard
society as imposing itself on the individual from the time of his

---

[1] Few articles and books published in English deal with the French
child's socialization. Attention is called to these: Lawrence Wylie, *Village
in the Vaucluse* (New York: Harper & Row, 1965); Rhoda Metraux and
Margaret Mead, *Themes in French Culture: A Preface to a Study of the
French Community* (Stanford, Calif.: Stanford University Press, 1954).
The files of the *American Sociological Review* contain one article on the
subject—Paul-Henri Chombart de Lauwe, "The Interaction of Person and
Society," Vol. 31, No. 2 (April 1966), 237–248. Literature in French
is abundant, and references to much of it appear elsewhere in footnotes in
this chapter.

origin) seeks ways by which the individual will "gradually emerge" from society.[2] Therefore, socialization is not as great a consideration for French sociologists as it is for American ones.[3] The French perspective is global, and it directs attention more toward relationships among persons, and between persons and groups.

French psychology is not in agreement concerning the original nature of the child's relationship to society. Jean Piaget, for example, viewed socialization as the principal formative process in society, and regarded the child not as being born social but as becoming social eventually. He denied the existence of "social instincts," contending that socialization is something that is attained after birth, deriving from the child's relations with other children and adults. For Piaget the child is socialized beginning with his first days of existence and is conditioned from the first by his *milieu*.[4] Piaget contended that socialization operates by imitation. Socialization of thought depends on exchange and cooperation, implying the reciprocity and equality of partners. He argues that the different steps in the evolution of a child's thought are relative to the diverse forms of collective thought contained in societies in evolution.[5] Different relationships exist between the activities of individuals and group coordination, and for Piaget it was a case of techniques, scientific thought, sociocentric ideologies, and the construction of certain general structures for the accommodation of socialization. For Henri Wallon, however, the individual and society are related to each other

[2] Chombart de Lauwe, 238.

[3] Chombart de Lauwe, 238.

[4] See Jean Piaget, "Pensée égocentrique et pensée sociocentrique," *Cahiers internationaux de sociologie,* 10 (1951), 34–49.

[5] Perhaps not too much should be made of the Piaget-Wallon controversy. Those interested might examine Jean Piaget, "Pensée égocentrique . . . ," and Henri Wallon, "Étude psychologique et sociologigue de l'enfant," *Cahiers internationaux de sociologie,* 3 (1947), 3–22. Piaget writes that he presented essentially the same theory as Wallon but "under different terms." He states that Wallon dissociated the biological and the social, "being a victim of the school of Durkheim." Wallon states that he had never separated them, since they are "closely complementary in man from birth."

intimately from the beginning.[6] The group is the initiator and vehicle of social practices, surpassing purely subjective social actions. Within the family group, the child—occupying a given place among parents and brothers and sisters—lays in his apprenticeship for the development of certain relationships and social feelings. As he grows, more and more groups become available to him. Around the third year in his life he discovers in groups the different kinds of relationships that result in his being united with or opposed to his society.[7]

Socialization involves exposure to multiple environments; one is physical, the other human. The physical environment comprises climate, terrain, and temperature. The human environment includes those persons around the individual, the groups to which he belongs, and the complex of social conditions that relate to him directly and indirectly. These multiple environments usually harbor elements of compatibility and incompatibility. Whenever elements of contradiction exist, there usually is some effect on socialization. The family, for example, represents one environment, acting upon the child from birth and normally accompanying him in his development until he achieves maturation. In France that environment is relatively closed; it also is hereditary and ranked. The school represents another environment, which in France is made available to the child suddenly and intrusively at the age of three or four.[8] This environment is broad and hierarchical. Elements of compatibility and incompatibility will derive from the interaction of family and school environments.

Socialization, then, consists of the individual passing through different levels and states. Conscious at first primarily of his physical environment, the child then becomes increasingly aware of himself and those elements of balance and imbalance

---

[6] Wallon, "Étude psychologique . . ."; see also Henri Wallon, "Les groupes et la psychogenèse de l'enfant," *Cahiers internationaux de sociologie,* 16 (1954), 2–13.

[7] Wallon, "Les groupes et la psychologenèse de l'enfant."

[8] See M. Debesse, "L'adolescence est-elle une crise?" *Enfance,* 4–5 (December 1958), 287–302, and by the same author, "L'enfant et le milieu. L'action du milieu sur l'enfant," *Bulletin de psychologie,* Vol. 16, Nos. 19–21 (May 1963), 1121–1138.

that confront him. This marks a further step in his evolution. After having integrated in the family, he is exposed subsequently to environments that are broader than the family and which require further integration by him. Adaptation to that equilibrium demands of him considerable personal effort.

Socialization is reciprocal. The French child until the ages of six or seven has more of a place in adult than in juvenile society. After that, he gravitates toward his contemporaries and is initiated in the processes of reciprocity. The group is a social magnet which attracts the child because it satisfies one or more of his needs (although he may find the members not particularly to his liking; he usually supplements this relationship with relations with friends and neighbors). He achieves reciprocity sometime between his tenth and thirteenth year when he learns to supply the group with what it wishes from him, in turn getting from it what he wants. The group performs at this time a role that is both moral and intellectual, for presentation and exchange of opinions now gain considerable significance in it.[9] Until this time the individual had complied principally with norms that had their origins primarily in the family, school, and play groups.

The group acts as a socializing instrumentality, contributing to formation of the child's personality. The child needs the group. It contributes to his liberation from maternal dependence. Should the child be unacceptable to a given group, he may turn to one or more other groups for identification. Should he find outside his family that he is unacceptable to other groups, this is a reflection of his nonfacility for adaptation. The reasons for his inadaptation may derive from himself or his family environment, or both, and they may be psychological or physiological or biological, or combinations of these variables.[10]

Adolescent groups help fulfill a child's need for autonomy. These groups usually are of spontaneous origin. They absorb individual aggression, enlisting it in behalf of their own expression. They sop up and accommodate feelings of inferiority and

---

[9] See R. Cousinet, *La vie sociale des enfants* (Paris: Éditions du Scarabee, 1958).

[10] R. Fau, *Les groupes d'enfants et d'adolescents* (Paris: Presses Universitaires, 1952).

guilt, acting as a compensatory device. Their roles are dependent upon the extent to which their members can achieve adaptation. Individuals exhibiting high degrees of adaptation usually associate with socializing groups; individuals exhibiting low degrees of adaptation may be led to find membership in regressive groups. If the group's socializing role is established, it helps the individual to make the transition from family to society.

When individual maturation finally is accomplished, the individual often abandons youth groups—primarily because his needs have been served and fulfilled already. Dufrasne's study of youth attitudes relative to youth groups over a period ranging from 1944 to 1962 concludes that such groups respond to individual needs, offering contacts, multiple activities, direct action, and participation.[11] He found that these needs were prevalent primarily in the industrialized regions of France, where children in their daily lives are permitted little initiative.[12] Such groups, he concludes, allowed them to assume responsibility, providing them with a method of affirming and taking cognizance of their real capacities.[13]

Socialization during adolescence to some extent is dependent on the degree to which elements of the individual's old and new environments are in harmony with each other. Full integration with the new society is achieved gradually, the speed being relative to the individual himself. Influencing individual maturation are the individual's position in the family environment, his position relative to the economic and social structures of society, and his responses to stimuli received from the technical environments in which he resides.[14] During this period the individual must learn to adhere to a multiplicity of roles. They must be varied in content and he must develop sufficient flexibility to pass from one role to another. Château notes that some individuals retain a certain "ambiguity" and resist this transforma-

[11] C. Dufrasne, *Étude sur les attitudes des jeunes à l'égard des mouvements de jeunesse de 1944 à 1962.* Unpublished thesis, 3d cycle. (Paris: University of Paris, 1963).

[12] Dufrasne, *Étude sur les attitudes des jeunes.* . . .

[13] Dufrasne, *Étude sur les attitudes des jeunes.* . . .

[14] See Georges Friedman, *Où va le travail humain?* (Paris: Gallimard, 1956).

tion, waiting as late as the age of twenty-five before accomplishing it.[15] Isambert-Jamati observes that the threshold of entry into adulthood usually occurs sooner in large French cities and later in small ones, and earlier among the working class and later among the middle class.[16] Larrue and Malrieu state that socialization is earlier and more complete in the city than in the country due to the existence there of a more intense social life. Exposure to media of communications, such as books and movies, also is greater in the city than in the country.[17]

During adolescence many individuals "slip into" some occupational slot in the society. In fact, "slipping in" is the case only too often. A study by Rousselet shows that there exists in France a lack of guidance and information for adolescents seeking employment in the job market. He concludes that for many of them settling into a job is influenced heavily by their associates, and that there is a lack of real imagination in choices of profession.[18] Another of Rousselet's studies estimates that 30 to 35 percent of French adolescents abandon the possibilities of secondary or technical schooling in order to find immediate salaried employment in commerce or industry. Rousselet attributes this to various factors: (1) geographical origin, whether the area is favored or disfavored economically; (2) family balance, whether the parents are divorced—divorce contributing often to the adolescent's early entrance into the job market; (3) the number of children in the family, this being a factor of early employment, and (4) rank in the family, which leads to the eldest child often being put to work prematurely.[19]

Relationships between parents and children in the French

[15] See Jean Château, *L'enfant et ses conquêtes* (Paris: Vrin, 1960).

[16] V. Isambert-Jamati, "Éducation et maturité sociale dans la France contemporaine," *Cahiers internationaux de sociologie,* 31 (July–December 1961), 129–144.

[17] J. Larrue and P. Malrieu, "Enquête sur l'éducation à la ville et à la campagne," *Enfance,* 1 (January–February 1958), 31–63.

[18] J. Rousselet, "Quelques aspects des ambitions sociales des adolescents," *Enfance,* 3 (1962), 291–308.

[19] J. Rousselet, "Influence des facteurs socio-économique sur la mise au travail des la fin de la periode de scolarité obligatoire," *Enfance,* 4–5 (1958), 407–418.

family are shaped by the physical and social environments in which they live. Studies by Chombart de Lauwe contend that the child who lives in a rural environment enjoys great liberty in almost all areas; he rarely is isolated and generally he benefits from a good family equilibrium and a rather regular family routine.[20] Other studies show that the rural child receives less attention than the urban one, that his parents show less familiarity with him and exercise less intervention in his life.[21] The French Institute of Public Opinion concludes that "If the rural family knows fewer open conflicts, its cohesion is often only on the surface. It is the fruit of a coexistence or of a cohabitation without real dialogue. It is also the most closed to the outside world —and the most depoliticized." [22] Among workers' families the child is affected by the bad conditions of his parents' lives and suffers generally from a lack of companionship. According to de Lauwe, workers' families are "the most sensitive receptors to economic dislocations and social imbalance." The worker's family is preoccupied with maintaining a certain level of existence and constantly is questioning how it can emancipate itself from the difficulties of daily existence. Diet (meat particularly) and housing are of great concern and provide in family gatherings an issue climate which undoubtedly has an affect on the children.[23] In intellectual *ménages,* housing conditions are better, the child has many social contacts—particularly with people outside the family—but sometimes the child is affected by certain irregularities in the life of the family.[24]

The father's presence in the French household and his behavior there are of great importance to the child's socialization. The father's behavior is shaped by what was the performance of

[20] P. H. Chombart de Lauwe, "Études comparatives du comportement des parents envers l'enfant," *Information sociales,* 7 (July 1954), 803–810.

[21] P. Rossi-Brochay, "Parents et nourrissons en milieu rural," *Enfance,* 4 (September–October 1957), 483–489.

[22] Jacques Duquesne, *Les 16–24 ans* (Paris: Le Centurion, 1963), p. 100.

[23] P. H. Chombart de Lauwe, *La vie quotidienne des familles ouvrières* (Paris: Éditions du CNRS, 1956).

[24] Chombart de Lauwe, *La vie quotidienne. . . .*

his father. French psychologists and sociologists concede that one must have had a good father in order to become a good father. If one's father played his "role" properly, then a certain identification is established and assumption of the role by the son is that much easier.[25] Second, the relationship between the father and mother is of great importance to the child.[26] If they both enjoy a satisfactory and reciprocal relationship and perform well in their respective roles, the child will be that much better off as a consequence. If the household lacks a father, the role of the mother is important in relation to the images she assumes and conveys to the child—and they can either harm or better the process of identification. The absence of a father from the family is a variable that plays a dominant role, being exercised in different ways. Hamon, Vergez, and Honore have written convincingly about children who run away from their homes, pointing out that this occurs most frequently in those from which a father is missing.[27] Launay concludes that children who suffer from psychological difficulties often are those who were subjected to maternal domination and insufficient attention by the father.[28] However, presence of the father in the household is in itself not enough to guarantee that the family will function effectively as a unit, for it is fairly common for the father to "resign" from the family while continuing to live inside the family dwelling. Fatigued by his work chores, only too often is he inclined to delegate paternal responsibilities to the mother, and eventually there is confusion and ambiguity relative to his "role" in the family.[29]

The child's rank within the French family is related to his

[25] J. Blanjan-Marcus, "Carences paternelles," *Cahiers de l'enfance* (May 1959), 45–52.

[26] S. A. Dos Santos, "Troubles de la conduite et milieu familial," *Enfance* (1949), 93.

[27] J. Hamon, R. Vergez, and B. Honore, "Problèmes socio-èducatifs dans les collectivites familiales militaires," *Le groupe familial,* 11 (April 1961), 3–16.

[28] C. Launay, "Le role des parents dans la genèse des maladies mentales chez l'enfant," *L'hygiène mentale,* 5 (1959), 233–253.

[29] S. A. Dos Santos, "Troubles de la conduite et milieu familial." The author concludes that the most stable homes are those in which the mother frequently undertakes some form of professional activity.

psychological development and socialization. Mauco and Rambaud, in their study of 791 French children (treated at the Centre psycho-pédagogique of the Academy of Paris), conclude that juvenile inadaptation occurred most frequently among single-child families. Their difficulties often derived from lack of social contacts and family overprotection, being reflected in school in the form of a sense of insecurity. In families having more than one child, instability occurred most frequently (38 percent) with the eldest child. The eldest son went through the Oedipus conflict and fear of castration with difficulty. The eldest and intermediary daughters were the victims especially of family conflicts. Frequently the intermediate son experienced sentiments of inferiority. The eldest of both sexes had difficulty especially when followed by a brother, the intermediary when he had an older brother, the intermediary girl when sandwiched between two sisters, and the "favorite child" especially when there was in the family another child of the same sex. With the birth of another child, jealousy appeared especially when the age difference between the two was less than five years.[30] Descombey and Rocquebrune examined the relationship between the child and his positioning in the family, and concluded that the principal mistake committed by parents of an only child consists in sudden changes in their behavior, in "tightening up" or "clamping down" after the appearance of initial difficulties. Among some of the children they studied such changes provoked a reaction of retreat and passive opposition. They concluded that in families with two children those kinds of behavior that are to be avoided are relative to whether it is an elder child or a newborn infant. The eldest child often is affected by a change that takes place in parental behavior from the time of the birth of the second child. With reference to the younger child, the major error consisted of trying to maintain him in an infantile state and in close dependence upon the family, with the eldest becoming an example to follow or avoid. The authors observed that these two types of parental behavior contributed sometimes to extreme cases of inadaptation, the youngest remaining infantile and the eldest

[30] G. Mauco and P. Rambaud, "Le rang de l'enfant dans la famille," *Revue française de psychanalyse*, 2 (1951), 245–268.

becoming inhibited. The authors concluded that the attitudes of the parents carry influence more or less according to those physiological factors that affect the character of the child. They concede, however, that in each case of juvenile inadaptation to brothers, sisters and the family *milieu,* the character of the subject and those of the sister or brother also are important.[31]

Failure of socialization, or inadaptation, which is the result of discord between the individual and French society, is related to different factors which are biological and physiological, and to mechanisms related to psychological development. Whatever the child's biological and physiological condition, society imposes on the child certain demands, transforming them into norms to which the child is expected to conform. Chombart de Lauwe has studied urban environments in Paris and Bordeaux; after observing several thousand children not suffering from organic problems and all under the age of fourteen, he concluded that environment encourages or discourages hereditary tendencies. He submits that often it is fruitless to argue about the influence of heredity and environment, and that it would be preferable to study relationships between the two areas. A major difficulty exists, however, in attempting to determine such relationships. Social isolation, for example, is a major source of mental illness; however, in such cases determination of the illnesses' hereditary origins can constitute a most difficult task.[32]

HOUSING AND SOCIALIZATION

French housing is difficult to come by, and for years construction has lagged far behind the needs of French society. According to the Fédération patronale du bâtiment, France constructed between 1951 and 1960 on an average of fifty-four living units for every 1000 of population. The average for European countries during the same period was sixty-seven, and for the coun-

[31] J. Descombey and G. Rocquebrune, "L'enfant caractériel parmi ses frères et soeurs hypothèses relatives à l'influence de la situation de l'enfant dans la fratrie sur son comportement," *Enfance,* 5 (1953), 329–368. See also G. Rocquebrune, "L'enfant caractériel parmi ses frères et soeurs," *Enfance,* 5 (1956), 1–33.

[32] M. J. Chombart de Lauwe, *Psychopathologie sociale de l'enfant inadapté* (Paris: Éditions du CNRS, 1959) pp. 35–103. See particularly chaps. II and III dealing with urban ecology and housing.

tries of the European Economic Community, seventy-two. During those years France ranked eleventh in construction of dwellings, surpassing only Italy, Portugal, and Spain.[33] An inquiry conducted in 1961 by the Ministry of Construction produced a dramatic comment on the low estate of French housing. Seventy-six percent of the dwellings examined (all were nonagricultural) were more than twenty-eight years old; 60 percent of the apartments antedate 1914, and 27 percent were constructed before 1870. In the Paris region apartments built in and around 1914 constituted more than 50 percent of the total, whereas those constructed after World War II represented 16 percent of the total. The ministry described only one unit of every three among the 15,000 as being correctly equipped with sanitary equipment—about 16 percent were without water, approximately 16 percent were with water but without a toilet, and 33 percent had water and some sort of water closet but no recognizable sanitary equipment. The ministry described 17 percent of the units as being overcrowded and 8 percent as "critically overpopulated," averaging three persons per room (in the Paris region overpopulation of units was put at 25 percent). Those affected most by this congestion are people who live in the Paris region where the housing situation is critical, and those who can afford to pay only low rents. In 1966 United Nations studies placed France eighth in Europe, with 8.4 units constructed for every 1000 inhabitants. (Ahead of France were Sweden with 12.5, Switzerland 10.1, Germany 10, USSR 9.5, Holland 9.4, Spain 9 and Denmark 8.5. Only Italy is inferior, with 7.5 per 1000.)[34] In 1967 the annual budget was the first since World War II to recognize a slowdown in construction of dwellings, causing astoundment in some social circles. During that year the state financed only 345,000 dwellings (as against 357,000 the previous year), illustrating the "stagnation of French construction."[35]

---

[33] *Le Monde,* March 5–6, 1967, p. 2. Despite these and other figures Premier Georges Pompidou told the nation in 1966 that France is ahead of all Western nations in development!

[34] *Le Monde,* March 5–6, 1967, p. 2.

[35] *Le Monde,* November 9, 1966, p. 1; it should be recognized that French expectations in housing are modest and that the French are not likely to react as strongly against substandard housing as residents of

Having cited data illustrative of the bad condition of French housing, attention is turned now to its effects on French society. The consequences relative to the physical health of the society are well identified, producing in measurable quantities imperfections in physique, increased mortality rates, and greater incidence of contagious diseases. Too often neglected, however, are its effects on the mental health of the society. Studies by Chombart de Lauwe show that the indices "number of persons per room" has a determining role on the behavior of French families and interpersonal relations, and that generally the psychological problems of children tend to increase when they reside in over-congested conditions of housing—particularly when two to three persons occupy a single room. He concludes that there is a "clear elevation" in nervous, violent, and aggressive children when the population of dwellings attains 2 to 2.5 persons per room, and that under such conditions parental repressiveness is inclined to increase. Two thirds of runaway children come from dwellings characterized by at least two inhabitants per room. Chombart de Lauwe also has discovered that difficulties systematically appear more frequently when occupation of a room in a dwelling exceeds more than two persons.[36]

A study by Hausknecht has inquired into the influence of housing conditions on parent-child relations.[37] Children from primary schools situated in the department of the Seine were studied; they had been suffering from psychological disorders and were sent to the Center of Observation in Vitry (Seine) for periods of three to five months for treatment. The ages of the children ranged from four to twelve years, all IQ's were superior

some other countries. See for example "Une république de mal-loges," *Le nouvel observateur,* 120 (March 1–8, 1967), pp. 20–24, reporting an inquiry by the French Institute of Public Opinion in which 5 of every 10 respondents disapprove of the government's housing policy, and yet 8 of every 10 consider themselves satisfied with their lodging (although more than 2 million families fall within the discontent category).

[36] M. J. Chombart de Lauwe, *Psychopathologie sociale. . .* ; see also P. H. Chombart de Lauwe, *La maladie mentale comme phénomène social, Études de socio-psychiatrie,* Monograph No. 7 (Paris: Institut national d'hygiene, 1955), pp. 11–36.

[37] A. Hausknecht, "Conditions de vie et troubles du caractère d'enfants admis au centre d'observation," *Journées internationales des Centres psycho-pédagogiques de langue française,* 5 (July 1954), 119–126.

to 85, and 500 dossiers were studied over a period of two and a half years. The standards of living of the families from which the children came were low. Approximately 40 percent of the children came from Paris, the locale for some of the most inadequate housing in the nation. Thirteen percent of the children lived in one-room dwellings; only 38 percent slept alone in a bed. About half of the children came from families in which the family head was a manual worker. Interviews with some of the parents revealed that more than half felt that poor housing conditions influenced directly parental "nervousness" relative to their children. The study concludes that the importance and gravity of the sanctions employed by the parents appeared to be related directly to the nature of their housing, subject in turn to certain modifications deriving from *milieu* and the presence or non-presence in the dwelling of the wife during the day. Aggressive external behavior tended to increase with increases in housing density. Although the author of the study was unable to verify the preponderant influence of bad housing on mental health, he did raise questions and possibilities which demand further research.[38]

Bad housing definitely is a factor in juvenile delinquency. A study by Lamotte shows that in Rennes 60 percent of the delinquents came from overpopulated homes.[39] In Montpellier the figure was 73 percent, and in Angers 70 percent. However, the Regional Association of Rennes also was forced to conclude that "the importance of the dwelling in the inadaptation of the young appears secondary in relation to other factors relating to a general deficiency in the family environment," and the Marseilles Société de patronage remarked on the great difficulty of extricating family from social factors and assessing the respective influences.[40] It appears that housing is a factor of juvenile delinquency but that only rarely is it a determinant of it and the unique element of imbalance. The family environment plays a primary role in inadaptation, and bad housing has an influence on the child in that it disturbs this *milieu*.[41]

[38] Hausknecht, "Conditions de vie. . . ."

[39] M. Lamotte, "Logement et délinquance," *Cahiers de l'enfance,* 5 (March 1954), 47–63.

[40] Lamotte, "Logement et délinquance."

[41] Lamotte, "Logement et délinquance."

"THE 16–24-YEAR-OLDS"

Les 16–24 ans is the result of a study authored by Jacques Duquesne under the auspices of the French Institute of Public Opinion.[42] Fifteen hundred young people, all within the ages of sixteen and twenty-four, who lived in 127 different parts of the nation and who belonged to all social categories, were surveyed. The report helps to explain the feelings and attitudes of the younger generation in France. The results are relatively easy to describe. This group appeared to be apprehensive of the future, serious, and conformist, and rarely among those interrogated were there any "signs of revolt." [43] Confidence appeared to decrease according to the professional categories to which they belonged, among farmers, workers and salaried employees being more limited than among others. Paradoxically, high salaries were a reason for concern; many acknowledged their fear of crisis and wondered if affluence would remain. The primary concern among the respondents appeared to be that of sustaining their health, and after that their next concern was with money.[44] Risk taking appeared not to be one of their preoccupations; considerable weight was given to prudence. When asked "If you had the choice of professions which would you choose?" they expressed their preferences in the following order: technicians, journeymen workers, the liberal professions, engineering, and chemistry. The occupations of farmers, civil servants, office workers, and businessmen were given low priority, ascending in that order from the bottom of the list. Noticeably absent was a preference for adventurous and dramatic professions such as the military, air, navy, and exploration, these being midway on the list.

Political indifference was particularly strong among the group—20 percent being completely disinterested in politics, 47

[42] Duquesne, *Les 16–24 ans.*

[43] Duquesne, pp. 207, 235. They were asked to cite "the three things of which deprivation would be most serious"—43 percent responded health, 18 percent money, 13 percent love, 7 percent liberty, 5 percent work, 4 percent religion, and 3 percent friends. Insofar as the phenomenon of socialization is concerned, the 3 percent accorded "friends" should not be ignored.

[44] Duquesne, pp. 207, 235.

percent greatly disinterested, and only 3 percent being very interested. Young workers, in particular (they formed 28 percent of the group), appeared to be exposed relatively little to the exterior world; they were less attached to traditional values and more integrated in the modern world, however, than agricultural workers. Marxism appeared to have made little headway among them. The young employees who were interrogated appeared to be "tuned in," insofar as the world is concerned, and students, although not necessarily "tuned in," had greater access to communications media and, consequently, were more open to the outside world. Political disinterestedness was greater among females than males. The group's disinterest in politics should not be equated with rejection of collective action, however, for 61 percent favored union action, and 43 percent indicated that they already favored and belonged to a union, or that they favored unions and intended to join one.[45] Such responses suggest receptiveness to economic action more than to political action.

The religious identification of those interrogated was in almost nine out of every ten cases Catholicism (3 percent were Protestant, 8 percent "no religion").[46] Among the group existed the conviction, however, that "dechristianization" is coming—only 7 percent thought religion more important for their generation than for their parents' generation, while 47 percent thought it less important (a belief that tended to be prevalent more in

[45] Duquesne, pp. 138–141.

[46] Duquesne, p. 221. The study classified the respondents in four categories: (1) regularly practicing Catholics, constituting about one-third of the group, there being three females for every two males, with better representation in the country than in the city; (2) occasionally practicing Catholics, representing about 37 percent of the entire group, there being about the same number of females as males, with former students of primary schools and people in cities ranging from 2000 to 100,000 inhabitats numerous in this group; (3) nonpracticing Catholics, constituting about 18 percent of the entire group, there being three men for every two women. Industrial workers and employees of average and large-size cities are well represented in this group; (4) members of other religions and "no religion," constituting 3 percent Protestants and 8 percent "no religion," with equal representation of men and women. Individuals over twenty-one years of age were more numerous in this group. For every 100 persons in the "no religion" group, 29 were children of industrial workers, 23 of employees, 16 of merchants, and 12 of agricultural workers.

large than in small population centers). In the rural areas only 16 percent fell into the "nonpracticing" and "no religion" categories. Industrial workers appeared to be the most "dechristianized," 37 percent falling in the "nonpracticing" and "no religion" categories. It appears altogether that religious practice had not a determinate influence on the attitudes of the majority. The study concludes that practicing Catholics gave a priority to material things and showed little interest in "spiritual values"— "For them, Christianity is more an *ensemble* of exterior values, of moral rules—from which they tend to liberate themselves progressively—than a life." [47]

The study conveys the preoccupation of the subjects generally with material things, their disinclination to assume responsibilities, their sense of individualism and the slight importance they extend to friends, and their greater concern with comfort than love. The study concludes that this youth collectively is not very youthful, being endowed instead with "the attitudes of an old man." [48]

Les 16–24 ans contains interesting data concerning participation in youth groups. Only 22 percent of the 1500 respondents belonged to youth groups, and only 6 percent belonged to several.[49] Half of those who belonged to youth groups were affiliated with movements or institutions whose activities are cultural, educational, professional, tourist, political, and so on. Cultural and educational organizations comprised 12 percent of the individuals, whereas student organizations accounted for 2.5 percent, scouting 2.2 percent, and professional organizations 1.4 percent.[50] Political organizations accounted only for 1.1 percent, confirming the slight interest of youth in political groups. Who joined these various clubs? The largest single category consisted of students, followed by employees, workers, and agricultural workers. Agricultural workers appear to have been attracted primarily to cultural and educational organizations, but scarcely to political ones. Workers exhibited a preference for sports clubs, and to a lesser extent for educational and cultural

[47] Duquesne, p. 231.
[48] Duquesne, p. 231.
[49] Duquesne, p. 216.
[50] Duquesne, p. 216.

associations—but hardly for political clubs. Finally, more women than men participated in youth organizations.

The study concludes that membership in youth groups is "rather rare," and it interprets this phenomenon as the consequence of the "refusal of commitment, flight from responsibilities, and concern with independence." [51] Further inquiry into levels of participation revealed them as having been low-level.[52]

EDUCATION AND SOCIALIZATION

There are different types of educational systems. One type, the traditional one, is based on the authoritarian school. Another type, the democratic one, is based on the liberal school; it accepts the child as a juvenile, contributing various of its efforts to his socialization. A third, the libertarian type, is based on the *laisser être* school (not *laisser faire*); it is divorced from the adult world and generally free from all reference to the future. The French educational system, which is of the first type, also incorporates within it elements of the second type. No part of the French educational system is of the third type. Private schools which fall within the second type are few in number. For example, the Petite école du Père Castor, situated formerly in Paris and located now in Sceaux (a *commune* approximately four miles south of Paris), attempts to combine on the primary level elements of intellectual and manual effort accompanied by relatively relaxed supervision and discipline. By French standards it is classified as progressive, "new," or "active"; by American standards it is less than progressive and other than conservative.

By and large, the French school plays a selective role, bearing an undeniable relationship to the social structure of the country. Its socializing role is played more within class than among classes. The American public school, or "common school" attended by all, has been much criticized by some Europeans for

---

[51] Duquesne, p. 216.

[52] Duquesne, p. 216. Participation in church organizations exceeds participation in educational associations (some educational associations are Catholic, however). Within cultural and educational clubs, 12 percent were practicing Catholics, 6 percent occasional practicers, 5 percent non-practicers, and 4 percent were without religious preferences.

its academic "watering down" and its social-leveling tendencies. Whatever its inadequacies, it has played, nonetheless, a significant role as an intrumentality of socialization, doing that job rather well and serving as a unit of nation building (although not in all respects, for instance, racial relations). France never has had one "common school." For a long time the elite was educated one way, and "the others" in other ways. The elite received a training that was classical, and the others obtained whatever they could (vocational education, for example, was not introduced until 1919).

Before the French Revolution secondary education was dispensed by Jesuits to only a few; primary education was given by the Christian Brothers' Order to not many more. In 1789 approximately half the society was illiterate. After the Revolution, education—although defined by the Constitution of 1791 as "common to all citizens"—remained for a long time limited and elitist. *Lycées* and secondary colleges were created by Napoleon for the training of civil administrators and military officials drawn from the middle class. State primary education was later created by the Third Republic, as a vehicle for educating the popular class. Technical education was introduced subsequently for the purpose of training workers. Related to the creation of these different types of schools were certain aspects of social class. "In the 19th century each of these schools developed a distinct closed sector having as its mission to teach its own particular clientele and to recruit it on social rather than scholastic criteria. Instead of following each other, the educational sectors paralleled each other." [53] All three systems from time of introduction were of separate origin, an individuality they retain to the present day. Lacking among them are paths of continuity, the separate establishments being noncomplementary. All are under the Ministry of Education, but due to the trilateral nature of the system coordination is resorted to only on a limited scale and efforts frequently are duplicative. State educational services are supplied free of cost or at nominal cost, the presumption being that financial considerations will not preclude student participa-

---

[53] W. R. Fraser, *Education and Society in Modern France* (London: Routledge, 1963), p. 21. Fraser is quoting a publication of the Ministry of Education, 1957.

tion in any level of the system (a questionable presumption in a society in which class differentiations are common and in which the distribution of wealth is limited).

Bound up with French education is the idea of *culture général;* literature, history, science, philosophy, and the arts are all viewed as being characterized by a certain discipline of intellect. The vehicles are classics and mathematics, and when the graduate of the system has long forgotten the details, he will retain, theoretically, a residue of logic.[54] Associated also with the history of French education is a cultural tradition that professes to contain and transmit to the student certain humanizing and liberating values. This tradition is expected to be sustained and passed on to others, both inside and outside France. It is presumed that it will be retained by the recipient of formal education long after he has concluded his schooling. It is based on the conviction that the very best of that which is cultural has its roots in things French. This view permeates French society, being by no means confined to but several segments of it. The late Léon Blum, for example, who was broad, humane, and an internationalist, frequently and with great pride derived his standards from sources which were almost exclusively French. And the French newspaper *Le Monde,* when opposing some years ago a rise in overseas postal rates, protested, for example, that the decision, in effect, would amount to a denial of French culture to subscribers in other countries (this, undeniably, was a slap also at the Gaullist regime, calling it to task on the basis of one of the General's favorite themes).

French education is structured so that elementary or primary education continues from the age of six until the student goes to a secondary *collège* or *lycée,* or to a technical school, or to work. The age of fifteen represents that critical stage in a student's life when many aspects of his ultimate destiny are decided. If he enters a *lycée* or *collège,* he embarks upon the path of academic training in pursuance of the baccalaureate; if he secures the *bac,* he may then enter the university. If he enters a technical school, he begins training for a profession, and his destiny will not be tied to the university. According to Fraser, secondary schools, technical schools, and supplementary courses

[54] Fraser, p. 21.

(given for limited periods of time in primary schools to their graduates) receive 85 percent of the children of members of the liberal professions, senior civil servants, and administrators; 68 percent of the children of industrialists; 55 percent of the children of junior civil servants, clerks, and foremen; 39 percent of the children of shopkeepers and artisans; 20 percent of the children of industrial workers; and 12 percent of the children of farmers and agricultural workers.[55] Higher education trains fewer people than lower education. Those who fail to go on to higher education, that is to say, the great mass, remain undereducated. The result is waste of a great resource which the nation needs but which it fails to utilize. The fact that the educational system fails to supply some needs of French society was acknowledged in 1956 by the Sarrailh committee, when it verified that the needs of agriculture, commerce and industry then exceeded the number of technicians available.

Education reforms passed in 1960 seek to remedy some of the inadequacies of French education. They prescribe that every child should be educated commensurate with his abilities. Children are to be differentiated and relegated to one of three educational categories: (1) those qualifying for the long course of education leading to the university; (2) those qualifying for a long course of education comprising few abstract concepts and theories; (3) those not qualifying for a long course of education who will prepare for an occupation and leave school at the minimum age.[56]

---

[55] Fraser, p. 54.

[56] See La documentation française, *France* (Paris: Georges Lang, 1964), pp. 104–109. The educational categories and sequences are as follows: (1) *Ages two to six, nursery school*. (2) *Ages six to eleven, elementary school*. Curriculum includes French, reading, writing, mathematics, science, history, geography, civics, moral and physical education, art, music, crafts. (3) *Ages eleven to thirteen, Course of Observation*. Follows elementary education and lasts two years. At the end of first quarterly term a Guidance Council makes first report to parents, recommending course of study for the child. The parents must then decide whether the child continues or changes to another course and possibly another school, if the course is available only elsewhere. At the end of Course of Observation parents may send the child to type of school recommended by the Guidance Council, or select a course of education other than that recommended by the Guidance Council, for which the

The French educational system expects students to learn at diverse rates; it recognizes that some learn better than others. A priority is extended to intellectual performance and contributions. Each student in the school is on his own, for better or for worse, and there is little emphasis on the student body as a collective entity. There is no conviction that all form "one large group." In fact, among students there is slight affinity for group affiliation, "pairing off" being more the tradition. Consequently, atomization is regarded not as unusual but as a way of life. Stress within the curriculum on cultural education is extensive but related only slightly to *the group,* or *groups.* Henri Chatreix, writing in 1946, commented that "the school is not designed with a view to the productivity of the group, nor even to its

---

child may qualify by passing an entrance examination. (4) *Ages thirteen to eighteen, five different courses possible:* (a) *Final State of Elementary Education,* involving two years of the Course of Observation plus three years of general education, leading to preparation for positions in agriculture, crafts, commerce or industry, granting *Certificate d'études primaires élémentaires* which cites the work for which the recipient has been prepared. (b) *Short Course of General Education,* involving two years of the Course of Observation plus three years given in Colleges of General Education (*Collèges d'enseignement général*), training for lower-level nontechnical supervisory positions and entrance to teachers colleges, granting a *Brevet d'enseignement général* (General Education Certificate). (c) *Longer Course of General Education,* dispensed in classical, modern and technical secondary schools known as *lycées,* involving after two years of the Course of Observation four years of study in one of the several sections, followed by a preliminary examination, and another year of study in one of five sections—philosophy, experimental sciences, elementary mathematics, mathematics and technology, human and economic sciences. Completed by granting of baccalaureate. (d) *The Shorter Course of Vocational Education,* involving training of skilled workers in a three-year course, which may be preceded by a one-year preparatory class, which follows the period of Observation, and granting the *Certificat d'aptitude professionnelle* (certificate of professional aptitude). (e) *The Longer Course of Vocational Education,* starting after the period of Observation, training skilled technicians in four years and granting them *agent technique breveté,* and middle rank management personnel technicians in five years, granting them *technicien breveté.* Final stage of technician training leads to *technicien supériêur breveté.* (5) *Over eighteen, the university.* (6) *The Great Schools.* Exist parallel to the universities and differ from them in that they prepare for important professions.

cohesion, it is designed for the integral development of each individual." [57]

Despite some recent reforms, democratization of education remains relatively insignificant in France. Duquesne's *Les 16–24 ans* revealed that, among those interrogated in his survey, 55 percent of the children of agricultural workers and 42 percent of the children of industrial workers terminated their studies at or before the age of fourteen.[58] Children of bourgeois parents remained, however, in educational institutions on an average until the age of eighteen. His respondents evidenced a kind of "fatalism"; some believed that their lot in life derived from circumstances imposed on them by the national social structure.[59] That attitude was prevalent particularly among the sons of industrial and agricultural workers.[60] And when asked the question, "Have you undertaken the studies you wanted?" 29 percent responded *tout a fait* (completely), 38 percent said "in part," and 33 percent answered negatively.[61] The study concludes that "access to knowledge and culture remains closed to the great majority of young French for reasons of a material and financial nature." [62] A majority of the respondents (59 percent) had begun work at or around sixteen years of age.[63]

The *lycée,* known for its selectivity, both of teachers and students, and the way in which it trains students hard and well, remains an object of common criticism because of the narrowly restricted social clientele to which it caters. Among its instructional staff rests the conviction that different types of education exist justifiably for different types of intelligence. Classical education is offered to those invested with and capable of express-

---

[57] Henri Chatreix, *Au-delà du laicisme* (Paris: Éditions du Seuil, 1946), p. 112; see also Fraser, 53, who quotes M. C. Brunold, Inspector-General of Secondary Education: "We must recognize that the Frenchman is, generally speaking, not given to cooperation. . . . This distaste is due in part to the fact that we have insufficiently developed the community spirit in a youth whose activity is sometimes marked by an excessive individualism."

[58] Duquesne, p. 17.
[59] Duquesne, p. 18.
[60] Duquesne, p. 18.
[61] Duquesne, p. 18.
[62] Duquesne, p. 37.
[63] Duquesne, p. 37.

ing theoretical intelligence; the locale for this is the *lycée,* that place for the "highly gifted." However, those endowed with good but nonetheless practical and nontheoretical minds are fit best for modern or technical education, while those of limited intelligence can do themselves and others a service by not attempting more than primary school education.[64] It is not that *lycée* teachers are infested with a strong antidemocratic bias. Most argue that democratization of education is desirable, and generally they concede that the institutions in which they teach are restricted to a very limited social selection. In fact, many would prefer as *lycée* students more sons of farmers and workers; yet it is questionable whether many would welcome a large influx of such social categories, for many of them feel that this would lead to a leveling down of the *lycée* and subsequent destruction of its high standards. These instructors cannot be described as social snobs who do not wish to associate with large numbers of less-favored social categories; nevertheless, they offer some resistance to large-scale social mobility when it is at odds with *their image* of the best in academic standards.

While recognizing fully the quality of its academic instruction, the *lycée* constitutes, nonetheless, a barrier to socialization, playing a role that accentuates certain divisions in French society. Receiving only those who are defined as "gifted," the decision as to who is and who is not gifted is made at so early an age that often such valuations are based more on social background and origins than on intelligence and aptitudes. Many children from farmer and worker social categories offer considerable intellectual resources but they are diverted into production at an early age and deprived of the instruction that would develop their potentialities.[65] Nonetheless, the *lycée* continues to educate its elites, and the French educational system continues to undereducate the popular class, irrespective of the potentialities of some of its members, despite the fact that they are entitled to free education and equality of educational opportunity, all of which become less meaningful and more theoretical at

[64] Viviance Isambert-Jamati, "La rigidité d'une institution: structure scolaire et système de valeurs," *Revue française de sociologie,* Vol. 7, No. 3 (July–September 1966), 315.

[65] André Philip, *Pour un socialisme humaniste* (Paris: Plon, 1960), pp. 41–42.

advanced levels when accessibility to them is determined primarily by social and economic rather than intellectual phenomena. A state that is noticeably stratified socially cannot realistically presuppose the absence of financial barriers blocking the path of students seeking to continue their educations.

Lycée instruction is associated with the idea of *lente imprégnation* (slow impregnation), a concept that is of aristocratic perspective. The brochure of the Société des agrégés states that "secondary instruction has this profound originality in that it constitutes a long and patient initiation in advanced instruction." Students are prepared at a certain pace for integration in the middle class, but not for their integration in French society as a whole. Finally, there is no indication that the *lycée* is prepared to deviate from its chosen course. Professor Isambert-Jamati views the *lycée* as an institution that defies change and fears *démantelement;* she cites the way in which in the modern age it holds on to classical education as an effective method of resisting *primarisation.* Her study of 500 prize award speeches delivered in *lycées* over a 100-year period shows by them an increasing trend toward cultural impregnation objectives, a tendency, she states, that may be interpreted as a reaction to educational reforms.[66]

Pierre Bourdieu describes the French school system as a factor of social conservation, "legitimizing" social inequalities and giving its sanction to a "cultural heritage" and social gift it treats as "natural." A son of a high civil administrator has eighty times more chance of entering the university than the son of an agricultural worker, and twice that of the son of a middle-level civil administrator. Bourdieu concedes that only three out of every ten families prefer to send their children to *lycées,* but he contends that those families of popular and lower middle class origin who decline this preference do so because to do otherwise would be to wish for the impossible. He argues that the statement that the *lycée* "is not for us" is based only too often on the knowledge that "we do not have the means." [67] He concludes

---

[66] Viviane Isambert-Jamati, p. 317.

[67] Pierre Bourdieu, "L'école conservatrice: Les inégalités devant l'école et devant la culture," *Revue française de sociologie,* Vol. 7, No. 3 (July–September 1966), 331.

that the system, although it pretends to neutrality, is a perpetu-
ator of social inequalities—that it treats socially conditioned
aptitudes "as inequalities or gifts of merit" and makes them into
law. In other words, his contention is that the system deals with
social and economic differences in qualitative terms, legitimizing
transmission of the cultural heritage enjoyed by but one segment
of society.[68] He concludes that the system functions so as to enable the elite to justify being what it is, and less privileged classes
are allocated elsewhere because it is assumed that it is "natural"
for them to be "what they are." [69]

ATTITUDES AND EDUCATION

According to the studies of Lobrot, the attitudes of diverse social
categories vary relative to education. Socially and economically
favored categories display more of a liberal and cooperative attitude toward education, whereas less favored social categories
exhibit toward it an attitude that is more repressive and less
cooperative. On the doctrinal level, however, favored social
categories display toward education convictions that, paradoxically, are unusually rigid. Lobrot suggests that the authoritarian attitudes of less-favored social categories relative to education might possibly be explained by great anxiety due to the
tensions working on them, reflecting on the child by the intermediary of educational attitudes.[70]

In some social *milieux* entrance into school gives rise to
certain negative attitudes by the parents relative to education.
Studies by Lanneau and Malrieu, for example, show that parents
who reside in the country generally hope for their children's educational success, and yet they are inclined sometimes to consider
educational work as other than "real work" and not a contribution to the progress of their farms. Frequently they provide little
real stimulation for the child; often such children are led to

---

[68] Bourdieu, "L'école conservatrice. . . ," p. 342.
[69] Bourdieu, "L'école conservatrice. . . ," p. 342.
[70] M. Lobrot, "Sociologie et attitudes éducatives," *Enfance,* 1
(January–February 1962), 69–83.

imitate their parents in "sterile fashion." A child of twelve or thirteen frequently is expected to act not as a child but as an adult—not just any adult, however, the image actually being that of the father. Rural exhibitions which exhort the child to "get up there and drive the tractor like papa" are frequent. Thus, although entrance into school may provide such a child with a certain autonomy from the family, inculcation in the child within the autonomous area of certain attitudes may produce a conflict with those expressed in the home by the parents.[71]

On the other hand, well-to-do social categories are preoccupied often with their children's scholarly attainments. In fact, studies show that the more elevated the category, the greater the concern. This is not to say, however, that the preoccupation necessarily is substantive insofar as education itself is concerned. Often it is with the trappings of formal education, and in different ways bound up with class. A well-to-do bourgeois family with a background of formal education, may feel, for example, social embarrassment if their child is unable to qualify for entrance into the *lycée*. That means that the child is destined for a technical school and that he may never enter the university. While in the technical school he will be associated with colleagues of worker origins. Sometimes the university-educated father is inclined to view this turning as a "tragedy," and perhaps it will be seen that way even by the *fils à papa* himself. The hiring of tutors and frequent admonitions of "What's going to happen to you if you don't get into the *lycée?*" are not unusual in well-to-do bourgeois families. The pressures on such children are great, and in some cases they have led to real rather than imaginary

[71] G. Lanneau and P. Malrieu, "Enquête sur l'éducation en milieu rural et en milieu urbain," *Enfance,* 4 (January–February 1958), 465–482. This study was conducted in the Toulouse region. The authors noticed gaps among student educational performance in rural, urban and social *milieux.* They conclude that children in large cities do better than children in small cities and rural areas, and that children from families of the intellectual *milieux* and liberal professions do better than children of workers in industry and agriculture. They also contend that the child who comes from a family comprising few children, when long intervals exist between their births, does better than children who are less isolated in the family complex.

tragedies. Considerable criticism of the educational system resulted some years ago from a small child's suicide after he had failed to pass his educational examinations.

LES GRANDES ÉCOLES

Existing alongside the universities are the *grandes écoles,* or great schools, which differ from the university in that they prepare people for important positions in the upper ranks of the civil service, education, commerce, industry, army, navy, and public health services. Entrance is by competitive examination and acceptance is available only for a limited number of those who qualify. The great schools are all work, and practices sometimes followed in the universities are not tolerated (for example, doing a "bit of reading" and preparation in the spring for end-of-the-year examinations). Examinations are difficult and frequent, and attendance is compulsory (which, unlike the university, usually precludes the student's taking outside work). The great schools comprise less than 15 percent of the total student population. In them the rate of failure is low, being under 3 percent; they receive the elite to start with, and they produce top scientists, engineers, and technocrats. Approximately 150 such schools exist in all of France. The two which undoubtedly are the most famous are the École polytechnique and the École normale supérieure; in a sense, both comprise the elite of an elite. The École polytechnique trains army officers and military and civilian engineers. The École normale supérieure, although designed originally to train secondary school teachers, confers the *licence* and *agrégation* and represents one of the best paths to university teaching and research.[72] Other famous great schools are the École nationale supérieure d'ingénieurs (ENSI), for the training of engineers, the École nationale d'administration (ENA), for the training of high civil servants, and the École des hautes études

---

[72] The *licence* is a university degree intermediate between the bachelor and doctoral degrees. The *agrégation,* granted after participation in a competition, declares the *agrégé* competent to teach in a *lycée* or *faculté.*

commerciales, the Institut national agronomique, and the various Instituts de sciences politiques, and so on.[73]

Despite their high-caliber training programs and enormous prestige, the great schools fall short of producing for the nation enough technical leaders. The Boulloche committee, which sought in 1961 to "define the conditions of development, recruitment, functioning and sitting of the *grandes écoles*," stated that they were not turning out a sufficient number of engineers, and that it was necessary to create in the provinces additional schools of engineering (somewhat more than 40 percent of engineers were then trained in the Paris region, resulting in neglect of the provinces). The committee also was critical of requirements for entrance into the great schools, suggesting that school records instead of competitive examinations suffice, a recommendation to which Prime Minister Pompidou, partisan of the competitive examination, took exception. Finally, the committee called attention to the need for engineering schools to involve themselves more with practicality, communications, and team training.

French education is concerned with the training of elites. However, one look at the great schools should convince the observer that French education has not enlarged its elites sufficiently to supply the greatest needs of the nation. France is a nation of high production; it lacks, however, enough people to exercise leadership in fields of production. That could be achieved by educating a larger number of elites, or by mass production of

[73] See Chapter 9 for comments on the ENA, or National School of Administration; The Pompidou cabinet, created April 15, 1962, which included in addition to the prime minster, five ministers of state, two ministers delegate, fourteen ministers, and seven secretaries of state, contained eight graduates of the old École libre des sciences politiques (predecessor of the present Institut d'études politiques of the University of Paris), and three graduates of the École normale supérieure. Other schools represented were École d'études supérieures de droit (1), École nationale des langues orientales (2), École des hautes études commerciales (1), École du Louvre (1), Oxford University (1), École de Grignon (1), Academy of International Law at the Hague (1), École nationale de la France d'outre-mer (1), École polytechnique (1), École nationale d'administration (2), Centre des hautes études administratives (1), École des arts et métiers (1). For details see Ambassade de France (Service de presse et d'information), "The Composition of the Pompidou Cabinet," No. 136 (April 19, 1962), pp. 1–7.

elites. Various proposed educational reforms acknowledge the need, but the process is difficult to implement in a society geared so long to the idea of producing restricted elites. It also is difficult to achieve in a country which only recently has become highly industrialized with a market of mass consumers. Many reforms have been promulgated recently in French education, but few foresee drastic overhaul of the system in order to remedy this imbalance. It now appears that the Ministry of Education is not yet prepared to address itself fully to the necessities of educating *for* national existence.[74] High-level specialists must be educated in sufficient number so that the society may cope fully with technical, social and psychological problems of contemporary existence.

CIVIC EDUCATION

France gives little attention to civic education—and few Frenchmen complain about its neglect. Civil-mindedness is not a French preoccupation, for the Frenchman's sense of community is less than well developed. This is not to say, however, that he is necessarily anticommunity. It is only to say that the Frenchman sees himself as an individual and others as individuals too, not as a collective entity. Few societies have developed so deeply among their citizens this attitude of "I am as I am. Accept me or reject

---

[74] See P. Dandurand, *Essai sur l'image de la société dans les manuels de lecture au cours moyen* (Paris: University of Paris, 1962), unpublished doctoral dissertation, Faculty of Letters. The author concludes that there are undeniable discrepancies between social reality and the images of reality presented in primary school texts and manuals, which he attributes to resistance to or ignorance of a technical and industrial society. He studied the texts and manuals used in primary schools between 1930 and 1961 in order to determine the images they seek to develop. He noticed that over the thirty-year span there occur increasing references to "life in the country"; that during this period the principal institution was always the family, but greater significance was extended to it in 1961 than in 1930; that an increasing importance is attributed to the middle class, often at the expense of the working class; that there occurs a steady evolution in the direction of what is described as moral neutrality and that encounters with moral themes occur with diminishing frequency, although some new ones appear as old ones disappear; that the image of the adult remains relatively fixed and stable, although the portrait of the child becomes increasingly less idealized.

me, but don't try to make me over." When this outlook becomes exaggerated, it takes the form of isolated individualism and its influence on social atomization is correspondingly greater.

The slight attention extended to civic education is not at odds with the Frenchman's image of community. Nor has its neglect necessarily much to do with the French lack of *civisme*—unless one believes that *civisme* results from teaching facts about French government and telling students what they owe to society and what it owes to them.[75] Civic education has been a fact of American public and private instruction for many years, emphasizing democratic values and behavior, and yet it would be difficult to prove that it has succeeded in producing a "nation of democrats." In French education, the real lack insofar as *civisme* is concerned is in the absence from the school of groups which contribute to the molding of social cohesiveness. In fact, their absence drives students toward social isolation. French education has yet to recognize that existence means group existence. The American student body may offer some humorous examples of rhetoric and behavior; nonetheless, it does encourage and make available to students groups and the channels by which group affiliations can be established. A multiplicity of groups, from the stamp club to the athletic team, cover a wide range of possible interests, accommodate diverse tastes, and draw to themselves even those with complicated antisocial tendencies, modifying those tendencies in the process.

When considering French education, one should not be turned away from its real problems and diverted to such themes as the authoritarianism of its teachers, the haughtiness of their behavior, and the ruthlessness with which they allocate educational honors and prizes. Although such images have been exploited for years in American literature, the fact is that many French teachers differ little from their American counterparts. Many are not obedient "children of Descartes" who seek to hammer into the child a rationalistic positivism without regard for other approaches and considerations. These teachers are not held ruthlessly in the grip of the syllabus of the Ministry of Education. These teachers are, however, part of a "system" which owes its

---

[75] *Civisme* is that "civic spirit" which is charactertistic of the responsible citzen, in distinction to the isolated and irresponsible citizen.

origins to a great militarist and which is administered in rigid bureaucratic fashion from that immovable stone building known as the Ministry of Education. Like any number of American teachers confronted with their own local "ministries," or boards of education, they also want change and more freedom to determine the standards of their own trade. Any number of these teachers regard the child as both a social being and an educable person. They acknowledge that education proceeds at diverse rates, and they would like the ministry to be aware of it too. Too often are these teachers judged by the pronouncements of the Ministry of Education—and this can be as shortsighted as judging American teachers by the statements of some of their boards of education. Wylie acknowledges in his study of Peyrane discrepancies between the directives of the ministry and what the teachers actually do: "After all, the teachers are French and consequently recognize the gap that usually separates laws and regulations on the one hand from actual practices on the other." [76] He concedes that in practice the educational program is "far from being as rigid and impersonal as it seems." [77]

An increasing number of French teachers are demanding in the educational system inclusion of some form of "training for life." In the elementary school learning usually is by rote and removed from the realities of existence. The technical high school does not "train for life"—it trains students occupationally and gives them bits and pieces of a few academic subjects. The *lycée* does not "train for life"; in fact, it does an extraordinary job of teaching middle-class students to write and speak as other social categories do not. If, however, the educational system wishes truly to "train for life," it could take a big step in that direction by transforming itself and bringing within it on a full and unrestricted basis children from all social categories. One of the best ways to "train for life" is to come face to face with it, and at the very beginning of the educational process itself. "Training for life" could be furthered also by encouraging the formation of groups early in the student's education. Such groups presently are meager in number. Some efforts have resulted in creation of a limited number of groups in student gov-

[76] Wylie, p. 70.
[77] Wylie, p. 70.

ernment, but usually they are found on the level of the student's class in the school and not on the level of the entire student body. In fact, there is in the French school generally no "student body." Experiments in student government at the class level often take on the appearance of "guided democracy," the faculty supervisor never being too far removed from them. Finally, there is reason to believe that the Ministry of Education is not enthusiastic about the formation of such groups, particularly if they promise to take on a social and political character. During the events of May 1968 some *lycée* students did organize groups and proclaim their opposition to the regime. Even in a remote part of the mountains of the Haute-Loire students in a private *collège* proclaimed their sympathy with the workers and "occupied" their own dormitory (they were led, incidentally, by an American).

Wylie comments in his essay in *In Search of France* on the great amount of national and local history and geography required of students in French schools. The child, he says, is expected to learn the identity of those forces that formed him and the world around him "in order to act in accordance with it." [78] In geography, says Wylie, the major principle is that it is the environment that produces man, and although he may adapt it to his needs, he may not transform it "fundamentally" nor "alter the fact of his relationship with it." [79] Wylie concludes that a child growing up in this system feels less capable of controlling his future than a child less informed about such forces.

Let us examine here—solely for purposes of information, clarification, and illustration—one history text used in many tenth grade, or *troisième,* classes.[80] This book ranges from the beginning of the eighteenth century to 1870. The student is first introduced to world civilization at the beginning of that century, and then in greater detail to European civilization. France is then examined in relation to its position in the European context.

[78] Lawrence Wylie, "Social Change at the Grass Roots," in Stanley Hoffmann ed., *In Search of France,* pp. 159–234. The quotation is from p. 213.

[79] Wylie, "Social Change at the Grass Roots."

[80] R. Girardet, P. Jaillet, A. Jardin, and J. Monnier, *Histoire: La naissance du monde contemporain* (1715–1870). Collection Jean Monnier. (Paris: Fernand Nathan, 1966).

Also included are some chapters on Britain and the United States. One of the two chapters dealing with the United States examines American history from 1789 to 1865. The student is introduced to the Revolutionary War, the rise of the federal government, introduction of the Bill of Rights, the War of 1812, westward expansion, population growth, economic development and growth, social and political transformation, the Democratic party in power between 1829 and 1861, the slavery issue and the Civil War. Two short documents are appended to the second chapter, "The Yankee and the Virginian," and "The State of Spirit of the Pioneer." Questions at the end of this chapter ask the student: (1) to compare New York in 1789 and 1860; (2) to determine the land surface of the United States in 1789 and 1860; (3) to establish the principal differences between the north and the south in 1860; (4) to compare American and Russian expansion and determine if they exhibit common traits which distinguish them from European colonization. If this text is parochial, it is because of its specialization and selectivity, for it gives a great amount of space to French history and not too much to non-French historical phenomena. At the same time, there is in the text no evidence of distortion of materials; nor do the authors fall short of their purpose—to produce a "precise and simple text" that is not "a superficial recitation of facts nor too scientific." [81] It seems also that the authors fulfill their purpose and "avoid abstract and premature explanations that would run the risk of turning the student away." [82] The text is used very profitably in many tenth grade classes. Nor is the treatment given in it to the French Revolution in line with Duverger's comment that the history of the French Revolution—as it is taught in France—teaches resistance to the state.[83]

POLITICAL SOCIALIZATION
AND THE ACQUISITION OF PARTISANSHIP

How does an individual acquire political partisanship? How does he become a communist? or socialist? or conservative?

[81] Girardet *et al.,* p. 3.
[82] Girardet *et al.,* p. 3.
[83] Maurice Duverger, *The French Political System* (Chicago: University of Chicago Press, 1958).

Which forces work on him from birth and contribute in varying degrees to the molding of his political partisanship? Of what significance in this process are family, social category, religion, historical tradition, region, and subjective identification?

The French family did exhibit for many years a very well-defined form, being more highly insulated than the family in many other western countries. That development turned its face away from certain aspects of societal existence. Its membership tended to retreat inside itself in pronounced bourgeois fashion, isolating themselves from the community and its organs of collective expression. The family acted as a promoter of community secession, inhibiting its members from participating in community life, and discouraging access to itself by outsiders.

The French family now is in a state of transformation. *Le foyer,* or the moral environment of the home, which in other years was described as the "center of love," now is described by the French Institute of Public Opinion as the "center of convenience." No longer is it that physical and moral place which preserves indissoluble family ties, and now the lives of its members are characterized by growing isolative tendencies. Philip Converse and Georges Dupeux have discovered among French respondents that only 26 percent could even identify their fathers' political party affiliation or political tendency (an additional 3 percent were able to identify the fathers' orientation as "variable" or "apolitical").[84]

At the same time, the family still retains a sense of identity and it continues to transmit to its members a sense of class. That feeling of class is furthered by segregation of housing along class lines (not legally, of course). The family usually occupies a *quartier* populated by families who belong to the same social category. This physical separation furthers lack of interclass communication among diverse social categories.

French society is a class society. Stendhal, sometimes called the greatest of all French novelists, describes in *The Red and the Black* the nature of nineteenth-century bourgeois orienta-

---

[84] Philip E. Converse and Georges Dupeux, "Politicization in France and the United States," *Public Opinion Quarterly* (Spring 1962), 1–24.

tion.[85] Stone walls play in his novel a most prominent role; they keep the bourgeois within his world and workers and peasants outside of it. Julien Sorel is of proletarian origin but he manages to penetrate the walls. Sorel soon realizes how incompatible his way of life is with life within the walls. Sorel is gifted; yet in his former world such gifts were not of any particular significance. If they are to mean anything, they must be exercised within the bourgeois world. Once Sorel has scaled the walls, he discovers that there are always new ones that still must be attempted. Moreover, in bourgeois society Sorel is "different." To the aristocratic Marquis de la Mole, he even is "frightening." That, says the Marquis, is because of "the impression that he makes on everybody." The Marquis concludes, therefore, that "there must be something real about it." And there can be no doubt whatsoever that for the Marquis the "difference" is "real" —he "feels" it, and it must be so. The barrier is both social and psychological. Julien Sorel manages to secure within the walls certain privileges, but he pays a dear price for their acquisition, going to his death as a consequence.

Relationships between bourgeois and working class categories have, of course, been modified greatly since the time of Stendhal. At the same time, they continue to retain some elements of Stendhal's century. In a recent study of the French Institute of Public Opinion, 50 percent of the respondents stated that they consider themselves members of a social class—that is, members of a social stratum defined by its level of existence, income, collective beliefs, and consciousness of itself as a group.[86] Approximately 44 percent believe that the class struggle is a reality, this belief being particularly apparent among workers and lower middle-class elements of the population.[87]

Bourgeois and worker families frequently exhibit toward each other negative feelings. Working class families show considerable irritation with bourgeois families, primarily because of the latter's often higher incomes and greater social privileges. In turn, bourgeois contempt for worker families is well known.

---

[85] See the penetrating analysis in Martin Turnell, *The Novel in France* (New York: Vintage Books, 1951), pp. 144–165.

[86] Institut français d'opinion publique, "La vie politique de mai 1966 à décembre 1967," *Sondages,* Vol. 2, No. 1 (1968), 44.

[87] "La vie politique de mai 1966. . . ."

Bourgeois families with earnings inferior to those of some worker families guard their "way of life" and seek to escape from slipping into the working class. Some lower middle-class shopkeepers cling, for example, to enterprises productive of but marginal income; their loss—even if employment elsewhere as a worker would yield greater income—would involve these individuals in a downward step into a "lower" social category and involvement in a different kind of life.

Material differences between bourgeois and working classes have in recent years declined, being in no way as strikingly apparent as they were in the nineteenth century. With the elevation of the purchasing power of the worker and the coming of the mass consumer society, distinctions between bourgeois and worker no longer are readily demonstrable in matters of dress and ownership of some material conveniences. The worker's blue jeans and blue coat are a declining phenomenon on weekends. Some workers drive *deux chevaux,* that curious and efficient little two-cylinder car designed by Porsche when he was a prisoner of war and which is sometimes called—because of its styling—"Porsche's revenge." Yet, despite growing material convergences between the classes, no love is lost between them, even if among some young workers there is evidence of a decline in awareness of worker orientation.[88]

All of French population is distributed among certain social categories. The working class, which internally ranges from unskilled manual workers to highly skilled technicians, contains more than 8 million people. Agriculture, which includes individual proprietors, tenant farmers, agricultural workers, and sharecroppers, comprises about 3 million people. The middle class comprises more than 8 million persons. Social category has been and continues to be an important determinant of political partisanship (but not the only one). The social category most closely tied to the Communist party is the working class. Although worker affiliation with the Communist party is on the decline, more than 30 percent vote for it.[89] Birth within a Com-

[88] Duquesne, p. 141.

[89] See Mattei Dogan, "Political Cleavage and Social Stratification in France and Italy," in Seymour M. Lipset and Stein Rokkan, *Party Systems and Voter Alignments: Cross-National Perspectives* (New York: The Free Press, 1967), pp. 129–195.

munist "ghetto" means that the son of a Communist worker generally will be reared within an insulated and relatively homogeneous community that sets barriers against assimilation to other orientations. If this type of encirclement makes other orientations less readily accessible, it also makes them less desirable. In this environment the individual creates relationships that involve long-range affiliations and continuation in a certain "way of life" from which departure can cause all kinds of traumatic reactions.

If membership in a given social category is often a determinant of political partisanship, it is not, however, the only one. If approximately 55 percent of the working class is oriented toward communism and socialism, 45 percent is not. Subjective identification with a given social category is important in the determination of political partisanship. As Dogan says, if two individuals of the same profession and rank do not associate themselves with the same social class, the odds are that they will vote differently. If, however, two individuals of different professions and different incomes associate themselves with the same social class, generally they will vote the same way.[90] Dogan shows, for example, that membership in the working class is for some workers not equivalent to membership in the "poor class," a psychological distinction that may account for the political partisanship of these workers.[91] On the other hand, the fact also remains that any number of workers choose not to identify themselves at all with the working class. In identifying with other social categories, they often adopt the political partisanships favored by some constituent units of these categories.

Normally, agriculture is not productive of strong support for communism; during the 1950s this social category produced not more than one third of all the Communists and Socialists in the republic. Yet during these years communism was a major phenomenon in several agricultural regions. The two most Communist departments in the entire nation were the agricultural Corrèze and Creuze. Both departments contained a type of agriculture restricted to small individual holdings. In 1951 the Corrèze produced a Communist vote slightly in excess of 40

[90] Dogan, p. 172.
[91] Dogan, p. 173.

percent; in 1956 the agricultural Creuze returned a Communist vote of 46 percent, exceeding the Communist vote in the worker areas of the Pas-de-Calais and the "red belt" of Paris. As Jacques Fauvet notes, both departments contained small agrarian exploiters who had a difficult time making a go of it; in reacting against oppression and authority, they developed extreme Left political partisanships.[92] They lived, moreover, in departments in which the Left tradition is the oldest in the nation and in which clericalism is not of any particular significance.

François Goguel is of the opinion that social structure plays less of a role in the determination of political partisanship within certain regions of the nation than certain political traditions which are "intellectual and sentimental, and sometimes very old." [93] If Goguel is correct, François Mitterand's vote in the 1965 presidential election derived less from social structure and economic factors than from tradition, which led in about a fourth of all the departments to votes for him. Goguel interprets much of the Mitterand vote as being tied closely to the history and some of the political institutions of the nineteenth century. Goguel finds tradition to be more prevalent in a rural *milieu* and in underpopulated departments often in decline, rather than in a worker *milieu* and urban areas.

Political partisanship varies among members of the middle class; moreover, there are different middle classes: lower middle class, middle middle class, and upper middle class. Salaried lower middle-class people such as clerks and lower civil servants supply in the cities much of the support for the Communist party.[94] Members of the independent lower middle class such as shopkeepers and artisans generally develop conservative partisanships and show from time to time antirepublican tendencies and occasionally an affinity for fascism. Although of radical tendencies at the turn of the century, this group supplied under the Fourth Republic nearly half the support for the Poujade movement.[95]

[92] Jacques Fauvet, *La France déchirée* (Paris: A. Fayard, 1957), pp. 86–89.

[93] See François Goguel, "L'élection présidentielle française de décembre 1965," *Revue française de science politique,* 16 (April 1966), 221–254.

[94] Dogan, p. 150.

[95] Dogan, p. 155.

The middle middle class (Dogan's classification includes more than twenty socioeconomic groups) develops partisanships toward the Center and Center Right; hardly more than 20 percent affiliate with the extreme right, and perhaps 16 percent with socialism and communism.[96] If it is republican, that does not preclude it from flirting periodically with Bonapartism. Members of the upper middle class affiliate only slightly with socialism and communism, and infrequently with fascism.

There is a relationship between political partisanship and objective social category; there also is a relationship between political partisanship and perception of social category. The relationship between political partisanship and objective social category is more clear among worker elements than among nonworkers.

The extent to which religion influences and molds a person's political partisanship is affected in large part by whether the person is a practicing or nonpracticing Catholic (see Chap. 3). The more practicing the Catholic, generally the more conservative is his political partisanship. Religious adherence is more elevated among females than males, and so the former tend to be of more conservative political partisanship. Workers are little concerned with religion; religious practice is elevated among members of the agricultural category. For the great majority of the French, however, the church and its dogmas are known only in a superficial manner. Although more than 90 percent of the French are reared in a Catholic religious atmosphere, they "appear to love God more than their Church," and this attitude is increasing among the young.[97]

The Catholicism of the French is influenced primarily in early childhood by the religious attitudes of the father more than those of the mother, and by private Catholic education (60 to 70 percent of all practicing Catholics are educated in such institutions).[98] Families who give their children a religious education do so primarily for reasons of family tradition. A study of the French Institute of Public Opinion shows that only 22 percent of the families interrogated sent their children to a Catholic

[96] Dogan, p. 156.

[97] Institut français d'opinion publique, "Religion et politique," *Sondages*, 2 (1967), 13.

[98] "Religion et politique," 11.

school so that they will believe in God.[99] The institute states that for three quarters of the French, religion is a matter of moral order or of principles of education: "Religion for the majority is not a matter of belief but more simply a respectable practice, a conformist attitude. We raise our children in the Catholic religion so that they will conform to the norm, so that they are serious." [100] The institute also concludes that if the French easily abandon the church at the age of twelve, the religious idea or belief tends to remain with them despite the absence of practice.[101]

The church does not prescribe any precise political partisanship, but its catechism does state that Catholics should "vote for capable men, and if possible good Christians." [102] Yet, as Dogan shows, Burgundian Catholics are very conservative, but not because they are very religious. In Alsace, Catholics are religious but not very political. In eastern France Catholicism is connected with a progressive working class orientation, while in Brittany, Catholicism is peasant and reactionary.[103]

Finally, certain types of political partisanship have often meant different things at different times in French history. As Thomson shows, affiliation with a revolutionary tradition meant at the beginning of the Third Republic something far different from what it means now. Adherence to that tradition was associated in 1875 with peasant proprietors and small property holders—although theory was deferred to all kinds of checks and institutions to make sure that a revolutionary doctrine was not applied.[104] Adherence to a republican tradition meant before 1875 commitment to a revolutionary tradition. However, after 1875 adherence to the republican tradition meant for some newly conservatized republicans defense of the regime and a hands-off policy relative to private property. Adherence to a

[99] "Religion et politique," 14.
[100] "Religion et politique," 14.
[101] "Religion et politique," 18.
[102] Jean Meynaud and Alain Lancelot, *La participation des français à la politique* (Paris: Presses universitaires, 1965), p. 73.
[103] Dogan, p. 181.
[104] David Thomson, *Democracy in France: The Third and Fourth Republics,* 3d edition (New York: Oxford, 1958), pp. 42–43.

revolutionary tradition in the late 1940s generally meant adherence to the Communist party, whereas in this era it is associated primarily with some student elements and some small splinter groups.

CONCLUSION

Socialization involves exposure by the individual to multiple environments, which usually harbor elements of compatibility and incompatibility. Contradictions usually inflict some effect on socialization. Socialization consists of the individual passing through different levels and states. It also involves reciprocity. The group attracts the child, eventually satisfying various of his needs; in turn, the group expects something from him. The group is a socializing instrumentality. In France the group plays less of a role as a socializing agent than its counterpart in the United States.

The child who lives in a rural environment appears to reside in a cohesive family unit; generally, however, that cohesion is only on the surface. The rural family often is the most closed to the outside world and the most depoliticized of family units. The worker's family frequently is affected adversely by economic and social imbalances. Middle-class families often are the recipients of pressures different from those experienced by other social categories.

The presence in the household of a father is of great importance to a child's socialization, as is also the relationship between the father and mother, the child's rank within the family, and conditions of the family's housing.

Les 16–24 ans, the most recent comprehensive study of French youth, explains their feelings and attitudes. This generation appears apprehensive of the future, serious, conformist, and rarely does it evidence "signs of revolt." It is not given to risk-taking, and it gives considerable weight to prudence. It appears to be strongly indifferent to politics, but not to forms of collective economic action. It is not greatly concerned with religion and group affiliations.

The French educational system exercises a selective role which is related to the social structure of the country. It plays more of a role socializing within class than among classes. Children of middle class parents have easier access to education than children of workers and peasants. This results in a great loss to the nation, that of a badly needed resource. The *lycée* constitutes a barrier to socialization, accentuating divisions in French society. It educates its elites, while other parts of the educational system undereducate the popular class—irrespective of the potentialities of its members. The *grandes écoles,* or the great schools, train their elites but fall short of producing enough technical leaders for the nation.

Civic education receives little attention, a phenomenon that is not at all at odds with the Frenchman's less-than-well-developed image of community. Development of groups is not encouraged by French education. However, French education should not be associated now with an intense rationalistic positivism, for that is associated more with the France of the past than with the France of the present. Certain changes considered desirable by many teachers are precluded by that great stone building of conservatism, the Ministry of Education.

Acquisition by the individual of political partisanship is affected more or less by the individual's family, social category, religion, region, subjective identification and historical tradition. Family life is characterized by growing isolative tendencies by its individual members. However, the family continues to transmit to its members a sense of class, and generally that feeling is furthered by segregation of housing along class lines. Membership in a given social category often is a determinant of political partisanship; it is, however, not the only one. Subjective identification with a given social category is important too. François Goguel argues that social structure plays in the determination of political partisanship within certain regions of the nation less of a role than certain political traditions. Generally, religion is not often a determinant of political partisanship; nevertheless, the more practicing a Catholic, the more likely that his political partisanship will be conservative. Finally, some kinds of political partisanships mean different things at different time in the history of the nation. What was radical at the turn of the century is at midcentury generally conservative.

THREE
THE INDIVIDUAL AND THE STATE
Themes of political culture

Some aspects of French thought reflect exaltation of the individual and distrust of authority; other aspects of it exalt authority and distrust of the individual. Alain, or Émile Chartier, the late philosopher of radicalism, described the former orientation brilliantly in his *Le citoyen contre les pouvoirs*. He remained convinced that for Frenchmen "resistance to the powers is more important than reformatory action." [1] He tells in his work how Frenchmen felt it their responsibility to elect their deputies, and to see then that those deputies did not let the ministers and civil servants follow their "natural inclinations" and abuse their positions. He describes how they resorted to actions calculated to weaken the state by resisting its powers, and how those actions derived from feelings that had their origin in years of resistance to monarchy, church, Napoleonic regimes, and republics asso-

---

[1] Alain, *Le citoyen contre les pouvoirs* (Paris: Éditions du Sagittaire, 1925); see also Nathan Leites, *Images of Power in French Politics,* Vol. 1 (Santa Monica, California: The Rand Corporation, 1962), p. 4. Leites, who examines self-interest as a dominant theme in French politics, states that there is a disbelief in "any preestablished harmony between the pursuit of individual interests and public service." Unfortunately, Leites develops the theme with no small amount of exaggeration.

ciated with suspicion and distrust. The latter orientation, or exaltation of authority and distrust of the individual, is associated with an approach to power known as Jacobinism. The term, which derives from the time of the French Revolution, is associated with those who claim a deep and unobstructed relationship between the individual and the state. During the Revolution Jacobinism was a reaction against excessive individualism, being apprehensive of pluralism lest it revive a society of privilege. Talmon, who explains Jacobinism's meaning well, states that for it the Revolution meant simply "the Republic one and indivisible, and the defence of the welfare of the masses." [2] It embraced the conviction that the Revolution made it possible for the revolutionists to go the entire distance toward achievement of their grand design, and it rejected a "theory of balance." In fact, the Jacobins tended to disregard the idea that there could exist legitimately multiple and conflicting moralities. If things were to be gotten on with, they had to be carried out without any intermediaries diverting the doers from their accomplishments. If for historical reasons it would be misleading to call this type of thought "totalitarian," it would be shortsighted not to recognize in French history its long-range and often authoritarian implications. Such thought, understandable in 1789 considering the cleavage structure that then existed in French society, crops up from time to time in the public expressions of modern leaders. Michel Debré, de Gaulle's first prime minister, who held the post between 1959 and 1962, brought to it a passionate Jacobin love of the state and deep contempt for the opposition. He told the National Assembly in his inaugural address of January 15, 1959, that "Our beings are nothing and our institutions themselves have no meaning except in the measure that they serve the state." [3] He brought to the post also the conviction (explained previously in his book *Ces princes qui nous gouvernent*) of the need in France for depoliticization and limited participation in political affairs, mentioning in his initial speech to Parliament the need to "depoliticize the vital problems" and asserting that "The

[2] J. L. Talmon, *The Origins of Totalitarian Democracy* (New York: Praeger, 1960), p. 79. See also pp. 69–131.

[3] Pierre Viansson-Ponté, *Les Gaullistes: Rituel et annuaire* (Paris: Seuil, 1963), p. 101. See pp. 101–107 for biography of Debré.

depoliticization of the national essential is a major imperative." [4] That thesis, well known in French ideology, is particularly prominent in times of crisis (in 1919, for example, with leagues like *la démocratie nouvelle* that emphasized the necessity of positioning the state above political parties). [5]

If some Frenchmen prefer weak political regimes, they also want stable regimes. They know, therefore, that they must periodically sacrifice one in order to realize the other. Since 1958 Frenchmen have seen considerable governmental stability, and many are inclined to admit that it is preferable to weak regimes and constant bickering that threatens to make untenable all government whatsoever. Frenchmen saw that happen to the Fourth Republic. Whatever their suspicions of de Gaulle, many Frenchmen hesitated to vote for de Gaulle's opposition for fear that in government these persons might again engage the country in a series of hopeless ministerial crises that might terminate in the destruction of yet another republic. Many of those who voted for de Gaulle and for the political party that professed to follow his directives are seized with mixed sentiments. Resenting de Gaulle's frequent exercises of personal authority, [6] and the methods he employed to get over his policies, many of these people voted for de Gaulle nonetheless, because of the weaknesses of his opposition, and the potential political chaos that that opposition might have ushered in if installed in government. Whatever the magnitude of the Frenchman's distrust of authority, many prefer in government the mixture of Bonapartism and Jacobinism known as Gaullism to its uncertain alternative.

THE REPUBLICAN TRADITION

Doctrines are a common part of French political life. Some offer an abstract and general scheme of things; others are exposi-

---

[4] Jean Meynaud and Alain Lancelot, *La participation des français à la politique* (Paris: Presses universitaires, 1965), p. 104.

[5] Meynaud and Lancelot, p. 104.

[6] Institut français d'opinion publique, "La vie politique de novembre 1964 à avril 1966," *Sondages*, 1 (1966), 37. In the institute's polls 60 percent viewed de Gaulle as having installed in France a regime of "personal power."

tions, or word and phrase bundles, that are calculated to attract to certain associations people who may not be attracted to them by other considerations. All doctrines have less value than their proponents claim for them.

An important segment of French political thought subscribes to certain social and political convictions known collectively as the republican tradition. No one interpretation has earned legitimacy in the state. The multiple interpretations vary, but generally all proponents agree that the offices of the state ought to be elective, suffrage universal, church and state separate, and participation in policy determination by ordinary citizens possible as a result of qualifying for such through established orderly processes ratified previously by the citizenry. No one economic doctrine is associated exclusively with the republican tradition. There are socialist republicans and private enterprise republicans, although in each camp more than a few complain periodically that republicanism is incomplete and inadequate if prevailing economic practices are at odds with their own economic convictions.

Republicanism has been a fragile thing in France, having been but a minority belief for some years after the republic became a reality. For some time after the creation of the Third Republic both republicans and antirepublicans frequently called attention to the fact that the constituent assembly which produced the Constitution of 1875 contained not a republican but a monarchical majority, and it was surprising that the regime had taken subsequently a republican form. And even as late as World War I, a famous Sorbonne professor still could not bring himself to refer to the regime as other than "the bitch republic." After World War I, however, the political environment changed greatly. Practically all politicians identified themselves as republicans, and—irrespective of how reactionary their proposals —almost all identified themselves in the public eyes as proponents of "democracy." Votes were to be won, and those who ventured into the public arena dared not refuse to invoke democracy's symbols. In his addresses to the nation, former President de Gaulle justified on the basis of republicanism even the most antirepublican of acts, concluding his orations always with *vive la république*.

THE LEFT, THE RIGHT,
AND THE REPUBLICAN TRADITION

The term "Left" now is a hazy classification that once signaled commitment to the idea of a republic, opposition to monarchy, organization of the state along secular rather than clerical lines, subordination of property to the general welfare (whether the interpretation favored public or private ownership), equality of citizens and not their hierarchical ordering, popular sovereignty rather than elitism, and the preferability of liberty to authority. The term "Right" now is also a fuzzy term. Originally it was associated with monarchical restoration, clerical organization, a privileged position for property, inequality (both social and legal), and authority. The distinction between Left and Right— once well established—now has relatively little significance. The terms themselves retain very little of their original meaning. Today the republic is a fact; moreover, conflicting conceptions of its internal organization are seldom as far apart as they once were (in fact, they have in common more than is presumed generally). Clerical and monarchical restorations now are out of the question, and proposals infrequently made in their behalf are detached profoundly from reality. Equality of citizens is guaranteed by law, and any serious challenge to it is lacking. Some argumentation persists relative to the "republican virtues" of "government by assembly" and the "Bonapartist pretensions" of presidentialism, but within the ranks of both camps are many "good republicans." Catholics, once noted for their opposition to the republic, no longer live outside its fold; nor do the Communists, who have undergone in recent years a reintegration that is both political and social, which is bound to have a deep effect on the political thought and behavior of the future. The theme of the "two Frances," locked in everlasting battle with each other (in the process inflicting on French society internal divisions that precluded real progress in various areas of human effort), is a theme that belongs more to another century than to this one. France has its internal divisions, but their existence does not lead to such consequences. Some social categories are less well off than others, but this does not produce social paralysis and consequent immobilism. The France of today is many doctrines and divisions removed from the France of twenty years ago. Casting all ideological pretensions aside, French politicians now are in sufficient agreement to concede to the state an important role in the determination of economic and social affairs. There are economic differences among organized groups but these, too, are undergoing considerable reduction. Socialists and Independents remain far apart, it is true, and both have difficulty in entertaining similar budgetary considerations (the Independents representing the old France of small entrepreneurs, medium- and small-size property holdings, and regressive tendencies). Economic differences do not present an insurmountable barrier, however, to Socialists and Gaullists, for the latter represent a new France that is not hamstrung by a clientele derived from regressive and static parts of the economy. It is evident that the Gaullists also are not afraid of economic and financial innovations, nor of governmental excursions into the economic life of the community. They do not fear reform, and although they are not advocates of nationalization, they do not place against it great doctrinal barriers.

CONFLICTING INTERPRETATIONS OF EXECUTIVE AUTHORITY

For many decades Republicanism meant commitment to limitations upon executive authority; consequently, republicanism and presidentialism were considered to be antithetical. Nor was that conviction without foundation, for earlier in French history, whenever the republic was threatened, the menace presented itself often in the form of a threatened increase in executive authority. Consequently, "custodians of the Republic" acted like vigilant Gambettas, viewing presidentialism as unheedful of restraints and productive ultimately of Bonapartism. That perspective—which persisted throughout the Third and Fourth Republics—exists today in some quarters.[7]

---

[7] Bonapartists advocate a strong executive, highly centralized government, heavy emphasis on the state and its "role," acceptance of popular sovereignty but frequent usage of the plebiscite. Just before the beginning of the present century, various Bonapartists showed a flair for

In recent years many republicans have been forced to revise their conceptions of executive authority, knowing that they must shift their ground and present a new arrangement of public powers if they would combat Gaullism effectively. Consequently, in the last half-decade many of these people have laid classical parliamentarism quietly to rest and accepted a form of restricted presidentialism. This is not to say, however, that they believe, like the Gaullists, that the republic of the future will depend more on presidentialism and less on parties; they believe, rather, that the parties which they support should support presidentialism, not the Gaullist version of it, but one that is responsible and capable of acquiring prestige in a system that is stable and balanced.

A growing number of members of republican Left parties now concede that France should continue with a presidential regime—but that it should be responsible and not based on personal power. Nevertheless, Gaullist publications such as *La Nation* like to assert that the Left has not yet evolved enough in its thought to accept presidentialism fully. They like to remind the Socialists, in particular, that the late Socialist leader Léon Blum once pronounced in favor of presidentialism, and that the SFIO is guilty of betraying the beliefs of its former secretary-general in not accepting this organization of public powers. Blum

the use of violence as a means of "solving" problems; one of the best examples of a threatened increase in executive authority with potential dictatorial results occurred in 1877 when President MacMahon attempted to dissolve the Chamber of Deputies, having sent to it a letter in which he emphasized his responsibility, and having delivered his *Message au peuple français* of September 19 in which he accused the Chamber of Deputies of having challenged his leadership and authority. "They say," he stated, "that I want to bring down the Republic, don't believe it." The Republic then was still very weak, and MacMahon's actions were considered by Republicans as but an affirmation of personal power. Although MacMahon sought to picture himself as but a soldier without party who was guided simply by love of country, this threat to the Republic was put down. Later, in 1923, when President Millerand departed from constitutional neutrality and asked for creation of a stronger presidential power, his actions united the Left and resulted in dissolution of the Chamber of Deputies and the forcing of his resignation by the newly elected majority.

did not hesitate to acknowledge that the parliamentary regime is not the only form of democracy, it is true, and that much was to be said for presidentialism: "I incline, for my part, toward systems of the American or Helvetic type which are founded on the separation and the equilibrium of powers, and consequently on the sharing of sovereignty, and assuring to the executive power, in its own sphere of action, an independent and continuing authority." [8] It should be noted, however, that Blum, after his release from a Nazi prison, modified his views considerably, and came to regard the presidential system as difficult to reconcile with the situation that then existed in postwar France. In fact, Blum emphasized the differences between an American and French presidentialism, stating that under no circumstances can the American president dissolve the legislature as a consequence of being in conflict with it, and that under even as strong a president as Roosevelt presidential power was not personal, nor of a Caesarian essence. He conceded that the creation and maintenance of a separate executive power is entirely defensible for a republican, but that Gaullism goes beyond acceptance of this, foreseeing the elimination of political parties. Gaullism, he argued, seeks to establish the clear superiority of the executive over the legislative authority, not in the republican tradition, but purely in the tradition of Bonapartism. Blum said that "in our country and in the times in which we live, the strongest objection against the presidential conception exists in General de Gaulle himself. His person is the principal reason for those who oppose the system that he upholds." [9] Under de Gaulle, Blum added, France would be a "monocracy." [10]

According to General de Gaulle, effective executive authority can derive only from the president of the republic, not from the Parliament. That idea was never accepted fully by many members of the first legislature of the Fifth Republic (1958–1962), who regarded it as proceeding from themselves—despite de Gaulle's attempts to convince them that they were incapable of

---

[8] Léon Blum, *L'oeuvre de Léon Blum,* Vol. 1 (Paris: Éditions Albin Michel, 1958), p. 469.

[9] Blum, p. 469.

[10] Blum, p. 469.

governing without him (and despite his paradoxical assurances early in 1959 that Michel Debré would form a "government of the legislature" and nothing else). However, in subsequent years more and more people came to favor presidentialism and reject "government by assembly." Exceptions are the Communist party, which remains committed to a form of classical parliamentarism (viewing all proposals for presidentialism as "antidemocratic"), Mendès-France, and Guy Mollet.[11] Mendès-France, despite his pleas for the adoption of "a modern republic" (the title of one of his books), continues to cling obstinately to a conception of government that has much in common with the forms assumed by parliamentarism under the Fourth Republic. That, however, is not to say that Mendès-France holds any brief whatsoever for the misworkings of that system, it being common knowledge that

---

[11] Mitterand was in 1965 ambivalent relative to the choice between presidentialism and "government of the legislature." Obviously, this was shaped by his desire to retain the support of proponents of both types, in the Federation of the Left and in the country. See "Les Quinze points de Nevers," *Le nouvel observateur,* 120 (March 1–8, 1967), 10–11, in which he stated, "I do not make a choice between the presidential regime and the parliamentary regime, which to me appears to be a school quarrel as long as Gaullism is in existence." Compare this with his statement in "L'avenir selon Mitterand," *L'Express* (March 20–26, 1967), pp. 53–54, "For my part, I am not hostile to the presidential regime in principle. One can prefer the presidential style to the parliamentary style and be not less of a good republican . . . As for me, I am more readily receptive to the regime . . . which is close to the German system: the President of the Republic remains an arbiter . . . and it is the first minister, chief of the executive, who is the expression of universal suffrage." And in the same interview, "We are closer to some of the institutions voted in 1958 than General de Gaulle himself. He himself has destroyed, in fact, the institutions that he had promulgated." In 1969 Mitterand's Convention of Republican Institutions (CIR) endorsed presidentialism. The program of the Federation of the Left, reproduced in *Le Monde,* July 16–18, 1966, p. 4, stated, "It is a case in effect of a program of government of the legislature." On Mendès-France see, for example, his statement to the newspaper *Dauphine libéré* reproduced in *Le Monde,* November 8, 1966, p. 7, in which he pronounced in favor of the principle of government by legislature: "It is the principle of government of the legislature which avoids the excess of disorder of the IVe, the excess of authoritarianism of the V^e, and the excessive centralization of both."

his regard for that regime was not of the highest. His conviction is that traditional or classical parliamentarism is best for France and that, moreover, it can and will work effectively there. He wishes to restore Parliament to the center of things, giving it a role in appointing and constituting the government, and enabling it to freely challenge, question and, whenever necessary, censure it. According to Mendès-France, Parliament must be responsible for transferring the "nation's will into law"—however, he concedes that Parliament must allow for delegations of legislative authority to the government if the political system is to function effectively.[12]

One need not go beyond the Bayeux Constitution of 1945 for a clear description of de Gaulle's conception of executive authority: "It is obvious that the executive power cannot emanate from a Parliament, composed of two chambers, exercising the legislative power, without risk of leading to a mixing of powers in which the government would soon be only an assemblage of delegations." In that same speech de Gaulle questioned how this executive authority could emanate from the legislative power that it must balance without jeopardizing the unity, cohesion and discipline of France. He asked how a member of the government could be "at his post only the holder of a mandate from a party," and he stated that "The executive power must, therefore, emanate from the Chief of State." [13]

There once was some mystery associated with the constitutional views of General de Gaulle; this, however, was not the case in recent years, when he clearly articulated his position on constitutional powers. He was convinced that "internal political struggles have no profound reality." [14] Any organization of

[12] Pierre Mendès-France, *A Modern French Republic,* trans. by Anne Carter (New York: Hill & Wang, 1963), pp. 60–62.

[13] The proposal takes its name from the town in which it was delivered. Pierre Viansson-Ponté, "Il y a vingt ans à Bayeux," *Le Monde,* June 16, 1966, pp. 1, 8. The author states that de Gaulle, for whom everything has a symbolic value, chose Bayeux because it was the first French city liberated by the French after the invasion of the Continent in World War II.

[14] French Embassy (Press and Information Division), *Major Addresses, Statements and Press Conferences of General Charles de Gaulle,* May 19, 1958–January 31, 1964 (New York: 1964), p. 245.

constitutional authority that delivers power to the discretion of the political parties could only detract from effective handling of both domestic and foreign affairs. He said "That is why the spirit of the new Constitution, while retaining a legislative parliament, consists of seeing to it that power is no longer a thing of partisans, but that it emanates directly from the people, which implies that the Head of State, elected by the Nation is the source and holder of this power." [15] In rejecting "government of the legislature," he contended that under it the National Assembly cannot bring down a government without setting the stage for its own dissolution, thereby removing the head of state from any possible intervention. In turn, this gives the political parties the opportunity to appoint the prime minister, to influence the composition of his cabinet, and to engage in political maneuvers. He warned constantly lest the deputies employ their know-how, and prevent crises in the legal form from leading to a dissolution for the purpose of returning France to the system of "government by assembly."

Although a partisan of presidentialism, de Gaulle criticized those who want in France a presidential system of the American type, one with a president in full charge of executive power, and a parliament dominated by the political parties exercising legislative power "in its entirety." [16] This arrangement, stated de Gaulle, would allow each of the two powers to be tightly enclosed in their own domains, with "the President not being able to dissolve, nor the Parliament to overthrow." [17] "Neophytes," said de Gaulle of those persons who would like to see French government concentrated in the hands of one person, "not divided between a President and a premier," with a parliament that "would be untouchable, voting or not voting the laws and budget as it sees fit." [18] De Gaulle felt that this system is undoubtedly satisfactory for the United States, but that it would fail to work in a highly centralized France with its numerous political parties. Perhaps this system is entirely unfit for France, and

[15] French Embassy, p. 246.
[16] French Embassy, p. 246.
[17] French Embassy, p. 246.
[18] French Embassy, p. 247.

perhaps de Gaulle is correct about its inapplicability there, but his description of French government as consisting during his reign of a division between the president and the prime minister should be examined carefully. De Gaulle proclaimed orally that "it must evidently be understood that the indivisible authority of the State is confided entirely to the President by the people who have elected him, that there exists no other. . . ," [19] and "it is for him to adjust the supreme domain in order to maintain a distinction between the function and field of action of the Chief of State and that of the prime minister." [20] In fact, between 1958 and 1964 the transformation in his conception of the office was considerable. On September 4, 1958, he referred to himself as "above the political struggles, a national arbiter." On October 20, 1962, he called himself "Chief of State and guide of France," entrusted with the "destiny of France and that of the Republic." Then, finally in January 1964 he became "the man of the nation," and the "source" of all power. Did this lead in French government to a "division" between President de Gaulle and the prime minister—and, if so, where exactly was the other half?

De Gaulle ordered for France a system in which the president at his own discretion may dissolve the National Assembly whenever he feels that it is necessary to resolve conflicts between it and the prime minister. However, it was in the nature of things that most of the conflicts which appeared to be between the National Assembly and the prime minister really were conflicts between it and President de Gaulle. The ministers, including the prime minister, were not truly independent but subordinate to General de Gaulle. What defense was there for the National Assembly under this type of system? Its powers are meager, and even when it exercises these it risks dissolution. Moreover, this system professes to a separation of legal powers. How, however, can the powers be balanced in a true republican regime if the president has the power to dissolve the National Assembly whenever it is in disagreement with him?

Although some observers view the power of dissolution as

[19] French Embassy, p. 248.
[20] French Embassy, pp. 248–249.

incompatible with a real presidential regime, the influential Club Jean Moulin (hardly a Gaullist association) views dissolution as an institutional device not contradictory to presidentialism. Its image of a presidential regime is much broader than de Gaulle's, and it suggests five reforms as preconditions of a true French presidentialism: [21]

1. Elimination of the post of prime minister, with the president of the republic acceding to the post, with the ministers named by him and responsible to him

2. Elimination of the right of the president to dissolve the National Assembly without terminating his own term

3. Setting the term of the president of the republic to be equal to the period of time served by the legislature

4. Creation of a vice-president, elected at the same time as the president of the republic

5. Extension of the powers of the Constitutional Council in matters of control of the constitutionality of the president's acts, particularly his recourse to the referendum and use of Article 16

THE POLITICAL FAMILIES

The periodical *Réalités* published in September 1966 statements by Georges Pompidou, Giscard d'Estaing, and François Mitterand on the "art of governing." All had been asked to define in advance the "political families in France." Pompidou gave these groupings: the "Gaullist family"; the Communist party ("the nostalgic left of 1848 or of the year 2000"); the PSU (Unified Socialist party); the political clubs, "the reactionary Left which consists of the SFIO and the Radical party"; the "European" Right comprising the Democratic Center, and the "nationalist" Right, including Tixier-Vignancour ("both for an American protectorate"). D'Estaing replied that they are the extreme Right, the moderates, and the Center (comprising two thirds of the Radicals and three quarters of the MRP), the non-Communist Left (that *famille à l'esprit compliqué*), and the Communist

---

[21] Club Jean Moulin, *L'état et le citoyen* (Paris: Seuil, 1962), p. 25.

party. Mitterand replied that they consist of communists, social democrats, liberal democrats, and conservatives.[22]

Gaullism

In his work, Edmond Michelet, long-time associate and admirer of de Gaulle, describes Gaullism as a "political doctrine adapted to the history of our country for the second half of this century." It is, he says, a sentiment shared with de Gaulle of "a certain idea of France," which is not herself "without *grandeur*." [23] Michel Debré, de Gaulle's former prime minister, states that the first principle of Gaullism is "the existence of the French nation; its first objective is the independence, progress and prestige of the nation." [24] Fellow Gaullist Christian Fouchet states that Gaullism is a belief which is European, calculated to encourage European cooperation and Europe's strength, which can best be secured by a strong France. It also is "socialist," he states, with an economic and social Left orientation, capable of going as far on some points as the Communist party, but not "indebted to or dependent on a foreign power." [25] Jacques Soustelle, first a Gaullist and later a militant opponent of de Gaulle, sees Gaullism as a body of doctrine, but one which is different from what de Gaulle espoused when the two men worked with each other before their break in the 1960s.[26] "Pure Gaullist" Lucien Neuwirth characterizes

[22] Quoted in *Le Monde,* September 9, 1966, p. 5.; Mitterand's classification is essentially the one adopted by Guy Mollet. See Mollet's statement to *Le Monde,* September 4–5, 1966, pp. 1, 6. "We believe that the French are classified in four great families. The social democrats, attached to . . . political democracy . . . collective security and arbitration . . . in transfers of sovereignty to some organizations . . . The Communists . . . not believing—or believing little—in political democracy, and generally hostile to transfers of sovereignty. The liberal democrats, partisans of political democracy and supranationality but generally hostile to transfers of sovereignty. The liberal democrats, partisans of political economy. . . . Finally, the conservatives, defenders of a capitalist regime, attached to nationalism and often ready to renounce political democracy." He adds, "As for the Center, it is essentially the economic problem which separates us."

[23] See Edmond Michelet, *Le gaullisme, passionnante aventure* (Paris: Arthème Fayard, 1962).

[24] See Michel Debré, *Au service de la nation* (Paris: Stock, 1963).

[25] *Le Monde,* December 18, 1962, p. 7.

[26] Jacques Soustelle, *L'espérance trahie (1958–1961)* (Paris: Éditions de l'Alma, 1962).

Gaullism as a guide to action, unfixed and always evolving.[27] Passeron says that Gaullism is not a doctrine but a pragmatism whose rules were formulated and expressed clearly over thirty years ago in *Le fil de l'épée*.[28] Jacques Baumel, secretary general of the Gaullist Union of Democrats for the Fifth Republic (formerly the UNR-UDT) states: "Gaullism exists and it will for a long time . . . for Gaullism is . . . a doctrine for today and for tomorrow, a new style, founded on efficacy and stability, a positive program of concrete realizations equipped with dynamic and competent men." [29]

It is impossible to find a systematic body of doctrine which might qualify as Gaullism. For years Gaullism consisted of advice and directives divulged on a regular basis by the General to his followers, and their responsibility was to apply these to existing and future circumstances (even if the General contradicted today what he said yesterday). Gaullism could not be divorced from the person of the General.[30] Now the General has departed; nonetheless, there still exists a "Gaullist family." Is it destined to disappear, too, soon after the disappearance of the General from the presidency, or will it retain enough cohesiveness to sustain itself as a relatively permanent feature of the French political scene? Will it remain on, offering the basis for creation of a great modern force comprising conservative and liberal elements, or is Gaston Defferre correct when he says that the departure of de Gaulle eventually will set off the Gaullists like a live grenade and redistribute their pieces all over the political map? The question, of course, is unanswerable at this time, but studies of the French Institute of Public Opinion show public opinion to be doubtful about the future of the Union of Democrats for the Fifth Republic. One of their studies made in 1964

[27] Department of Political Science, University of California, Berkeley. *Fifth French Republic* (Berkeley, Calif., 1960), p. 29.

[28] André Passeron, *De Gaulle parle des institutions, de l'Algérie, des affaires étrangères, de la communauté, de l'économie et des questions sociales* (Paris: Plon, 1962).

[29] *Le Monde*, May 28, 1963, p. 3.

[30] Institut français de l'opinion publique, "La vie politique de novembre 1964 à avril 1966," *Sondages*, 1 (1966), 37. In the Institute's poll 60 percent of the respondents viewed de Gaulle as having installed in France a regime of "personal power."

showed that 46 percent of the respondents believed that it will not play an important role after de Gaulle passes from the scene.[31] In fact, 39 percent said that they did not wish to see it play an important role (35 percent said that they did).[32] Whatever the future of the "Gaullist family," the Union of Democrats for the Fifth Republic in recent years engaged in making future preparations for the period "after de Gaulle." In 1966, in its seminar directed by the public relations organization *Services et méthodes* in Poigny-la-Forêt, the name of de Gaulle was played down while full attention was given to the theme that "after de Gaulle there are the Gaullists." [33] The fifty-page manual distributed there contained only one reference to the General, and its instructions dealt with suggestions on how to "reassure the Right," how not "to discourage the Left," how to stress the word "peace" "because it makes a very strong impression on the *milieux* of the Left," and how to propagate the idea that the Gaullists are the France of the future, whereas the opposition is the France of yesterday.[34]

Socialism and communism

Socialism originated in the nineteenth century as a psychological and sentimental protest against the gross inequalities fashioned by the rationalization of capital.[35] Its rapid growth was stimulated greatly by the chaotic social effects of the industrial revolutions of that era. Many interpretations of socialism evolved but all had in common rejection of capitalism. Some socialist "schools" antedated Marx; nonetheless, the arrival of Marx in France presented socialist thought with more rigorous systematization, greater dependence upon empiricism, and an orientation that was "scientific." He did not have too much to do, however, with the development of socialist action in France, for that was primarily the work of Jean Jaurès (1859–1914), who transformed the movement, bringing it out of the wilderness,

[31] "La vie politique de novembre 1964 à avril 1966," 41.
[32] "La vie politique de novembre 1964 à avril 1966," 41.
[33] *Le Monde,* November 27–28, 1966, p. 6.
[34] *Le Monde,* November 27–28, 1966, p. 6.
[35] See Élie Halévy, *Histoire du socialisme européen* (Paris: Gallimard, 1948).

propelling it squarely down the path of direct political action and involvement in the affairs of the republic. In turn, his efforts were aided by a republic which provided socialism with an environment in which it could express itself freely, and in which it could work openly in its efforts to become a significant force in French political life. As for Jaurès, who sought to substitute for capitalism socialization both of production and distribution, although he failed in that quest, he did contribute to the ultimate acquisition of certain objectives, setting the stage for the subsequent adoption of the eight-hour day, a minimum wage, a weekly rest day, and a progressive tax on income.

Jaurès was instrumental in 1905 in loosely uniting most socialist elements in one political party, the Unified Socialist party. That party's internal cohesiveness was more myth than reality, however, and various of its factions constantly were in disagreement on questions of ministerial participation in government, reformism, revolution, and relations with the Socialist Second International.[36] Militant interaction continued within it until the Russian Revolution wrought changes that completely transformed the party. The majority faction sought adherence to the Communist Third International and its revolutionary program, the center faction preferred continued affiliation with the Socialist Second International, and the right faction continued to pledge reformism and cooperation with bourgeois elements. A complete party rupture occurred in 1920, when in the Congress of Tours the Leninist majority pledged affiliation with the Communist International, reconstituting the organization as the Communist party of France. Most members of the center and right factions then left the organization, reconstituting themselves as the French Socialist party, SFIO, and affiliating with the Socialist Second International. Soon the Communist party realized that the break had led to a rupture in the Left vote and subsequent success at the polls by many of the Communist party's opponents. At first the Communist party tried to recapture that vote, but its efforts were unsuccessful; then, in 1922, it adopted the tactical policy of the United Front, calling for coordinated

---

[36] See *Le parti socialiste, la guerre et la paix, toutes les résolutions et tous les documents du parti socialiste du juillet 1914 à fin 1919* (Paris: Librairie Humanité, 1918), pp. 110–112, 120.

cooperation of Communists and Socialists.[37] During the 1920s, numerous calls were issued by it to Socialists calling upon them to join in opposition to reaction. During the 1930s the Communist party urged the Socialists to join it in united opposition to fascism and war, a policy that was in keeping with that of the Communist International which called everywhere for action by Communists, Socialists, and democrats "in a common front against fascism." [38] Finally, in 1934, both Communist and Socialist parties concluded with each other limited agreements on the attainment of predesignated objectives (excluding, however, fusion of the two parties and use of violence).[39] These agreements served as preconditions of the subsequent Popular Front agreement of 1936, and the government which bore its name (staffed with Socialists and Radical Socialists, and upheld in the Chamber of Deputies by the Communist party). That government lasted until 1937, and after its termination the Socialist party again viewed Communist proposals with suspicion, particularly those that called for mutual coordination of tactical policies. In subsequent years Communists and Socialists generally went their separate ways, a condition that lasted until 1962 when in the legislative elections of that year both parties entered with each other a limited number of electoral agreements between the first and second ballots.

Division of the French Left into both Communist and non-Communist elements is a key theme in French politics. Members of the Communist Left are all found within one political party, whereas members of the non-Communist Left are distributed among diverse political parties (such as the French Socialist

[37] See Communist International, *Verbatim Report of the Negotiations between the Second and Third Internationals on the Question of Supporting the Heroic Struggle of the Spanish Workers* (London: 1934), p. 39. Reproduced here is a copy of Lenin's speech of 1922 in which he explains the necessity for a United Front, that "cunning mechanism of two fronts in the whole of international politics, for the sake of this we have adopted the united front tactics and will pursue them to the end."

[38] *Verbatim Report. . .* , p. 39. See also Alfred Spire, *Inventaire des socialismes français contemporains* (Paris: Librairie de Medicis, 1946), p. 156.

[39] See Parti socialiste, *XXXIe congrès national, tenu à Toulouse les 20, 21, 22 et 23 mai, 1934. Compte rendu sténographique* (Paris: Librairie populaire, 1934), p. 37, for copy of resolution.

party, SFIO, the Unified Socialist party, PSU, the Radical Socialists). Within the non-Communist Left beliefs range from rigidly
constructed versions of Marxism to flexible interpretations of
welfare statism, and to that which is not other than conservatism
(particularly among some Radical Socialists). Some of its
Catholic components seek to achieve a synthesis with Marxism,
while other of its Catholic elements expend efforts that reflect
diverse degrees of anti-Marxism.

Defining its relationships with the Communist party always
presents the non-Communist Left with grave problems. The
Communist party makes constant overtures to it; seldom are
they very fanciful, stressing always that which is practically
attainable, and presenting cold, hard, realistic possibilities which
hardly can be ignored by the non-Communist Left. It always is
difficult, however, for parties of the non-Communist Left to determine exactly how they may work with the Communist party in
pursuance of common objectives without endangering their own
organic independence and liberty. Familiar with the Communist
party's insatiable appetite, they wish to be certain that any
agreements that they may conclude with that party do not result
in their being swallowed by it. Knowing the innumerable nuances
Communist tactical policy always harbors, they must weigh
whether common agreements which appear initially to enhance
the objectives of all the Left are worth the price. In other words,
the non-Communist Left always must carefully deploy its own
tactical policy so as not to play into the hands of the Communist party.

A problem confronting the non-Communist Left is the
large claim that the Communist party has on the electoral force
of the Left. That claim is capable of being exercised positively in
electoral situations, but subsequently it has little carryover either
to the creation of a government or of a responsible opposition.
The Communist party threatens to produce instability in any
coalition government in which it participates, and its presence
there often is a hindrance rather than an aid to non-Communist
government parties, stimulating the concentration and coordination of both Center and Right forces, depriving the non-Communist Left often of chunks of its Center electorate.[40] The presence

[40] See Club Jean Moulin, *Un parti pour la gauche* (Paris: Éditions
du Seuil, 1965) pp. 24–35, for excellent discussion of this point.

of the Communist party creates uneasiness, moreover, among elements who share with it consolidated opposition. However, the non-Communist Left knows that it is difficult to ignore the Communist Left if it wishes to entertain serious pretensions to power. In turn, the Communist Left needs the non-Communist Left if it would come to power. Finally, one alternative to governing with the Communist Left is for the non-Communist Left to conclude alliances to its right and to return to a form of tripartism similar to that in which it participated during certain times in the Fourth Republic. Seizing that alternative presents, however, certain problems for the non-Communist Left, involving programmatical sacrifices and the implementation of policies that are other than its own.

The extent to which the Communist Left and the non-Communist Left can coordinate their activities for purposes of common action is always a question of lively speculation. Both forces take different positions relative to different problems. In 1954 the French Institute of Public Opinion made an extensive inquiry into Left opinions. More than 200 persons of all ages, sex, and social categories were questioned and tested in order to clearly solicit reactions of Left identification. The institute discovered that the Communist Left was preoccupied with existing problems, such as the functioning of colonialism and the economic condition of the workers, whereas the non-Communist Left was taken up more with problems of principle. The Communist Left was oriented toward action, while the non-Communist Left was inclined to verbalize its problems. There is no doubt that in those tests both categories viewed and assessed the social order in different ways.[41] Other studies made since that time continue to show that opinions displayed by electors of the extreme Left often are very different from those held by electors of the moderate Left. Homogeneity relative to certain questions is characteristic of the Communist Left, whereas lack of it is on many questions characteristic of the non-Communist Left (areas of disagreement being pronounced, and often precluding much real agreement). In their study of 10,000 electors, Deutsch, Lindon,

---

[41] The study is republished as "La gauche," *Les temps modernes,* 112–113 (1955), 1576–1625; see also Jacques Fauvet, *Les forces politiques en France: Étude et géographie des divers partis* (Paris: Éditions Le Monde, 1951), for excellent discussion of the non-Communist Left.

and Weil discovered that the non-Communist Left is on the problems of free schools, nationalization, and loss of colonies a great distance from the Communist Left—being on these issues closer to the Center and Right. They conclude that the only issues on which the Communist and non-Communist Left agree are the preferability of socialism and French independence from the United States. They conclude the absence of a common ideology among the electors of the non-Communist Left, and they state that its lack is "perhaps the cause—or an expression—of this *crise de la gauche.*" [42]

Deutsch, Lindon, and Weil examined also the views of the Communist Left and non-Communist Left relative to political parties (utilizing the results of the SOFRES public opinion inquiry of 1966). They show that while the Communist Left had a strong preference for the Federation of the Left (a late electoral union consisting of the Socialist party, SFIO, and the Radical Socialists), fewer members of the non-Communist Left accepted it (59 percent). Among members of the non-Communist Left, no political party succeeded in receiving more than 33 percent approval. The Federation of the Left was revealed, however, as having great potential among members of the non-Communist Left, receiving from it greater support than other electoral unions and parties. However, a real problem existed when the non-Communist Federation of the Left received from the non-Communist Left less support than the Communist party received from the Communist Left. The authors conclude that the Federation

> just "had not" developed a natural clientele. . . . Its leaders "had" a profound problem—its electoral clientele, the moderate Left, "was" deeply divided on ideas. It "was" thus hard for them to propose a program that rallies together the voters of the moderate Left. Its electoral alliances "were" hard to conclude. Electors who "were" more disposed to conclude alliances with it "were" generally extreme Left. But it "was" with the center that its own electors "prefer" to ally. And the center "was" attracted more by an alliance with the right.[43]

[42] E. Deutsch, D. Lindon, P. Weil. *Les familles politiques aujourd'hui en France* (Paris: Éditions de Minuit, 1966), p. 38.

[43] Deutsch *et al.,* p. 50.; see also Institut français d'opinion publique, "La vie politique de novembre 1964 . . . ," 44. The institute asked

Electors of the Communist and non-Communist Left total approximately 35 percent of the electorate. That total can unite to a very marked extent behind a candidate or candidates, but after doing so serious problems arise in maintaining a united condition. If, however, a united condition were created and then maintained, a united Left still would have to search elsewhere, in the Center, for example, in order to recruit a majority. What are the chances for a united Left to dip into that Center and take away from it enough votes to create a majority? The answer to this question demands examination of the Center, as well as subsequent determination if any part of it can be recruited electorally by the Left.

Most estimates place the Center at around 40 percent of the voting electorate. Deutsch, Lindon, and Weil noted over a two-year period some political tendencies among the French electorate that are remarkably stable—16 percent extreme Left, 19 percent Left, 41 percent Center, 17 percent Right, and 7 percent extreme Right.[44] They discovered also that on many problems electors of the "Center" had opinions close to those of electors of the Right (particularly on issues such as limiting the right to strike, sympathy for the army and the *force de frappe,* or independent nuclear deterrent), but that half of this group was without opinions on a majority of political problems. In fact, the authors found it difficult to describe it as having a "political temperament." [45] Deutsch, Lindon, and Weil conclude that most people overestimate the political importance of the Center—confusing it with the *marais,* that sodden swamp or bog, which, according to their estimates, constitutes about 32 percent of the electorate, and which has no real opinions, being inspired in its voting by "sentiments, demagoguery, or personalities." They contend that the "*marais* is not any closer to the Center than it is to other families. It is attracted even more to entrenched positions of extreme parties than it is to nuanced opinions and pragmatic ones of the Center." [46]

---

electors if it is preferable for Socialists to ally with political parties of the Center or of the Left, including the Communists; 43 percent preferred the Center, 27 percent the Left, 30 percent declined to answer.

[44] Deutsch *et al.,* pp. 13–14.

[45] Deutsch *et al.,* p. 39.

[46] Deutsch *et al.,* p. 82.

To come by a majority, the Left first must unite, and then subsequently acquire the support of a portion of the *marais*. Deutsch, Lindon, and Weil conclude that a future majority is for the Left "not impossible because theoretically the *marais* is politically neutral and it has no incompatibilities of opinion with those of the left." [47] They state that the *marais* often is discontent with its economic situation and expresses that discontent by voting with the opposition; "but just now they are . . . rather favorable to the UNR which offers them a guarantee of stability and continuity." [48] They add, "To conquer the *marais* the Left must make its own unity and promise the *marais* an amelioration of their conditions of life and appease the fears they have of the Communist party, and furnish real guarantees of political stability." [49] Therefore, although they conclude that nonunity of the Left will probably perpetuate for some years the existing majority formula axised on the electorate of the Right and of the Center, Deutsch, Lindon, and Weil readily recognize that this may not always be the case and that a future Left majority is possible. If this be the case, does the future belong to the Center (as is sometimes contended), or does it belong to those who are able to retrieve periodically from what only appears to be the "Center" enough votes to make their own majorities? [50]

In recent years—particularly in the period between 1964 and 1966—public opinion has softened its outlook on commu-

[47] Deutsch *et al.*, p. 39.

[48] Deutsch *et al.*, p. 72.

[49] Deutsch *et al.*, p. 72.

[50] The *marais* was made capital of by de Gaulle, who exploited its fears and continued to contribute to its lack of political education. As far as he was concerned, the greater the reaction against political parties and the greater the subsequent growth of the bloc of the partyless, the more secure his position as chief of state. Perhaps there would be grounds for optimism if de Gaulle had attempted to induce these people to become real supporters if not members of the Union of Democrats for the Fifth Republic, thereby laying the foundations for a real future majority. One man will not always suffice for the getting of a majority, as de Gaulle discovered on the first ballot in the presidential elections of 1965, a lasting one being dependent upon a firm structured basis. However, the President of the Republic would have none of this. To have taken this tack, the Union of Democrats for the Fifth Republic would have had to become more than it was, perhaps even a real political party.

nism and the French Communist party. A study conducted by Alain Duhamel under the auspices of the French Institute of Public Opinion shows that six out of every ten people inter-rogated believe that the Communist party has become more con-ciliatory, and that this belief is greater even among Socialist and Radical Socialist voters (71 and 76 percent, respectively).[51] Approximately 55 percent of the Center Left voters now believe that unity of action with the Communist party is easier to achieve than it was ten years ago, and receptiveness to participation of Communist party ministers in government increased in two years from 31 to 38 percent.[52] This wish by the French for rein-tegration of the French Communist party in national political life is not to be equated, however, with preference for a Commu-nist regime. Only one in six wish to see the Communist party entrusted with control of the Ministry of Foreign Affairs, and most prefer non-Communist control of the Ministries of the Interior, Education, Economic Planning, Agriculture, and Labor.[53] Finally, few people regard seriously the Communist party's chances for taking power in France.[54]

Liberalism and conservatism

Liberalism is associated historically primarily with rejections of monarchism and clericalism, and with many sentiments and ideals expressed in 1789 in the Declaration of the Rights of Man and the Citizen.[55] Later, its efforts were consecrated to the win-ning of the republic and, after it was attained, protecting it from regressions and against attacks by antirepublicans. However, after the republic eventually became an established fact, liberal-ism then settled down into a little-changing doctrine while

---

[51] Alain Duhamel, "L'image du parti communiste," *Sondages,* 1 (1966), 61.

[52] Duhamel, 62.

[53] Duhamel, 62.

[54] See for discussion of this Maurice Duverger, "L'objectif No. 1," *Le Monde,* November 3, 1966, p. 6.

[55] The statement recognizes the interest displayed in liberalism by monarchists such as Constant and Chateaubriand. Their attention had been turned, however, primarily to the English version, of which Con-stant acknowledged the futility of trying to get the French to understand.

around it the world continued its transformation. Soon it became a facade for those who resisted governmental interference in those portions of the economy with which they equated their own interests. Individual rights came to be emphasized more than responsibilities, and affiliation by the doctrine with causes of property holders rather than with those of the non-propertied became prevalent. Nevertheless, the doctrine never renounced its identification with the ideal of popular sovereignty, although many of its proponents have not hesitated to use it as a brief for some individuals in society rather than for society itself. Negativism became one of its earmarks, and often it was employed by those interested in constructing barriers against state action; its resistance to change became an attraction to some class interests. As Kingsley Martin has observed, this creed, created in a struggle against eighteenth century institutions, an instrumentality employed to secure individual liberty in a "comparatively simple agricultural society," could prove hardly adequate as the basis for a complex industrial society.[56] "The men of the Revolution . . . could not . . . know that their championship of individual liberty against Church and State would be used to justify the commercially powerful in oppressing the weak." [57]

Conservatism is associated historically with themes and forms of social and political organization that serve to safeguard the institutional and juridical bases of private property. All interpretations of conservatism (and there are many) are related in some way or another to religion, the magnitude of that affiliation varying among the diverse "schools." Some interpretations reflect versions of strutting nationalism, and others appear to have broken finally with it (such as those who favor adoption of a United States of Europe). Conservatives, for example, who were militantly nationalistic were Paul Déroulède (1846–1914), who was obsessed with notions of extracting revenge from Germany, and Maurice Barrès (1862–1923), enemy of reason and of the democratic republic, who wanted to substitute for the

[56] Kingsley Martin, *French Liberal Thought in the Eighteenth Century* (New York: Harper & Row, 1963), p. 3.
[57] Martin, p. 304.

latter a Napoleonic republic, reconstruction of France's national greatness, and elevation to primacy of the ideal of "the nation." Yet another form of conservatism was expressed by Joseph de Maistre (1753–1821), "the prince of reactionaries," whose orientation was monarchical, clerical, opposed to all reform, and scornful of human reason. His thought was somewhat similar to that of Louis de Bonald (1754–1840), who wanted a Catholic regime presided over by a monarch responsible only to God. On the other hand, Hippolyte Taine (1828–1893) and Alexis de Tocqueville (1805–1859) were conservatives and partisans of decentralization, monarchy, and individualism.[58]

It was long in coming, but now most interpretations of conservatism finally have made their peace with republicanism. At the same time, no interpretation displays for it any great unbridled enthusiasm. Attitudes currently associated with the diverse forms of conservatism are defense of private property, marked hostility to socialism and communism and Russia, the United Kingdom, and, lately, the United States.[59] Some conservatives are staunch partisans of the army, and only a few years ago many were ardent proponents of the cause of Algérie française. Conservatives refer often to the "Christian legacy," but now they seldom equate it solely with Catholicism.

The extreme Right and fascism

The rightist group most highly publicized in recent years was the Secret Army Organization (OAS) which practiced terrorism, doing whatever it could to prevent a cease-fire in Algeria and prospects for the emergence of a sovereign and independent Algerian State. The OAS was created in February 1961 as the result of a series of agreements concluded in Madrid among opponents of the Fifth Republic. Its leaders insisted that it was not a political organization but a vehicle designed to save France from Gaullism, communism, and the loss of Algeria. Its leaders,

---

[58] See for discussion of various types of conservatism Hans Kohn, *Making of the Modern French Mind* (New York: Van Nostrand, 1955), pp. 50–59. Kohn classifies Taine and de Tocqueville in the liberal tradition.

[59] The growth in 1957 of anti-Americanism among conservatives in Lille was particularly noticeable.

many of them militarists, lauded the French army until they came into subsequent conflict with it; after that, they claimed the necessity for destroying certain of its elements whenever they jeopardized chances for their own success.

The basic plan of the OAS was expressed clearly in the directives of the ex-General Salan seized in Constantine and Algiers in February 1962, which demanded the creation of *maquis,* the necessity for constant provocations, elimination of the Moslem elites, creation in Algeria and metropolitan France of definite zones of insurrection against the Fifth Republic, creation of a revolutionary climate in the great urban centers, violence against the police and the Republican Guard, utilization of the methods of the streets and deployments of crowds so that they could be used for the acquisition of OAS ends, the assassination of all Moslem intellectuals friendly to the rebel National Liberation Front (FLN), and stimulation of the prospects for civil war in France. The directives emphasized that undesirable acts also should be resorted to whenever possible and attributed to the Communist party and the Unified Socialist party, so as to create in France the image of an impending communism.[60]

During those months after March 19, 1962, when the cease-

---

[60] See *Le Monde,* April 24, 1962, p. 4, for a description of the directives; the case of ex-General Salan is perplexing. A Socialist and known at the age of forty-five as a "General of the Left," Salan wore the highest decorations of the Republic. A *protégé* of the late Georges Mandel, he had been sent to Algeria by a Socialist government and was considered by it to be strictly in the "republican tradition." Later, even when in revolt, Salan articulated sentiments in defense of republican institutions, protesting against the "dictatorship of the Fifth Republic," saying that he wished to "mobilize the French on the essential terrain of fundamental liberties, social justice and national territory . . . ," and collaborating with but keeping some distance from, it is said, Susini, Lagaillard, Ortiz and Argoud, all men of fascist or near-fascist tendencies. However, with the appearance of his February directive, calling for assassinations and the like, Salan made the transition from full republicanism to full reaction. As with Georges Bidault, the Salan story defies full explanation. Both men had never been collaborationists, and had risked death to resist the Nazis. There is no way of explaining what prompted them to destroy so many years of good service and throw their weight to a mad adventure that required the use of methods once repugnant to them. Raoul Salan was amnestied in 1968, after serving a lengthy prison term.

fire concluded between France and the rebel FLN was in effect, the OAS participated in maneuvers against the Fifth Republic: included in its efforts was massacre of Moslem hospital patients and destruction of individuals by plastic bombs. The most telling thing about the OAS campaign of terror, however, was that it never had the least chance of success. The OAS could not have prevented the emergence of an independent Algeria, even had it been able to seize both Algeria and metropolitan France (which, of course, was out of the question). If the Fourth and Fifth Republics could not retain Algeria there was no reason to believe that that could have been achieved by the OAS. Nevertheless, the OAS continued its mad policy long after the game had been lost, destroying lives and engaging in repeated attempts to assassinate President de Gaulle. A few years later, some OAS elements negotiated with the regime and succeeded in obtaining from it a general amnesty. Only then did the conflict cease. Remnants of the OAS exist still today, but they no longer present a threat to individual lives and the regime.

Disgraced previously by its pro-OAS tendency and crushed in the legislative elections of 1962, the extreme Right made a partial revival in 1965. Included in its efforts were defense of a treaty of amnesty for imprisoned or exiled people of Algérie française persuasion, strong opposition to General de Gaulle (the man "who betrayed the revolution of 1958"), refusal of French aid to former French possessions, particularly Algeria, and in some cases support in the presidential election of 1965 for the candidate of "national opposition," Jean-Louis Tixier-Vignancour. The extreme Right's distaste for Gaullism, which succeeded to some extent in pulling it together, did not succeed, however, in uniting it.

The extreme Right comprises numerous organizations. Some are significant; others merit scant attention.[61] All of these organizations are far from power, and their prospects for taking it appear to be negligible. The Féderation des étudiants nationalistes (Federation of Nationalist Students) is of some importance. Created in 1960, it supports a strong nationalism and persistent

---

[61] See the helpful article by André Laurens, "Nouveaux visages de l'extrême droite," *Le Monde,* February 27, 1965, pp. 1, 7; March 2, 1965, p. 8; March 3, 1965, p. 6.

anticommunism, opposing to Marxist materialism its own "spiritual conceptions." Democracy is viewed as having sacrificed the personality of man to the principle of equality. Man is to be defined by his nation, race and religion. A "new elite" must dispense authority and defend the ethnicity of the French.[62] After 1964 the Féderation des étudiants nationalistes coordinated activities with Europe-Action. Committees established in Paris, Lyon, Toulouse, and Marseilles distribute the propaganda of Europe-Action, and membership in them often is held by members of the Fédération des étudiants nationalistes, the Parti patriote révolutionnaire (led by the lawyer Biaggi, who was arrested in 1958 while armed with hand grenades), and the Parti nationaliste.

Many former members of the Jeune nation were absorbed by the Fédération des étudiants nationalistes after the former organization was dissolved in 1958 by the regime; nevertheless, the directors of Europe-Action claim important differences with the Jeune nation (the Jeune nation was founded in 1949 by the Sidos brothers, its themes being antiforeignism, antiparliamentarism, and anti-Semitism). They state that the nationalism of Barrès now is dated and that a broader conception of nationalism must be acquired by affiliating with nationalists of other countries (European), and accepting certain aspects of a nationalism common to Europeans. Their aim is to obtain recognition of the superiority of European civilization and to combat all conceptions of liberty and equality. Committees of Europe-Action supported and spent considerable money in 1965 on the electoral campaign of Tixier-Vignancour, acknowledging that the campaign offered them slight chance for success but an excellent opportunity to distribute their propaganda and to unite further the "Nationalist opposition." [63]

Georges Bidault, former foreign minister of France and associated later with the OAS (which he denies) and who until recently was in exile, heads the monthly publication *Esprit public*.[64] This publication, which resents being identified as rightist, claims that its social program is Left-oriented, that it defends a

---

[62] Laurens, "Nouveaux visages. . . ."
[63] Laurens, "Nouveaux visages. . . ."
[64] Laurens, "Nouveaux visages. . . ."

United States of Europe, that it deplores racism, and that its foreign policy is identical with that of the former Popular Republican party, MRP. In 1964 the directors of *Esprit public* formed the Rassemblement de l'esprit public, an organization whose basic unit is the cell, announcing that its struggle for "Algérie française has been purely defensive and that it now is a case of going over to the offensive on the political plan, to take power by legal channels." [65] It stated that it does not hope to bring down the Gaullist regime but that its action is reserved for "after Gaullism." It also stated that "After de Gaulle, we want to participate in power." [66] The Rassemblement's "parallel hierarchies," comprising five to twenty people each, have been installed in various cities and villages. At this time, however, the Rassemblement is very reserved, probably because it is so discredited and because Bidault is hoping to gain clearance from provisional release.

Action française, presided over by Bernard Mallet, is one of the oldest antirepublican associations. Opposed to all versions of universal suffrage, it states that "our first hope is to utilize all the forces at our disposal and to work for the reestablishment of monarchy." [67] During the presidential election of 1965 it supported Tixier-Vignancour, but only with the understanding that this would not prevent it from continuing to focus on the attainment of monarchy. Its candidate for the throne is the Count of Paris, whose views often are contrary to its own. The count is articulate and capable, and various of his articles find their way periodically into serious publications, including those of Mendès-France orientation.

Pierre Poujade, President of the Union et fraternité française, is a veteran at combating all forms of republicanism. During the Fourth Republic he led in the National Assembly a delegation of deputies, but the legislative elections of November 1958 deprived his group of all representation. Poujade is anti-parliamentary and anti-Semitic (which he denies), and was formerly of Algérie française orientation. His appeal is to small

---

[65] Laurens, "Nouveaux visages. . . ."
[66] Laurens, "Nouveaux visages. . . ."
[67] Laurens, "Nouveaux visages. . . ."

proprietors plagued by high taxes, inflation, and the rise in France of large corporate bodies. His popularity under the Fourth Republic was greater than it is now, but he continues to boast that he leads the "only organized movement from Dunkerque to Perpignan" which is outside the classical political parties.[68] At his disposal are a newspaper and publishing house.

Poujadism began as an antitax movement concentrated in the locality of Saint-Ceré, where Poujade owns a stationery store. It spread from there to the departmental level, and, finally, to the national scene. Poujade claims that until 1954 his movement had confidence in the Fourth Republic, but that it then realized that it is impossible to defend small enterprisers without attacking the technocrats of the regime, who wish to make distribution in France exclusively the property of the great trusts.[69] Publications defending Poujade describe him as being opposed to all ideology, and interested not in ideas but "in action." One of his own propaganda tracts describes Poujadism as consisting of "defense of little people," and it refers to him as "the man who stopped controls [fiscal], the Robin Hood who rushed out of the night with his bows, his band, his big laugh, and scattered the archers of the king." [70] Poujadism once claimed 800,000 adherents, but it has today the support only of a fraction of that figure.

In 1964 diverse organizations of the extreme Right established a coordinating agency to support Tixier-Vignancour in the presidential election of the following year (the bureau de liaison de l'opposition nationale).[71] Nevertheless, the extreme Right found itself at a great disadvantage in its attempts to attract the French to defense of its main themes. Ultraconservative French who resent the devaluation of the French army, the understanding that De Gaulle achieved with many Communist countries, the loss of Algeria, and the abandonment of what once was an empire are also preoccupied with maintaining a strong sense of national independence; they do not want a

[68] Laurens, "Nouveaux visages. . . ."

[69] Publications défense de l'Occident, *Le Poujadisme,* 33 (Paris: Les sept couleurs, 1956), 18.

[70] *Le Poujadisme,* p. 13.

[71] Laurens, "Nouveaux visages. . . ."

United States of Europe, and they favor retention of the *force de frappe*. These are phenomena for which Gaullism stands too, and so their ability to derive satisfaction from some of its policies detracts from the growth of the extreme Right.

CHURCH, STATE, AND CATHOLICISM

The conflict between church and state has given to the French political process a certain contour. Anticlericalism influences the doctrines and actions of the Left; clericalism influences the activities and beliefs of the conservative forces. However, the magnitude of that influence now is diminishing among elements both of the Left and Right.

Church-state conflict derives from the French Revolution, that time in French history when the state proclaimed new ideals and institutions opposed to those previously created, shaped and dominated by the church. The Revolution was directed against many aspects of the Old Regime; in particular, it announced its dependence upon rationalism rather than Catholicism as a means of solving the problems of society. Consequently, for many years after 1789 the church adopted a distinct antirepublican attitude, combating that form of political organization and continuing to value the idea of reestablishing its hegemony over the French nation. The conflict reached all the way to the Vatican, papal authority being enlisted to denounce the "atheistic republics." [72] During the early years of the Third Republic both hierarchy and priesthood engaged periodically in attempts to bring down the republic. During the Dreyfus affair, for example, efforts were undertaken by members of the church to coordinate anti-Semi-

[72] Pius IX, for example, regarded by liberal Catholics Lord Acton in England and Dollinger in Germany (who later was excommunicated) as an unfortunate event in the history of the papacy, issued in 1864 his famous "syllabus of errors" in which he condemned republicanism, free inquiry, and liberalism. Later, in 1877, the French bishops demanded of the state that it recognize the temporal authority of the Pope and his government. In 1904 the French government withdrew from the Vatican diplomatic recognition, an act that intensified church-state controversy in France, leading within the nation to incidents of violence. World War I slowed down the conflict, and subsequently it evolved into one centering on the relative merits of Catholic versus secular education.

tism and antirepublicanism in a calculated drive against the regime. The Jesuit societies, who formed a regime within the regime and who sought to bring down the republic, never succeeded in their quest.

Both monarchy and the church failed in their collaborative effort to destroy the republic. Later, after the republic had been consolidated, a new relationship evolved between Catholics and propertied elements, and this time the enemy became socialism. That relationship was subsequently transformed, too, after movements within the church began to suggest that Catholicism was not dependent for its existence on capitalism, and that it could prosper better in a socialist environment. Consequently, annual conferences in which Catholic and socialist elements seek to determine how a synthesis of the two can be effected have become commonplace.

It is easy—when examining the church-state controversy— to forget that Catholicism is the religion of members both of the Left and the Right. The electorate of the French Left identifies itself as being two-thirds to four-fifths Catholic, and among the parties of the Left those who identify themselves as being "without religion" form only a minority (29 percent Communist; 17 percent Socialist, SFIO; 11 percent Radical-Socialist).[73] However, practicing Catholics, who form approximately 2 to 11 percent of the electorate of the Left, constitute about 28 to 45 percent of the electorate of the Right.[74] With reference to religion, the distinction between the Left and the Right is not Catholicism and non-Catholicism, but between a Catholicism that is practiced more and one that is practiced less. Those who practice Catholicism on a regular basis tend to be more conservative politically and economically than those who do not.[75] Practicing Catholics voted heavily for de Gaulle in the presidential election of 1965, casting approximately 66 percent of their ballots for him (and about 20 percent for Lecanuet and 8 percent for Mitterand).[76]

Ninety percent of all French citizens are baptized, take

[73] Institut français d'opinion publique, "Réligion et politique," *Sondages,* 2 (1967), 48.

[74] "Réligion et politique," 48.

[75] "Réligion et politique," 48.

[76] "Réligion et politique," 51.

communion, and are married in the Church. Nevertheless, only one fourth practice Catholicism regularly.[77] Dominant traits of practicing Catholics are a preponderance of females, a strong proportion of people more than fifty years of age, and slight representation among working class elements.[78] The nonpracticing population is characterized by a preponderance of males, an average age slightly inferior to the average national age, a strong proportion of workers, and meager representation among people engaged in agriculture.

French Catholicism is not ready to abandon its alliance with conservatism and form a new affiliation with the Left. Studies by the French Institute of Public Opinion show that such a break is less than imminent, and that the Left will for a long time continue to enjoy minority status among Catholics. Nonetheless, studies do demonstrate the flow to the Left of more Catholics than ever before, indicating that an evolution is in progress and that some Catholics are revising and reformulating their versions of conservatism, all the time adopting on issues positions that are less conservative than heretofore. Their struggle against the republic is associated now with the past. Their campaign against socialism is not waged strongly any more. Even their crusade against communism no longer is approached ferociously. No longer can the extreme Right offer very much to Catholics, and only a small minority is attracted to it. Catholics who would not think of voting for the Communist party or the late Federation of the Left do not hesitate to vote massively for the Union of Democrats for the Fifth Republic and less heavily for the Center and its Catholic candidates. Segments of the young clergy now preach support of unions, international cooperation, and unity in French politics; the curricula of private and public schools no longer are so different that they offer strongly competing conceptions of existence and organization.

Both Catholics and Communists have "evolved"; their integration within the republic now is real rather than theoretical. Both remain adversaries, but they now are both societally integrated. In the France of the future, controversy between

---

[77] "Réligion et politique," 7.
[78] "Réligion et politique," 10.

them very well could flow along the lines of established republican competition. And—should this become the case—what would be the rationale, then, for continued existence of the Center? Was not the Center an instrumentality that played its role best in those times when it mediated between polar extremes, and made possible the creation of governments that could not have existed otherwise? What, however, would be the role of the Center in a France in which Catholics are not alienated and Communists are not isolated? Clearly, this is not the time for the creation of two great coalitions, one of the Left and one of the Right, one exercising power responsibly, the other constituting a responsible opposition, but if someday that possibility is available, it may be at the cost of the Center. Just now there are signs that some elements of the populace are already prepared to make this transformation (more so than some outmoded political parties, with their heavy *apparatus* and established sentiments of "patriotism of party" who are not anxious to yield to this change).

Convergence between Right and Left is occurring now with greater frequency than heretofore, and gaps between practicing and non-practicing Catholics no longer are so great as to preclude the shaping of a minimum consensus that will enable them to engage each other in orderly competition and rotation in office. Political action with Communists is regarded by Catholics as no longer impossible; the French Institute of Public Opinion reveals that among the practicing Catholics it interrogated, 47 percent are prepared to engage with Communists in common action.[79] Among all those interrogated, including both practicing and nonpracticing Catholics, the affirmative response to common action with Communists was 53 percent.[80]

It cannot be said that the church-state controversy has been solved completely in contemporary France, or that it has failed to leave an imprint on political habits and thought. On the other hand, who can deny the conflict's deintensification and its

[79] "Réligion et politique," 50.
[80] "Religion et politique," 61. The question asked was, "According to you, is it possible for a Catholic to engage with a Communist in common political action?"

resultant contribution to the making of a better France? This evolution represents considerable progress in a nation whose inhabitants in times previous killed each other because of this issue. In fact, among the citizenry, it is difficult to detect evidence now of preoccupation for or against religion of a magnitude sufficient to give to social and political behavior a definite coloration.[81]

POLITICAL VIOLENCE AND REVOLUTION

The observer of French affairs cannot help but be aware of the prevalence in French history of the seizure of power and revolution. Nor can an observer fail to note the obvious pleasure taken by the French in describing themselves as a revolutionary people —even if in everyday life French society evidences relatively few signs of valuing violence.

The French think that they are a revolutionary people; and, in fact, they do resort occasionally to this form of expression. However, the fact that the French also are a very conservative people probably accounts for their ability to retrieve after such upheavals out of apparent disintegration some amount of integration and an operable order. Historians have noted in French political history the way in which great transformations have been followed by compromises between forces that previously seemed antithetical. The destruction of the First Empire was followed by the creation of a semiparliamentary system; the revolution of 1848 was followed by a regime based on some elements of consent; and the bloody Paris Commune uprising of

[81] Take, for example, the United States of Europe movement, which comprises Catholics and members of other religions, as well as socialists and conservatives. Years ago some socialists were inclined to view the movement as a "Jesuit conspiracy," whereas conservative Catholics, contrary to Vatican policy, frequently saw it as an instrument of potential socialist domination. These attitudes rarely are found today; among some Protestant communities of the south sometimes more concern is evidenced relative to church-state relations than is the case among Catholics. Protestants once were subjected to terrible persecutions. Perhaps the apprehensions of this minority are understandable. Nevertheless, their assessments appear to be shaped sometime by what the church-state relationship *was,* instead of what it now *is.*

1871 was followed by the creation of the Third Republic, yet another regime based on compromise. The destruction of the Fourth Republic led in 1958, however, to the creation of a regime that subordinated the Assembly entirely to the domination of a strong executive, and which, as the years went on, became increasingly unheedful of public opinion and criticism. In May 1968 a large segment of the populace addressed itself to certain imbalances in the regime.

FROM *RÉVOLUTION À LA GO-GO* TO NATIONAL PARALYSIS

May 1968 was the tenth anniversary of the Gaullist republic. The regime in anticipation of it prepared a number of presentations and public relations overtures calculated to congratulate the French for being so fortunate as to have General de Gaulle as their national leader, Georges Pompidou as their prime minister, and the Union of Democrats for the Fifth Republic as their party of "stability and continuity." The opposition forces prepared counterbriefs, seeking to convince the French that it was time for a change in regime. Numerous students at the Sorbonne prepared their own *manifestation* against Gaullist educational policies, one which evolved quickly from a Latin Quarter demonstration to the status of a student version of *révolution à la go-go*.[82] The *quartier* became the locale for street fighting between students and police [83] (all of the trees on historic *Boul'mich* were cut down to construct barricades). Soon there was established on the Left Bank a "juvenile commune" comprising Marxist-Leninists, Trotskyites, anarchists, and other diverse categories. The movement, which was oriented initially toward educational reform, soon broadened and claimed societal

[82] The crisis began with the arrest of students who were protesting in the vicinity of the Sorbonne against a university they had come to regard as one of the great bastions of bourgeois society.

[83] *Le Monde,* May 16–22, 1968, *Sélection hebdomadaire,* p. 4, states that many bourgeois parents were more indignant with the behavior of the police than with that of their offspring. Various residents of the *quartier* descended to the streets to give medical aid to the students. And there were reports of garbage and potted plants being thrown at the police by some residents from the upper floors of dwellings.

reform, expressing its sympathy with the workers and urging them to occupy the factories. Revolts occurred elsewhere in the university system, as well as in some *lycées* and *collèges*. The country's work force responded, and as many as ten million people struck their employers, plunging the nation into weeks of economic paralysis. The financial loss to the nation was calculated at many millions of dollars per day.

This is an era in which political scientists assess almost all behavior in terms of elite phenomena; nonetheless, the events of May 1968 appear to have taken place *despite the elites*. Both the elites of the "majority" and those of the opposition lacked real control over the movement. The movement was in origin spontaneous, touched off first by the students, caught up then by the workers, and accepted finally by elements of the middle class. When it was at its peak, the president of the republic and the prime minister were without institutions or segments of the populace effectively to whom they could turn for aid. The wrath of much of the country was turned temporarily against both the president of the republic and the prime minister. Article 16, which allows for emergency dictatorship when the safety and institutions of the nation are threatened, hardly was capable of being invoked by the president—can a president apply emergency powers to eight or ten million people who decide to remain away from their jobs indefinitely, and thereby get them back to work?

The man who had overcome the army and who pushed the traditional political parties into the shadows of obscurity and who for years had lectured the people like a stern papa, in May 1968 became temporarily the victim of his own paternal overprotection. Instead of using his years in office to bring more elements of the populace into participation in his regime— preparing it thereby for exercise of the responsibilities that go along with a mature citizenry—de Gaulle had kept it in a juvenile state, asking of it only that it follow. And for years it did follow; de Gaulle, however, resorted periodically to exercises of behavior that did not hide his contempt for it. A populace that had given so much could not continue to be treated that way without ultimately reacting. It would be presumptuous to claim that the France of Alain temporarily was reborn in May 1968; at the same time, it probably is accurate to say that ten years of the Gaullist regime had not succeeded in divesting the French of their distrust of the flamboyant usage of authority. France is a country in which authority must be employed—nonetheless, those who use it must do so with some sense of restraint and with some reservations about its deployment. To employ it in haughty fashion is to invite many Frenchmen to engage in personal searches for pins with which they can prick the balloon of authority. Devaluating overconfident and pompous leaders is an old French pastime.

The results of the legislative elections of June 1968 show that the French are not averse to chastising an authority without abandoning it. Although the Gaullists were returned in great numbers to the National Assembly, it would be inaccurate to describe their victory as blind affirmation of them by the populace, and proof of its susceptibility to de Gaulle's arguments of an impending "red totalitarianism" in France. Prior to the elections the Gaullists promised the country future reforms of a major nature—such as pay raises of at least 10 percent, educational transformation, and liberalization of enterprise. They offered the country an attractive package if it would return to work, and they told it that the best way to realize that package was by returning the Gaullists to power in the legislative elections of June 1968. The country did precisely that, producing for the Union of Democrats for the Fifth Republic a legislative majority, the only homogeneous one ever recorded by a political party in all of French history. Those French who ordered that package then waited for its delivery. The contract has been "signed" and then the question was whether the promises would be implemented. The coming months would bear testimony to the ability of the Gaullists to keep those promises. There could be no reasonable alibi for not doing so; the Gaullists asked for the majority, and they received from the populace exactly what they requested. No longer did they lack the legislative means with which to translate their promises into realities. The results of the legislative elections of 1968 did not end the crisis of Gaullism; they signaled a new stage in its evolution. The populace found in May 1968 that it can bring to its knees any authority unheedful of its welfare. During that month that populace was in France the greatest decision-making force of all (it was also the greatest "collective bargainer").

What were the "lessons" of the May 1968 disorders? First, by 1968 the Gaullist regime had taken its existence so much for granted that it had become increasingly heedless of public opinion and its demands. Moreover, it had become downright contemptuous of the opposition. For many years the populace had been told repeatedly that it could not possibly do without the Gaullists. That contributed to a growing public resentment against the Gaullists and determination by some segments of the populace to teach the regime a "well-deserved lesson." Second, for too many years President de Gaulle had been "above it all," giving scant attention to domestic affairs while he busied himself with the things "that really count," or the great areas of international diplomacy. When the rioting erupted, he was not in the country but abroad in Rumania.[84] His prime minister was in Iran. Later, when street fighting and economic stand-still had reached their peaks, de Gaulle spent the day investigating the possible utilization of his services in the Vietnam peace talks then in progress between representatives of the United States and North Vietnam. Third, the President of the Republic, "safe" until the expiration of his mandate in 1972, and the government of Georges Pompidou, "secure" as the result of its composite majority in the National Assembly, failed to realize until late in the game how much the executive and legislative organs of the Gaullist regime were out of tune with the tenor of public opinion. A populace "turned on" for weeks brought those organs virtually to their knees, as it participated in behavior unprecedented in western Europe in the twentieth century. No Georges Sorel led it in a general strike, and organized political parties did not guide its actions. Millions of people simply walked off the job, teaching the Élysée Palace, the Matignon, and the Palais Bourbon that "authority" has its source not in them but in the people. By 1968 the Gaullist regime had become drunk

---

[84] *Le Monde*'s headline of May 18, 1968, played up the occupation of factories in Lyon, the extension of strikes, and student disturbances. Also on page one was a feature article on de Gaulle, who was telling Rumanian citizens at that very time that "We hope to make Europe from one end to another without an iron curtain."

on the arguments that it had manufactured for itself in its own cellars; however, public action during the second quarter of that year did much to "sober it up."

After May 1968, it was obvious that President de Gaulle and a Gaullist government would not again be as contemptuous of and as far detached from public opinion as they were before May 1968. No longer could they refuse to listen and write off as "communist propaganda" demands of large segments of the populace. No longer could de Gaulle perform as he did in previous years, lecturing the French like children from that set paternal posture. The Élysée Palace was back on the Rue Saint-Honoré (where it belongs), and not on Olympus (where once its occupant mistakenly thought it was). Finally, France had changed again, and now the question was whether President de Gaulle and the forces arrayed around him were capable of changing with it? De Gaulle adapted himself to certain roles which were instrumental in pulling him through many crises during the period between 1958 and 1968; nonetheless, he would have to dig further into his arsenal of roles in order to address himself effectively to post-1968 exigencies. His future performance would be determined in large part not by the number of seats won by the Union of Democrats for the Fifth Republic in future legislative elections, but by the way in which elements of the populace reacted to him.

PROGRAMMATIC IMAGES AND PREFERENCES AMONG THE POLITICAL PARTIES

The Communist party proposes the nationalization of monopolies in key sectors of industry, nationalization of the large banks, full employment, aid to industrially underdeveloped regions, augmentation of the purchasing power of workers and amelioration of their conditions of life (no salary or pension being inferior to 600 francs per month). It also favors return to a forty-hour week, partial indemnization for unemployment, no restrictions on the right to strike, reimbursement for medical and pharmaceutical expenses at a minimum of 80 percent, elevation of the incomes of agricultural workers, lower retirement ages, guarantees for a minimum income of 250 francs per month for aged persons, construction of 600,000 housing units per year, reduction of consumption taxes, increased exemptions from income tax for lower income categories, equal salaries for women, reduction in the term of military service to twelve months, development of closer relations with the Soviet Union, "substitution for the military blocs of a system of European collective security," adaptation of the *force de frappe* (independent nuclear deterrent) to nonmilitary ends, prohibition of further nuclear testing, condemnation of colonialism and of the American "aggression against the people of Vietnam," repudiation of presidential "personal power," and creation of a government which "must be responsible before the National Assembly" and "elected by proportional representation." Finally, the party endorses programmatically union of the parties of the Left realized on the basis of a common program that would become the basis of a "contract of government" for a future majority, extension of departmental and communal liberties, separation of church and state and laity of the schools, and a new set of regulations for radio and television.[85] This is the program on which the Communist party presents itself to the populace, and when it does special efforts are made by it not to become involved in Marxist or Leninist theory. The approach is hard, cold, and closely tuned to existing realities. Marxist and Leninist theoretical excursions are reserved for conferences and presentations by special figures. If the Communist party wishes to get to the people, it must sound like the people.

The Unified Socialist party (PSU) presents itself as the "protector of power of the workers." It regards the Fifth Republic as having placed the economy at the service of the well-to-do, increasing unemployment, retarding production, and neglecting the housing crisis. It proposes wage increases, return to a forty-hour week, reduction of the retirement age from sixty-five to sixty, larger retirement pensions with a minimum guarantee of at least 250 francs per month, an apartment for each family according to its needs and at a price compatible with

[85] All aspects of the program cited in this paragraph are from Parti communiste français, *Selon que vous serez banquier ou salarié* (Paris: *Éditions L'Humanité,* March, 1967), pp. 1–5.

its resources, construction of 550,000 dwelling units per year, rent controls, reductions in consumption taxes, higher progressive taxes on capital and luxury items, elevation to eighteen years of the age at which one may leave school, creation of a lay and democratic "National Service of Education," reduction of voting age to eighteen years, free medicine for all, establishment of real equality for women and abrogation of female restrictive legislation, more of a share by peasants in the national revenue, increases in French economic expansion of at least 5.5 percent per year, salary guarantees for workers who change profession or region, more money for research, and vesting in the nation the means of production "each time that this appears necessary" (particularly the great banks, steel, oil, nuclear industry, naval shipworks, chemistry, pharmacy, aviation, and publicity). Politically, the PSU wants a "government of the legislature," and substitution for the Senate of an economic assembly which would play a role in the execution of the "Plan." The PSU also proposes greater local autonomy, elimination of nuclear testing, a permanent police force for the United Nations Organization, disarmament, abandonment of the *force de frappe,* reductions in the size of the armed forces, an independent Europe "free from American domination," the end of the Atlantic Pact, and repudiation of presidential "personal power." [86]

The program of the French Socialist party (SFIO), adopted by the party's National Council on May 19–20, 1962, which was the result of three years of work, takes cognizance of "modifications since 1945 in the functioning of the capitalist regime and in the relations among peoples." The "permanent objectives" of the party are: (1) Man must be liberated from all spiritual and material oppression. (2) The capitalist system is founded on the accumulation and abusive utilization of surplus value. Socialism seeks to remain between capitalism and Sovietism. Individual property must be safeguarded when acquired by individual work. (3) The SFIO is reformist and revolutionary. (4) Colonialism and imperialism are indefensible. (5) Political

[86] All aspects of the program cited in this paragraph are from Parti socialiste unifié, PSU, "Élections législatives de mars 1967," *Tribune socialiste,* pp. 1–4.

democracy must be accompanied by economic and social democracy. Economic and social democracy must be accompanied by political democracy. (6) Government must be stable and the state must be secular.[87]

The program of the Federation of the Democratic and Socialist Left (to which the SFIO and the Radical Socialist party adhered until 1968) emphasized during the legislative elections of 1967 that "the myth of Gaullist stability" finally had been shattered, and that the Gaullists were fragmenting, "some of them have already abandoned the ship." France—the federation argued—was already in the period of post-Gaullism. The federation emphasized political stability but not on the basis of one-man rule, aid to education, real equality for women, a just share of the national revenue for workers, decent pensions for the aged, condemnation of the *force de frappe,* a "socialism adapted to France," and a "return to democracy." The federation's conceptions of the future regime and its opposition to Gaullism were contained in detail in its common agreement of February 24, 1968, with the Communist party, which is described in detail in Chapter 5.

The Radical Socialist party program expresses opposition to presidential "personal power," and approval of the creation of a new majority. In the party's sixty-third Congress held in Marseilles in November 1966, it was stated that "It gives its approval fully and completely to the program and orientation of the Fédération." [88] The Radical Socialists reject the idea of an "isolated France" and endorse a United States of Europe.[89] However, whatever its programmatical orientation, the Radical party always is a "party of contradictions." While its program invariably is to the Left, many of its members hope for the success of the Center. In fact, in 1962, until the people of the Queuille-Morice tendency broke with the organization, their preference was Algérie française and pro-OAS.[90] In the majority

[87] The entire program is summarized in *Le Monde,* August 23, 1962, p. 2.

[88] *Le Monde,* November 22, 1966, p. 8.

[89] *Le Monde,* October 1, 1963, p. 3.

[90] Jean François Kesler, "Actualité du radicalisme," *Perspectives socialistes* (August–September 1962), 22–29.

motion voted by the party in its Lyon Congress of 1965, the party endorsed François Mitterand, praised Gaston Defferre, and saluted Jean Lecanuet! [91]

The program of the Democratic Center emphasizes the growing economic insecurity in France, particularly the fact that with 400,000 idle France has its greatest unemployment in almost a decade and a half. The Center is critical of the decline in French domestic investments and lack of expansion in the economy. The tendency of the Center is to support the mainte-nance of existing political institutions, asserting that an effective political system is impossible without a "strong executive." The party supports the Constitution of the Fifth Republic but condemned the fact that under President de Gaulle it belonged no longer to the nation, "but to a man, a party, a clan." The Center supports full employment, guarantees for housing and construction of at least 600,000 dwellings per year, guarantees for the aged of a decent life, equal treatment for women, mod-ernization of education, guarantees for commercial property endangered by Gaullist projects, greater economic expansion and purchasing power increases, tax reductions for people in lower income categories, lower taxes for investments promoting eco-nomic growth, reduction of interest rates, construction of more highways and introduction of a plan for traffic control, modern-ization of telecommunications, construction of more hospitals, creation of a United States of Europe, and a real Supreme Court. Finally, the Center states, "The choice is not between stability and a return to the past. It is between a policy of stagnation which disturbs the country and a new policy of expansion in a United Europe." [92]

The "Gaullist family" (UNR-UDT, Républicains indé-pendants, Gauche Vᵉ République) went into the legislative elections of March 1967 with a program that was almost purely defensive. It did not emphasize what it intended to do when in government, dwelling instead on what it had achieved, and advancing itself as the best means of "barring the road to the

[91] *Le Monde,* October 24–25, 1965, p. 7.
[92] All aspects of the program cited are from Centre démocrate, *Élections législatives de mars 1967, 17 circonscription, 15ᵉ Arrondisse-ment, Paris.*

Communists and the nostalgics of the Fourth Republic." It presented itself as that "majority which upholds de Gaulle," saying that citizens could hardly refuse to continue in power those who had reestablished the international prestige of France, restored French money to one of the best in the world, and assured the success of the European Economic Community. A special effort was made to present the "Gaullist family" as non-sectarians who were being confronted by "the extremists of the Right and of the Left." Pleas were extended for no return to the regimes of the past and their crises, instability, and inflation: "Choose. 1946–1958, in 12 years of the Fourth Republic, 22 governments. 1958–1967, in 9 years of the Fifth Republic, 2 governments!" In the legislative elections of 1968 the Gaullist formation presented itself as the barrier against "Red totalitarianism," the foe of disorder, and the guarantor of great impending reforms.[93]

The Independent party's program supports strengthening of the family, the "Christian legacy," and defense of small and middle-size property holders. It stands also for militant opposition to communism, socialism, Gaullism, and most forms of state economic planning. Identification of what the Independents oppose usually is more revealing than inquiry into what they support. Now that the era of "after de Gaulle" has arrived, the Independents are hoping that the "Gaullist family" will fragment so that they can pluck from it elements which they feel are truly closer to themselves.[94]

---

[93] All aspects of the program reproduced in this paragraph are from Comité d'action pour la Vᵉ République, Élections législatives des 5 et 12 mars 1967, XV arrondissement, 17 circonscription, Paris, March, 1967, pp. 1–2.

[94] See interview with Antoine Pinay by *Paris-Match* reproduced in part in *Le Monde*, November 5, 1965, p. 1. Pinay "astonished" some people by stating that he agreed with most aspects of the domestic and foreign policies of the Pompidou government. Independent party leader Pinay knew that no conservative candidate could beat de Gaulle in the presidential election of 1965, and that Independent candidates would fare poorly in competition with Gaullists in legislative elections. It appears that M. Pinay, like a professional boxer confronted with a hard-hitting adversary, was "moving in close for protection." Why "slug it out toe to toe" if it means certain annihilation?

COMMUNICATIONS MEDIA

The press

Few books have been written on the French press. Among the most prominent is the early work published by Georges Weil, *Le journal: Origines, évolution et rôle de la presse périodique.*[95] In 1963 the late Jacques Kayser brought out his *Le quotidien français,* a work concerned primarily with the development of techniques for systematic study of the press, which must be regarded as a highly commendable effort.[96] What is needed, however, are more studies which explore the extent to which the citizenry seeks to inform itself as a result of its utilization of this medium of communication and education.

Like the press in the United States, the French newspaper world has been undergoing great contraction. In 1874 Paris alone counted forty newspapers; by 1962 that figure had been reduced to twelve. In 1874 the provinces comprised 179 newspapers—and only ninety-six by 1962.[97] Cities which previously had more than one newspaper now find themselves only with one (although newspapers from other cities and departments may readily be available there). On the departmental level, fourteen departments have been without any newspapers of their own since 1874. Local news within these areas frequently goes unreported, and in the *communes* citizens rely on oral communications for information. This absence of newspapers has occurred more commonly in the south, in those parts of the nation usually referred to as underdeveloped, whereas the far north has been the locale for greater development of this medium of communications.

Whatever the real orientation of French newspapers, they exhibit little inclination to identify themselves openly as political or ideological organs. Jacques Kayser discovered in his study that in the whole nation only one newspaper classifies itself as

[95] Georges Weil, *Le journal: Origines, évolution et rôle de la presse périodique* (Paris: A. Michel, 1934).

[96] Jacques Kayser, *Le quotidien français* (Paris: A. Colin, 1963).

[97] Kayser, p. 17.

a *journal politique;* four in Paris and fifteen in the provinces describe themselves as having a political or ideological orientation; six use the word "democracy"; one calls itself radical, two socialist, and three communist; three identify themselves as party presses (*Le Populaire,* Paris, SFIO; *L'Humanité,* Paris, and *La Liberté,* Lille, Communist). *La Croix* presents an interpretation that clearly is religious.

In all, the tendency for newspapers to identify their orientation was greater in the past than it is today. Each day newspaper policy is influenced more and more by the necessity of recognizing that sales and advertising are dependent upon ability to appeal to a broad consumer market. Consequently, there is an inclination to shape presentations so as to concentrate on delivering up versions of the news which contain fewer personal convictions. Even so doctrinaire a publication as *L'Humanité* is heedful of not penetrating certain sensitive areas. *L'Humanité* has considerable advertising from cleaners, liver pills, and certain department stores, and it has no desire to drive these subscribers elsewhere. Newspapers must find advertisers and sell copies. *L'Humanité* also exists to sell communism. *L'Humanité* tries to do both of these things.

All of the foregoing is not intended to suggest that coverage of political phenomena has decined in the French press; all that is suggested is that the way in which political information is handled has been subjected to refinement and new techniques in an age of mass consumption. Increasingly, it is the policy to run more information of more general interest, toning down that which divides and broadening that which does not. Consequently, in this kind of environment the decline of "newspapers of opinion" is something to be expected.

The metropolitan daily *Le Monde* is in a class by itself, being perhaps the greatest newspaper in the world. *Le Monde* does not hesitate to express its opinions through various signed articles, which seldom are worth ignoring. The editor presents his views in editorials, and people such as Jacques Fauvet, Maurice Duverger, Raymond Barrillon, Pierre Viansson-Ponté, and many others express their convictions in special articles that appear either on a daily or weekly basis (Fauvet sometimes appears on a monthly basis). There is no prescribed ideological format for *Le Monde,* and diversity of opinion is regarded by the publication as normal. Some of the paper's articles are examples of lengthy research. It is not the policy of the paper to run photographs, and with very few exceptions it has successfully resisted this practice. Straight news releases are handled with scrupulous accuracy. Finally, it is difficult to know how on a daily basis *Le Monde* consistently can squeeze so much valuable information into approximately twenty pages (and far more than appears in the columns of one American newspaper whose Sunday edition sometimes exceeds 300 pages).

With few exceptions, French newspapers give the reader generally what he wants. According to the surveys of the French Institute of Public Opinion, readers' interests run more to local news dealing with domestic and foreign policies. Fewer than half of the readers read editorials.[98] Most newspapers exhibit a general tendency to present raw information, insignificant facts, and anecdotal situations in the field of politics.[99]

French publications discovered decades ago that photographs increase circulation. Leading the way in exploiting this technique, Jean Prouvost increased the sales of the daily *Paris-Soir* by almost a million and a half copies in the period between 1931 and 1933.[100] Today *Paris-Match* and other publications increase their circulation by extensive use of photography. A recent newcomer to the slick market is *Adam,* which is similar to the American publication *Playboy.* It contains articles dedicated to diverse themes—including politics (it also contains touched-up nude photography, and so it is difficult to tell how many people buy it for its literary content).

For a country that contains so many diverse brands of public opinion, paradoxically, there are few opportunities for expressing them in the press. Two Paris newspapers contain space for letters to the editor (*Paris-Jour* and *Paris-Presse*). *Le Figaro* and *Libération* provide space periodically, as does *Le Monde.*

Two weekly news magazines circulate extensively in the

---

[98] Meynaud and Lancelot, p. 37.
[99] Meynaud and Lancelot, p. 39.
[100] Meynaud and Lancelot, p. 36.

metropole and overseas. *L'Express* is like the American *Time* and the German *Der Spiegel*. It capsulizes the news, reviews plays, movies, and books, and gives information on political personalities. Ten years ago it took a very firm stand on controversial issues (which probably lost it some readers), and identified itself closely with the views of Pierre Mendès-France (although it gave one-page coverage to the *Bloc-notes* of François Mauriac, until his pro-Gaullism led to his resignation from the publication). *L'Express* adopted a new approach in 1964, fashioning itself after popular contemporary news magazines, minimizing opinions and emphasizing "objectivity" as a theme. That transformation enabled it to increase its circulation greatly. *France-Observateur* also underwent change in the 1960s. The organ of the classical Left was "retooled," adopting a new name (*Le nouvel observateur*) and a broader and more modern Left perspective. Editorial policy was refashioned. Claude Bourdet, Oxford graduate, brilliant polemicist, and the author of editorial appeals that sometimes were more relevant to the nineteenth than to the twentieth century, left the direction of the publication. Today *Le nouvel observateur* remains doctrinaire, discovering each week the great conspiracies of the Right and fighting the great battles of the Left; nevertheless, now it pays attention to phenomena that once it ignored.

Table 3-1 presents a list of Paris dailies, showing increases or decreases in their circulation between July 1949 and March 1957.

Radio and television

State and private radio stations both existed in France before World War II. In 1945 broadcasting was named a natural resource and defined as a state monopoly. Abuses, however, soon entered into the use of this resource, as various governments saw in it an effective vehicle for public indoctrination. Such behavior became characteristic of governments in general, irrespective of their political orientation; and whenever crises developed the airwaves witnessed more lavish efforts at propagandization. In 1956, after the outbreak of the Algerian war,

**Table 3–1   Increases and decreases in circulation
of Paris daily newspapers, July 1949 to March 1957**

| Name of Daily | Daily Circulation | | Difference |
	July 1949	March 1957	
Morning papers			
Le Parisien libéré	437,000	836,000	+399,000
Le Figaro	401,000	489,000	+ 88,000
L'Aurore	323,000	474,000	+151,000
L'Humanité	252,000	215,000	− 37,000
Franc-Tireur	245,000	89,000	−155,000
Ce Matin	194,000	failed	
Libération	140,000	115,000	− 25,000
Combat	97,000	59,000	− 38,000
L'Époque	66,000	failed	
Le Populaire	52,000	14,500	− 37,500
L'Aube	46,000	failed	
Evening Papers			
France-Soir	573,000	1,331,000	+758,000
Paris-Presse	402,000	183,500	−218,500
Ce Soir	246,000	failed	
La Croix	166,000	156,000	− 9,500
Le Monde	161,000	202,000	+ 41,000

Source: Robert Chapuis, L'Information, 1959, reproduced in Meynaud and
Lancelot, p. 34.

political "information on the war" bore, for example, great
similarity to the Mollet government's aspirations. The introduction in France of television subsequently enlarged the government's opportunities for manipulated political persuasion.

In 1959 the state addressed itself to reform of radio and
television service (known as ORTF). Although autonomy appeared to have been granted to both under the authority of
the minister of information, senior appointments to the service
remained, nonetheless, at the discretion of the government "to
whose pressures their holders were subject." [101] The subordinate

[101] P. M. Gaudemet, "Le régime de la radio diffusion et de la
télévision en France," International Review of Administrative Sciences,
Vol. 31, No. 1 (1965), 15.

staff was given a recognized status, and newsmen attached to the organization were defined as civil servants. The changes affected did not preclude the organization from remaining under the control of the government. Later, in 1964, a new law sought further reforms in the radio-television service (the Act of 1959 was not repealed but only amended by the Act of 1964). A directing office was established under a supervision other than that of the minister of information with the idea of granting to the service more autonomy, a board of directors was created, and certain parliamentary checks appeared to have been imposed on the operation of the entire organization. However, care was taken to see that the majority of appointees to the board are state representatives, and that the board plays only a small role in management. The parliamentary controls instituted had the effect only of limiting the board's financial independence. *Le Monde* describes the 1964 "reform" as creating an "instrument more efficient and more docile." [102] A committee "to safeguard the ORTF" was established for the following "reason" (according to the minister of information): "In certain regions the opposition has a quasi-monopoly of the written press; it is perhaps the role of television that will reestablish the equilibrium, of giving opinion that is not dispensed by papers not in the habit of expressing freely." [103] Thus, the "reform" of 1964, in giving the impression of having reduced greatly the control of the government over the ORTF, reduced only the powers wielded over it by the minister of information. In the meanwhile, the service continues to act as a creature of the government. Programs of excellent quality appear periodically both on radio and television, but political information is carefully regulated and censored. In fact, even some taped television interviews have been subject to subsequent editing (as was the case with an address by Immanuel d'Astier in 1967). Certain political candidates and opposition holders of public offices have had great difficulty, in getting access to the service (paradoxically, during the presidential election of 1965 the ORTF offered opposition candidates broadcasts of a length that was considered excessive

---

[102] "Bilan du septennat," *Le Monde,* November 26, 1965, p. 3.
[103] "Bilan du septennat," p. 3.

by some!).[104] Being underfinanced, the ORTF embarked in 1968 upon a system of commercial advertising as a means of raising revenue (construed by some as having also a second objective—getting at the advertising of the newspapers, which, in the majority, are anti-Gaullist).

Undoubtedly it is too early to determine effectively the influence of television on electoral campaigns; thus far, few systematic studies have examined this area. However, one inquiry contends that the influence of television on the vote in the referendum of October 1962 was slight, and that most voters had arrived already at their decisions before the opening of the campaign.[105] Nonetheless, the author concedes that the "information" broadcast by the ORTF is considered by the populace generally as "official" and that, therefore, this outlook undoubtedly will play in the future a non-negligible role "in a great number of cases." [106] René Rémond and Claude Neuschwander regard French television as showing definite promise of becoming a political force. They note that it fit well the character of President de Gaulle—particularly his deliberate creation of a style based on his direct relationship with the citizens, uncomplicated by the existence of any intermediaries whatsoever.[107]

Electronic electoral machinery

Synthesis and rapid distribution of political information has been aided greatly by new types of electronic electoral machinery

---

[104] "Bilan du septennat," p. 3; see also Maurice Denuziere, "La télévision et la politique," *Le Monde,* April 6, 1966, p. 5; see G. Rochecorbon, "Le contrôle de la campagne électorale," *Revue française de science politique,* Vol. 16, No. 2 (April 1966), 355–371. The author describes the presidential election of 1965 as one in which mass media replaced traditional methods of propaganda, the campaign as having been dignified, the Control Commission's directives as having been exemplary, and the government's performance as having won more than it lost.

[105] Guy Michelat, "Moyens d'information et comportement électoral", *Revue française de science politique,* Vol. 14, No. 3 (June 1964), 877–905.

[106] Michelat," p. 903.

[107] René Rémond and Claude Neuschwander, "Télévision et comportement politique," *Revue française de science politique,* Vol. 13, No. 2 (June 1963), pp. 35–347.

which are indispensable for storing political information, exploiting statistics, examining the results of public opinion inquiries, and making rapid comparisons of theory and practice. The drive in the direction of making serious and scientific electoral studies began after the presidential election of 1965 when efforts at simulation sought to predict the political composition of future National Assemblies and voting behavior according to different hypotheses, attitudes of candidates in relation to the groups from which they derive, and so forth. All such efforts without the existence of machines would have required prodigious activities and years of research. However, the general public has been slow to realize the full advantages that derive from the use of such equipment, and it is not unusual to hear among it such criticisms as "They represent man's mastery by the machine." Some elements of the populace were delighted when between the first and second ballots in the legislative elections of 1967 the machines mistakenly predicted on the second ballot an overwhelming victory for the Gaullists. Later, some newspapers mistakenly referred to the error as a "breakdown in the machinery," whereas inadequate attention had been given to the quality of programming and the content of what had been fed to the machines. The French public seems to be less than well-informed on the real nature of such machinery and what it seeks in the way of accomplishments; nor does there seem to be any real awareness of its potential.[108] There is evidence of a feeling of awe.

CONCLUSION

Some aspects of French thought exalt the individual and distrust authority; other aspects exalt authority and distrust the individual. The radicalism of Alain is illustrative of the former; Jacobinism and Bonapartism reflect the latter—having in French history long-range and often authoritarian implications. The French probably prefer weak political regimes; however, they like stable

---

[108] See Roland Sadoun, "L'ordinateur dans la vie quotidienne," *La Nef*, 32 (1967), 175–181. Sadoun states that those who resist the "machine" are the same ones who ten years ago resisted "the pill."

ones too, and sometimes they sacrifice the former in order to realize the latter. The Gaullist regime offers them stability, even if under President de Gaulle it was characterized by frequent exercises of "personal power."

Republicanism, which was for years a fragile thing in France, eventually became an established national theme. The "Left" and the "Right" are now hazy classifications, and distinctions between them are not as many as in former eras. Catholics and Communists, once noted for their opposition to the Republic, now live within its fold. The "two Frances," both continually at war with each other, belong now more to the past than to the present.

Republicanism once was tied closely to limitations on executive authority; for many years republicanism and presidentialism were considered antithetical. That conviction—although it has receded since the coming of the Gaullist regime—continues to persist today in some quarters. At the same time, a growing number of members of Left political parties are coming to endorse the presidential system. Many Left conceptions of executive authority now are associated with defense of a responsible presidentialism based on political parties.

General de Gaulle's conception of executive authority was presented at Bayeux. As far as he was concerned, executive authority could not derive from Parliament. Domestic political differences had for him "no profound reality." Political parties were for him vehicles of destruction.

Gaullism is "a certain idea of France" associated with national grandeur. It is not a body of systematic doctrine but a collection of directives and advice divulged periodically by the General to his followers. In addition to Gaullism, there is also a "Gaullist family." Its future remains uncertain. Is it destined to pass on with the General, or will it manage to survive and become a regular feature of the French political scene?

Socialism, in the words of Halévy, is a psychological and sentimental protest against the gross inequalities fashioned by the rationalization of capital. Communism is a protest against capital, spurred by the Russian Revolution of 1917. Existence within the French Left of separate Socialist and Communist components is a major feature of French politics. Mending the rift between the two is a constant theme among Left elements. The extent to which the Socialist and Communist Lefts can coordinate activities always is a matter of lively speculation. Both categories view the social order in different ways. Electors of the Socialist and Communist Lefts total approximately 35 percent of the electorate. Even if these components were to unite the Left still would have to search to the Center in order to come by a majority. The Center appears to be around 40 percent of the electorate. Nevertheless, Deutsch, Lindon, and Weil argue that a large part of the Center is not center at all but the *marais,* or the swamp, that force that often appears to be center but which is frequently attracted to extreme positions. A united Socialist-Communist force would have to dip into this category in order to shape up a majority in the country.

Liberalism and conservatism have settled down in relatively fixed positions; meanwhile, the world around them continues its transformation. Nevertheless, liberalism is republican, and by now most versions of conservatism are republican too. The extreme Right, disgraced by its pro-OAS tendency and crushed in the legislative elections of 1962, has undergone a partial and relatively ineffective revival. While Gaullism hardly can be classified as conservative, it attracts a number of conservative voters who are receptive to Gaullism's emphasis on national sovereignty, opposition to a United States of Europe, acceptance of the *force de frappe,* and so on. Consequently the extreme Right is unsuccessful in retrieving from Gaullism elements that are in some ways closer to it.

The church-state controversy has not been completely solved, and its history has left a definite imprint on political habits and thought. Nevertheless, the conflict has been greatly deintensified, and this has contributed to the making of a better France.

French history is filled with examples of seizures of power and revolution. The French proclaim themselves a revolutionary people, even if in their daily lives they give few signs of valuing violence. Periodically they resort to revolutionary expression. The French also are a very conservative people, and after revolutions they seem able to reconstruct some amount of integration and an operable order. Consequently, the post-revolutionary product often is a compromise. The regime created in 1958 was other than that, and ten years later, in what undoubtedly was the greatest mass demonstration in French history, a huge segment of the population addressed itself to imbalances in the regime.

French newspapers show little inclination to identify themselves as political or ideological organs. Their policies and appearance are shaped primarily by their need to appeal to a mass consumer market. Therefore, political information is handled and dispensed in ways which avoid that which is divisive while stressing that which is nondivisive. Consequently, the reader often is given what he wants. Finally, a radio-television monopoly has enabled the French state to use this resource as a vehicle of public indoctrination. And, as several authors have noticed, this medium of expression did fit well the personality of de Gaulle when he was President of the Republic.

FOUR
A NATION
OF SMALL
COMMUNES
Local and
national politics

Innumerable small *communes,* many relatively unimportant
arrondissements and cantons, twenty-one districts of regional
action, and almost a hundred units called departments serve as
juridical forms of French territorial administration.[1] *Communes*
and departments date in organization from the end of the eighteenth century to the beginning in 1875 of the Third Republic.
The *commune,* which served as the natural unit of organization
when the great majority of the French lived in rural villages, is
today primarily a public utility area, providing in a given locale
gas, electricity, water, housing and other services (other public
economic responsibilities there are the responsibility of other
juridical levels, being assumed by the department and the central
government).

The *commune* is the smallest territorial unit in the nation,
there being almost 38,000. Many are small villages, others are

---

[1] The administrative hierarchy is the ministry, the territorial departments, the *arrondissements* (about 450), the cantons (about 3000),
and the *communes.* The position of the twenty-one districts of regional
action in the hierarchy is somewhat ambiguous at this time; the regime
has stated that their creation does not alter the basic structure of French
administration.

towns, some are good-sized cities—however, fewer than thirty-five contain populations in excess of 100,000. Only 300 *communes* are in excess of 2000 residents each. The census of 1962 established the existence of 37,962 *communes* with populations as follows: [2]

32 have	100,000 or more	inhabitants
51 have	50,000 to 99,999	inhabitanst
199 have	20,000 to 49,999	inhabitants
305 have	10,000 to 19,999	inhabitants
590 have	5,000 to 9,999	inhabitants
1,904 have	2,000 to 4,999	inhabitants
3,670 have	1,000 to 1,999	inhabitants
7,248 have	500 to 999	inhabitants
13,179 have	200 to 499	inhabitants
7,361 have	100 to 199	inhabitants
3,423 have fewer than	100	inhabitants

PROFILE OF A *COMMUNE*

Most *communes* are situated off the "main line" in diverse stages of relative isolation. Those that are part of large suburban complexes form exceptions. The *commune* of Bourg-la-Reine, for example, which is situated on main highway 20, only ten minutes by car from the Porte d'Orléans (the "south gate" of Paris), is large, modern, and sometimes described as the *plus agréable* part of the *banlieu*. Its ties with the Paris area are great, for most of its inhabitants work there, but it also has a life of its own, with a busy shopping area, an interurban train station, and various municipal activities. Some minutes away from it by automobile (not by bus, for connections with it are very poor) is Wissous, the *commune* about which the Andersons have written. Wissous is part of the Paris suburban complex but, unlike Bourg-la-Reine, it constitutes an exception, being relatively isolated. Its "old city" might as well be many miles away from Paris. The Andersons report a Wissous baker as saying to them, "Wissous is very self-contained. I never would have thought it possible so close to Paris. It is as though we were living many years ago

[2] Reported in *Le Monde*, March 4, 1965, p. 7.

. . . You would not know there was a world beyond." [3] Nonetheless, residents of Wissous dependent upon public transit can "break out" and get access to Paris if they are willing to suffer the bad connections involved in getting there. Those residents who have their own autos are not subject to such restrictions. They can be in Paris within fifteen minutes, heavy traffic and all. Le-Chambon-sur-Lignon is, on the other hand, located high in the mountains of the Haute Loire and detached as a *commune* from almost everything. Approximately forty miles away is Valence, a good size active city located on a major railroad artery and referred to by its residents as the "gateway to the Midi." Off in another direction, fewer than 100 miles from Le Chambon, is Saint-Étienne, a locale for industry and frequently the site for militant worker's movements.[4] Le Chambon might as well be thousands of miles away from both Valence and Saint-Étienne as far as its residents are concerned.[5] Le Chambon has fewer than 2000 inhabitants, a main street, few automobiles, a handful of small business enterprises, and the usual town square. To one side of the square is the Casino supermarket (a revolutionary innovation already taken much for granted by residents). Elsewhere on the square are several *cafés*. One is tiny and inhabited sparsely by elderly peasants (most residents of the *commune* shun it). The other, the *café* of the Hotel Central, is a popular place to visit for an *apéritif* or a glass of wine (perhaps it would be more popular were its proprietors not Catholic, but Le Chambon is in that part of France that is Protestant and the locale for a minority that once was persecuted). The Central's *café* offers a place for local residents to socialize (not to consume large amounts of alcohol; moreover, excessive drinking is

[3] Robert T. Anderson and Barbara Gallatin Anderson, *Bus Stop for Paris: The Transformation of a French Village* (New York: Doubleday, 1965), p. 15.

[4] Boulangerism, for example, had its birth in the industrialized areas of Saint-Étienne, Marseilles, and Toulon. Initially, it was associated with leftist workers, and only later did it become a movement of the Right, antiparliamentary and racist. General Boulanger (1837–1891) led an anti-republican movement that failed after some initial successes. He committed suicide in 1891.

[5] Infrequent exceptions are "visiting the relatives" in Saint-Étienne. Ties with Valence appear to be even more remote.

expensive). Talk is easy and conversations are not difficult to initiate, for villagers know each other and require no introductions. Visitors from the "outside world"—whether French or foreign—find conversatioinally that it does not take long to break the ice; issues and areas of discussion are diverse, but locals are not likely to give much attention to discussion of politics, not because it is unimportant, but because the *café* offers relaxation, some humor, and association with others, and nobody is interested in "spoiling" things. The *café* represents a "place to go," providing some people with a welcome escape from monotony.

There are many things to complain about in Le Chambon (the *commune* is not wealthy, it is unlikely that it ever will be, and its people are not getting very much out of the new affluent world), but in the *café* discussion of divisive issues is generally absent. Frequenters of this small communications center are selective about what they communicate to each other. The *café* also is largely a man's world. Escorted women occasionally enter it, particularly for refreshments after a Sunday outing; otherwise its clientele is almost exclusively male. During the day a card game often is in progress, for M. Chaillet likes to play with his customers. On hand are Madame and several assistants to do the cooking for the hotel restaurant, make the beds, and clean the rooms; a barman who has been in the *commune* since 1946 and who is tight-lipped about what he hears; and a sixteen-year-old boy who sets and waits on table and helps out in the kitchen and the hotel. He is learning "hotel management" and someday he hopes to move elsewhere, to one of the "big prosperous hotels." If, however, one does not wish to go to the *café,* there is the municipal cinema which projects popular films two nights a week—or, if one has a television set, one can watch the late evening movie transmitted from Paris. There is no municipal swimming pool, but there is the river which is used frequently by townspeople during the summer months (on one bank is an attractive grassy area). There also is a municipal athletic field for the youth of the *commune*. Scattered throughout the surrounding mountains are many paths which can be used for walks when the weather permits. "Blue buses" connect Le Chambon with Valence and other *communes,* picking up riders twice daily. Also available is "the machine," a curious little train connecting with

Saint-Étienne. However, residents travel out of the *commune* only infrequently (except to work), for it is expensive and not many budgets can accommodate it. Finally, a small enterprise makes available newspapers, and a bookstore contains practically any book published in France. Information relative to the "outside world" is relatively easy to obtain, but local residents only are vaguely familiar with what goes on "out there." One soon acquires the feeling that they are hardly a part of it. The *commune* is "their world" and like so many of their countrymen, they live in a state of relative isolation. Finally, important events occurring outside of the *commune* attract little attention from the townspeople unless they have an effect on Le Chambon itself.

Like all *communes,* Le Chambon has its mayor (larger *communes* have one or more assistant mayors) and an elected municipal council.[6] The council elects the mayor, who serves as its head, is charged with executive implementation of its decisions, and cannot be dismissed by it. He registers marriages, births, and deaths, inquires into violations of law, exercises police power in order to apprehend lawbreakers, and exercises other lesser functions of the state in the *commune.* In a sense, he is a "little prefect." [7] His executive powers are considerable, and he is the only representative of the state in the *commune.* His municipal council meets only for approximately three months of the year, during which time it arranges its budget, makes provision for necessary services such as fire and health protection and other services not specifically prohibited by law. The council—

[6] Members of municipal councils are elected by universal suffrage for terms of six years each. Under the Fourth Republic all *communes* with populations in excess of 9000 employed proportional representation as the method of election, whereas those with fewer than 9000 used list voting on a majority basis. In 1958 the Fifth Republic passed a series of measures calculated to reform aspects of municipal elections, electing municipal councillors by list voting on a majority basis in *communes* whose populations did not exceed 120,000 and by proportional representation in those in excess of that number. The law was altered again in 1965 and its present status is discussed elsewhere in this chapter.

[7] See Charles Vanhecke, "Qu'est-ce qui courir M. le maire?" *Le Monde,* November 2, 1966, p. 15. This article gives an excellent description of the daily operations of a local mayor (M. Louis Grenier) in the small *commune* Coulonges-sur-Sarthe.

although local—always is under the supervision of the central government administration. It may be dissolved if, in the judgment of the central government, it fails to protect communal interests. The departmental prefect may annul a council decision if he feels that it is illegal or in excess of the council's powers. Moreover, his power of removal extends also to its personnel should they show evidence of dereliction of duty (as defined by law), if they are excessively absent from council meetings, or if they lack eligibility for their posts. The municipal council is free to formulate policy but it is precluded from intervening in municipal administration.

COMMUNAL REORGANIZATION

The existence of so many tiny *communes* has become a serious problem both on the national and local government levels. More and more people are going all the time from the country to the cities; consequently some *communes* are growing and others are diminishing in size. Nonetheless, all continue to have their expenses. Therefore, the central government is trying to encourage certain communal transformations which will diminish the costs of this relocation. Central government policy encourages the *communes* to reorganize according to different options. *Communes* whose lives are economically and socially complementary may coordinate their activities and merge, if they wish; or they may form together syndicates which perform multiple activities; or they may form urban or rural districts which will enable them to undertake solutions that a sole municipal administration could not provide by itself. The basic idea here is to allow units to form larger ones and thereby implement projects often too costly for small ones. Sometimes these transformations lead to complete change in the communal political map.[8]

The central government has embarked upon a vast program of public relations in order to cultivate local receptiveness to its proposals. A *bureau d'information des maires et conseillers*

[8] See André Passeron, "Le regroupement communal. I.-Depuis deux ans, trois mille communes ont fusionné ou constitué un syndicat ou un district," *Le Monde*, March 4, 1965, p. 7.

généraux (office of mayors and local councillors) has been created in Paris by the minister of the interior, and a bulletin is sent regularly from it to the mayors in order to call their attention to some of the aspects of the program. From time to time the minister of the interior holds meetings for representatives of municipal councils. In 1964, 6000 mayors traveled to Paris to hear Interior Minister Roger Frey explain the reasons and advantages of communal reorganization. Mayors were invited irrespective of political affiliation, with one exception—Communist mayors were excluded. Opposition mayors, including Antoine Pinay, responded to the invitation and participated in the sessions.

Between 1962 and 1965 almost 3000 *communes* affected some kind of reorganization. By January 1965, 222 intercommunal syndicates performing multiple tasks had been created; involved in the entire operation were 2426 *communes.* Forty special districts had united 273 *communes,* and 118 mergers in forty-five departments involved 253 *communes,* leading to the elimination of 135.[9]

Special procedures are required for implementation of communal mergers. Required first is an affirmative vote by the involved municipal councils. The central government ordinance of January 5, 1959, states that when *communes* merge their councils must do so also. A *commune* that is in the process of being absorbed must drop from its council certain members. The regulation is that those dropped are members who obtained fewer votes than their colleagues in the previous council elections. Consequently, room on the new council is left for mayors, their assistants, and some members of the absorbed councils. Representation on the new council is proportionate to the respective populations.

Some *communes* have expressed some doubts about "taking in" other *communes* when the merger threatens increased costs for the absorbing *commune.* Possible tax elevations are a cause of particular anxiety. However, the central government decree of October 14, 1963, made to the *communes* certain concessions, guaranteeing a minimum tax to absorbing units

[9] Passeron, "Le regroupement communal."

(comparable to what would have been implemented in the poorer *communes* had they not merged). The central government gives priorities in state equipment subsidies also to absorbing *communes* (decree of August 27, 1964). Therefore, a municipality deciding to undertake local construction that would involve an expenditure of one million francs, for example, could look forward to a possible subsidy of 40 percent. Should several *communes* decide to engage jointly in construction for the same sum, they could benefit, for example, from a subsidy as great as 53 percent.[10] On the other hand, the central government has clarified that it does not wish to encourage mergers simply because *communes* wish greater subsidies, having cautioned them not to attempt them solely with this purpose in mind.

The ends sought by communal mergers are improvements in local administration, easier acquisition of equipment, and a rational approach to local financing. Tiny *communes* tend to be underadministered, lacking, sometimes, even basic clerical services. Thirty-one thousand *communes* with fewer than 1000 inhabitants each lack resources to maintain efficient administration. Moreover, as equipment costs soar, mergers can bring together greater numbers of contributors to participate in their purchase. Nonetheless, the central government acknowledges that the options offered the *communes* are designed not to solve their problems entirely; however, the options do propose at least to do something about them, particularly in the areas of investments and equipment, and to initiate action by the *communes* themselves.

SAINT-CHAMOND: EXAMPLE OF A COMMUNAL MERGER

On March 14, 1964, the *commune* of Saint-Chamond merged with the adjacent *communes* of Izieux, Saint-Martin-en-Coailleu, and Saint-Julien-en-Jarez.[11] The fusion, which was desirable economically, geographically, and socially, was the pet project

[10] Passeron, "Le regroupement communal."
[11] The author wishes to express his indebtedness to André Passeron's excellent article "Le regroupement communal. II-Une fusion réussie: Saint-Chamond double sa population," *Le Monde*, March 5, 1965, p. 8.

of Antoine Pinay, mayor of Saint-Chamond since 1929 and a former president of the Council of Ministers during the Fourth Republic. Saint-Chamond—prior to the fusion—was the real center of the complex of *communes,* with local businesses concentrated in it and the financial services of the canton situated there. It was the locale also for the only train station, the one *lycée* (more than half its students live outside Saint-Chamond), and the sole hospital. The three *communes* adjacent to Saint-Chamond chronically were in financial difficulty and unable to provide certain of their needs. Periodically conflicts occurred between them and Saint-Chamond because of the higher prices charged their citizens for the use of municipal services there. Eventually the matter came to a head over the question of accessibility to burial in the Saint-Chamond cemetery (residents of the adjacent *communes* sought its services because of the lower fees obtainable there).[12]

The procedures employed to achieve the merger finally were implemented, but not without some initial difficulties. The motion for fusion carried by a vote of twelve to nine in the municipal council of Izieux; some of the resistance encountered there was due to Communist, Socialist (SFIO), and Unified Socialist party (PSU) opposition to Saint-Chamond mayor Antoine Pinay, long time leader of the Independent party.[13] The four communal mayors approved the fusion, and one municipal council replaced all four old ones. Fourteen municipal councillors from Saint-Chamond (the last thirteen elected on the list for the old council were dropped) were joined by the mayors and councillors who were carried over from the absorbed *communes* (nine for Izieux, four for Saint-Julien, four for Saint-Martin). The new council totaled thirty-one members.

As a consequence of the merger, the population of Saint-Chamond increased from approximately 17,000 to 36,000 inhabitants, and the city now is one of the largest in the department. Additional dwellings have been constructed, traffic control has been improved, and tax uniformity has been established. Some additional expenses have devolved upon Saint-Chamond (particularly in water), but reductions have been realized by the

---

[12] Passeron, "Le regroupement communal."
[13] Passeron, "Le regroupement communal."

former residents of Izieux, Saint-Julien and Saint-Martin. Moreover, to his great satisfaction, Mayor Pinay is able to tell now precisely where Saint-Chamond begins and ends, something he was unable to do prior to the time of the merger.

THE DEPARTMENTS

Between the central and local governments is a chain of command that originates in Paris with the Ministry of the Interior and other government ministries, continuing down through the regional and departmental prefects into the *communes* and their mayors. The system is centralized and hierarchical, and consequently there always is some question as to whether units of organization below the central government level really deal very much with the business of governing. In fact, perhaps it would be more accurate to describe their functions as essentially administrative in nature. Local officials, although elected by their municipalities, are representatives of the national authority, entrusted by it with the exercise of certain functions and charged with their implementation. Each mayor, departmental prefect, and regional prefect must look upward to the government in Paris for orders. This elaborate administrative apparatus, bolted down on the entire territory from above, is the result of factors relative to France's historical development. Absolutist pre-Revolutionary regimes viewed the structure as best suited for maintaining their hegemony; after the Revolution, the Napoleonic regime consolidated it further in efforts to extend its control. Post-Napoleonic regimes have seen no compelling reasons to alter drastically its basic structure.

The territorial unit of administration known as the department serves to coordinate public and private efforts in certain areas of activity, particularly production and distribution; it undertakes investments, engages in transportation, and exercises many other activities. Within each of the departments is a general council whose members are elected by universal suffrage for six-year terms.[14] Each district, or *arrondissement,* within a de-

---

[14] Election is on a majority basis, half of the members retiring every three years. One ballot suffices if a majority is earned. Constituencies are based on the canton.

partment is allowed one seat on the general council. The council is headed by the prefect, the central government's representative in the department. Two annual sessions (approximating six weeks) are considered sufficient for the general council to determine and handle the few services it performs. In all, the powers of the general council are feeble. It passes on the departmental budget submitted to it by the prefect, and he is then responsible for its implementation. By the laws of the regime certain expenditures which are expected of the department can be inserted in its budget by the department prefect, whether the general council of the department approves them or not. On the other hand, should the general council provide in its budget for expenditures to which the department prefect takes exception (for reasons of law)—as, for example, departmental subsidies to parochial education, or imposition of a direct tax—the department prefect can subject these to his veto. The departmental general council is supposed to act as a mechanism for expression of views of its population, give impetus to certain of their common interests, make available services which are necessary but which are not local in nature, and serve as a connecting link between citizens and the state. However, as Duverger comments, the orientation of the councillors, like that of the senators, "represent the mentality, preoccupations, and interests of a France passed up by evolution. The underrepresentation of cities is stronger at the departmental level than in the Senate. More than 60 percent of the councillors are elected in cantons of fewer than 10,000 people; 19 percent only are elected by cities of more than 30,000, in which are contained about 28.5 percent of the French. Inside each council the urban populations are deprived of action." [15] The social composition of the general councils in 1966 was 18.3 percent from agriculture, 20 percent industrialists and merchants, and 11.7 percent employees, workers, and foremen.[16]

The department prefect is mentioned in the Constitution only in a very general way; he is responsible for administration in his department, for the national interest, and for respect for the laws of the republic. Nominated by the Ministry of the

[15] Maurice Duverger, "La démocratie régionale," *Le Monde*, June 9, 1966, pp. 1, 7. The average age was then fifty-six years seven months.

[16] Duverger, "La démocratie régionale."

Interior, his appointment comes from the president of the republic, announced through the Council of Ministers. The prefect's responsibility is to control his department as best he can, and to transmit to the central government knowledge of what is going on there.

A series of new administrative reforms seek to achieve departmental administrative coordination, and to remedy what often is described as "departmental anarchy." Various of these reforms center on the departmental prefect, pushing him forward as the sole representative of the government in all state activities performed within his department.[17] All state services are under his responsibility, with exception of military service (he remains responsible for nonmilitary aspects of national defense), judicial services, national education (particularly with reference to pedagogical questions and administration of personnel), activities deriving from the Ministry of Finance, and inspection of work and of social laws in agriculture. Save for these services, all others are placed under his direct authority.

The departmental prefect must operate in an extraordinarily vast terrain. The newly adopted reforms seek to further facilitate his performance. Newly developed communications media have been placed at his disposal so that he may deal more effectively with technical services, with the ministers, or with local collectivities (for instance, a new central courier service with advanced photocopy facilities now is available to him). Delegations of his authority are possible now on a greater basis than was the case heretofore. A reform has made a juridical distinction between his "delegation of power," and "delegation of signature." Delegations of his power involve total transfer of his authority and competence to the recipient; in turn, this establishes the responsibility of the latter. This procedure is reserved generally only

[17] See André Passeron, "La réforme administrative," *Le Monde,* February 12, 1964, pp. 1, 6; February 13, 1964, p. 6; February 14, 1964, pp. 1, 6. See also *Le Monde,* September 4, 5, 1963. That is to say, the departmental prefect now is the direct representative of each of the ministers, assuming in his own department authority over each of the heads of all their local branch services. Moreover, the prefectural civil service corps has been unified and means have been provided for circulation of personnel between central and local government services.

for services of the most technical nature, such as creation within the economy of certain markets. If the prefect wishes not to delegate his authority, he is free to give his reasons for not doing so. If he delegates his authority, he may not retrieve it except by an "act of express revocation." Delegation of signature, on the other hand, is a simple procedure, restricted alone to the prefect's signature and not to his powers and attributes. Once delegated, it may be recalled at any time.

The new administrative reforms stress *déconcentration,* passing along to the departmental prefect powers of decision making which belonged previously to a minister, or ministers, in areas which deal primarily with public investments—particularly educational construction, rural electrification, water resources, agrarian education, and telecommunications. Consequently, the majority of ministers have delegated already to their department services decision-making authority which required only a few years ago always the signature of the minister or ministers. Certain local budgets, particularly those of chambers of commerce, professions, and agriculture, now have less national significance and require no longer the signature of a minister.

INTERREGIONAL DEVELOPMENT

New reforms at the departmental level deal only with some of the problems of French administration. The department itself is too small as an administrative unit, and so, realistically, efforts have provided for the adoption of a new regional structure. For too long various government ministries concentrated primarily on certain geographic districts, implementing their technical services within them, while they gave less attention to others. The longer that condition continued, the more difficult it became to redress chronic regional imbalance. Almost a hundred departments, each with a prefect, no longer qualify as viable units for coordinating economic and social action.

The government decree of January 7, 1959, required the diverse administrations to harmonize their departments with new plans of economic development. In 1960 another decree created twenty-one districts of regional action (*vingt-et-un circonscriptions d'action régionale*). These twenty-one districts each comprise from two to eight departments (Fig. 4–1). Departments showing for each other certain economic affinities are grouped together so as to allow regional action and management programs to operate there efficiently in a plan of development. The effort here is to correct regional disequilibriums. However, each of the twenty-one districts is not intended to constitute a new administrative level. According to Louis Joxe (then minister of

Figure 4–1 The 21 districts of regional action

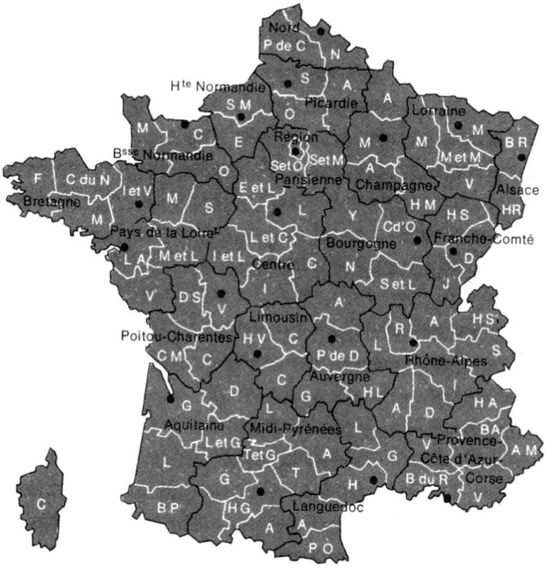

Source: *Le Monde*, March 22–23, 1964, p. 8.

state in charge of administrative reform), "It is a connecting link between the central power and the department." [18] M. Joxe stated that it is necessary "to simplify, to coordinate the structures of administration, to decrease duplication, and to reorganize the already too numerous public services." [19] He added that it is necessary to encourage the descent of authority and

[18] *Le Monde*, March 22–23, 1964, p. 8.
[19] *Le Monde*, March 22–23, 1964, p. 8.

responsibility towards the provinces—"Too many matters come to Paris which can be taken care of and decided on the spot. Too many decisions wait which can be accelerated." [20]

The districts of regional action are endowed with new administrative organs; for example, the regional prefect, the regional administrative conference, and the regional commission of economic development. The regional prefect is selected from among all the prefects of those departments that comprise his region. He is responsible for his region; his job is to inspire economic thought and decision making and coordinate policy in the economic area. He is concerned particularly with investments, presiding over requests made for them by the regional services, and shuttling along those requests, whenever feasible, to the competent ministers. The work of the regional prefect centers, in other words, on preparation and implementation of "the Plan." In the area of equipment, he is the power at the regional level, and all existing commissions are subject to his jurisdiction and powers. For all of these duties he needs an administration—and an economic team, too, one that is staffed with civil servants—an inspector of finance, an engineer of bridges, an economist, and a statistician, who serve for him as an "economic brain." An "interdepartmental conference" brings together periodically all prefects of the departments within his region, as well as the general inspectors of the national economy and treasury services. This organ is consultative, and is at the disposal of the regional prefect. A "regional commission of economic development" exercises a consultative role, purporting to assure representation to local collectivities and various economic interests. It is staffed with at least twenty members, and it may comprise as many as fifty—half are representatives of professional activities and syndical interests, a fourth are representatives of local collectivities (municipalities and cantons) designated by the local councils, and a fourth are personalities designated by the prime minister for reasons of competence.[21] If this organ is to operate in a consultative capacity, the government prefers that it do so in an economic rather than a political

[20] *Le Monde,* March 22–23, 1964, p. 8.
[21] *Le Monde,* March 22–23, 1964, p. 8.

manner. It designates its president and vice-president but it is convoked by the regional prefect, who creates its secretariat and establishes its *ordre du jour.* Thus far, there is no indication that the regional prefect is a "superprefect"—although he might become one eventually.[22] He is responsible to Paris and he presides over structures based as closely as possible on the correspondence of regional and economic areas. His region has been made large enough to provide vitality, but efforts have been made to confine it to a size that will not exceed his controls. His regional action domain is new in the administrative history of France.[23]

One of the new twenty-one regional districts is the District of the Region of Paris, charged with coordinating the development of the entire Paris region and consisting of a General Delegation (to which powers of several ministries may be delegated), a Board of Directors, and a Consultative Economic and Social Council. The former department of the Seine has already been transformed into the administrative areas, or departments, of the Seine-Saint-Denis, the Haute-de-Seine, the Val-de-Marne, and the City of Paris; the Seine-et-Oise has been converted into the Val-d'Oise, the Yvelines, and the Essonnes departments. The department of the Seine-et-Marne remains unaffected by the transition. Until the reorganization of 1964 the Paris region covered 4700 square miles; it contained 8.5 million inhabitants, one quarter of the country's employees, almost 19 percent of the total population of the nation, and about 65 percent of the nation's regional offices. The rationale for this broad reform was the region's underadministration.[24]

[22] Jean Hourtiq, "La vie administrative dans les circonscriptions d'action régionale," *International Review of Administrative Sciences,* Vol. 31, No. 1 (1965), 8–12. See also Maurice Le Lannou, "La région et le citoyen," *Le Monde,* March 16, 1967, p. 9; Michel Philipponneau, *La gauche et les régions* (Paris: Calmann-Levy, 1967); and Robert Lafont, *La révolution régionaliste* (Paris: Gallimard, 1967).

[23] See Marcel Waline, "La réforme de l'administration dans les départements et régions (décrets du 14 mars 1964)," *International Review of Administrative Sciences,* Vol. 31, pp. 13–14.

[24] Henry Puget, "Les nouvelles structures de la région parisienne," *International Review of Administrative Sciences,* Vol. 31, No. 1 (1965), 1–7.

At the top of the administrative structure described here are the government departments. Their nature and structure involve inevitable problems in communications and supervision due to their extensive external services, the magnitude of those services, and their juridical and practical relationships with the departments. The ministries are situated in Paris, but less than 5 percent of their personnel are employed there, being distributed throughout the nation in diverse branches of external services. These services are deconcentrated—not decentralized—so as to enable the ministries to maintain firm control over them. Thus, administration is direct, rather than indirect, and authority is delegated to these units on a state or geographical basis. Within the government departments, numerous divisions entrusted to technicians carry out the performance of functions. No overall departmental blueprint exists for purposes of organization, however, and so it varies from department to department. In all, a ministry performs numerous and diverse functions.

FURTHER TIES BETWEEN LOCAL AND NATIONAL LIFE

There are obvious ties between national and local political life, differentiations between the two levels often being less than what they appear to be. All national elections take place physically on terrain that is indistinguishable from that of the localities; all national elections contain some issues that are of significance in some local areas. In turn, some local issues are related to some degree to national elections.

Both municipal and departmental councils presently are in a state of anguish because of their feeling that the central government holds them to services and expenses too great for them to assume legitimately. They claim, moreover, that their protests are not given just recognition by the central government.[25] Some recent administrative reforms have triggered reactions by elected members of departmental and municipal councils who insist that they were not consulted seriously in relation to the decrees that prepared the reforms. They claim that the staffing

---

[25] See François Goguel and Alfred Grosser, *La politique en France* (Paris: Colin, 1964).

of organs of regional administration reflects the whims of the regime and the presence of many people who are there simply because they agree with the prime minister. Protesting the "undemocratic nature of the reforms," they argue that while the government's theory is to encourage at the local level decision making by local authorities close in proximity to those people affected by such decisions (particularly in areas of personnel management, procedure, and investments), the government's practice acts to deny rather than to encourage liberties for the local collectivities. Some departmental and municipal electees contend that enlargement of local liberties is meaningless unless supplemented by additional financial resources by the central government.[26] Such arguments, when presented by Antoine Pinay, Pierre Pflimlin, Auguste Laurent, and other old ornaments of the Fourth Republic, sometimes bear the earmarks of some older conflicts, being suggestive of other days, of another republic, and of other and older interactions on the national level between executive and legislative forces. That struggle, which has since shifted, is enclosed now within new forms in the new republic. In other words, local elective bodies now serve as the terrain on which many of the representations of classical political parties find expression, and such representations resemble the old struggle between majority and minority. The opposition—frustrated and thwarted on the national level and constantly rebuffed in the National Assembly—finds, however, not too many listeners these days, even if its pleas are not negligible; the fact remains that the *communes* need monies in order to supply essential services. Some *communes* are getting funds, others are not. Over all of this hangs a heavy political element, and it would be interesting to know precisely how *communes* with opposition mayors and councils (particularly Communist, Socialist,

---

[26] Although the central government contributes to the *communes* revenues derived from taxation, and although central government policy encourages among *communes* voluntary mutual activities, granting them subsidies (for equipment, for example), these subsidies are usually insufficient for the *communes* to meet their financial responsibilities. *Communes* juridically have access to other funds, being allowed by the Plan to qualify for state loans at reduced rates from the Deposits and Consignment Fund, or from private loan bodies.

and Unified Socialist) have fared as the recipients of such aid. There are suspicions that there are times when it "pays" to have a Gaullist mayor and council.[27]

Finally, one complaint voiced by some members of the municipal and departmental councils is that the regional prefect should not serve simultaneously as the prefect of a department, because this prevents him from carrying out impartially his role of arbiter. Seldom, however, does the government reply directly to this complaint, contending, instead, that the functions required of him are not so onerous that they cannot be handled equitably by a capable high civil servant.

POLITICAL PARTIES: INTERMEDIARIES
BETWEEN THE NATIONAL AND LOCAL LEVELS

Certain political parties serve as intermediaries between the national and local levels, providing ties between them. The Communist party's structure in the country—based on the cell—is an efficient unit of organization for coordination of local and national issues. Its shortcoming, however, is that transmission and articulation are exercised more often on urban than rural lines, primarily because Communist pockets of support are distributed that way. The positioning of cells is almost always occupational rather than geographic, and articulation is restricted, therefore, in areas where cells are limited in number. The Socialist party (SFIO), which currently is engaged in a process of shrinkage from the national level to certain regional fiefs, is strong still in the departments and major cities of the Bouches-du-Rhône, Pas-de-Calais, Nord, Seine, and Haute-Garonne, and to a lesser extent in the Aude, Haute-Vienne, Var, Gironde,

---

[27] As of 1966, the only large city in the provinces with a Gaullist mayor was Bordeaux; see *Le Monde,* July 28, 1966, p. 6. SOFRE directed an inquiry to 5000 mayors, asking "To which political tendency do you feel closest?" and received 1485 replies: 3 percent Communist party, 3 percent PSU, 14 percent SFIO, 10 percent Radical Socialist, 11 percent MRP, 29 percent Independents (CNI), 6 percent d'Estaing Independent Republicans, 12 percent UNR-UDT, 2 percent Tixier-Vignancour, 10 percent imprecise. See *Le Monde,* November 27–28, 1966, p. 7, and complaints at the Fiftieth Congress of Mayors—for example, how the *commune* is treated only as an economic unit rather than a center of life, how its personality must be safeguarded, and similar reproaches.

Hérault, and Seine-et-Oise (all federations falling within these departments accounted in 1965 for 66 percent of the votes in the Socialist party annual conference). And in departments where Socialist militants are fewer than elsewhere, the Socialist party maintains many important posts on the municipal and cantonal levels. The Radical Socialists retain many positions in rural areas, and there their influence often is stronger than it is on the national level—particularly in the Midi and southwest. Nor are their local-national ties weak in the Paris basin. Their coordination of national and local levels leads frequently to acts in local administration dedicated to preservation of the status quo. The Union of Democrats for the Fifth Republic, an upside-down party with stronger development on the national level, is of limited influence on the local level.

THE MUNICIPAL ELECTIONS OF 1965

The electoral law applied in the municipal elections of 1965 varied according to whether cities contained more or fewer than 30,000 inhabitants. In cities in excess of 30,000 people, there were two ballotings with voting by bloc lists. Any list receiving on the first ballot an absolute majority of the votes cast and one quarter of the registered voters automatically was elected. On the second ballot the list with a relative majority was elected. Voting was restricted to but one list per ballot. The second ballot contained only those lists that claimed on the first ballot at least 10 percent of the votes cast. All fusions, both of lists and candidates, were prohibited between the two ballots. Lists, therefore, were required to appear on the second ballot exactly as they had appeared on the first.

Voting procedure in cities with fewer than 30,000 inhabitants was different, resting on majority voting with two ballots, possible *panachage,* preferential voting, possible fusion of lists, and allowance of presentation of candidates between ballotings.[28]

[28] *Panachage* allows voters to choose, if they wish, among several lists, each choice constituting a fraction of one vote. In voting a given list, the voter can strike off certain candidates and substitute for them candidates from another list or lists. Or, if he wishes, he can write his own list. There is no voting for more names than there are seats, but one may vote for fewer names than there are seats.

Candidates appearing on the first ballot needed an absolute majority of the votes cast for election, as well as one quarter of the registered voters. Seats were distributed after the second ballot as the result of having obtained a relative majority.

The electoral law successfully sought sharp reductions in both the number of candidates and lists presented. In cities of 100,000 or more inhabitants there were only half the number of candidates who appeared on lists in the elections of 1959.[29] The electoral law also was calculated to polarize the vote and to favor the government.[30] Attention was concentrated almost completely on Paris and its suburbs, Marseilles, Nice, Le Havre, Toulon, Nantes, and Angers, and little campaigning took place in *communes* comprising fewer than 2000 inhabitants each. In all of France 470,414 council seats were at stake, and two thirds of the electors were registered in *communes* comprising fewer than 30,000 inhabitants each (Table 4–1). Standing for council seats were sixteen members of the government, 400 deputies, and 198 senators. *Le Monde* counted in all 130 different types of alliances and coalitions.[31]

Approximately two thirds of the cities with more than 30,000 inhabitants each elected their municipal councils on the first ballot, as incumbent mayors and their lists generally won reelection.[32] After the second and final ballot, the Union of Democrats for the Fifth Republic almost doubled its seats for the whole of France, while the National Center of Independents continued its great decline, dropping from almost 80,000 to approximately 25,000 seats. The Communist party declined,[33] as did the

[29] *Le Monde,* March 12, 1965, p. 1.

[30] François Goguel, "Les élections municipales des 14 et 23 mars 1965," *Review française de science politique,* 16 (April 1966), 911–917; Gaullist propaganda denied that the law was designed to advance its cause. Gaullist Alexandre Sanguinetti argues, for example, that it was designed to get rid of the "parasitical lists and old formations inherited from the Fourth Republic." See his article, "Quatre tendances et deux conceptions," *Le Monde,* March 31, 1967, p. 7.

[31] *Le Monde,* March 16, 1965, p. 1.

[32] *Le Monde,* March 16, 1965, p. 1.

[33] *Le Monde,* March 23, 1965, p. 1. The Communist party managed to salvage itself on the second ballot, after a discouraging experience on the first, as a strong push in its behalf developed in the Seine, Le Havre, Nîmes and Alès—often at the expense of the SFIO.

Socialist party (SFIO), the Radical Socialists, and the Popular Republican party (MRP). The newly created Independent Republicans captured almost 17,000 seats. In cities with more than 30,000 inhabitants each, the Union of Democrats for the

Table 4–1   Results of election of municipal councillors on March 1965

	Cities of more than 30,000 inhabitants		Communes of 9000 to 30,000 inhabitants		All of France	
	Seats held pre- viously	Seats won	Seats held pre- viously	Seats won	Seats held pre- viously	Seats won
ALIM	602	679	25	43	125,160	200,523
Communist party	993	996	72	71	19,872	16,254
Extreme Left	168	197	10	9	20,637	12,998
SFIO	894	975	114	111	51,992	40,029
Radical Socialists	228	220	30	28	41,202	24,868
Left Center	380	458	50	53	68,558	61,256
UNR	663	684	61	63	20,089	39,427
Independent Republicans	129	172	32	31		16,964
MRP	688	614	43	44	33,482	25,096
CNI	521	512	38	23	79,058	25,255
Extreme Right	36	17	1	0	1,751	738

Abstentions	
France	Paris
1st ballot—21.8%	34.2%
2d ballot—29.22%	36.1%

ᵃ The ALIM ("Local Action and Municipal Interests") is not a political party but a complex of local coalitions.

Source: Le Monde, March 24, 1965, p. 8. These figures were released by Interior Minister Roger Frey.

Fifth Republic showed light gains, as did the Communist party and Independent Republicans, while the Independents showed light losses, and the SFIO registered more than moderate gains. In *communes* ranging from 9000 to 30,000 inhabitants each, the Union of Democrats for the Fifth Republic, the Communist party, Radical Socialists, MRP, and SFIO just about held their own, whereas the Independents again registered losses.

François Goguel concludes that in the majority of cases the municipal elections demonstrated relative satisfaction by electors with affairs in their *communes*.[34] A public opinion poll taken during the first months of 1965 showed that 51 percent of those interrogated wanted reelection of their municipal councils (23 percent wanted another, 26 percent had no opinion).[35] It would be difficult to see in the results of those elections any evidence of hostility to the government.

CONCLUSION

Between the central and local governments exists a chain of command which originates in Paris and reaches all the way down into the smallest *communes* of the nation. New reforms seek modifications in this centralized and hierarchical structure.

The number of *communes* is too many; their needs often exceed their resources. The central government seeks to encourage *communal* reorganization. This may take the form of mergers, syndicates, or urban and rural districts. These options do not offer a complete solution to communal problems but they do constitute at least a step in the direction of their amelioration.

Departments are too small individually and too numerous to allow for effective administrative coordination. A new regional structure has been adopted. Twenty-one districts of regional action, each district comprising from two to eight departments exhibiting economic affinities for each other, allow regional action and management programs to operate in a plan of development with the intention of correcting regional disequilibriums. Each district serves as a connecting link between the central government and the departments. In each district a regional prefect works primarily on preparation of and implementation of the "Plan." He is not a "superprefect," but he could become one eventually.

[34] Goguel, p. 917.
[35] Goguel, p. 917.

Municipal and departmental councils often protest that the central government holds them to expenses and services which exceed their capabilities. They frequently insist that the funds allocated them by the central government are inadequate. Over the allocation of such monies hangs what is undeniably a heavy political element.

Adjustments in municipal electoral laws in 1965 reduced both the number of candidates and party lists. According to one prominent observer, the results of the municipal elections of that year demonstrated relative satisfaction by electors in the affairs of their *communes* and little hostility toward the central government.

FIVE
POLITICAL
"CHAPELS"

The party system

THE "POVERTY OF COLLECTIVE LIFE"
AND THE CREATION OF POLITICAL "CHAPELS"

In his brilliant essay *Partis politiques et réalités sociales,*
Georges Lavau notes that the French have had little experience
with collective responsibilities, that they have fewer associations
than other Western societies, and that those associations that do
exist operate less intensively than their counterparts elsewhere.[1]
He notes that during part of the Second Empire worker's clubs
were active, bourgeois political "circles" existed, and rural life
was characterized by some organizational activities, but that
group activities subsequently gravitated toward a "style of bourgeois life" turned toward the "inside" and the exercise of "family virtues." [2] The result was what Lavau describes as a "legendary individualism." Why, asks Lavau, did the Frenchman—in
searching for guarantees for individual liberty—exclude himself

---

[1] Georges Lavau, *Partis politiques et réalités sociales* (Paris: Colin,
1953), p. 155.
[2] Lavau, p. 156.

from groups? Why did he emerge with this version of "isolated individualism"? Why is his allegiance to groups or even to a social class so weak? Why does he show so little need to adhere to a political party or a political movement?

Lavau states that for Frenchmen "party is . . . first a doctrine, a system, or sometimes simply a state of spirit, never a social group playing a precise role in economic progress or social life." [3] Lavau describes this outlook as "unrealistic." He is of the opinion that the lack of realism in French political life is the consequence of nonparticipation in groups and lack of exercise of responsibility within them. The one area that could provide the very best source of political training, says Lavau, is infrequently resorted to and used. "Deprived of their education," the French consequently are led to the abstract and in politics tend to be moralistic. Lacking prior training in problems of the concrete, and without prior exposure to the "politics of the concrete," the Frenchman tends to be ignorant of the concrete. He forgets the "worldliness of politics" and "makes a morality of the absolute. His options hinge on ideas." [4] This "unrealism"— which has its origins in the poverty of community life—results in a chapel-like image of party.

THE PARTY SYSTEM

The French party system contains at least eight well-defined parties, as well as some federations that comprise parties. The parties are the Communist party, the Unified Socialist party (PSU), the French Socialist party (SFIO), the Radical Socialist party, the Democratic Center, the Union of Democrats for the Fifth Republic, the Independent Republican party, and the Independent party. The Federation of the Left included the Socialist (SFIO) and Radical Socialist parties; the Union of Democrats for the Fifth Republic includes various Gaullists; the Democratic Center includes former members of the Popular Republican party (MRP), and Center and Left Center adherents.

The party system postdates by many years the evolution of French political development along multifactional lines; never-

[3] Lavau, p. 157.
[4] Lavau, p. 157.

theless, the system has absorbed many of these elements. The system operates within a country where different regions have evolved differently, where the vote is dominated by traditions and interests, and where, as Raymond Aron says, people entertain different "politico-metaphysical" convictions.[5] The system has been shaped and transformed by, and in the backwash of, numerous historical phenomena, among them the Revolution of 1789, the Industrial Revolution of the last century, the Russian Revolution of 1917, and the Gaullist seizure of power of 1958. The system has been shaped by republicanism and its history of ups and downs. The system was for years relatively open—that is, new parties had little difficulty breaking into it. The system until recently was not hard on smaller parties, affording them for a variety of reasons conditions which enabled them to hang on in the party arena. Some, like the Radical Socialists, for years managed to obtain in the legislature a number of seats far out of proportion to its limited numerical strength in the country. The system appeared until 1968 to be completely unreceptive to one party obtaining a unified and homogeneous legislative majority—until that was achieved that year by the Gaullists. The system has produced political parties which generally have lacked sufficient power to exercise securely and effectively over sustained periods governance of the nation. The system comprises parties that failed generally to recruit members and supporters on a mass basis (exceptions are the Communist and Socialist [SFIO] parties), and, consequently, for years parties like the Radical Socialists and the Independents operated as cadre organizations with large executive heads and minuscule membership bodies. The discipline of these parties was ineffective in Parliament, and various of their deputies often voted with other undisciplined deputies for the purpose of bringing down cabinets. Such deputies had little to fear, knowing that the strength that they enjoyed in their own fief-like electoral districts would protect them against their own political organizations. These deputies were members of organizations based on a nineteenth- rather than a twentieth-century conception of party.

The system did in some eras give government the means,

[5] Raymond Aron, *Immuable et changeante* (Paris: Calmann-Levy, 1959), p. 67.

however, to govern. That was so during times in the life of the Third Republic. As Duverger states:

> . . . all this did not work as badly as we have been told . . . Between 1875 and 1920, the Third Republic was one of the best political systems of Europe. I shall always gladly defend this statement, for it was a republic which, albeit in a somewhat peculiar style, was able to create a State, to dispose of an opposition that originated in the struggles of the previous century, and to preserve great internal freedom.[6]

In other eras, however, the system contributed to governmental instability, or inhibited governments from entering some areas of policy making. That was the case during the Fourth Republic, when the poison of the Algerian conflict spread throughout French society and governments often abandoned the making of policies relative to it. A "good" party system maintains conditions for effective governance in times good and bad, in crisis and noncrisis. During the Fourth Republic the system frequently was inadequate for this task.

MULTIPARTISM

Maurice Duverger describes the multiparty system as the result of the "noncoincidences of the main cleavages in opinion." [7] The system arises, he says, from the mutual independence of sets of antitheses, and it presupposes different sectors of political activity to be relatively isolated and sealed off from each other. The two-party system, says Duverger, is "natural." Whenever the factions within both parties no longer can find common ground, the tendency toward dualism is defeated and the transition to multipartyism is made. Duverger gives as an example the Radical party, whose gradual formation in the nineteenth century divided the Republicans and produced Conservatives, moderate Republicans, and Radicals. Various of those splits gave

[6] Maurice Duverger, "The Development of Democracy in France," in Henry W. Ehrmann (ed.), *Democracy in a Changing Society* (New York: Praeger, 1964), p. 71.

[7] Maurice Duverger, *Political Parties* (New York: Wiley, 1954), p. 234.

rise to Center parties. Unlike Duverger, Leon Epstein views multipartyism as perhaps "more natural" in a modern pluralist society.[8] He argues that if one begins not with two sides but rather with the existence of a variety of interests and opinions, then one would expect multipartyism "unless unusual circumstances channeled the variety into only two parties."[9] He asks, very plausibly, why "should all the inevitable cleavages coincide with respect to such diverse issues as welfare, civil rights, foreign policy, religious education and the nature of government authority?"[10] There is, indeed, no reason why they should, and it is not often that they do. On the other hand, as Raymond Aron says, the multiplicity of ideological families, various electoral laws, and economic and social diversities certainly do not raise an insurmountable barrier to a system of a few parties.[11]

COMPETITION IN MULTIPARTY AND TWO-PARTY SYSTEMS

Components of the two-party system normally articulate and aggregate interests; components of the multiparty system normally articulate interests but fail to aggregate them. Epstein describes each of the parties in a multiparty system as being more like a "large interest group," undertaking functions that are exercised in two-party systems only by interest groups.[12] Nevertheless, insofar as the workability of a multiparty system is concerned, Epstein states that "It seems safest to regard multiparty competition, like two-party competition, as a workable democratic method."[13] He adds, "This is another way of saying that the difference between the two forms of competition does not appear so fundamental as do the circumstances making for one form or another."[14] Epstein concludes that "In multi-party situations, all that can be shown is that the cohesive parliamentary party has become usual (but not universal) in

[8] Leon D. Epstein, *Political Parties in Western Democracies* (New York: Praeger, 1967), p. 70.
[9] Epstein, p. 70.
[10] Epstein, p. 70.
[11] Aron, p. 67.
[12] Epstein, p. 70.
[13] Aron, p. 76.
[14] Aron, p. 76.

most nations and that is especially prevalent when multipartyism verges on two-partyism." [15] With reference to this observation, it should be noted that the French multiparty system contains under the Fifth Republic some cohesive parliamentary parties, for example, the Union of Democrats for the Fifth Republic, the Communist party, and the Socialist party SFIO. The system also has recently witnessed reductions in the number of its parliamentary parties, and at the time of this writing such eliminations have not been characteristic of its cohesive ones.

THE COMING OF BIPARTISM?

Is the reduction in the number of political parties indicative of an evolving trend toward bipartism? This question continues to preoccupy and puzzle students of French electoral behavior. Maurice Duverger believes that it is, and that each day France comes closer to bipartism. Guy Mollet thinks that it is possible. Gaston Defferre thinks, however, that it is not; he finds it difficult to believe that the Communist party will ever be prepared to participate in the democratic game and work with Socialists and Radical Socialists in a true federation of the Left. Moreover, he is convinced that the departure of de Gaulle eventually will explode the Gaullist majority like "a live grenade," resulting in new alliances that will drain off elements from the Left and multiply groupings of the right center.

There is no doubt, however, that a further simplification of French political life has already occurred. The elimination contest is under way, and the list of vanquished political parties may well increase in the years to come. The once-powerful Popular Republican party MRP fell by the wayside in September 1967, when its executive group announced that it would function no longer as a political party but as a political club undertaking political studies and maintaining ties with Christian Democrats in other countries. The Popular Republicans had contributed to the Fourth Republic five prime ministers and two foreign ministers, and its ministers had participated in almost all of the twenty cabinets of that regime. After 1958 most MRP leaders came into opposition to the Gaullist regime, and yet many MRP electors

[15] Aron, p. 333.

found in that regime sources of strength and stability and supported it.[16] After 1962 the MRP fell into a kind of political isolation, having been caught between a unified force both to its left and right. The party arrived at the point where it had no place to go, and its electors continued to redistribute themselves among other political formations. The party system was in a process of contraction, and the party fell victim to it. After the MRP's dissolution, some of its elements flowed to the Democratic Center of Duhamel and Lecanuet, which suffered defeats in the legislative elections of 1967 and 1968, pushing it from the mainstream of French politics. Then, in the legislative elections of 1968, the Left was badly mangled, the Federation of the Left being one of the real victims of the defeat. The Federation of the Left was dissolved later that year. Are the Gaullists correct when they contend that France eventually will be reduced to but bipartisan contests between Gaullist and Communist parties? As of 1968, the trend still was more toward bipolarization. On the second ballot of the legislative elections, five of every six contests were two-way "duels."[17] One party, or pole, of extraordinary size emerged. Is there, nonetheless, also a trend toward bipartism, and is it presently in the making?

MULTIPLICITY OF PARTIES AND EFFECTIVE GOVERNMENT

Ineffective government, a characteristic of the Fourth Republic, derived not so much from the multiplicity of parties as from

[16] One of the MRP's last acts was of dubious distinction. Jacques Soustelle, activist and OAS member in exile, was nominated by it for an Assembly seat in Lyon. "Ghost candidate" Soustelle did not appear publicly in the campaign; for the attraction of MRP electors to de Gaulle, see, for example, *Le Figaro,* June 19, 1964, p. 2, for report on public opinion surveys of the French Institute of Public Opinion, especially those of May 22 and 31, 1964, in which 58 percent of MRP sympathizers said that they would vote for de Gaulle in the coming presidential election. It appears that the MRP was a party more conservative than its leaders allowed it to become. For discrepancies between MRP leaders and electors, see Jacques Moreau, "Le choix du MRP," *Revue française de science politique,* Vol. 15, No. 1 (February 1965), 67–86.

[17] *Le Monde,* June 29, 1968, p. 1. Second ballot contests were confined to 316 seats, of which 270 were "duels." Of the 270 confrontations, 242 were between a Gaullist and a member of the Left opposition.

their nature. The parties of that regime succeeded in establishing over a period of many years ties with government but not with the populace. They failed to become mass organizations capable of serving as pipelines that could transmit popular opinions from below so that they could be converted into governmental policies from above. As Almond and Powell state, "the conversion processes in the Fourth Republic were often blocked. Demands . . . piled up and were not converted into policy alternatives or enacted into law." [18]

THE PARTY SYSTEM
IN THE FIFTH REPUBLIC

The Fifth Republic's political system, when dominated by De Gaulle, purposely closed all doors against the accessibility of political parties to "conversion processes." De Gaulle repeatedly accused the political parties of incompetence and inadequacies that ranged from responsibility for the fall of France in 1940 to responsibility for the destruction of the Fourth Republic. The party system failed to qualify even as a stepchild of his regime. It was more like an abandoned child to whom the President of the Republic denied any legitimacy whatsoever. He did all that he could to keep the parties as far as possible from government, including even the party that is Gaullist and which claimed for the first time in French legislative history command of a unified and homogeneous majority. This party called itself a party, it tried to look like one, and yet it was not always that it acted like one. It was actually a giant formation of presidential supporters who took time along the way to be elected to the legislature. It had a limited hand in implementing "conversion processes." In the meanwhile, the other components of the party system yearned for power but were kept a great distance from it by the President of the Republic and the structures he created in 1958.

In the Fifth Republic many of the parties continue to play limited roles in developing ties with the populace. Despite some recent loud declarations in behalf of pluralist democracy, the designation of very important party candidates continues to be

[18] Gabriel Almond and G. Bingham Powell, *Comparative Politics: A Developmental Approach* (Boston: Little, Brown, 1966), p. 264.

the result of manipulations by small numbers of influential people. Gaston Defferre's candidacy in 1964 for the presidency of the republic, for example, was thrust on the populace by Jean-Jacques Servan-Schreiber's group after first being called to its attention in the press organ *L'Express.*[19] And after Defferre's retirement from the race, a series of conferences among leaders of different parties of the Left subsequently led to the presentation of François Mitterand as his replacement. Jean Lecanuet secured the support of his *Centre démocrate* and entered the presidential race of 1965 without having undergone a previous competition.

There have been, however, some changes among the parties of the Fifth Republic that merit attention. One important change has come about in the decline of "local notables" who can become deputies without dependence upon a national political party. Candidates for legislative seats now must run generally under the banners of a national political party. Second, the parties recently have adopted some of the modern techniques of political persuasion applied effectively by political parties in other countries. The Union of Democrats for the Fifth Republic implemented in 1966 local polls in approximately fifty electoral districts prior to the meeting of its national council in Poitiers. The public relations firm Services et méthodes, counterpart of Whittaker and Baxter, and Research Services, Ltd., helped Jean Lecanuet create on television an image that was both persuasive and amiable during the presidential campaign of 1965, to become what Pierre Viansson-Ponté describes as a kind of French James Bond. In 1967 the same organization conducted seminars for the Union of Democrats for the Fifth Republic, teaching it how to make the most of its public appeal. Moreover, parties of the Left now have discovered that political clubs serve for pur-

[19] It is remarkable that so small a group was able to launch Defferre's candidacy and carry it so far. One of his final acts was to seek the nomination of his own SFIO in a congress. He secured it but the "victory" was illusory. Many militants resented the way in which he sought to force himself on his party; and Secretary General Mollet, who supported him publicly, privately did everything he could to defeat him. Defferre's candidacy, paradoxically, "ended" when he "received" the nomination. His second candidacy, in 1969, was hollow and never did receive real support from Mollet and many SFIO members.

poses of recruiting, organizing, and carrying through on political campaigns. The only Left party offering great resistance to this innovation is the Communist party, which is gravely suspicious of such unorthodox ventures.[20] Within the Gaullist majority there also are Giscard d'Estaing's political groups, known as Perspectives et réalités, which are similar to the political clubs of the Left, and which were created to bolster support for his type of thought. There has been a change too in political party campaign costs, with expenses rising all the time. Now a candidate for a legislative seat can expect to pay perhaps 25,000 francs for his campaign in the Paris district, and probably twice that amount in the suburbs or provinces, while a national political formation can expect to pay 20 to 25 million francs for assistance, physical facilities, and electoral analyses.[21]

Finally, another change among the parties (although not without precedent [22]) has been in the rise of federations, as for example, the late Federation of the Left. The Federation of the Left included the French Socialist party, SFIO, and the Radical Socialist party. The agreement establishing the Federation was more than electoral, foreseeing parliamentary and, eventually, governmental collaboration. However, the participating parties did not lose their identity in the federation, preserving in it their organic uniqueness. Early in 1968 the Federation of the Left signed electoral agreements with the Communist party (described elsewhere in this chapter) which did not go as far as the parliamentary and governmental stages of collaboration. The Democratic Center comprises members of the former MRP, as well as other Center and Left Center elements. The Union of Democrats for the Fifth Republic is a federation comprising the UNR-UDT, the Independent Republicans, and other elements, having realized among its participants agreements that are electoral, parliamentary, and governmental. It remains a federa-

---

[20] Pierre Viansson-Ponté, "Prélude à la campagne. II. Le nouveau parti," *Le Monde,* July 7, 1966, p. 6.

[21] Viansson-Ponté, "Prélude à la campagne . . ."

[22] For example, the *Cartel des gauches,* which began after the beginning of the twentieth century and which, after transformations in the party picture, was sustained at times by Socialists, SFIO, and Radical Socialists after the first World War.

tion only because the Independent Republicans of Giscard d'Estaing vigilantly guard their organic separateness while working within it.

SOCIAL CATEGORIES AND THE PARTY SYSTEM IN THE FIFTH REPUBLIC

To which political parties do the diverse social categories of the nation give their support? How is this support distributed among the parties? [23] The Communist party electorate is predominantly male (61 percent). Its electorate is the youngest of all party electorates, only 12 percent being more than sixty-five years, and 65 percent being less than fifty years of age. More than 50 percent of the party's supporters derive from the working class, and about one fourth from the middle class. The average age in the party is approximately thirty-eight. The membership composition does not differ greatly from that of its supporters in the country. Communist voters usually earn more than Radical Socialist, SFIO, Democratic Center, and Independent Republican voters. It is not, as Duhamel says, "the bottom of the working class but its aristocracy" that often votes Communist. The French Socialist party SFIO is predominantly a male party (63 percent). Its electors tend to be of advanced age. Though it is sometimes called the "party of civil servants," many affiliate with it, but the party nevertheless draws support from all social categories. Workers supply about a third of its voters. Voters comprise salaried employees, persons in middle management, and people in agriculture (15 percent). Electors are divided between large- and middle-size cities; generally, they tend not to be rural or Parisian. The Radical Socialist party's electorate is predominantly male, aged, and rural. Workers comprise about a fourth of its voters. No longer is agriculture heavily represented among its supporters. The party's strength is greater in rural *communes* than in large cities. The Union of Democrats for the Fifth Republic draws its strength from all social categories. Its clientele comprises more females than males. Only 24 percent of its

[23] All data appearing in this section are drawn from Alain Duhamel, "La structure sociologique de l'électorat," in "La vie politique de novembre 1964 à avril 1966," Vol. 2, No. 2, *Sondages* (1966), 3–9.

voters are under thirty-five years of age, and 12 percent are over sixty-five. This party refers to the opposition parties as the "old parties," but in terms of the ages of its own supporters, this party is truly "old." Its clientele includes 27 percent workers. Approximately 13 percent of its supporters are in agriculture. The party's occupational group support includes employees, persons in middle management and the liberal professions, industrialists, merchants, and others. Its voters tend to be better off financially, being outdone in earnings only by Independent party electors. Its electorate is more urban than rural and is well distributed geographically. The Democratic Center's electorate is more female than male. Youth is not greatly attracted to the party. Approximately 25 percent of its voters are in agriculture; another 25 percent are workers. Employees and middle-management persons are well represented in its electorate. Representation is greater in the provinces and smaller cities; the Center's representation is not great in the Paris region. Earnings of its electors tend to be slight. The Independent party's electorate is now more masculine than female and of an elevated age. The party comprises among its electors people who are self-employed and members of the liberal professions. Twenty percent of its electorate is in agriculture and 20 percent are workers. In the Independent Republican party electorate there is about equal distribution of males and females. Its voters are young. Industrialists, merchants, employees, and middle-management persons are well represented in it. People in agriculture support the party more than they do the Union of Democrats for the Fifth Republic. Nevertheless, the party is not a rural party, being well represented in the large cities. The party's electorate is not rich.

DE GAULLE AND THE MISTAKES
OF THE PARTIES OF THE LEFT

President de Gaulle had a genius for putting the Left parties on the most difficult terrain whenever they engaged him in conflict; invariably, this resulted in his assuming the best possible ground. For example, during the referendum of October 28, 1962 (which proposed to elect the president of the republic by direct, universal suffrage rather than by an electoral college, and which, as a proposed constitutional amendment, was presented to the populace by a procedure clearly in violation of Article 89 of the Constitution), de Gaulle came off as the defender of direct, universal suffrage and the parties were pictured by him as defenders of restrained, indirect suffrage. He argued that his opponents feared universal suffrage because they did not want to part with the privileges of the "political class." [24] And when de Gaulle promised to return home to Colombey if his proposal did not receive a majority in the referendum, SFIO Secretary General Mollet told him, "Vous n'avez pas le droit de partir si le suffrage universel s'est prononcé" (You don't have the right to leave if universal suffrage is declared).[25] During that conflict, the parties concentrated first on the unconstitutional aspects of de Gaulle's referendum, but soon afterward they abandoned this effort and turned their attention to other things. In moving to new ground they had to concede (privately, of course) in French political circles that constitutionality never has been a strong plea. However, the Left parties, in initially assuming a position that was strictly constitutional, disadvantaged themselves by placing themselves on the side of an argument that was decidedly unpopular. They succeeded only in publicizing their unwillingness to share in a broader distribution of suffrage in the France of 1962, a position that came off as very old fashioned in a modern era. Their contentions of "Bonapartism" were obscured by the fact that the election of the president by universal suffrage and not by an outmoded college of "notables" undoubtedly is the most democratic solution that can be provided for staffing the office. From its own viewpoint, the body politic hardly can regard its opportunity to elect the president of the republic as an example of dictatorship. It must be assumed that de Gaulle had won this battle in advance, and it is somewhat surprising that the referendum did not carry by more than 46 percent of the registered voters.

The Left parties approached the referendum of October 28, 1962, convinced that de Gaulle would win it, and then lose the subsequent legislative elections of November 18 and 25. The Left parties did little prior to the referendum to convince

[24] *Le Monde,* September 23–24, 1962, p. 3.
[25] *Le Monde,* September 23–24, 1962, p. 3.

the populace that it should vote negatively, standing generally on the proposition that an *oui* vote would lead indisputably to further personalization of the regime, and that a *non* vote was a step toward constitutionality. Tactically, the parties and people who adhered to the *cartel des nons* offered potential political combinations that lacked popularity and which were identified with shabbier aspects of the dead Fourth Republic—campaigning for the reestablishment of parliamentary prerogatives, creation of an equilibrium between Parliament and president, and the necessity for the president to bring more members of Parliament into government. And, although the presidential office was not up for election, the Left parties essayed no real solutions relative to de Gaulle's replacement.

The Left parties made the mistake of believing that the termination of the Algerian war would force de Gaulle to choose between retiring and being retired. Therefore, they pictured him as but a temporary phenomenon who would disappear when things "righted" themselves. Earlier, however, major elements of the Left—in agreeing with the proposition that only de Gaulle could end the war and that any interference with his Algerian policy would intensify and lengthen the conflict—had helped cast de Gaulle in a powerful image, furthering the conviction of elements of the populace that the only man who could solve the war could be very useful in addressing himself to problems in the subsequent postwar era.

The weakness of the Left parties was reflected in de Gaulle's willingness to *force* a showdown with them whenever the opportunity presented itself. When, in 1962, the National Assembly brought down the Pompidou government, thereby paving the way for its own dissolution and subsequent national elections, the Assembly did precisely what de Gaulle had wanted it to do. After the Assembly voted censure of Pompidou's government, de Gaulle acted before the Assembly could act again, putting to the test its contentions and inviting the country to go to the polls and prove it wrong—which the country did. In return, he received a legislature with a Gaullist composite majority and succeeded in strengthening his own support within it. That conflict between de Gaulle and the National Assembly differed from a traditional one between a government and an outgoing parliamentary majority, being waged instead between the president and the elected representatives of the people. De Gaulle succeeded in putting the contest on that ground, and during the campaign he made it clear that the issues to be ruled on were between him and the people—not between him and the parties. In fact, outgoing Prime Minister Pompidou went even so far as to refer to the censure vote as a "plot against de Gaulle."

To some extent de Gaulle succeeded in tying the Left parties tightly to the Fourth Republic, contending that they died with the latter. Pleas by the Left parties that they too wish to avoid a return to the Fourth Republic have not succeeded in attracting full popular recognition. The Fourth Republic was truly the regime of parties—the same Left parties, in fact—and they have not been able to get the public to cast aside completely this identification. Some Left spokesmen acknowledged that perhaps it was best to wait for de Gaulle's system of "personal power" to run its course and terminate in the creation of a Fifth Republic that would make a "reformed Fourth" seem preferable. This proposition was not a very convincing one however, being suggestive of the plea, "We promise to reform the political structures if you promise to give us just one more chance." Nonetheless, everybody knows that these people had their "chance," and that a decade before they made a very bad job of it. Moreover, President de Gaulle never missed the opportunity to tell the populace that this was the case, and that a rejection of the Fifth Republic and acceptance of the Left opposition parties automatically would herald a return to the Fourth Republic and the conditions that attended it.

The theme of "no return to the Fourth Republic" became for President de Gaulle a most convenient device once many issues previously important had been resolved. Early in the history of the Fifth Republic he argued that he was the only one who could shield the populace from military dictatorship. Sometime later he argued that he had to remain on because he was the only man who could terminate the Algerian war.[26] After the

[26] See *Le Monde,* September 27, 1961, p. 1, and de Gaulle's argument that unless the parliamentary majority held, he would be forced to dissolve the National Assembly, thereby setting the stage for parliamentary elections that would strengthen the extremes and make it even more

end of the war he stated that he was the only one who could furnish French leadership on the world scene. Then he said that he was the only one who could prevent France from returning to the Fourth Republic. The argument was a very compelling one—even if it was specious—for by then the parties of the majority and of the opposition both were opposed to a restoration of the Fourth Republic. Nonetheless, de Gaulle continued to orate that the parties of the Left really did not mean what they said, and numerous voters placed no small amount of credence in this contention.[27]

THE COMMUNIST PARTY

Although committed to revolutionary action, evidence is slight that the Communist party today really believes in it or is willing to participate in it. There is no doubt that it wishes for it, as is evidenced by its rhetoric, although that too has undergone modification in recent years. No longer does it employ lavishly epithets such as "fascist" and "social reptile." The Communist press continues its "doctrinal dance," and theoretical "zigzags" continue to provide a source of confusion, but there is no doubt that the fire has gone out of many of its assertions.[28] The Communist party itself still is very "different," being other than an ordinary political party, but it is part of a France that is now in

difficult to find a majority—in which case he would have been obliged to go home.

[27] During the mass paralysis of May 1968, de Gaulle presented himself as a barrier against "totalitarian communism."

[28] That press, by the way, is in bad financial condition. See *Le Monde*, February 9, 1965, p. 7, for report of the Communist party conference on the state of the Communist press. It was reported that for the newspapers *L'Humanité, Liberté, L'Écho du centre, La Marseillaise,* and *Le Petit Varois,* daily circulation did not exceed 400,000, in contradistinction to 800,000 for fourteen papers ten years before. *L'Humanité* was reported as having increased its daily circulation almost 25,000 in one year, but it remains in poor financial straits. Price per issue in 1965 was fourteen centimes, whereas the cost of putting it out was fifteen centimes. In the Atlantic part of the Loire, a region without a Communist paper, perhaps 3.5 percent of the Communist electors read *L'Humanité,* and in the Alpes-Maritimes, the number of Communist electors who read *Le Patriote* was estimated at 25 percent.

transition. It, too, must undergo change. The party's clientele is not that of ragged and pauperized workers, alienated from society and desperately dedicated to destroying the environment in which they live, but a clientele that has been integrated in the society of a highly industrialized nation. Consequently, irrespective of how revolutionary the Communist party may attempt to appear, its behavior is affected in no small measure by its dependence upon social categories that are less than revolutionary.

The Communist party's electoral strength hovers constantly around 20 percent; its seating in the legislature was greater under the Fourth Republic than it has been under the Fifth (in the legislative elections of the Fourth, it captured in elections consecutively 166, 106, and 150 seats; in those held under the Fifth, it has returned 10, 41, 73, and 34 seats). Its limited seating now is due primarily to an electoral law that is directed against it, taking advantage of the way in which Communist votes pile up in urban and industrialized pockets, and inability, in the elections of 1968, to maintain strong discipline among its electors.

Despite its great demands for maintenance of internal discipline, the Communist party's life has been a series of crises and tensions. Competition over its leadership has been a common phenomenon, expressing itself primarily in terms of tendencies rather than individuals. That was the case during the secretary-generalship of the late Maurice Thorez, who first came to the post in 1930 (as the result of a crisis). Most leadership crises have turned on one theme—the relationship of the Communist party to other elements of the Left, and the desirability of participating with them in some form of united action or "united front." [29] In 1961 another crisis arose, and the Thorez-Rochet tendency won out over the Servin-Casanova and Kriegel-Valrimont tendency concerning tactical policy relative to the Gaullist regime (the latter group was accused of wanting to compromise with Gaullism). Now that Thorez is dead, Waldeck-Rochet leads the party along lines similar to those traveled by "Maurice." The party remains opposed to the "trusts" and

[29] Jacques Fauvet describes this in his excellent article "Le parti communiste et ses crises cycliques," *Le Monde,* February 1, 1961, p. 1.

"monopolies" of the Gaullist regime, and was critical of de Gaulle's "personal power," but it did not describe de Gaulle's foreign policy as "aligned with American imperialism." After Soviet and Gaullist foreign policies evidenced some convergences and compatibilities, Communist leadership from time to time even said some nice things about Gaullist foreign policy (as de Gaulle pretended not to listen).

The Communist party boasts that it commands among its four million voters and some 400,000 militants discipline and cohesiveness that will allow it to respond to various domestic crises. Such claims are exaggerated; the discipline—which is greater, of course, among the militants than the voters—often breaks down. During the crisis of May 13, 1958, Communist party demands for a general strike generally went unheeded, and job abstentions among workers were only slightly above normal (loss of a day's work during periods of high prices and inflation can be a serious thing). In November 1958, when the Communist party asked for a *no* vote in the referendum on the Gaullist Constitution, approximately 2.5 million Communist electors found reason to vote in the affirmative. Again, in 1965, during the first presidential election held under universal suffrage, some Communist electors joined that part of the 14 percent of the Left that threw its vote to de Gaulle. Losses again occurred during the 1968 elections.

The Communist party attracts all kinds of voters; some are Communists, some are not. A small minority of those who vote Communist want the introduction in France of a true communist system. Some Communist votes are due to protests against the existing order, while others are cast by workers who may not wish to vote Communist but who feel it is impossible to vote non-Communist because of the party's hold over the General Confederation of Labor (CGT), and their fear that negative votes might have an adverse effect on their wage increases. Finally, although Communist and non-Communist electors tend to see the social order in different ways, and although the former are more inclined to action than the latter, the lack of a strong socialist party with some real relationship to socialism probably results in some gains in Communist voting strength. There is no doubt that *some* sources of Communist party strength derive from the weaknesses of the French Socialist party, SFIO.

THE UNIFIED SOCIALIST PARTY

The Unified Socialist party PSU owes its origin to frustration by some former Socialist party SFIO members with that organization's inability to cope with the Algerian war, reaction by them to the conservative policies of SFIO Secretary-General Guy Mollet, and resistance by them to his unwillingness to tolerate dissent within his own party. The PSU was formed after the crisis of May 13, 1958, first as the Autonomous Socialist party, PSA, and reconstituted shortly afterward as the Unified Socialist party. Initially, it comprised those men who had formed a minority in the SFIO, men who had set out to capture its apparatus and who had failed in their efforts to unseat Mollet. After its creation, it set out to become a party situated somewhere between the Communist and Socialist parties.

The PSU is truly socialist; and at one time as many as six distinct conceptions of socialism competed for power within it. One stood for complete opposition to the regime on all terrains; another wished the PSU to become a middle-class party and work with bourgeois elements; one desired an approach to problems of the regime based on a broad "union of the left"; one favored Trotskyism; one represented a tendency that was "progressive and lay"; and one endorsed a policy of searching for the support of new social categories in the country.[30] However, by 1963 those divisions had been reduced to two, and a majority and minority already had evolved within the PSU (for example, in the Congress of Grange-aux-Belles, the subject of orientation of the party carried by 54 percent, and the party program by 52 percent).[31]

The end of the Algerian war hurt the PSU membership drive. Today the party comprises some 20,000 members, and in late 1969 won a seat in the National Assembly. The party continues to talk about uniting Marxists and Christians on the

[30] *Le Monde,* January 25, 1963, p. 3.
[31] See *Le Monde,* November 13, 1963, p. 6, for description of activities in the Congress of Grange-aux-Belles.

lay issue, how it can acquire a worker's base, and how it can become a real force in the country.

THE FRENCH SOCIALIST PARTY

The French Socialist party, or SFIO, as it is commonly called, is a party of paradoxes, with a revolutionary jargon, a Marxist doctrine, and behavior that is very orthodox. The Socialist party would like to be socialist and work for the advent of socialism but circumstances simply will not permit it to do so. Consequently, it rocks along (not too steadily at times) being whatever it can—which means generally it approximates the status of a very ordinary political party. This "advocate of socialism" votes in the National Assembly usually in behalf of capitalist proposals. Colonialism and imperialism infuriate it, and its parliamentary party usually protests vehemently against such adventures, except when Socialist governments find opportunities to engage in similar ventures of their own (a Socialist party president of Council of Ministers, Guy Mollet, in 1956 ordered French troops to the invasion of Suez). Militarism, too, is repugnant to the SFIO's doctrine, and yet frequently its parliamentary party votes in the National Assembly for military appropriations.

If in Parliament the Socialist party's behavior is less than dramatic, that "conventionalism" is more than compensated for within the SFIO by the interaction of its diverse tendencies. This legacy of multiple internal tendencies was transmitted to the SFIO by its precursor, the old Unified Socialist party, which, after its creation in 1904, fell short of achieving their synthesis. Between 1904 and 1914, Socialist leader Jean Jaurès sought but failed to bring all of these tendencies comfortably within one house. His assassination in 1914 deprived the party of a great force who had worked for its internal cohesion. Further and greater divisions occurred after the Russian Revolution, terminating in 1920 in an authentic party rupture. Left elements of the party subsequently reconstituted themselves as the Communist party of France, while center and right elements reformed as the SFIO. Into the new Socialist party poured certain of the internal groups which had plagued the old Unified Socialist party—

groups which persist to this day, although not in the form, of course, in which they presented themselves in 1904. Within the SFIO today are old-style socialists who support traditional parliamentary forms and types of nationalism associated with older times. Some are ferociously anti-Communist (at least one, Deputy Le Bail, made of it a profession). There also are "Europeans" who favor a United States of Europe and compromise with bourgeois elements, and "revolutionists" who endorse versions of socialism that range from tired Trotskyism to archaic anarchosyndicalism. All of these are within the Socialist party, and many of them present an interesting study in how the language of the Left frequently is employed in pursuance of objectives that have nothing to do with socialism.

Socialist leader Léon Blum used to distinguish between *l'exercice du pouvoir* (the exercise of power) and *la conquête du pouvoir* (the conquest of power). The former is evolutionary and the latter is revolutionary. The Socialist party exercised ministerial responsibility for the first time in the Popular Front government of 1936, settling for an approach to political power that is evolutionary. That policy has been sustained by it since that time. However, the Socialist party's policy toward government was not always traditional; after the party was founded in 1920, it immediately declared its opposition to Socialist ministerial participation in bourgeois coalition cabinets. That was merely a continuation of the policy adopted previously by the Unified Socialist party in its declaration of 1905. Nonetheless, that policy was modified before the 1920 Congress of Tours. During World War I, Socialists Blum, Thomas, Guesde, Sembat, and others participated in the wartime government, justifying their experience on the ground that the war was an "exceptional circumstance" and that socialist participation in governments already had been accepted elsewhere in Europe by major social-democratic parties. Clemenceau's acceptance of the prime ministership in 1917 alienated the left wing of the Unified party and resulted in the issuance by the party of a manifesto prohibiting Socialist participation in his cabinet. Had the right-wingers retained their positions on the permanent administrative committee of the Unified party, Clemenceau's offer of participation probably would have been accepted. After that decision, Blum anonymously published articles suggesting future Socialist participation in government.

Early in 1924 the SFIO Congress witnessed growing sentiment for Socialist entrance into government (the Federations of the Rhône, Var, Hérault, Vaucluse, and Tarn had already voted for it). When a special congress of the SFIO investigated the possibility later that year, Moutet, Varenne, and others argued that it was time for the SFIO to "share in governmental power." The final resolution put off the question of participation in government, but it was agreed that it could be reopened if "exceptional circumstances should arise." Later, in 1926, when the special SFIO congresses of Japy and Bellevilloise determined the conditions for the exercise of socialist power, Socialist participation in government still was precluded by the historical tradition of the SFIO and the questionable success of ministerialism at that given time. The party refused to accept participation in government until it was able to recruit in the Chamber of Deputies a unified and homegeneous Socialist party majority. After 1926, however, it was only a short time before the party cast aside one of its last vestiges of revolutionary behavior and entered government. The Socialist parliamentary party wanted to form a coalition government with the Radical Socialists in 1929, but it was restrained by the party's permanent administrative committee. Later, in 1932, Blum informed the Socialist congress that the SFIO would participate in coalition government with the Radical Socialists if that party would include in its program provisions favorable to the SFIO.

While "late" in participating in government, the SFIO had given its support much earlier in the Chamber of Deputies to progressive bourgeois governments, a policy that allowed the parliamentary system to function effectively, presenting a viable alternative to rightist rule. Adherence to that policy enabled the party prior to 1934 to meet the test of practically all parliamentary conditions. After 1934, however, the French nation was confronted with new circumstances. Ambitious antiparliamentary forces made their appearance, altering the traditional parliamentary picture. Moreover, the SFIO, as a result of the legislative elections of 1936, became the largest political party in the Chamber of Deputies. Its success on the electoral terrain then brought it face to face with the question of its participation in government. The largest party in the Chamber hardly could continue to function as it did in previous years, attempting to influence the majority and directing it toward the acquisition of socialist ends. Moreover, the parliamentary system itself was at stake, a fact that no tactical formula could evade. Lacking in the Chamber of Deputies a unified and homogeneous majority of its own, the SFIO cast aside one of the major struts in its tactical policy when in 1936 it entered the Popular Front government.

Gustav von Noske used to say that Socialist governments nearly always make a determined effort to placate the opposition, "instead of rendering him harmless as they elected to do." Blum's Socialists displayed in government little of the audacity they had revealed earlier when in opposition. Sharing the cabinet with Radical Socialist ministers, and depending upon a Socialist–Radical Socialist–Communist majority in the Chamber, Blum found himself incapable of bringing about the introduction of a broad financial and economic transformation in the country. His role as prime minister became different from his position as party chieftain. His address to the Socialist congress on May 31, 1936, resembled a farewell as he told its members that the life of the SFIO was to go on apart from that of the government. His party, although it unanimously approved assumption of ministerial responsibility, proclaimed that it was toward complete socialism that it would direct the course of its own activity.

The importance of the SFIO's participation in government was one thing; the impact of that participation on the SFIO was yet another. Its participation in government bridged the gap in the fabric of the Third Republic, as yet another party gravitated toward the traditional political order, making possible the continuation of government and helping to sustain the republic. The effect on the SFIO of that participation in government remains debatable. Participation payed some short-range dividends, strengthening the SFIO's popularity during the first "100 days." On the other hand, participation produced some long-range deficits, due primarily to the fact that the party had assumed office when its chances for real power were negligible, when it lacked a unified and homogeneous majority behind it in the Chamber. Consequently, its influence on authority when in government was perhaps less than what it had been when in opposition. In the government, representatives of a party that advocated socialism gave their efforts to implementation of a nonsocialist program, illustrating in practice what Robert Michels once described as "the socialism of nonsocialists with a revolutionary past." Thus, the party settled down to traditional conflict on traditional terrain. No longer was it an energetic party of the Left. Had it sought to manitain its position on the Left, the Communist party might have been in subsequent years less than it is now.

Guy Mollet, who has held the post of secretary-general of the SFIO for more than twenty years, came to it first in 1946 as the result of the party congress held in Montrouge (a suburb of Paris) and of the attacks that he launched there against the conservative leadership of "archaic" Léon Blum and Daniel Mayer. Mollet was then the "new man of the Left," the one who was "best equipped" to bring the party out of its lethargy and restore it to the revolutionary mainstream. Once invested, he led the organization into adventures in conservatism that transcend most of those in which it participated when it was under the direction of the old leadership. Mollet leads the SFIO today. He is a socialist, and there is no doubt whatsoever that he wants socialism in France—nonetheless, he undertakes very few efforts to achieve it.

Mollet has fashioned for himself an image as "savior of the Republic." According to him, he entered the Gaillard government in 1957 because continuation of republican government was impossible without SFIO participation in that cabinet. In 1958 he entered General de Gaulle's revolutionary cabinet after —he states—"turning the country from civil war and saving the Republic," having been the first among all the anti-Gaullist opposition leaders to alter his position and make possible a "legal" assumption of power by the General. "Saving the Republic" is for Mollet a frequently exercised vocation, and if he is correct, his efforts have been instrumental in preserving "two fifths" of French Republicanism.

The SFIO has been in a state of decline for many years. That recession, which began under the Third Republic, was accentuated during the Fourth. There have been no signs of its recovery during the Fifth. The party has settled down, claiming in national elections approximately 13 percent of the total vote. That disabling illness of political parties—regionalism—now is characteristic of its membership strength in the country. Figure

Figure 5–1 Membership in the SFIO by department in 1962

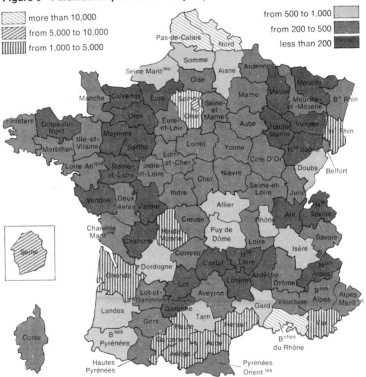

Source: *France-Observateur,* June 6, 1963, p. 6.

5–1 depicts its severity.[32] Only three departments, the Nord, Pas-de-Calais, and Bouches-du-Rhône, serve as SFIO bastions. As of 1962, in no department did the number of SFIO members exceed 11,000 (for recent developments see p. 443, note 6).

[32] *France-Observateur* (June 6, 1963), p. 6.

FROM THE SOCIALIST-DEMOCRATIC FEDERATION TO THE FEDERATION OF THE DEMOCRATIC AND SOCIALIST LEFT

The Socialist-Democratic Federation (Fédération démocrate-socialiste) originated as an idea during the early 1960s. Its aim was to affect a radical reorganization of the Left. It sought to synthesize some Left parties and to present them to the voters in the form of one great political formation. Its presidential candidate in 1965 was to be Gaston Defferre, Mayor of Marseilles and long-time member of the French Socialist party, SFIO. That federation died in 1965, at the hands of the very parties Defferre sought to amalgamate, and Defferre withdrew his candidacy from the presidential race. Another federation was formed almost immediately, the Federation of the Democratic and Socialist Left (Fédération de la gauche démocrate et socialiste), headed by François Mitterand, deputy from Nièvre and long-time member of the UDSR (Union of Democratic and Socialist Resistance). This federation was very different from Defferre's, being an electoral union composed of the Socialist, SFIO, and Radical Socialist parties, which looked forward to parliamentary and governmental alliances, and in which the sovereignty of the participating parties was guarded jealously. In fact, there was some question as to whether it was a true "federation."

Defferre argued for the adoption of a new and modern political party. His Socialist-Democratic Federation sought absorption of some of the old parties, ranging from the Unified Socialist party, PSU, on the left, to the Popular Republican party, MRP, on the right. It also proposed to draw to it youth elements not previously involved in politics, groups in favor of socialism who had refused to join the SFIO, and unions and political clubs. Defferre's project had originated with the political clubs, in fact, those small associations who seek both an alternative to Gaullism and classical parliamentarism. Among the most important were the Club of Jacobins (founded by Charles Hernu and oriented strongly towards Mendès-France), the Club Jean Moulin (which comprises numerous high civil servants and some of the most illustrious names in France), the Citoyen 60 (led by Roger Jacques, oriented toward Catholic social action, and having close ties with scoutism), the Cercle Tocqueville of Lyon, the Clubs démocratie nouvelle of Marseilles, and the Club Position of Vichy. All of these clubs, united in the first Congress of Clubs which convened in Vichy in 1964, endorsed Gaston Defferre's candidacy for the presidency.

Among the leading figures who supported Defferre was Jean-Jacques Servan-Schreiber, who worked for him tirelessly and who was instrumental in pushing Defferre's personality before the public. Editor of the mass circulation weekly *Express,* Servan-Schreiber had quit the publication and moved to Marseilles in order to conduct Defferre's campaign for the presidency and support his efforts to construct a new Left, one that was tuned to the realities of modern existence and could provide a viable alternative to de Gaulle and lead the way to the reconstruction of French democracy.

Many of Defferre's ideas are presented in his book *Un nouvel horizon,* published in 1965, in which he set his goal as "definition of the great options of a policy of progress." [33] That work was part of his effort to rally the partisans of a "modern France." In it he described the stability of the Gaullist regime as illusory, and its parliamentary majority as disunited and not cemented together by any common conception: "The stability of the State reposes presently in one man. But this man is mortal and the permanent causes of disorder and of impotence always are present." Divisions have multiplied, he argued, during the long absence of democracy from France. "France has never attained the vital minimum of democracy: a strong power, an effective popular control. General de Gaulle hides these divisions; in eluding all control, in refusing all contestation, in discouraging all participation of citizens in the affairs of the state, he has succeeded in lasting—but a modern democracy will be no more satisfactory as a plebiscitarian monarchy than an anarchy of clans." Stability, said Defferre, is not synonomous with immobilism, and "A policy which stagnates in a society which changes necessarily engenders discontent, disorder, violence. . . ." [34]

Defferre said that as president he would retain the 1958

[33] See Gaston Defferre, *Un nouvel horizon,* Collection idées (Paris: Gallimard, 1965).

[34] *Defferre,* p. 91.

Constitution (which offended some elements of the Left), but that, unlike de Gaulle, he would apply it; that he would abolish the "reserved sector" treasured by de Gaulle; that he would modify Article 16, the Constitutional Council and usage of the referendum; that he would take decision making from the president of the republic and restore it to the prime minister; and that he would dissolve the National Assembly so as to obtain a majority to go along with the new president.[35] The president of the republic and the deputies would be elected on the same day. The parliamentary term being five years, the president could resign at the time of its expiration—for if the National Assembly is dissolved and the president remains, that would set the stage for the possible existence of two majorities, one that elected the president and the one that elected the deputies. The president would be an arbiter—namely, in three kinds of cases: (1) in case of discord in the government; (2) in case of discord in the parliamentary majority; (3) in case of discord between the government and Parliament that resulted in a ministerial crisis, in which case the act of arbitration performed by the president would consist of dissolution of the National Assembly.[36] Defferre's image of Europe was one that had a "socialist character," rather than being outright socialist. He wanted a "federated Europe with a parliament and government capable of acting in its name. . . . A Europe powerful and unified," that could "become the artisan of a lasting *rapprochement* between the East and the West."[37] He opposed the French *force de frappe,* acknowledging, however, that he was sympathetic to a European one (nonetheless, he refused to come to a definite commitment on the latter).[38] He articulated his support for general disarmament and promised, if elected, to give first priority to national education.[39]

Defferre pointed to divisions within the Left and the paralysis of action that they had produced. Seeking to shake the Left from its lethargy, he indicted its policy of waiting for de

---

[35] *Le Monde,* January 14, 1964, p. 1.

[36] *Le Monde,* February 11, 1964, p. 5.

[37] *Le Monde,* December 12, 1964, p. 12.

[38] *Le Monde,* February 11, 1964, p. 5, February 7, 1964, p. 4.

[39] *Le Monde,* February 12, 1964, p. 12.

Gaulle to disappear as a precondition of coming to power in France—a policy, he argued, which could convert the Left into but a simple force of opposition for the following twenty years. One of Defferre's major tactical concerns was with the Communist party and discovering ways in which he could secure the votes of its supporters without becoming its captive. He described Communist electoral potential as having been sterilized since 1920; he acknowledged, however, that without that vote, the rest of the Left and Center Left were doomed to the status of permanent minorities. Everything changes, said Defferre, except the French Communist party, which is out of touch with both France and the USSR, clinging to an outmoded mythology and not daring to lead its followers out of "their ghetto." Defferre proposed creation alongside of the Communist party of a more dynamic and powerful formation, one that would provide a source of Left leadership and compel the Communist party to come along with a new tide of renovation. The condition of such a *rassemblement* was to bring together all partisans of change, all those dissatisfied with society as it is: "From the MRP to the Communist party, from the CGT to management, the number of those who search is beginning to surpass the number of those who have, once and for all, stopped searching." [40]

Defferre's wish was to lead the Left away from its innumerable internal divisions and endless doctrinal interactions; he asked all partisans of change to rise above the sovereignty of and loyalty to party in order to join in the construction of a broad movement fashioned along modern lines. Defferre's effort represented an attack on the classical Left conception of party, leading to a series of reactions among traditional Left politicians, particularly by the leader of Defferre's own SFIO, Guy Mollet. Consequently, Defferre became a "marked man," and soon he paid the price for trying to modernize the party system. That price was extracted from him by many of his fellow SFIO members, whose narrowly construed "patriotism of party" precluded support of his policy. Although he had the support of such men as Gazier, Jacquet, Pineau, Metayer, Chandernagor,

[40] Defferre, p. 34.

and others, there were many others who opposed him, not daring, though, to come out publicly and say so. He secured the endorsement of his party for his presidential candidacy in the February 1964 special Congress, but the "support" given him there by Mollet was something of a *cadeau empoisonné*. After paying tribute to Defferre's republicanism, Mollet questioned the risk involved in Defferre's candidacy, stating that Defferre had to distinguish his policy sufficiently from de Gaulle's so as to bring along with him all republicans (some aspects of his and de Gaulle's policy did converge). Mollet expressed reservations about Defferre's possible endorsement of the presidential regime, and succeeded in influencing the resolution adopted by the Congress—that the SFIO would avoid a presidential system and seek the election of a president who would not refer to the "reserved sector." The resolution, which stated that "This regime will be neither the presidential type nor the classical parliamentary type," was distinctly a "compromise." [41] Later, during the following year, in the Socialist congress which convened in Clichy, Mollet moved against Defferre, proposing a "small federation," ranging from the Unified Socialist party, PSU, to the Radical Socialist party. Defferre countered that Mollet's plan represented "slow death," that the PSU would not enter any federation from which the Communist party was excluded, and that the Radicals would stay out if the Popular Republicans were not included.[42] He described Mollet's policy as being strictly of the "Maginot line" variety.[43] Within the congress it was apparent that many Socialists were fearful of doing anything that might limit their party's independence of decision making. There were those who felt that a broad federation of the type proposed by Defferre constituted an attack on the SFIO itself. This time Secretary-General Mollet had his way. Mollet stated that he had been in 1963 a sincere defender of Defferre's candidacy but that now he felt compelled to challenge Defferre's socialism, not for what it included but for what

[41] *Le Monde*, February 4, 1964, p. 1. Anybody who doubts Mollet's tactical competence should consult this issue of *Le Monde* for description of the way in which he approached the resolution.

[42] *Le Monde*, June 5, 1965, p. 1.

[43] *Le Monde*, June 5, 1965, p. 1.

it excluded—that it was not revolutionary but reformist, and that the party should defend the definition of socialism adopted by it on February 24, 1964, and refuse to cooperate with those who reject it.[44] Mollet was supported by Augustin Laurent, secretary-general of the Federation of the Nord, and Claude Fuzier, leader of the Federation of the Seine. Laurent told Defferre, "I don't know where you are going," and accused him of tendencies toward presidentialism, of wanting to cooperate with conservatives, supporting a vague reformism, pressuring his own party, wanting a "pseudo-socialist federation," and being guilty of "doctrinal revisionism." [45] Fuzier charged that Defferre was leading the party "toward reactionary forces" and setting the stage for the replacement of socialism by industrial capitalism.[46]

The conflict within the SFIO between the Defferrists and Molletists involved issues that went beyond the impending presidential election. The Defferrists were critical of SFIO leadership (this was somewhat reminiscent of the 1956–1958 conflict when André Philip and his asociates worked for internal reforms and tried to remove the unshakable Mollet from the secretary-generalship).[47] In January 1966, after the presidential election, and long after Defferre had withdrawn his candidacy, the Defferrists launched an attack on the tactical policy of the SFIO and "the methods of a leadership too personalized." [48] They described the party as "enfeebled," of being "closed to innovations." [49] They were answered by the majority letter to the militants which referred to those "troublemakers" in the party who were determined to "get Mollet," "the man who has always abided by the statutes of the party." [50]

[44] *Le Monde,* June 5, 1965, p. 1.

[45] *Le Monde,* June 5, 1965, p. 1.

[46] *Le Monde,* June 5, 1965, p. 1.

[47] Philip was expelled in March 1958. He remembers, as he told the author, when—years before—he told Mollet that he had to be less timid and more forceful if he were to succeed in politics!

[48] *Le Monde,* January 25, 1966, p. 10.

[49] *Le Monde,* January 25, 1966, p. 10.

[50] *Le Monde,* January 25, 1966, p. 10; see *Le Monde,* December 31, 1965, p. 7 for earlier remarks of Defferre that irritated the Molletists, particularly his comment that certain revolutionaries of the Left are revolutionary only in language.

It should not be concluded that Defferre's own SFIO alone was instrumental in defeating his proposed federation, and retiring him from the presidential race. Despite earlier declarations of sympathetic sentiments, other political parties of the Left simply were not ready then to immerse themselves in such a federation. Nor were some prepared to go along with Defferre's empiricism and slight regard for doctrine. The Unified Socialist party, PSU, rejected his project; PSU Assistant Secretary-General Gilles Martinet pictured Defferre as a centrist candidate who sought integration of the worker movement in neocapitalism, as well as a splitting of the Left. He accused Defferre of being too subservient to the Popular Republican party, MRP, and too much of a proponent of "Atlanticism." [15] However, if the PSU regarded Defferre's federation as nonsocialist, the Popular Republican party viewed it as being too socialist. The MRP repudiated the federation, after criticizing the laicism of the SFIO, its collectivism, and its relations with the Communist party.[52] MRP leader Lecanuet stated that federation had been possible only with a part of the SFIO, not with all of it, that nobody had given Defferre much of a chance, but that few had wanted to say so publicly.[53] The real MRP preference was not for a social-democratic federation but for a center of democrats, one that could attract voters of the Center and Right, not one that would isolate the Right. Moreover, the MRP was completely opposed to any alliance whatsoever with the Communist party; the MRP knew that Defferre was not receptive to such an alliance either, but it was uneasy because Defferre preferred not to block the path toward a possible dialogue with the Communist party.[54] The MRP also knew that its participation in such a federation would subject it to controls by nonconservatives, and it was opposed to that. Finally, certain of the MRP leaders were opposed to the federation from the first.

The defeat of Defferre's proposed federation was furthered by its lack of a common program (in fact, it hardly had one at all), and existence among members of Left parties of an image of party that was very different from the one advanced by

[51] *Le Monde,* June 9, 1965, p. 1.
[52] *Le Monde,* June 11, 1965, p. 1.
[53] *Le Monde,* June 20–21, 1965, p. 8.
[54] *Le Monde,* June 1, 1965, p. 1.

Defferre. Defferre's opposition came primarily from party traditionalists, men who hold the organization before the cause, and refuse to yield to any merger that threatens to decrease their organization's power. These men hold important posts in their organizations and dominate the apparatus. Defferre's support came largely from militants, from people removed from the executive and administrative bureaucracies of their parties. Irrespective of how modern was Defferre's conception of party, it had little effect on party leaders, who had developed interests peculiar to themselves. Giving away a little autonomy is one thing; sacrifice of structure and position, however, is really too much to ask. This time "the men of the Fourth" behaved as though they were really of the Fourth Republic.

Defferre withdrew from the presidential campaign in June, 1965 (just five months before the election), stating that the defeat of his proposed federation had forced him to retire,[55] and that he had no intention of making an appeal "to the people against the political parties."[56] He said that he had regarded his task only as that of strengthening the democratic parties and uniting them, in order to attract new generations to public life and to provide a simple and solid basis for democracy.[57] He

[55] *Le Monde,* June 26, 1965, p. 1. See also Gaston Defferre, "De Gaulle and After," *Foreign Affairs* (April 1966), p. 436. Defferre states, "My object was to create at least two large political forces, one left of Center, the other conservative. The Communists and the extreme Right would remain outside these groups. Since I did not succeed in this, the natural, honest, and moral thing was for me to withdraw. I considered it my duty to withdraw in order to save the idea. Though I did not succeed, once the idea had been launched it was taken up in a narrower form, that of the Federation of the Democratic and Socialist Left." Defferre appears to be "pushing things" in this statement. Both his idea and his federation were different from what subsequently followed.

[56] *Le Monde,* June 26, 1965, p. 8; see "La vie politique de novembre 1964 . . . ," 1, 42. This study of the French Institute of Public Opinion concluded in 1966 that the public hardly believed in the possibility of Defferre's federation. Only a minority said that they could vote for him if he ran for the presidency. However, in favor of the chance to federate were 60 percent of the SFIO electors interviewed, 40 percent of the Radical Socialist electors, and 37 percent of the MRP electors. See also p. 9 of the same study, in which only 24 percent of the respondents favored Defferre's reelection to the mayorship of Marseilles (17 percent were opposed, 59 percent had no opinion).

[57] *Le Monde,* June 26, 1965, p. 8.

conceded that eventually the federation would find a candidate who would unite all those "reform democrats" who do not want personal power or communism.[58]

Questions have been raised relative to the manner in which Defferre conducted his campaign. Aspects of his program bore definite resemblance to the program of de Gaulle; the Communist party charged him with practicing "Gaullism without de Gaulle," thereby alienating some prospective supporters. His conception of the president as an arbiter was not too far removed from a real presidentialism, and yet he hesitated to say so, approaching it obliquely and proceeding slowly, as though Left voters were incapable of adjusting to new political perspectives. During the campaign he appeared somewhat reticent to explore publicly all the convictions that he might have had. That was understandable, considering the diverse forces that he was seeking to recruit to his support, but it also was disappointing for many of his listeners and potential voters. In fact, in February 1964 he said that his intentions were not to say what he would do if elected, and that by maintaining this position he could avoid demagogic promises and count on the positions he took on a day to day basis in order to combat Gaullism.[59]

Finally, Defferre's proposed federation was complicated by the question of whether the parties of the Left would be willing to give it real power and a competent organization, or whether it would be only an association on which participant parties would seek to impose their own domination. Subsequently, as events unfolded, the discussions which involved the leaders of potential participant parties showed more concern with the federation's future tactics and strategy than with endowing it realistically with the means to become a great, modern political party. Controversies in the discussions focused on the question of whether alliances should be with the Communist party or with the Center. Competing with each other were the Center alliance views of Defferre and the alliance with the Communist party tendencies of Mitterand. The centrists insisted that an alliance with the Communist party was undesirable because it would lead to future losses in legislative elections; they wanted

[58] *Le Monde,* June 26, 1965, p. 8.

[59] See *Le Monde,* January 14, 1964, p. 1; and February 7, 1964, p. 4.

cooperation with the MRP and those Independents who supported the Democratic Center's Jean Lecanuet as a means of finding an end to Gaullism. The Mitterand group argued that this strategy could lead only to duplication of periods of political conservatism of the type dominated in 1956 by Guy Mollet. However, a telling point about the discussions was the way in which they were confined to the leaderships of the parties of the Left—and deliberately withheld from certain illustrious citizens who might have preferred to have had something to say about them. In fact, precautions were taken early by these leaderships so as to ensure that membership in the federation would be on the basis of organizations and not of individuals. Nor could anything have been done about changing that structural phenomenon. Mollet not only wanted it, he insisted on it—and his domination of the SFIO constituted assurance that membership would continue to be defined on that basis.

The defeat of Defferre's Socialist-Democratic Federation was followed by the creation of yet another federation, the Federation of the Democratic and Socialist Left. This organization was hastily created. After the legislative elections of 1967, Mitterand's Federation of the Democratic and Socialist Left stepped in the direction of the "road to *rapprochement*" with the Communist party when on February 24, 1968, both organizations entered into a common agreement relating to their conceptions of the future regime and opposition to Gaullism (the agreement, a lengthy one occupying almost two pages in *Le Monde,* was the result of eight months of bargaining and discussions among representatives of both organizations).[60] The agreement did not lay down anything resembling a Federation–Communist party "common program of government"; instead, it established a consensus concerning what each may do, exposing it to considerable clarification. The agreement constituted a departure by the Communist party, moreover, from its usual practice of "putting aside that which divides" in order to "retain that which unites," establishing and describing instead those areas

[60] See *Le Monde,* February 22–28, 1968, *Sélection hebdomadaire,* pp. 8–9, for full text of the agreement. For assessments of it, see, in the same issue, Raymond Barrillon, "L'accord Féderation–Parti Communiste," pp. 1, 9, and Jacques Fauvet, "La gauche et son programme," p. 1.

in which both parties acknowledged opposing views. The main lines of the agreement were as follows:

1. Condemnation of personal power and abrogation of those constitutional articles which make it possible, particularly Article 16 (the Communist party also wants transformation of Articles 54, 56, and 61).
2. Votes of censure by the National Assembly should lead automatically to its dissolution.
3. The right of initiative in matters of the referendum should belong to Parliament.
4. Parliament must be convened when the conditions prescribed in Article 29 of the Constitution are satisfied.
5. A government's majority should be tested by the prime minister fifteen days after he has been named by the president.
6. Both a Supreme Court and Higher Council of the Magistracy should be established independent of the executive.
7. The "blocked vote" should be modified.
8. In all cases of constitutional revision Article 89 should be adhered to strictly.
9. The presidential term should be reduced from seven to five years.
10. Radio, television, and press should be democratized.
11. The right of *habeas corpus* and rights to information and culture should be established in the Constitution.
12. Local collectivities should be given autonomy.
13. The federation wishes a true separation of powers between the executive and legislative organs, and the discard of all forms of "government by assembly" "that lead to instability." (The Communist party maintains its attachment to an Assembly retaining strong controls over the government, and its opposition to all forms of presidential government. Unlike the federation, the Communist party endorses proportional representation.)
14. Salaries and pensions should be increased.
15. More housing should be constructed.
16. In foreign policy the federation endorses arbitration by the United Nations and other international organizations that support peace; disarmament; construction of a European political *ensemble* in which the Europe of the Six would form the nucleus, so as to assure independence

of *les grandes;* admission of the United Kingdom to the political *ensemble* (described as "a common political power elected by universal suffrage"); no rupture with the Atlantic Alliance (in foreign policy the Communist party states that national independence is fundamental, and that France must remain outside the two military blocs; supports international arbitration "designed to maintain the peace," with application of the United Nations Charter as one of the means; urges nonrenewal of the Atlantic pact).

17. Criticism of the European Economic Community as dominated by cartels, trusts, and international pressure groups, and demands for its democratization and detechnocratization, as well as representation in it of more social categories.

18. Opposition to German nuclear rearmament.

19. End of the *force de frappe.*

20. Further cooperation with the "Third World."

21. Further nationalizations (although federation and Communist conceptions of breadth and magnitude differ).[61]

The Federation of the Left, which suffered crushing defeat in the legislative elections of 1968, winning in the National Assembly only fifty-seven seats, was dissolved later that year.

THE RADICAL SOCIALIST PARTY

Earlier in French history—particularly when republics were threatened or in doubt—the Radical Socialist party equated itself with the republic itself. It was, said Édouard Herriot (the late mayor of Lyons, and for many years "Mr. Radical Socialist" himself), the "infantry of the Republic." It would be more accurate, however, to identify its strongest republican pretensions with the Third Republic.

Léon Gambetta, one of the great figures of radicalism, stated in 1869 that the program of radicalism consisted of separation of church and state, free primary education (mandatory and secular), universal suffrage, freedom of speech, assembly

[61] This summary by the author includes only the agreement's most important points; great length precludes its full reproduction here.

and association, suppression of armaments, abolition of the Senate and elevation of the Chamber of Deputies, election of judges, and emancipation of workers from the cruel conditions of their material existence.

Until 1877 radicalism was almost entirely an urban and Parisian phenomenon, after which it became provincial and spread throughout the nation. During the Dreyfus affair it played a great role, drawing together the forces of the Left to combat anti-Semitism, clericalism, and nationalism, even though internally it displayed substantial disunity.[62] By 1902, for example, although it was by then an organized political party, Radical Socialists sat in the Chamber of Deputies and Senate not as one parliamentary group, being distributed instead among the Radical Left and Radical Socialist Left factions. Until 1910 its deputies were allowed to belong to two or more parliamentary groups. In 1913 the party achieved "loose unification" as the result of exclusion from it of some of its most difficult dissidents. "Loose unification" remains to this day a decided Radical Socialist party characteristic.[63]

The "Radical Republic" was terminated by 1912; nonetheless, for many years after that the party was never too far removed from power. Between World Wars I and II Radical Socialists presided over thirteen of forty-two governments, and after the Liberation, although the party generally was discredited, nine governments of the Fourth Republic served under its direction. Displaying a genius for making the most of its votes in the

[62] Captain Alfred Dreyfus was sentenced in 1894 for having sold military secrets to Germany. Dreyfus, who insisted on his innocence, became the target of the army, church, antirepublicans, and anti-Semites. Dreyfus was defended by some republican elements. The case became a conflict between antirepublican and republican forces. Eventually it was revealed that Dreyfus had been railroaded by those who had actually committed the espionage—high military officers who had picked him as a scapegoat because he was the only Jew on the general staff. Many years later, when Charles Maurras was tried by the state for having collaborated with Germany during the second World War, he exclaimed, "It is the revenge of Dreyfus." See Ernst Nolte, *Three Faces of Fascism* (New York: Holt, Rinehart and Winston, Inc., 1966), p. 85.

[63] Jean-François Kesler's article, "Le radicalisme et les radicaux," *Perspectives socialistes,* 50 (May 1962), 29–43, gives a good picture of the early years and background of radical socialism.

country, the party claimed in the legislature often more seats than those won by other parties claiming superior support at the polls.

The Radical Socialist party embraces internally many different interpretations of radicalism. All of these claim a philosophy of history, defense of science and utilitarianism, a rationalist and naturalist tradition founded on the search for happiness, and a theme of solidarity which seeks to reconcile individualism and collectivism. All of this does not conceal the fact that the Radical Socialist party is, however, never far removed from defense of property. It is not by chance that Jacques Fauvet refers to it as the most bourgeois of bourgeois parties, concerning itself primarily with the holdings of small property owners in small cities.[64] There are some differences among the radicalisms of the Côtes-du-Nord, Seine-Maritime, Eure-et-Loir, and the Charentes, but they all spell one thing—conservatism. There are radicalisms of the right bank of Paris, the Alpes-Maritimes, Indre, Nantes, Bouches-du-Rhône, and the Seine-et-Oise, but generally they all come down to antireformism. There also are radicalisms of the Rhône, Drôme, Vaucluse, and east and southwest Champenois, which profess to be based on internationalism, tolerance, and progressive nationalism. Pierre Mendès-France once tried to do something with this type of thought, asking it to support a modern political movement that could thrust both Marxism and conservatism into the background. After asking that it support the introduction of a modern capitalism, he discovered subsequently that many of the Radical Socialists were concerned not with modernism but with a static economy and the retention of devices that best protected their modest holdings. Mendès-France gave up on radicalism late in the history of the Fourth Republic; it would be difficult to say, however, that radicalism gave up on him. It probably is more accurate to say that it never gave him a chance.

The decline of the Radical Socialist party in French politics was helped along by the deintensification of the church-state controversy and the resultant reduction in clerical and secular anxieties, the costly state financial scandals in which periodically

---

[64] Jacques Fauvet, *La France déchirée* (Paris: Fayard, 1957), p. 23.

various Radical Socialist ministers and deputies were involved, and the Great Depression that antiquated so many of its economic views. A good indication of the party's bleak future was revealed when in the elections of 1919 it won only eighty-six seats in the Chamber of Deputies. Sliding downhill all the time, the party managed—by a clever tactical policy and searching for majorities both to its right and left—to sustain itself as a major force until 1932. After the elections of that year the party discovered that it could no longer scurry back and forth between Left and Right claiming working majorities wherever they could be found. Rejected by the Right, the party then became dependent upon the Socialist party, SFIO, entering cabinets which the Socialists supported but in which the Socialists refused to participate.[65] Tarnished by many years of having exercised power, and now a lesser force in French politics, the party learned to settle periodically for whatever it was able to claim in the way of an occasional ministry. Now, however, the Radical Socialists are not able to claim even that, for the party is in opposition to the Gaullist regime.[66]

The Radical Socialists are a "party of generals" who appear sometimes to be seemingly oblivious of desertions from all quarters within their ranks. Some of these "generals" are capable, but they can achieve little with their forces so diminished on the national level. Some, like Edgar Faure, after inventorying the Radical establishment, have "crossed over" to where the business is and have affiliated with the Gaullists (Faure was rewarded in 1966 with the Ministry of Agriculture, if that ministry can be considered a "reward," and later with the Ministry of Education). Time, though, is running out for the Radical Socialists, and now the party is much less than what it was—nevertheless, it remains on, extracting from the political environment whatever it can, which often is not very much.

---

[65] Because of the absence of a unified and homogeneous Socialist majority in the Chamber of Deputies.

[66] *Le Monde,* November 22, 1966, p. 8. In its sixty-third congress held in Marseilles, the party declared its opposition to "personal power" and its support for the creation of a new majority, of which the Federation of the Left will be the axis: "It gives its approbation fully and completely to the program and the orientation of the Federation."

Faure has fled already to the Gaullists; Mendès-France has left for the PSU, but Félix Gaillard stays on in the family establishment. Who knows how many Radical Socialist leaders agree with Robert Frost's feeling that home is where you go when no other place will take you in.

THE DEMOCRATIC CENTER

The Democratic Center (Centre démocrate) was created in 1966 by MRP member Jean Lecanuet and associates of his from the same political party. The Center owed its origins to Lecanuet's showing as an opponent of Gaullism in the presidential election of 1965, and to MRP efforts to block Left attempts to monopolize and profit possibly from anti-Gaullist electoral coalitions. The Center sought to throw a wedge between two great forces on either side of it, in order to prevent either one from gaining a clear victory in national legislative elections. Once achieved, the Center then would have been in a position to have bargained with one of the forces, and to have inflicted upon it various demands as a condition of completing its legislative majority. Proper positioning and being "just large enough" to be effective are characteristics of this operational policy. There were several flaws, however, in Lecanuet's approach. It did not raise any great excitement among some of the MRP leaders, and it failed to attract the Radical Socialists away from the Left; allies to the right of the Center proved, moreover, hard to come by, and in the 1967 national legislative elections the Center was not able to field enough of its own deputies to put itself in a real bargaining position. In fact, there was some question as to whether the creation of the Center compensated for the prior dissolution of the MRP. Finally, although Lecanuet attracted great attention in the presidential election of 1965, he had great difficulty in sustaining his image in subsequent months. At first he was witty, charming, and downright attractive, but word soon spread of his extraordinary efforts to create through public relations media a fixed public image of himself. Elements of the populace came to regard him as being one of the best actors on the national television (that is, when he was able to get on the screen), and some public resentment set in. Confronted on both sides with great electoral coalitions, the future of Lecanuet and the Democratic Center obviously is limited. Running under the title of the CPDM, the Center was crushed in the legislative elections of 1968 and reduced to but twenty-nine deputies in the National Assembly.

FROM THE UNION OF THE NEW REPUBLIC TO THE UNION OF DEMOCRATS FOR THE FIFTH REPUBLIC

The UNR (Union pour la Nouvelle République), which was created in 1958, after the Gaullist seizure of power, won in the legislative elections of that year enough seats to become the largest party in the National Assembly. During its first days it looked more like a large formation than a political party, recruiting solely on the basis of fidelity to General de Gaulle. Roger Frey, its first secretary-general, explained in 1958 that the UNR's mission was to "follow the example of General de Gaulle" and remain "faithful to the social and national philosophy of Gaullism; these are the lines along which the General must guide us." Paradoxically, the formation created by revolution sought to present itself as a moderating force in French politics, as "neither to the Left nor the Right." From the first, one of its clearly expressed objectives was to drive the Communists from those elective posts that they held on both the national and local levels.

All sorts of personalities were attracted to the UNR during the first months in its existence. Among its first parliamentary party were a number of deputies who were either classical militarists or old soldiers with a clear dislike for politics and a preference for colonialism. Others were "pure Gaullists," blindly obedient to the dictates of the General. Others were liberals, some were adventurers, and a few were none other than fascists. All however, accepted nationalism and demonstrated great faith in the ability of the General to solve France's problems.[67]

The UNR represented one of a number of distinct efforts made by General de Gaulle over a period of twenty-five years to achieve leadership of France. Those efforts began with his lead-

---

[67] "L'UNR telle qu'elle est vue de Claude Bourdet à André Stibio," *Le Monde,* December 9, 1958, p. 3.

ership of the Free French during World War II, his creation in 1947 of the Rally of the French people (Rassemblement du peuple français), his acceptance in 1958 of leadership of the successful revolutionary movement against the Fourth Republic and, during the same year, his introduction of a "new formation," the UNR. The UNR was launched October 1, 1958, in the office of Information Minister Jacques Soustelle, as a federation of movements describing themselves all as Gaullist (the Convention républicaine, the Union pour le renouveau français, the Centre national des républicains sociaux). Among these, Soustelle's Union pour le renouveau français had as its primary objective retention of Algeria by France. One month after its creation the UNR claimed as its responsibility maintenance of "French Algeria," and it stated that it would be guided in this task by directives referred to it periodically by General de Gaulle.[68]

Although ostensibly a formation of fierce fidelity to de Gaulle, soon after its creation the UNR witnessed considerable interaction among its internal groups. "Up to the declaration of General de Gaulle, the 16th of September 1959, on the self-determination of Algeria, the struggle of tendencies over Algerian policies was disguised in the UNR in a quarrel over the organization of the movement."[69] After de Gaulle's historic pronouncement, Jacques Soustelle, principal UNR opponent of Algerian self-determination, then adopted within the party a "new policy" of influencing its action in the direction of Algeria's *francization*. On October 14, 1959, Léon Delbeque and eight other UNR deputies of Algérie française persuasion resigned from the party. Soustelle remained in the UNR until his expulsion from it April 25, 1960, Prime Minister Michel Debré informing him that for the UNR only one policy was "admissible" for Algeria—the policy defined by General de Gaulle.[70]

Internal crises occurred with regular frequency within the UNR between 1958 and 1962, during which time the party used

[68] *Le Monde,* November 15, 1958, p. 3.

[69] Jean Charlot, *L'UNR: Étude du pouvoir au sein d'un parti politique* (Paris: Colin, 1967); *Cahiers de la fondation nationale des sciences politiques,* No. 153, p. 49.

[70] Charlot, p. 83.

up five secretary-generals and five presidents of the parliamentary group. After 1962 fewer changes were implemented in the party's administrative posts and charter, and stronger discipline was imposed on its parliamentary group (although Article 22 of the statutes adopted September 23, 1960, affirmed that "Inside the group liberty of expression and of the vote are complete"). The reason for those crises was that during these years all of the men of the UNR did not view their organization through one common perspective.[71] Members Jacques Soustelle and Léon Delbeque were at odds with de Gaulle on his Algerian policy, and they came to feel that the UNR should have established itself independent of both de Gaulle and the government. Later, after their departure, Secretary-General Albin Chalandon (not of Algérie française persuasion) suggested that the party acquire a "political personality" not totally equatable with that of the government, a suggestion that was supported quietly by Chaban-Delmas, president of the National Assembly, and Raymond Schmittlein, president of the parliamentary party. Chalandon's decline began soon after, and before long he was removed from the post. Michel Debré and Georges Pompidou submitted that the leaders of the UNR were President de Gaulle and his prime minister, and that the policy of the party was that of the government. Their "explanation" was relatively simple—President de Gaulle created the government, and was the source of its power; the UNR is a party of fidelity to General de Gaulle, therefore it must uphold the government.[72] The role of the secretary-general then underwent "political devaluation" (that is, no more Chalandons), becoming that of an administrator whose job is to keep an eye on candidacies and arbitrate some differences among diverse party groups.

[71] See Jacques Soustelle, "Pour une opposition unié," *Le Monde,* July 31–August 1, 1966, p. 5, for his description of the tendencies in the UNR. He refers to the "heavy infantry of the UNR" (the orthodox Gaullists), the Gaullists of the Left (to guard against social and economic reaction), the Giscard d'Estaing Independent Republicans (the moderates), Emmanuel d'Astier and others ("the light cavalry of the Parisian extreme Left"), the neo-Gaullist Radicals of Edgar Faure, and those Gaullists who are "Poujade-like."

[72] Charlot, p. 70.

After 1962 the UNR became very different—in some ways —from what it was in 1958 when first it was formed. The party still had Chaban-Delmas, Michelet, Debré, and Frey; however, no longer did it have those figures who were separated from it by de Gaulle's self-determination-for-Algeria statement of September 16, 1959—men like Soustelle, Delbecque, Béraudier, Dronne, and Biaggi, all of Algérie française persuasion. Some had been expelled from the organization, others had quit it (and seldom were any of these people subsequently successful in French politics). That separation increased the internal cohesiveness of the party; that is not to say, however, that it resulted in the introduction to the party of members who all thought alike. Within the organization different generations and types of Gaullits often saw things in different ways; yet most of these people were united in one belief—trust in de Gaulle's leadership, looking to him for revelation of "a certain idea of France." Most believed in uniting behind the "restorer" of French grandeur and national unity, that "injector" of the primacy of the common good in those participating in French politics, that "guide" who enabled the populace to see clearly the uselessness of those "perpetrators" of national disasters, the classical political parties. Among such men were such diverse types as Michel Debré, France's "first Jacobin," René Capitant, who aspires to the creation of a Gaullist social left, and Louis Terrenoire, who searches constantly for the "common good." [73] In 1962 the UNR merged with the Democratic Union of Work (Union démocratique du travail), or UDT, at the request of de Gaulle and against the wishes of a number of conservative Gaullists who were chilled by having to associate with what they consider as the "PSU of Gaullism." The UDT represents an old kind of Gaullism, the kind that dates from the Resistance (having "paid its dues from the first") and which, socially, is of Left orientation. After being brought into the UNR, these "reserves" of Gaullism periodically have expressed reservations about the UNR's drift to the right.[74] In 1966 some electors of the Left who supported de Gaulle wanted creation of a parliamentary group distinct from the UNR. They hoped that they would be joined in that effort by certain

[73] Charlot, p. 70.

[74] Charlot, p. 109. Capitant stated in February 1966, "I don't wish a scission, but I don't fear it."

MRP deputies, some nonparty affiliates, and by René Capitant's UDT. Pompidou fought that trend successfully.

The UNR-UDT in 1967 was renamed the Union of Democrats for the Fifth Republic (Union des démocrates pour la Vᵉ République). The party also was reorganized. The Action Committee for the Fifth Republic was designated supreme federal organ of the Gaullist formation presided over by the prime minister, leader of the majority. This instrumentality serves to "discipline" the different branches of "the family," and it gives to the public an image of the UNR-UDT as flanked on each side by Giscardian Independent Republicans and "Gaullists of the Left." [75] Nonetheless, there was no indication that the reorganization satisfied certain members of the Gaullist Left. Both René Capitant and Louis Vallon, former directors of the UDT, continued their criticism of Georges Pompidou, describing the policy of his government in social and economic matters as a "policy of the Right," particularly in the areas of incomes and investments.[76] Capitant warned the majority in 1967 of a possible future worker's revolt against the regime, and Vallon referred to the existence in France of "profound social discontent." [77] He is critical also of the Committee for the Fifth Republic for having denied various of its internal groups the freedom of action it "allows" to the Independent Republicans of Giscard d'Estaing.

The reorganization in 1967 of the "Gaullist family" was due neither to a tightening up by the Pompidouites nor to the subsequent imposition by them upon the *entire formation* of greater discipline. It was due instead to concessions made grudgingly to the Independent Republicans by the Pompidou group. The reorganization marked the growth within the formation of demands for greater internal freedom of action by one of its groups. Giscard d'Estaing announced as the reorganization took place that he had no intention of joining the Pompidou cabinet, that in the future he intended to be more demanding, and that he wanted the government to modify the "blocked vote" and restrict its application to only the most important measures (the "blocked vote" obliges the deputies to vote in the National As-

---

[75] See Pierre Viansson-Ponté, "La nouvelle gauche gaulliste," *Le Monde,* October 11, 1966, p. 10.

[76] *Le Monde,* March 18, 1967, p. 6.

[77] *Le Monde,* March 18, 1967, p. 6.

sembly for or against a government bill as a whole, denying them the opportunity to amend or consider the bill article by article). Moreover, d'Estaing gave scant attention to de Gaulle's directive that "the majority must be united and solid." [78] He refused to integrate his Independent Republicans in a unified Gaullist bloc in the National Assembly, creating instead a separate parliamentary faction.[79]

Before the reorganization of 1967, the Gaullist parliamentary party had been decreasing in its willingness to engage in conciliation and to share broadly in the majority with other elements in the National Assembly. "Why share the victory?" and "We are large enough to make our own majority" were the views of some members of the group. Such sentiments, if not arrogant, were *then* at least unrealistic. D'Estaing's Independent Republicans were treated by them with some contempt. Perhaps the Gaullist parliamentary group believed that d'Estaing would surrender to it unconditionally and docilely bring along his group to complete the Gaullist majority in the National Assembly? If that was their assessment of his future behavior, they were mistaken. D'Estaing was willing to cooperate, but he lost no opportunity to clarify that in completing the majority that he was anything other than an "unconditional" ally of Gaullism. He soon became known as *M. mais, oui. Yes* he was willing to cooperate, *but* it could not be achieved unconditionally.

The elections of March 1967 marked a new phase in French political history. The loss within the Gaullist formation of forty-seven seats by the UNR-UDT, and the acquisition of nine additional seats by d'Estaing, placed in his hands *for the time being* the keys to the majority and made of him the real arbiter of the parliamentary situation. The majority then was smaller than it was previous to the March 1967 elections, but within that majority d'Estaing's group was larger. Pompidou consequently had to be increasingly cautious in his dealings with d'Estaing.[80] Michel Debré once said that nothing is more desir-

---

[78] *L'Express,* March 20–26, 1967, p. 55.

[79] *Le Monde,* March 16, 1967, p. 8.

[80] D'Estaing himself achieved in the legislative elections of 1967 an impressive victory on the first ballot, receiving on it 5000 more votes than he had won in the legislative elections of 1962 (29,600–24,400). See description of his victory in *L'Express,* March 6–12, 1967, pp. 10–11.

able than a narrow majority to wake up those who sleep within it; that statement might have been entirely appropriate after the legislative elections of 1967 had the objectives of de Gaulle and d'Estaing been the same. However, everybody knows that they differ on some points. As Jean Lecanuet says, "M. Giscard d'Estaing believes that it is possible inside the majority to obtain some modification of the policy of General de Gaulle." [81] D'Estaing says himself that "It is a common problem in all modern democracies to explore the manner in which we can inflict political action without demolishing the majority. The majority of the future must go from traditional moderates as far as the current of Christian democracy." [82] Moreover, when the Action Committee for the Fifth Republic was created, the text of its invitation to all French to unite around de Gaulle "for progress, independence, and peace" recognized such support could come from "diverse horizons." [83] A concession was made to the Giscardians by stating, "Independence, what is it? Assuredly not isolation nor narrow nationalism." [84] And later, when in April 1967 the Pompidou government faced a confidence vote, d'Estaing stated, "The government is asking for a delegation of powers. It must justify it, and it is in the light of these justifications that the Independent Republicans will state their position." [85]

Although d'Estaing's group voted for the delegation of

---

[81] *Le Monde,* September 14, 1966, p. 8. Lecanuet made this statement on the TV program *Face à face.*

[82] *Le Monde,* September 16, 1966, p. 7.

[83] *Le Monde,* October 2–3, 1966, p. 6.

[84] *Le Monde,* October 2–3, 1966, p. 6.

[85] This involved a bid by de Gaulle to rule France by decree on social and economic matters for a six-month period. Pompidou asked the National Assembly to relinquish until October 31 debate and voting on certain economic and social matters which the government sought to convert into law. Pompidou did not consult the Independent Republicans in advance. D'Estaing replied to the snub by boycotting the meeting of the Gaullist majority in the Assembly May 9. D'Estaing's demand for an explanation by Pompidou went unanswered, and Pompidou then left on vacation. Gaullist Edgar Pisani, minister of equipment and lodging, resigned from the Pompidou cabinet in protest against the decree bid and accused the government of violating the spirit of the Constitution. He stated that Pompidou believes that the majority's only role is to follow.

powers, it did clarify that it is unlikely that it can vote that way again. D'Estaing has said repeatedly that the majority must be given a "content of political liberalism," that his group will not tolerate the imposition of "one party" surrounded by satellites, and that the "institutions of the Fifth Republic are not the property of one person." [86]

The Independent Republicans met in their first federal council under the leadership of President d'Estaing in September 1966. There they identified themselves as a reorganization of the "family of Independents who, having known power in the recent past under the impetus of Pinay, was scuttled in 1962. Today the liberal moderates must organize anew for they represent a profound tendency of French public opinion without which the present majority would not be other than ephemeral." [87] They submitted that the UNR-UDT represented 30 percent of the electorate and that the Independent Republicans could complement them "durably." They defined their task as that of playing a decisive role in a difficult epoch of French history, being the ones who will remedy the "fragility" of the Fifth Republic by supporting a government that is "moderate and evolving." They placed particular emphasis on their wish to "represent in the body of the majority an element which is centrist, liberal, and European . . . The Independent Republicans are liberal in the political sense of the term. . . . It is a case of a democratic liberalism, that is to say, conscious of assuring concretely a real participation of citizens in public life and dedicated to untiring effort in favor of social justice. . . . The Independent Republicans are European, for Europe is for us more than a probability, it is a choice and a conviction." [88] They went on to say that Europe cannot be a juxtaposition of states nor a superstate, but an "organized *ensemble* born progressively of research and construction." [89] They completed their remarks by saying that Parliament will have a role to play in the France of the future, that the tendencies represented in the majority must remain free, that cohesion will be found not in constraint but only in *persuasion,*

[86] *Le Monde,* July 3–4, 1966, p. 7.
[87] *Le Monde,* September 15, 1966, p. 8.
[88] *Le Monde,* September 15, 1966, p. 8.
[89] *Le Monde,* September 15, 1966, p. 8.

and that they view party discipline as applicable only to the fundamental policy and action of the government.[90]

Prime Minister Georges Pompidou was immensely relieved when the legislative elections of June 1968 produced so large a majority for the Union of Democrats for the Fifth Republic that it no longer was necessary for him to rely on Giscard d'Estaing and his Independent Republicans to complete the Gaullist majority. He immediately set about the business of telling the Union of Democrats for the Fifth Republic that he expected from it tight discipline and unanimous support for the government during the life of the newly constituted National Assembly. This was a warning to d'Estaing's sixty-four Independent Republicans, and public acknowledgement by Pompidou that d'Estaing no longer held the keys to the majority. Consequently, Giscard d'Estaing was no longer *M. mais, oui,* and Gaulist governments need bargain no longer with him and his group in order to sustain themselves. Consequently, d'Estaing's influence now is less than heretofore; nevertheless, he still retains the means to focus attention upon himself and his group. He knows too that someday things will change again, and so he continues to restrict his maneuverability because of considerations that have more to do with the future than the present. D'Estaing never fears any crisis that promises to improve his own position. He would like someday to be president of the Council of Ministers, or president of the republic itself. And should he depart subsequently from the Gaullist majority, he probably will see to it that the act of separation is furnished by it and not by himself.[91]

THE INDEPENDENT PARTY

In 1952 Maurice Duverger stated that "Except under unusual circumstances there do not exist in France—at least to the

[90] *Le Monde,* September 15, 1966, p. 8.

[91] *Le Figaro,* July 2, 1968, p. 4. Pompidou stated, "We have all been elected under the banners of the Ve Republic and its leader . . . the government originates with the President of the Republic and not with the Assembly. Thus, there is a profound solidarity between the President of the Republic and his first minister. Those who seek to distinguish between their adhesion to the government deceive themselves and play the game of adversaries of our institutions."

right of the Radicals—political parties worthy of the name." [92] Shortly after that essay was published, a conservative party worthy of consideration did come into prominence—the Independent party.[93]

The National Center of Independents, CNI, was created in 1948 by Roger Duchet for the purpose of coordinating the activities of the conservative associations known as the Republican Group of Peasant and Social Action. After 1951 the National Center succeeded in concluding some electoral agreements with the MRP, RPF, and some Third Force groups to the right of the Socialist party, SFIO. After the legislative elections of 1956 the Independent party mustered in the National Assembly more than 100 deputies, playing there the game of systematic blockage and, with the voting aid of their Communist party opponents, contributing to a series of government crises. Between May 1957 and April 1958, the Mollet, Bourges-Maunoury, and Gaillard governments all fell when the Independent party gave support to their opposition (67 voted against Mollet, 63 against Bourges-Maunoury, and 100 against Gaillard).

The parliamentary system of the Fourth Republic was "made to order" for the Independent party, not because the Independents displayed toward parliamentarism itself any particular affection, but because in that divided regime that vehicle afforded the Independents numerous opportunities to block proposals disadvantageous to their own interests. Under the Fifth Republic, however, the Independent party started that regime by first supporting President de Gaulle. Antoine Pinay, former president of the Council of Ministers, Mayor of Saint-Chamond, and "M. Conservative" himself, became Michel Debré's minister of finance—a relationship that was terminated in 1960. Dis-

---

[92] Maurice Duverger, "Public Opinion and Political Parties in France," *American Political Science Review* (December 1952), 1072.

[93] The author does not consider the Gaullist party classically conservative or, for that matter, necessarily conservative. Those *elements* of conservatism exhibited by it seem to be associated with its nationalism. On the domestic level, it is interventionist in the economy and willing to undertake there innovations that would repel a conservative party. In fact, there seems to be some likelihood that someday Socialists and Gaullists will be capable of working together in some areas of domestic economic policy.

pleased with the financial and foreign policies of the Gaullist regime, the Independents then went into opposition to it (although Pinay supported Pompidou in the presidential election of 1969).

Independent party claims to "respectability" usually center on Antoine Pinay, its thoroughly competent and well-liked leader, who now lives in semiretirement. After Pinay, however, it is less than rewarding to conduct popularity contests in Independent leadership circles. During the Algerian war a number of Independent deputies were identified with the Algérie française theme, and Pétainist factions came out of the shadows during some Independent conferences and blended into Independent ranks.

The statement attributed to Maurice Duverger at the beginning of this section is no longer "dated." The 1967 legislative elections "did in" the Independent party, reducing it to approximately 6 percent of the national vote and only twenty-five seats in the National Assembly. Five years prior to those elections, Giscard d'Estaing had contributed prematurely to that "doing in" by splitting with the National Center of Independents and taking his Independent Republicans into support of de Gaulle. The 1968 legislative elections all but completed the rout of the Independent party.

PARTY ORGANIZATION

As Maurice Duverger states, "The organization of political parties is certainly not in conformity with orthodox notions of democracy. Their internal structure is essentially autocratic and oligarchic; their leaders are not really appointed by the members, in spite of appearances, but co-opted or nominated by the central body; they tend to form a ruling class, isolated from the militants, a class that is more or less exclusive." [94]

The basic organizational unit in the Communist party is the cell (of from three to thirty members), established usually on an occupational and infrequently on a geographical basis, with a bureau that is responsible to the cell and also to the next

[94] Maurice Duverger, *Political Parties* (New York: Wiley, 1963), p. 422.

higher organizational unit, the section. Sections form departmental federations that send delegates to the national congress, which elects a Central Committee of approximately seventy-five members; theoretically, that committee is the highest party organ but in reality it is secondary to the Political Bureau, the Secretariat, the Control Committee, and the Finance Control Committee. The Political Bureau is the only organ that may speak for the party, and both the Control Committee (which maintains "party purity") and Secretariat are under its domination. Members of the parliamentary party sign "resignations" in advance of entering Parliament, being compelled to adhere to party decisions and surrender their parliamentary salaries to the party, receiving in return a living allowance. Organization of the Communist party is "total," and members are expected to belong entirely to its world and not share it with any other.

The basic organizational unit in the French Socialist party (SFIO) is not the cell (for it has none), but the section, organized on a geographical rather than an occupational basis. In each department of France sections elect delegates to a departmental federation. A national congress seats delegates of federations that contain at least five sections or 100 members. A National Council comprises one delegate from each departmental federation. Power in the Socialist party is concentrated in the executive committee, or *comité-directeur,* which is staffed with thirty-one members elected by the national congress delegates. The annual congress of the party in fact is dominated by four large federations who account almost automatically for at least a third of all the votes cast in the congress. In order of size, these federations are the Bouches-du-Rhône, Pas-de-Calais, Nord, and Seine, and their leaderships are the key to the placing of members on the *comité-directeur.* The secretary-general of the SFIO is sustained primarily by the federations of the Pas-de-Calais and Nord. Members of the parliamentary party are subject to tight discipline. Those who fancy the SFIO as offering an excellent *milieu* for free expression should examine exclusions of members who have appeared before the party's *comité d'exclusion* after attacks on the "Mollet machine."

The Radical Socialist party's basic units, organizationally, are local committees, followed by federations, and then by the

National Congress. A National Council presides over the organization. Organization of the Radical party is loose, and so is its discipline, members of its parliamentary party behaving sometimes as though they had not heard of it. A cadre association that has known better days, its elites operate as clubs within "the club." Its organization must be loose enough to accommodate this style—and, were it not, there could well be no Radical party. Radicalism is synonymous with faction; and this party is true to its tradition. Real efforts undertaken to truly unite it could lead to its destruction (which some observers feel would benefit entirely the French political process).

The Independent party belongs to the CNI, or the National Center of Independents (once known as the Independent and Peasants' party, but since modified). The National Center attempts to articulate the activities of its internal groups, but for this cadre association, looseness, and disunity are characteristic of its organization (its statement of 1951 described itself as "the only group which leaves total liberty to vote to its members, who vote according to their convictions and conscience"). In recent years, however, the Independents have tightened somewhat their organization, and no longer is there the presumption that total liberty to vote is left to members. The Independent Republicans are the party of Giscard of d'Estaing and an offshoot from the Independents, breaking off from them in 1962 to support de Gaulle and retaining a type of organization similar to that of the Independents.

The Gaullist party is an oddity—little organization, big vote. In each department of France federations are under the control of a congress. No truly significant organization has been achieved on the grass-roots level.[95] This party was built from the top down.

---

[95] In 1959 Secretary-General Frey warned the UNR against mass recruiting which he described as "badly controlled and dangerous for the unity and reputation of the movement." The quotation is reproduced in Charlot, p. 116. However, see *Le Monde,* March 2, 1965, p. 6, for later statement by Frey at the UNR Information Conference at Asnières, in which he announced that the UNR will become the center or nucleus of a great organized party—"A mass party along Anglo-Saxon lines." Without mass recruiting, M. Frey?

The MRP, or Popular Republican party, which was dissolved in 1967, organizationally had the section as its basic unit; in turn, sections formed federations. An annual congress elected its president and secretary-general. Party leaders controlled the National Executive Committee, which endorsed candidates.

CONCLUSION

The French have had little experience with collective responsibilities and have fewer associations than many other Western countries. Slight participation in groups leads to a "legendary individualism" and gives to their politics a certain "unrealism." Their image of party, according to Georges Lavau, is chapel-like.

The party system has produced parties lacking generally in sufficient power to exercise securely and effectively over sustained periods governance of the nation (except in one era of the Third Republic). With but several exceptions, these parties have failed to recruit members and supporters on a mass basis. Such organizations are based more on a nineteenth- than a twentieth-century conception of party. During the Fourth Republic, the party system inadequately met the problems that confronted it. Ineffective government derived not so much from the multiplicity of parties as from their nature.

The political system of the Fifth Republic—which is drastically different from that of the Fourth Republic—closes the door on the accessibility of political parties to government and utilization by them of the "conversion processes." In this regime the party system is like an abandoned child whose legitimacy was contested daily by de Gaulle when he was the president of the republic. Cut off from government, the parties continued, nonetheless, to maintain limited ties with the populace.

Whenever the parties engaged President de Gaulle in competition, de Gaulle displayed a genius for putting them on the most difficult and least tenable terrain. De Gaulle succeeded in tying the parties closely to the Fourth Republic, contending that they died with it, despite contrary pleas by the parties that they too wish to avoid a return to the Fourth Republic.

The Communist party is committed to revolutionary action, but evidence is slight that it wishes to participate in it or really believe in it. The party still is "different," but it also is a party in a France in transition, and its dependence is upon social categories that are less than revolutionary. The Unified Socialist party, PSU, is a small organization which professes "workerism" and which has few members. Its future appears hazardous. The Socialist party, SFIO, is a party of paradoxes with a revolutionary jargon and a behavior that is not other than orthodox. Internally, its life is complicated by the interplay of diverse "tendencies," a legacy of the socialist movement earlier in this century. The party is led by Guy Mollet, who has guided it into various adventures in conservatism. The party has been in a state of decline for many years, being now a victim of the crippling political disease of regionalism.

The Socialist-Democratic Federation of Gaston Defferre sought radical reorganization of the party Left, attempting to synthesize some Left parties and to present them to the voters in the form of one great political formation. That effort was a victim of "patriotism of party" and the unwillingness of Left party directors to amalgamate. The Federation of the Democratic and Socialist Left, unlike Defferre's federation, was an electoral union of Socialists, SFIO, and Radical Socialists, which looked forward to eventual parliamentary and governmental collaboration. In this federation, the sovereignty of the participating parties was guarded jealously. The federation entered an agreement with the Communist party in 1968, one which stressed conceptions of the future regime and opposition to Gaullism, but which did not lay down anything resembling a "common program of government."

The Radical Socialist party, described by Jacques Fauvet as the most bourgeois of bourgeois parties, has been in decline for years; that descent was furthered by the lessening of the church-state controversy, party involvement in financial scandals, and various of the party's dated views. The Democratic Center, successor to the MRP, attracted some attention in the presidential election of 1965 but suffered greatly in the legislative elections of 1967 and 1968. The Gaullist Union of Democrats for the Fifth Republic has evolved since its creation in 1958, retaining some of its internal "tendencies" but becoming increasingly cohesive. The Independent Republicans have cooperated with the Gaullists but d'Estaing refuses to integrate his organization with the Gaullists in one unified bloc in the National Assembly. Independent Republican orientation is described by the party as centrist, liberal, and *European*. Despite their convergences with Gaullism, the Independent Republicans have some differences with it too, being more European in outlook and less interventionist in the economy than the Gaullists. D'Estaing would like to be a future president of the council or of the republic, and if he plays his cards correctly his aspirations may become realities in the era "after de Gaulle." Finally, the Independent party is a casualty of the Fifth Republic and but a shadow of its former self, with only 6 percent of the national vote and slight representation in the National Assembly.

SIX

THE ELECTORATE SPEAKS

The political sociology of France

ELECTIONS*

Participation in voting has been unusually high in Fifth Republic referenda and national legislative elections (see Table 6–1). (Participation in both ballotings tends to be similar; however, if after the first ballot a candidate's success appears certain, participation tends to decrease on the second ballot.) Participation in national elections generally is greater than in contests for the departmental and municipal councils.[1]

---

* This chapter is supplemented by Appendix B, which makes an intensive examination of voting returns during the Fifth Republic by means of thirty-eight electoral maps. Each map displays, in considerable geographic and other detail, information on a particular aspect of these returns.

[1] Although national voting generally is greater than local voting, studies of some *communes* show turnouts that sometimes exceed national ones. A major problem involved in accurately comparing national and local turnouts derives from the French practice of reporting national statistics on a complete basis and local statistics on a fragmentary basis (only those of the largest *communes* are reported in full). An interesting study, in sharp contrast with traditional opinion, has been made by Mark Kesselman, "French Local Politics: A Statistical Examination of Grass

Table 6–1   Voting in legislative elections first ballot

| | Nov. 23, 1958 | | Nov. 18, 1962 | |
	Number	Percentage	Number	Percentage
Registered voters	27,236,491		27,533,019	
Votes cast	20,999,797	77.1	18,931,733	68.7
Valid ballots	20,484,709	75.2	18,329,986	66.6
Abstentions	6,236,694	22.9	8,603,286	31.3

| | March 5, 1967 | | June 23, 1968 | |
	Number	Percentage	Number	Percentage
Registered voters	28,291,838	79.1	28,171,635	
Votes cast	22,392,317		22,539,743	80
Valid ballots	21,897,483	97.84	22,138,657	78.58
Abstentions	5,404,687	19.10	5,631,892	19.99

Large numbers of votes are not synonymous with high participation in electoral campaigns; during the national legislative elections of 1958, the French Institute of Public Opinion reported, for example, that 89 percent of the people they inter-

---

Roots Consensus," *American Political Science Review,* Vol. 60, No. 4, (December 1966), 963–973. Kesselman concludes that contrary to general belief, in most *communes* turnout for voting is higher for local elections than for national elections. He also concludes that cleavages in a *commune*'s local voting behavior appear to parallel cleavages in its national voting behavior, but that there is little direct relation between cleavages in national and local elections; that in national elections turnout increases as the size of the *commune* increases, and that in local elections turnout diminishes as the size of the *commune* increases. He states, too, that "Political scientists generally assume that turnout varies in response to the closeness of an election. Yet study of French local elections suggests that there is no necessary link between electoral turnout and competition. Given the low competition in local elections, why is turnout high? Why, in fact, is particularly low competition in local elections associated with high turnout?" It should be said here that competition has tended to increase in view of the growing tendency of the Gaullist opposition to concentrate on capture of municipal councils. Beginning in 1958, the Gaullists sought to chase the Communists off the councils; the Communists dug in to retain their seats. Since then other anti-Gaullists have intensified their quest for seats at the local level. *Communes* witnessing such interaction can hardly be described as locales of "low competition."

Table 6–2   Seating in the National Assembly

Party	1958	1961	1967	1968
Communists	10	41	72	34
Socialists	44	65	76 ⎫	
Radical Socialists				57 Federation of Left
and affiliates	23	42	40 ⎭	
MRP	57	36	40 ⎫	27 Center (CPDM)
Conservatives	133	28	⎭	
Gaullists	198	229	190 ⎫	358 Gaullists
Gaullist Con-				(UD V^e + Indep. Repubs.)
servatives	—	20	40 ⎭	
Others	—	4	12	

viewed had not participated in a political meeting, 35 percent had not heard the radio reports, and fewer than one in five had read articles about politics in the newspapers. One authority places approximately 45 percent of the voters in "a low state of political participation." [2] The interest of the French in politics— as Meynaud and Lancelot state—"is generally mediocre and so is their information in this area. All surveys establish the general indifference of the French. . . ." [3]

THE ELECTORAL LAW
AND LEGISLATIVE ELECTIONS OF 1958

The electoral law of November 1958 regulated the first legislative elections to the National Assembly under the newly created

[2] Georges Dupeaux, quoted in Jean Meynaud and Alain Lancelot, *La participation des français à la politique* (Paris: Presses universitaires, 1965), p. 18.

[3] Meynaud and Lancelot, pp. 9, 11. The authors state that "lacunae are probably more grave for international than domestic problems." See also Institut français d'opinion publique, "Les élections législatives . . ." *Sondages,* 15. The Institute discovered in 1967 that 45 percent of its respondents mistakenly thought that the Communist party belonged to the Federation of the Democratic and Socialist Left; out of 100 electors intending to vote for the Communist party, 54 percent declared mistakenly that the Communist party was a member of the Federation of the Left; out of 100 electors intending to vote for the federation, 51 percent thought (erroneously) that the Communist party belonged to the federation.

Fifth Republic. Voting in metropolitan France was confined to single-member constituencies, two ballots required if no candidate was elected by a majority on the first, a plurality sufficing on the second.[4] Election districts each comprised approximately 93,000 electors. All departments were entitled to at least two deputies. The thinly populated Basses-Alpes could claim only two, whereas the heavily populated department of the Seine had fifty-five.

The electoral law prohibited the filing of new candidacies between the two ballots (this restriction minimized the number of "deals" candidates could make after the first and before the second ballot; it was calculated not to interfere with the emergence of a stable governmental majority). Candidates could run only in one election district; only those candidates who received on the first ballot at least 5 percent of the total votes cast could run on the second; each candidate's 1000-franc deposit was reimbursed if the candidate acquired at least 5 percent of the total vote cast; candidates had to be of French citizenship, at least twenty-three years of age, and could be of either sex. Those ineligible for candidacies included people deprived of their civil rights as a result of conviction for criminal acts, certain cate-

---

[4] Four hundred and seventy-five deputies were elected in metropolitan France and the Overseas Departments and seventy-one in Algeria, constituting the total membership of the National Assembly at 546. The method of voting in Algeria and the two Saharan departments was by list, with one ballot. The Overseas Departments of Guiana, Guadeloupe, Réunion, and Martinque were divided into single-member constituencies, one for Guiana and three for each of the others, and there applied there the same electoral procedures and rules that applied in metropolitan France. In subsequent years the total membership of the National Assembly was reduced because of Algeria's independence and a decrease in overseas possessions. For the end of the parliamentary mandate of the Algerian deputies, see *Le Monde,* July 15, 1962, p. 4. Their disposition was decided by ordinance, and 68 deputies and 34 senators simply were removed from their seats. The decision, taken by the prime minister and transmitted to the president of the senate, who communicated it to the Parliament, raised certain questions relative to its legality. One criticism heard was that if deputies represent the nation rather than their constituencies, why abolish only the seats of the Algerian deputies—why not dissolve the National Assembly instead? The precedent for the removal of the Algerian deputies was furnished in the cases of the Alsacian and Lorraine deputies, who left on March 1, 1870, as a consequence of the law relating to peace with Germany.

gories of civil servants, and certain appointed officials whose prestige in an election district "might exert pressure on the voters." All parliamentary groups presenting a minimum of seventy-five candidates were eligible for reimbursement of campaign expenses. Parliamentary groups that joined together in electoral coalitions were not required to present seventy-five candidates each, that figure sufficing for all. All candidates were required by law to designate alternates, to replace them after election in the event of death, resignation, or appointment to the Constitutional Council, the cabinet, or a government mission in excess of six months' duration, or acceptance of paid employment as an official of a professional association.[5] Thus, when balloting for a candidate, the voter cast also for his alternate.

The system of majority voting with two ballots originated with General de Gaulle, who contended that it offered simplicity, clarity, and a chance for continuity in French politics. In reality, the law was calculated to weaken the controls over candidates by the political parties in the new election districts, and to reduce drastically Communist party representation in the National Assembly by isolating in a limited number of electoral constituencies its densely and tightly concentrated voters. At first glance it appeared that the law possibly would favor the Socialist party, SFIO, because of the distribution of numerous Socialist electors in many small *communes,* but that possibility did not materialize. The electoral law wanted and obtained by de Gaulle was opposed (although not openly) by the UNR and some elements of the moderate Right, for its intent was to deal not only with the Communist party but with all parties in order to reduce de Gaulle's dependence on any of them.[6] The law did take care of the Communist party, reducing drastically its representation in the National Assembly. It was not the first time that an electoral law of this type had been used. In 1889 the "republicans" isolated Boulangerism in its urban and industrial strongholds by constructing an electoral law that prevented it from

---

[5] In cases when a deputy goes to the cabinet and his replacement refuses his seat, no partial election can be held and the seat is left vacant if the event takes place in the year which precedes the renewal of the National Assembly.

[6] Charlot, p. 257.

extending its control into other parts of the nation and dominating the Chamber of Deputies. The same electoral law can display both republican and nonrepublican virtue.

In the legislative elections of 1958 only thirty-nine deputies were elected on the first ballot by an absolute majority. Between the first and second ballots the Communist and Socialist parties failed to conclude with each other enough electoral agreements to support certain candidates in common.[7] Nonetheless, their opponents were able to conclude among themselves agreements that enabled them to elect a large number of deputies to the National Assembly. The UNR exceeded all of its electoral expectations (see Table 6–3). The Radical Socialists slipped to about three percent of the vote on the second ballot, the Socialist party, SFIO, declined to 14 percent, and the Communist party, although it accounted on the second ballot for 21 percent of the vote, saw its representation in the National Assembly (Table 6–2) reduced to but ten deputies because of the nature of the law regulating the elections.

It is unlikely that the conclusion of even a satisfactory number of electoral agreements among Left parties could have saved the Left in the elections of 1958. The elections were a "one-man show," and voting tended to gravitate around General de Gaulle. The decline of almost all the classical parties was shattering, and the elections of 1958 represented for some of these groups the beginning of the end, especially for those that had already demonstrated their ineffectiveness and their inability to operate the Fourth Republic and resist those forces who had brought about its destruction. However, it was not surprising that the one component of the classical party system which survived the elections was the Independent party, returning on the second ballot a large percentage of the vote and 120 deputies to the National Assembly. The Independents had achieved previously an anti-Fourth Republic reputation, having been instrumental in toppling some of the last governments of that regime.

Although it was known to some, most elements of the populace did not realize in 1958 that the old party system was *permanently* injured, and that its radical transformation was

---

[7] Approximately thirty such agreements were concluded.

Table 6–3   Political party percentages in legislative elections

Year	Party or federation	First ballot (%)	Second ballot (%)
1958	UNR	17.60	28.1
	Communists	18.90	20.5
	National Independents' Center	13.70	15.4
	Socialists	15.50	13.8
	Popular Republicans	9.10	7.3
	Radicals	4.80	3.3
	Moderates	6.20	3.1
	Left Republican rally	3.50	2.4
	Republican center	3.02	2.4
	Christian Democrats	2.05	1.8
	Extreme Right and Poujadists	3.03	1.0
	Miscellaneous Left	1.04	0.8
1962	UNR	31.9	40.5
	Communists	21.8	21.3
	Socialists	12.6	15.2
	National Independents' Center	9.1	7.4
	Popular Republicans	8.9	5.3
	Independents	4.4	1.6
	Left Center	3.8	2.8
	Radicals	3.7	4.2
	Extreme Left	2.4	1.2
	Republican Center	0.5	0.4
1967	Union of Democrats for Ve Republic and Affiliates	37.8	42.6
	Federation of the Left and Affiliates	21	25
	Communists	22.4	21.4
	Democratic Center	12.8	7.1
	Others	6	3.9
1968	Union for the Defense of the Republic and Gaullist Affiliates	43.65	48.8
	Federation of the Left and Affiliates	16.50	21.6
	Communists	20.03	19.9
	CPDM (Center for Progress and Modern Democracy)	10.34	8.1
	Others	9.48	1.6

necessary if it were to mean anything in the new republic. For years some men had reiterated the theme that the classical parties were antiquated vehicles of the nineteenth century ill-adapted to the realities of the present era. The events of May 1958 furnished dramatic evidence of the validity of that contention—nonetheless, it was one to which few people had listened.

THE LEGISLATIVE ELECTIONS OF 1962

The referendum of October 1962 and the legislative elections of the following month must be considered in relation to each other. Both had much to do with a conflict between the President of the Republic and the National Assembly elected in 1958, a conflict that had already been in progress for many months. On October 4, 1962, the National Assembly engaged in a heated debate on the Pompidou government, during which the state television (ORTF) gave 1½ minutes each to two leaders of the opposition, and half an hour to the prime minister.[8] A vote of censure carried, 280 out of 480 deputies voting in its behalf. This represented the first ministerial crisis of the Fifth Republic —being, however, more of a conflict between the President of the Republic and the deputies, and less one between the government and the deputies.[9] The crisis centered on the illegal methods used by President de Gaulle to amend the Constitution, and his snub of the National Assembly by denying its right to vote on the new method proposed by de Gaulle for electing the president of the republic by universal suffrage. After the Pompidou government fell, President de Gaulle dissolved the National Assembly, setting the dates for the referendum (to elect the president of the republic by universal suffrage) and subsequent legislative elections. During both contests state TV gave scant

[8] See *Le Monde,* October 6, 1962, p. 1., for details.

[9] *Le Monde,* October 6, 1962, p. 1. Pompidou accused those who signed the petition of censure of engaging in a "plot against de Gaulle." The 280 included 10 Communists, 43 SFIO, 33 Entente démocratique (of 37), 50 MRP (of 57), 109 Independents (of 121), 3 UNR (of 176) and 32 others. In the vote of censure 4 UNR voted in the affirmative and were subsequently expelled from the party.

attention to the opposition. The referendum carried by 62 percent of the votes cast (approximately 25 percent of the electorate declined to vote), and approximately 46 percent of the total registered voters. In the legislative elections of the following month, although abstentions and invalid votes constituted approximately 30 percent, the Gaullist group returned to the National Assembly the largest number of deputies ever assembled there up to that time under the banners of any political party (a large number of candidates were elected on the first ballot). Many prognosticators had expected de Gaulle to win the referendum and lose the legislative elections. He won both, and in the November elections the success of the Gaullist UNR was astounding.

Among the candidates appearing on the first ballot, four distinct types were noticeable—Gaullists, Communists, "men of the Fourth Republic," and activists of the Right. The Gaullists accumulated 31.9 percent of the first ballot vote and claimed 51 of the 96 deputies elected. The Communists claimed a sizable percentage of the vote also, registering 21.8 percent and electing 9 deputies. In increasing its vote on the first ballot to 21.8 percent, the Communist party registered a gain of approximately 120,000 electors, a gain that was not too important, considering that the party had lost between 1956 and 1958 approximately 1,600,000 voters. Thus, the Communist party was able to increase its electoral support by only 3 percent in four years. The gain in no way could compare with that registered by the UNR between the first ballot of 1958 and the first ballot of 1962; a gain that amounted to 14.4 percent. Therefore, contentions that the first ballot of 1962 resulted in a victory for the extremes are exaggerated. In fact, the Communist party succeeded in regaining but a bare fraction of the many voters that it had lost previously. As for the other parties, the first ballot results for them were less than encouraging. The SFIO received 12.65 percent and 1 deputy, the Radicals and affiliates 3.71 percent and 3.85 percent, respectively, and 9 deputies, the MRP 8.92 percent and 13 deputies, the Independent Republicans 4.36 percent and the Independents 9.06 percent for a total of 15 deputies. The classical Right received a sound defeat, and the extreme Right was crushed. Abstentions on the first ballot were numerous, constituting 31.25 percent of the registered voters and exceeding all those recorded in legislative elections since 1881 (strongest in the Massif Central, where they usually are greater than elsewhere; abstentions were great in all districts, particularly in Brittany, the north, and Alsace, areas where voting tends to run high). Finally, Paul Reynaud and Pierre Mendès-France, two of the best-known figures of the Fourth Republic, were defeated on the first ballot.

The most striking result of the second ballot was the overwhelming victory won by the UNR-UDT; having garnered 229 seats in *métropole,* the UNR-UDT became the largest group to be seated in the national legislative body. Still lacking a unified and homogeneous majority, the party was assured of a working majority, however, due to the support given to it by dissident Independents, MRP, and other elements. For the first time in its history, Paris elected all of its deputies from one party, the UNR-UDT, canceling the effect of some losses registered elsewhere, in the Gironde, the Nord, the Puy-de-Dôme, Vienne, Saône-et-Loire, and the Lot-et-Garonne. The UNR-UDT took all of the seats in the Bas-Rhin, 6 of 7 in the Finistère, and 8 of 10 in the Rhône. The party's strength was sustained in those areas in which it was strong previously, for example, the Haut-Rhin, Calvados, Vosges, and Doubs.

Of importance in the 1962 elections were the agreements concluded between the first and second ballots by Communist, Socialist, SFIO, and Radical Socialist parties, agreements which benefited these three parties, thereby preventing the UNR-UDT from achieving even greater representation in the National Assembly. The SFIO was the beneficiary, as Communist electors maintained discipline, assuring the SFIO of victory in six straight fights with the UNR-UDT. For the first time in Communist party history, some of its candidates, more favorably placed arithmetically, retired in order to allow Communist electors to support Socialist, Radical Socialist, and PSU candidates.[10] In straight fights between the Communist party and UNR-UDT, however, the latter won 90 of 103 such duels. In 58 similar contests

[10] One exception was in the Bouches-du-Rhône, where the Communist party, although it retired its candidate in favor of Gaston Defferre, opposed the candidacy of François Leenhardt, SFIO member and militant anti-Communist. See *Le Monde,* November 22, 1962, p. 1.

between the UNR-UDT and the SFIO, the latter won 35. This electoral agreement among Left parties, or the *cartel des nons,* saved the day for the SFIO. Without that agreement, the SFIO would have returned to the National Assembly only 25 deputies instead of 65. The agreement, erroneously referred to between the first and second ballots as "the Guy Mollet error," fell short of being a true "Popular Front" arrangement. Participation in the *cartel des nons* signified only that both Communists and Socialists and other participants were in agreement in opposition to de Gaulle, and that both wished the reestablishment of some parliamentary prerogatives and the restoration of an equilibrium between the president of the republic and the Parliament. That did not prevent Prime Minister Pompidou from accusing Mollet of complicity with the Communist party,[11] to which Mollet replied that the Gaullist Rally of the French People, RPF, had stood side by side with the Communist party in the National Assembly during the Fourth Republic, and that a slight increase ing the number of Communist deputies was meaningless and preferable to an increase in the size of the UNR-UDT delegation.[12] Forced to the wall during that election, Mollet had to resort to every tactical trick in order to save his party from extinction— a task in which he succeeded.

The results of the second ballot signaled yet another step in the evolution of the Fifth Republic, burying deeper some of the classical formations held over from the Fourth. The Independents, for example, sustained a crushing defeat, losing everywhere to the UNR-UDT, Socialist, and Communist candidates, and undergoing approximately a two-thirds reduction in its parliamentary representation. Independent losses were great even in areas considered previously as their bastions, such as the Côte-d'Or, Vendée, and Brittany. Particularly telling was the defeat of those Independent candidates who had affiliated with Algérie française and OAS tendencies. Moreover, the decline of the MRP also was the sharpest it had known since its creation in 1945, particularly in the Moselle, the Nord, and Alsace, as many of its electors switched allegiance to the UNR-UDT.

When reviewing the 1962 election, one cannot fail to notice

---

[11] *Le Monde,* November 23, 1962, p. 2.
[12] *Le Monde,* November 23, 1962, p. 2.

the way in which it moved in the direction of shaping up a cleavage between two rival camps. Of the 369 electoral districts in which a second ballot took place, nearly half the total number of voters casting ballots had a choice between but two candidates (the UNR-UDT had also retired some of its candidates in favor of some others better placed on the second ballot). In 227 electoral districts only two candidates competed.[13] In 130 districts there were three candidates each, in eleven districts there were four candidates each, and in one district there was only one candidate. In those 227 districts there were 192 "duels" between the UNR-UDT and representatives of other parties (95 Communist, 2 PSU, 58 SFIO, 18 Radical Socialists, 6 MRP, 13 Independent, and 35 involving other parties). The cleavage carried over to the new National Assembly. The Gaullists were more numerous than before, but so was the opposition stronger than it had been in the preceding legislature. Now more than a hundred were clearly hostile to the Gaullist regime. Yet, the Gaullists now could present behind the executive a working majority, and give the regime a more "democratic" appearance. Consequently, the question arose as to whether the defeats administered to the classical conservative parties would contribute to the creation of a great modern conservative formation, more in the English than in the French tradition. Were conservatives who had played at one time or another with Poujadism, the RPF, and the MRP now prepared to settle down with the UNR-UDT and remain with it? And, finally, would the UNR-UDT take the best advantage of this situation and construct seriously an organization of lasting durability?

THE LEGISLATIVE ELECTIONS OF 1967

The legislative elections of 1967 were by direct universal suffrage with all French citizens twenty-one years of age and over eligible to vote. Two ballotings, on successive Sundays, were scheduled. Candidates were elected on the first if they received an absolute majority of the votes cast and a total number of votes equal to

---

[13] For complete description, see *Le Monde*, November 25–6, 1962, p. 2.

a quarter of the registered voters in the election district. If no candidate won on the first ballot, a relative majority of the votes cast sufficed on the second. Requirements for appearing on the second ballot were appearance on the first and receipt in it of votes equal to at least 10 percent of the registered voters in the election district. This new rule requiring 10 percent instead of 5 percent (as in 1962) eliminated from the second ballot 600 of the 2190 candidates who had appeared on the first ballot (151 Democratic Center, 80 PSU, 74 Federation of the Left, 52 Communist party, 36 ex-Gaullist dissidents, and 20 others. In two districts of Corsica [Bastia], 8 of 11 candidates were eliminated, setting the elimination record for the first ballot).[14] The number of deputies elected in France was increased from 465 to 470, due to creation of five new election districts in the Paris region. Overseas Departments and Territories elected 16 deputies, giving to the National Assembly a total membership of 486. Election districts were calculated on the basis of 1 deputy for every 93,000 inhabitants, with each department entitled to at least 2 deputies. Campaign expenses were provided by the state as long as candidates attained 5 percent of the votes cast on the first ballot.

Of these 79 candidates elected on the first ballot, 63 were under the banners of the Gaullist formation. The Gaullists accounted on the first ballot for 38 percent of the vote. During that first ballot, the strongholds of Gaullism remained generally what they had been during the elections of 1962 (East Alsace, West Brittany, and some departments of the Center and Bas-Rhin). The Democratic Center of Jean Lecanuet was a casualty of the first ballot, losing at least a quarter of the votes it had received from the MRP and Independents in 1962. The Center did badly even in those departments in which Lecanuet had obtained his best results in the presidential election of 1965 (Mayenne, Haute-Loire, Maine-et-Loire, Manche, Calvados, Orne). The Communist party received on the first ballot approximately 800,000 more votes than the Federation of the Left, causing the federation considerable anguish relative to its future leadership of the Left. Prior to the first ballot, various federation

---

[14] See *Le Monde,* March 7, 1967, p. 2, for further details.

leaders had expressed the hope that their organization would so clearly establish its electoral superiority that the Communist party would be forced to fall automatically in its tow. However, the Communist party's numerical advantage, and the consequent dependence by the federation on the Communist party to defer on the second ballot to federation candidates (those arithmetically more favorably placed), gave the Communist party great importance on the second ballot. Moreover, the results of the first ballot demonstrated also to the federation the unrealistic nature of any thoughts that it might have had of absorbing the Communist party. The Communist party had entered into agreements with the federation but it remained wary of any initiative by it that related to fusion (the Communist party has its own tradition, structure, and militants; it took years for it to build that organization, and for it fusion is feasible only on its own conditions).[15]

One surprise of the election was the Gaullist's inability to

[15] Some leaders of the federation also were wary of fusion; see *Le Monde,* September 4–5, 1966, p. 4, and Mollet's statement that the federation only is a "federation of three formations. It is normal that the common program is a synthesis of the preoccupations of each" and "Entretien: L'avenir selon Mitterand," *L'Express,* March 20–26, 1967, pp. 53–54, for Mitterand's views relative to the federation: "It can be a real federation or a fusion. For my part, I am receptive to the first solution." It should be noted here that the Communist party is changing, having become flexible to the extent of making agreements with other parties of the Left, and that it now is out of the wilderness in which it lived for so many years. However, it still has not come down to a definite position, and it remains at this moment poised somewhere "in between." If it is not what it was, it still has not made clear what it intends to be. A number of roads are open to it. It could return again to a policy of hard systematic opposition to all bourgeois regimes, but that hardly would be profitable for it—resulting, undoubtedly, in a Poujadism of the Left devoid of a future. Or, the party could undergo a revolutionary toughening, and risk being transformed into a thoroughly outmoded vehicle. If, however, it evolves along a "third road," that of social-democracy, its version is bound to be different from traditional *embourgeoisé* interpretations of it—particularly those offered by the Socialist party, SFIO. As *Esprit* notes (quoted in *Le Monde,* November 13–14, 1967, p. 7), the party continues to be characterized by a naive and sincere conviction that it is "right" in its relations with adversaries and allies alike.

make significant progress between the first and second ballots. Their performance on the first had been outstanding; why, then, was it so slight on the second? Gaullist overconfidence undoubtedly played a role here, leading on the second ballot to less intensive campaigning. The ability of the Left to unite electorally on the second ballot played its part, too, but the factor probably most influential in the Gaullist's lack of progress on the second ballot was their inability to claim from the Center more votes. Center voters, confronted often with having to choose between a Gaullist and a leftist, voted for the leftist more often than had been foreseen by electoral statisticians. According to the studies of CFRO (Centre français de recherche opérationnelle), in Paris 25 percent of the voters of the Democratic Center abstained on the second ballot rather than vote Gaullist.[16] Finally, lack of Gaullist progression from the first to the second ballot was not in any way due, however, to abstention by Gaullist voters, for during the second round all abstentions amounted only to 19 percent of the registered voters. Inability to progress significantly between the first and second ballots did not prevent the entire Gaullist operation and affiliates from winning 244 seats, however, and emerging with a narrow victory. Yet, within that operation the UNR-UDT won 40 seats fewer than it had won in the elections of 1962. The UNR-UDT was unable to take advantage of both a second ballot that had been greatly simplified by a reduction in the number of candidates who had appeared on it, and the number of straight fights they entered into with the Federation of the Left. Previously the claimant of all 31 seats in Paris, Gaullist representation was reduced there to 21. A total of 7 seats were lost in the Nord (-3) and the Pas-de-Calais (-4). Gains were registered in the Ain, Jura, Somme, Lot, Mayenne, and Bas-Rhin, but losses were recorded in the Finistère, Haute-Garonne, Haute-Loire, Haute-Saône, Vaucluse, Belfort, Yonne, Gard, Lot-et-Garonne, Cher, Ardennes, Moselle, Gironde, Var, and Alpes-Maritimes. The results of the second ballot illustrated very clearly the slender hold on the majority manifested by the Gaullists, for 52 deputies representing both the majority and the minority each were elected by fewer than 1000

---

[16] *Le Monde,* March 16, 1967, p. 8.

votes. Finally, within the Gaullist majority, Giscard d'Estaing, the questionable ally of *mais, oui,* now claimed 43 seats, a progression of 9 over the number his group had received previously in the legislative elections of 1962. This had the effect of entrusting Giscard with the keys of the majority.

The Left returned a vote of 46 percent in the legislative elections of 1967. Despite some prior apprehension about the electoral agreements concluded between the Federation of the Left and the Communist party, this maneuver proved to be both feasible and profitable. The federation claimed on the second ballot 25 percent of the vote, the Communist party 21.4 percent. Collaboration on the second ballot produced for the Communist party 32 additional seats, 25 more for the federation, and 3 for the PSU. A divided Left had registered in the elections of 1958 a total vote of only 40 percent. This electoral reunification probably was the most spectacular development in Left politics and strategy since the Popular Front experience of 1936.[17] The Left vote of 46 precent gave rise immediately to discussions centering on how that vote could be stretched subsequently to 51 percent. Within the Left various schools of thought continued to subscribe, however, to different policies relative to the attainment of this objective. The followers of Gaston Defferre continued to argue that a Left majority is impossible without capture of a segment of the Center vote. Mitterand's followers viewed a united Left comprising the Communist party as a precondition of a Left victory. The followers of Mendès-France saw the problem as essentially a tactical one, contending that victory can be achieved only after the Left first has evolved a "creditable" and realistic program for the nation's governance, and that the Federation of the Left and the Communist party first must prove to the nation that they are competent to go beyond just an electoral victory. Long after the election had been concluded, there remained within the Left leaders with diverse "answers" to this problem.

The legislative elections of 1967 produced two chiefs of the

---

[17] At the same time, one inquiry by the French Institute of Public Opinion showed that 17 percent of Communist electors interviewed showed a "certain favor" toward Gaullist candidates. See Institut français d'opinion publique, "Les élections législatives . . . ," 26–27.

majority, Pompidou and d'Estaing, and two chiefs of the opposition, Mitterand and Mendès-France. Pompidou remained leader of a majority that comprised d'Estaing and which was dependent upon his willingness to sustain it. Meanwhile, his ties with d'Estaing were strained. D'Estaing held the keys to the majority, but he did not wish to break it and thereby risk personal responsibility for having opened a crisis. Mitterand, leader of a united Left, held the difficult position of being considered expendable by certain of his "supporters" who wished to see the Left led by Mendès-France. Nevertheless, the time was not propitious for a real competition between these men, for that would have detracted from the newly found unity of the Left.

Members of the Pompidou government who ran for seats in the National Assembly did extremely well on the first ballot, electing 11 of 23 candidates. Prime Minister Georges Pompidou was elected a deputy for the first time (in Cantal). Another member, Edgar Faure, was elected in a district where he was presented for the first time (Doubs). Nine members of the government were elected in districts where they had served already as deputies. Five members who stood as candidates for the first time were obliged to run again on the second ballot. Ten members were forced to stand on the second ballot in districts in which they had not been elected previously. Two members chose not to run as candidates. Twenty-two members of the government were elected. Among the four members defeated, Couve de Murville lost by only 245 votes, Sanguinetti by 166 and Charbonnel by 417.[18] Pierre Messmer suffered the only decisive defeat, going down by 2410 votes.

The legislative elections of March 5 and 12, 1967, took place in an environment that differed greatly from that which had existed during earlier elections of the Fifth Republic. The

---

[18] There is no way of telling if Sanguinetti's fantastic earlier hypothesis figured in his defeat. He stated that de Gaulle, if elected president of the republic, could then dissolve the National Assembly if it proved hostile, and if the newly elected Assembly proved to be hostile, too, de Gaulle could then invoke Article 16, or the "dictatorship article," and rule by it. It should be noted that Article 16 may be invoked only when the institutions of the state are endangered. Was Sanguinetti suggesting that a hostile legislative majority would endanger the institutions of the state? For details of his speech see *Le Monde,* November 17, 1966, p. 8.

Algerian war was over, having been terminated in 1962, the OAS was gone and domestic violence had disappeared, and the country was at peace. Foreign policy was not a great divisive factor, being endorsed by a majority of the nation, and the economic and social situation—although incapable of inspiring great optimism—did not give rise to noticeably dramatic differences within the society. During the first ballot voters were aware of a transformation in habits and conditions. References to the "majority" and the "opposition" were articulated frequently, a new phenomenon in French politics. The election, instead of comprising innumerable political parties of varying sizes, included instead 4 great formations—the Gaullists, the Communist party, the Federation of the Left, and the Democratic Center. And when the first ballot had been completed, the number of formations had been reduced from 4 to 3 as a consequence of the destruction of the Democratic Center.[19] The trend in the direction of bipartism caused observers to wonder if this was the result of the de Gaulle-Mitterand rivalry and the presidential election of 1965. If it was, that exactly was what the Left had worked previously to obtain. Although the 1967 electoral campaign officially had opened in March, 1967, the Left had worked previously for fourteen months to convince the voters that the legislative elections of 1967 constituted the "third ballot" of the presidential election of 1965.[20]

THE LEGISLATIVE ELECTIONS OF 1968

The legislative elections of 1968 followed on the heels of the Pompidou government's inability to deal effectively with the demonstrations, strikes, and national paralysis of May 1968. President de Gaulle dissolved the National Assembly on May 30 (no censure had ben voted), and the country balloted for new deputies on June 23 and 30. The electoral law remained the same as the one which had regulated previously the legislative

[19] For details see *L'Express,* February 27–March 5, 1967.
[20] Institut français d'opinion publique, "Les élections législatives . . . ," pp. 14, 34. The institute remarks that this effort appears to have been successful, and that a noticeable stability of opinion carried over to the subsequent legislative elections.

elections of March 1967. Voting was in 470 districts of the *métropole,* ten districts of Overseas Departments, and seven Overseas Territories. The following political formations were participating in the elections: the Gaullists, running under the banners of the UDR (Union pour la défense de la République), which comprised the UD V^e (Union of Democrats for the Fifth Republic) and the RI (Independent Republicans); the CPDM (Centre progrès et démocratie moderne), or the Center of Lecanuet and Duhamel; the FGDS, or Mitterand's Federation of the Left; the Communist party, the PSU, or Unified Socialist party; the M. Ref. (Mouvement pour la réforme) of former Gaullist Minister Pisani; and the I et D (Club technique et démocratie), and some Gaullist dissidents.[21]

The three-week electoral campaign at first was characterized by apathy and indifference, and later by noticeable alarm on the part of the populace.[22] During the campaign the President of the Republic dissolved some student groups, giving the impression that they were controlled by the Communist party. *Le Monde*'s correspondent, Pierre Viansson-Ponté, noticed creation of "a climate of fear which undoubtedly left some mark on the vote." [23] President de Gaulle warned the country of an impending "red totalitarianism," National Assembly President Chaban-Delmas warned that if civil war occurred, the Communist party undoubtedly would leave its mark on the country, and Premier Pompidou told the nation, "If you want to turn back subversion, if you want to block the road to a totalitarian party who threatens our liberties, give your votes . . . to the candidates invested by the Union for the Defense of the Republic." [24] Giscard d'Estaing was one of the few Gaullists who remained free from this type of campaigning, stating that he refused to accept the "alibi" that the crisis began "because of a Chinese invasion during the night." [25]

[21] *Le Monde,* June 23–24, 1968, p. 1.

[22] *Le Monde, Sélection hebdomadaire,* June 13–19, 1968, p. 1.

[23] *Le Monde, Sélection hebdomadaire,* June, 13–19, 1968, p. 1.

[24] *Le Monde, Sélection hebdomadaire,* June 13–19, 1968, p. 2; for similar comments by Pompidou, see *France-Soir,* July 2, 1968, p. 24.

[25] *Le Monde, Sélection hebdomadaire,* June 13–19, 1968, p. 2. D'Estaing was referring, of course, to Maoism.

The Gaullist "fear campaign" undoubtedly scored votes. Viansson-Ponté reports an opposition candidate remarking, "Each barricade costs me a hundred votes," and a Gaullist saying, "Some more red and black flags and I'll be reelected on the first ballot. Why should I schedule meetings, why give explanations?" [26] Surprisingly, the elections were relatively calm, marred only by some isolated incidents of violence. Soon after the polls opened, it became apparent that the vote was being returned with great speed. In Redon, for example, 20 percent of the registered voters had cast their ballots by 9:30 A.M. [27] Participation in voting was high in all regions (rain or shine)—even in the Midi, noted for its abstentionism. The Vosges was up 8 percent, Belfort 7 percent, the Haut-Rhin 5 percent, the Bas-Rhin 5 percent, and the Moselle 3 percent. [28]

Results of the first ballot

The first ballot produced an extraordinary victory for the Gaullists, as they progressed from 37.8 percent in 1967 to 43.65 percent in 1968 (to which must be added the 4.14 percent of d'Estaing and other moderates). [29] The Communist party dropped from 22.4 percent to 20.03 percent, and the Federation of the Left from 21 percent to 16.50 percent. The Center declined from 12.8 percent to 10.34 percent. Among all of the elements of the Left, only the PSU profited from the vote, passing from 2.21 to 3.9 percent. Two new formations, M. Baret's Technique et démocratie and M. Pisani's Mouvement pour la réforme, failed to survive the first ballot. Low-vote records were set in Paris in the third district, fifth *arrondissement,* by M. Griffon (Club des égaux) who received one vote, and in the sixth district, eighth *arrondissement,* by M. Bismuth (Union de la

[26] *Le Monde, Sélection hebdomadaire,* June 13–19, 1968, p. 1.

[27] *Le Figaro,* June 24, 1968, p. 7.

[28] *Le Figaro,* June 24, 1968, p. 7.

[29] *Le Monde, Sélection hebdomadaire,* June 20–26, 1968, p. 1; *Le Monde,* June 22, 1968, p. 3. Total number of candidates on the first ballot was 2267 (470 Communist, 325 extreme Left, 431 Federation of of Left, 35 Left of other diverse categories, 462 UDR Gaullists, 267 Center (CPDM), 28 Mouvement pour la réforme, 79 Club technique et démocratie, 143 Right or diverse categories, 17 Extreme Right).

jeunesse et d'externité), who did two times better.[30] General de Gaulle, not a candidate but always in the best of form, balloted in his home town of Colombey-les-deux-églises and committed a light infraction of the voting regulations when he handed the mayor Madame de Gaulle's elector's card.[31] Thirteen candidates in the Latin Quarter were not on hand for the vote, having been detained temporarily by the Ministry of Justice.[32]

The first ballot saw the Gaullists score heavily in all parts of the country, penetrating deeply into even the bastions of the Communists, Socialists, and Radical Socialists. In the Nord and Pas-de-Calais, Gaullist votes increased from 36.8 to 44.5 percent, and from 33.4 to 45.22 percent, as voters frequently abandoned the Left.[33] Elsewhere—in what was supposed to have been Mitterand country (Nièvre, Hérault, Var, Alpes-Maritimes, Rhône, Isère, Gironde, Somme, Vienne, Ain, Dordogne)—votes piled up for the Gaullists. And if the Union of Democrats for the Fifth Republic did well, the Independent Republicans, the other half of the Gaullist formation, did even better (that is, in relation to the number of candidates they ran). Never was there any evidence that they were being "carried" by their partners.[34]

The Left's retreat on the first ballot was great, so much so that some of its members could describe it only as "shocking." The Federation of the Left lost everywhere, as did the Communist party, which went in the Department of the Nord from 26.04 to 24.3 percent and in the Pas-de-Calais from 28.5 to 26.48 percent. The Federation dropped in the Pas-de-Calais from 32 to 28.02 percent. In Paris, the Communist party went from 22.31 to 18.83 percent, and there the federation dropped from 11.36 to 7.64 percent. The Gaullist position improved greatly in Paris, going from 42.98 percent in 1967 to 44.50 percent in 1968. Duhamel and Lecanuet's Center did well also in Paris,

---

[30] *France-Soir,* June 25, 1968, p. 3.

[31] *France-Soir,* June 25, 1968, p. 3.

[32] *France-Soir,* June 25, 1968, p. 12. More than 500 candidates were eliminated on the first ballot for receiving a number of votes inferior to 10 percent of the registered voters in their electoral districts; those detained were being held because of charges filed against them during May 1968.

[33] *France-Soir,* June 25, 1968, p. 3.

[34] *France-Soir,* June 25, 1968, p. 3.

receiving 16.08 percent against its 14.11 percent in 1967. The first ballot represented for the Left another step in its continuing decline. The Gaullists elected in all 470 districts of the *métropole* 152 deputies on the first ballot (against 63 in 1967), the Communists returned 6, and the Center 5 (without Gaullist competition). Eight of the 10 deputies elected in the departments and territories of the *Outre-mer* were Gaullists.

Leading figures of the majority enjoyed on the first ballot almost complete success. Georges Pompidou received 80.09 percent in the Cantal, Marcellin 81.50 percent in Morbihan, and d'Estaing 61.36 percent in Puy-de-Dôme. Among those ministers standing election, 21 were elected, and only 7 were forced to go on to the second ballot. The showing of the leaders of the Federation of the Left was on the first ballot dismal. François Mitterand did 43.9 percent in Château-Chinon (dropping 300 votes in Clamecy, where even unemployed workers went heavily for Gaullism), a decline by 5000 votes from his performance there in 1967. Guy Mollet was down 2700 votes, and Defferre 2000.

The second ballot

Abstentions increased to 20 percent on the second ballot, exceeding slightly those that had occurred on the first ballot (some of these were important in Paris, where 30 of 31 seats were claimed by the Gaullists with fewer votes than they had received in 1967; the Left vote in Paris was light, challenging the "rule" that moderate electors are the ones who abstain).[35]

The Center's Jean Lecanuet (laughing all the way to defeat) summed up the huge Gaullist second-ballot victory, "It's marvelous, for, after that, they can't do anything except decline."[36] For the first time in all of French republican history one formation, the Gaullist UDR, claimed in the National Assembly an absolute majority, winning 358 out of a total of 487 seats; the Union of Democrats for the Fifth Republic claimed 294 of these, and the Independent Republicans 64.[37] Throughout the country the UDR carried close to the same proportion of votes, claiming in

[35] *Le Figaro,* July 2, 1968, p. 4.
[36] *France-Soir,* July 2, 1968, p. 8.
[37] D'Estaing claims 64; some credit him with 56.

thirty metropolitan departments exclusive representation (no longer could the Left claim that in any department).[38] Seven members of the government were elected on the second ballot.[39] Some close races were recorded on the second ballot, but they were fewer than those that had occurred in 1967.[40]

As a consequence of the elections, Mitterand's Federation of the Left could claim in the National Assembly only 57 seats; all of the deputies from his Convention des institutions républicaines (the clubs) were eliminated, including Charles Hernu, a vice-president of the Federation of the Left who was defeated in Châteauroux. Surviving leaders include Mitterand, SFIO Secretary-General Guy Mollet, Marseille's Socialist mayor Gaston Defferre (only by 400 votes), and Radical Socialists Félix Gaillard and Maurice Faure.[41] The Communist party acquired 34 seats (losing 7 seats that they had won in Paris in 1967, and 7 in the suburbs). The PSU (which had progressed on the first ballot) witnessed in the National Assembly the elimination of all of its representation.

Assessment of the vote

Throughout the nation voters frequently deserted the Left to vote for Gaullist candidates. Communist losses were apparent early in the contest, as on the first ballot some of the party's voters abstained, and others went to the PSU.[42] The Communist party's worker votes continued to diminish after the first ballot, and Gaullism was able to profit from this defection in industrial areas such as Amiens, Perpignon, Périgueau, Lens, and Rouen.[43] In Grenoble, in one of the most watched races in the nation, Gaullist candidate Jean-Marcel Jeanneney defeated PSU candidate Pierre Mendès-France—who subsequently told the press

[38] *Le Figaro,* July 2, 1968, p. 4.

[39] Only one member of the government, Yon Morandat, Secretary of State for Social Affairs, was defeated in the entire race.

[40] Jeanneney defeated Mendès-France by 132 votes, Louis Mermaz won over David Rousset by 81, Modiano won over Pierre Cot by 98, Pierre Jalu won over Millet by 15, and Didier over Arrighi de Casanove by 1. A total of 49 seats were won by fewer than 1000 votes each.

[41] Right-wing Radicals clearly did better than left-wing Radicals.

[42] *L'Express,* June 24–30, 1968, p. 5.

[43] *L'Express,* June 24–30, 1968, p. 5.

that he had lost his race in the working class *communes* of Saint-Martin-d'Hers and Échirolles because of the inability there of the Communist party to deliver the vote.[44] Communist votes were instrumental in electing three Gaullist candidates in Marseilles, and in Aubusson some Communist electors supported a Gaullist against federation candidate Chandernagor. The situation was similar in Lyon, where Gaullist candidate Couste received on the second ballot 10,000 more votes than he had received on the first. In his case, however, Federation rather than Communist votes went to him. In the Department of the Nord, Federationists sometimes voted Gaullist rather than cast in behalf of the Communist candidate. And to the south, in Orange, Communist candidate Marin (who received in 1967 on the second ballot approximately 1500 new votes) lost on the second ballot some 3000 electors who had voted for him on the first ballot. In the "red bastion" of Saint-Denis, the Communist candidate was unable to acquire from the non-Communist Left electors more than 1300 of 5300 votes.

Where in the 1968 elections was the "unity of the Left"? It had existed in the elections of 1967. The *désistements* (retiring candidates and pledging collective support to a single candidate) were respected by the directorates of the Communist party and the Federation of the Left, but not by various of their respective electors. Some electors of traditional Left orientation simply would not vote for Communist party candidates, and some candidates of the Federation expressed publicly their hostility toward the Communists, costing the latter seats in some instances.[45]

[44] *France-Soir,* July 2, 1968, p. 8; *Le Figaro,* July 2, 1968, p. 14D. Jeanneney received on the second ballot 31,059 votes, Mendès-France 30,927. Abstentions on the second ballot were 20,027. The vote on the first ballot was Jeanneney 22,707, Mendès-France 19,567, Jean Giard (Communist) 10,715, Jean Vanier (Gaullist dissident) 6559, Armand Boissenot (Right) 2071. Vanier and Boissenot, who were eliminated for failing to win 10 percent of registered votes, informed their electors that they favored Jeanneney.

[45] See for earlier evidence of irritation by Communist electors because of Mitterand's attitudes toward them, Institut français d'opinion publique, "Les élections législatives . . . ," 21; *Le Monde,* June 5, 1968, p. 5. The Communist party on the first ballot presented only its

The defeat of the Left in the elections of 1968, of course, was due to more than the Left's inability to maintain its unity. First, the Left was unable to bite from the Center chunks of the vote comparable to the size it had taken from it in the elections of 1967. In 1968, Center voters frequently had their eyes on Gaullist candidates, and their flow away from the Left in some regions was massive. Second, one of Mitterand's favorite hypotheses is that the entire electoral experience of 1968 was manipulated psychologically by the Gaullists, and that the French voted not on issues but on an emotional basis in response to Gaullist "fear propaganda." Even if one rejects Mitterand's hypothesis, it must be acknowledged that the closeness of the vote to the disorders of the previous month did make the environment more propitious for the deployment of anti-Left propaganda. Third, although the Left had pressed for months for dissolution of the National Assembly, it could not—as Maurice Duverger states—have gone into a national election at a worse time, that is, being sure to lose in the Center because of the latter's fear of the Communist party.[46] Yet, as Jacques Fauvet says, "If the Communist party paid the price for the barricades, its role in them did not exist."[47] During the month of May both the Communist party and the CGT expressed solidarity with the student demonstrations, stating the movement's "natural convergence with the worker's struggle," but both organizations did not lead the movement. In fact, they regarded the students as "adventurers," and the CGT's Georges Séguy's aversion to Daniel Cohn-Bendit (one of the student leaders) was common knowledge.[48] The students (the "real" revolutionaries of France, and perhaps the only ones) regarded the Communist party and the CGT as having capitulated to the system and capitalism. *L'Express* reports some revolutionary Latin Quarter students as expressing their delight with Communist party defeats on the

---

own candidates, refusing to practice *désistements* until completion of the first ballot.

[46] Maurice Duverger, "La restauration," *Le Monde*, June 23–24, 1968, p. 4.

[47] Jacques Fauvet, "La peur et l'espoir," *Le Monde, Sélection hebdomadaire*, June 20–26, 1968, p. 1.

[48] *Le nouvel observateur*, June 26, 1968, p. 5.

first ballot.[49] These students believe that the Communist party loves the word "revolution," but not revolutionary action. Fourth, if the Communist party entered the elections appearing revolutionary to the middle class, it was in the eyes of some members of the extreme Left not revolutionary enough. As *L'Express* states, the Communist party, a party of revolution, met its enemy—revolt. *L'Express* quotes Roger Chonaval, writing in *France-Nouvelle,* weekly of the Central Committee of the Communist party, "It is remarkable . . . that the most sensitive losses of the Communist party and all the Left were found generally around the hottest points of the events of May. In general, the abstentions were most numerous in the municipalities held by the Communists . . . Some workers did not vote." [50] The Communist party appears in 1968 to have been caught between what it is and what it did not do. Finally, it is entirely possible that the Federation of the Left suffered in 1968 some losses due to the inability of people to distinguish its organic separateness from the Communist party.[51] Fear of Communism and disorder played its part in this election—and people fearful of black flags and red flags, and of anarchy and disorder and Communism occasionally blend all of these into one great nightmare. Political scientists are only too familiar with the fact that people decide things often not on the basis of what really exists, but, rather, on the basis of what they think exists. Whatever the reasons for the great Gaullist victory of 1968, the results put to rest (at least temporarily) speculation as to whether Gaullism is a phenomenon of a developed France, and Leftism one of an underdeveloped France. Gaullist voters popped up everywhere in the elections of 1968, and in doing so they junked the old line of demarcation between a North which was "Gaullist and developed," and a South which was "Leftist and underdeveloped." Moreover, the magnitude of the Gaullist vote transformed Gaullism from the status of what previously was an urban

[49] *L'Express,* July 1–7, 1968, p. 13.

[50] *L'Express,* July 1–7, 1968, p. 13.

[51] See Institut français d'opinion publique, "Les élections législatives . . . ," 15. As indicated elsewhere in this piece, this confusion extended in 1967 to approximately 50 percent of those people interrogated by the institute.

phenomenon. During the elections of 1968 Gaullism's progress among small peasants was considerable; the increase in Gaullist electoral strength was in excess of 20 percent in France's 200 most rural districts.[52]

Two final comments on the elections of 1968 are in order here. First, d'Estaing's Independent Republicans continued their drive upward in those contests, and his group now is the second largest in the National Assembly—and it may achieve even further progress in coming months. No longer has d'Estaing the importance on the parliamentary plan that he once had—nonetheless, he may have an opportunity to regain it sometime in the future. Second, the Federation of the Left was forced to re-evaluate its position in French political life. The Federation collapsed later in the same year.

THE PRESIDENTIAL ELECTION OF 1965

The presidential campaign of 1965 aroused enthusiasm among people who hoped for a renovation of the Left, particularly those who sought to unite Left voters on other than a traditional political party basis and to attract to the conflict people previously uncommitted or isolated in various clubs of study and political education. Two Left candidacies were advanced during the campaign, the first by Gaston Defferre and the second by François Mitterand. Defferre's candidacy was unique in French politics. He was portrayed first to the public by the weekly news magazine *L'Express* as "M. X," the "ideal candidate" of the opposition. The style of that introduction was well-received by public opinion and appreciated less by those members of his own Socialist party, SFIO, who were not attracted to his methods of

---

[52] *L'Express,* July 1–7, 1968, p. 8.; *Le Monde,* June 30–July 1, 1968, p. 3. These districts are distributed among 22 departments (Gers, Creuse, Cantal, Lozère, Lot, Vendée, Dordogne, Mayenne, Tarn-et-Garonne, Deux-Sèvres, Lot-et-Garonne, Landes, Manche, Aude, Corrèze, Orne, Aveyron, Haute-Loire, Côtes-du-Nord, Vienne, Indre, Morbihan). The Gaullist increase in these districts (25.8 percent) was greater than in the whole of France (14.3 percent). These districts elected 79 Gaullists on the first ballot, as against 37 in 1967; *Le Monde,* June 5, 1968, p. 5. Minimum agricultural wages were revised upward by the government (to three francs per hour) shortly before the elections of 1968.

Table 6–4 The presidential elections December 5 and 19, 1965

	First Ballot	Second Ballot
Registered voters	28,913,422	28,902,704
Votes cast	24,502,957	24,371,647
Abstentions	4,410,465 (15.25%)	4,531,057 (15.67%)
Invalid votes	248,403 (0.85%)	668,213 (2.31%)
Valid votes	24,254,554	23,703,434

Votes obtained by	Number		Valid Votes		Registered Voters	
	First Ballot	Second Ballot	First Ballot	Second Ballot	First Ballot	Second Ballot
Charles de Gaulle	10,828,523	13,083,699	44.64%	55.19%	37.45%	45.26%
François Mitterrand	7,694,003	10,619,735	31.72%	44.80%	26.61%	36.74%
Jean Lecanuet	3,777,119		15.57%		13.08%	
Jean-Louis Tixier-Vignancour	1,260,208		5.19%		4.35%	
Pierre Marcilhacy	415,018		1.71%		1.43%	
Marcel Barbu	279,683		1.15%.		0.96%	

Source: Ambassade de France (Service de presse et d'information, *Re-election of General De Gaulle as President of the French Republic and Composition of the New Pompidou Cabinet*, 186A (January 10, 1966), French Affairs, p. 1.

investiture (he asked his party for the nomination). During his campaign he remained somewhat aloof from the political parties, especially the Communist party, which he hoped to bend to his support. In fact, he sought to elevate himself above party and ride to the presidency on the shoulders of a great wave of public opinion. He also tied his candidacy to a project of federation which he tried to construct along the lines of an American political party, and which he hoped would absorb eventually his own SFIO, Radical Socialists and the MRP. That project failed, his candidacy subsequently disintegrated, and he withdrew then from the race. He was succeeded by François Mitterand who, unlike Defferre, first negotiated with the traditional political parties and their apparatus before participating in the contest. It is said that Mitterand secured Mollet's approval after engaging with him in private conversations. A member of a small and relatively uninfluential group (the Union of Democratic and Socialist Resistance, or UDSR), Mitterand's candidacy was more attractive than Defferre's to the large political organizations of the Left. Mitterand was a "last-minute" candidate who accepted the nomination in the belief that he never had a chance to defeat de Gaulle. The Socialist party, SFIO, supported his candidacy, as did the Communist party. The MRP decided, however, to go along with its own presidential candidate, Jean Lecanuet.

François Mitterand's candidacy came as no great surprise. Available and "ready," he had been around the political arena for more than twenty years. Undoubtedly he would have liked the nomination to have gone originally to him instead of to Defferre; nonetheless, he was happy to accept it when it finally became available. Mitterand was born in Jarnac in Angoumois on October 26, 1916. During part of World War II he was in a prison camp; subsequently he served in the Resistance. After the war he was a member of the 1947 Ramadier government. Later he served as minister of justice, and in 1954 he acquired a reputation for being sympathetic to French retention of Algeria (never, however, was he of Algérie française persuasion).[53] In 1959 his political career came close to destruction

---

[53] His 1954 views on Algeria are reproduced in part in *Le Monde*, September 30, 1965, p. 8, especially his "*L'Algérie, c'est la France.*"

as a consequence of the "affair of the Observatoire." Mitterand claimed that an attempt had been made on his life in Paris' Rue Observatoire. Some people claimed that Mitterand had arranged the incident for reasons of personal publicity. The case was dropped when all witnesses disappeared. Mitterand is something of a mystery. Secretive and cool, he inspires little personal confidence, and often he creates the impression of having convictions other than those which he displays in public.

Mitterand entered the race with the support of a team staffed with men who had spent years in French politics, but who did not qualify as propaganda specialists. He was aided by Charles Hernu, a former Radical deputy from Saint-Denis, who also is anti-Mollet and a presidentialist.[54] Another supporter was Georges Brutelle, former assistant-secretary of the SFIO and anti-Mollet. Others recruited were Georges Suffert, former supporter of Defferre and secretary-general of the Club Jean Moulin, Claude Estier (journalist), André Rousselet (industrialist), Dayon (councillor of state), Legatte (Mendés-France's former chief of cabinet), Aubert and Tron (senators), and some high civil servants whose identities were kept secret. Colloques socialistes, a society dedicated to the orientation of French society toward socialism, and Colloques juridiques, an association seeking definition of a new approach to the Left, both gave Mitterand their support, as did also many of the political clubs who had supported Defferre in his earlier bid for the presidency. Contacts with the Communist party were made through Jules Borker (in order to determine the extent of its support). Newspapers supporting Mitterand were *Le Populaire* (Socialist, SFIO), *Combat* (independent Left), and *L'Humanité* (Communist, Paris). Other publications coming to his defense were *France-Nouvelle, Humanité-Dimanche, La Terre, Démocratie 65,* and *Le nouvel observateur.* Both the influential *Le Monde* and the witty *Canard enchaîné* gave accurate coverage of his campaign.

---

[54] Claude Manceron, *Cent mille voix par jour pour Mitterand* (Paris: Robert Lafont, 1966), p. 103. Hernu declared in 1961: "Why not work for the future for the preparation of a presidential parliamentarism? . . . a power strong and responsible, finding its source in the people, that must be one of the principal preoccupations of men of the Left."

During the campaign Mitterand emphasized the theme of returning the republic to republicans:

> I am a man with free hands . . . I wish to be able to create some psychological conditions which are free from the thought patterns and discussions of parties. I have no apparatus, I am almost alone, but I shall have arrived, the 6th of December, if I am able to unfold a new state of spirit, that is to say, if I manage to make the people important, if, by my action, the citizens are more apt than yesterday to become responsible.[55]

Mitterand's program as presidential candidate was shaped along the following lines: [56]

1. Creation of a parliamentary republic and installation of a president "without abusive powers"
2. Restoration of fundamental liberties
3. Creation of a United States of Europe including the United Kingdom
4. Retention of nuclear power but its conversion to peaceful purposes
5. Democratization of economic planning, involving worker consultation
6. Creation of higher salaries, better housing
7. A "radical democratization" of national education, providing equal educational opportunity and training for positions of one's own choice
8. Support of the Atlantic Alliance

"François Mitterand is a man of the left, but it is certainly understood that he is not a Communist and on numerous points he has conceptions that differ from those of our party," stated the Communist party in 1965.[57] Why, then, did the Communist party support Mitterand in the presidential race of 1965? The answer lies in the fact that while Mitterand failed to satisfy all of the Communist party program, he did, nonetheless, satisfy

[55] *Le nouvel observateur,* September 25, 1965, p. 4.
[56] *Le Monde,* December 2, 1965, p. 4. This is the way Mitterand defined his program in response to specific questions put to him by *Le Monde.*
[57] *Le Monde,* September 25, 1965, p. 2.

enough of it to gain its support. Moreover, he was able to convince the Communist party that the presidential election was not the primary issue involved, and that more important was the paving of the way toward a popular *rassemblement* as a precondition of curbing personal power—and that he was the man who best could do this.[58] He favored constitutional revision of those articles that furthered personal power, he then favored governmental responsibility before the parliament and not presidentialism, he favored an economic planning dedicated to a more equitable distribution of wages, and he was willing to give a priority to the demands of national education (none of these positions being in real conflict with those of the Communist party). The Communist party recognized that if Mitterand spoke in behalf of phenomena which they opposed, such as a United States of Europe, the European Economic Community, and the Atlantic Alliance, he did oppose the *force de frappe,* he articulated the necessity for reexamining the NATO treaty, and he assured the Communist party that in no way would he seek to alter the existing *détente internationale.* Although a supporter of a United States of Europe, he convinced the Communists of his opposition to the Europe of cartels and technocrats, upholding a Europe of producers and workers.[59] As for his position on NATO, the Communist party stated, "We never presented retreat of France from the Atlantic pact

[58] *Le Monde,* October 17–18, 1965, p. 6. Guy Mollet revealed similar sentiments in an interview with *Le Monde.* He said that he was supporting Mitterand and that "The presidential election is not, in our eyes, the major event. We are preparing for the conquest of legislative power." He said that even if Mitterand were not elected, it would be a "victory" if he "remobilizes" the Left.

[59] *Le Monde,* January 6, 1966, pp. 1, 6. René Piquert, member of the Central Committee of the Communist party states that although the Communist party is opposed to the idea of the European Economic Community, it must recognize that the organization exists. Consequently, it should not "be made an object of irreducible conflict among the parties." In the meeting of the Central Committee in Saint-Ouen, Piquert stated that the parties of the Left must unite on a minimal governmental program—"But we do not present our project of program as one to take or leave in totality. We are ready to discuss jointly on this project some propositions contained in the programs of other parties of the Left and some political options formulated by François Mitterand."

as a condition of our participation in common action with the Socialist party and the other democratic parties." [60] Consequently the Communist party found certain "points of convergence" between its policy and his. The Communist party concluded:

> In short, despite the divergences that exist, we believe that it is possible to uphold a common policy on the condition that we orient it toward a policy of peaceful coexistence and *détente* aimed at cooperating among all the countries of Europe without discrimination and towards the reduction of armaments and general controlled disarmament . . . We state that the options presented by Mitterand more so in domestic policy than in foreign policy, comprise numerous objectives that figure in the program of the Communist party. [61]

It is doubtful that Mitterand would have been underwritten by the Communist party, however, had he shown the least drift in the direction of the Center or Right. The Communist policy constituted a step in the direction of reuniting the French Left—accepting that which unites, casting aside that which disunites. Its objective was "the development . . . of unity of action between socialists and communists, the gathering together of all the working forces, democratic and national." [62]

Mitterand's television campaign commenced in stony inflexibility and ended in what was interpreted by some observers as an imitation of de Gaulle (Mitterand was far from providing as dramatic a show as candidate Marcel Barbu, who appeared on television as the "nonvoice" of the "many nonvoices of France," who stated that he had been criticized for looking like a "beaten dog" but that this was appropriate inasmuch as France is "full of beaten dogs," and he was their representative). Mitterand sought to convey the impression that like his opponent de Gaulle, he, too, was not a captive of party: "I am not a man of a party, I am not a man of a coalition of parties, I am a candidate of all the Left." He dealt lightly with the theme of succession, saying that when the time came de Gaulle would leave and probably

[60] *Le Monde,* September 25, 1965, p. 2.
[61] *Le Monde,* September 25, 1965, p. 2.
[62] *Le Monde,* September 25, 1965, p. 2.

deliver to the French people an unknown successor, leader of "an anonymous syndicate of interests and intrigues." [63] He de-emphasized doctrine, stating, for example, "What is the Left? . . . it is simply the knowledge by the methods of science, of technique, of statistics, of what the world will be in ten years." [64] Nor did he find himself in disagreement with de Gaulle on all issues, agreeing that there were positive aspects of Gaullist foreign policy, for example, application in Southeast Asia of the accords of Geneva and opposition to American foreign policy in Latin America. [65] Finally, in a bid for the female vote that played so large a role in electing de Gaulle, Mitterand pledged abolition of the then existing anti-birth-control law. [66]

At first it appeared that President de Gaulle did not intend to campaign in the presidential race, and he did so only after the first ballot, after having received on it but a minority of the vote. Although he altered his principles in no way, he did soften his style, particularly on television where he spoke to the electorate more like a gentle *papa* than a seasoned competitor. He told his viewers that he was aware of his elderly age and that he did not pretend to know everything, but that a vote for him was a vote for the continuation of progress and protection for the future. [67] However, Michel Debré did not modify his approach. He told the nation that Mitterand's success would make France the prisoner of Washington, and that a defeat for de Gaulle would be a defeat for France. Debré referred to the Alsatian who gave as his reason for voting de Gaulle, "Je vote la France." [68]

During the presidential campaign six candidates were presented to the public; they were Charles de Gaulle, incumbent, François Mitterand, candidate of the Federation of the Left, Jean Lecanuet, candidate of the Democratic Center, Senator

---

[63] *Le Monde,* December 5–6, 1965, p. 1.

[64] *Le Monde,* November 24, 1965, p. 2.

[65] *Le Monde,* November 6, 1965, p. 3.

[66] Introduced in 1920 and repealed in 1967, the law prescribed six months in prison and fines ranging from 100 to 5000 francs for "prescribing, divulging, or offering to reveal the proper procedures or facilitating the use of such procedures."

[67] *Le Monde,* December 19–20, p. 1.

[68] *Le Monde,* December 19–20, p. 1.

Marcilhacy, Jean Louis Tixier-Vignancour, symbol of the extreme Right, and Marcel Barbu.[69]

Participation in the first ballot

Participation was 85 percent of the total number of registered voters, with seventeen of every twenty qualified voters casting ballots (Table 6–4). The turnout, which was the highest recorded in French history, surpassed the vote in the legislative elections of 1936 (where 15.6 percent abstentions were registered) and the referendum of September 28, 1958 (15.44 percent abstentions). In all of France, few electors absented themselves from the polls, convincing the pollsters that electoral participation was not in a state of steady decline. Also reversed was the old "law" which suggests that abstentions are greater in the Midi, "to the south of an arc of a circle which goes from Charentes to Jura, passing by the Sologne and delimiting the France of the Left." [70]

[69] Prior to the first ballot, *Le Monde* asked Lecanuet, Tixier-Vignancour, and Marcilhacy three questions: (1) "Would you tell why you criticize the regime and how you would act if elected?" (2) "What conditions are necessary among the Six?" (3) "What measures would you apply to the economy?" Lecanuet replied that (1) de Gaulle exercised too much personal power and that the authority of one man had been confused with the unity of the State, (2) the president of the republic should not substitute for the government, (3) that he would be the guardian of the Constitution, (4) that he would return to Brussels and construct a new Europe, (5) that he would reduce inequality of incomes, (6) that he would introduce a better system of traffic control, (7) that he would provide greater economic expansion, and (8) that he would adopt a more liberal housing policy. Tixier-Vignancour replied that (1) he would eliminate personal power, (2) that the government should be responsible before the chambers and that they should be vested with co-equal powers, (3) that he was for a united Europe in alliance with the United States, (4) that he was for private initiative and opposed to state planning, (5) that he would end inequality of incomes, and (6) that he would end the housing crisis. Pierre Marcilhacy replied that (1) he would apply the 1958 Constitution "to the letter," that (2) inasmuch as the Treaty of Rome opens the door toward a United Europe it is impossible for France to reject "all ideas of supranational power," (3) that he would provide more housing, and (4) that he would liberalize the economy further. The responses of all these personalities are reproduced in *Le Monde,* December 2, 1965, p. 4.

[70] *Le Monde,* December 7, 1965, p. 1.

This area was under the Fourth Republic traditionally the area of "no." More than 90 percent of those registered voted in thirty-two departments, many of which were situated in the Massif Central, the Pyrénées, and the Alpes. Among these, the Pyrénées-Orientales, the Haute-Vienne, and the Isère are departments in which high abstentions normally are recorded. Nonetheless, other departments normally of high participation did not exceed them in voting. Blank and null votes were the lowest in French history, indicating that those who called for this kind of response exercised virtually no influence over the voting (the editing circle of *L'Humanité,* pro-Chinese, had asked for a null ballot).

The first ballot and the de Gaulle vote

The number of votes received by General de Gaulle was the least he had ever received in any vote carried on under the auspices of the Fifth Republic (if one can employ the referenda of October 1962 and September 1958 as constituting votes for or against the President of the Republic because of the way in these contests that he consistently tied his personality to the device. In the referendum of 1958 he received approximately an 80 percent affirmative vote, and in October 1962 approximately 62 percent). President de Gaulle received an absolute majority on the first ballot only in 13 departments (having received an absolute majority in forty-three in 1958 and seventy-six in October 1962). Those thirteen departments are traditionally of Gaullist persuasion (Haut-Rhin, Bas-Rhin, Moselle, Vosges, Meuse, Ille-et-Vilaine, Morbihan, Orne, Manche, Haute-Marne, Lozère, Corsica, and Vendée). Nonetheless, de Gaulle did lead the voting in seventy departments, although those departments in which Gaullist deputies held seats were of no particular aid to him.

The first ballot and the Mitterand vote

François Mitterand received probably more votes than he expected, exceeding de Gaulle in twenty departments of the Pyrénées, Massif Central, and the Mediterranean Midi. He accumulated in his own department of Nièvre 52.49 percent of the vote. However, only in one other department did he accomplish an absolute majority, that being Ariège, where he received 50.10 percent of the vote. Mitterand was at his weakest in the Gaullist strongholds of Alsace and the Manche.

The first ballot and the Lecanuet vote

Jean Lecanuet extracted his vote from the Independents, the MRP, some Radical Socialists, and even from some people who were adherents of Poujade, Soustelle, and Antier. A majority of his votes came from agricultural regions. Lecanuet was able to drain off from Gaullist strongholds enough votes to prevent de Gaulle's reelection on the first ballot. In fact, Michel Debré accused Lecanuet of being responsible for preventing de Gaulle's success the first time around, to which Lecanuet replied that his candidacy "was a necessity," proving "that there exists a current which is democratic, social and European. I estimate that from now on that it will be possible to create a corresponding movement."

Results of the first ballot

On the first ballot President de Gaulle won approximately 44 percent of the vote, Mitterand 32 percent, Lecanuet 16 percent, Tixier-Vignancour 5 percent, Marcilhacy 2 percent, and Barbu 1 percent. The presence of Jean Lecanuet on the first ballot prevented de Gaulle from winning the election on it, thereby requiring a second ballot.

On the first ballot de Gaulle was able to cut into the worker's vote, frequently in regions predominantly of Communist persuasion. In Montreuil, Nanterre, Pierrefitte, and Bonneuil, for example, *communes* that in the spring of 1965 gave the Communists municipal council victories on the first ballot, this tendency was observed. Moreover, in Saint-Denis, Mitterand was not able to exceed 53 percent, although its voters had elected a Communist mayor just six months previously. A similar tendency operated in the Paris suburbs, the Nord, Pas-de-Calais, and in Marseilles, where Mitterand carried the vote but lost many workers' votes to de Gaulle.[71] The French Institute of Public Opinion noted that 13 percent of the electors who

[71] *Le nouvel observateur,* December 8–14, 1965, p. 8.

vote habitually for the three parties of the Left voted for de Gaulle on the first ballot.[72]

The Société française d'Enquête par sondages, or SOFRES, as it is commonly known, published in December 1965 the results of a study of voter motivation in the presidential election. SOFRES discovered two reasons for which people voted for de Gaulle on the first ballot—because "He represents France better," and "In order to prevent a return to the disorder of yesterday." [73] Moreover, a public opinion survey conducted by the French Institute of Public Opinion shortly before the first ballot revealed that 76 percent of those interrogated clearly approved of de Gaulle's foreign policy (although his domestic policy succeeded in securing less than a majority approval).[74]

One of the objectives of de Gaulle's opposition was to prevent him from winning on the first ballot, forcing him to undergo the "humiliation" of having received less than a majority and hoping that he would then refuse to carry through on the second ballot and depart abruptly from the presidential office. Had this happened, the first ballot would have been annulled and the Constitutional Council could have called then for new elections on the basis both of Article 7, which directs the Council to address itself to cases of "presidential vacancy," and Article 58, which compels it to "ensure the regularity of the election of the President of the Republic." That possibility never materialized; de Gaulle stayed in the race and participated in the second ballot.

The second ballot and the presidential election

All other candidates having been eliminated as a consequence of the first ballot, de Gaulle and Mitterand faced each other in the run-off second ballot. De Gaulle received 55.19 percent of the votes cast (45.26 percent of the registered voters); Mitterand received 44.80 percent of the votes cast (36.74 percent of the registered voters). De Gaulle was proclaimed president of the republic by the Constitutional Council on December 28, 1965.

[72] Reproduced in Jacques Fauvet, "Regroupements et élections," *Le Monde,* February 8, 1966, pp. 1, 14.

[73] *Le nouvel observateur,* December 29, 1965, p. 4.

[74] Reproduced in *Le Monde,* December 28, 1965, p. 5.

President de Gaulle received an absolute majority in 66 departments, and in twenty departments in excess of 60 percent of the vote. Only in Gers was his vote inferior to 35 percent. His strongholds remained generally the same—Alsace and Lorraine, the interior of the west, Normandy and Brittany, and some departments of the Center, such as Cantal, Haute-Loire, Lozère, Haute-Marne, Bas-Rhin, Haut-Rhin, Manche, and the Moselle. In regions in which the centrist vote normally is strong—in the Maine-et-Loire, Haute-Loire, Mayenne, Orne, and Calvados—de Gaulle managed to retrieve many of these votes on the second ballot.[75] In these departments a majority and sometimes two thirds of the electors voted for him.[76] De Gaulle profited from the strong majority support given him by female voters, although he was in the minority among men. Both de Gaulle and Mitterand received about the same magnitude of support from persons thirty-five years of age and under, but de Gaulle's strength was greater among advanced age categories, claiming heavily among these groups.[77] De Gaulle was favored heavily by retired persons, merchants, industrialists, and members of the liberal professions. However, the peasantry did not favor him as a group.

Gaullist Alexandre Sanguinetti argues that the Mitterand vote was a phenomenon of the France that is underdeveloped and poor, while the de Gaulle vote was one of a France that is modern and industrial.[78] There is no doubt that the Mitterand

[75] Institut français d'opinion publique, "L'élection présidentielle de décembre 1965," *Sondages,* 4 (1965), 20. Approximately 6 of every 10 Lecanuet votes went to de Gaulle on the second ballot.

[76] *Le Monde,* December 16–22, 1965, *Sélection hebdomadaire,* p. 1.

[77] *Le Monde,* January 1, 1966, p. 6.

[78] See François Goguel, "L'élection présidentielle française de décembre 1965," *Revue française de science politique,* 16 (April 1966), 221–254. Goguel concludes that Mitterand's support came from primarily "the persistence of an old historic tradition solidly rooted which led the majority of electors in about one fourth of the departments to vote Left." He states that the "France that voted Mitterand . . . is the France which remains faithful to a style and to some political institutions constituted at the end of the XIX, and the beginning of the XX century which some appear to consider no longer applicable to the needs of the present epoch and to the tasks which today have devolved upon the state." See also Michel Bosquet, "La ligne de clivage," *Le nouvel observateur,* December 29, 1965, p. 6.

vote came from pre-industrial and rural regions which are old and stagnant, for in the twenty departments that gave Mitterand more than 53 percent of the vote, conditions are not among the best in France. In eleven, the average salary for all occupations (excluding workers) is less than 8000 francs per year (compared to almost 14,000 in the Paris region). In Gers, where Mitterand received approximately 65 percent of the vote, the average salary is 6884 francs per year (excluding workers, who averaged 5628 francs). Sanguinetti's argument weakens, however, when one considers that in twenty departments in which de Gaulle received more than 60 percent of the vote, ten have average salaries inferior to 8000 francs per year. Only in three of the twenty departments which are most heavily Gaullist is there an elevated standard of living (two Alsacian departments and the Haute-Savoie). Moreover, some of the departments that voted Mitterand have elevated incomes, too—as, for example, the Bouches-du-Rhône, Haute-Garonne, and the Basses-Alpes.

Mitterand was able to gain new votes on the second ballot, but they came primarily from moderate areas, not from those habitually voting Communist—demonstrating that Mitterand suffered greatly from his inability to increase his Left vote between the first and second ballots.[79] Many of the Left votes Mitterand was unable to win went to his adversary, President de Gaulle, demonstrating the invalidity of the Left contention that a vote for de Gaulle was a vote for the Right. Mitterand did succeed, however, in increasing his centrist vote, now that Lecanuet had been eliminated on the first ballot. The French Institute of Public Opinion estimates that on the second ballot 38 percent of Lecanuet's votes went to Mitterand, increasing his vote by 10 percent in such traditional Catholic strongholds as the Bas-Rhin and Haut-Rhin (where he received almost half of Lecanuet's votes). Noticeable increases also were registered by Mitterand in the rural areas of the west and *centre*. A large number of Tixier-Vignancour votes also went to Mitterand. The Mitterand vote revealed several important things about both the Catholic centrists and extreme Right Tixier votes. It showed that the anti-Gaullist centrist vote can and did go in

[79] *Le Monde*, February 8, 1966, p. 1.

large numbers to a candidate who had solicited and received Communist votes, demonstrating that fear of the Communists had disappeared appreciably in contemporary France. It also provided evidence that the extreme Right—which was solidly Tixier on the first ballot—in throwing its votes to Mitterand on the second ballot was not particularly fearful that the electoral union of the Left would lead to the subsequent creation of a Popular Front government. Had it thought that, it hardly would have voted Mitterand. In giving to Mitterand so overwhelming a vote, the extreme Right demonstrated its lack of fear of the Left and its hatred of de Gaulle.[80] Curiously, Mitterand ended up receiving more conservative and extreme Right votes than de Gaulle received Left and extreme Left votes.

SOFRES' study of voter motivation revealed that among those who voted for de Gaulle on the second ballot "fear of disorder" was followed by "in order to prevent the Communists from coming to power" (particularly among those beyond the age of 30.) [81] SOFRES discovered that few voters balloted to "eliminate the old parties." Mitterand's supporters gave as their reasons for voting for him: "because he's a candidate of the Left," "because he's a real democrat," "because he wants to modernize the country," "because de Gaulle isn't concerned with the well-being of the French." [82] According to SOFRES, the motivation of those who voted Mitterand on the second but not on the first ballot appeared to consist primarily of concern for de Gaulle's disregard for the well-being of the French, and because Mitterand was the opposition candidate with the most votes. SOFRES concluded that the issues of laity and birth control had very little influence on the votes cast by Mitterand supporters.

During the three-week electoral campaign, General de Gaulle's support fell from 61 percent to as low as 43 percent, Mitterand's rose from 25 to 27 percent, and Lecanuet increased his support from 7 to 20 percent. The floating vote was estimated to have been at times as great as 29 percent. Electoral statisticians appear to have underestimated the Left vote, a

---

[80] *Le nouvel observateur,* December 22, 1965, p. 8.
[81] *Le nouvel observateur,* December 29, 1965, p. 4.
[82] *Le nouvel observateur,* December 29, 1965, p. 4.

common inclination because of their conviction that many supporters of a minority candidate tend to modify their views as the election comes in sight, casting finally for the most favored candidate. However, up to the last minute the fluidity of the electoral body injected in the election elements of uncertainty.

Sixty percent of the Left electorate carried from the first for Mitterand; de Gaulle's electorate diminished during this period, primarily because of the candidacy of Lecanuet, to whom almost half of the centrist electorate went. After the first ballot the electorate stabilized itself, settling down and clearly establishing its preferences. General de Gaulle had a majority among females, a minority among males (49 percent). Among persons under 35 years of age, preferences were equally distributed between de Gaulle and Mitterand. However, the greater the age category, the more likely its sympathy for de Gaulle. Between the two ballots (candidate preferences having been clearly established already), television viewers spent little time listening to candidates not of their choice. After the first ballot, former supporters of defeated candidates quickly made their choice between de Gaulle and Mitterand. Polls conducted by the French Institute of Public Opinion before and during the elections established clearly the image in which General de Gaulle was held by an important part of the electorate. Prior to the first ballot, 38 percent wished to see de Gaulle defeated, 10 percent wanted to see him elected only after two ballots, 10 percent wanted him elected on the first ballot but only "with a feeble majority," and 26 percent wished to see him elected on the first ballot with a strong majority. Between the two ballots, 49 percent wished for his election, 37 percent for his defeat. A fraction of the electorate who had voted on the first ballot for other candidates and who gave their votes to de Gaulle on the second ballot appeared to be opposed to his winning an easy victory, preferring that the success of the President of the Republic be modest. Fifty-one percent of the people interrogated between the two ballots voted for de Gaulle "because he inspires confidence" (only 20 percent of those who favored Mitterand voted for him for that reason). Only 18 percent of those who voted de Gaulle did so because they "approved of his ideas." Thirty-eight percent estimated that de Gaulle was the person most likely to find and apply solutions (35 percent attributed this characteristic to Mitterand). Only 52 percent believed that the capacities of the President of the Republic were superior to those of Mitterand (48 percent favored Mitterand). In the areas of international relations and French prestige, de Gaulle was far ahead of Mitterand (but voters interrogated between the ballots gave to Mitterand superiority in dealing with social questions, particularly salaries and prices). Those who gave their votes to Tixier-Vignancour on the first ballot believed in the majority that de Gaulle would lose the election (64 percent), whereas only 23 percent thought that he would win.[83]

REFERENDA

Nine referenda have been conducted between the Liberation and 1968. Three were conducted by the Fourth Republic, all having been instrumental in the creation of that regime. The others have been conducted by the Fifth Republic (one of these was fundamental to its creation. Another was restricted to Algeria when it still was part of France).

The first referendum, that of October 21, 1945, asked electors if they wished the Assembly elected that day to be a constituent one, and whether they wished the temporary organization of public powers to conform with that recommended by the government bill until the new Constitution came into force. Both questions were answered in the affirmative. The second referendum, that of May 5, 1946, requested electors to vote on the text of the Constitution adopted previously by the Constituent Assembly. The text was rejected. The third referendum, that of October 13, 1946, asked the electors to vote on a second constitutional text, which subsequently was accepted by slightly more than one million votes.

The first referendum conducted by the Fifth Republic was held on September 28, 1958, and was a constituent referendum concluding the existence of the Fourth Republic and creating its successor, the Fifth. The constitutional text was drawn up by

---

[83] All data in this paragraph are from Institut français d'opinion publique, "L'élection présidentielle . . . ." A summary of this study appears in *Le Monde,* January 1, 1966, p. 6.

the de Gaulle government that had been invested June 1, 1958, and submitted to the electors for their vote. The referendum also asked electors in Overseas Territories to choose between real independence and membership in a new organization called the French Community. The Constitution was accepted by a massive vote. In response to the second question, only Guinea opted for independence. The second referendum, that of January 8, 1961, asked the electors to approve or reject the government bill submitted to them by the President of the Republic concerning the self-determination of Algerians, as well as the organization of public powers proposed for Algeria prior to self-determination. Both questions carried affirmatively. The third referendum, that of April 8, 1962, called for approval of the government proposals of March 19, 1962 (which had resulted in a Franco-Algerian cease-fire), and authorized the President of the Republic to implement the legal instruments for Franco-Algerian cooperation after the creation of an independent Algerian nation. The referendum asked that the President of the Republic be given either by ordinances or decrees enacted in the Council of Ministers the right to take all measures relative to leading Algeria to independence. The fourth referendum, that of July 1, 1962, asked voters in Algeria only to answer *yes* or *no* to the question, "Do you want Algeria to become an independent State cooperating with France under the conditions defined by the declarations of March 1962?" Answered massively in the affirmative, Algeria shortly thereafter became a sovereign, independent state. The fifth referendum, that of October 28, 1962, asked the populace to vote *yes* or *no* to one question, "Do you approve the project of law submitted to the French people by the President of the Republic relative to the election of the President of the Republic by universal suffrage?" The response was affirmative, and since then France has elected its president by direct, universal suffrage (rather than by an electoral college, which was the case in the Fifth Republic previously, or by a legislative body, which was the case in the Third and Fourth Republics). The sixth referendum, that of April 27, 1969, asked the populace to answer *yes* or *no* to the question: "Do you approve the bill submitted to the French people by the President of the Republic relative to the creation of regions and the transformation of the Senate?" The response was negative, and on the evening of April 27 Charles de Gaulle announced his retirement from the presidency, effective the following day.

The referendum of September 28, 1958

This referendum was participated in by qualified voters in metropolitan France, Algeria, and Overseas Departments and Territories (Table 6–5). All were asked to vote *yes* or *no* on the constitutional text proposed for the Fifth Republic, and all Overseas Territories were asked whether they wished to enter the French Community or establish outside of it their own sovereign independence. The referendum had different meanings in the metropole and the overseas areas. The metropolitan French were asked: (1) if they approved the Constitution proposed by de Gaulle's government and its version of the organization of

Table 6–5 The referendum of September 28, 1958

	Metro-politan France	Algeria and the Sahara	Overseas Depart-ments	Overseas Territories
Registered voters	26,603,464	4,694,270	373,135	14,151,288
Votes cast	22,596,850	3,751,522	246,988	9,911,327
"Yes" votes	17,688,790	3,589,876	218,187	9,211,585
"No" votes	4,624,511	121,920	24,933	623,606
Abstentions	4,006,614			

Source: Ambassade de France (Service de presse et d'information), *The Referendums in France since World War II,* 135 (April 1962), French Affairs, p. 3.

public powers; (2) if they were willing to "legitimize" by their *yes* vote de Gaulle's coming to power by revolutionary means, assuring him by their vote, moreover, that they wished him to remain chief of state; (3) if they favored a new external association (almost exclusively Franco-African) called the French Community (of which the Fifth Republic would be a member). People voting in the metropole were given a reasonably clear idea of what they could expect subsequently if they voted *yes;* prospective *no* voters were given the opportunity to reject de Gaulle and his proposed organization of public powers and run, thereby, the risk of committing the society to subsequent alternatives that ranged from anarchy to naked military dictatorship. The referendum asked of those overseas: (1) if the Overseas Territories wished to form a new Community with France or break every tie with her; (2) if the Moslems of Algeria wished to be French; (3) if the Africans were willing to enter a Franco-African Community.

The referendum endorsed the Constitution by almost 80 percent of those who voted, being declined only in the African Territory of Guinea, which thereby refused membership in the French Community. All departments in metropolitan France returned positive majorities, and in five departments over 70 percent of the registered vote was *yes*. One of the most striking aspects of the vote in metropolitan France was that almost two thirds of the French working class voted affirmatively. Approximately 1.5 million Communist electors voted *yes,* despite the campaign undertaken against the Constitution by the Communist party, the General Confederation of Labor, CGT, almost half of the Socialist party, SFIO, deputies, other Left associations, and figures such as Mendès-France and Daladier. The vote carried in Communist Jacques Duclos' constituency of Montreuil, in the "red belts" of Paris, Lille, Grenoble, and Marseilles, and in the red pockets of Vitry, Saint-Denis, and Ivry. Only one *commune* (Bagnolet) in the whole of France voted against the Constitution.

The referendum of January 8, 1961

President de Gaulle announced on December 20, 1960, that subsequently the French people would be asked to express in a referendum their views relative to Algerian self-determination. The referendum, held on January 8, 1961, contained two questions, passed first by the Council of Ministers in the form of a decree. It asked the populations of metropolitan France, Algeria, and the Overseas Departments and Territories: "Do you approve the Government bill submitted to the French people by the President of the Republic concerning the self-determination of the Algerian populations, and the organization of public powers in Algeria before self-determination?" The government bill stated that the Algerian population also would be asked to state its own views later on self-determination—after the creation in Algeria of satisfactory security conditions. Prior to this, the Council of Ministers would determine by decree the organization of public powers in Algeria. Thus, voters were expected to respond but one time to two distinct questions. The referendum carried in the affirmative (Table 6–6). In metropolitan

Table 6–6   The referendum of January 8, 1961

	Metropolitan France	Algeria	Saharan Departments	Overseas Departments	Overseas Territories
Registered voters	27,184,408	4,470,215	291,692	398,099	175,819
Votes cast	20,791,246	2,626,689	193,018	241,174	134,786
"Yes" votes	15,200,072	1,749,969	168,563	211,376	117,688
"No" votes	4,996,474	767,546	18,970	23,157	11,628

Source: Ambassade de France (Service de presse et d'information), *The Referendums in France since World War II*, 135 (April 1961), French Affairs, p. 3.

France—despite his apparent "great reversal" on Algeria's destiny—de Gaulle was able to pull along with him electors in those eastern and western parts of the nation traditionally of religious and conservative orientation (the *yes* vote exceeded 60 percent of the vote cast in eight departments of the east and thirteen of the west). In the departments of the Pas-de-Calais and Nord, areas which are industrial and which then were normally of Socialist orientation, the referendum carried by more than 60 percent. Elsewhere, in two distinct parts of the country, both economically regressive and of Left orientation, the *no* vote dominated.[84] The *yes* vote won in the department of the Seine, although in the red suburbs a heavy *no* vote was returned. Rightist attacks on the referendum by Jacques Soustelle and Roger Duchet were unsuccessful (Duchet, Mayor of Beaune [Côte-d'Or] saw "his town" vote *yes* by five to one).

[84] One was formed by the departments of the Indre, Cher, Nièvre, Saône-et-Loire, Allier, Puy-de-Dôme, Corrèze, Creuse, and the Haute-Vienne. The other consisted of the Var, Basses-Alpes, Isère, Vaucluse, Bouches-du-Rhône, Gard, Hérault, Aude, Pyrénées-Orientales, Haute Garonne, Tar-et-Garonne, Lot-et-Garonne, Gers, and Ariège.

Like all Gaullist referenda, this referendum offered something to almost all of the diverse categories comprising the electorate. It suggested to the metropolitan elector that his *yes* vote constituted a step in the direction of peace in Algeria; it promised the rebel Moslems of Algeria the possibility of self-determination; it promised "loyal" Moslems of Algeria, or the *Beni-oui-oui*'s, in exchange for a *yes* vote creation of Algerian executive and legislative organs calculated to serve as long as lack of security conditions prevented a vote of self-determination; for the non-Moslem Algerian settlers, or "Europeans," a *yes* vote promised some guarantees for their protection; and to the army (which was then undergoing "depoliticizing") the referendum promised that its role in the "new era" would not be insignificant. Thus, although the referendum offered something to almost all categories of prospective voters, few could vote in it without feeling some frustrations. The arrangement whereby one could respond but once to what essentially were two questions posed for some people grave difficulties. Voters who wanted Algerian self-determination but who opposed de Gaulle knew, for example, that their *yes* vote would grant even more far-reaching powers to a president of the republic who had already great personal powers. Moreover, the elector who did not want Algeria to exercise self-determination knew that his *no* vote—even if it contributed to a majority—probably would not change de Gaulle's position relative to Algeria's future. The very people who had been instrumental in bringing de Gaulle to power for the purpose of keeping Algeria French knew by then that de Gaulle was not going to be deterred from pursuing self-determination to the very end. In fact, de Gaulle admitted several months after the referendum of January 8, that the Algerian insurrection had merely confirmed his own thoughts on self-determination—ones to which he subscribed, he said, as far back as the Conference of Brazzaville!

The referendum of April 8, 1962

The powers conferred by this referendum on the President of the Republic were great, although limited in their objective—that is to say, to his application to the Algerian war of the peace agreements of Evian. Prior to the referendum he had called for the nation to confer upon him "the means of settling, with the least possible delay, the problems that we shall face as we proceed with implementation." A *yes* vote in this referendum meant that until the time Algeria acquired sovereign existence, the President of the Republic could—by ordinances or decrees adopted in the Council of Ministers—take legislative or regulatory measures consistent with the government declarations of March 19, 1962 (the Evian peace agreements).

During the referendum, most of the political parties favored a *yes* vote. The Independent party left its members "liberty of the vote." The PSU urged a null vote as a way of saying *yes* to the peace and *no* to the Gaullist regime. Among those persons urging a *no* vote were rightists Pierre Poujade, Colonel Trinquier, Jean Paul David, André Morice, André Marie, and Roger Duchet. The Algerian deputies (Regroupement national pour l'unité de la République, a parliamentary group, not a party) recommended abstention, describing the referendum as "unconstitutional and illegal."

Voting in the referendum (Table 6–7) was 75.34 percent.

Table 6–7   The referendum of April 8, 1962

	Total	Metro-politan France	Over-seas Depart-ments	Over-seas Terri-tories
Registered voters	27,582,072	26,997,743	406,541	183,788
Votes cast	20,779,303	20,401,906	237,620	139,777
"Yes" votes	17,866,423	17,508,607	228,247	129,569
"No" votes	1,809,074	1,795,061	5,566	8,447
Abstentions	6,802,769	6,589,837	168,921	44,011

Source: Ambassade de France (Service de presse et d'information), *The Referendums in France since World War II,* 135 (April 1962), French Affairs, p. 7.

Null and blank votes were more frequent than usual, more of these appearing than in all the referenda since 1946.[85] The strongholds of *yes* were the traditionally conservative and re-

[85] Null votes were frequent but it would be difficult to say that this was due to PSU influence. In two strong PSU constituencies, Alfort and Antony, null votes were 966 out of 19,330, and 1203 out of 17,307.

ligious east Lorraine and Alsace and Brittany. However, heavy support also was secured in traditional Left country, particularly in Corrèze and Creuse, where large abstentions normally are commonplace. Departments recording the greatest number of *yes* votes were the Haut-Rhin, Bas-Rhin, Moselle, Morbihan, Finistère, Côtes-du-Nord, and the Ille-et-Vilaine. Only two departments, Gers and Creuse, cast less than 55 percent affirmative votes. The *no* vote was reduced generally to the extreme Right; however, all of its leaders saw their own constituencies vote *yes*. Rightist *no* votes were recorded in the Garonne valley, and in that part of the Mediterranean coast running from Marseilles to Nice, areas populated by repatriates from Algeria. Rightist Roget Duchet urged abstention, and this time 2 percent of the voters of "his town" of Beaune obliged him by staying away from the polls. In the department of the Seine abstentions rose but the *yes* vote was a massive 90.49 percent, as Communist electors and numerous workers joined in it (particularly in red Ivry, Saint-Denis, and the XXe *arrondissement*).

It must be concluded that the *yes* vote was a way of saying *no* to the OAS and its terrorism, as well as providing a method for paving the way toward peace. It must also be concluded that de Gaulle's success in this referendum was relatively greater than that of the UNR-UDT, whose leaders in Right constituencies failed to come in with overwhelming *yes* votes.

The referendum of July 1, 1962

This referendum was confined to Algeria, asking electors to vote *yes* or *no* to the question: "Do you want Algeria to become an independent State cooperating with France under the conditions defined by the declarations of March 19, 1962?" The answer was a massive *oui,* the percentage in relation to the votes cast being between 97 percent and 99 percent. Voting was calm and unmarked by terrorism, as approximately 85 percent of the registered electors voted. Nonvoting generally was confined to settlers of European extraction, and abstentions in the European *quartiers* of Algiers ran as high as 75 percent. In Oran and its general region, particularly in Sidi-bel-Abbès (former home of the Foreign Legion), heavy European voting caused—as *Le Monde* observed—the only surprise of the referendum.

Algeria shortly afterwards became a sovereign, independent state.

The referendum of October 28, 1962

This referendum proposed a constitutional reform, asking the electors to vote yes or no to the question: "Do you approve the project of law submitted to the French people by the President of the Republic relative to the election of the President of the Republic by universal suffrage?" The referendum passed

Table 6–8   The referendum of October 28, 1962

Registered voters	28,185,478	
Votes cast	21,694,563	
Valid ballots	21,125,054	(74.95% of registered voters)
"Yes" votes	13,150,516	(62.25% of valid ballots)
		(46.66% of registered voters)
"No" votes	7,974,538	(37.75% of valid ballots)
		(28.29% of registered voters)
Abstentions	6,490,915	(23.03% of registered voters)

Source: Ambassade de France (Service de presse et d'information), *Results of the Referendum of October 28, 1962,* 145 (November 10, 1962), French Affairs.

(Table 6–8), the *yes* vote constituting 62.25 percent of the ballots cast and 46.66 percent of the registered voters. The *no* vote was 37.75 percent of the votes cast and 28.29 percent of the registered voters. Abstentions were fewer than those recorded in the two referenda which preceded this referendum, but greater than those recorded in the referendum of November 1958.

The *yes* vote cast in the referendum of October 1962 declined in relation to those *yes* votes cast previously in the referenda of 1958, 1961, and April 1962. The affirmative vote in Bas-Rhin, Haut-Rhin, Manche, Moselle, and Meuse exceeded 80 percent of the votes cast—lesser but still strong *yes* votes were recorded in Alsace, Lorraine, West Brittany, and the Vendée. However, a new trend appeared, one that had not emerged in three preceding referenda, when fifteen departments of the Mediterranean part of the Midi, center and southwest contributed *no* majorities (Allier, Basses-Alpes, Ariège, Aude,

Bouches-du-Rhone, Gard, Haute-Garonne, Gers, Hérault, Lot-et-Garonne, Tarn, Tarn-et-Garonne, Var, Vaucluse, Corrèze). Electoral analysts were challenged by the positioning south of the Loire of all of the *no* departments—thirteen of these departments from the Midi and part of country that is underdeveloped, agricultural, peasant, and traditionally of republican orientation. This *no* vote raised certain questions. Did it represent a *no* of the Left? Was it representative of the reappearance of the old traditional France—one divided between Left and Right, according to regions of Left and Right orientation? Was not the *yes* vote concentrated in two areas, both of them traditionally conservative and clerical (Normandy and Brittany)—was not the *no* vote in a zone traditionally Left and anticlerical? Was not the *no* vote recorded in that part of the nation that is underdeveloped and materially inadequate and was not the *yes* vote registered in a France that materially is well off? This argument is very seductive but it breaks down when one notices that the *yes* vote also was in the majority in Paris and the Nord—parts of the nation which normally are of Left and republican orientation. Or, does the argument have merit and only appear to break down? Was it a case not of one but of two Lefts, one peasant and contemptuous of referenda, and the other industrial and less critical of such devices? Or are these arguments only illusory and but fanciful products of the minds of ideologues?

Complicating the referendum of October 28 was the manner in which it was undertaken by the President of the Republic. The question put to the populace proposed a constitutional amendment; however, Article 89 of the Constitution states very clearly that the initiative for constitutional amendment "shall belong both to the President of the Republic on the proposal of the Premier and to the members of Parliament," and that all government or parliamentary bills for amendment must be passed first by identical motions of a majority of the memberships of the National Assembly and Senate, after which they shall become law if they receive popular approval in a referendum. An alternative to submitting a proposed amendment to a referendum is for the president of the republic to submit it to a Parliament convened in a Congress, in which case the proposed amendment—in order to become law—must be accepted by a three-fifth majority of the votes cast. However, in this case President de Gaulle went completely outside of Article 89, bypassing the National Assembly and Senate and submitting the referendum directly to the people for their vote. President de Gaulle "explained" that Article 11 justifies this procedure. Article 11 does say that the president of the republic may submit to a referendum any bill dealing with the organization of "governmental authorities," or with the approval of a Community agreement, or with the authorization to ratify a treaty—however, Article 11 does not allow for a constitutional amendment; nor, for that matter, does it preclude a constitutional amendment. It simply says nothing whatsoever about constitutional amendments. The procedure for amending the Constitution is included in Article 89, where it is stated clearly and without any ambiguity. Nonetheless, the referendum was held, the Constitution was amended as a result of utilization of Article 11, and the Constitutional Council—after being asked by Senate President de Monnerville to rule on the amendment's "regularity"—ruled that it was incompetent to receive the question (Article 60 states that "The Constitutional Council shall ensure the regularity of referendum procedures.").[86] Consequently, the new constitutional amendment provided for a president of the republic elected by universal suffrage for a period of seven years. After the referendum de Gaulle addressed the nation on television and told it that the vote of October 28 confirmed the right that the Constitution gives to the president to submit to the country by referendum all projects of public law relating to the organization of public powers—and that now his was the chance to be a "real chief of state," thanks to the mandate he had received.[87]

In the meanwhile, angry and frustrated deputies and senators complained bitterly about the "shortcut" employed by

[86] *Le Monde,* November 8, 1962, p. 1.
[87] *Le Monde,* November 9, 1962, p. 2; See *Le Monde,* July 19, 1962, p. 2. In discussions reported on this date the Senators viewed constitutional reform by other than the assemblies as a *coup d'état.* See *Le Monde,* March 2, 1962, p. 5. When attention was given earlier to a proposal to modify constitutionally both the composition and powers of the Senate, Senate President de Monnerville argued that it was not possible without Senate agreement (nor by Articles 11, 16, or 45).

the President, and yet they did nothing significant to combat it, ignoring Article 89 and the use they might have made of it themselves in order to attempt a reconstruction of the Constitution (Article 89 does allow them the initiative for constitutional amendments too).

De Gaulle's methods of achieving the constitutional reform constituted another step by him in the direction of personal power. Aiding him, however, was the political situation that then existed in the country. A *no* vote in the referendum might have opened yet another political crisis, one that might have driven him out of office and acted to the benefit of the OAS. Although the Algerian war had been terminated by then, the OAS still was practicing terrorism on a substantial scale—and it would have relished the opportunity to seize on any events in order to drive him into retirement (if it did not succeed in assassinating him first). De Gaulle's lack of respect for the Constitution was, therefore, but part of an overall problem on October 28; his contempt for constitutionality was aided greatly by the anticonstitutional activities of members of the OAS and the terrorism they then were engaged in throughout the nation. Complaints by weak deputies and parties against de Gaulle's unconstitutional practices could command little attention in times such as those.[88] Finally, de Gaulle's proposed constitutional amendment also was aided by what it offered substantively to the populace, giving to it rather than to members of the professional political class the opportunity to elect the president of the republic. When has a populace been rewarded so well for looking away from constitutionality?

The referendum of April 27, 1969

The referendum of April 27, 1969, asked the voters to reply

[88] *Le Monde,* October 6, 1962, p. 1. From within the National Assembly the late Paul Reynaud accused de Gaulle of having broken his promise to revise the Constitution only as the Constitution prescribed, that is by Article 89. Reynaud asked, "Where in the free world can you find a regime as extravagant and dangerous as this?"; *Le Monde,* July 19, 1962, p. 2. When Senator Courrière asked Secretary of State Pierre Dumas, "Do you admit that the only procedure of revision is that of Article 89?" Dumas replied, "It is not for the government to say which is right."

yes or *no* to a single question, "Do you approve the bill submitted to the French people by the President of the Republic relative to the creation of regions and the transformation of the Senate?" The bill, which was lengthy and complex, incorporated sixty-eight articles in approximately 8000 words, and sought modification or replacement of nineteen articles of the Constitution of the Fifth Republic. The bill proposed administrative decentralization along regional lines, transformation of both the Senate and the Economic and Social Council and their merger in one body, and amendment of the law of presidential succession so as to enable the premier rather than the president of the senate temporarily to assume the presidency in the event of disability or vacancy.[89]

---

[89] Ambassade de France (Service de presse et d'information), "The Referendum of April 27, 1969," No. 1231, pp. 1–14. The region would have been superimposed on the departments and communes; its council would have been a federation of local communities. Each regional council would have included elected members and representatives of socio-occupational groups. The regional councillors would have been: (1) the deputies of the National Assembly elected by universal suffrage in the departments composing the region; (2) territorial councillors elected in each department by indirect universal suffrage by the General Councils (whose members are themselves elected in each department, with 1 councillor per canton), and by municipal councillors or their delegates. The socio-occupational councillors would have been designated for six years by bodies most representative of economic, social and cultural life of the region. The number of territorial councillors and socio-occupational representatives would have varied according to the size of the population in the region and in the following proportions—(1) a minimum of twenty territorial councillors and one additional territorial councillor per 250,000 inhabitants; (2) socio-occupational councillors equal to two thirds of the elected councillors, being 40 percent of all members of the Regional Council.

The number of seats for senators would have been 323—173 "territorial senators" elected for six years by territorial units (160 for metropolitan France, seven for Overseas Departments, six for Overseas Territories), their seats renewable by halves every three years; 150 representatives designated for six years by socio-occupational bodies (146) and by French living abroad. All senators would have been elected on a regional and not on a departmental basis, except in the Paris region, which would have been divided into three districts. The college electing the senators would have included the deputies of the departments included in the region, general councillors of the departments, delegates from the municipal councils, and regional territorial councillors.

President de Gaulle, who insisted that a *yes* vote was necessary in the referendum in order to avoid national disaster, announced several weeks before the referendum that he would resign from the presidency if the voters rejected his proposals: "There cannot be the slightest doubt on this subject. Upon the answer that the country will give to what I ask will obviously depend either the continuation of my mandate or my immediate departure . . . what kind of a man would I be if I . . . sought to maintain myself ridiculously in my present functions?"

In calling for the referendum, de Gaulle resorted to Article 11 of the Constitution (not Article 89), denying that he was using improper means to achieve constitutional amendment: "The quarrel that was given me in 1962 and that is given today, concerning the use of the referendum in accordance with Article 11 of our Constitution, is therefore a false quarrel of prejudices and routine." [90] The Gaullist argument for passage of the referendum ran as follows: (1) The Senate needs transformation; its powers are but illusory and the body is not representative of modern France. The new Senate would represent the local territorial communities, departments, *communes,* and regions in a more equitable fashion than is presently the case. There would be territorial senators and senators designated by the economic and social organizations, thereby eliminating the need for retention of the Economic and Social Council; "Thus the Senate will be truly representative of all the active forces of the country." [91] The Senate's powers on legislative matters presently are only theoretical, for it is the National Assembly that always has the last word. Once the Deputies decide, that is it. The Senate's "mission" would be to "formulate its opinion and to propose amendments" in advance of discussions in the National Assembly, thereby increasing its influence. (2) The creation of a new unit, the twenty-one regions (added to the territorial units that exist already, for example, communes, departments and Overseas Territories), would complement the Senate. Each of the twenty-

[90] Ambassade de France (Service de presse et d'information), "Major Excerpts from the Televised Interview of General de Gaulle, President of the French Republic, with Michel Droit, at the Élysée Palace, 1224, April 10, 1969," p. 3.

[91] "Major Excerpts . . . ," p. 1.

one regions would have a council consisting of elected and socio-occupational representatives. The regional councils would vote their budgets and eventually their taxes. The powers of the regions would comprise investments in all areas except those of great national interest, for example, roads, public works, schools, hospitals, urbanization, and the like. This, said the Gaullists, would assure at the regional level direct participation in management of affairs. Moreover, they stated that regionalization would not add to further centralization of government authority, that regional prefects would not become "superprefects," and that there would not be increased expenses and heavier taxes.

De Gaulle rejected the charge that his proposed reform of the Senate was tantamount to its destruction as a legislative and political assembly. He argued that his reform would enable the Senate to recover by "giving it the new composition and attributions which will give it back weight and prominence." [92] The Senate, said de Gaulle, is capable of receiving drafts only after the Deputies of the National Assembly "have taken their decisions, so it arrives weaponless after the battle." [93] Moreover, de Gaulle said, the Economic and Social Council, comprised of representatives of the occupational groups, is consulted only on what is submitted to it, making for "a veritable waste of resources and competences." [94] By bringing together both bodies in a transformed Senate which would publicly discuss bills in the presence of ministers and which would submit its opinion and proposed amendments before the Deputies have decided on the matter in the National Assembly, the Senate would acquire new importance and enable social and economic groups to participate directly in the preparation of the laws. Finally, the creation of new regions and transformation of the Senate were for de Gaulle intimately related and formed one "whole." There should be, he stated, a direct relationship between territorial communities and the Senate.

The bill regulated by the referendum was not submitted to Parliament for debate; once approved by the populace, said de Gaulle, it would then be examined at length by the govern-

[92] "Major Excerpts . . . ," p. 5.
[93] "Major Excerpts . . . ," p. 5.
[94] "Major Excerpts . . . ," p. 5.

ment, studied by the territorial economic and social bodies, discussed in the National Assembly and Senate, and perfected after consultation with the Council of State. And Premier Couve de Murville stated that the bill established "nothing definitively" and that "Every modification" would "be possible subsequently by the ordinary legislative path." [95] Nonetheless, de Gaulle told the populace that "it is in keeping with common sense that each Frenchman . . . leave to the President, the Government and their Councils the care of deciding on its details." [96]

The President of the Republic appealed on television and radio during the week of the referendum, asking for an affirmative vote. He approached the populace on a personal basis, calling on it to have confidence in his ability to cope with the future. As far as he was concerned, to believe in him was to believe in his proposals. Before the balloting began it was obvious that it was to be more of a contest for or against a man rather than for or against his proposals. Instead of educating the populace to the desirability of his proposed reforms, de Gaulle attempted to overshadow the issues of the referendum and pegged its passage to his retention as president.

A public opinion survey conducted by COFREMCA, from March 6 to 21, showed that a majority of respondents were favorable to the creation of regional assembles (54–20 percent), their election by universal suffrage (42 percent for, and 34 percent for their election by intermediary bodies), and for furnishing them with adequate resources (51 percent–27 percent). People between the ages of 21 and 24 years favored the reform by 63 percent, whereas those 65 years of age and older rallied to it by 45.5 percent.[97] Another inquiry, conducted by SOFRES, showed, on the other hand, that the majority of their respondents thought that the project of regionalization and reform of the Senate was more properly the concern of the Parliament.[98] During the last days of the campaign, voters in the 35- to 49-year

---

[95] Ambassade de France (Service de presse et d'information), "Excerpts on Regional Reform and the Transformation of the Senate from the Statement Made by Premier Maurice Couve de Murville in Lille, on April 14, 1969," 1229, p. 3.

[96] "Major Excerpts . . . ," p. 7.

[97] *L'Express,* April 28–May 4, 1969, p. 53.

[98] *L'Express,* April 28–May 4, 1969, p. 53.

category who intended to vote *no* constituted a majority.[99] The SOFRES survey, conducted from April 23 to 24, showed the referendum as losing supporters in virtually all areas.[100]

The results of the referendum (Table 6–9) suggest that a

**Table 6–9   The referendum of April 27, 1969
(metropolitan France only)**

Registered voters	28,656,494	
Votes cast	23,091,019	(80.57%)
Valid ballots	22,458,888	
"Yes" votes	10,515,655	(46.82% of votes cast; 36.69% of registered voters)
"No" votes	11,943,233	(53.17% of votes cast; 41.67% of registered voters)
Abstentions	5,565,475	(19.42%)
Blank or null votes	632,131	(2.20%)

Source: Le Monde, April 29, 1969, p.1.

great number of French did exactly what de Gaulle had hoped that they would do—that is, they voted more on the basis of him than on the merits of his proposed reform. The difficulty, however, was that more voted against de Gaulle than for him. The *non* vote won by 53.17 per cent to 46.82 percent. Four of every five electors voted, and abstentions were less important than predicted. The *non* vote was distributed throughout the country (Fig. 6–1)—carrying in sixteen of the twenty-one regions, in seventy-one departments, and in Paris (a *non* majority existed in every *arrondissement*), Lyons, Marseilles, Bordeaux, Rennes, Nantes, Nice, Reims, Cherbourg, and Bar-le-Duc. Some cities situated in those departments in which the *yes* vote carried returned a *no* majority; nevertheless, the positions of departments and cities generally were in agreement. In the Gaullist bastions, the *yes* vote—although still in the majority—was greatly reduced:

[99] *L'Express,* April 28–May 4, 1969, p. 53.

[100] *L'Express,* April 28–May 4, 1969, p. 53. SOFRES estimated the vote as 51 percent *no* and 49 percent *yes*. It estimated male support 44 percent, female support 53 percent, peasant support 58 percent, the liberal professions 48 percent, employees 47 percent, workers 40 percent, voters in the 21 to 34 year category 46 percent, those 35 to 49 years 44 percent, and those 50 to 64 years 48 percent.

Alsace (67.93 percent), Brittany, part of the Loire, Corsica, lower Normandy, and Lorraine.[101]

Electors of the Communist party and of the late Federation of the Left voted heavily against the referendum, particularly those who are male workers and under 35 years of age. However, people in industry, business, and the liberal professions who

Figure 6–1 The *no* vote in the referendum of April 27, 1969

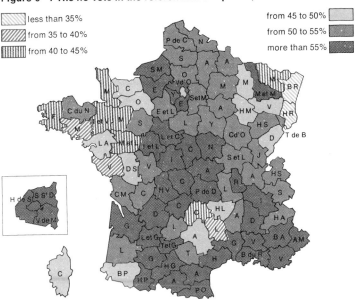

Source: Le Monde, April 29, 1969, p. 2.

supported the referendum fell to a minority. It was the *marais,* nonetheless, that force that never can be discounted and out of which de Gaulle had previously extracted so many votes, that cost de Gaulle a victory in the referendum. This time the *marais* had little to fear, and a good chunk of its electorate reversed its

[101] For complete coverage of results of referendum in metropolitan France see *Le Monde,* April 29, 1969, pp. 1–12.

field and voted *non*. Perhaps de Gaulle forgot that the *marais* is not only nonpolitical but also nonloyal? The worn-out pitch, "To vote *no* or to abstain is to vote for the Communist party," appears to have had little effect on the vote.

Several features of the referendum deserve comment here. First, the law proposed by the referendum was lengthy and complex and therefore hardly attractive to voters. Second, the law was presented by General de Gaulle to the populace on an arrogant "Take it or I'll go home to Colombey" basis. The behavior of the General—in what promised at first to be a tight vote—did not make for the best public relations. Third, de Gaulle had had in May 1968 ample warning to take greater heed of the country's social and economic problems; moreover, in June 1968 the country gave to the Gaullist party in the National Assembly a majority and thus the legislative means to do exactly what the Gaullists said they wanted to do. Although the Gaullists subsequently made some economic and social changes, the domestic inflation continued, eating up recently acquired gains and endangering further areas of social existence. It was in this kind of environment that the General presented to the country in April 1969 lofty political reforms that appeared to take precedence over social and economic reforms. When de Gaulle did that, he assumed in the public eye the image of a man who takes great pride in his contributions to the realm of the "purely political" and who is preoccupied with the most complex political problems of state. Perhaps the General assumed once too often that political reform is an effective substitute for economic and social reform and delivery by the Gaullists of the goods ordered by the populace one year earlier in May 1968. Defeated in the referendum, General de Gaulle resigned from the presidency on May 27, 1969.

Some considerations about de Gaulle's referenda

Objections to the referendum as a democratic device are difficult to raise if the questions asked of the populace are clear and free from ambiguity, and if each question asked allows freely for a clear response. These possibilities were not characteristic of de Gaulle's referenda. Voters often were asked to reply but once to a package containing multiple and diverse questions. Had he wished, de Gaulle could have provided in each referendum for as many responses as there were questions asked. However, de Gaulle never offered that accommodation. Voters generally had to give to the regime something in order to get something from it. Second, questions in a de Gaulle referendum often were characterized by an ambiguity that precluded the voter from knowing exactly that to which an affirmative vote would lead. Only too often voters were asked to express their confidence in de Gaulle's ability to employ methods known only to him in order to find a solution to some problem. Third, de Gaulle's referenda seldom allowed for getting advance views of important bodies in French life on the questions involved. Issues seldom were explored pro and con freely on television and radio, for Gaullist control of these media often precluded proponents of *no* from airing their views before the populace. Fourth, a de Gaulle referendum usually was tied closely to his own personality, and questions were put to to the populace asking it to vote for or against a man, rather than for or against the institutions that the man proposed. And the Chief of State frequently threatened to "go home to Colombey" if after the vote the *no*'s outnumbered the *yes*'s. The way in which the General always attained close personal identification with a referendum suggests that he believed that he was the only person in the whole of France capable of implementing its proposals.

CONCLUSION

High participation in elections and referenda of the Fifth Republic should not be equated with high participation in politics. Both participation (beyond the act of voting) and interest in politics tend to be low.

The laws that regulate national legislative elections—based on two ballotings, a majority sufficing on the first, and a plurality on the second—are calculated to weaken political party controls over the candidates, and to reduce drastically Communist representation in the National Assembly.

The legislative elections of 1958, the first held under the new Fifth Republic, constituted the first in a series of defeats administered the classical political parties, representing for some the beginning of the end. The sole exception, the Independent party, began its decline some years later, in the elections of 1962. In 1958 it was difficult to realize that the old party system was permanently injured, and that its electorate would be reduced drastically in coming years. By the time of the legislative elections of 1962, the new Gaullist UNR-UDT, although lacking still in the National Assembly a unified and homogeneous majority, had become the largest group ever to be seated in any national legislative body under any republic. The results of that election signaled yet another step in the evolution of the Fifth Republic, burying still deeper some of the classical formations held over from the Fourth. That election also moved in the direction of shaping up a cleavage between two rival camps.

The legislative elections of 1967, conducted in an atmosphere different from that of legislative elections that preceded it, now that the Algerian war was terminated, witnessed a recession in the UNR-UDT segment of the Gaulist formation; nevertheless, those elections increased the strength of Giscard d'Estaing's section, entrusting him in the National Assembly with the keys to the majority. The ability of the Communist and Socialist parties to conclude on the second ballot common electoral agreements bolstered Left strength in the National Assembly.

The 1967 legislative elections—instead of comprising innumerable political parties of varying sizes—included instead four great formations. When the voting had been completed, the number had been reduced from four to three, and observers wondered if a trend towards bipartism was in progress.

The legislative elections of 1968 followed unusual circumstances, coming shortly after the great demonstrations of May 1968 and the Pompidou government's inability to deal effectively with them. The campaign was attended by frequent Gaullist warnings of an impending "Red totalitarianism." The elections produced a huge Gaullist victory, a unified and homogeneous majority for the Gaullist formation in the National Assembly, and one of the heaviest defeats for the Left in all of French history. Left unity was missing from this election. The Left was unable to claim from the Center too many votes. The election transformed Gaullism from predominantly an urban phenomenon to one that is both urban and rural. Finally, the Gaullist section of the Union of Democrats for the Fifth Republic attained more than a majority in the National Assembly and succeeded in divesting d'Estaing and his Independent Republicans of the keys to the majority.

In the presidential election of 1965 de Gaulle was held to a minority vote on the first ballot; he claimed an easy victory on the second ballot. The frequently repeated hypothesis that the de Gaulle vote was typical of a France that is modern and industrial and the Mitterand vote characteristic of a France that was underdeveloped and poor does not appear tenable. De Gaulle secured many votes from regions that are both developed and underdeveloped. He also secured a considerable number of Left votes. Mitterand managed to secure almost 40 percent of the Center vote, and a great number of votes of the extreme Right.

De Gaulle's referenda were characterized by the inclusion of multiple and diverse questions to which the voter could give but a single *oui* or *non*. Referenda were constructed so that they did not allow for a response to each of the questions posed. To get something from a de Gaulle referendum the voter had to be prepared frequently to give in return his approval to another often contradictory question. The questions asked in de Gaulle's referenda often were ambiguous. De Gaulle's referenda were tied closely to his own personality. Often the populace was asked to vote for or against a man, rather than for or against the institutions he proposed. Staking all on the outcome of the referendum of April 27, 1969, de Gaulle lost and resigned from the presidency the same day.

SEVEN
THE POLITICS
OF INTEREST
Groups, interests,
and cleavages

Gabriel Almond points out that French interest groups are undifferentiated from political parties—that both do not form autonomous political subsystems. The General Confederation of Labor, CGT, is tied to the Communist party, the French Confederation of Trade Unions, CFDT, to the Democratic Center, and the Worker's Force, FO, to the French Socialist party, SFIO. They "interpenetrate each other," says Almond, and consequently some political parties "more or less" control interest groups. Almond believes that "When parties control interest groups they may, and in France do, inhibit the capacity of interest groups to formulate pragmatic specific demands; they impart a political ideological content to interest group activity." [1] Lack of an "autonomous, secular interest group system" leads to inadequate supervision between the political system and the society. Consequently there is a high incidence of anomic interest articulation; interest groups are unable to

[1] Gabriel Almond, "Introduction: A Functional Approach to Comparative Politics," in Gabriel A. Almond and James S. Coleman, *The Politics of the Developing Areas* (Princeton, N.J.: Princeton University Press, 1960), p. 38.

299

take demands from the society and transform them into "aggregable claims," shuttling them on to the "party system, legislature, cabinet, and bureaucracy from which they may emerge as impacts on public policy and regulation." [2]

Almond's contention concerning the limitations of a system with undifferentiated subsystems fails to explain the inability of French unions to secure from the system certain nonideological goals, such as wage increases and reductions in working hours. This inadequacy, according to Epstein, may be due not to the interpenetration of unions and parties but to "particulars of the French system." [3] Epstein points to the success of British unions in obtaining such goals; their example would make it very difficult to demonstrate that their connections with the Labor party have interfered with their ability to secure from the political system such concessions. Moreover, that relationship is organic, not autonomous at all. French union inadequacy with respect to this issue probably has much to do with the nature of party in France, and its inability to pass on demands effectively, and to the existence of a multiparty rather than a two-party system. Moreover, the fact that labor is in the majority organized in Britain and not in France also has bearing on this question. Finally, one cannot discount either that labor is in Britain relatively united while in France it is divided. A relatively united labor force organized in unions with organic ties with a political party can prove to be a productive rather than a limiting relationship.

In France the term *interest group* was for a long time pejorative. The term had essentially moral implications, as the French differentiated between groups working to further their own personal ends (designated as interest groups) and those working toward the general welfare (which they placed in another category).[4] However, the distinction broke down after the development of French political science and devaluation of Rous-

---

[2] Almond.

[3] Leon D. Epstein, *Political Parties in Western Democracies* (New York: Praeger, 1967), p. 146.

[4] No definitive list of interest groups exists. The leading work on French interest groups by Jean Meynaud, *Les groupes de pression* (Paris: Colin, 1958), cites at least 306 organizations.

seauean and other democratic myths. Today French political scientists identify interest groups on other than the criterion of whether they succeed or fail to establish compatibility of their ends and those of the "general welfare." [5] Some interest groups' ends may be compatible with the common welfare; others may not, being in nature restricted and partisan. Some interest groups methods are in keeping with established and legal modes of operation, while others are not. However they choose to operate, interest groups are vehicles of representation which serve as intermediaries between citizens and instrumentalities in both the public and private sectors; their existence has more or less of an effect on the communications and resource allocation processes of society.

Interest groups result either from the inability of other existing associations to implement certain interests, or from the inability of those associations to implement interests as fully as some people would desire. Interest groups seek to inflict pressures wherever they promise to be productive. Political parties are normally a particular target of interest groups whenever they are of importance and have access to the centers of decision making. The French Socialist party offered under the Fourth Republic an example of the successful application of pressure by a group to a political party. Civil servants voted in large numbers for this party; a considerable number comprised its membership. Seldom did the party fail to respond to the demands of the groups formed by this occupational category, being particularly heedful of the treatment of *les fonctionnaires* and seldom failing to rank pay raises for them high among its programmatical priorities.

The accessibility of interest groups to the state is related to whether the target is the Parliament, or the ministers and administration. When Parliament is the hunting ground, accessibility to it generally is greater than to the ministers and administration. Nonaccessibility of interest groups to the state can set the stage for irresponsible behavior by them. That was the case

[5] See discussion by Georges Lavau, "Political Pressures by Interest Groups In France," in Henry W. Ehrmann (ed.), *Interest Groups on Four Continents* (Pittsburgh, Pa.: University of Pittsburgh Press, 1958), pp. 60–95. One of the best essays available on French interest groups.

during the great riots of May 1968. For years the state had by-passed meetings with various student and professional education groups; they were denied even the opportunity to talk with the regime. The old French saying that the opposition—when not in a representative assembly—usually is in the streets, finally came true as various groups took to the thoroughfares after having been long rebuffed by a ministry of education that per-haps had come to consider itself as impregnable.

Coalition governments generally tend to distribute favors among more interest groups than do noncoalition governments. Coalition governments exhibit less cohesiveness than noncoali-tion governments and plucking here and there ministers from them is a relatively easy task. Such governments usually contain ministers whose parties have previously established ties with interest groups. However, this is not to say that noncoalition governments always are more resistant to interest group efforts —in fact such regimes may prove to be easier game than coali-tion governments.

Interest groups exert special efforts to influence communica-tions media, particularly journals of opinion and newspapers. The great amounts of money expended may or may not be allocated effectively. A new area for interest group expendi-tures was opened in 1967 when the President of the Republic pushed for and Parliament voted the introduction on state television of paid advertising, a medium from which private interests had been excluded previously (for years the greatest propagandist on State television and radio was the state itself).

AGRICULTURAL INTEREST GROUPS

The agricultural interest group of primary importance is the FNSEA (Fédération nationale des syndicats d'exploitants agri-coles), which comprises subsidiary units that reach almost into all aspects of French agricultural specialization. Its most impor-tant subsidiary is the CNJA (Centre national des jeunes agricul-teurs), which in 1957 transformed its own status to that of a union. The CNJA, which is inclined to regard the parent organi-zation as lethargic, is typical of an agrarian association which has undergone transformation with the rise of new generations of agriculturalists. It owes its creation to the Catholic action movements, and it wishes to liberate the agrarian movement from the domination of old men and patriarchal families who have manipulated the parent association for years, handing down their seats in it on a father-to-son basis. The CNJA's young elite wishes to integrate in the modern world, seeking for itself a technical competence that will enable it to transform methods of production. The young members, unlike their fathers, are inclined to view government price supports as not the solution to agrarian problems, and they acknowledge that too often their fathers regarded state intervention favorably—if only *d'assurer une juste rémunération des produits*.[6] Another interest group in agriculture is the APPCA (Assemblée permanente des présidents des chambres d'agriculture), which is a public assembly elected by different types of farm operators, owners, and agricultural workers; ties between it and the FNSEA are noticeable at both leadership levels. The CNMCAA (Confédération nationale de la mutualité, de la coopération, et du crédit agricoles) is concerned with agricultural questions, as are the MODEF (Mouvement de défense des exploitations familiales), which is of Left orientation, and the CFCA (Confédération française de la coopération agricole), which is of conservative persuasion. Efforts at coordination of the diverse agricultural associations have not been successful (although a movement in that direction shaped up in 1966).

Although worker and managerial unions remained relatively inactive during the presidential campaign of 1965, the peasant unions entered the campaign directly and identified themselves with an anti-de Gaulle position. The FNSEA repudiated the agricultural policy of the Pompidou government, a strategic move that was regarded with some surprise, considering the fact that both the directors and militants of the FNSEA are distributed among practically all of the political formations. The direct participation of the FNSEA had much to do with conducting a program of information for the agricultural and non-

[6] See Yves Tavernier, "Le syndicalisme paysan et la cinquième République," *Revue française de science politique*, Vol. 16, No. 5 (October 1966), 869–912; see also Meynaud, *Les groupes de pression . . .* , pp. 672–697.

agricultural associations, however, informing both of the nature and magnitude of peasant problems. It also was undertaken because all other methods of pressure had failed. In retrospect, it appears that it pays, when classical methods have been unproductive, to abandon them and participate directly in the political arena, for the FNSEA's performance in this instance produced considerable dividends—for example, permission to distill more inferior wine for the market, raising milk and beef prices, and cancellation of the tax on wheat and barley. Finally, the peasant associations also have rediscovered the fact that there are times when only violence pays, and lately they have utilized it. Yves Tavernier and Henri Mendras conclude that although it still is too early to assess them fully, the peasant demonstrations of June 1961 did produce a change both in ministers and agricultural policies.[7]

LABOR INTEREST GROUPS

The unionization of the total labor force probably does not exceed 35 percent. This restricted organization limits the effectiveness of French unions. Moreover, the organized element of the labor force is distributed among diverse organizational vehicles, cutting into the ability of unions to engage effectively in coordinated activities. A "Charter of Amiens" mentality has cost French unionism dearly, precluding it from making effective allies of political parties (it might also be said that French political parties have not benefited from this separation either, and that they might be stronger today had they cultivated earlier relations with the unions). Finally, it must be concluded that the noise generated by French unions outstrips greatly their achievements; those oral bombardments in which they so frequently engage are the result often of frustrations which derive from their inability to engage management in fruitful negotiations.

The CGT (Confédération générale du travail) has approximately 1.5 million members; the CFDT (Confédération française et démocratique du travail) numbers perhaps 450,000; and the

---

[7] See Mendras and Tavernier, "Les manifestations de juin 1961," 647–691.

FO (Force ouvrière) about 600,000.[8] Other organizations bring the total unionized labor force to approximately 2.5 million members. The CGT had almost two million members in 1920, and approximately five million in 1936, having undergone since its creation numerous internal schisms which have not aided its recruiting. The key ministries of the CGT are Communist dominated; however, other posts within the CGT are held by non-Communists. The CFDT is essentially Catholic, being known until 1964 as the CFTC (Confédération française des travailleurs Chrétiens). Its size is inferior to that of the CGT but its reputation for "toughness," particularly in agrarian parts of the nation, exceeds sometimes that of the CGT. It is not uncommon, in fact, for some French managers to proclaim that they prefer to negotiate with the CGT rather than with the CFDT. The FO largely is a paper organization insofar as nonsalaried workers are concerned; its ties are primarily with certain categories of civil servants who are concentrated mainly in the posts, telephone, and telegraph (PTT) services.

French syndicalism from the time of its creation was in competition with socialism. The unions, while admitting to the necessity of political action by parties, but not by themselves, regarded the socialist parties as outside of and subordinate to themselves. In turn, socialist parties regarded unions as potential auxiliary associations. Consequently, there evolved between the two a kind of coexistence marked periodically by relations that were less than peaceful. Marxism never was able to subordinate the unions fully to party. In turn, the unions never came up with a "British solution," domination of a labor party by them —moreover, they never wanted that kind of relationship. What resulted was a union movement ill at ease with political parties (despite the existence in earlier years of various people who were members simultaneously of the CGT and the SFIO; and despite the existence of people who belong today both to the CGT and the Communist party). This barrier between unionism and socialism weakened the SFIO (which owed its birth to a worker's movement, which originally was a worker's party, and

[8] Especially recommended and a "must" on French labor is Val R. Lorwin, *The French Labor Movement* (Cambridge, Mass.: Harvard University Press, 1954).

which today continues to proclaim its "workerism," although real workerism has been absent from it for many years), and detracted from the power of the Communist party, precluding it from getting over the CGT controls even more far-reaching than those presently held by it.

The Charter of Amiens adopted in 1906 by the CGT Congress prescribed preparation by the unions for integral emancipation of society; this was to be realized by expropriation of capitalism and the method was to be the general strike.[9] The unions were viewed as future units of production and distribution, constituting the basis for a future form of political organization. The "bosses" of tomorrow were to be the unions, the directors of enterprise. In each enterprise, workers were to be their own masters, forming associations somewhat analogous to cooperatives. The cooperatives then were to be federated in order to coordinate production and exchange. Overall direction was to be assumed by an assembly of cooperators headed by a responsible director, with ultimate choice over distribution of benefits. All this was calculated to secure economic democracy. This was the early version of syndicalist doctrine.

After the end of World War I another and more realistic vision of the future made its appearance in CGT ranks. Its principal component was nationalization, favored until then only by socialists and certain radicals. The Fourteenth Congress of the CGT, meeting in Lyon in September 1919, affirmed that "The impotence of the directing class and of the political organizations" was increasing "more and more each day," and the Congress prescribed as the goal of the CGT nationalization of the great services of the national economy under the control

---

[9] See Raymond le Bourre, *Le syndicalisme français dans la Vᵉ République* (Paris: Calmann-Levy, 1959), p. 176, for copy of Charter of Amiens. The Charter declares the CGT to be "outside all political schools;" that it recognizes on the economic terrain the class struggle, and exploitation and oppression, both material and moral, of workers by the capitalist class; that capital must be expropriated; that the method of action is the general strike; that the unions will be in the future the unit for organization of production and distribution and social reorganization; that unionism attains its maximum effect in economic action, and that political parties can, if they wish, "follow" the unions in the societal transformation (reflecting here indifference, suspicion, and disdain).

of producers and consumers. That idea subsequently was reaffirmed in 1934 in *le plan de la CGT,* when nationalization and a directed economy were tied closely to each other. The industries constituting the bulk of economic direction were to be nationalized first, particularly credit, followed by the nationalization of key industries, those concerned with the extraction of primary elements, particularly sources of energy, methods of transportation, armaments, and so on. However, as the years went on, the CGT, although not repudiating the objective of nationalization, came to recognize that private aggregates of capital, instead of disappearing, were growing in number, and so the CGT then fell into the habit of employing nationalization less as an objective and more as a tactical device. When the CGT employs the term today, the odds are that it is doing so to push for a change in existing conditions—that is to say, for a return to greater autonomous action (usually the CGT tends to identify the latter as a fundamental precondition of economic democracy), or for the acquisition of a new tactical position.

Study of French unionism involves careful sifting of reality and mythology, and sometimes the two become so intertwined that some confusion on the part of the inquirer is inevitable. The CGT's Charter of Amiens, for example, prescribes economic action and precludes political action; nevertheless, the key posts in the organization are dominated by the Communist party. The CGT pays lip service to the efficacy of the general strike, yet few of its members regard this instrument as a realistic weapon of action. Occasionally the CGT speaks programmatically of the final organization of society along economic lines in syndicates of production and distribution, and yet various of its members undeniably are attached politically to the parliamentary republic—even if its forms are contrary to those forms favored by the CGT, and even though parliamentarism demonstrated woefully its inadequacies under the last republic. Finally, the "nonpolitical" CGT with its key posts dominated by members of the Communist party ought to reveal somewhere along the line dependence upon Marx. The Marxian conception of the relationship between a union and a political party remains, however, distinctly contrary to the CGT's charter. Moreover, the major influence on the CGT is Proudhon, whose practical imprint on the organization exceeds that of Marx in practically every respect. As J. Hampden Jackson states:

> The influence of Proudhon's ideas was naturally most direct and enduring in France . . . All French working-class organizations were Proudhonist in 1865, and when trade unions were at last fully legalized in 1884 it was by Proudhonist workers that the new, large, peaceable industrial syndicates as well as the small, revolutionary craft unions were built up . . . By the first years of the twentieth century Proudhonism had prevailed in the French trade-union movement. It had abandoned some of the master's ideas on tactics, rejecting, for example, his anti-strike views. It had been inspired by new teachers, particularly Georges Sorel whose *Avenir Socialiste des Syndicats* (1897) reaffirmed the anti-State, non-political principles of Proudhon. The victory of the Proudhon tradition came at the Amiens Congress of the *CGT* in 1906, when a charter was adopted separating the trade unions from the political movement. . . . Before the Second World War, French trade-unionism had turned to politics and was becoming the prey of parties and sects, but if one asks oneself in what respect trade unionism in France differs from trade unionism in other West European countries, the answer must be in the influence of Proudhon's ideas.[10]

BUSINESS INTEREST GROUPS

The most prominent business interest groups are the CGPME (Confédération générale des petites et moyennes entreprises) and the CNPF (Conseil national du patronat français).[11] The latter is associated with large enterprise, while the former is associated with small activities and holdings. The CNPF has ties throughout the nation and a high-level influence on the economy. It is not hostile to *le plan*, for it influences it and derives from it certain advantages. Among CGMPE members, however, there is considerable suspicion of the CNPF, increased grumbling

[10] J. Hampden Jackson, *Marx, Proudhon, and European Socialism* (London: English Universities Press, 1957), pp. 166–168.

[11] The best study of business interest groups is by Henry W. Ehrmann, *Organized Business in France* (Princeton, N.J.: Princeton University Press, 1957).

about the rise of giant corporations and bigness in the French economy, and resentment against the Gaullists for favoring the growth of *les trusts*.

THE POLITICAL CLUBS

Political clubs are "societies of thought" and "groups of political interests."[12] Georges Lavau states that the clubs are a relatively new innovation, there being few before 1955 and many after 1957.[13] The rise of the clubs is testimony to the futility of the political parties at the end of the Fourth Republic, the frustrations created by the war in Algeria and, later, reaction to the "constitutional" revision of 1962. The clubs represent an attempt to redress the void created by the partial breakdown of the traditional political party system, and they seek to lay the groundwork for a network of communications that will enable people to identify and learn about political problems and do something about them. The clubs are an understandable response to the anxieties caused by the machinery introduced by the Gaullist regime, although originally they were a response to the inadequacies of the machinery of the parliamentary system of the Fourth Republic. Basically, the clubs are a phenomenon of the non-Communist Left and Left Center, being found primarily among the opposition to the Gaullist regime and less frequently among those forces and elements associated with it. Georges Lavau and Roland Cayrol observe that the clubs and their positions are very diverse, and that they constitute at least three types (and possibly more): (1) those who refuse to participate in immediate political combat or opt for a definite political camp (*Rencontres, Positions*); (2) those who are committed politically (Club of Jacobins); (3) those who wish for change but who will enter political battles only under "certain carefully chosen conditions" (Cercle Tocqueville, Club Jean Moulin, Citoyens 60).[14]

[12] Georges Lavau, "Les clubs politiques," *Revue française de science politique,* Vol. 15, No. 1 (February 1965) 105.

[13] Lavau, p. 111.

[14] Roland Cayrol and George Lavau, "Les clubs devant l'action politique," *Revue française de science politique,* Vol. 15, No. 3 (June 1965), 555–569.

The clubs seek to convey to those willing to listen views and information denied the general public by the screens and airwaves of the state dominated television-radio service (ORTF). The newspaper *Le Monde* devotes considerable attention to their activities, as do the publications *Combat* and *La Revue politique et parlementaire*. Various political personalities, primarily of the non-Communist Left, appear periodically before the organizations, and to a lesser extent representatives of the CGT, FO, and FEN. The Communist party, however, is distinctly cool to the clubs.

Two large conventions of clubs were held in 1964, one at Vichy (thirteen clubs) and the other at the Palais d'Orsay (fourteen clubs). The Vichy convention created a permanent committee and a secretariat. Common characteristics of the clubs participating at Vichy were religion, all being predominantly Catholic, noninclusion of the "political class" (they were not invited), and agreement that the clubs should be either training organizations or activity associations (most appeared to want something in between). What distinguished the Vichy meeting from the gathering at the Palais d'Orsay was the attendance at the latter of many political celebrities and members of Parliament, as well as a movement there on the part of the *Convention républicaine* to create a *grand parti*. Contacts between the participants in both conventions were occasional and some memberships were overlapping.[15]

Aside from acting as organs of education and communication, as of now the future of the clubs is not entirely clear. Will they be training organs for civic education, or will they branch out to become more than that—namely, political formations? There is at present a slight trend in the latter direction. At Vichy, for example, the participant clubs sought to lay down "new

---

[15] Lavau, "Les clubs. . . ," 105. Lavau notes that localization of the clubs who participated at Vichy is a distinct phenomenon. *Positions* is active only in Moulins, the *Club Jean Moulin* in Paris, the *Cercle Tocqueville* in Lyon and Grenoble, *Démocratie nouvelle* in Marseilles and Aix-en Provence. *Citoyens 60* has branched out somewhat into several cities. Formalization of ties is lacking among the majority of clubs; see *Le Monde*, November 6–7, 1966, p. 6, for meeting of *Convention républicaine* and pressures exerted by it on the Federation of the Left.

modes of action," while at the Palais d'Orsay the clubs sought to define commitments and those institutions that appear to be desirable in a modern republic.[16]

Clubs created by the Gaullists are designed to give to the public the impression that there exists an effective counterclub network. The Convention of the Fifth Republic Left (*Convention de la gauche Vᵉ République*), which met in Paris in October 1966 and which comprised the *Front du progrès,* the *Association nouveau régime,* the *Centre de la réforme républicaine,* and the *Clubs Vᵉ République,* seeks to siphon off votes from the Left and to provide a coordinating vehicle for the diverse "left" groups associated with Gaullism. In that October meeting the convention endorsed the foreign policy of President de Gaulle.[17]

CONCLUSION

French interest groups frequently are not clearly differentiated from political parties; that is, interpenetration of parties and interest groups has precluded the formation of autonomous subsystems. Almond says that this interferes with the ability of interest groups to transform demands from the society into "aggregable claims" which ultimately can produce impacts on public policy. Nonetheless, considering the success in the United Kingdom of the Labor party and its organically related unions, the inadequacies of certain French interest groups, such as the major unions, may derive more from particulars of the French system rather than from lack of autonomous subsystems.

The direct intervention of the FNSEA in the presidential campaign of 1965 was illustrative of the fact that other methods of pressure utilized previously by it had not been productive. On the other hand, its change in tactics produced some clearly identifiable dividends. Other agricultural interest groups have come lately to the conclusion that the employment of violence occasionally pays.

Labor interest groups are limited by their inability to

[16] *Le Monde,* November 6–7, 1966, p. 6.
[17] See *Le Monde,* October 11, 1966, p. 10, for report of the conventions.

organize a majority of French labor. Moreover, union unwillingness to work fully with the political parties probably has lost
both parties and unions some definite gains.

The CGT is the strongest union in the country, followed
by the CFDT and the weak FO. The CGT is close to the Communist party, the CFDT is close to the Catholic elements found
once in the left wing of the old MRP and now affiliated with the
Democratic Center, and the FO is close to the French Socialist
party SFIO. The major influence on French unionism is not
Marx but Proudhon.

Business interest groups are characterized by considerable
antagonisms between those affiliated with large enterprise and
those connected with small enterprise.

The political clubs are relatively new, being in part an
attempt to fill certain voids created by a weak party system, and
a way of improving political education and communications in
the Gaullist state. The clubs are basically a phenomenon of the
non-Communist Left and Left Center. The path of their future
development is uncertain.

EIGHT
ELEVEN YEARS OF REPUBLICAN MONOCRACY
Policy-making roles and structures

Parliament—having reached its peak under the Fourth Republic—did a poor job of sustaining that regime. That performance convinced many people that an assembly-dominated form of parliamentary organization is ill-suited for France. In contradistinction, some segments of the republican force continue to promulgate the idea that a strong Parliament remains the best safeguard of the democratic tradition. This belief now is associated, however, more with an older generation than with younger people; among the latter are various defenders of presidentialism who advance the idea that it and Bonapartism are not necessarily synonymous, and that one need not lead to the other.

PARLIAMENT IN THE FIFTH REPUBLIC

Parliament consists of the National Assembly and the Senate. The constitutional powers of both houses are almost identical. However, the Senate, unlike the National Assembly, may not censure the government and force its dissolution. Nor may the

Senate, unlike the National Assembly, be dissolved by the president of the republic.

The Fifth Republic's version of republicanism is very different from the one accepted by its predecessor, the Fourth Republic. The roles of Parliament and government are now different from what they were under the Fourth Republic. Relationships between the two instrumentalities are also different. Parliament took the lead in legislation under the Fourth, with the government intervening, only as a secondary measure, generally when Parliament failed to make a decision, or when Parliament instructed it to act, delegating to it its authority for that specific purpose. In the Fifth Republic the picture is totally different: Article 34 of the Constitution defines those areas in which Parliament may legislate, and Article 37 reserves to the jurisdiction of the government all other matters. The government's statutory powers are broad and frequently independent of Parliament, enabling the government to modify and amend laws which previously were within the province of Parliament. Now the government has assumed the lead as major legislator, and behind it Parliament runs a poor second. Government legislation may enter even the area open to Parliament, and the government may utilize Article 38 to suspend parliamentary legislation for an unspecified period of time (with parliamentary approval).

The traditional notion in French law until the advent of the Fifth Republic was that all laws were the result of having been acts of Parliament, in accordance with procedures defined by Parliament, with no restrictions whatsoever on content (with exception of constitutional ones). Now, limitations on the lawmaking power of Parliament are numerous, and they are supplemented by others which allow the chief of state in exceptional circumstances to act for an unspecified period of time as lawmaker. Moreover, he may act also as an originator of law, submitting propositions of law in a referendum to be voted directly by the people, a possibility that applies not only to ordinary laws but to constitutional ones as well.

Parliament's powers now are restricted narrowly in areas of lawmaking. In some areas Parliament may legislate fully and in detail, areas (which are described in Article 34 of the Constitution) which include all aspects of the electoral system, civil rights, creation of the judiciary and status of judges, inheritances, gifts, marriage contracts, creation of public institutions, nationality, currency, eminent domain, and nationalization. In other areas Parliament may legislate in principle but not in detail, areas which include labor legislation, civil law, local administration, education, property rights, social security, and organization of national defense. Subjects exclusive of all of the foregoing areas may be handled by the government by means of executive orders. Thus, in certain areas Parliament may not legislate at all—and should Parliament seek to exercise in the lawmaking realm power in areas denied it by the Constitution but allowed to the government, the government may amend simply by executive order such bills (subject to the requirement that the Constitutional Council verify that the Parliament has exceeded its constitutional powers).[1] Under the Gaullist regime, the Constitutional Council has ruled frequently against Parliament's intervention in the executive power, as, for example, in 1960, relative to the disputed ordinances of 1958 dealing with finances and war damages. However, government decrees which have stretched over into the area reserved by the Constitution to the Parliament seldom have been interpreted by the Constitutional Council in a manner that has spelled trouble for the government.[2]

THE STATUS OF THE NATIONAL ASSEMBLY UNDER THE FIFTH REPUBLIC

The Gaullist regime—almost immediately after its creation—clarified that the National Assembly was to be one of the less

[1] Article 41 of the Constitution states, "In the event of disagreement between the Government and the President of the Assembly concerned, the Constitutional Council gives a ruling, at the request of either party, within a week."

[2] *Le Monde,* March 6, 1962, p. 1. Jacques Fauvet states that although in his speech to the Council of State on August 27, 1958, Debré said that the creation of the Constitutional Council signifies the will to subordinate the law to the superior rule of the Constitution, the Constitutional Council judges these days acts which are of a legislative rather than an executive nature, concentrating on whether Parliament has exceeded its law-making powers and on whether Parliament's rules of procedure are constitutional.

significant institutions in French political life. In the special session of January 1959, when the deputies sought to adopt rules of procedure that would have resulted in an increase in their parliamentary prerogatives, the Debré government granted them only minimal concessions and turned the deputies aside when they sought to have oral questions followed by debate and the voting of resolutions. During April of the same year the deputies discovered that although they could present oral and written questions to the government, discussion with the government of a problem is very difficult if the government wishes to evade the issue. The deputies soon realized that motions of censure deposited against the government by one tenth of their number is one way in which they can attempt to force the government to come face to face with them over a problem it wishes to avoid. They also realized that it is difficult for them to function effectively if they can disagree meaningfully with the government only by defeating it by a vote of censure. The "moment of truth" came to many deputies in 1960 when 287 of their number, a majority of the National Assembly, petitioned for a special session in response to demands by constituents who hoped that its convocation would enable the deputies to pressure the government to take emergency measures relative to easing the agrarian crisis. The request was denied by President de Gaulle, who stated publicly that the special session would result only in partisan minorities essaying efforts detrimental to the majority; that is to say, he refused to meet the demands of a majority of deputies because he thought that they would convene for the purpose of speaking only for a minority in the country! Later, in September 1961, when the presidents of the National Assembly and Senate requested a special parliamentary session for the purpose of examining agrarian problems, they were told by President de Gaulle that he would not prohibit the convocation as long as Parliament did not have a "legislative objective." The constitutional provision allowing Parliament to meet in extraordinary session at the request of the prime minister or at the request of a majority of its members, only when the president of the republic allows it, is a sharp departure from the practices both of the Third and Fourth Republics. The Constitution of the Third Republic obligated the president of the republic to convoke the chambers in extraordinary session, whenever between sessions that was requested by an absolute majority of the members of the chambers. Under the Fourth Republic convocation simply was at the discretion of the National Assembly's bureau. Under both the Third and Fourth Republics convocation of Parliament at the request of a majority of members was automatic, and something over which the presidents of both regimes lacked discretion.

The National Assembly was a victim of May 13, 1958. After that, the Assembly became the victim of circumstances which continued until the termination of the Algerian war. The first National Assembly seated under the Fifth Republic contained initially a large bloc of deputies who appeared happy to rely on directives transmitted to it by the President of the Republic. That legislature also contained Left elements—who wished to strengthen the prerogatives of the National Assembly but who hesitated lest they also strengthened those deputies who professed to be "Gaullist" but who were considerably to the right of de Gaulle. Many of these "Gaullists" were militant proponents of Algérie française. Elements of the Left had every reason to suspect—and rightly so—that certain Gaullist deputies entertained conceptions relative to the Algerian question that went far beyond those harbored by de Gaulle. Why, then, they reasoned, should they seek to enlarge the prerogatives of the Assembly and risk furthering the importance of elements that they opposed more than de Gaulle himself? Second, during those first months in the life of the Fifth Republic, elements of the Left opposition in the Assembly, although apprehensive of de Gaulle's personal power and his conception of an excessive presidentialism, hesitated to offer very much opposition to him because they knew that the possible alternative to him was the army. Therefore, they were unwilling to do anything that might have resulted in his displacement by it. Third, after de Gaulle's historic pronouncement of September 16, 1959, promising Algerians self-determination, elements of the Left opposition in the Assembly then sought to do nothing that would have prevented him from carrying through on this aspect of his foreign policy. They came to regard de Gaulle as the only man capable of achieving peace in Algeria. Parliamentary prerogatives hardly can be strengthened under circumstances as complicated as these.

The National Assembly that sat between the elections of 1958 and 1962 was not devoid, however, of all activity. Most of its time was taken up with debates on the Algerian war; it did deal with the *force de frappe,* France's relationship with Europe, the agrarian law, and the investiture of two prime ministers. It disposed of the Algerian issue, rejecting first Algeria's integration in the Republic and, subsequently, it gave its approval to de Gaulle's policy of self-determination, allowing the government on February 2, 1960, special powers to deal with Algeria. The *force de frappe* led to various attempts at votes of censure by the opposition deputies but the vote carried and a nuclear project was created at Pierrelatte. Subsequent attempts at votes of censure received only slight legislative support. Lively debate and some sparring with the government was engaged in by some deputies who behaved as though they had not heard of May 13 and its consequences, but by 1961 the National Assembly presented a picture of futility, and deputies' activities in it had diminished greatly due to the tutelage in which the National Assembly had been placed in relation to the cabinet. In the session of June 28, 1961, some deputies feebly attempted blockage when they refused to examine the business included by the government in the order of the day. However, the following day things returned to "normal" and the deputies then went back to the performance of the few functions allowed them.

Once the Algerian war was terminated, de Gaulle acted swiftly so as to prevent the National Assembly from reacting against him and the government. The majority (which had changed since 1958) was then subjected to a series of presidential tactical maneuvers calculated to force the dissolution of the National Assembly and the return to it of a Gaullist majority. The chief weapon in the President's arsenal was the referendum. In proposing the election of the president of the republic by universal suffrage, rather than by an antiquated electoral college, de Gaulle knew that the constitutionally questionable means he employed would lead the majority in the Assembly to oppose the proposed amendment. The Assembly—snubbed by the President of the Republic, and excluded from the amending procedure in a clearly unconstitutional manner—reacted by calling attention to the illegality of the referendum.[3] In doing so it placed itself in an impossible position, opening itself to charges by de Gaulle that it was concerned less with legality and more with precluding the populace from exercising popular control over the election of the president. De Gaulle's maneuver forced the Assembly to take the bait, committing it thereby to a conflict with the President of the Republic and necessitating its subsequent dissolution. According to de Gaulle, the purpose of the new constitutional amendment was to pave the way for the presidential succession —and who could object if it also took care of a National Assembly that was showing signs of getting "out of hand"?

The legislative elections of 1962 returned to the National Assembly the largest single group that had ever been seated until then in the history of the Republics, and the UNR-UDT with some additional support gained an easy working majority in the chamber. Demonstrating fidelity to the chief of state and to his representative, Prime Minister Georges Pompidou, the Assembly was transformed into an even more docile and servile body. Debate became somewhat irrelevant and parliamentary initiatives declined. Ministers were subject to few of the pressures known by members of governments when facing vigorous legislative bodies. Now the President of the Republic and the prime minister were men who came not from the parliamentary ranks or traditional political formations, but from the army and the high civil administration. "Government stability" set in—or was it merely an illusion, created as a consequence of parliamentary immobilism?

The legislative elections of 1967 also returned a large number of Gaullist deputies to the National Assembly; nonetheless, this time they found their working majority there not altogether certain. Giscard d'Estaing and his Independent Republicans assured the President of the Republic that they were not to be taken for granted by the Gaullists (his precise ideas—partic-

---

[3] *Le Monde,* July 19, 1962, p. 1. The Senate's position was presented by Senate President Gaston de Monnerville who held that no constitutional revision was legal without the vote of both assemblies of Parliament—or, if both houses reconstituted and sat as a Congress, as prescribed by Article 89 of the Constitution, the proposed amendment could not be presented to the people in the form of a referendum.

ularly in finance—made of him an uncertain ally). In the Assembly, in the meanwhile, the opposition parties continued to oppose the government, but the latter gave little attention to their efforts. Their influence on the government in debates was minimal, and understandably they behaved at times in ways that were apathetic and practically aparliamentary. Nonetheless, they stayed in there, recognizing that debates could be of some value if they gained outside of Parliament in media of mass communications publicity for the opposition (not on radio and television but in the columns of certain influential newspapers). As Professors Goguel and Grosser state: "The talent and the competence with which the author of an oral question exposes his point of view and with which the representative of the government answers him is in general of more importance than the question of knowing if the Assembly has or has not the faculty of adopting finally, as a result of debate, a motion summing up with more or less clarity the opinion of a majority of its members." [4] And Goguel and Grosser conclude, "If the Parliament no longer has a monopoly of the exercise of sovereignty, what counts above all in the parliamentary debates is the contribution they make to the information of the electors—that is, the measure in which they can make and contribute to serious opinion, which they can then translate into legislative votes, referenda and presidential elections." [5]

The foregoing considerations aside, the devaluated status of the National Assembly acts today as a deterrent against participation by deputies in its sessions, and their personal appearances there become consistently less frequent.[6] Some say that participation does not pay because the Assembly means nothing any more, while others claim that they have other functions as mayors, general council presidencies, and so on. As Pierre Viansson-Ponté states, "Some arrive from the provinces Wednesday morning and go home Thursday night. Marcel Dassault, for example, makes two or three appearances per year." [7] A constitutional provision

---

[4] François Goguel and Alfred Grosser, *La politique en France* (Paris: Colin, 1964), p. 173.

[5] Goguel and Grosser, p. 173.

[6] Pierre Viansson-Ponté, "Prélude à la campagne. III. Le nouveau député," *Le Monde,* July 8, 1966, p. 7.

[7] *Le Monde,* July 8, 1966, p. 7.

requiring legislators to attend the Assembly on a regular basis has not been implemented. Base pay for legislators is supplemented by attendance pay, and a legislator absent from one third of the balloting in a month is supposed to forfeit one third attendance salary, two thirds if he misses more than half, and all if absent for a month. Absence from three consecutive committee sessions is supposed to constitute basis for dismissal from the committee, and reduction of additional salary by one third until the beginning of the parliamentary session the following October.[8]

The new and drastically reduced field of action of the National Assembly is in keeping with the methods of operation of the new technocratic state, one which proceeds on the assumption that economic matters are handled poorly by a parliament that is but a place for the colonization of partisan minority interests. Not receptive to parliamentary control over economic phenomena, the Gaullist republic handles this area by experts in both the public and private domains who generally are outside of Parliament. The Gaullist state is part of a modern world which is bypassing parliaments increasingly, viewing them as bodies which came into being when the intervention of governments in the economy was less than now, and restricted generally to the fixing of tariffs and the voting of budgets. Conditions now are different, and today real decision making in the economic area is made most often outside of Parliament. Therefore, the Constitution places upon the deputies definite limitations in fiscal matters, and in this area the initiative has been taken over by the government which presents most propositions of fiscal law. The Constitution prevents deputies (and senators) from introducing either by propositions of law or amendments measures calculated to increase or decrease public expenditures. This trend, which began before 1958 under the Fourth Republic (when the chambers allowed the government broad leeway in fiscal matters), has been completed by the Fifth. The difference, however, is that the

---

[8] Another constitutional provision prohibiting members of Parliament from receiving specific instructions on voting has been ignored. Designed originally to modify control of the Communist party over its deputies, such a provision, which is as antiparty as it is anti-Communist, could be deployed to threaten any political association seated in Parliament.

chambers allowed the government this leeway under the Fourth Republic, whereas under the Fifth the Constitution allows the chambers few fiscal prerogatives. Should Parliament decide to amend the finance law, finance committees in both houses must determine the receivability of amendments and rule on them. Should the parliamentary iniative threaten an increase or decrease in expenditures and yet be passed by both houses, the prime minister is empowered to request that the Constitutional Council examine the pending law and, if necessary, forbid promulgation of any part of it that it rules unconstitutional. Occasionally, deputies are able to get through amendments to projects of law when initiated by the government. Some are adopted as a consequence of being recommended by the *rapporteur général* of the finance committee, and sometimes their adoption is dependent upon which political party presents them. Such amendments usually are confined, however, to details and not major issues. The voting by Parliament of finance laws is regulated by an organic law allowing for a possible delay of seventy days, after which— if Parliament has not adopted or rejected the law—the government may promulgate it by ordinance.

Although they may originate in either chamber, most bills have their origin with the government (a trend characteristic more of the Fifth than of the Third and Fourth Republics, now that executive domination is so complete). Government bills may first be presented either to the National Assembly or Senate (with the exception of finance bills which are given first to the Assembly), and such bills, as well as private member's bills favored by the government, are accorded priority consideration in the receiving chamber. Once introduced in Parliament, bills then go to a legislative committee—either to a permanent or standing one, if the government wills it, or to a special committee created by the government itself. Bills sent to standing or special committees must come to the floor within three months. After having reached the floor, bills occasionally are recommitted to committee for additional revisions—or, they may be subject to amendments proposed by ministers or members of the chamber.[9] However, once debate has begun, the government may

[9] Despite the Constitution's separation of legal powers, ministers have rights of amendment equal to those enjoyed by deputies. This means that texts of propositions of law when passed are not necessarily those

object to discussion of any amendment not submitted previously to committee or, if it wishes, the government may demand that the chamber accept or reject by only one vote "the whole or part of the Bill or motion under discussion, together with such amendments as have been proposed or accepted by the Government" (a procedure for which no precedent whatsoever existed under the Third and Fourth Republics). Thus, during discussion of a bill by the chamber concerned, the government may or may not allow separate inquiry into each of the bill's articles and possible amendment thereof. When a single vote is demanded by the government (known as the *vote bloqué,* or blocked vote), this is the government's way of telling the chamber to accept or reject the package as a whole. It is understandable that the government usually gets its way.

After the chamber has approved the bill, it goes then to the other chamber and if passed by it the bill then is forwarded to the government and either promulgated as law or held up temporarily by the president of the republic (within fifteen days of its transmission to the government, in which case the "veto" enables him only to ask Parliament for a reconsideration of the law or of certain of its articles. The Constitution states that this reconsideration may not be refused). In some cases, however, the bill goes straight from the Parliament to the Constitutional Council for a ruling on its constitutionality. Should the bill pass the National Assembly but fail the Senate, the government may then create a special committee consisting of an equal number of members of both houses. However, means for more rapid expedition of the bill are at the disposal of the government, and it may decide after the bill's first reading that it be sent instead to a special committee if the prime minister feels that it requires "special consideration." In such cases, the special committee, after it finishes its work, then sends the bill to the government which returns it to both houses with no amendment possible if the government is unwilling to agree to such. If the Senate refuses to vote the bill and it is approved by the National Assembly, the government can ask the National Assembly to rule

---

produced previously by the competent committee of the legislature—their contents correspond generally to the demands of the government inasmuch as the government has the last say over them.

definitively on the bill, in which case the National Assembly may accept the special committee version, its own, or its own plus the amendments made by the Senate. If both houses reject a bill, the government cannot do much to offset the move.

The government has absolute control over the *ordre du jour* and all propositions of law whose discussion it judges necessary. With respect to timetables, priorities, and area of performance, the Parliament is boxed in by the government and can do little except tag weakly along behind it. However, one weapon that the National Assembly has cannot be taken lightly—that is its power of censure. Motions of censure against the government (signed by one tenth of the deputies and filed forty-eight hours in advance of the beginning of formal censure proceedings) may be received by the National Assembly during normal sessions of Parliament (even if Article 16 is in effect), but not during short or special sessions, according to a ruling made by National Assembly President Chaban-Delmas.[10] Between 1958 and 1965, ten motions of censure were presented by the opposition in the National Assembly. Four of these dealt with the *force de frappe,* and none were successful. One of the ten motions was successful, the one of October 5, 1962, which received 280 votes (241 were required). The government resigned immediately (as is required by the Constitution, Article 50). That censure resulted from the procedure employed by President de Gaulle to amend the Constitution. After the resignation of the Pompidou government, de Gaulle dissolved the National Assembly, sending the country to new elections; after the seating of the new Assembly, de Gaulle then reappointed Pompidou prime minister.

Membership in Parliament, whenever incompatible with other positions held by the electee, is covered by a procedure adopted in 1962. The new member has fifteen days in which to resign from the incompatible post or posts. Should there be doubt relative to the compatibility of his seat with any other

[10] *Le Monde,* September 20, 1961, p. 1; *Le Monde,* September 15, 1961, p. 1. The Constitutional Council, after being asked by the Assembly president to rule on his decision, declared itself incompetent to receive it. The Constitution, by the way, nowhere mentions that the voting of censure during short or special sessions of Parliament is prohibited.

post that he may hold, the bureau of his assembly, the minister of justice, or the deputy himself may put the question of compatibility to the Constitutional Council for final disposition. Should the Council decide that there is incompatibility, the mandate of the deputy can be revoked by the Council if the deputy does not comply with its decision.[11] Those occupations which preclude a person from holding a legislative seat simultaneously are directorships of nationalized or state subsidized enterprises, those which involve making legal representations in behalf of enterprises suing the state, and those involving directorships of organizations concerned exclusively with the execution of state contracts.

Members of Parliament may not be prosecuted, sought, arrested, detained or tried as a consequence of opinions or votes expressed by them in the exercise of their functions. No member of Parliament may, during Parliamentary sessions, be prosecuted or arrested on criminal or minor offenses without authorization of his assembly, except in cases of *flagrante delicto*. When Parliament is not in session, no member may be arrested without authorization of the Secretariat of his assembly, except in cases of *flagrante delicto,* or of authorized prosecution, or of final conviction. Detention or prosecution of a member of Parliament shall be suspended if requested by his assembly. In the case involving the immunity of the ex-deputy Le Pen, a fascist activist who sought to support de Gaulle during the first days of May 1958, but whose services were rejected by the General, the request for the lifting of his immunity came first from the minister of justice after Le Pen declared on November 16, 1961, in a meeting at the Maison de mutualité in Paris that "The Declaration of war has been made." The statement was interpreted as an expression in behalf of OAS terrorism. The request for deprivation of his immunity, according to the rules of the National Assembly, then was taken up by an *ad hoc* committee of 15 of its members named by the Assembly (staffed according to proportional representation—6 UNR, 4 Independents, 2 MRP, 1 SFIO, 1 Entente démocratique). The committee then heard representations by the deputy (in his absence, they may be presented by a rep-

[11] *Le Monde,* January 2, 1965, p. 5.

resentative), it made its recommendation, and the National Assembly then voted the question in the affirmative. Pierre Lagaillard's parliamentary immunity was lifted December 8, 1960, after his participation in the Algiers' insurrection of the first of that year. Marc Lauriol lost his immunity after his involvement in the army revolt of April 1961. Georges Bidault was extended similar treatment when the National Assembly, in July 1962, by a vote of 241 to 72, raised his immunity after ex-General Salan named him as his successor to the leadership of the terrorist OAS.[12]

The role of parliamentary committees is less now than what it was under the Fourth Republic. Permanent committees are restricted to six in each house. However, additional committees can be created at the discretion of the government; this is done occasionally, particularly when the government wishes a report to complement the report of the permanent committee charged with the responsibility. Efforts by deputies and senators have resulted in both houses in subdivision of permanent committees for the purpose of conducting more specialized inquiries. This arrangement sometimes bears resemblance to the committee structure under the Fourth Republic.

In the National Assembly elected in March 1967, members of the teaching profession and medicine formed the two largest categories (67 teachers, ranging from beginning grades to the university, and 48 members of the medical profession). Also in the body were 45 high civil servants, 34 lawyers, 34 representatives of agriculture, 32 workers, 32 lower civil servants and employees of the state, 27 businessmen, 25 engineers, 20 journalists, 20 commercial brokers and representatives of commercial interests, 18 industrialists, 11 members of the judicial profession who were other than lawyers and magistrates, 3 diplomats, 3 magistrates, and 3 artisans. Unlike the legislature elected in 1958, representation of the military was slight, there being in the Assembly only 4 military men. Ages represented in the Assembly ranged from twenty-six years (Alain Terrenoire, Loire, Gaullist) to eighty-five (Hippolyte Ducos, Haute-Garonne, Federation of the Left, who still is a youngster alongside of the Senate's Marius

---

[12] For details see *Le Monde,* July 7, 1962, p. 1.

Moutet, SFIO, who first was elected to the legislature in 1914). Of the deputies elected, 11 were women (6 Gaullist, 4 Communists, 1 Federation of the Left).[13]

In the legislature elected in June 1968, members of the *grands corps de l'état* (56) and the teaching profession (8 higher education, 24 secondary and technical education, 23 primary education) formed the two largest categories. The medical profession fell to third place in representation (38 doctors of medicine; but also in the Assembly are 15 pharmacists, 4 dentists, and 8 veterinarians). Other categories represented are 41 leaders of enterprise, 31 representatives of agriculture, 28 lawyers, 23 members of the liberal professions, 18 journalists, 12 ministerial officers, 11 businessmen, 11 workers, 11 engineers, 7 employees, 6 artisans, 5 military, 4 "retired," 1 national railway director, 1 employee of the national railways, and 8 women (5 Gaullist, 2 Communist, 1 Federation of the Left). Hippolyte Ducos still is the *doyen* of the Assembly.[14]

THE STATUS OF THE SENATE
UNDER THE FIFTH REPUBLIC

The Senate of the Third Republic had powers coequal with those enjoyed by the Chamber of Deputies. However, legislative chambers with coequal powers seldom are willing to be coequal, and each chamber strives for superiority over the other. Constant struggles over finance were commonplace between the Senate and the Chamber of Deputies, resulting finally in some compromises never adjudged fully satisfactory to both houses. Compromises also were worked out relative to the means of extracting and sustaining ministerial responsibility. During that regime, the Constitution allowed both chambers the right to withhold confidence from the government, a system which functioned frequently in unsatisfactory fashion.[15] The Third Republic's suc-

[13] All data in this paragraph on the 1967 Assembly are from *Le Monde,* March 14, 1967, p. 4.

[14] All data in this paragraph on the 1968 Assembly are from *Le Figaro,* July 2, 1968, p. 5.

[15] Constitutionally, the president of the Third Republic could dissolve the Chamber of Deputies with Senate consent. The Senate could

cessor, the Fourth Republic, solved the problem posed previously by the existence of the Senate by creating a second house, the Council of the Republic, endowed with little power. Whenever the Council acted as a brake on the National Assembly, that action only was momentary. It was what some members described realistically as a "Council of Reflection," its powers extending to examination of bills voted by the National Assembly, to requests that the Assembly give a second reading to those bills with which the Council disagreed, and to calling to the attention of a relatively powerless president of the republic acts of the National Assembly it believed unconstitutional.

Constitutionally, the "powers" of the Senate of the Fifth Republic almost are identical with those enjoyed by the National Assembly. It votes the laws in the same fashion in which they are voted by the Assembly. However, it may not censure the government and bring it down, and it may not be dissolved by the president of the republic. Should legislative disagreement arise between the Senate and the National Assembly, the prime minister may, if he wishes, employ methods to coax the Senate along by establishing a committee comprising an identical number of deputies and senators, asking it to reach an agreement acceptable to both houses.[16] Should both houses fail to approve the suggested compromise and continue to differ with each other, the prime minister may, if he wishes, request the National Assembly to decide the question. Therefore, although the Senate may consistently oppose the government and the National Assembly (which it has), its ability to continue as an obstructive force on legislation is limited sharply, and it is able to go only

---

not be dissolved. In 1877, when President MacMahon attempted to dissolve the Chamber, that effort was interpreted as a Bonapartist maneuver, and subsequently dissolution (as well as the presidency) fell into disuse. Cabinets then were left without a weapon to employ when in conflict with the chambers, and presidents became the servants of Parliament.

[16] *Le Monde,* January 13–14, 1963, p. 1. In January 1963, after reaching a compromise between both houses, Parliament gave its approval to the *Cour de sûreté de l'état,* which replaced the military court of justice and the military tribunal. This marked the first time in an important situation that a mixed committee of deputies and senators evolved a compromise.

so far before being put out of the game of the prime minister, should he resort to the device of asking the Assembly to rule definitively on the issue. Moreover, this relationship among government, National Assembly and Senate makes procedural conflict among them relatively insignificant. The government decides alone just what it is willing to "tolerate" from the Senate and how long it wishes to accommodate it; yet it should be noticed that whenever the political complexion of the government and Senate are similar (which they have not been), the government, if it wishes, is in an excellent position to see the Senate perform as "an instrument of prevention" in opposition to any National Assembly that may prove to be hostile to the government. During the first ten years of the Fifth Republic, the government was in a position to release the brake whenever the Senate sought to apply it to legislation. The one exception was constitutional reform, which requires that amendments must be voted by both chambers by identical motions. This is applicable, of course, only if the Constitution remains operative, and as long as the president of the republic does not take the path to constitutional reform "allowed" by Article 11.

The electoral law regulating the election of senators is calculated to throw the weight of representation into the small *communes,* rural areas, and less densely populated departments, so much so that at first some observers referred to the Senate as the "Chamber of Agriculture." [17] Most senatorial electors come from small *communes* comprising fewer than 1500 people each, ones that represent a little more than 30 percent of French society. Cities whose populations exceed 10,000 people each, and which comprise somewhat more than 40 percent of the total population contain little more than 20 percent of the senatorial electors. The law in heavily populated urban departments is proportional (allowing for representation of rural minorities),

[17] Senators must be at least thirty-five years of age, and meet, otherwise, requirements that are the same as those that apply to the National Assembly, including designation of an alternate. Election is for a nine-year term, and one third of the membership of the body is renewed every three years. Election is on the basis of the department, and each department is entitled to at least one senator, as well as any additional senators as justified by additional population.

whereas in lightly populated departments the majority system employed there underrepresents the cities. The first elections to the Senate of the Fifth Republic produced in it a large gathering of "old ornaments" of the Fourth Republic (eighty-five Independents among them). Receptive at first to the Gaullist regime, the Independent members soon went into opposition to it and the Senate acquired a reputation for hostility to the regime. The elections conducted in 1965 in thirty-one departments of the *métropole,* and in one department and two territories overseas, for the purpose of filling ninety of the 274 Senate seats, modified only slightly the political composition of that body. The returns showed a slight MRP and Gauche démocratique increase (the Gauche démocratique is a force comprising Radical Socialists of diverse tendencies: Valoisians, independent Radicals, RGR, UDSR), obtained generally at the expense of moderates and the UNR-UDT. Of the thirty-one departments, nineteen did not change political affiliation.[18]

After the election, representation in the Senate was as follows:

Table 8–1   Party representation following the September 1965 elections

Party	Seats
Communist	14
SFIO	52
Gauche démocratique	50
MRP and Democratic Center	38
UNR-UDT	30
Independents	64
Peasants	17
No party	9

The former president of the French Senate, Gaston de Monnerville, for some years engaged in a continuing battle with General de Gaulle, accusing him of lack of proper respect for the Constitution (which seems reasonable), creation in France of

[18] See *Le Monde,* September 28, 1965, pp. 1–6, for election returns.

concentration camps (which is absurd), and responsibility for the dismissal of civil servants and judges because of their protests against de Gaulle's violations of the Constitution.[19] Consequently, de Monnerville was "boycotted" by President de Gaulle and the ministers, a "boycott" which extended beyond de Monnerville to part of the Senate itself. In May 1965, the Council of Ministers prohibited the ministers from participating in the debates of the Senate, stating that they would be represented there instead by secretaries of state.[20] In 1963, when receiving some members of the Senate at the Élysée Palace, de Gaulle expressed the hope that the Senate will play its role "conforming to the Constitution"! That reception was marked by the absence of de Monnerville, Goguel (secretary-general of the Senate), and Communist and Socialist party senators.[21] Some senators acknowledged the irresponsibility of some of de Monnerville's charges, but they also regarded Élysée behavior as childish. In the meanwhile, rumors—originating undoubtedly in the Élysée Palace—alluded frequently to a possible constitutional amendment which would abolish the Senate or merge it with the Economic and Social Council.[22]

THE EXECUTIVE

The presidency under the Fifth Republic

The Third Republic's presidential office was divested of all real powers in 1877 when the republicans prevented the dictatorial President MacMahon from dissolving the Chamber of Deputies creating, thereby, a precedent for subsequent presidential inactivity. After the end of the Third Republic and subsequent to

[19] *Le Monde,* October 3, 1963, p. 1.

[20] *Le Monde,* May 8, 1965, p. 10.

[21] *Le Monde,* January 1, 1963, p. 10.

[22] The Economic and Social Council comprises more than 200 members who serve five-year terms and is staged by professional associations and the government. The Council serves in a technical capacity; its advice may be sought by the government (solicitations are becoming less frequent all the time), or it may offer it whenever it has definite suggestions relative to economic and social phenomena, particularly ones which relate to "the Plan."

the Liberation, the Fourth Republic sustained the devaluation of the presidency and attempted to concentrate decision making in the National Assembly.

Under the Fifth Republic, the most important powers of President de Gaulle derived from him and not from the Constitution. *Constitutionally,* the powers of the president are as follows. He appoints the prime minister and the other ministers on the proposal of the premier; he heads the armed forces; he appoints and receives ambassadors; he promulgates laws voted by Parliament and can request it to reconsider bills within two weeks of their having been passed; he presides over the Council of Ministers and high councils of the armed forces; he gives his signature to decrees; he appoints officers of the armed forces and high civil servants; he ratifies treaties, exercises the power of reprieve, and can send messages to the National Assembly. For all of the powers described previously, constitutionally the president needs the countersignature of the prime minister and such other ministers as may be involved (with the exception of sending messages to Parliament and appointing the prime minister). Other constitutional powers of the president are as follows: whenever a constitutional amendment is proposed by the government to Parliament, he may decide not to submit it to a referendum if Parliament gives the amendment its authorization (the method is to submit it to a joint meeting of both chambers of Parliament); he may dissolve the National Assembly but he is restricted only to one dissolution in twelve months; he may send on to the voters in the form of a referendum bills relating to the organization of public powers or ones concerned with treaties. He may invoke Article 16 and rule by decree whenever the institutions of the State are endangered. Finally, Article 5 charges him with responsibility for seeing that "the Constitution is respected" (a provision that President de Gaulle undoubtedly found relatively ambiguous).

At the disposal of the president of the republic is a large administrative office comprised of four distinct divisions. A military establishment consists of a commander of the guard of the presidential palace, a general in charge of *gendarmerie,* a military general staff, and military aides. A civil establishment consists of a personal cabinet, and a General Secretariat staffed with technical councillors and *chargés de mission* who are re-cruited both from inside and outside the civil service. The tasks of the civil cabinet are primarily political, while those of the general secretariat are primarily administrative. Finally, an over-seas division comprises the General Secretariat for Community and African Affairs (which was an area of special interest for President de Gaulle).

Electing the president of the Fifth Republic

The Fifth Republic has employed two methods of designating a president of the republic; the first was elective and indirect, restricted to approximately 80,000 voters, whereas the second is elective and based on direct universal suffrage. The electoral law that obtained between 1958 and 1962 prescribed the election of the president of the republic for a seven-year term by an elec-toral college comprising members of Parliament, departmental General Councils, Assemblies of the Overseas Territories, and elected representatives of the Municipal Councils (the number varying proportionately according to the populations of the *communes*).[23] In October 1962, the French people approved the election of the president of the republic (in a referendum passed by 61.75 percent of the votes cast), and since that time France has elected its president by direct universal suffrage.[24]

---

[23] The electoral law of 1958 designated the representatives of the Municipal Councils as follows: (1) the mayor for *communes* of fewer than 1000 inhabitants; (2) the mayor and deputy-mayor for *communes* of 1000 to 2000; (3) the mayor, first deputy-mayor and one municipal councillor selected according to the order of appearance on the council lists for *communes* of 2001 to 2500; (4) the mayor and first two deputy-mayors for *communes* of 2501 to 3000; (5) the mayor, the first two deputy-mayors and three municipal councillors selected according to the order of appearance on the council lists for *communes* of 3001 to 6000; (6) the mayor, the first two deputy mayors, and six municipal councillors selected to the order of appearance on council lists for *communes* of 6001 to 9000; (7) all the municipal councillors for *communes* of more than 9001; (8) Additional delegates in *communes* of more than 30,000 inhabitants at the rate of one delegate for every 1000 inhabitants ex-ceeding 30,000 elected by the municipal councillors by proportional rep-resentation based on the rule of the highest remainder.

[24] *Le Monde,* October 26, 1952, p. 8. Former Prime Minister Georges Pompidou states that direct election gives the president the

The Electoral College that met on December 21, 1958, elected General de Gaulle president of the republic by 79 percent of the votes cast by its 81,764 electors. An absolute majority was gained by de Gaulle on the first ballot, making a second ballot unnecessary. The Electoral College was similar to the one that elects the Senate, and in it the weight of authority was vested in electors who came from *communes* comprising fewer than 300 people each. The referendum of October, 1962, superseded the electoral law of 1958. Now the president is elected by direct universal suffrage by an absolute majority of the votes cast; if that majority is not obtained on the first ballot, the two leading candidates carry over and run off against each other on the second ballot. The election must be conducted between twenty to thirty-five days before the powers of the incumbent expire. Should the office fall vacant by death or other cause (such as impeachment), as verified by the Constitutional Council, the President of the Senate assumes the office temporarily (if he is unable, the government then exercises the functions), and a regular election must be held within the prescribed twenty to thirty-five days. During any period of presidential vacancy, the Constitutional Articles 49, 50, and 89 cannot be exercised. The procedure for establishing candidacy for the presidency is relatively simple. A candidate must be nominated by at least 100 citizens who are members of Parliament, of the Economic and Social Council, general councillors, or elected mayors. A candidacy cannot be established unless among the 100 sponsors

---

power and prestige necessary for him to exercise his functions and that the president cannot address himself satisfactorily to the "excesses of the political parties" unless he has the public's confidence; *Le Monde,* August 31, 1962, p. 1. De Gaulle decided that the president of the republic should be elected by universal suffrage in order to "assure the continuity of the State." The decision, revealed first to the Council of Ministers, was explained in his broadcast of September 20, 1962. Each minister was asked to bare his attitudes relative to the proposal and requested to resign if he objected to the method employed. The decision was contrary to the views of most of the political parties. Mollet described it as "inconceivable and inadmissible" and said, "I still can't believe my ears. What is the value henceforth of the constitutional guarantees?" The political commission of the UNR-UDT approved the decision, stating that it would "bring the people and the public authority closer together."

there are represented at least ten departments or overseas territories. No person can become a presidential candidate without first giving his consent. The Constitutional Council verifies the list of candidates eighteen days before the first ballot, and the list is published by the government fifteen days in advance of the first ballot. Finally, the law provides no reimbursement of campaign expenses for those candidates who fail to receive at least 5 percent of the votes cast.

The "style" of de Gaulle as president

Opponents of General de Gaulle occasionally referred to him as a "Maurrassian," or disciple of Charles Maurras, a long time critic of French democracy who was racist, anti-Semitic and fascist. The reference, of course, is erroneous, for de Gaulle is not racist or fascist.[25] Unlike Maurras, de Gaulle never rejected legal equality or held it to be incompatible with progress; nor, like Maurras, was he opposed to the republic, and it was largely through his efforts that the republic was restored in France after the Pétain period (during part of which the Marshal claimed strong popular support). In fact, in the first days after the Liberation, de Gaulle could have possibly established a dictatorship in France, and yet he spurned that opportunity. It is true that de Gaulle is opposed to traditional conceptions of French democracy, equating them with weakness and viewing them as being destructive of the republic, but unlike Maurras, he has never felt the destruction of French democracy to be a precondition of stability. His contempt for the sovereignty of the National Assembly is well known, and his disgust with political parties is legendary; and he believes that previous forms of French government have allowed private interests to corrupt public ones— but these convictions have not led him to denounce democracy

---

[25] As to whether he is anti-Semitic, his famous press conference of November 27, 1967, throws some light on this. See Ambassade de France, "Sixteenth Press Conference held by General de Gaulle as President of the Fifth Republic in Paris at the *Élysée* Palace on November 27, 1967," *Speeches and Press Conferences,* 276, 4, in which he referred to the Jews as having "remained what they had been down through the ages, that is, an elite people, sure of itself and dominating. . . ." Anti-Semitic, yes, but not Maurrassian.

as a form of anarchy, as did Maurras. If he successfully clipped the power of the National Assembly and reduced it to the status of an ineffective organ—subordinating it entirely to executive leadership reinforced by a separation of legal powers—he did not tamper with universal suffrage and he did respect the verdict of popular elections. Admittedly, he did show a deep preference for the referendum, and the questions posed by him there were selectively paradoxical, making it difficult for voters to register negative votes. However, he is not a Maurrassian, but a very crafty politician with noticeable Bonapartist tendencies who always tried to appear a democrat. And if there were times when he did not succeed too well, then his behavior was often described by opponents as scandalous. Like most any politician, de Gaulle did what ever he could to warp existing institutions to his own ends; seldom, however, did he bend them to the point of extinction.

Before and shortly after May 13, 1958, de Gaulle made all sorts of contradictory promises to numerous figures high in military echelons; consequently, he could have used the army to undo the republic and install in its stead a military dictatorship. He spurned that possibility and in subsequent years neutralized the army and reduced its importance in French political affairs.[26] He disbanded the Legion and transferred its

[26] During the Algerian war the army was both a military vehicle and pressure group, and its subsequent "depoliticization" and subordination to the civil authority was not an easy task. Between June and December 1958, the five trips made by de Gaulle to Algeria had a dual function—to isolate the army from the activists of Algérie française, and to restore it to civil jurisdiction. In June de Gaulle ended the activities of "committees of public safety" which comprised both military and civil figures. This was followed by replacement of General Salan by a high civil servant representing Paris in Algeria, and shortly afterwards by appointment of a minister in charge of military affairs and the transfer of national defense to the *domaine réservé* under President de Gaulle. The army then was reorganized and many of its activist elements distributed among isolated French posts around the globe. The taming of the army, particularly in a period of war, must qualify as one of de Gaulle's most remarkble feats (many of his rightist opponents contend that it represents instead an extraordinary example of treachery). For a good account of the French army, see *Une histoire politique de l'armée* Vol. I, 1919–1942, by Jacques Nobecourt, and Vol. II by Jean Planchais,

elements elsewhere. Some high-ranking officers were prosecuted for plots against the republic, and the man who came to the leadership of France with the support of the army came to know hatred and by some of its figures various assassination attempts upon his life. Instead of using the army to rule, de Gaulle restricted it to military phenomena and broke its political back. The devaluation of that army in French political life was largely the work of a man who is a military man and who never professed to be a strong democrat but who succeeded in doing what the Gaillards, Bourgès-Maunourys, and Mollets could never achieve. Gaillard was powerless before the army during the bleak, early days of 1958; his predecessor, Bourgès-Maunoury, went out of his way not to offend it; Bourgès-Maunoury's predecessor, Guy Mollet, suffered the indignity of seeing his Resident Minister to Algeria Robert Lacoste become the creature of some of the most antirepublican elements in the French army. Other considerations aside, men who are most critical of de Gaulle often are ones who wanted but were unable to do to the French army what de Gaulle succeeded in doing to it.

(Paris: Seuil, 1967). The French army has had a long history of association with reaction, Maurrassianism, monarchical preferences, and opposition to democracy. For years, however, it refused to intervene directly in politics, remaining obedient to various regimes but exhibiting sympathy for diverse antirepublican forces—particularly in 1934. In the African army after 1943 pro-Pétain elements remained strong. Generally, highly politicized militarists often waited for retirement before speaking out against the regime. Marshal Juin, for example, after his retirement spoke out against the Fourth Republic and later, after becoming disenchanted with de Gaulle, took issue with the Fifth. After their retirements, General de Castelnau founded the rightist Union nationale catholique, and Marshal Lyautey chaired meetings of the fascist Phalanges universitaires. During the second World War the army became particularly fond of Vichy. Finally, repeated involvements by the republic in colonial adventures and war reoriented the army from indirect to direct involvement in politics. See, for example, *Le Monde,* March 25–26, 1962, p. 1, for Marshal Juin's letter addressed to General Salan in praise of the OAS and his reference to "ideas and sentiments that we share." In the letter he cautioned against the use of violence in France lest it "discredit your generous movement and expose you to false accusations of fascism. Many of us admire your courageous efforts. God help you and protect you."

De Gaulle never acknowledged affiliation with the plots and revolution whose consequences carried him to power shortly after May 13, 1958. He conveys the impression that he then was above those events and that he merely responded to the call, being the only man who could prevent civil war and restore France to stability and order. He prefers to appear as the savior who stood to the side and watched events unfold, the one who years before had repeatedly warned his countrymen of the inevitability of the situation they were witnessing. Whatever de Gaulle's relationship to the events of May 13, the fact remains, however, that he was close to the scene once the military went into revolt and repudiated the premier and his cabinet. On May 15, he did respond to a call by the revolting militarists, not closing the door on a possible return to power, and again on May 28 he was in contact with the insurgents, at least to the extent of indicating his willingness to be invested as president of the Council of Ministers. He did much, undoubtedly, to channelize and orient the movement, with an eye to his eventual return to power. However, four years later in a speech on Algeria he referred to 1958 as a "plot of usurpation." [27] The picture had changed. Many of the "heroes" who had helped carry him to power in 1958 were by 1962 anti-Gaullists and "traitors" in a state of revolt against the regime. Many of these architects of 1958 failed to survive the republic they had been instrumental in creating, going subsequently into exile, dishonor, or prison.

What was "the case" for de Gaulle? Why did so many support him? First, as president of the republic he did implement successfully probably the most sweeping decolonization in modern history, making statehood possible for approximately twenty African communities. That was done without violence or bloodshed, in a transition that was entirely peaceful. Second, he succeeded in bringing an end to the Algerian war, giving statehood to Algeria and establishing subsequently with her cooperative ties. In doing so, he eliminated a grave problem that had brought down the Fourth Republic and which at times threatened

[27] French Embassy (Press and Information Division), *Major Addresses . . . de Gaulle,* p. 185. "When in 1958, we came to grips with the affair, we found—who has been able to forget it?—the powers of the Republic drowned in impotence, a plot of usurpation being formed in Algiers . . ."

to kill its successor, the Fifth. Third, he neutralized the French army, terminating its political power, subordinating it to civil authority, and eliminating its potential antirepublican threat. Fourth, he succeeded in shaping the peaceful integration in metropolitan France of approximately 800,000 settlers from Algeria, calming them politically and seeing to it that they did not open wide some grave political divisions in French society. Fifth, he promulgated a statute for conscientious objectors, and helped shape a general amnesty both for former supporters of Algérie française and its opponents. Sixth, he introduced a foreign policy which sought to modify and humanize differences between the United States and the USSR, arguing that the destiny of Europeans should be primarily in their own hands. He maintained a firm opposition to both American and Soviet hegemony over Europe, and he succeeded in opening a corridor to the East and creating better relationships with nations situated there.

There also was "a case" against de Gaulle. Some citizens advanced the following as reasons for voting against him. First, by emphasizing the "Europe of States," or confederation, he did irreparable damage to the idea of true European federation —and at a time when so many Europeans appeared to be most receptive to this type of organization.[28] Second, by demanding

[28] In 1962 the periodical *Communauté européenne* published results of an inquiry into public opinion relative to Europe. Four Institutes of Public Opinion participated in the effort. The results showed that opposition to European unification is slight, feeling being that it would better protect the peace, individual well-being, and values of civilization. Only 8 percent of French workers stated that they were opposed to the Common Market. In all, 72 percent of the French interrogated favored European unification. The results of this survey are published in *Le Monde,* December 15, 1962, p. 4. Later, in 1966, the French Institute of Public Opinion released the results of its survey of June, 1965, showing a large segment of the French as being in favor of the idea of European unification. To the question, "Do you think it possible to create a European community comprising men of different languages and cultures?" 78 percent replied *yes* and 8 percent *no.* Those under fifty years of age were more favorable than those over fifty. Partisans of a European federation (38 percent) outnumbered partisans of a "Europe of States" (30 percent). In each age and professional category federationists outnumbered defenders of national sovereignty. Results of this survey are reproduced in *Le Monde,* January 23–24, 1966, p. 5.

that France have an independent nuclear deterrent, he squandered huge sums and denied badly needed funds to various social services—particularly those of education, housing, social security and health. Third, he did not solve the agrarian crisis, and the plight of the farmer achieved only slight improvement during his reign. Fourth, he gave Algeria its independence, he refused to defend there the interests of approximately 8.5 million French settlers, and the promises he made to keep Algeria French subsequently were abandoned by him. Fifth, he betrayed the men who were instrumental in bringing him to power, using duplicity and all kinds of subtle moves to bring them to dishonor. Sixth, he devaluated the French army and disgraced the Legion, the cream of the French military. In doing so, he pushed out of the mainstream of French life what heretofore was one of its most important instrumentalities. Seventh, he specialized in the employment of political techniques that dismayed even some of his strongest supporters, even denying the opposition representation on radio and television. He considered himself above criticism. His flair for personal power allowed him to take lightly various constitutional considerations and restraints, and at times he operated from positions which were undeniably illegal. Eighth, he attributed to the political parties all kinds of sinister practices and objectives, and he refused to recognize that a republic and its practices depend upon the existence of these intrumentalities for its performance.[29] Ninth, in his support of corporatism, he damaged numerous small entrepreneurs and ruined many others.

---

[29] "La vie politique . . . ," pp. 37–38. This survey of the French Institute of Public Opinion shows 59 percent of these interrogated as believing that political parties are necessary for the proper functioning of a democratic regime; as Meynaud and Lancelot point out, the renovation of French political parties is, "in the eyes of the majority of observers . . . the most important point; it is a case of giving life to the network of parties and political movements. These formations suffer today from a detestable reputation, but they remain indispensable to the game of democracy." See Jean Meynaud and Alain Lancelot, *La participation des français à la politique* (Paris: Presses Universitaires, 1965), p. 119; see *Le Monde,* December 17, 1965, p. 1, and report on de Gaulle's television address in which he indicted the parties, charging them with "disorder," stating, "The parties cannot lead France, it is too hard, and it is why, moreover, after my return in 1945, when the parties had reappeared, all against me, understandably, I left, and they did no more, except to make twenty-three ministerial crises."

He was the enemy of the small operator. Tenth, he over-emphasized the importance of one-man leadership and in doing so he prepared the way for the abdication of personal responsibility by others and the subsequent introduction of possible chaos in French political life after he retired from the scene. He consistently gave the impression that only one man is qualified to exercise effective leadership and determine French destiny.

The cabinets of the Fifth Republic

Cabinet instability was a phenomenon of French parliamentary life during the sixty-five-year span covered by the Third Republic; its frequency, however, was greater during periods when the country was confronted with crises. Between 1876 and 1881, for example, the country had eight governments, whereas between 1899 and 1909, only five governments existed—and of these three lasted two and one-half years each. Between 1920 and the end of the Third Republic, the life of a government averaged six months. During the entire course of the Third Republic (1876–1940), 119 governments each averaged eight months in duration.

The Fourth Republic attempted to concentrate decision making in the National Assembly. Deputies regarded cabinets as meddlers who were dealt with best by constantly being kept off balance and outside the periphery of decision making. Cabinets pursued shifting majorities with diminishing success, their positions weakening as the years went on. As the problems accumulated, cabinets avoided the most important ones because they knew that they could do nothing about them. Consequently, many simply were passed along from successor to successor. Governmental paralysis set in, the situation bordered on anarchy, and the political environment then became especially fruitful for exercises of decision making by extraparliamentary forces. The army, untroubled by the existence of instrumentalities of restraint and off its leash, mastered the knack of making major policy decisions of its own. It made its most important one in May 1958, allowing that further existence of the Fourth Republic no longer was necessary.

In looking back on the Fourth Republic, one notices during its last years both cabinet instability and ministerial stability. Frequently the same personages acted as ministers in successive governments. Time and again well-established deputies experienced no difficulty in finding a spot in a good share of these. Both cabinet instability and ministerial stability became facts of French parliamentary life. The system induced hardened politicians to indulge in exercises of self-interest, picking off here and there a ministry whenever they could. Its operation also encouraged a considerable amount of continuity in policy determination—which took the form of the same old ornaments of the Fourth Republic deciding repeatedly in successive cabinets that little could be done by them in the realm of policy determination.

The Fifth Republic has greatly transformed the "cabinet game." Mendès-France likes to remind the regime that it has achieved since 1958 both governmental stability and ministerial instability (although not in the premiership; between 1958 and 1968 only Michel Debré, Georges Pompidou [three times], and Couve de Murville had served in the post). Mendès-France's contention is confirmed by the numerous ministerial shufflings that occurred after 1958. Between 1959 and 1965 France had seven ministers of education, seven of information, four of the interior, justice, PTT (post, telephone, telegraph), and three of agriculture, health, public works, industry, veterans affairs, and finance.

French cabinets generally comprise approximately twenty-five members. Within the cabinet is the prime minister, ministers who are heads of departments (the number of ministries generally is about fifteen),[30] ministers of state, and ministers delegate

[30] The Pompidou cabinet created April 15, 1962, comprised 29 members—the prime minister, five ministers of state, two ministers delegate, fourteen ministers, and seven secretaries of state. The ministers of state headed: cultural affairs; cooperation; overseas departments and territories; Algerian affairs; scientific research, atomic and space affairs. The ministers delegate headed: relations with parliament; regional planning. The ministers headed: justice; foreign affairs; interior; armed forces; finance and economic affairs; national education; public works and transportation; industry; agriculture; labor; public health; construction; war veterans and war victims; post office and telecommunications. Secretaries of state headed: information; civil service; foreign affairs; repatriation; foreign trade; domestic trade; public works. Ambassade de France (Service de presse et d'information), "The Composition of the Pompidou Cabinet," 136 (April 19, 1962), French Affairs, 1–2.

of the prime minister. Beneath these are secretaries of state (the Fifth Republic has not appointed under-secretaries of state). Secretaries of state oversee the activities of a section of a department (subordinate to the minister himself), and seek coordination among the departments. In the Fifth Republic membership in the cabinet has devolved more and more upon civil servants, approximately two thirds of all positions being staffed this way. The presence there of a large number of such people is due primarily to President de Gaulle and his technocratic convictions, as was his appointment to the premiership of Georges Pompidou, a former high civil servant himself.

When the cabinet meets with the president of the republic serving as its presiding officer, it is known as the Council of Ministers, and such meetings are attended only by the president of the republic, ministers and secretaries of state. When the cabinet meets without the president of the republic and with the prime minister as its presiding officer, the convocation is known as a Council of Cabinet and is attended by all members of the cabinet.

The prime minister is appointed by the president of the republic; he and his cabinet are responsible to the National Assembly. This means that he and his cabinet must retain the National Assembly's confidence in order to remain in existence. When by majority vote the National Assembly withholds confidence from him, he and his cabinet must then resign (the president of the republic can then dissolve the National Assembly and send the country to new elections—if he wishes—but not within the year immediately following general elections). Questions of confidence may originate not only with the National Assembly, however, but also with the prime minister, should he on program or policy seek to pledge the responsibility of his cabinet. Should he stake his cabinet's responsibility on a legislative text, that text —once it has received an affirmative vote—is considered passed. The prime minister may be censured by the National Assembly only if the action is preceded by a motion of censure signed by one tenth of the deputies filed by them at least forty-eight hours in advance. Between 1958 and 1968 only one government underwent censure. On October 5, 1962, by a vote of 280, thirty-nine more than the minimum number of votes required, the government of Georges Pompidou suffered defeat. However, President de Gaulle then dissolved the National Assembly and sent the country to national legislative elections; the newly elected Assembly contained a Gaullist majority and Georges Pompidou was then reinvested as prime minister.

According to the Constitution, "The Government shall determine and direct the policy of the nation," and the "Premier shall direct the operation of the Government." This, when de Gaulle was president, was one of the nation's leading jokes, for in his regime the cabinet determined only some lesser aspects of the policy of the nation. If the prime minister "directed" national policy, it always was under the continued supervision of the president of the republic. The prime minister had to achieve cohesion within the cabinet, however, although this to a very great extent was already secured by the relationship of its personnel to the president of the republic. He had to coordinate its various divisions and administrative departments. His role also was that of arbiter when confronted with conflicting demands for resources by department ministers. He appeared periodically in Parliament and participated there in discussions of importance, performing in that body more as a generalist than a technician (although Pompidou was more of a technician than a generalist). He carried messages periodically to the public on the national radio and television (this was made easy by manipulation by his own government of media of telecommunications; his opposition often was precluded from appearing there).

The prime minister is charged with implementation of laws and issuance of regulations and decrees that require his signature, and with the making of appointments to civil and military positions not made by the president of the republic. He is second in command in the nation, but was in de Gaulle's regime greatly inferior to the president of the republic (not because of the Constitution but because of the way in which the system operated). A prime minister of the Fourth Republic carried real importance, but de Gaulle's prime ministers of the Fifth were truly subordinate, or subexecutive. Finally, the prime minister need not be elected previously to the National Assembly. However, if he is elected to it, he must—because of the existing "separation of powers"—resign his legislative seat in order to accede to the post of prime minister.

The prime minister has the right to initiate legislation, although the voting of all laws is the sole prerogative of the National Assembly and Senate. Government bills are considered first in the Council of Ministers (presided over by the president of the republic) and require consultation with the Council of State, after which they are filed with the Secretariat of either the National Assembly or Senate (appropriations bills are sent only to the Secretariat of the National Assembly). The prime minister must take bills before Parliament, and "in the order set by the government," they have priority on the agenda of the assemblies. Therefore, he holds in his hands the ability to determine the sequence of future debates. And, moreover, when he demands it, he may compel the assembly before which the bill appears to vote but only one time on all or part of the text. When this method of voting is invoked (the Gaullist regime states that the "blocked vote" merely is for the purpose of "expediting" matters), this clears from his path any discussions or amendments that might otherwise be disadvantageous to him and his government. Consequently, only those amendments proposed by him or acceptable to his cabinet are passed. Once a government bill has been approved (or a parliamentary bill too), the prime minister must then forward it to the other assembly, and should the bill be rejected there, the prime minister may then call for the creation of a mixed committee consisting of an identical number of senators and deputies who then are charged with responsibility for drafting a text acceptable to both assemblies. If the mixed committee fails to achieve this feat, the prime minister then may request the National Assembly to rule once and for all on the text. If it rules in the affirmative, the text then becomes law.[31]

The prime minister may request members of Parliament to

[31] If, after a bill appears to have satisfied all requirements for becoming a law, the prime minister believes that the bill may be unconstitutional, he may, if he wishes, refer it to the Constitutional Council for a ruling on its constitutionality. He may secure also from the Economic and Social Council, if he wishes, opinions and studies that may result in bills or lead to implementation of texts. The Council, which is supposed to give its opinions on bills, programs and plans of an economic or social nature, may not give its opinions on appropriations bills.

sit in closed committee (members may do so on their own initiative providing that it is requested by one-tenth of the members of the assembly concerned). He may request special sessions of Parliament (as may the members of Parliament themselves, subject to approval by the president of the republic). Once a special session has been convened, cloture is enforced when the agenda has been completed or, at the latest, twelve days after the beginning of the convocation. Should the prime minister wish a further special session, he may request it prior to the end of the month following cloture.

Under the terms of the Constitution, the prime minister is identified as being responsible for national defense. The president of the republic is designated by the Constitution to head the armed forces and preside over national defense high councils and committees. He commands the armed forces. Between 1958 and 1962 the prime minister exercised some controls over general directives relating to national defense. At least that was Michel Debré's interpretation when he served in the post. After 1962, however, the prime minister was declared to be the guardian of coordination of defense policy, and the minister to the armed forces was entrusted with responsibility for planning and conducting military affairs. The prime minister is responsible for seeing that decisions are carried out. The organ in which defense policy is determined is the Council of Ministers; its presiding figure is the president of the republic, and under de Gaulle the policies adopted there were his.

The reorganization of 1962 was the result of innumerable quarrels between the services at the disposal of the prime minister and those which belong to the minister of the armies. Although Prime Minister Debré had acquired previously some authentic controls over national defense (for instance, his nomination of General Puget to replace General Olie in September 1961), the reorganization of 1962 eliminated them and allowed for even more direct control over national defense by the president of the republic and strengthening of the technical attributes of the minister of the armies.[32]

[32] See *Le Monde,* December 5, 1961, p. 1, for details of earlier Fifth Republic reorganizations of defense; see *Le Monde,* April 27, 1962, p. 3, and July 13, 1962, p. 1, for detailed description of changes in national defense.

The prime minister and his cabinet are aided by Article 34 of the Constitution which limits the legislative area and precludes the Parliament from exercising lawmaking in some domains. The means by which laws are implemented are determined exclusively by the cabinet. If Parliament votes the laws, it does so in the shadow of a cabinet which generally introduces them and which determines the means by which they will be effected. And during his presidential reign de Gaulle overshadowed both the cabinet and the Parliament.

The prime minister and his cabinet may employ Article 38 as a "little Article 16." Article 38 allows the Parliament to authorize the cabinet to undertake ordinances that fall normally within the jurisdiction of Parliament. Parliament, having been reduced to inconsequential status, can usually offer little resistance to such demands. When he was president of the republic, de Gaulle had little difficulty in getting powers for the cabinet and determining their content. For example, when on February 2, 1960, the Parliament voted the cabinet special powers for one year's duration, enabling it to deal with threats to the state, law and order, and "pacification and administration of Algeria," the ordinances, although "decided on" officially in the cabinet, really had their origin in the presidential office. In that crisis, the president decided, the cabinet demanded, and the Parliament gave—after the prime minister assured it that it would keep its budgetary, censure, and legislative powers, and that it would continue to "control the government"!

Decisions, however, fall to the cabinet for implementation, whether they originate within the presidential "reserved sector" or within the cabinet's own "second sector." When they originated with de Gaulle, they were executed promptly and seldom with any evidence of papa having been challenged by his children. As Viansson-Ponté states, "To criticize a decision is to lose one's usefulness and depart from the cabinet—like Soustelle or d'Estaing or the MRP ministers. Whatever the case and irrespective of the type of ministers, the cabinet approves." [33] When decisions originate within the cabinet's rule making, or decree making authority, they take immediate effect (a decree

[33] Pierre Viansson-Ponté, *Bilan de la Ve République: Les politiques* (Paris: Calmann-Lévy, 1967), p. 124.

deals with a regulation of a general nature or an appointment, which must be adopted by the entire government in the Council of Ministers and signed by the president of the republic, prime minister and any other ministers who may be involved). When they originate in the form of an ordinance, the effect also is immediate (an ordinance is the result of a delegation of parliamentary power to the cabinet authorizing it to legislate on specific matters; it must be approved by both the Parliament and the cabinet). If, however, the cabinet issues an ordinance in order to secure the eventual implementation of an "organic law" (a law not considered to be within the realm of ordinary legislation but in fulfillment of a constitutional article or articles), the organic law must be voted by Parliament within a specified time and be reviewed by the Constitutional Council for constitutionality (in the event of Senate disagreement with the National Assembly, the Assembly can then pass the proposed law by absolute majority, although any organic law that refers to the Senate must pass both houses by the same kind of majority).

Concentration of decision making in the hands of President de Gaulle had the effect of freeing Fifth Republic cabinet ministers from chores previously considered traditional by ministers of the Third and Fourth Republics. Ministers no longer needed to sally forth into the legislature in order to recruit and sustain support, as did ministers of earlier republics. Consequently, ministers were free to go more often to their government departments and serve more extensively in administrative supervision. Yet, if ministers enjoyed some freedoms not enjoyed by their predecessors, from time to time they had to identify also with decisions that did not originate with them but with President de Gaulle—on which they as ministers had to pass and for which they ultimately were responsible. "Getting at" the President of the Republic because of his decisions defied a direct path—getting at him through the ministers offered members of Parliament one of the few channels available to them for his criticism. Thus, ministers often had to bear criticism for decisions that were identified with them but which did not originate with them. Moreover ministers defended regularly and publicly presidential decisions that they did not necessarily endorse themselves, causing some deputies to remark that some men will say anything in order to remain government ministers.

Aiding the prime minister are certain government services; he deals with some directly, and with others indirectly by delegations of his power to ministers or secretaries of state. Ministers of state are in charge of the civil service, cultural affairs, overseas departments and territories, relations with Parliament, scientific research, and atomic and space affairs. A General Secretariat of the government, created in 1936, aids him in carrying out his duties, and is headed by a senior civil servant who always attends with him meetings of the Council of Ministers (that civil servant writes the proceedings of each of its meetings). The senior civil servant and his aides are responsible for restricted committees, committees, and working parties that are under the supervision of the prime minister. The secretariat's sections, which are administrative, legislative, economic, and financial, are fundamental to the prime minister's performance. The service performs also the function of verifying the legality of and carrying to the ministers the implementing texts for ministerial countersignatures and subsequent publication in the *Journal Officiel* (which is under the service's supervision).

A government minister has at least three kinds of administrative organs available to him: these are the ministerial cabinet, the inspectors general, and advisory bodies. The ministerial cabinet is staffed with technicians who are an important part of French administration. All are the product of specialized training, and they derive primarily from the civil service. Their job is to aid the minister and to help him obtain what he seeks. Therefore, their activities have much to do with arbitration and coordination within the administration. Outside of the administration, they must deal with all those organized interests which seek to bring pressure to bear upon the minister, and with those pressures that members of Parliament seek to inflict upon him. The inspectors general are civil servants who play a supervisory role relative to the activities of the administration, reporting to the minister and supplying him with needed information. Advisory bodies may aid the ministry on an overall basis, or deal only with a division or divisions within it.

The Debré and Pompidou cabinets: 1958–1968

During its first years—particularly between 1958 and 1962—the Debré government remained in power primarily because of the Algerian war and because the deputies were loath to bring it down and witness a possible replacement of the Gaullist regime by a military one. Prime Minister Debré rested his authority during this period on General de Gaulle, and the deputies went out of their way generally to avoid ministerial crises. During this same period, many people believed that the institutions of the Fifth Republic were tied solidly to its founder, and that the republic would vanish once the General disappeared. However, after 1962 a second era in French political life was introduced. President de Gaulle managed to subdue the army (if that is the word for it) and terminate the Algerian war, and in the elections of 1962 a Gaullist majority was introduced in the National Assembly. For the first time, there evolved what may be described as an era of "parliamentary Gaullism." The government still lacked a homogeneous and unified majority in the National Assembly, but it did rest its authority on a composite majority and it managed to achieve greater stability. In the meanwhile, those changes that had resulted in 1958 in executive omnipotence at the expense of legislative authority were joined by others, and executive authority was strengthened still further. Now that the war was over, the government was exposed to opposition by unions, parties of the Left and Right, and many of the forces that had been instrumental in bringing the Gaullist regime into being in 1958. The "internal depoliticization" that had been prevalent previously among the body politic began to disappear. Many of the men of the Fourth Republic climbed out of their political graves and public opinion again became relatively articulate.

Only three men held the premiership between 1958 and 1968. Michel Debré held it three years and three months, between 1959 and 1962. He assumed the post shortly after his fiftieth year. He had served previously as a senator (Indre-et-Loire), as a member of the Comité général de la Résistance, and in the Félix Gaillard cabinet (1957–1958). He had opposed the European Defense Community and denounced Euratom as a "plot against France." A chronic attacker of the Fourth Republic, he subsequently served as de Gaulle's constitutional adviser, playing an important role in the drafting of the Constitution of the Fifth Republic. Before becoming premier he was a partisan of Algérie française, and even after he became president of the Council of Ministers rumors continued to circulate about his close attachments to various of the men who had gone into revolt against de Gaulle and his regime. As prime minister, he was a rigid determiner of the parliamentary agenda and generally precluded oral questions from leading to debate.[34] During his first year in the premiership he developed the habit of referring to the opposition in the National Assembly as the "anti-France," treating the Assembly like a delinquent child and subjecting it to various indignities. This earned him the name of the "angry one" (a title given to him by the opposition deputies). An SFIO assistant secretary-general once described him as the "Fifth Republic's nastiest person," and even loyal Gaullists report having received from him memoranda challenging their competence. When Debré left the premiership in 1962 (his letter of resignation comprised approximately twenty-five pages), it was rumored that he had wanted President de Gaulle to dissolve the National Assembly and order the country to new legislative elections, and that de Gaulle declined his request.[35] Defeated for a National Assembly seat in the legislative elections of 1962, Debré then went temporarily into eclipse. Subsequently he returned to the National Assembly as a result of having won a seat from Réunion Island, and again became one of the leaders of the Gaullist majority. Later he became Premier Georges Pompidou's minister of finance and earned in that post the reputation for being a tireless worker. After the dissolution of the National Assembly in May 1968, he was named minister of foreign affairs in the new de Murville government created by de Gaulle—bringing to that post a militant and strutting anti-Americanism that offered a contrast to the easygoing style of his predecessor (Couve de Murville).

[34] Viansson-Ponté, *Les Gaullistes* . . . , p. 103. The author notes that Debré was heavy-handed and domineering, but curiously reticent before "forces who need to be commanded"—for example, the army.

[35] Bromberger, p. 9.

Georges Pompidou, premier between 1962 and 1968, is in his fifties. Pierre Viansson-Ponté describes him as one-third banker, one-third civil servant, and one-third pedagogue.[36] Pompidou states that his desire was to become a professor. Author of various studies (one is entitled *Britannicus,* another is of Taine and Malraux and is designed for secondary school instruction), he completed in 1963 an anthology of French poetry. Pompidou once served as director of the banking house of Rothschild Brothers (René Mayer occupied that position before going to the premiership) and as administrator for different important associations. His diploma is in *sciences po* and he also was in the Council of State. He was a member of the post-Liberation cabinet of the provisional government which preceded the creation of the Fourth Republic, and in the administration of the last cabinet of the Fourth Republic, the one created by de Gaulle for the purpose of abolishing that regime. He was named in 1959 by de Gaulle to a nine-year term in the Constitutional Council, and subsequently undertook for de Gaulle efforts to achieve a peaceful solution to the Algerian war. His reputation is that of a careful politician, articulating nothing that might serve to his disadvantage and remaining ever heedful of what the General thinks.[37] In fact, "discreet" is the word for Georges Pompidou, and seldom will he allow his opponents to catch him out in the open so as to allow them to get a clear shot at him. He is a man who always was careful about his affiliations. During World War II he was not a Pétainist or a collaborator; nor did he belong to the underground or the Free French. After the war he was an active participant in most of the important meetings of the RPF (Rally of the French People), although he never joined that organization. He participates today in many of the activities of the Gaullist Union of Democrats for the Fifth Republic, but there is no evidence that he holds a membership card in it. A nonjoiner who manages to be in on most things, he says, nonetheless—paradoxically, so it seems—"I am not made for active politics. They rather disgust me."

---

[36] Viansson-Ponté, *Le Gaullistes . . . ,* p. 167.

[37] See Institut français d'opinion publique, "La vie politique de novembre 1964 . . . ," p. 36. The institute asked electors if they would like Pompidou or Debré to play the most important role in French political life. Pompidou ran far ahead of Debré.

It is said that Georges Pompidou never wanted the presidency of the Council of Ministers; however, it also should be observed that he never appeared ready to surrender the position to another person. Never a party man, nor a minister or a member of the National Assembly (until his election to it in 1967), his was exactly the background that de Gaulle sought in a president of the Council of Ministers—a top-echelon technocrat with extensive ties in the high administration and its specialized committees who never had liaison with the traditional political forces and formations. Moreover, if Debré was as prime minister a "martyr of fidelity" to de Gaulle, Pompidou probably was even more of a one—his docility before the President was legendary.

The appointment in 1962 of Pompidou to the prime ministership constituted a precedent, being the first time in French Republican history that charge of a government was assumed by a man who was a civilian, nonparty, and a nonmember of any parliamentary assembly. Two military men had served previously in the premiership without having served in the legislature—de Gaulle in 1945 and 1958, and de Grimaudet de Rochebouet in 1877 (who was appointed by Marshal MacMahon but who resigned three weeks later). Pompidou's first government acquired a "parliamentary appearance" when he added to it eight more parliamentarians (in addition to the thirteen holdovers from the Debré government), but that resulted in no way in restoration of parliamentary prerogatives.[38]

---

[38] *Le Monde,* April 17, 1962, p. 1; See Viansson-Ponté, *Les Gaullistes.* . . . Aiding Pompidou when he came to the premiership, although not as members of the cabinet, were men such as Roger Frey, Olivier Guichard, Jacques Foccart, and Jacques Chaban-Delmas, men known for their loyalty and faithfulness to de Gaulle. Frey, former secretary-general of the Social Republicans and later of the UNR, was a close associate of Jacques Soustelle until their break in 1961. His background prior to his entrance into the RPF in the 1950s is somewhat obscure. Born in Noumea in 1913, he saw wartime service in the Pacific. He was a member of missions during the war to MacArthur, Mao-Tse-tung, and Chou-En-lai, and served also in the Italian, German, and French campaigns. He was a member of de Gaulle's group in London and later was in the administration of his cabinet in Paris. His early career in the RPF was uneventful, and in 1952 his real introduction into politics was brought about by Soustelle, being elected first to the National Assembly and subsequently to the post of councillor of the French Union. In 1958 he was one of the men

Pompidou's opposition in the National Assembly seldom missed an opportunity to remind him that in terms of the "powers" vested in him by the Constitution he was less than

who left Paris for Spain and Algiers, authoring messages of a clandestine nature during the weeks of the crisis. Along with Soustelle, he played a large role in the creation of the UNR, going subsequently to the ministerships of information and interior. His progress was retarded momentarily in 1960, certainly by Debré and probably by de Gaulle, and possibly for reasons which had to do with his relationship with Soustelle. As Minister of the Interior he was blamed for various acts of terrorism which plagued the regime but he survived his critics. Olivier Guichard entered the RPF in 1947 and in 1951 became chief of cabinet for General de Gaulle, serving him with an attachment that was not less than religious. In 1955 he became press *attaché* of the Commissariat of Atomic Engergy. Guichard was the contact man for de Gaulle with, it is said, knowledge of all existing plots on May 13. In 1958 he became assistant director-general of the cabinet of the President of the Council, the director being Georges Pompidou. He has never risen to a cabinet post and there is considerable speculation as to why he has been "passed over" but no definite explanation. Rumor has it that this offspring of a Pétainist family has gone as high as he can in the Gaullist regime. Jacques Foccart, it is said, is the former head of the Free France network. He is a specialist in secret service and, therefore, not too much of his life is public information. Member of the Resistance and of the RPF, a councillor of the French Union and in 1954 its secretary-general, in 1958 he went to de Gaulle's cabinet, and in 1959 to the general secretariat of the president of the republic. In 1960 he became for the Élysée secretary-general for African affairs. He has contacts at all levels with the police. It is said that he has never been photographed. Jacques Chaban-Delmas, one time Radical deputy and director of the RPF, served also as minister to Mendès-France, Mollet and Gaillard. He is a man who has had his feet in camps that are both traditional and Gaullist, parliamentary and nonparliamentary, being close to many former presidents of the Council of Ministers, as well as to de Gaulle. It is rumored that he collaborated with anti-Fourth Republic military plotters when he served as minister of information. The mayor of Bordeaux, he has close contacts there and considerable support. Sometimes he presents a double image, one which is Gaullist and one which is somewhat Left. When he combats Mollet, he probably is on good terms with the head of the SFIO federation of the Gironnde. He has great charm and appears to the public as *trés sportif,* being a former tennis champion of France. A member of the reserve, he also has ties in the military. He was the minister of defense who gave the "go ahead" to the French air corps to bomb the Tunisian station of Sakhiet in 1958. Soustelle always said that de Gaulle never had any love for Chaban-Delmas.

a "real premier." This was one of the favorite themes of François Mitterand and deputy Paul Coste-Floret. Coste-Floret attacked Pompidou and de Gaulle in April 1964, asking the National Assembly, "Who governs today? The government or the President of the Republic? In effect, is it necessary to ask the question? Ask the first person you meet in the street!" [39] He recalled to the Assembly the resignations of five MRP ministers in 1962, and he quoted the statement made in 1961 by the Secretary General of the MRP, "We are not consulted on affairs, neither in the 'Parliament' . . . nor in the Council of Ministers—which is inadmissible and contrary to Article 20 of the Constitution".[40] He continued, "We know that there is no more authority, even ministerial, which does not proceed from the Chief of State, even though in August 1958 a Constitutional Committee affirmed that the first minister governs, the President of the Republic arbitrates." [41] During the same debate Coste-Floret maintained that Pompidou's decree of January 14, 1964, giving the president of the republic power to reorganize national defense, including nuclear power, was rigorously unconstitutional, violating Article 34 of the Constitution.[42] Article 21, he said, clearly designates the premier as being in charge of national defense but—he argued—Pompidou allowed by his decree the president of the republic to be personally responsible for commitment of the *force de frappe*.[43] Coste-Floret and his supporters took the position that this power and other lost powers belong to the government which is responsible for them before the National Assembly.[44]

Pompidou's reply is described here, not because it focuses additional light on constitutional legitimacy, but because of his interpretation of the way in which government proceeded in the France of de Gaulle. He told the National Assembly that President de Gaulle was not wielding personal power, and that all decisions taken by the government were the result of long de-

[39] *Le Monde,* April 26–27, 1964, p. 2.
[40] *Le Monde,* April 26–27, 1964, p. 2.
[41] *Le Monde,* April 26–27, 1964, p. 2.
[42] *Le Monde,* April 26–27, 1964, p. 2.
[43] *Le Monde,* April 26–27, 1964, p. 2.
[44] *Le Monde,* April 26–27, 1964, p. 2.

liberations first between the President of the Republic and the premier, subsequently with the ministers who were properly involved, and, finally, with the entire government.[45] He described the power of President de Gaulle as being subject to "precise limits," stating that with the sole exception of Article 16 the president is incapable of acting without the agreement of the government:

> Without doubt there are other possible regimes: the American system . . . or the British system. But, neither one nor the other fits the France of today. We have chosen an intermediary system: the chief of state draws his authority from universal suffrage, but he cannot exercise his functions without a government that has the confidence of Parliament. This regime supposes, in order to function effectively, a large identity of views between the President of the Republic and the first minister, assuring the homogeneity of executive power and giving in the fullest sense the responsibility of the government before the Assembly. . . . This cohesion of government, and its leader and the President of the Republic, makes only a formality of the question of knowing if the chief of state can revoke the premier.[46]

However, two years later, on the television program *Face à Face,* Pompidou presented a more restricted interpretation of the premiership and an image of a presidentialism whose magnitude was greater than he had described in 1964. When asked, "Who is the real chief of government? Is it you or General de Gaulle?" Pompidou replied, "We are in a regime which is neither presidential nor parliamentary. The President of the Republic defines the general lines of policy, chooses a premier, names the ministers in order to apply this policy and answers to the Assembly which has the right to reverse them." [47] He continued, "The first minister, who is, between the President of the Republic and the Parliament, the constitutional intermediary, is forcefully in very close liaison with the majority . . . *it is the majority of the President of the Republic, since it is the*

[45] *Le Monde,* April 26–27, 1964, p. 2.
[46] *Le Monde,* April 26–27, 1964, p. 2.
[47] *Le Monde,* March 30, 1966, p. 6.

majority that upholds what he has defined and what has been approved by the people who elect him." [48]

From Pompidou to Couve de Murville, third prime minister of the Fifth Republic

After having served six years and three months as prime minister, and after participating with other Gaullists in the greatest victory won by any political party in the history of the republics, Georges Pompidou left the premiership in July 1968. President de Gaulle requested his resignation, Pompidou complied, and de Gaulle then expressed regrets at Pompidou's "decision" to leave the post. Nonetheless, he gave Pompidou assurances that "Wherever you will be, I would like you to know, dear friend, that I intend to maintain particularly close links with you. Finally, I hope that you may be ready to carry out any missions and to accede to any mandate which may one day be entrusted to you by the nation." One rumor had it that de Gaulle had pulled Pompidou out of the political mainstream for the purpose of grooming him as his successor. Another had it that General de Gaulle, like the Roman Emperor Thrasybulus, had trimmed the garden in order to prevent one growth from outdistancing all the others. And yet another had it that Pompidou simply had outlived his usefulness as prime minister—and that like his predecessor, Michel Debré, who hardly was the man to serve after the Agreements of Evian as one of the architects of peace with Algeria, Pompidou was not the man to serve as premier in what de Gaulle foresaw as a great new era of social and economic transition.

Maurice Couve de Murville, who was appointed prime minister by de Gaulle in July 1968, was born in Reims in 1907. His formal education includes a degree in literature, a diploma from the old École des sciences politiques (now the Institut d'études politiques), and a doctorate in law. Early in his career he served as an inspector of finance; during the second World War, after three years affiliation with Vichy, he abandoned the *métropole* and went to Algiers where he joined the French government in exile. He served after the war as director general of political affairs in the foreign ministry, ambassador to Rome,

[48] Italics added.

Cairo, Washington, and Bonn, and permanent delegate to NATO. He was Pompidou's foreign minister, and briefly his minister of finance. His bid in 1967 for a seat in the National Assembly in the Seventh *arrondissement* of Paris was defeated on the second ballot by a joint rightist-leftist surge (he had led on the first, but Left votes deployed on the second ballot to prevent as many Gaullists as possible from winning gave the seat to Rightist Frédéric-Dupont). Couve subsequently was successful in his second try for the National Assembly.

Couve de Murville is strictly a negotiator; as prime minister he faced a very difficult period in which negotiations will play a primary role. Among most of the French politicians, he is the one least likely to antagonize people. The French Institute of Public Opinion discovered in 1967 that Couve ran second only to Giscard d'Estaing as the one whom respondents picked to play the most important role in the majority.[49] And in another of the institute's surveys, the public ranked Couve behind only d'Estaing and Debré in popularity (Pompidou's name was excluded from the list given to respondents).[50] Finally, the institute found that Couve inspires among people little controversy and few opponents (respondents were submitted a list of seven politicians—d'Estaing, Mitterand, Mendès-France, Pompidou, Mollet, and Soustelle all ran behind Couve).[51]

In his general policy statement before the National Assembly, July 17, 1968, Couve de Murville defined the guidelines of his government. He told the Assembly that the losses and cost increases resulting from the crisis of May will take the nation perhaps eighteen months to redress, and that certain changes in "the Plan" now are inevitable. He warned against the perils of inflation, underemployment, and unemployment. He acknowledged the need for major transformations in France, "not to say revolutions," in order to "adjust France to the modern world, particularly in the areas of education (such as new relations be-

[49] Institut français d'opinion publique, "La vie politique de mai 1966 . . . ," *Sondages,* 1, 30.

[50] Institut français d'opinion publique, "Les élections législatives . . . ," *Sondages,* 20.

[51] Institut français d'opinion publique, "Les élections législatives . . . ," *Sondages,* 42–43.

tween students and professors, greater student participation), in political and administrative organization, in local government (further decentralization of central government power), and in the relations between management and labor." At the same time he warned that "no one can contest that a business should be managed and that this management belongs to those who are responsible," a warning to the workers that the regime foresees reform, not revolution. Finally, he referred to the radio-television (ORTF) service and the need for its reorganization and adoption of expanded and "objective information." [52]

CONCLUSION

Parliament reached the peak of its development under the Fourth Republic. The position of Parliament in the Fifth Republic is totally different. The cabinet does not derive its authority from it; its statutory powers are broad and frequently independent of Parliament. Parliament has been devalued by the regime; in certain areas it may not legislate at all. Consequently Parliament is one of the less significant institutions in French political life. It is truly a victim of May 13, 1958. However, the National Assembly does retain one important weapon—the power of censure. Its presence gives to the regime more of a "parliamentary" appearance.

The Senate's powers are coequal with those of the National Assembly; however, the Senate may not censure the government —nor may it be dissolved by the president of the republic. The law regulating the election of senators was designed to throw the weight of representation into the small *communes,* rural areas, and less densely populated departments. Consequently the first elections of the Fifth Republic produced in the Senate a large number of old ornaments of the Fourth Republic. Many of these men soon went into opposition to the Gaullist regime. For years President of the Senate Gaston de Monnerville engaged the President of the Republic in a running controversy, authoring

[52] Ambassade de France (Service de presse et d'information), "General Policy Statement by French Premier Maurice Couve de Murville before the French National Assembly on Wednesday, July 17, 1968," 1114 (July 17, 1968), 1–9.

arguments that sometimes were responsible and sometimes irresponsible. Rumors originating in the Élysée Palace suggested for years a pending constitutional revision that would abolish the Senate or merge it with the Economic and Social Council.

So much of the story of the Fifth Republic was the story of President de Gaulle. The most important of his "powers" derived primarily from him and not from the constitution. As pointed out above, opponents sometimes referred to him as a "Maurrassian," or a disciple of Charles Maurras, long-time critic of French democracy. De Gaulle opposed traditional conceptions of French democracy, but never did he feel the need, as did Maurras, for the destruction of democracy as a precondition of stability. The former President of the Republic was not a Maurrassian but a very crafty politician with noticeable Bonapartist tendencies who tried hard to pass himself off as a democrat. There was a case "for" de Gaulle, just as surely as there was a case against him, but the *bilan,* or balance sheet, is not easy to construct.

De Gaulle's republic greatly transformed the cabinet "game." The Constitution talked about the cabinet determining and directing national policy, and the prime minister as directing the operation of the government, but every man in the streets knew who really directed the French state. Prime ministers of the Fifth Republic truly were subordinate to President de Gaulle. As Viansson-Ponté says, ministers did not criticize de Gaulle's decisions, they simply approved them.

Michel Debré and Georges Pompidou, the Fifth Republic's first two prime ministers, were "martyrs of fidelity" to President de Gaulle. Couve de Murville, appointed prime minister in 1968, is strictly a negotiator. He also was a prime minister in the Gaullist tradition, faithfully following the dictates of the President of the Republic until de Gaulle's departure from the post in April 1969.

NINE
THE GENERAL AND THE GENERAL WILL
The policy-making process

PRESIDENT DE GAULLE AND POLICY MAKING

President de Gaulle—who was cast in the Rousseauean tradition—viewed himself as having a direct link with the populace.[1]
Intermediaries, particularly Parliament and the political parties,
were treated by him with contempt. They obscured his vision
and prevented him from seeing what the populace needed (what
it wanted is another thing—but then, he knew that segments of
it frequently want "everything"). He, as President of the Republic, was best equipped to identify it. Why should he not have
been able to exercise this function? He was not nominated by
a political party for the presidency, he did not have a political
party (although one claimed him), and his views were based on
something "higher" than party. So was his regime, which stood
for a refutation of party—in fact, its workability was true testimony to the "insignificance of party." De Gaulle presumed to
stand above party as a free being with his gaze concentrated
exclusively on the true national interest. He stood for the "real
France," the France on and beyond the France of partisan inter-

[1] Sirius, "En toute conscience," *Le Monde,* October 26, 1962, p. 1.
The author states that nothing, absolutely nothing, must come between
de Gaulle and the people—not even the constitutional rules.

361

ests and their selfish interaction. He knew that his power came from the people (did not the referendum of September 28, 1958, confer upon him an imperative mandate, and did it not entrust him with the "indivisible authority of the State?"). Did he ever refute the idea that his authority stemmed from the people, and did he ever fail to acknowledge its origins before proceeding to tell the people—in the name of that authority—anything that he wanted to tell them (moreover, they were expected to believe it)?

Although de Gaulle stated repeatedly that the Élysée Palace is "above" the political struggles, its position generally was other than that of an Olympus suspended over the earth below it. To listen to the Chief of State orate, one would have presumed that his detachment from things political was so great that he seldom descended to earth in order to lift a wing to defend himself politically. In November 1962 he did not hesitate to ask the populace to vote for certain deputies; in 1965 he demanded that the people choose between him and anarchy; in March 1967 he took to the television and radio to ask the people to vote for the Gaullist formation. During the crisis of May 1968 he went to the people to warn them repeatedly of an "impending Red totalitarianism." Whenever the competition was intensified, the Chief of State did not hesitate to descend into the political arena in order to scratch away at his opponents.

In his address given at the Place de la République on September 4, 1958, de Gaulle explained that he, as president of the republic, was "accountable in the case of extreme danger, for the independence, the honor and integrity of France and for the safety of the Republic." Emergency powers described in Article 16 of the Constitution allow the president of the republic to take the necessary measures to deal with threats to the republic, its institutions, and territorial integrity "whenever the regular functioning of the constitutional public authorities has been interrupted," after he has consulted with the prime minister, the presidents of the National Assembly and Senate, and the Constitutional Council. President de Gaulle told the Consultative Constitutional Committee on August 14, 1958, that "The exercise of these powers is tied to a situation entirely abnormal, characterized essentially by the inability of the public powers to function properly." Later, on August 27, 1958, Michel Debré informed the Council of State that Article 16 is an "exceptional responsibility of the head of state in a tragic period." Malfunctioning of the public powers (and presumably existence of a "tragic period") allow the president of the republic to invoke Article 16.[2] Implemented for the first time during the Army revolt of April 1961, Article 16 was not revoked until September 30 of the same year (its duration originally was thought to be twelve days; de Gaulle had informed the nation initially that it would be enforced until the conclusion of the Algerian war).[3]

In his Place de la République address, General de Gaulle explained the president's role as that of a "national arbiter—far removed from political bickering, elected by the citizens who hold a public mandate, charged with the task of insuring the normal functioning of the institutions, possessing the right to resort to the judgment of the sovereign people. . . ," a description, however, that hardly conforms to the role played by

[2] When in effect, Article 16 allows the minister of the interior and the prefects to create zones of "special protection," interning those involved in or encouraging subversion; they may also prohibit mobility and political meetings and make night arrests. Article 30 of the Penal Code, which requires normally that a person stand judicial inquiry forty-eight hours after detention, is modified when Article 16 is in effect, and a person may be held fifteen days before transfer to a judicial court. Invocation of Article 16 allows for requisition by the state, whenever necessary, of persons and property, in conformity with the laws of July 6, 1877, and January 7, 1959. The president of the republic may not use Article 16 to dissolve or suspend Parliament (although there is nothing that can prevent him from first dissolving Parliament, ostensibly for the purpose of holding new elections and then invoking it)—nor can he use it to amend the Constitution (so it is believed).

[3] Invocation of Article 16 led on April 27, 1961, to creation of the High Military Court (Haut tribunal militaire), and later, on May 3, 1961, to establishment of the Military Court (Tribunal militaire). The High Court was abolished May 27, 1961, after delivering its decision in the case of the renegade ex-General Raoul Salan. On June 1, 1961, a Military Court of Justice (Cour militaire de justice) with no right of appeal, and consisting only of general officers and lesser militarists was created. On October 19, 1962, however, after the trial of André Canal, the Council of State annulled the ordinance which had created the military court; among the reasons for the decision was denial by the court of recourse to appeal.

President de Gaulle in the Fifth Republic. In fact, his presumed prerogatives in decision making and his determination to be more than an arbiter, were revealed in 1959 in his letter to Michel Debré, first prime minister of the Fifth Republic, defining for the latter the limits of cabinet action. The idea of the president as an impartial arbiter was not consistently applied by de Gaulle, and the area reserved by him for presidential action existed from the first. "Dialogue, cooperation, and equilibrium" between executive and legislative organs never really came off; "The greater his impatience with the representative features of the system, the more de Gaulle became convinced that his role was that of guide." [4] Later, de Gaulle went even farther, describing himself as the "man of the nation" and "the source" of all power!

Policy making frequently originated with the executive in de Gaulle's republic. The primary decision-making force within the executive in areas of importance was President de Gaulle; decision making in areas of lesser importance was exercised by the cabinet. The Constitution, although it defines the President as more of an arbiter than decision maker, did not preclude de Gaulle from exercising decision making in areas denied the president of the republic by it. The Constitution charges the prime minister with directing the action of the government, and the government with determining and conducting national policy, but everybody knew that President de Gaulle determined and conducted the main lines of national policy. De Gaulle decided, and only infrequently did the ministers disapprove. De Gaulle's excursions into areas in which the cabinet is supposed to be competent made a mockery of the cabinet's decision-making pretensions. It should be understood, however, that de Gaulle's influence over decision making originated with his stature and nature, and not with the Constitution. The strength of the office's occupant, and not the strength of the office itself, allowed for such exercises of power.

At times the influence of de Gaulle over decision making was so great that he was virtually the government itself. He arbitrated periodically between cabinet and Parliament, as re-

[4] Henry W. Ehrmann, "Direct Democracy in France," *American Political Science Review* Vol. 57, No. 4 (December 1963), 891.

quired by the Constitution, but more often he intervened in behalf of the cabinet in order to support various of its "decisions" that originated previously with him. His behavior relegated the cabinet to a position that frequently was but advisory and ratificatory. It was part of the executive, but only in a very subordinate way. De Gaulle's decision making was not restricted to the areas described in 1959 by Chaban-Delmas, president of the National Assembly: "The Presidential sector covers Algeria . . . the Community, foreign affairs and defense. The second sector covers the rest. . . ." De Gaulle's inclination was to ride high in certain presidential sectors, but he did not hesitate to intervene in the "second sector" whenever he thought it profitable and desirable. When he "delegated" decision making, it was with the understanding that it had not been given away and that it was capable of being revoked. During the meetings of the Council of Ministers, the President of the Republic always was on hand to rule on any differences that arose among the ministers; seldom was he out of position. When his arbitration did not suffice, he was available to them as a guide; and if that did not serve its purpose (that is, if he risked not getting the "right decision"), he was there to exercise his own determination. Arbitration, guidance and personal determination all were not separate but overlapping functions; if one did not work, perhaps another would—sometimes one was intensified, and the others deintensified. All three, however, were part of but one approach, and seldom were they allowed to fall into disuse. Hanging over this entire performance was a conception of government that began and ended with General de Gaulle.

Because of de Gaulle's conception of and performance in government, the cabinet could not be described as a consistent decision-making authority in his republic. The president, stated de Gaulle, should be separate from the prime minister, "being the only one to hold and to delegate the authority of the State," not being absorbed in matters that are political, economic and administrative, tasks for which the prime minister is best suited. Nonetheless, de Gaulle argued also that watertight compartments do not separate those levels at which the functions of president and prime minister are exercised—"the councils and meetings exist to permit the Head of State to define step by step the orientation of national policy and to permit the members of the Cabinet, starting with the Premier, to make known their viewpoints, and to specify their action and to give an account of their acts." De Gaulle then explained that "Sometimes the two levels merge," when "it is a matter of a subject whose importance involves everything and, in this case, the President distributes the responsibilities as he deems necessary." He concluded that "the individual authority of the State is entrusted completely to the President by the people who elected him, that there is no other authority—either ministerial, civilian, military or judicial—which is not entrusted and maintained by him." Therefore, de Gaulle believed it his duty to adjust his office with the offices he entrusted to others, and to exercise— as a result of a power of interpretation and judgment conferred upon him by the Constitution—constant contact with the prime minister.[5] De Gaulle was careful to argue, however, that in "ordinary times" the functions and field of action of the president and prime minister are to be kept separate. If the presidency and premiership were vested in one man and one office, the incumbent, in the event of parliamentary opposition, would be precluded from appealing to the populace; in turn, Parliament would be powerless to overthrow him, resulting in "chronic opposition between the two untouchable powers." That, stated de Gaulle, would lead either to pronunciamentos or conversion of the president into a docile and powerless follower of the legislature. This argument was a slap at those who champion an authentic presidential system; he stated that they simply do not know what they are doing, and that such constitutional innovations would lead France only to "political disaster."[6]

Cabinets in de Gaulle's republic were staffed exclusively on the basis of loyalty to him, and rotations in their personnel were primarily if not exclusively at his discretion. In 1960 certain of Finance Minister Antoine Pinay's policy positions collided with those of President de Gaulle, and as a result Pinay left the cabinet. Soustelle, Debré's first minister of information,

---

[5] *Le Monde,* September 27, 1961, p. 16. See for Mollet's criticisms, particularly that the President's responsibility is not to interpret the Constitution but to apply it.

[6] See French Embassy, *Major Addresses . . . de Gaulle,* pp. 246– 249, for all of de Gaulle's views reproduced in this paragraph.

favored policies that proved to be repugnant to de Gaulle's, and he left the cabinet too. In May 1962, five MRP ministers resigned from the cabinet immediately after a press conference given by President de Gaulle in which he closed the door on European integration. The ministers were Pflimlin, Schuman, Buron, Bacon, and Fontanet. Their resignations, which came after Simmonet, Dorey, Colin, and Lecanuet of the MRP reacted to what they considered as insults by de Gaulle to their defense of European integration, constituted the first collective resignations under the Gaullist Republic.[7]

Although certain ministries and "big appointments" were considered to be more closely under the tutelage of President de Gaulle (such as foreign affairs, national defense, interior, finance, cultural affairs), strong loyalty was demanded by de Gaulle of those who occupied lesser ministries and appointments. The ministers were the president's ministers (including the prime minister). If, occasionally, an exception "appeared" to occur, it did not represent any reduction whatsoever in the influence of de Gaulle over the cabinet. In August, 1961, the "unconditional Gaullist" Edmond Michelet was dismissed from the Ministry of Justice by Prime Minister Michel Debré. Both Debré and Michelet entertained different conceptions of the Algerian conflict. Michelet had been associated with a "soft" outlook relative to how he thought the conflict could be terminated, and Debré is reported as having said, "I do not want an FLN minister of justice." [8] Michelet then was assigned by de Gaulle elsewhere in the government (there is every reason to

---

[7] See Le Monde, May 17, 1962, p. 1, for report on MRP press conference; Le Monde, May 18, 1962, p. 1, states that the departure of the ministers indicated that they had refused to accept the idea of unconditional agreement simply by virtue of membership in the government. Le Monde states that de Gaulle had given the Ministers the choice of "renouncing their portfolios or their Europe."; Coste-Floret, however, states that the cause of the resignations was that the ministers had not been informed on de Gaulle's foreign policy decisions or the manner in which they were to be formulated. His statements appear in Le Monde, May 17, 1962, p. 1.

[8] Merry Bromberger, "Le destin secret de Georges Pompidou," Le Monde, July 17, 1965, p. 9. Bromberger reports that Debré said, "Je ne puis pas admettre d'avoir un garde des sceaux FLN. Ce sera lui ou moi!"

believe that his views on the Algerian solution were closer to de Gaulle's than to Debré's).

Seldom did de Gaulle show faith in the cabinet's ability to engage in decision making when crises were in progress. The Algerian settler mutiny of January 1960 had been in progress only five days when the President intervened in order to restore peace. During the insurrection's first days, the cabinet seemed unable to do anything in the way of terminating it— and when it received "emergency powers," they came as a consequence of de Gaulle having "commanded them."

Cabinet meetings—as a consequence of de Gaulle's great influence over decision making—occurred now less frequently than under previous regimes. Cabinet ministers also were restricted from serving simultaneously as members of Parliament (a constitutional provision that contributed to the disentangling of ministers and parties, thereby allowing for greater gravitation by ministers around the president of the republic). Finally, de Gaulle's influence over the cabinet's decision making was furthered by his appointment to it of technicians, rather than professional politicians, who would have served in the state bureaucracy in other regimes (this also extended his control over top-level bureaucrats).

EXAMPLES OF POLICY MAKING

Policy making relative to the French Community and the Algerian conflict originated solely with de Gaulle himself. That also was the case with policies created by de Gaulle in pursuance of Article 16. In France's dealings with NATO de Gaulle was the exclusive formulator of policy. There are other areas of policy making, however, in which de Gaulle did not play a dominant role and in which policy making was participated in by other persons and groups. Nuclear power, for example, had its origin under the Fourth Republic, becoming at de Gaulle's insistence a reality of the Fifth. Subsidization by the state of private schools offers an example of involvement in the policy-making process by executive, legislative, and administrative organs of government, as well as by various interest groups. Consideration of some aspects of the Fourth Plan involved the participation of groups other than those exclusively of the regime. Various case studies—particularly those conducted by Harrison, Andrews, Macridis, Brown, and Sweetman—are helpful in assessing so difficult an area as policy making.

De Gaulle and the French Community

In 1960, when the African territories of France pushed for sovereign independence, de Gaulle told them that they could achieve it and still remain within the French Community. De Gaulle was not restrained by the fact that relations between France and the Community were then regulated by Article 86 of the Constitution which did not provide for simultaneous independence and membership in the Community. It was only later that Article 86 was amended so as to allow members of the Community to be sovereign while belonging to it. And when the machinery of the Community became obsolete, de Gaulle went ahead unilaterally and terminated the existence of certain of its organs. In the case of the Senate of the Community, he informed Prime Minister Debré of its dissolution.

De Gaulle and Algeria

In his efforts to solve the Algerian war, de Gaulle determined policy unilaterally and succeeded in keeping it beyond the grasp of forces outside of himself. While holding these forces off, de Gaulle managed, nevertheless, to make use of them. His speech in Constantine in 1958 was a bid for the support both of the French settlers and the Algerian Moslems. His statement that the results of the 1958 referendum "mutually and forever pledge" France and Algeria together was designed for settler ears. His promises for modernization of Algeria, distribution of thousands of acres of land to Moslem farmers, access by Moslems to government positions, new educational opportunities for Moslems, and construction of new ports, roads and housing obviously was a bid for Moslem support.[9] He simultaneously bid for the support of those who wished Algeria to be integrated in the metropolitan framework, the same figures who had been instrumental in bringing him to power in 1958.

[9] See *Le Monde,* October 4, 1958, p. 1, for reproduction of speech.

Maurice Duverger reported in 1958 in *Le Monde,* for example, that some people interpreted the discourse of Constantine as "having commenced the application of integration", and that some people viewed the General's views as being those of Jacques Soustelle.[10] Soustelle announced publicly that the Plan of Constantine was what "I had recommended . . . since 1955, in a proposition that was formerly called the Soustelle Plan." [11] The Committee of Public Safety of Algeria and the Sahara (dissolved shortly thereafter) viewed the speech of Constantine as "the equivalent of complete integration." [12] And Algérie française Marshal Juin stated publicly that he had only the greatest confidence in de Gaulle's desire to implement integration.[13] While tucking policy determination securely beyond the reach of those who had brought him to power, de Gaulle also succeeded for a time in convincing them that their desires were his. It was only later, by a step-by-step process, that he disentangled himself from Algérie française elements around him and in the army. He was ready by September 1959. During that month he announced publicly his famous proclamation inviting the possibility of future self-determination by Algerians. Some revolts followed, a civil one in Algiers, and an uprising by the French military in Algeria, but after many trying months negotiations were realized with the rebel FLN, or the National Front of Liberation. Algerian independence finally was secured in 1962.

During the whole of the Algerian conflict the Left political parties were unable to get their hands on Algerian policy. They did, however, support de Gaulle's policy (but not his domestic policy). De Gaulle was well aware that that support restrained the Left parties from exerting efforts to overthrow the Gaullist Debré government. Between 1959 and 1962 those parties frequently backed away from a conflict with Debré lest they weaken him and interfere with de Gaulle's efforts to get a solution to the conflict.

[10] Maurice Duverger, "Le feu rouge," *Le Monde,* November 28, 1958, p. 1.

[11] *Le Monde,* November 21, 1958, p. 6.

[12] *The New York Times,* January 11, 1959, p. 16.

[13] *Le Monde,* November 15, 1958, p. 2.

During the Algerian conflict de Gaulle succeeded also in keeping the public a safe distance from policy. He exposed them to numerous of his departmental visits, imploring the populace repeatedly to have confidence in him. Periodically he presented the public with referenda containing tidbits that satisfied its multiple appetites. He also told it that the alternative to him was "chaos."

During the Algerian conflict the Parliament was unable to get close to the policy process. It did debate and vote Debré's statement on Algerian policy but that was as far as it was able to go. The cabinet was kept away from Algerian policy too, despite earlier attempts by some of its elements to reshape de Gaulle's policy. They soon were removed, including Soustelle who had spoken out in disagreement with the policy. De Gaulle solicited counsel from the cabinet but there is no evidence that he made use of it. His creation of a Committee for Algerian Affairs pushed the cabinet even farther out of the picture. In fact, de Gaulle's pronouncements on Algeria sometimes came to cabinet attention simultaneously with their public announcement. Algerian policy was from the beginning and until its end strictly a one-man show.

De Gaulle and Article 16

Martin Harrison's study of the one exercise by President de Gaulle of Article 16 shows that the public was well-prepared for it, the Élysée palace having leaked in advance reports of its pending invocation.[14] The decision to employ Article 16 was made by de Gaulle on April 23, 1961, after the commencement of the French military insurrection in Algeria. The President resorted first to constitutionally recommended consultative procedures before informing the public of his action. Earlier, however, de Gaulle had dealt with the 1960 settler's revolt in Algiers by receiving from Parliament power to legislate by ordinance under Article 38 of the Constitution. In 1961, however, de Gaulle invoked Article 16 so as to free his decisions from having

---

[14] Martin Harrison, "The French Experience of Exceptional Powers: 1961," *The Journal of Politics,* 25 (February 1963), 139–158. The author expresses his indebtedness to Mr. Harrison.

to go through the cabinet.[15] Article 38 states that "The Government may, in order to carry out its program, ask Parliament to authorize it to issue ordinances, for a limited period, concerning matters which are normally in the domain of the laws." [16] Article 38, a "little" Article 16, was not "big" enough for this crisis. During the whole time Article 16 was in effect—from April 24 to September 30, 1961—de Gaulle undertook eighteen decisions in its behalf. Although the revolt in Algeria was put down in four days, de Gaulle continued for months afterwards to hold tightly to Article 16. In fact, only three decisions were taken in pursuance of Article 16 after June 15. Those decisions that were taken generally banned certain groups and publications and initiated action against some military and police personnel. Disloyal elements were removed from the army and the police. Some critics charged that some of the actions taken were designed also to reduce surplus personnel and provide more flexible retirement privileges—considerations that have little to do with an emergency and threats to the state. Attempts by the Parliament to induce the Debré government to define the duration of Article 16 proved fruitless.

Peasant demonstrations opened some months after the invocation of Article 16. Some peasant groups demanded a special session of Parliament. When Parliament finally convened de Gaulle informed it that its session could not have a "legislative outcome." In other words, Parliament was told that it could meet—that it could aid the government and the President, but that it could not legislate. Debate was allowed but Parliament was forced to pull up short of lawmaking. The President of the National Assembly informed Parliament that relationships between the Assembly and the government—when Article 16 is in effect—differ from times when it is not in effect.

Termination of Article 16 was followed by yet another nine months of state emergency powers. As Harrison says, "The propriety of exercising these powers after Article 16 had been withdrawn is questionable. Almost certainly it was not strictly necessary since Parliament could have been asked to pass legislation in the normal manner. The precedent may one day serve

---

[15] Harrison, "The French Experience . . . ," pp. 139–158.
[16] Harrison, "The French Experience . . . ," pp. 139–158.

to justify extending even wider powers for even longer after the formal ending of the emergency."[17] On the night that de Gaulle invoked Article 16, although he asked, *Français, aidez-moi,* his pronounced hostility to intermediary bodies precluded realization of that possibility.[18]

De Gaulle and NATO

William G. Andrew's study of French policy toward NATO shows de Gaulle's control of that policy and how all decisions relative to the organization were made by de Gaulle himself.[19] Some of his decisions never were publicized to the cabinet; nor was the cabinet asked by de Gaulle to consider and make decisions relative to NATO. NATO was the object of discussions in the National Assembly and in the Foreign Policy Committee, although de Gaulle never submitted a NATO question to them. Attempts by Parliament to consider NATO questions were unsuccessful, resulting in three abortive censure motions. The National Assembly's "European Manifesto," which supported European integration and rejected Gaullist policy on it, and which requested European and American equality in the North Atlantic Treaty Organization, was signed by 293 deputies; it resulted only in the Assembly's dissolution and subsequent election of a new National Assembly more sympathetic to Gaullist policy. When de Gaulle decided finally in favor of French withdrawal from NATO, the decision was his alone. Without prior consultation with the cabinet or the Defense Council, de Gaulle informed the American, British, German, and Italian leaders of France's determination not to participate any longer within the organization. Personal letters to these leaders preceded by hours the report of his action to the cabinet (which then approved the action unanimously). The decision was transmitted to the National Assembly without debate, although later, on April 13, 14, and 19, there it was the object of discussion and of an unsuccessful censure motion. Subsequently the Senate Committee

---

[17] Harrison, "The French Experience . . . ," pp. 139–158.

[18] Harrison, "The French Experience . . . ," pp. 139–158.

[19] William G. Andrews, "De Gaulle and NATO," in Roy C. Macridis, ed. *Modern European Governments: Cases in Comparative Policy Making* (Englewood Cliffs, N.J.: Prentice-Hall, 1968), pp. 92–115. The author wishes to express his indebtedness to Mr. Andrews.

on Foreign Affairs, Defense and the Armed Forces expressed its reservations about de Gaulle's decision. However, as Andrews notes, Parliament was "involved" in the decision only after it was made; and when it finally gave its endorsement it did so only "passively and by implication." [20] The political parties, with the exception of the Gaullists, Communists, and Unified Socialist party, generally opposed de Gaulle's policy. On the other hand, public opinion appears to have favored it. Andrews concludes that "NATO policy in the Fifth Republic has been de Gaulle's policy . . . he has conceived it . . . decided it and implemented it in a highly personal manner. He has done so, however, with the acquiescence of the other major political institutions." [21]

France and nuclear policy

Roy Macridis' study of the French *force de frappe* shows very clearly that policy decisions leading eventually to its adoption preceded by some years de Gaulle's return to power.[22] Implementation of policy fell, however, eventually to the Fifth Republic. His study is in part an examination of commitments made by the Fourth Republic which subsequently were included in the policy of the Fifth Republic. Macridis determines how the policies were formulated and implemented, the extent to which the elites and the public were brought into decision making, and the roles played by the executive and Parliament. He notes under the Fourth Republic that prevalence of cabinet instability and lack of cohesiveness among its parties did not preclude the governments from producing a disarmament policy and various agreements that led subsequently to production by the Fifth Republic of the atomic bomb. Macridis states that the elites and public opinion both favored under the Fourth Republic disarmament and nuclear production. During that regime a small group of decision makers supported atomic power without

---

[20] Andrews, pp. 92–115.

[21] Andrews, pp. 92–115.

[22] Roy C. Macridis, "The French Force de Frappe," in Roy C. Macridis, ed. *Modern European Governments,* pp. 68–91. The author expresses his indebtedness to Mr. Macridis; see also the excellent study by Lawrence Scheinman, *Atomic Energy Policy in France under the Fourth Republic* (Princeton, N.J.: Princeton University Press, 1965).

interruption and without attracting too much attention to their activities. Ostensibly, they did so for its peaceful use. Some military men, scientists, ministers, and members of Parliament quietly concentrated on the executive agencies and Parliament in order to secure appropriations. Costs were kept down and never under the Fourth Republic was the issue made into a political one. Parliament had four separate opportunities to look carefully at the issue but failed to extend it serious consideration. Communist party efforts in the National Assembly to push for the adoption of an amendment restricting atomic power to non-military use were fruitless. As Macridis says, twelve years of decisions preceded the actual decision to make the bomb, and during that time France had seventeen premiers, nineteen different ministers of defense, and more than 200 cabinet ministers. Parliamentary majorities ranging from Left to Right supported nuclear legislation, as did cabinets—the basis of support being scientific rather than military. When, finally, it became clear that disarmament was doomed and that France was entering yet another era in world diplomacy, it was easy to make the transformation from peacetime to military nuclear power objectives. In 1956 and 1957 French officials began to state that atomic power was to have military as well as peacetime application. After 1958, when de Gaulle became leader of the nation, atomic power for military purposes then became established policy. It then became a political issue. Before the advent of the Fifth Republic, when it was dealt with quietly and in another form during the regime of the Fourth, it was not an issue. The atomic program today devides the elites and threatens to become a truly divisive force in the nation.

The Fifth Republic and the *loi Debré*

Bernard Brown's study of *loi Debré*—which provides state subsidies for private schools—shows participation in the policy process by government, Parliament, civil service, and special-interest groups.[23] Before the law was enacted, various interest groups had access to those in charge of the policy process. The

[23] Bernard E. Brown, "The Decision To Subsidize Private Schools," in James B. Christoph (ed.), *Cases in Comparative Politics* (Boston: Little, Brown, 1965), pp. 131–153. The author expresses his indebtedness to Mr. Brown.

secular Ligue française de l'enseignement and the Catholic-school-oriented Secretariat d'étude pour la liberté de l'enseignement et la défense de la culture, the two most important organizations involved in the game, both had extensive ties with political parties and other groups. The Ligue had access to civil servants in the Ministry of Education who were of secular orientation and to Left parties similarly predisposed. The Secretariat had access to the Parliamentary Association for Liberty of Education, or APLE, which works in defense of private education and whose council comprises parliamentary deputies and senators. The results of the 1958 elections and the heavy Gaullist victory swelled APLE's membership to 380 deputies and 160 senators. The government—sympathetic to state subsidies but mindful of public opinion—assigned a select committee to the issue. APLE, in the meanwhile, managed to get a motion before the Parliament. However, that soon was withdrawn. After the committee completed its report, some of its controversial provisions led APLE to an attempt to shape a compromise between the government and private school representatives. The controversy then moved to the cabinet level where de Gaulle attempted to goad the cabinet on to policy formulation. Finally, another compromise friendly to private school interests was evolved in the form of a government bill. That bill was submitted to the National Assembly. However, the Secretariat and its numerous deputies still were not satisfied. Members of the parliamentary majority met again with de Gaulle and the bill was altered. The Secretariat remained dissatisfied with the bill's version, as was the minister of education, who offered his resignation. Assembly debate of the bill was concluded in one day, and then the bill passed the Assembly and the Senate.

As Brown points out, organized groups played in the game less of a role than they had played in 1951 when the question of state subsidies to private schools resulted in earlier legislation on the subject. In the case of the *loi Debré,* the government was sympathetic to state subsidies for private schools (as well as state controls), as was de Gaulle, who exerted his influence to secure support from the parliamentary majority. Brown shows that both the Ligue and Secretariat sought the support of public opinion, of the executive power, and of deputies sympathetic to their cause. The Secretariat, bolstered by the new regime and the inclusion in it of a great number of deputies friendly to its cause, enjoyed at the parliamentary and cabinet levels greater success than its rivals. If the Secretariat failed to secure all that it sought, it obtained, nonetheless, many concessions. The secular Ligue received far less than what it had pressed for, and it vowed that it would continue to seek changes in the law.

Policy making and the Fourth Plan

L. T. Sweetman shows in his study that the Fourth Plan (1960–1964) was from the first "thoroughly discussed." [24] He also notes that the prior plans were formulated in "what amounts to a vacuum accessible only to the bureaucrat and his brainy cousin the technocrat." [25] The First and Third Plans never were submitted to Parliament. Sweetman quotes Quermonne who noticed prior to the Fourth Plan that the regime was not "interested in observing the niceties of consulting interested parties, indeed the nation as a whole, when proposing internal administrative reforms." [26] However, the Fourth Plan was different from its predecessors; regional divergences and consequent regional imbalance compelled it to make use of regional factors. Its creators avoided local control over the regional plans, but in approaching the problem of regional development they did encourage local interests. Dialogue did take place between organs of state administration and regional level interests, with various suggestions being offered.

Examples of direct policy making by de Gaulle are numerous. His approach to the French Community, Algeria, and Article 16 illustrates that very clearly. Yet it would be preposterous to believe that all policy making originated with de Gaulle; whatever the desires of the former President of the Republic, it would have been impossible for one man to handle so large an area entirely on his own. Government, Parliament, and the civil service also played roles in policy formulation.

[24] L. T. Sweetman, "Prefects and Planning: France's New Regionalism," *Public Administration* (London) 43 (Spring 1965), 15–30. The author expresses his indebtedness to Mr. Sweetman.

[25] Sweetman, "Prefects and Planning . . . ," 15–30.

[26] Sweetman, "Prefects and Planning . . . ," 15–30.

Brown's study of the *loi Debré* illustrates, for example, their activity and some aspects of their influence. In the France of de Gaulle the President of the Republic carved out for himself certain important areas of policy making, and in these his wishes were paramount. In lesser areas the cabinet, Parliament, and civil service acted as policy determiners. Finally, the pressures generated by interest groups on the policy process are not to be discounted. Although the Gaullist regime claims that its strong executive is the best barrier against interest group pressures, Brown notes that the administration's "hard line" on this matter has not precluded it from yielding to diverse demands in areas such as wages, agriculture, pensions, taxes, or drugs. At the same time, Brown also notes early successes by the Fifth Republic in withstanding the demands of alcohol lobbies, an area in which the Fourth Republic was particularly vulnerable.[27] It appears that interest group influence on the policy process has not been reduced drastically by the strong executive of the Fifth Republic.

THE BUREAUCRACY AND POLICY MAKING

The precursor of the French civil service was an ill-defined group of individuals who assisted pre-Revolutionary monarchs in the practice of state services. In the sixteenth century this group was replaced by *commissaires* who were appointed by the monarch and who were responsible to him (and replaced by him whenever necessary). From this arrangement there emerged a hierarchical administration headed by ministers. Later, in the nineteenth century, a code of rules was adopted, regulating civil servants and recognizing the profession as a special service entitled to certain rights. Nonetheless, as late as the Third Republic the merit principle was implemented only within the ministries and bureaus, and lacking was a general statute defining rights and obligations of civil servants, as well as a commission to supervise the service. The service still was an example of favoritism and diverse standards. Attempts at reform initiated

[27] Bernard E. Brown, "Pressure Politics in the Fifth Republic," *The Journal of Politics,* 25 (August 1963), 509–525.

from within the service requested adoption of uniform standards and a general statute applicable in the same way to all of its members. Those efforts met with opposition in the Chamber of Deputies. After the Liberation some reforms were implemented by the Provisional Government of General de Gaulle. A new office called the Direction of the Public Service supervised the service and reorganized it. Civil servants were divided into two general classes and four categories.[28] Codes were introduced prescribing rights, privileges, and wage scales related to existing realities. A charter of the civil service finally was introduced by the law of October 19, 1946, granting to civil servants the right to form unions (and recognizing the right of unions to plead before all jurisdictions), the right to further training and accessibility to higher categories in the service, and the right to appeal against administrative regulations and individual decisions relating to personnel that might affect "the collective interest of civil servants." Also created was a Superior Council of the Civil Service (headed by the premier or his delegate and consisting of twenty-four members appointed by decree in the Council of Ministers, twelve of these on recommendation of the civil service unions), which performed advisory functions and which influenced considerably decisions that led to the creation of

---

[28] A distinction was made among those engaged in policy making (civil administrators), those carrying out policies (secretaries of administration), and those performing lesser functions (administrative assistants and clerical aides). Civil administrators are recruited through the National School of Administration (ENA). This class is distributed among five ranks. Advancement is through merit and convenience, and not by seniority. Only 10 percent of this category may come from other than the National School. The secretaries of administration are selected from among graduates of secondary schools by competitive examinations. This class is distributed among four ranks. Promotion is by merit, but within each rank seniority determines one's position. Those gaining access to this rank without qualifying by competitive examinations are limited to 10 percent of the rank itself. Civil administrators aid in the overall governmental policy, drafting directives and legislative proposals, and acting as coordinators of the public services. Executive secretaries are technicians distributed among the different agencies for the purpose of carrying out specialized functions. See Jerzy S. Langrod, "General Problems of the French Civil Service," in Raphaeli Nimrod, *Readings in Comparative Public Administration* (Boston: Allyn & Bacon, 1967), pp. 106–118.

committees concerned with improvement of promotions, ratings, efficiency, recruitment, and standards for determining minimum wages for civil servants. Most of the rights enjoyed by civil servants today were bequeathed to them by the Fourth Republic.[29]

What qualities should a civil servant bring to the service? Most literature dealing with this question consists of assertive essays in which are set forth qualities that go to make the "perfect human." Take, for example, the textbook used in the course on rules of conduct of the civil servant given to students in the Institut études d'outre-mer.[30] The civil servant should have a national feeling, not something that simply is a synonym for patriotism or nationalism, but a consciousness of national unity, a sense of preeminence of the nation. He should have a sense of progress, and an awareness of evolutionary possibilities. His should be a general and continuing culture. His professional qualities should be honesty, regard for others, modesty, willingness to carry through and finish his tasks, courage, prudence, altruism, and a sense of work in common, or an *esprit de corps.*

---

[29] Rights and responsibiliites of civil servants generally are as follows. For those of his official acts which result in litigation, the civil servant is not responsible, these being the responsibility of the state; those of his acts that are personal and exercised outside of or beyond his official duty are his responsibility, not the state's. His right to strike is assured by law (if other than a policeman or public prosecutor), subject, however, to the somewhat ambiguous provision that said act is not of political significance, that it will not affect other public services, and that it will not terminate continuation of essential services. He may participate in politics, subject to the restriction that he may not publicize his membership in the service, nor utilize in politics such information as he may acquire as a consequence of his state position. He is free to hold any political or religious belief, but is expected to be loyal to the state. He may assume elected office, subject to the restriction that he do so after taking leave from the service. While in the service he is precluded almost in all cases from accepting other paying positions. He has tenure and in this is secure; his position may be taken from him only as a result of disciplinary action, after hearings are properly conducted and opportunity is given for appeal, or if his position has become obsolete, in which case the state is obligated to place him elsewhere in the service or provide him with compensation for his losses.

[30] See Robert Catherine, *Le fonctionnaire français* (Paris: Editions Albin Michel, 1961).

He should have a technical and specialized knowledge related to the particular tasks with which he is entrusted. He should be able to anticipate, organize, command, coordinate, and control. He should demonstrate qualities of leadership, particularly a sense of being, prestige, character, competence, will, and energy. Finally, he should demonstrate certain attitudes—namely, a great reserve, confidence, ability to explain and persuade, and to hold to his decisions. He should be forceful but objective, and show an ability to "bounce back" from temporary setbacks.

The French civil service is a hierarchical structure which comprises approximately a million and a half employees, topped by an elite corps which represents less than 1 percent of the entire body and which helps to originate and implement policy. This elite is known as the *grands corps de l'état*. It is recruited on the basis of competitive examinations, its members having been educated previously in schools such as the École nationale d'administration, the École polytechnique, the Instituts d'études politiques, and the law faculties of the universities. Its members tend to be of bourgeois origin and orientation. The École nationale d'administration was created by the Fourth Republic for the purpose of providing further training for qualified members of the service with five years previous experience. It gives a three-year course, pay is provided by the state, and the program of instruction consists of four branches—juridical and administrative subjects, social subjects, economics and finance, and international relations. The candidate is introduced also to practical administration by subsidiary work in statistics, business management, accounting, organization and methods, and two modern languages. In all, the school is considered to have somewhat of a limited field of concentration, as well as a rigid structure, and generally there is agreement that it is in need of modernization.[31]

The member of the *grands corps* generally states his belief in the general interest and his responsibility to contribute to its furtherance. That is to be achieved by means that are other than political; therefore, it is understandable if the member of the *grands corps* exhibits at least externally some contempt for the

[31] François Gazier, "L'École nationale d'administration: Apparences et réalités," *International Review of Administrative Sciences,* Vol. 31, No. 1 (1965), 31–34.

politician whom he regards as a symbol of partisan interests and an exponent of ideology. At the same time, it would be absurd to regard all members of the *grands corps* as enemies of all partisan interests and pursuers of the good society through its rational organization. Half of the directors of the central administration do collaborate in one way or another with a minister, and more than 30 percent come from a ministerial cabinet.[32] There are diverse partisanships among members of the *grands corps*—however, they are diverse, and thus far no one brand has been able to dominate the service completely. Instead, the tradition is for different factions to dominate different parts, and consequently certain ministries and agencies are known for the preferences they show toward certain interests. Finally, ministers who are both strong and superbly informed are hard to come by. Ministers must lean on members of the *grands corps* for advice, and these technocrats often have at their disposal means which enable them to disguise their political acts.

Bernard Gournay suggests that members of the *grands corps* do subscribe to a common ideology. He states that in contributing to a certain form of the state, members of the *grands corps* resist those forces which threaten to modify its structure, and that whenever proposals are made for creation of certain political structures, such as provincial political assemblies, they are likely to see their prerogatives endangered. Their "common doctrine," states Gournay, consists of maintaining the authority of the state. And maintaining that authority involves preserving its existing form. Although modern in orientation, members of the *grands corps* tend to be reactionary in their organizational preferences, states Gournay, and their defense of a conservative structure often is tantamount to setting the brake against change.[33]

Members of the *grands corps* lack that magnitude of common cohesiveness that would qualify them as a separate category in themselves. They exhibit certain divisive qualities, as has been stated previously, as a consequence of internal com-

---

[32] Bernard Gournay, "Un groupe dirigeant de la société: Les grands fonctionnaires," *Revue française de science politique*, Vol. 14, No. 2 (April 1964), 221.

[33] Gournay, "Un groupe dirigeant . . . ," 242.

petition, intracorps rivalry, the existence of diverse age categories, and different political affiliations of administrators. Different divisions of the administration have different objectives, and those policies evolved by governments usually are the result of compromise among their diverse demands.

During the nineteenth century and after the beginning of the twentieth, members of the *grands corps* for a time were recruited primarily from high elements in society, such as the Parisian and provincial aristocracies and upper bourgeoisie in business and the liberal professions. Recruiting since then has undergone transformation, and now elements of the middle class and lower middle class have increased in that body. Nonetheless, sons of workers and peasants remain difficult to find in it, and any "democratization" affected in this area has played primarily to the advantage of the middle class.

Persistent in French society is the belief that former students of the National School of Administration, or the ENA, go on to constitute in French administration an elite that is both homogeneous and influential. Existing studies show, however, that their "power" generally is less than what it is supposed to be, and that despite factors that make for internal cohesiveness, there are among them some substantial differences. Jean-François Kesler describes them as having "a limited but not negligible influence." [34] He finds among them existence of a common point of view—that is to say, a modern style, a planning perspective, a pragmatic mentality, and a group consciousness. Seldom are they reactionary. Infrequently they are political party militants; rather they are sympathizers. Usually, they are more party-oriented when they arrive at the school, rather than after they have been in it for some time. After a time their preference is for the political clubs rather than the political parties. Products of the modern state, their concern with traditional ideology is not great.[35] Those who come to the ENA from the Institutes of Political Science bring with them a training that is empirical and

[34] Jean-François Kesler, "Les anciens élèves de l'École nationale d'administration," *Revue française de science politique,* Vol. 14 (April 1964), 245.

[35] Kesler, "Les anciens . . . ," 246. Kesler says that Keynesian theory serves as their guide in economics.

pragmatic, having spent little time with juridical theories and more with the actual performances of political regimes. Most of those who manage to make it to the *grands corps* after graduating from the ENA came originally to the latter as former students of political science (in excess of 80 percent), whereas those who come to the ENA as civil servants and who subsequently go on to the *grands corps* constitute less than 15 percent of that elite.[36] Those admitted to the ENA from the civil service tend to be less bourgeois in origin than those admitted from the Institutes of Political Science and other schools; between 1951 and 1962, there were among them, however, only 4.8 percent who were sons of workers (in contradistinction to the students, among whom only 0.9 percent were sons of workers).[37] Civil servant recruitees generally are older than student recruitees. Student recruitees gravitate primarily toward the political parties and political clubs after graduation, whereas civil service recruitees tend to go in the direction of the unions.[38]

Few of France's prefects are graduates of the ENA, but two of every three underprefects of economic affairs and regional programs come from it. Therefore, it is understandable if graduates of the ENA have perhaps their greatest influence in the financial and economic domains. Approximately 25 to 35 percent of the graduates of the ENA are found among the personnels of ministerial cabinets.[39]

Former students of the ENA come from other than diverse social origins. Approximately 70 percent come from the middle class, being the children of parents who work at higher levels (higher than foremen) in industry, commerce, the liberal professions, the civil service, and farming. Since 1945 approximately 30 percent have come from "popular" social categories, being the children of artisans, shopkeepers, lower civil servants, employees, and industrial and agricultural workers (although only 2.5 percent of the candidates admitted to the school between 1952 and 1961 were sons of workers).[40]

[36] Kesler, "Les anciens . . . ," 248.
[37] Kesler, "Les anciens . . . ," 251.
[38] Kesler, "Les anciens . . . ," 258.
[39] Kesler, "Les anciens . . . ," 263.
[40] Kesler, "Les anciens . . . ," 261.

CONCLUSION

President de Gaulle prided himself on having a direct link with the populace. Intermediaries got "in his way," interfering with his communicating with the people in unobstructed fashion and preventing him from seeing what they "really" needed. President de Gaulle pretended to be above all internal political struggles, and yet he did not hesitate to intervene in them whenever the competition became intensified. Although he described himself in 1958 as a "national arbiter" far removed from "political bickering," that idea was never consistently applied by him. Subsequently he referred to himself as a "guide." Later, he modified that position too, and described himself as the "man of the nation" and the "source" of all power!

Policy making originated frequently with the executive in de Gaulle's Republic. President de Gaulle was the primary decision-making force within the executive. In areas of lesser importance, decision making was exercised by the cabinet. Because of de Gaulle's conception of government, the cabinet could not be regarded as a consistent decision-making authority.

De Gaulle's approach to the French Community, Algeria and Article 16 (when it was in effect) provided numerous examples of unilateral policy making. It would be out of the question, however, for all policy making to have come from de Gaulle, although often it was tempting to believe that it did. Studies by various authors show the government, Parliament, the civil service, and interest groups playing roles in policy formulation.

The influence on policy by the *grands corps* is considerable. That body, recruited almost exclusively from other than worker and peasant social categories, exhibits an orientation that reflects its social origins.

TEN
A ROMAN LAW COUNTRY
**French courts
and judges**

In May 1962 in its Congress in Dijon the National Chamber of
Solicitors (Chambre nationale des avoués) revealed the results
of its inquiry into popular impressions of the French legal system. "What do you think of when I pronounce the word *justice?*"
was one of the many questions asked of slightly more than a
thousand people drawn from 167 *communes* and all walks of life.
Only 171 credited it with exercising a useful role; 271 gave replies such as "injustice," "too expensive," "not very just," "too
complicated," "too slow," "badly functioning," or "something you
buy." Four hundred and seven persons recognized its necessity
but remain critical of its expense, slowness, and complexity; some
viewed it as "disgusting" and "revolting." The inquiry showed
clearly the tendency of people to refer to a court only as a last
resort. Slightly more than one in every four stated that they
knew nothing about French law; 31 percent equated justice with
"the police." Few of the respondents wished to steer their children in the direction of the legal profession, giving as their reasons the profession's bad reputation, its corrupting influence on
honesty, and the like. In all, the results of the inquiry were less
than encouraging.[1]

[1] All data in this paragraph are reproduced from Jean-Marc Théolleyre, "Une justice dans sa nation," *Le Monde,* May 11, 1965, pp. 1, 14.

The judiciary is confronted presently with multiple problems. First, demands upon it never have been greater than they are today, a condition due primarily to the great population increase, the growing concentration of people in urban areas, the development of business, and the difficulty of judiciary recruitment (there is a growing conviction that the judiciary is losing prestige). Second, the judiciary's independence is modified by the fact that its advancement is at the mercy of the political power (the Conseil supérieur de la magistrature now plays a quasi-consultative role).[2] It remains the "third power," but that expression is employed now with some reservations. "However equal to the legislative and executive powers it may appear to be, and assured of a total independence because of a separation of powers, this theory is seductive and symmetrically elegant—but *dépassé*."[3] Third, more and more is there the tendency to accept the idea that "A bad arrangement is better than a good trial."[4] Different enterprises, particularly large ones, are utilizing arbitration increasingly in order to avoid the hazards and delays of judicial procedure.[5] Anyone doubting these complaints had an opportunity to observe them when the Congress of Magistrates met in Reims in May 1967.

Because of the large size of the French judiciary, sometimes it is presumed (erroneously) that France has a sufficient number of judges. In fact, the number of magistrates has decreased by 30 percent in fifty years—and during the same time the

[2] The executive's discretion over advancement is great. Advancement depends upon a *commission du tableau d'avancement* comprising two magistrates, the first president and the procureur général of the Court of Cassation, and the directors of the Ministry of Justice. There are six others, three from the Court of Cassation and three magistrates from the courts and *tribunaux,* named by the minister of justice for three-year terms on a list established by the bureau of the Court of Cassation which includes twice the number of names for the appointments available. See also Denis Perier-Daville, "Le congrès de Reims a montré leur inquiétude," *Le Figaro,* May 29, 1967, p. 7. The author states, "But today the judicial power is no more than a dissertation theme . . . advancement is entirely in the hands of the political power and the *conseil supérieur de la magistrature* has been reduced to a quasi-consultative role."

[3] Théolleyre, "Une justice . . . ," May 14, 1965, p. 10. This is the second part of the article.

[4] Perier-Daville, "Le congrès . . . ," p. 7.

[5] Perier-Daville, "Le congrès . . . ," p. 7.

French population has increased many times. Moreover, the National Center of Judicial Studies (Centre national d'études judiciaires), which was created by the reforms of 1958 for the purpose of assuring future magistrates modern training and development of their personalities, independence, and impartiality, since 1958 has seen the number of its candidates decline. The CNEJ had 255 candidates in 1959, whereas by 1964, only five years later, the number of candidates had been reduced to ninety-eight.[6]

French justice is dispensed by judges on the basis of reference to codes which date primarily from 1804 to 1810 and which are revised periodically by parliamentary statutes. Civil, criminal, penal, commercial, and procedural codes are written in as precise a fashion as possible, and detailed in many articles. Theoretically it should be possible for any literate citizen to secure and understand the codes without difficulty, providing that they are simple, brief, and not too numerous. However, the accumulation of codes over a period of many years has made the exercise of that function exceedingly difficult, and professional guidance in interpreting the codes is almost always necessary.

French judges are civil servants who have qualified for their posts by passing competitive examinations, and who must be at least twenty-three years of age, have received a legal degree, and have had at least two years prior experience in certain aspects of the law. Judicial vacancies are declared by the Ministry of the Interior, and newly admitted members usually are assigned to them or to the lowest courts.

[6] Théolleyre, "Une justice . . . ," May 16–17, 1965, p. 8. (this is the third part of the article.) In the same article the author notes that the magistracy, on the other hand, no longer is what may be described as a caste, for these days more social categories are increasingly represented in it. Competition for entrance into the CNEJ in 1963 revealed among the candidates the following social origins: 10 percent magistrates families, fourteen percent families in the legal professions, 24 percent families of civil servants, 7 percent military families, 12 percent liberal professions (other than juridical), 11 percent artisans' and merchants' families, 11 percent foremen's and employees' families, 3.5 percent workers' families, and under one percent families of directors of enterprises. Clearly the judiciary is not the place to make money.

THE NATURE OF FRENCH LAW

French law originated in Roman law. As Peter Merkl states, the Roman conception of law was conservative, declining to set forth its form in written principles, and differentiating between matters public and private, secular and religious.[7] Rights such as life, liberty, property, opinion, and worship were respected as long as they did not lead to treasonable acts against the regime.[8] Codified in the sixth century in the Justinian Code, Roman law then went into eclipse until its revival in the twelfth century. Then it became —as Friedrich says—a boon to national unification and development, helping the kingdom absorb diverse local laws based mostly on custom, and containing principles friendly to the needs of an emerging commercial community.[9]

French and American legal conceptions vary as to the relationship between the individual and the state and between the individual and society. French law, like American law, considers some areas of individual existence to be outside its intervention, giving wide latitude to personal action. Legally, however, the French image of the pluralistic society is probably more restricted than the American one. The French state recognizes that juridical overemphasis on liberty could have disastrous consequences for a society which for so long viewed liberty as a weapon to combat public authority. Anglo-American law contains the right of *habeas corpus,* which French law lacks in any truly developed form. This right, too often taken for granted by Anglo-Americans, is one of the cornerstones of their personal liberties, precluding the state from practicing lengthy and unjustified detention of individuals. French law, like Anglo-American law, recognizes freedom of mobility, thought and expression, religion, assembly and association, inviolability of the home, and freedom from arrest and detention. Arrests must be preceded by warrants issued by a magistrate, although prefects of police can make arrests, search domiciles, and seize property as a conse-

---

[7] Peter Merkl, *Political Continuity and Change* (New York: Harper & Row, 1967), pp. 171–172, 315, 321.

[8] Merkl, pp. 171–172, 315, 321.

[9] Carl J. Friedrich, *Constitutional Government and Democracy* (Boston: Little, Brown, 1941), p. 14.

quence of actions directed against public security. The idea of due process is present in French law, and state instrumentalities are required to adhere to established procedures. *Ex-post facto* laws are prohibited. Each person has the right to trial. The right of asylum is granted those discriminated against for action in favor of freedom. With respect to civil liberties, the reader must remember that French law devolved from a state in which government once consisted of royal absolutism, whereas American law evolved in a state in which government initially was greatly limited. French law is the law of the state with consideration for the people, while American law is the law of the people with consideration for the state.

Anglo-American law is common law. It adheres to the principle of *stare decisis,* or the making of decisions based on precedents. Judge-made law, or case law, is the basis of its operation. This is law plus interpretation, and interpretations change as social and economic phenomena undergo transformation. On the other hand, French civil and criminal laws are codified, and in these areas the development of case law is precluded. Decisions in civil and criminal law apply exclusively to the case immediately under inquiry and do not form precedents which apply legally to other cases in which the facts are strikingly similar. This is not to say, however, that lawyers in civil and criminal cases are precluded from arguing on the basis of previous decisions of tribunals. They do, but such decisions guide rather than bind tribunals. Finally, if code law results in somewhat fixed decisions, equity—or justice founded on and dispensed on the basis of conscience—is not ruled out of existence. It definitely exists and decisions based upon it have been handed down in French courts.

French law comprises civil law, or the law of persons; criminal law, or the law which regulates crimes against the public order; administrative law, or the law which rules the actions and relations of state administrative units; and constitutional law, or law which is fundamental and paramount to other laws, and which is defined in scholarly legal treatises and in rulings made by the Council of State. Differences between French and Anglo-American law are not too apparent to observers insofar as most violations of law are concerned; they become most apparent in cases of noncriminal litigation within the realm of administrative law, in cases which involve relations between the individual and the state.

Private persons may sue the French state; its permission need not be secured. Administrative courts hear such actions. Administrative law, unlike codified civil and criminal law, is fundamentally case law—although it does have a written code which comprises principal regulations and laws but which excludes general principles applied by the courts. Weil defines administrative law as the "collection of rules defining the rights and obligations of the administration, that is to say of the government and of the administrative apparatus. . . ." [10] It is not and cannot be a law like other laws.[11] Administrative law is a form of limitation imposed by the state on itself. French administrative law is relatively young, having evolved slowly between the time of the French Revolution and the Second Empire. The reasons for its rise have more to do with French political history rather than abstract juridical theories. Before 1789 legal bodies sought to block both administrative and societal reforms proposed by the royal authority. Consequently in 1790 the Constitution deliberately prohibited courts from interfering with the administration—with the result, however, that the administration was removed from legal controls. Napoleon soon corrected this by creating the Council of State. This led to revival of administrative supervision, this time in the form of the administration itself. However, the Council of State did not play a strong role as the supervisor of administration until France entered the era of the Third Republic, that phase in her history when public policy was shaped by the bourgeois vision of private property. After the end of World War II and the introduction of the interventionist state and economic planning, certain ambiguities then entered the administrative law. Liberal doctrine was preoccupied previously with control of government, whereas in the postwar era emphasis was placed on the protection of the administration and allowance to it of the means to attain its ends.

Adminstrative law is autonomous from and independent of

[10] Prosper Weil, *Le droit administratif* (Paris: Presses universitaires, 1966), p. 7.
[11] Weil, p. 7.

civil law, as the Conflicts Court stated in 1873 in the *Blanco* case when it ruled on the liability of administrative bodies. The Court held that administrative bodies "cannot be regulated by the principles which are established in the Civil Code . . . it has its special rules." [12] However, now that state activities are bringing government and the economy closer to each other all the time, the distance between public and private law is narrowing. Consequently, similarities between civil and administrative rules often make it difficult to differentiate between the two. As Gaudemet says, the "borderline" between them still has to be fixed, and lacking is any sure criterion of administrative law.[13] The criterion for the application of administrative law is normally that of *service public*. When, however, the administrative authority acts as other than a public service, private law applies. Gaudemet gives the following as an example of the distinction between a public service and a nonpublic service. When a *commune* leases a vicarage to a vicar, no public service is involved and the lease is under the jurisdiction of private law; however, if the communal firemen extinguish a fire, it is a public service and under the jurisdiction of the administrative law.[14]

THE COURT SYSTEM

The French legal system has two branches: one constitutes the ordinary court system; the other forms the administrative court system. Conflicts which relate to which jurisdiction shall receive a case are resolved by the Conflicts Court.

The ordinary court system

The ordinary court system at the bottom level is founded on courts which entertain only certain types of litigation. Among these are labor courts (*conseils des prud'hommes*), commercial courts (*tribunaux de commerce*), and courts of rural equaliza-

[12] P. M. Gaudemet, "Droit administratif en France," in A. V. Dicey, *Introduction to the Study of the Law of the Constitution* (New York: St. Martin's, 1961), p. 49.

[13] Gaudemet, p. 481.

[14] Gaudemet, p. 481.

tion (*tribunaux paritaires de baux ruraux*). Labor courts judge labor-management disputes, exercising conciliatory and arbitral functions. These courts are staffed by election, the members hailing from interest groups (at least two from labor and two from management). Decisions are by majority vote and in the event of a tie, the judge of the local court of first instance (the next highest court in the judicial hierarchy) is called in to break the deadlock. Appeal may be made to the local court of appeal (providing that the sums of money in dispute exceed those sums over which the local court of first instance has jurisdiction). Further appeal may be made to the Court of Cassation on the grounds that there occurred previously an excess of jurisdictional powers. Commercial courts hear commercial disputes on the *arrondissement* level and are staffed by businessmen elected for two-year terms, and three or more judges who serve three-year terms (all have had previous experience as alternate judges for three-year periods). Decisions in disputes involving sums not in excess of approximately $300 are final, and should the sum exceed that amount decisions can be adjudged final if acceptable to the contesting parties. Finally, courts of rural equalization oversee rents in rural areas, containing as members renters, landlords, and a judge from the court of first instance.

At a level second from the bottom of the ordinary court system hierarchy are 457 local courts of first instance (*tribunaux de première instance*), one in each *arrondissement* capital, charged both with civil and criminal jurisdiction (over minor charges). Civil litigation is limited there to approximately $600 per person and approximately $1000 for joint claims. Civil decisions which do not exceed approximately $200 per person or approximately $300 for joint claims, and criminal decisions not in excess of approximately $12 or five days imprisonment, normally are final, although review may be exercised by the Court of Cassation under certain circumstances. Local courts of first instance comprise several judges who reside in the geographical area; decisions are delivered by one judge. These courts have replaced the justices of the peace who performed under the Fourth Republic cantonal functions that were conciliatory, administrative and judicial and who, as lawyers with competence over certain suits, were qualified to adjudge civil cases beneath certain financial limits, as well as misdemeanors (for which they could imprison).

At a level third from the bottom in the ordinary court hierarchy are the 172 major courts of first instance (*tribunaux de grande instance*) which are situated on a departmental basis, and which replace the Fourth Republic's 359 civil courts situated on an *arrondissement* basis. These courts are staffed by three judges and their decisions are accorded on a majority basis. A civil chamber of the court of first instance has in civil cases original competence (provided that the case has not been restricted already to an administrative court or special court), whereas its criminal chamber has appellate jurisdiction, hearing appeals from commercial courts, labor courts, and local courts of first instance. When hearing criminal cases, these courts sometimes receive from the involved parties civil claims growing out of the alleged criminal act.

At a level fourth from the bottom in the ordinary court hierarchy are the assize courts (*cours d'assises*), one in each department, staffed with three judges. Its president is from the court of appeal; the others are from a court of appeal if one exists in the immediate area or from the court vested with primary jurisdiction in the area where the case is tried. Assize courts try felonies, the indictment coming from the local court of appeal or from the Court of Cassation. Decisions are final, there being no right of appeal (although decisions may be reviewed by the Court of Cassation). Trial is by jury with nine jurors and three judges sitting in decision (conviction is by two-thirds majority; sentence is by simple majority).

At a level fifth from the bottom in the ordinary court hierarchy are the courts of appeal situated in twenty-seven judicial districts of the nation and endowed each with jurisdiction extending from one to seven departments. These courts receive and decide on appeals arising from courts within their jurisdictions, and cases submitted to them by the Court of Cassation whenever that court refuses to accept a decision by another court of appeal.

At the apex of the ordinary court pyramid is the Court of Cassation which is situated in Paris and which is separated into one criminal chamber and four civil chambers. The Court of Cassation is staffed with a chief justice, presidents of each of the five chambers, and sixty-three councillors. The responsibility of this court is to see that the law has been interpreted uniformly and correctly by inferior courts. Technically, the court does not try cases—instead, it tries decisions, although it need not accept a decision for review should it be so disposed. In any case in which it affirms a ruling by a lower court, it simply rejects the petition, thus securing the decision, but in any case in which it negates a ruling by a lower court, the case then is sent back to a lower court at a level at which the case originated (but not to the court which decided the case initially). Whenever the lower court's findings are contrary to those of the Court of Cassation, the latter—relying on a collective decision of at least thirty-three of its sixty-three councillors—then is empowered to rerefer the case to a lower court which then must rule as was found by the Court of Cassation.

Disputed jurisdiction

Disputes arise occasionally as to whether a case should be assigned to the ordinary or administrative court system. In instances of contestation, assignment to one of the systems is decided by the Conflicts Court. Few difficulties preclude definitive assignment, such problems being infrequent (a rare exception occurred in the 1920s which involved a jurisdictional dispute concerning a senator whose complaint finally was received by one of the court systems after years of personal effort and as the result of assignment by parliamentary statute). The Conflicts Court is chaired by the minister of justice, who presides over three councillors from the Council of State, three from the Court of Cassation, and two from either or both of these courts. The Conflicts Court may decide not only the assignment of cases but in some instances cases themselves. Its functions consist almost exclusively of assignment but it may, as a result of being ordered to do so by parliamentary statute, receive and decide a case—providing that both the ordinary and administrative court systems have refused it their jurisdictions.

The administrative court system

Separate from the ordinary court system is the administrative court system.[15] "The essential work of the administrative courts is to balance the means available to the public authorities for furthering the general interest with the rights of the citizen." [16] Administrative courts are separate not only in jurisdiction but also in personnel from the ordinary courts. They deal daily with actions by state instrumentalities and complaints that they have exceeded their powers and are guilty of "personal faults," damages inflicted by them on private property, and a broad range of other actions that involve relationships between individuals and the state.

Within the nation are approximately fifty administrative jurisdictions which comprise permanent courts, as well as courts which can be created or revived according to existing needs. At the bottom of the administrative court hierarchy are courts restricted to certain types of cases from which appeal may be made to the Council of State, which is at the top of the administrative court hierarchy. For example, the Court of Budgetary Discipline (*cour de discipline budgetaire*) oversees budgetary restrictions imposed on public personnel; Councils of Revision (*Conseils de revision*) entertain disputations relating to compulsory military service; the Court of Accounts (*Cour des comptes*) is entrusted with supervision of the accounts of public personnel; the National Education Council (*Conseil supérieur de l'éducation nationale*) is entrusted with school supervision and is the recipient of appeals resulting from decisions in education.

Second from the bottom in the administrative court hierarchy are thirty-one courts of general jurisdiction (*tribunaux administratifs*) composed of a president and several councillors (three members are obliged to sit for such a court to convene), who hear cases in which one of the parties must be a member of the administration whose rights and obligations are in dispute. Appeal from a court of general jurisdiction is to the Council of

[15] For additional information, see the detailed articles of Gerald L. Kock, "The Machinery of Law Administration in France," *University of Pennsylvania Law Review,* 108 (1960), 366–386, and Francis Deak and Max Rheinstein, "The Machinery of Law Administration in France and Germany," *University of Pennsylvania Law Review,* 84 (1936).

[16] Maxime Letourneur, "L'évolution récente de la jurisprudence administrative pour la protection des droits des citoyens," *International Review of Administrative Sciences,* Vol. 31, No. 1 (1965), 24–30.

State. Heading the administrative court hierarchy is the Council of State (*Conseil de l'état*), which entertains appeals from lower administrative courts.

Prosecution of criminal cases, preventive detention, and provisional release

Investigation and prosecution of criminal cases is by state lawyers in the Ministry of Justice, who form part of the *parquet* (office of public prosecutor) who are "standing," not "sitting," and who are attached to all except minor courts. Three kinds of offenses fall within French criminal law—petty, misdemeanors, and felonies. Three kinds of penalties are possible—petty, correctional, and criminal. Petty crimes may be punished by not more than two months' imprisonment and limited fines. Misdemeanors may be punished by not more than five years' imprisonment and limited fines. Felonies may be punished by death, imprisonment or deportation.

Criminal cases originate with a complaint (which may be accompanied by a civil damage claim) which, when accompanied by a claim, enable the judge to open his investigation. When a claim is not filed, the local prosecutor decides whether to recommend to the judge that he initiate an investigation. The investigation involves summoning the suspect and any witnesses the judge decides to call. The judge (*juge d'instruction*), after examination in private with the aid of counsel for the suspect, then decides whether the case is to be continued or dropped. Should the judge decide not to press charges, appeal may then be made to the local court of appeal by any private party or prosecutor who feels that his interests have been prejudiced. The preliminary investigation must decide the facts of the case and those grounds on which charges can be preferred. Should there be a case, the preliminary investigation must direct it then to the jurisdiction of a trial court. Suspected petty offenses are directed to police courts, suspected misdemeanors to courts of first jurisdiction, and suspected felonies to the indicting chamber of the local court of appeal and—if the decision is that the suspected felony be tried —it is sent to the Assize Court for trial within ten days. Sometimes the case is held by the indicting chamber for further investigation. Should the indicting chamber decide to drop the case, or should it decide that it is less than a felony, the indicting chamber may transfer it to a police or correctional court. Petty offenses tried by a police court summon parties by citation (although they may appear voluntarily), as a result of a petition prepared by the prosecutor or the accused. Procedure in misdemeanor cases is similar, most being received by the criminal chamber of the *tribunal de grande instance*. In open court (unless the court decides to go into private session), arguments are presented both by the prosecution and defense and the court then determines whether it has jurisdiction. Should the court decide that the case is not a misdemeanor but a felony, the court then sends the case to the appropriate judicial level for purposes of prosecution. Should the court decide that the case belongs not with it but properly within the competence of a police court, the court may send it on to one—or simply decide the case itself. If the court decides that the case involves a misdemeanor and that it belongs within its own judicial competence, the presiding judge decides the case. If civil as well as criminal charges have been preferred, the judge disposes of both. Appeal is to the local court of appeal. Assize courts try felonies, receiving them from the indicting chamber of the local court of appeal. The accused must have the aid of counsel, providing his own or having it appointed for him by the court. Trial at this level is by jury, and proceedings are public—unless the court decides that they are private. The right both of the prosecution and accused to present arguments is carefully safeguarded. The president of the court, judges, and jurors question the defendant (the latter when authorized to do so by the court president). The defendant in a criminal trial is presumed innocent and the burden of proof is clearly on the court insofar as conviction is concerned. The president of the court presses examination, and careful attention is given to the admissibility of evidence. Guilt or innocence is determined by secret ballots cast by the president of the court, judges, and jurors (conviction is by affirmative vote of eight of the twelve court members), and in the event of conviction, the court votes the penality by secret ballot. When the criminal charge is accompanied by a civil charge, the latter is ruled on by the three judges. In cases involving both criminal and civil charges, the court may find the defendant innocent criminally but guilty on civil grounds. Assize court decisions may not be appealed, although they may be reviewed by the Court of Cassation after a petition for review has been forwarded to it.

The Code of Penal Procedure provides for preventive detention and provisional release. Preventive detention may be invoked relative to an individual who is waiting for a verdict in a case in which he has been criminally charged; provisional release may be granted to an individual who is waiting for completion of proceedings in a case in which he has been criminally charged. The code defines preventive detention as "an exceptional measure," "justified by the frequent exigencies of public policies or by the quest for the truth," restricting it to cases involving misdemeanors or felonies—with the understanding that the court may, if it wishes, deduct the time spent in preventive detention from the final sentence. Article 138 of the Penal Code states that provisional release may be granted in a correctional case—"When the maximum penalty prescribed by law is less than two years' imprisonment . . . an *inculpé* domiciled in France cannot be detained longer than five days after his first appearance before an examining judge, unless he has been previously convicted of a crime or sentenced to imprisonment for an unsuspended term exceeding three months for an offense under the general law." [17] The code states also that "in every case where it cannot be claimed as of right, provisional release may be ordered by the examining judge . . ." Provisional release may be applied for by the defendant. The code refers to provisional release as "a matter of right" if "there are no substantial grounds for the belief that the *inculpé* may flee, exert pressure on witnesses, destroy evidence, commit new offenses, or disturb public order. . . ." Finally, by the code, "Preventive detention can only be ordered if there are both very serious indications of guilt and reasons to fear that the *inculpé* may misuse his provisional release," and that "as soon as one of these two conditions ceases to be fulfilled, the preventive detention must come to an end."

[17] Robert Vouin, "Provisional Release in French Penal Law," *University of Pennsylvania Law Review*, 108 (1960), 335–365.

Preventive detention is limited in duration but it can be renewed indefinitely—and renewal is but a formality.[18] This allows for lengthy detentions which are entirely permissible in French law. In periods of great crisis, as in the time of the Algerian war, preventive detention was invoked frequently, sometimes with obvious abuse. Interruption of provisional release may be ordered by the court if, in its opinion, it is warranted by the defendant's behavior. Persons granted provisional release are restricted to residence in the judicial area in which their cases arose, to possible house detention if they are aliens, and to possible bail which, in the event of forfeit, is used to allay costs and damages for both the accusor and the state.

The Council of State

Although the French Revolution prescribed the subordination of executive action to the domination of law, it did seek initially to box in the judges because of a fear of continuation of their hostility toward the administration (during pre-Revolutionary times the judicial corps was critical of royal administrations). This created a problem, however, whenever judicial jurisdiction could not be found to cover a violation of law, and in 1799 Napoleon introduced the Council of State to remedy this difficulty. It was called upon to resolve litigation questioning the decisions of the administration; it also drafted legal codes and played the role of counselor to the chief of state.

Over the years the Council of State played faithfully its role of overseeing the administration; eventually it achieved a reputation for not letting any executive act escape it. "Its function became over many regimes that of conciliating the exigencies of administrative action with the rights and liberties of the citizen." [19] Early in this century it upheld the separation of church and state, during Vichy it restricted anti-Semitic legislation, and in 1954 in one of its most famous decisions it declared in favor of the constitutional rights of a Communist denied

---

[18] Jean-Marc Théolleyre, "Une justice . . . ," May 11, 1965, p. 14. The author notes that "Sometimes a judge forgets to renew his mandate at the end of two months."

[19] Jean Rivero, "Le rôle du conseil d'état dans la tradition française," *Le Monde,* October 31, 1962, pp. 1, 14.

access to the National School of Administration. "It never departed from its line as defender of the liberty of individuals," and few would concede that it has failed in this job.[20]

Today the Council of State remains at the top of the administrative judicial structure, hearing from lower administrative levels appeals relative to the relationship between the state and its civil servants. It continues to act also in an advisory capacity to the government (the Constitution prescribes that legislative texts which the government wishes to modify by decree first must be the object of consultations with the Council of State, and that government bills must be discussed first with the Council before being filed with the secretariats of the National Assembly and Senate).[21]

An example of the important role played by the Council of State as the protector of personal rights of citizens occurred in October 1962 when the Council annulled an ordinance by which the President of the Republic had instituted in May 1961 a court of military justice.[22] The ordinance had been adopted as a consequence of Article 16 (de Gaulle had dissolved the high military court and replaced it with a military court of justice). After the withdrawal of Article 16, de Gaulle's ordinance of June 1, 1962, reestablished the court of military justice, an act that was authorized by the referendum of April 8, 1962, which gave to the president of the republic the right to ordinance "all legislative and regulatory measures relative to the application of the declarations of Evian." The court subsequently condemned six defendants.[23]

The Council of State did not question de Gaulle's right

---

[20] *Le Monde,* October 31, 1962, pp. 1, 14.

[21] Membership in the Council of State is slightly more than 150 persons; approximately sixty are auditors who do preparatory work for higher members of the court and who come to this body by competitive examination from the National School of Administration (ENA); approximately fifty members are masters of requests, three of every four recruited from among the auditors; approximately fifty members are councillors of state, two of every three recruited from among the masters of requests. The government has the right to appoint to the Council of State (with the exception of its lowest level) qualified members. However, the "path" to the Council generally is the ENA.

[22] *Le Monde,* October 21–22, 1962 p. 1.

[23] *Le Monde,* October 21–22, 1962, p. 1.

to create the military court; it questioned instead its "composition and procedure," which it felt were contrary to law, and the protection by it of personal rights (civil magistrates were lacking and the right of appeal was denied).[24] The Council of State announced that the general principles of law have constitutional validity, and that they do impose themselves on the executive power (it called attention to the preamble of the 1958 Constitution which refers to the Declaration of Rights of 1789).[25] President de Gaulle reacted to the decision as "abnormal," and the government's communiqué claimed that the decision "encouraged subversion." [26]

In January 1963 a committee created for the purpose of inquiring into possible reforms of the Council of State recommended that the government be given the power to transfer to the bureau of the Council certain cases (members of the bureau were to be government nominees), and that retirement ages be changed for members of the Council. However, after subsequent consideration, the government decided that both recommendations were not feasible for adoption.

The periodical *L'Express* claims that the evolution of the Gaullist republic has been instrumental in converting the Council of State into "a bastion of republican defense." [27] Perhaps that claim is somewhat exaggerated; there is every evidence, though, that the Council of State has no intention of becoming a "bastion of Gaullism." The council has indicated that it is receptive to legal suits arising from exercise by the president of the republic of emergency powers under Article 16, as well as legal actions having their origin in powers delegated to the president of the republic by referendum. Moreover, in the *Brocas* case the Council declared its accessibility to any elector who sought for legitimate reasons to question the government's electoral arrangements.[28] Many years ago the famous jurist

[24] *Le Monde,* October 21–22, 1962, p. 1.

[25] *Le Monde,* October 21–22, 1962, p. 1.

[26] *Le Monde,* October 21–22, 1962, p. 1. See for copy of the government communiqué and the decision of the Council.

[27] *L'Express,* April 23, 1964, p. 41.

[28] H. Parris, "The French Conseil d'État," *Government and Opposition,* Vol. 2, No. 1 (November 1966), 102.

Joseph Barthelémy praised the Council of State and the protection it offers individuals in their relationships with the state—the Council of State, said Barthelémy, is an instrumentality of the state which serves as the best judge against the state.

The Constitutional Council

The Constitutional Council—were it allowed to exercise all of the constitutional tasks prescribed for it—could be one of the nation's most important legal organs. The Constitution charges the Council with responsibility for seeing that executive and legislative powers remain within constitutionally defined bounds, and that the regularity of elections is ensured (including those for the presidency); the Constitution designates the Council as the recipient of any complaints that may relate to such elections. The Constitution also obligates the president of the republic to consult with the Council concerning the legality of any measures taken by him in times of emergency when Article 16 has been invoked. Moreover, should the government seek to modify laws by decree, the Council must declare them capable of being modified. Any organic law sought by Parliament must be verified by the Council. The Council checks the constitutionality of the rules of the assemblies and determines presidential disability. Only the president of the republic, and the presidents of the National Assembly and Senate may submit to the Council proposals of law. Opinions of the Council as to the constitutionality of proposed laws must be delivered in advance.

All Council decisions and opinions must be taken in the presence of seven or more of its members. No appeals are allowed as a consquence of Council decisions, inasmuch as the Constitution defines the Council as the final assessor of constitutionality. Membership in the Council comprises former presidents of the republic (ex officio for life), and nine other persons. The president of the republic and the presidents of the National Assembly and Senate each appoint to the Council three members for nine-year terms (no reappointment is possible). Members may not serve simultaneously in the government, National Assembly, Senate, or the Economic and Social Council; however, they need not relinquish their positions in the state service if they happen to be civil servants. Members of the Council cannot be appointed to any new public positions when serving as councillors. Every three years one third of the Council seats fall vacant (because three of the first appointees were named to three-year terms, three- to six-year terms, and three- to nine-year terms). The first Council appointed in 1958 averaged almost sixty-five years of age, and five of its eleven members exceeded seventy. Almost half had served as deputies or senators, and seven had legal degrees.

Constitutionally, the Council's competence is vast; practically, it is not in a position to see that its decisions are implemented. There is no guarantee that the president of the republic will consult with it when undertaking measures in pursuance of the emergency Article 16, nor is there any assurance that he will accept its advice after having consulted it. When Vincent Auriol, a former president of the Fourth Republic, announced in 1960 that he would sit no longer on the Council, he gave as his reason de Gaulle's unwillingness to submit to that body constitutionally disputable measures. Part of Auriol's attack was polemical, but there was some truth in his contention that the Council then was functioning more as a presidential than as a constitutional council. Moreover, in 1961, some eyes were raised when the Council declared itself incompetent to determine whether a motion of censure can be presented in the National Assembly during the application of Article 16 (after Assembly President Chaban-Delmas presented the question at the request of the Socialist party, SFIO).[29]

In his speech to the Council of State on August 27, 1958, former Prime Minister Michel Debré said that the creation of the Constitutional Council was illustrative of the will of the regime to subordinate the law to the Constitution; nonetheless, the Council's inclination has been to judge legislative rather than executive acts.[30] The Council has ruled frequently that Parliament has exceeded its lawmaking powers; and it has had no qualms about holding Parliament's rules of procedure constitutionally unallowable. And in the case of the highly controversial constitutional amendment of October 1962, which

[29] See *Le Monde,* September 16, 1961, p. 1; and September 19, 1961, p. 16.

[30] See the comments by Jacques Fauvet in *Le Monde,* March 6, 1962, p. 1.

changed the mode of election of the president of the republic, the Council refused comment on the grounds that the amendment had been effected already.

It may appear that the Constitution gives to the Council some basis for exercising a limited amount of judicial review, but that possibility is limited by the nature of things in the Fifth Republic. A strong limitation is the dominance of the political over the constitutional. Second, as Roger Pinto states, control over the constitutionality of laws is a difficult thing to introduce in France. Writing in 1959, he stated that the creation of a Constitutional Council by Title VII of the Constitution of 1958, "appears to open a new chapter in our constitutional history," but that "There's nothing to it." [31] He states that the constitutional commentators pointed out very clearly in 1958 that the Constitutional Council is not a superior jurisdiction like the United States Supreme Court or the Constitutional Court of the German Federal Republic, but a "juridical-political organ." [32] Its competence may be exercised on the initiative of the president of the republic or the prime minister, or of the president of either assembly. However, there was not then, nor is there now recourse to it by ordinary citizens in order to protect their individual liberties and fundamental rights. All of the procedures and mechanisms involved relate exclusively to the public powers. Finally, the composition of the Constitutional Council confirms its political character. Membership in it requires no particular legal competence, and in reality its first members represented proportionately the political groups then seated in Parliament. Pinto describes the council as a "council of tutelage." [33]

CONCLUSION

Although the French judicial system has developed a reputation for efficiency and easy accessibility, the study conducted by the National Chamber of Solicitors reveals that large numbers of

---

[31] Roger Pinto, "Le contrôle de la constitutionnalité des lois et la Constitution de 1958," in "Commentaires de la Constitution de la Vᵉ République," *Études juridiques et économiques,* 23 (November 1959), 30.

[32] Pinto, "Le contrôle . . . ," 30.

[33] Pinto, "Le contrôle . . . ," 30.

respondents regard the system as expensive, slow and "not very just." They also attribute to the legal profession other than a good reputation. The fact remains that the judiciary is confronted with great demands. Delays in litigation are common, for the size of the judiciary is insufficient for the satisfaction of contemporary demands.

French law is Roman law. Civil and criminal laws are codified, precluding within these areas development of case law. Administrative law, a form of limitation imposed by the state on itself, is autonomous from and independent of civil law. Unlike other laws, it is case law.

The French judicial system is divided into ordinary and administrative court systems. The ordinary courts handle civil and criminal actions. Administrative courts hear actions against the state by individuals. It is not necessary to secure the state's permission in order to sue it. The American judicial system does not include administrative courts. Suing the American state is dependent upon first securing its permission.

The Council of State—which oversees the administration—continues to play faithfully its role as defender of the liberty of individuals. It is today a first line of "republican defense." In the words of Barthelémy, it is an instrumentality of the state which serves as the best judge against the state. On the other hand, the Constitutional Council appears periodically as a line of "presidential defense." If, in the words of Michel Debré, the responsibility of the Constitutional Council is to subordinate the law to the Constitution, the role actually played by it in de Gaulle's Republic confirms its political character.

ELEVEN
THE THIRD
FORCE
The country's role
in world affairs

Foremost in de Gaulle's political thought was the nation-state, which he viewed as the loftiest vehicle attainable for the organization and expression of a people. The world consists of numerous nation-states engaged constantly in a competitive process of attempting to enhance their own interests and power.[1] France is one of these; her interest and power must be maximized, and this can be undertaken best by one man, the president of the republic, who can make France's foreign policy, advance her

[1] For de Gaulle, ideological expressions by national leaderships are but a facade for interests. See French Embassy (Press and Information Division), *Major Addresses . . . de Gaulle,* pp. 236–237, for his press conference in which he spoke about the ideological rupture between Peking and Moscow: "I will speak first about the ideological rupture, then about the realities . . . The break? Over what ideology? I refuse to enter into a valid discussion on the subject of the ideological struggle between Peking and Moscow. What I want to consider are the deeprooted realities which are human, national, and consequently international. The banner of ideology in reality covers only ambitions. And I believe that it has been thus since the world was born."

"real" interests (not just particular internal interests), and strengthen her position in the world. World order is realizable but it can be achieved only as the result of an equilibrium of powers. Some equilibriums are short-lived and dangerous, others are lasting and fruitful. The one that should exist is not the one that exists presently in today's world. Therefore, treaties and diplomatic efforts must lead to its transformation, and subsequently to the creation of a new equilibrium satisfactory to French interests and world peace.

DE GAULLE AND FRENCH SOVEREIGNTY

De Gaulle, who always was conscious of safeguarding French sovereignty, rebuffed all attempts that might possibly have resulted in its reduction or subordination to another power. He resisted, therefore, all moves to give to the Commission of the European Economic Community any functions that might have enabled it to exercise executive or supranational roles. He preferred to rely instead on discussions and negotiations conducted on a separate basis with the governments of countries having membership in the European Economic Community, or "Common Market." In 1965 he balked at that part of the Treaty of Rome which would have enabled the Council of Ministers of the Six to make decisions by majority vote. Although earlier he spoke (August 17, 1950) in defense of "European institutions proceeding from the direct vote of the citizens of Europe," he subsequently resisted election of the members of the European Parliament by universal suffrage and extension of the powers of the organization. He also refused ratification of the European Convention of the Rights of Man, which permits citizens of a member country of the Council of Europe to engage in litigation in the European Court as a result of a violation of these rights.

Diplomacy conducted along bilateral rather than multilateral lines was for de Gaulle the surest way of advancing French interests and not endangering French sovereignty. The North Atlantic Treaty Organization was viewed by him as an instrument of Anglo-Saxon hegemony, allowing freedom of action to both the British and Americans, and posing to a France bound to it threats to her independent action and sovereign existence.[2] De Gaulle's views of NATO were spelled out clearly over a period of years. In his famous "secret memo" of September 24, 1958 (described in *Le Monde,* November 11, 13, 1958, the contents being divulged publicly in de Gaulle's Grenoble address of October 7, 1960), which was addressed to Eisenhower and Macmillan, de Gaulle assessed problems relative to NATO and expressed convictions concerning its organization and policies. He conceded common responsibilities binding upon the alliance in time of war, while railing against inequality of armaments and decision making among its members. He urged that there be established within the organization a directorate consisting of the United States, the United Kingdom, and France, invested with the responsibility of devising a common military and political strategy of a global rather than a regional nature (the assumption being that all phenomena of war and peace are more than regional, being global). He urged joint use by the three of atomic weapons, and allied commands for all possible theatres of operation. His hope was for France to assume with the United States and the United Kingdom joint charge of global strategy, and, at the NATO regional level, charge of Atlantic problems. His effort also constituted an attempt to elevate France to a level no other European power could hope to attain. The memo contained the warning that France would reconsider her policy relative to NATO in terms of the responses of the United States and the United Kingdom. West Germany and Italy were irritated by the memo, and it was rejected by the United States. In turn, France withdrew from the NATO command her Mediterranean fleet in the time of war; she declined integration of her air defense within NATO, and prohibited construction of NATO launching pads and atomic stockpiling on her territory (inasmuch as French would have no control over

[2] French Embassy, *Major Addresses . . . de Gaulle,* p. 219. "To turn over our weapons to a multilateral force, under foreign command, would be to act contrary to that principle of our defense and our policy. It is true that we too can theoretically retain the ability to take back in our hands, in the supreme hypothesis, our atomic weapons incorporated in the multilateral force. But how could we do it in practice during the unheard-of-moments of the atomic apocalypse?"

them). De Gaulle then went ahead with his own nuclear bomb, contending that the only realistic defense is that which a nation wages at the national level.[3]

De Gaulle came to regard NATO generally as obsolete, and he argued that contemporary world conditions differed greatly from 1947, when the organization was created and when the need for it was great.[4] Nonetheless, de Gaulle always was opposed to its geographical and nonglobal limitations, the imbalance in its strategic and political organization, the denial to some of its partner nations of a greater share in policy planning and strategic decision making, and its being "over-integrated," "which would lead to excluding the nation from being responsible for the organization of its own defense."[5]

---

[3] Creation of nuclear power began with the Fifth Republic. Studies of nuclear power were begun under the Fourth.

[4] De Gaulle's decision to leave NATO if denied certain revisions in the treaty was made clear to the United States in 1964 when Ambassador Charles Bohlen and George Ball were the recipients of this information. See the remarks of André Fontaine in *Le Monde,* January 18, 1966, pp. 1, 3.

[5] Studies of the French Institute of Public Opinion conducted shortly before the coming of de Gaulle to power in 1958 show that public confidence in NATO then was declining at a fast pace. Four studies are worth examining. *NATO and Western Security,* December 24, 1957, and *NATO and the Defense of the West,* May 1957, both surveyed the views of more than 2000 respondents in different parts of the nation who commented critically on "powerlessness of the organization, rivalry and discord among the members." Neutralism had "reached a peak" and by then was "the majority school of thought in France." In the study of December 24, 1957, when asked the question, "At the present time, do you personally think that France should be on the side of the West, or on the side of the East, or on neither side" 51 percent replied "neither side." Fewer than one in five believed that France would stand on the side of the United States in time of war between the United States and the USSR; 62 percent stated that France in the event of such a conflict should not take sides. In response to the question, "Do you feel that France is treated [in NATO] as an equal partner of the United States?" 61 percent responded negatively. The third study, *Popularity of the United States and the USSR on the Eve of the Nato Conference,* December 20, 1957, repeated the previous question and the negative response rose to 66 percent. The study of December 24 showed also that French opinion was in the majority receptive to joint troop withdrawal from France. Yet another study, *The Reaction of Educated*

Finally, inasmuch as the need for NATO no longer existed, it was time to rely on a coalition of European armies, one that could be continued in an Atlantic Alliance, distinct from NATO, which need not rely on the United States for aid. In other words, for de Gaulle dependence could result only in domination, and in ten years he came all the way from arguing for equal participation in a real interdependence to a position of independence.

For de Gaulle the best safeguards of French sovereignty were a diplomacy conducted along bilateral lines—and a bomb.[6] He contended that the French nuclear defense constituted an effective deterrent, having against potential aggressors a moderating and even discouraging effect. Moreover, it is French and free from subordination to any multimember organization higher than the nation-state. It can be used by France when France wishes to use it; perhaps, more importantly, it can be withheld by France when the nation does not wish to use it. In any event, its possession places France in the "nuclear club," and among those sovereign powers known as *les grandes*. Therefore, the bomb has definite political connotations. It furthers French power in a state system whose members work tirelessly to enhance their own positions. Just having the bomb means something at the bargaining tables of *les grandes*. Its significance in peacetime is greater than its importance in wartime (being less potent than the nuclear bombs deployed by the United States and Russia). It exists, it cannot be ignored, and it can be enlisted in pursuance of the transformation in the equilibrium of power. And should a true political Europe be formed, de

---

French Respondents to American Foreign Policies, December 11, 1956, interrogated 1047 people over the age of 18 who had completed the baccalaureate. Two thirds expressed the view that the USSR was preoccupied with world domination; almost 50 percent attributed the same outlook to the United States. The "two colossi" so prevalent in the overview of the president of the republic, for them were an object of common reference.

[6] Two nuclear programs have been adopted. The first, 1960–1965, reserved approximately 15 percent of the military budget for the force of dissuasion. Despite sacrifices in traditional armaments, costs exceeded this figure. The second program, 1965–1970, foresees integration of traditional and nuclear units; France exploded her first hydrogen bomb in 1968.

Gaulle promised that he would "consider" how this deterrent force would be used within its framework.

De Gaulle entertained a vision of the community of nations that is hierarchical. There are those who qualify as *les grandes,* and they have a "world vocation." There also are those who are not among *les grandes,* and their vocation is regional. *Les grandes* are those who have the means to defend themselves against others—they are those who belong to the atomic club. France is one of these because she has the bomb.

When de Gaulle dealt with the United Nations, he assumed usually the position that the Charter must be applied as it was originally devised, with executive power vested in *les grandes* who are members of the Security Council. When dealing with disarmament, all depends on *les grandes.* If nuclear disarmament is capable of being negotiated, it can be achieved only by *les grandes,* or the nuclear powers themselves. Therefore, France refused to participate in the second disarmament conference which convened in Geneva on March 15, 1965, because the powers who formed the majority there were not nuclear ones. Moreover, de Gaulle refused to sign the Moscow Test Ban of August 5, 1963, because he considered it useless, and because China, a nuclear power, did not participate in it. In other words, all disarmament depends on *les grandes.*[7] A concert of *les grandes* is lacking just now. Perhaps some day it will exist, and perhaps then it will be capable of guaranteeing the peace. In the meanwhile, the precondition of that is reestablishment of cooperation among *les grandes.*

FRANCE, THE UNITED STATES, AND THE USSR

Although he did not hesitate to side with the United States in great crises like those of Cuba and Berlin, de Gaulle insisted that

---

[7] De Gaulle rejected the idea that European arms control can be achieved before the creation of global arms control. In fact, he regarded arms control in a limited geographical area as disadvantageous. See, for example, *The New York Times,* March 26, 1959, p. 8, for reproduction of a speech in which he states that no area for European arms control even is worth consideration unless its range is "as near to the Urals as it is to the Atlantic."

there is no guarantee that French and American interests necessarily will be harmonious or even compatible in other future crises. If, he said, France should rely solely on the United States for its defense, France would risk the possibility of going undefended as a consequence of a possible divergence between French and American foreign policy interests. De Gaulle had no objection to promulgating agreements with the United States, however, provided that they were bilateral, that they did not result in France's absorption in any integrated system, and that they did not result in France being placed in any way under American hegemony.[8]

De Gaulle felt that the equilibrium that presently exists between the United States and the USSR is potentially dangerous and incapable of offering a satisfactory solution to the peace of the world. In former years he argued that if the United States and the USSR are capable of undoing each other, in that same "showdown" they are capable of undoing all the others too. Later he suggested that both the United States and USSR are capable of putting aside mutually destructive designs and collaborating to establish over the world a joint hegemony that would be contrary to French and European interests.[9] In the meanwhile, under his direction French policy relative to the United States continued to be characterized by phases of opposition, *détente,* and cooperation. While French efforts to lure away from the United States other powers continued, each of the two countries

---

[8] *Le Monde,* January 2, 1965, p. 1. De Gaulle states that he refuses to associate with any system that "under the cover of integration or Atlanticism places us under American hegemony." De Gaulle views a United States of Europe as incapable of serving as a true federalism—it would be an artificial supranational regime with the United States arbitrating all "our conflicts" and the creature of American domination. See also *France-Observateur,* May 17, 1962, p. 14.

[9] French Embassy, *Major Addresses . . . de Gaulle,* p. 235. "And thus the United States which, since Yalta and Potsdam, has nothing, after all, to ask from the Soviets, the United States sees tempting prospects opening up before it. Hence, for instance, all the separate negotiations between the Anglo-Saxons and the Soviets which, starting with the limited agreement on nuclear testing, seem likely to be extended to other questions, notably European ones, until now in the absence of the Europeans, which clearly goes against the views of France."

received each other's representatives and both collaborated in some aspects of scientific and military technology.

In his *mémoires* de Gaulle refers to a Europe extending from the Atlantic to the Urals which perhaps the USSR eventually can be induced to join. In his speech of September 7, 1962, de Gaulle referred to a Europe "cut in two by the opposition and ambition of the Soviets" as capable of being reconstructed for the welfare of all. If the USSR wishes coexistence, that can be achieved by desisting from menacing actions and restoring to the satellites self-action.[10] In the meanwhile, inasmuch as the satellite countries now are in a process of evolution, it is profitable for France to make with them commercial and cultural agreements in order to speed that process along. Therefore, relations with Rumania—a country which has developed strong demands for independence from the USSR—were intensified. The "opening to the East" must be pursued at all times— and it was. In this geographical area Gaullist diplomacy succeeded in creating a bridge that other diplomacies had failed to erect.

THE EQUILIBRIUM

In practically all of his considerations both on the domestic and international levels, the theme of an equilibrium played for de Gaulle an important role. In the international arena "un autre ordre, un autre équilibre sont nécessaires." The equilibrium remains abstract but France's role within it would have been major. It was never truly shaped by de Gaulle—"Our hope is that the day will come when Europe plays an eminent role as an arbiter of the peace of the world." [11] The way that this was to be achieved was by creating first an equilibrium between a previously constructed European confederation and the United States,[12] and later an equilibrium between a Europe that was

[10] Ambassade de France (Service de presse et d'information), *President de Gaulle Holds Eleventh Press Conference* (February 4, 1965), Speeches and Press Conferences, 216, p. 12.

[11] Speech delivered in Guéret, May 19, 1962, quoted in *Le Monde*, November 28–29, 1965, p. 4.

[12] French Embassy, *Major Addresses . . . de Gaulle*, p. 78.

divided heretofore, one that ranges from the Atlantic to the Urals.[13] But in order to realize the European equilibrium, agreement was to be realized first on the German problem as a result of the "European peoples" ability to "examine together, regulate in common, guarantee jointly." [14]

Efforts at equilibrium were global, extending also to Asia. Communist China was recognized by France in 1964, and new technical and commercial agreements have been concluded between the two—as part of an effort to achieve China's emergence from isolation and her entry into the United Nations. In southeast Asia, where American policy is regarded as fruitless and dangerous to world security, de Gaulle proposed that the neutrality of Vietnam be achieved by return to the accords of Geneva of 1954 (on Indochina) and of 1962 (on Laos) calling for nonintervention in that part of the world. France proposed in January 1964 a treaty guaranteeing southeast Asian neutrality, asking for a new Geneva conference. In the meanwhile, agreements for cooperation with India and Pakistan were signed, a commercial treaty was concluded with Japan, and after 1963 both countries undertook periodic political consultations. Diplomacy was maintained with Seoul, Outer Mongolia was recognized, and signed agreements with Laos and Indonesia searched for the attainment of economic and cultural objectives. Paralleling all French efforts in Asiatic policy was publicization by de Gaulle of the independence that France enjoyed from the United States.

Efforts in behalf of the equilibrium continued also in other areas. Particular attention was paid to those nations now independent but who once were French possessions. They comprise part of what the French call the "Third World," which will be so important in the world of the future. Algeria, a former French possession which always is difficult to deal with, was treated gingerly lest "conflict with Algeria" ruin "the efforts of our diplomacy in the entire world." [15] Algeria has important contacts with the "Third World," and this channel of potential

[13] French Embassy, *Major Addresses . . . de Gaulle*, p. 78.
[14] French Embassay, *Major Addresses . . . de Gaulle*, p. 78.
[15] *Le Monde*, November 28–29, November 4, 1965, pp. 1, 4.

influence should not be endangered. Although diminishing, French financial aid to Algeria remains considerable (700 million francs in 1965), as does technical, educational, and military assistance. Morocco receives financial, military, and educational aid (financial aid is approximately 200 million francs per year). Strained relations with Tunisia result in less financial aid than was given to her before the crises of 1961 (Bizerte) and 1964 (nationalization of lands of French settlers) but cultural assistance continues. The African states and Madagascar received in 1966 cultural, military, and financial aid that amounted to 2274 million francs.

THE EUROPEAN CONFEDERATION

This was an old idea for de Gaulle, having been expressed by him in London on November 11, 1942, midway through World War II, when he referred to the necessity for France to lead in the making of a Europe whose needs, defense, and interests are hers in a way that is "practical and lasting." [16] In 1959 France requested of other members of the European Economic Community periodic meetings for purposes of political consultations among their foreign ministers, a practice that secured their approval but which fell into disuse after defeat of the United Kingdom's bid to join the European Economic Community (EEC). The following year a proposal for European political union culminating in a "vast confederation" was discussed by de Gaulle and German Chancellor Adenauer and plans were made for regular meetings and creation of committees for defense, policy, culture, and economics. European "summit" meetings followed in Paris and Bonn, and preparations were made for the creation of a treaty. A draft was evolved, but then France presented a substitute draft disputing some of the rights of her partners and refuting a clause proposing evolution of the union into a federation within a period of three years. The effort terminated April 17, 1962, but was followed by subsequent French efforts to establish with Germany political consultations in diverse areas in the hope of reviving the confederation.

---

[16] André Fontaine, "De Gaulle et l'Europe," *Le Monde,* October 28–29, 1962, p. 4. He referred again on September 21, 1951, to the necessity for a "Confederation of Europe."

De Gaulle believed that construction of a European confederation requires as its cornerstone a Franco-German entente —a belief that is very different from the views he held during the second World War when he opposed future German ownership both of the Rhine and the Saar, upholding future internationalization of the Ruhr and reestablishment in Germany of a unitary state. His views softened at the end of the war and he looked subsequently with favor on Adenauer's proposals for a Franco-German union and treaties of cooperation.[17]

The European policy of France continues to seek implementation of the goals of *"rapprochement* between France and Germany, greater economic development within the framework of the Common Market, and a greater share in world responsibilities for a firmly constituted political Europe." [18] With respect to *rapprochement,* the Franco-German agreement of cooperation of January 22, 1963, extends to matters that are military, cultural, and consultative. With respect to the European Economic Community, French policy is devoted to "creating among the Six an awareness of their European personality and bringing about, therefore, common action toward the rest of the world." [19] With respect to a political Europe, France seeks transformation of the European Economic Community into a European political community—however, under de Gaulle it had to be in the form of a confederation, not a federation, for

[17] De Gaulle did not view German reunification as urgent. Receptive to it on a basis of self-determination, he stated that it should be sought "as soon as possible," but it should be noticed that he advanced it as a long-term goal and that he was reluctant to press proposals for its attainment at this time. See *The New York Times,* March 26, 1959, p. 8, and his statement: "In awaiting the time when this ideal can be achieved, we believe that the two separate sections of the German people should be able to multiply between themselves links and relationships in all practical fields." At the same time de Gaulle made no move in the direction of recognizing East Germany. As far as he was concerned (although he certainly did not say so publicly), it is preferable for Germany to be divided and West Germany allied with France. This is the best defense against Germany becoming again a military threat to France. Moreover, in its present status, West Germany is a useful buffer between France and the USSR.

[18] French Embassy (Press and Information Division), *The First Five Years of the Fifth Republic of France* (New York: 1964), p. 19.

[19] French Embassy, *The First Five Years . . . ,* p. 20.

a France immersed in the latter would be bound to majority principles and unable to provide it with clear and unmistakable leadership.[20] In his press conference of May 15, 1962, de Gaulle said that "economic construction is not enough. Western Europe must form itself politically." [21] This was to be achieved in stages, beginning with the amalgamation of existing economic bodies. Former Prime Minister Pompidou said in his address in Copenhagen on August 26, 1963, that he is "convinced that we will arrive . . . one day even, at a confederation." [22] By creating this vehicle and shaping its policy, de Gaulle believed that Europe will attain someday "the role of equal partner in the free world with regard to America, the nonaligned countries, and the Eastern bloc." [23]

FRANCE, THE UNITED KINGDOM, AND THE EUROPEAN ECONOMIC COMMUNITY

In maintaining a close relationship with the United States and its foreign policy, the United Kingdom periodically supports programs of American origin with which the French find themselves completely at odds. However, a declining balance of trade and a gross national product that increased but 0.5 percent in 1966 compel the United Kingdom to seek additional alliances that might serve as a source of stimulation for the British economy. One such possibility is affiliation with the European Economic Community. The British are willing to enter the organization, but their Commonwealth obligations and commitments to preferential tariffs preclude them from meeting its entrance requirements. On the other hand, associate rather than

[20] French Embassy, *Major Addresses . . . de Gaulle*, p. 225. ". . . if the union of Western Europe—Germany, Italy, the Netherlands, Belgium, Luxembourg, France—is a capital aim in our action outside, we have no desire to be dissolved in it. Any system that would consist of handing over our sovereignty to august international assemblies would be incompatible with the rights and duties of the French Republic . . . In short, it appears essential to us that Europe be Europe and that France be France."

[21] French Embassy, *Major Addresses . . . de Gaulle*, p. 174.

[22] French Embassy, *The First Five Years . . .* , p. 20.

[23] French Embassy, *The First Five Years . . .* , p. 20.

full membership in the EEC might be possible for the British sometime in the future if they are willing to pay a price that would be more political than economic—that is to say, realigning their policy and orienting it away from Washington and toward Europe. In the meanwhile, the United Kingdom remains outside the EEC, the undeclared economic war between the United Kingdom and France continues, and prospects for the future of the British economy grow increasingly gloomy.

De Gaulle stated repeatedly that France is obligated to honor British membership in the EEC if at any time the United Kingdom decides to subscribe equally to the conditions of the Treaty of Rome. The French like to point out that on October 10, 1961, Heath informed the participant states of the EEC of British willingness to comply with this requirement, and that this was precisely what the British did not do when they participated for 16 months in the negotiations in Brussels. Heath made various concessions in that city and yet he defended tariffs, demanding for Canada aluminum and paper pulp exceptions. He also argued for guarantees for British agricultural exports, retention of some agricultural subsidies, and extension beyond 1970 of the transitory period for agriculture. Knowing exactly what they had to do in order to enter the EEC, the British had gone to Brussels in the hope that they would be able to negotiate there the concessions they sought.

President de Gaulle periodically liked to say that the United Kingdom would find it impossible to do in the EEC what the organization does itself, and that British membership would jeopardize the operation of the entire structure. He argued that the Six are continental and that the United Kingdom is not, being "tied beyond the seas" and "to the United States by all kinds of special agreements," making it impossible for her to "merge into a Community with set dimensions and rules." [24] Her agricultural situation is different too, said de Gaulle, and the United Kingdom depends on foodstuffs bought inexpensively throughout the world; her entrance into the EEC would affect adversely her balance of payments by levies, forcing her to raise the price of

[24] Ambassade de France (Service de presse et d'information), *President de Gaulle's Press Conference of May 16, 1967* (May 1967), p. 9.

her food (to price levels on the Continent), the wages of her workers, and the prices of her goods. De Gaulle's position was that "it is clear that she cannot do this. But if she enters the Community without being really subjected to the agricultural system of the Six, this system will thereby collapse, completely upsetting the equilibrium of the Common Market and removing from France one of the main reasons she can have for participating in it." [25] De Gaulle pointed also to the costliness of participation in the EEC and the fact that the British at that time could not see their way to allow capital to leave their country, whereas within the EEC capital circulates freely for the purpose of promoting expansion. Finally, he called attention to the less than promising future of the British pound, and commented that inside the EEC the British would be faced with growing isolation.[26]

[25] Ambassade de France, *President de Gaulle's Press Conference of May 16, 1967,* p. 10.

[26] Ambassade de France, *President de Gaulle's Press Conference of May 16, 1967,* pp. 10–11. De Gaulle's policy statement concluded, ". . . considering the special commitment that they still have in various parts of the world and which, basically, distinguishes them from the continentals, we see that the policy of the latter, as soon as they have one, would undoubtedly concur, in certain cases, with the policy of the former. But we cannot see how both policies would merge, unless the British assumed again, particularly as regards defense, complete command of themselves, or else if the continentals renounced forever a European Europe.

It is true that the British, as is very natural, envisage their participation as automatically leading the Community to become quite different from what it is at present . . . The British, moreover, make no secret of the fact that once inside they would undertake to obtain many revisions. As far as France is concerned, the condition in which she would then be as regards her industry, her agriculture, her trade, her currency, and, lastly, her policy would undoubtedly no longer have any relation to those that she now accepts within the Common Market.

Either recognize that, as things stand at present, their entry into the Common Market, with all the exceptions that it would not fail to be accompanied by, with the interruption of entirely new facts, both in nature and quantity, that would necessarily result from this entry, with the participation of several other States that would certainly be its corollary, would amount to necessitating the building of an entirely new edifice, scrapping nearly all that which has just been built."

FRANCE AND DECOLONIZATION

From the French Community to decolonization

The Fifth Republic in 1958 extended to all Overseas Territories attached to France by the 1946 Constitution an opportunity to choose among the following options: (1) retention of their existing status; or, (2) a change in status to that of Overseas Departments affiliated with the Fifth Republic; or, (3) to come in with the Fifth Republic as autonomous states within a new form of organization called the French Community; or, (4) to break all ties with France and assume independent status outside the French Community. The offer was valid for a six-month period subsequent to the introduction of the new Constitution of the Fifth Republic. In response to the offer, five territorial assemblies voted to maintain their existing status, twelve decided to become autonomous member states of the French Community, and the Overseas Territory of Guinea chose independence and nonaffiliation with the French Community. During the same six-month period members of the French Community were allowed to federate with each other (at their own discretion), or to secede from the Community and assume independent nonaffiliated status. Title XIII of the new Constitution enabled former members of the French Union and French Community an opportunity to return to it whenever they wish, thereby not closing the door on them completely (an opportunity to join the Community was made available also to any state wishing to enter it). Finally, the republic and the Community each were free to conclude agreements with any states who wished to associate with the French Community "in order to develop their own civilizations." [27]

---

[27] The machinery of the Community was as follows. The president of the Fifth Republic also was the president of the Community, presiding over its executive council, which comprised also the prime minister of the republic, the heads of the governments of member states, and ministers of the Fifth Republic concerned with the affairs of the Community, appointed to it by the president of the republic (they were free from supervision by the Parliament of the Fifth Republic). The Executive Council supervised general Community policies, jurisdictions in which the member states were not sovereign, and the administration and

Unforeseen developments led rapidly to separation and independent status outside the Community by many former French Overseas possessions. Soon the institutions of the Community had become obsolete. The French Empire had lasted many years; the French Union existed almost a decade and a half. The French Community survived for a year and a half.

The French Community never was able to get off the ground. When President de Gaulle convened the first session of the Executive Council on February 4, 1959, although he informed the participants that it was not in any way a counterpart of the Conference of Ministers of the British Commonwealth, he was confronted almost immediately by an independence versus nonindependence controversy among its members (in the sessions it took the form of differences among "federalists" and "nonfederalists"). The first session of the Executive revealed the

common policy budgets of the Community. The Executive Council was not responsible to the Senate of the Community. The Senate, constituted on the basis of one seat for every 300,000 inhabitants, with a minimum of three seats per state, examined acts, treaties, or international agreements relative to the Community; it was capable of being asked by the president of the republic for opinions on economic or financial policies common to the Fifth Republic and the Community voted by the Fifth Republic's National Assembly or by the legislative assemblies of member states. It exercised decision making as a result of powers delegated to it from the legislative assemblies of the member States.

The Senate met only twice and was abolished on March 16, 1961, when Prime Minister Debré informed the Fifth Republic Senate that the Senate of the Community had been terminated. A Court of Arbitration of the Community had jurisdiction over disputes among member states relative to the Constitution, Community agreements and conventions among the member states, and organic laws of the Constitution. The Constitution of the Community reserved to each member state local government administration, and sharing in common with the Fifth Republic jurisdiction of foreign policy, currency, defense, economic and financial policies, and strategic raw materials. The member states could through agreements create other common jurisdictions or transfer them from the Community to one or more of its members. The structure of the Community was focused juridically, however, on the president of the republic, who presided over its Executive Council, who headed its administration, who called the Senate into session, and who named the judges of the Court of Arbitration. In no way could the Community extract responsibility from the president of the republic.

strategy of the African members. Although solidly in favor of independence, they had voted in the referendum of November 1958 in favor of continued affiliation with France so as not to remove themselves from future French financial aid. By playing the game this way, they could qualify first for financial aid and later for independence. They achieved that independence within months, through access to Article 86 of the Constitution (". . . a member State of the Community may become independent. It shall thereby cease to belong to the Community."). Article 85 was amended to enable member states of the Community to change status simply by agreements concluded among themselves. The transformation—or decolonization—was peaceful and rapid. Madagascar's sovereignty was voted by the French Parliament, and transferred to the jurisdictions previously vested in the Community, after Madagascar promised in advance to conclude with the Republic certain treaties relating to finance, education, defense, and so on. Madagascar was followed by Mali, Senegal, Cameroun, Togoland, Ivory Coast, Dahomey, Niger, Upper Volta, transitions which in some cases were accomplished by treaties concluded among the Fifth Republic and the Parliaments of the different states. In the case of the Council of the Entente (Niger, Dahomey, Ivory Coast, Upper Volta), independence was made a precondition of signing future agreements with France (accomplished after independence but excluding all military ties).

The decolonization implemented by the Fifth Republic was orderly and satisfactory, providing an admirable image for the modern world. Not often has colonization had so desirable a conclusion. Later, termination of the Algerian war strengthened France's relations with her former African possessions who had favored Algerian independence. Today, these states are African, not French, but within them continuation of some pro-French cultural sentiment reinforces their continued association with France.

Failure of the Fourth Republic and the creation of the Fifth Republic

An understanding of the Fifth Republic requires understanding of its predecessor, the Fourth Republic, and the conditions that led to its destruction. The Fourth Republic ended in reality on May 13, 1958 (its "legal" end came some weeks later), when in Algeria and metropolitan France elements of the French military and various anti-Fourth Republic groups revolted against the regime, converging in their demands to call publicly for General de Gaulle's leadership of France. Years of war, ineffective attempts at decision making, and ill-concealed evasions of responsibility by its cabinets all hastened the demise of the Fourth Republic. During its last two years, the Fourth Republic was immersed in futility and near-governmental paralysis, verging at times on a state of near-collapse. Occasionally, it appeared even unlikely that successors could be found for defeated cabinets. Intrigue was at its zenith and public criticism of the "regime of parties" was widespread. The regime was not given the opportunity, nonetheless, to complete its own destruction. The military took matters in its own hands and banished it in May 1958. The Fourth Republic—which had satisfied so few of its social and political groups—was at the end supported by few people (one should not be misled by those who demonstrated in its behalf during the period May 13–June 1, 1958; many of those people acknowledged that the republic probably was not worth saving).[28]

The military's distaste for the Fourth Republic goes back to the early 1950s, when various of its members came to the belief that the French defeat in Indochina was the result of a

[28] Attention is called here to those authors who contend that the Fourth Republic was "not so bad," and that reports of its inadequacies have been exaggerated. The author takes sharp exception to these contentions, and asks what a republic must be in order to get a "bad" rating? The fact remains that the Fourth could not control the military, hardly any of its life was free from war, it could not end the war in Algeria, it could not control inflation, it was plagued by strikes, and toward its end it went more than two months before it could even recruit a government. The author interviewed in Paris in May 1958 several Left figures who had demonstrated against the Gaullist *coup*. One stated, "The only advantage is that the Gaullists did put an end to a very bad Republic." Finally, Mendès-France has never admitted it publicly, but was he not —although revolted by the Gaullists' methods—pleased with the destruction of the Fourth? Were not his demonstrations against the Gaullists in 1958 directed against them primarily and only vaguely with defense of the regime?

lack of support by the republic's governments. Well-known figures such as Marshal of the Armies Juin articulated publicly their contempt for the politicians at home. Some officers of the Army became convinced that civil cabinets in Paris irresponsibly ordered the army into conflicts without giving them subsequently the kind of support that would enable them to win. In the eyes of some of these men the Fourth Republic was the real enemy.

The Fourth Republic waged war in Indochina for nine years (1946–1954) in an effort to preserve her power there. The republic watered down its colonialism during that time with diverse democratic forms and fictions; nevertheless, France never was able to resolve the colonial issue itself. Nationalists, noncommunists, and communists banded together to coordinate efforts with the opposition Viet-Minh, while the French emphasized tirelessly the necessity of preventing communism from taking over the area. Never, however, were the French able to convince successfully both nationalists and noncommunists that they should abandon the communists and support the French. The French soon found themselves in an impossible position in Indochina. Both nationalists and communists came to be tied to each other. When the French struck against one, they were forced also to take arms against the other. The war dragged on and on, and the French continued to promise Indochina its independence—never, however, was a true version of it granted.

French governments at home recognized the futility of the war; some acknowledged it publicly. They knew that force was useless, and that the conflict evaded a military solution. Still they did nothing to terminate it until after the disastrous defeat at Dien Bien Phu when Prime Minister Mendès-France withdrew French forces from Indochina. The war had lasted nine years, thousands of lives had been lost, and more than 20 percent of the French officer class graduated from Saint-Cyr after 1945 had been destroyed. The French disaster in Indochina was not, however, the end of hostilities for the French army. In November 1954 rebellion broke out in Algeria, and the French army was dispatched there in another fruitless and costly effort to retain yet another French possession overseas.

Indochina was an example of a French colonial failure. Algeria was other than an example of that. The French contended that Algeria was not a colony but an extension of metropolitan France. Nonetheless, France had for years implemented there practices that normally are associated with colonialism, ranging from "assimilation" to "association." Assimilation sets standards which the local population presumably can attain and receive French citizenship; association sets citizenship not as the final stage, going beyond it to take the native population into the administration.

Efforts of different Fourth Republic governments to essay a solution to the Algerian insurrection were futile. Three of the last five governments of that Republic were helpless against it. Invested February 1, 1956, and in office until May 21, 1957, Guy Mollet's cabinet devised in search of a solution overlapping policies which it applied to the conflict: (1) long-term reforms in Algeria; (2) military pacification of Algeria; (3) contacts with leaders of the insurrection in hopes that they would lead to a negotiated solution. However, in 1956, when he and Eden ordered the invasion of Suez, Mollet probably saw the defeat of Nasser as contributing to the Algerian solution. Nonetheless, Nasser, as a consequence of the invasion, was not defeated but strengthened, as was the Algerian insurrectionist movement, the FLN, or the National Front of Liberation. A study of the Mollet government's approach to Algeria is a study of complete ineffectiveness—instead of terminating the war, Mollet contributed, perhaps, to its lengthening. Mollet's government was succeeded by the government of Bourgès-Maunoury which engaged in weak attempts to introduce new "framework" laws as a basis for the creation of new political institutions in Algeria subsequent to the end of hostilities there. These failed, too, and his successor, Félix Gaillard, found himself without means to deal with the rebellion. Gaillard, moreover, succeeded in alienating the army by effecting reductions in the military budget, prompting some officers to declare that the move was motivated by Gaillard's desire to prevent the army from restoring peace in Algeria. By March 1958 Gaillard had lost complete control of French military action in Algeria, and after the French bombing of the Tunisian village of Sakhiet (unauthorized by

Gaillard),[29] the political system—with respect to Algerian policy decisions—was subordinated to the military. Gaillard, having been unaware previously of the French decision to cross the Tunisian border, went before the National Assembly and there defended the action! By that time it was obvious that some of the republic's politicians were fearful of some of the republic's generals. Gaillard eventually was defeated by the National Assembly; two more cabinets subsequently were created but by that time the Fourth Republic was finished. Pierre Pflimlin was invested on May 13, the day that the army revolted in Algeria.[30] The last prime minister of the Fourth Republic was General de Gaulle, who was invested on June 3 —not to save the republic, but to abolish it and to devise another one in its stead.

Thousands of non-Moslem settlers occupied the government buildings in Algiers on May 13, 1958, urging the army to power and expressing their opposition to the newly invested President of the Council of Ministers Pierre Pflimlin. Leadership of the insurrection against the Fourth Republic passed first to paratroop General Jacques Massu (a tough soldier who cauterized his leg wound with a cigarette during the Suez invasion), and later to General Salan, commander of the French army in Algeria, member of the Socialist party, SFIO, and known for his "republican" sympathies. Salan immediately called for and end to the Fourth Republic and for creation of a new regime under General de Gaulle. Several days later, on May 18, General de Gaulle replied that he was willing to assume the premiership but only on condition that the National Assembly grant him emergency powers enabling him to create a new Constitution and another republic. The Assembly answered de

[29] "Authorized," it is said, by Chaban-Delmas, now premier of France.

[30] Pflimlin provided a dramatic example of how a cabinet can be secure and a republic in peril. Pflimlin never had a chance. It takes an army to put down an army, something that he did not have. It is said that early in the rebellion Pflimlin called the Admiral of the French Mediterranean fleet and directed him to retake Corsica from the military, and that he received but a one-word reply, *Merde*. What course other than resignation was open to Pflimlin? A government without an army is no match for an army without a government.

Gaulle by voting Prime Minister Pflimlin emergency powers (475–100), directing him to deal with the rebellion. Pflimlin waited until May 27 and then delegated some of the same powers to Salan—the action was bewildering to the populace inasmuch as Salan was at that time in insurrection against Pflimlin, his government, and his republic, as well! Pflimlin then returned to the National Assembly and told it that it had to choose between de Gaulle and him, and the Assembly again expressed its confidence in him. Supported by the National Assembly but confronted with a military coup against which he was powerless, Pflimlin resigned the premiership the following day. President Coty then entered the crisis and on May 30 told the nation that he was offering de Gaulle the opportunity to be invested as premier by the Assembly (Coty threatened to resign if the Assembly declined). The deputies knew that their vote heralded the end of the regime and the creation of another—but what else could they have done? Their rejection of de Gaulle would have exposed the country to the risk of army invasion and introduction of a military dictatorship.

Throughout most of the May crisis de Gaulle was opposed by the classical political parties; in fact, for a brief time it appeared that the National Assembly would refuse de Gaulle investiture as prime minister, if only to prevent him from coming "legally" to power. The first crack in the leadership ranks of the opposition parties appeared when Socialist party leader Guy Mollet decided that the only way to "save the Republic" was by pledging his deputies' votes in behalf of de Gaulle's investiture, thereby breaking the opposition line in the National Assembly and allowing the vote to carry (causing a deep rift in the SFIO parliamentary party). Invested by a vote of 329 to 224, de Gaulle then received from the National Assembly decree powers for six months' duration. He announced that soon a national referendum would allow the populace to approve or reject his blueprint for a new republic. On September 28 the constitution for a new republic was presented to the people in a referendum and approved by approximately 80 percent of those who voted in metropolitan France, Algeria, and Overseas Territories. Thus, de Gaulle's coming to power by revolutionary means was "legitimized." In the referendum the average voter was given the opportunity to vote *yes* relative to a very vague description of what the new republic was to be like; voters wishing to vote *no* were unable to vote for an alternative plan, and well did they know that naked military rule was distinctly possible if the referendum failed to secure popular approval.

The "men of May 13" who had brought de Gaulle to power generally were people who were dedicated to France's retention of Algeria; they thought that they saw in de Gaulle the means of guaranteeing that relationship. Nonetheless, during the first months that followed May 13 de Gaulle was curiously silent about Algeria's future, and speculation as to how the General really felt became a national game. Men such as Marshal of the Armies Juin did not hesitate to say that the General left no doubt whatsoever relative to Algeria's indissoluble ties with France, and Algérie française spokesmen like Jacques Soustelle assured listeners that the General soon would achieve what he had been brought to power to do. The General finally broke his silence on September 16, 1959, when he announced that in Algeria after the end of hostilities a referendum would allow the Algerians to exercise full self-determination or retention of their ties with France. The General finally had spoken, and now some of the men of May 13 began to lay plans for his destruction. There were some subsequent revolts, for instance, the revolt of Generals Zeller, Challe, Jouhaud, Salan, and Gardy, but these were put down with relative ease. The way finally was cleared for subsequent negotiations with the Algerian rebels, mutual cessation of hostilities, and acceptance of a treaty of peace. That was achieved by March 19, 1962, and when that happened the republic finally succeeded in coping with its greatest problem (for each additional day of insurrection endangered the Fifth Republic's stability still further). For more than seven years the republic and the rebels had fought each other to a standstill. The republic was unable to vanquish the rebels, and the rebels had been unable to expel the French from Algeria. A great state with a modern army had been checked by a guerrilla force with Algerian public opinion on its side. Recognition by the French came late that the Algeria of *Beni-oui-oui* had been dead for many years, and that Algeria was not French or Gaullist; nevertheless, recognition eventually did come, and primarily because of the efforts of a general who had been brought to the leadership of France to retain Algeria as a French possession. The war, when finally it halted, had consumed a republic, various governments, and thousands of French and Algerian lives.

CONCLUSION

Primary in General de Gaulle's thought was the nation-state, which he viewed as the highest vehicle attainable for the organization and expression of a people. The world order is that arena comprising states engaged constantly in the attempt to enhance their own interests and power. A new world order can be realized through creation of a long-lasting equilibrium of powers. Efforts must be undertaken to achieve by diplomacy and treaties transformations which will establish a world order satisfactory both to its own and French interests.

General de Gaulle rebuffed all attempts to reduce French sovereignty. Diplomacy conducted along bilateral rather than multilateral lines offered the greatest protection for French sovereignty. NATO was viewed as a threat to France's independence of action and sovereign existence, and dependence upon it could only result in France's domination by another power or powers. For de Gaulle, the best safeguards for French diplomacy were bilateral efforts and a bomb. Possession of the bomb placed France among those sovereign powers known as *les grandes,* or those who comprise the nuclear club, and enables her to wage diplomacy more effectively. *Les grandes* have a world vocation; those who are not among *les grandes* have a regional one. Perhaps some day a concert of *les grandes* will guarantee world peace; French efforts must be expended in behalf of this realization.

De Gaulle was convinced that the present world equilibrium should be replaced by another equilibrium, one that is better and more effective. A European confederation anchored in a Franco-German entente should be first constructed; later, an equilibrium should be constructed between it and the United States. And even later perhaps an equilibrium can be constructed between a European confederation ranging from the Atlantic to the Urals and other parts of the world. Special efforts must be given to bringing the "Third World" within this relationship.

France's refusal to accommodate British membership in the European Economic Community is based on any number of considerations. Whatever the narrowness of the French position, the fact remains that the United Kingdom can enter the EEC whenever she shows her willingness and ability to satisfy the conditions of its charter, the Treaty of Rome.

French decolonization was implemented by the Fifth Republic in an orderly and efficient manner, resulting in the satisfaction of self-determination demands by numerous peoples formerly of French juridical identification, and freeing France from multiple obligations which had become both overbearing and internally divisive.

The Fourth Republic was a regime of political futility. During its last two years that republic was immersed in near-governmental paralysis. The military slipped beyond civil control some months before the republic's destruction. Finally, in May 1958, the military banished the regime and brought to the leadership of France the man who they thought would guarantee French retention of Algeria. Under his leadership, Algeria achieved her independence in less than four years. By then many of the men who had brought de Gaulle to power were either in prison or exile. The end of the Algerian war terminated one of the Fifth Republic's greatest problems.

TWELVE
APRÈS
DE GAULLE?
**Summary
and conclusion**

Between 1958 and 1968 the Gaullist state took some steps toward economic modernization. Few people contested state intervention in social and economic affairs; many did contest the lack of vigor with which the state approached such considerations as housing, price levels, inflation, education, and the plight of descending social categories. Their concern came to a head in May 1968, when millions of citizens stopped work for weeks and negotiated their own collective bargaining contract for social and economic reform with a regime that had become increasingly unheedful, if not contemptuous, of public opinion. After May 1968 that populace looked to the Gaullists to deliver the great social transformations promised by them earlier. How far were the Gaullists prepared to go in reforming the tax system, capital-labor relations, distribution of national income, education, social welfare, technology? Was the "old order" passing, and was a new one preparing to supersede it, one that would defy all doctrinal classifications, such as "socialist," "conservative," even "communist," and reveal elements derived from all?

432

Was France truly on the threshold of great change? Would the Gaullists see to it that the more France changed, the more it *would not be* the same? Would the General be able to achieve this transformation? And if he failed, would other forces be willing and able to pick up the pieces and address themselves to implementation of this task?

Having witnessed defeat of the referendum of April 27, 1969, General de Gaulle retired that night from the presidency of the republic. Nothing obliged him to leave the post three years before the expiration of his term of office, and no constitutional question had been raised concerning his continuation in the presidency. De Gaulle left behind him a brief farewell, "I am ceasing to exercise the functions of the Republic. This decision takes effect at midnight today." His formal resignation was submitted the following morning to Gaston Palewski, President of the Constitutional Court. Premier Couve de Murville commented, "Tomorrow a new page in our history will be turned. General de Gaulle was at the center of our political and national life. We remain faithful to him. A difficult period, perhaps a period of trouble, now lies before us. For the moment, the government will assure the continuity of public powers in accordance with the Constitution. It will naturally do its duty."

France entered on April 28, 1969, the era of "after de Gaulle." The institutions and practices of the state had been tied for so long so closely to one man; his abrupt departure raised a host of new questions. Are the political structures of the Fifth Republic created in 1958 by the General only provisional, or will they continue to carry in the post de Gaulle era? Will the presidential regime be retained and utilized in future years by the Gaullists (providing that they survive the departure of the General) and non-Gaullists alike, or will it be replaced by a synthesized presidential-parliamentary system, or by "government of the legislature"? Will the Gaullist Union of Democrats for the Fifth Republic evolve mechanisms which will enable it to become a real political party in this new era "after de Gaulle"? What will be the nature of leadership in a France without de Gaulle? What will be the nation's appearance after his disappearance? Will the Left, which continues to regard itself as "revolutionary," continue to resist transformation and refuse to renovate its antiquated political parties, ones which have lost so much ground in recent years?

THE CONSTITUTIONAL QUESTION

In this new era "after de Gaulle" there probably will be considerable controversy concerning the form that republican organization should take. As Duverger says, if the presidential system is retained, the more entrenched will be the reaction of those who resist it, leading them to an even more vigorous defense of government by legislature. And as Macridis states:

> A sharp conflict over the institutionalization of the presidency . . . will not be an isolated affair. It will spill over into all other constitutional disagreements: the role of the prime minister, the electoral system, dissolution, constitutional reform, Article 16, use of the referenda . . . and make compromise difficult.[1]

It seems difficult to believe that the post de Gaulle era will be able to or even wish to avoid controversy concerning the allocation of presidential powers. Article 5, which allows the President to exercise arbitration probably will be contested. Article 11, which allows the President to submit to a referendum, on the proposal of the government, or on joint proposal of the two assemblies, any bill dealing with the organization of the public authorities or ratification of a treaty, probably will be exposed to demands for modification, for it has already been used in too plebisciterian fashion to avoid controversy. It also is possible that Article 11 might subsequently be entrusted, as the result of an amendment, solely to the initiative of the cabinet and Parliament and restricted exclusively to nonconstitutional projects of law. Article 12 certainly will be contested. This article allows the president of the republic to exercise dissolution of the National Assembly. MacMahon has been gone for almost

---

[1] Karl W. Deutsch, Lewis J. Edinger, Roy C. Macridis, and Richard L. Merritt, *France, Germany and the Western Alliance: A Study of Elite Attitudes on European Integration and World Politics* (New York: Scribner, 1967), p. 47.

a hundred years, and the republic is not threatened now as it was during his day; nevertheless, those who wish to modify Article 12 question the retention of the presidential power of dissolution, for they want to avoid the possibility of exposing a legislature to dissolution whenever it comes in conflict with the president of the republic. Article 16 is bound to be contested, perhaps even fiercely; some people will push for its abolition, and others may well demand that it be entrusted to the cabinet, with invocation dependent upon authorization by the Parliament.

Chances for adoption in the post de Gaulle era of a synthesized presidential-parliamentary system appear to be less than remote. Return to the political forms favored by the Communist party, the late Federation of the Left, and by diverse Left figures (a parliamentary system with executive power deriving from the legislature) seems unlikely. Guy Mollet may articulate loudly numerous protests against presidentialism, and Mendès-France may defend a system employed by a republic that was little to his liking, but it is a fact that the Left opposition now contains many presidentialists. If the late Federation of the Left supported government by legislature, François Mitterand, when he was its leader, did make a series of oblique references to receptiveness to a presidentialism close to the version provided by the Constitution—that is, a presidentialism in which the president would be strictly an arbiter and not an interpreter of the Constitution. Other figures within the Left offered for years an opposition to presidentialism that was primarily tactical, their criticisms being directed not so much against the system itself as against de Gaulle's perversion of it. The Left is a repository presently for both presidential and antipresidential convictions; consequently the post de Gaulle era may force the Left to achieve a synthesis of the two. Failing that, the Left will retain yet another division in its arsenal of divisions. It is entirely possible that the Center and those who presently are Gaullists will in this post de Gaulle era also be willing to strengthen the Parliament and push for the adoption of a synthesized presidential-parliamentary system. Conditions of political performance will be undergoing transformation in this post de Gaulle era, and the Gaullist force—if it survives the

departure of the General—may be able to derive from a synthesized system more than it can retrieve from other forms of
organization. The fact that the Communist party and the Independents continue to press for a government of the legislature
should not preclude attainment of a presidential-parliamentary
synthesis.

THE POLITICAL SYSTEM AND THE PARTY SYSTEM

In this post de Gaulle era, the operation of the constitutional
system probably will be restored to the party system—for who
can believe that this new era will produce yet another de Gaulle
and consequent nondependence upon party? Nonetheless, prospects for successful implementation by the parties of the political
system appear to be less than promising—not because maximiza-
tion of the role of parties is undesirable, but because of the
underdeveloped condition of French parties. If the parties hesitated during the time of de Gaulle to transform themselves and
undertake mergers with each other, what reason is there to
believe that they will do so in the era after de Gaulle? The era
of de Gaulle could have been for them a period of real revitaliza-
tion, with an eye toward the future, but things did not work
this way. The parties wasted their time rushing into conflicts for
which they were ill prepared, instead of devoting themselves to
reconstruction in preparation for the era after de Gaulle. Instead
of addressing themselves to the realities of politics, they frequently continued to play the game as though drastic change had
not attended the passage from the Fourth to the Fifth Republic.
Consequently they suffered reduction after reduction in their
public image. After the termination of the Algerian war, some
of the anti-Gaullist parties became identified with opposition for
the sake of opposition, an old French custom but one which
backfired on them repeatedly.

The time of Defferre's federation, back around 1964, was
that critical period when the opposition parties might have shaken
themselves loose from so many of their crippling inadequacies.
Yet nobody gave the federation much of a chance. Why? Not
because the federation was a "bad" idea in itself, but because
the federation required sacrifices not only by traditional men of
party but sacrifice of some traditional parties too. The SFIO,

Radicals, and MRP, who were not going anywhere individually, recoiled from the suggestion that they could go somewhere collectively. The defeat of Defferre's federation and its replacement by Mitterand's Federation of the Left signaled continuation of the old ideas and old ways by tired parties unalterably opposed to internal reforms and mergers with each other. Defferre's federation—although public opinion admittedly was ill prepared for its adoption—was killed by the convergence of the directorships of several traditional political parties. Ostensibly, the federation died because of the lay issue. In reality, it died because of Guy Mollet and his opposition to any change whatsoever that jeopardized the sovereignty of "his" party. The Mitterand federation was from the day of its creation never more than a mask for the directorships of tired Socialist and Radical parties. André Philip, who finally has abandoned the Left parties, more in sadness than in disgust, states that he lost all confidence in the Mitterand movement when in Lyon the federation decided to present as candidates in the legislative elections former Socialist and Radical deputies, refusing to extend any serious consideration whatsoever to young elements who had come from the political clubs. The federation, says Philip, tried to present "the dead" as candidates.[2]

The problem of transforming and revitalizing the parties is not confined alone to the Left opposition parties. Also involved is France's largest party, the Gaullist Union of Democrats for the Fifth Republic. The organization, less of a true party and more of a giant formation called into existence because of General de Gaulle's presence, has succeeded, nonetheless, in shaping up more than a small amount of internal cohesiveness. It has its own organization, and if it survives the departure of de Gaulle it must evolve internal mechanisms which will allow it to function as a true party. Now that the General is gone from the presidency, it will have to depend more on itself and less on signals from him. This may not be the way the General would want it, but in this era after de Gaulle the Union hardly can continue to be bound so strictly by his dictates.

The parties, then, will probably have the major say in

---

[2] André Philip, "Pour un dialogue efficace," *Le Monde,* May 28, 1966, p. 6.

operating the political system in the post de Gaulle era—for if they do not do it, who will? No person of de Gaulle's stature is likely to be on hand to play the kind of role he assumed in the Fifth Republic, and it is more than likely that his successor will be less powerful than he had been. Will the parties be equipped, however, for the task of operating the political system? Will they accomplish internal modernization before going on to it, or will they remain in their present condition and resurrect the "political class" and live off its machinations? If they do, the France of the future will prove a disappointment. On the other hand, in operating the political system the parties will not be confronted with Indochinese and Algerian wars; moreover, the parties now have the advantage of an army that has been tamed and restricted to indirect rather than direct political intervention. Yet, because of their limitations, the parties will not have an easy go of it—irrespective of whether France retains presidentialism, adopts a synthesis of presidentialism and parliamentarism, or settles for a return to government by legislature. Therefore, in this post de Gaulle era leadership will be all the more important. Fortunately, both the Gaullists and their opposition have in reserve some well-qualified men, Giscard d'Estaing, Edgar Faure, and Mendès-France, to name but a few. If none of these men is a de Gaulle, they are at least capable of commanding public trust. The problem with such men is not with their leadership but with the nature of the organizational machinery at their disposal. If Mendès-France, for example, wants *A Modern French Republic* (the title of one of his books), then he must find a modern party system that will bring it into being.

THE NEED FOR A VIABLE OPPOSITION

Earlier in this decade, Maurice Duverger frequently asked in his columns in *Le Monde* if the French would do eventually to de Gaulle what the English did to Churchill? He noted that in the United Kingdom there was an alternative to Churchill, but in France no alternative to de Gaulle.

The record of the Gaullist opposition is that of a long string of tactical errors and relatively impractical recommendations.

Early in the history of the Fifth Republic, efforts by the opposition to prepare for a return to "government by assembly" meant defense of a system that had demonstrated previously its ineffectiveness and from which public opinion had become alienated. Later, in 1962, the opposition's campaign against de Gaulle's "constitutional" amendment presented a study in confusion. There are many other examples of the opposition's inadequacies, but further listing of them probably is unnecessary. De Gaulle's regime was riddled with faults; however, despite its inadequacies, his opposition was unable to present a reasonable alternative to it. If his regime was immersed in personal power, his opposition was buried in impotence. So much of his "strength" derived from the weaknesses of his opposition. Why has the opposition been unable to devise a clear and simple program that satisfies the needs of the country? Why has it been unable to offer the stable government to which the country has become attached? If it cannot achieve these things, the opposition has little right to offer itself as a viable alternative to the existing regime. For years public opinion surveys consistently revealed resentment of de Gaulle's "style" of operation; however, those surveys also showed public unwillingness to vest very much confidence in the opposition's ability to implement an operable order. The French may like weak governments, but they also like stable ones. De Gaulle offered them stability and even managed its realization. His opposition offered the possibility of governmental instability and the threat of a return to the conditions of the past.

FOREIGN POLICY AND THE OPPOSITION

Now that France finally has passed from de Gaulle's control, the nation's foreign policy probably will undergo some modifications. Even if the Gaullists continue to dominate the organs of government, it is not unlikely that they will reevaluate foreign policy and strengthen somewhat France's ties with the United States and NATO. It also is likely that some changes will be effected in Middle East policy, particularly with respect to Israel. However, this is not to say that ties with the Arab world will be discarded. By and large, some main lines of de Gaulle's foreign policy will continue to be sustained and the French nation will keep an eye toward maintaining its independence from both American and Russian hegemony. Under the direction of the opposition, France would be closer to the possibility of membership in an authentic United States of Europe, bringing to an end the era of French dependence upon a "Europe of States" and an independent nuclear deterrent. The opposition would not purposely confuse real federation with participation in a European confederation which, for the Gaullists, is not a precondition of federalism but a barrier against it and a facade for Gaullist efforts to dominate European policy. However, when and if control finally passes to the opposition, there is no reason to believe that French foreign policy will be consciously and purposely subordinated to American foreign policy. Both Gaullists and anti-Gaullists agree that French foreign policy must not be an instrument of American foreign policy. When and if control finally passes to the opposition, chances for French and American cooperation in foreign policy probably will be improved— nevertheless, if thorough cooperation is to be obtained, the United States may very well have to speak in terms of a "true partnership."

IS THE END OF DE GAULLE
THE END OF THE GAULLIST REGIME?

The year 1968 was the "winter" of de Gaulle; he was denied the benefit of a full spring as his reign terminated in April of the following year.

De Gaulle is not only one of the great figures of this century; he may well be the greatest personage in all of French history. One recalls Chateaubriand's portrait of Napoleon: "This giant has not tied his destiny to those of his contemporaries. Men are in his eyes not more than a method of power, no sympathy exists between their goodwill and his; he isolates himself from them, he recoils from them."

If 1969 was the end of de Gaulle's career as president of the republic, it was not, however, the end of Gaullism. Now that de Gaulle is no longer president, how effectively and for how long can Gaullism survive?

POSTSCRIPT
THE PRESIDENTIAL ELECTIONS OF JUNE 1969

BACKGROUND

The presidential elections of June 1 and 15, 1969, were the consequence of General de Gaulle having staked his political life unnecessarily on the outcome of the referendum of April 27, 1969. De Gaulle had stated before the referendum, "Whether I stay in office or whether I withdraw immediately will obviously depend on the answer to the question which I have put to the country."[1] Technically, three questions were posed by the referendum (voters were asked if they wanted a regional reorganization of the nation, if they wanted a transformed Senate to be merged with the Economic and Social Council, if they wished the law of presidential succession to be amended so that the premier would become interim president in the event of presidential death or disability). The referendum asked a fourth question, however—one that was not written into it but which was on the minds of all electors. The French were asked if they wished to retain de Gaulle as president of the republic by voting affirmatively in the referendum, or if they wished to communicate to

---

[1] See *Le Monde,* April 12, 1969, pp. 2–3, for text of de Gaulle's declaration.

him their desire that he resign from office by voting negatively? The referendum was defeated decisively and de Gaulle then moved to Ireland until the termination of the pending presidential election, refusing to endorse anyone publicly and confirming the suspicion that he was relatively unconcerned with the choice of his successor.[2]

Important transformations within the Left opposition in 1968–1969 had an important bearing on the presidential election. The Federation of the Left fell apart late in 1968 and the agreement that had been concluded between it and the Communist party on February 24, 1968, was virtually junked. Left disunity—which was so clearly demonstrated in the legislative elections of June 1968—was accentuated further in 1969. The parties of the Left were unable to unite behind one presidential candidate; consequently they presented their own candidates (with the exception of the Radicals).

Polls taken in the spring of 1968 had given François Mitterand a good chance to succeed de Gaulle.[3] However, his disastrous leadership of the Left in the legislative elections of June 1968 led subsequently to a Socialist and Radical reaction against him and his performances in the presidential election of

[2] *L'Express,* 934 (June 2–8, 1969), p. 73. De Gaulle did send to Pompidou a *personal* letter of encouragement.

[3] Institut français d'opinion publique. "La crise de mai 1968." *Sondages,* 2 (1968), 22, 25. When in March of 1968 the French Institute of Public Opinion asked the question, "Whom would you vote for in the next presidential election on the first ballot?," 30 percent of the respondents replied Mitterand, 25 percent Pompidou, and 14 percent d'Estaing. The institute had recorded eight months earlier in response to the same question: 36 percent Mitterand, 21 percent Pompidou, and 16 percent d'Estaing. In response to the question asked in March 1968, "Whom would you vote for on the second ballot?," respondents gave Mitterand and Pompidou each 34 percent. In another survey conducted by the institute in 1968, one designed to test the popularity of twelve prominent politicians, Mitterand and Pompidou with 51 percent ran exactly abreast of each other (but behind Couve de Murville's 59 percent). The same survey showed opposition to Pompidou (28 percent) as exceeding opposition to Mitterand (26 percent). Negative percentages in excess of this were recorded only by Michel Debré and Waldeck-Rochet. Finally, in an institute scale, ranging from 1 to 10, Mitterand registered sixth (6.0) and Pompidou ninth (5.7) in popularity among a number of men of politics.

1965 and the legislative elections of 1967 were forgotten. Accused of *impopularité chronique,* the former president of the late Federation of the Left made numerous appearances in different cities, maintaining his identity with the theme of the necessity of Left unity, which—according to him—has not been destroyed and is capable of reappearing in future presidential or legislative elections.[4] Presenting himself as the "accuser" of those who had committed "a crime against the Republic" in making Left unity impossible, Mitterand designated Guy Mollet as one of his special targets,[5] for it was Mollet who decided in 1969 against endorsing with the Communist party and Mitterand's Convention of Republican Institutions (CIR) a presidential candidate in common.[6] Mollet used as his pretext the "re-Stalinization" of the Communist party and its return to rigidity after the Soviet invasion of Czechoslovakia—a thin pretext, indeed, for it was well-known that Mollet was sympathetic to the strategy of supporting on the second ballot a centrist candidate in order to defeat the Gaullist Pompidou.[7]

[4] *Le Monde,* April 24, 1969, p. 11.

[5] *Le Monde,* May, 6, 1969, p. 1.

[6] *Le Monde,* June 3, 1969, p. 5. See for discussion of Mollet's "reasons," *Le Monde,* May 6, 9, 1969, p. 1. During the presidential campaign Mollet also was involved in efforts to create a "new socialist party" comprising elements of the non-Communist Left. The "new party" met in a constituent congress in Alfortville in May; it was agreed that the party would be a reality by December 1969. The provisional executive committee at Alfortville mandated Pierre Mauroy, assistant secretary-general of the "ex-SFIO" to make "contacts with the Convention of Republican Institutions and the Union des groupes et clubs socialistes (UGCS)." Both organizations refused, however, to come to Alfortville. The provisional executive committee of the "new party" includes five former directors of the SFIO. The bureau, which has as its mission the creation of the "new party" is composed at the time of this writing exclusively of members of the SFIO. Roger Fajardie, SFIO, is in charge of the secretariat of the executive committee. At Alfortville the membership of the "new party" was given as 87,654, but it is known that the membership declined in the first weeks after the congress. Mollet sat at Alfortville as an "ordinary" member of the "new party." Of waning power, he remains in a firm position, however, at *cité Malesherbes* (SFIO headquarters).

[7] *Le Monde,* April 17, 1969, p. 6. Mollet said that collaboration with the Communist party was not possible until it clarified its attitude toward Prague.

THE CANDIDATES

Seven candidates appeared on the first ballot in the presidential election—Gaullist Georges Pompidou, centrist Alain Poher, Socialist (SFIO) Gaston Defferre, Communist Jacques Duclos, Unified Socialist party (PSU) member Michel Rocard, Trotskyite Alain Krivine, and rightist Louis Ducatel.[8] Following is a brief description of the backgrounds of the candidates—with the exception of Pompidou and Defferre, who are discussed at length in the main text and whose backgrounds do not require further attention here.

Alain Poher, sixty years of age, was born in Ablon-sur-Seine in the Val-de-Marne. He is a civil engineer who also holds a law degree and a diploma from the old École libre des sciences politiques. He began his career in the Ministry of Finance, rising to become in 1948 secretary of state for finance and the economy in the Schuman cabinet. During the same year he served as secretary of state for the budget in the Queuille cabinet. In 1952 he became a senator from the Seine-et-Oise, representing the MRP and serving subsequently as president of its senate group. For years Poher was affiliated with the assembly of the European Coal and Steel Community. In 1968 Poher was reelected senator for the Val-de-Marne, belonging in that body to the Center Union of Democrats for Progress (UCDP). On October 3, 1968, he was elected president of the Senate, replacing its long-time president Gaston de Monnerville. With the resignation of de Gaulle, Poher became interim president of the republic.

Poher is a very ordinary man who reminds one of the last president of the Fourth Republic, the late René Coty. A man who likes to play with words, his rhetorical creations usually are less than captivating. If he fails to resemble de Gaulle, this was for him an advantage during the presidential campaign. His regard for the primacy of the constitution differentiated him sharply from de Gaulle; moreover, his sincerity is incontestable. If under de Gaulle the Élysée Palace was inhabited by a notable of the regime, under Poher it would have been occupied by a

---

[8] For brief description of the candidates, see Ambassade de France (Service de presse et d'information), "The Presidential Elections of June 1, 1969," 1238 (May 1969), 1–14.

veteran politician noted for his resemblance to most other men in French society, one who never expected to be president of the republic but who would have performed as one as the consequence of the impulsive act of the General.

Poher had argued against the referendum of April 27, 1969. Although he is a partisan of regionalization, he had opposed the transformation of the Senate.[9] What is the value, he asked, of giving the regions more powers while suppressing the powers of the "Grand Council of Regions," the Senate? This kind of regionalization, he said, would be "no more than an illusion."[10] During the referendum campaign Poher criticized the government's manipulation of state radio-TV (ORTF) as producing lack of an "honest equilibrium."[11]

Jacques Duclos, seventy-two-year-old Communist party candidate, is an old ornament of this and other republics. Born in Louey in the Hautes-Pyrénées, Duclos wanted to become a teacher but was forced by poverty to take a job early in his life as a *pâtissier*. During World War I he served in the armed forces and was taken prisoner of war. In 1928 he made his "pilgrimage" to the USSR, returning "confident in the political judgment, foresight and tenacity of Stalin."[12] A member of the party's politburo, he first entered the legislative chamber as a deputy in 1926. In 1936 he served as vice-president of the Chamber of Deputies. For years he was assistant to the late party leader Maurice Thorez. With the coming of the Fifth Republic Duclos entered the Senate. Duclos is known as a man of absolute fidelity to his party.

Michel Rocard, candidate of the Unified Socialist party (PSU), is an official in the financial world who was known for years in PSU circles as Georges Servet. He is a Protestant and thirty-nine years of age. In 1967 he became secretary-general of the PSU. A graduate of the Institut d'études politiques and of the liberal arts section of the University of Paris, Rocard also is a product of the National School of Administration (ENA).

[9] *Le Monde,* April 4, 12, 1969, p. 7, p. 1.
[10] *Le Monde,* April 4, 1969, p. 7.
[11] *Le Monde,* April 14, 1969, p. 7.
[12] Alain Duhamel, "M. Jacques Duclos: Des prisons aux honneurs," *Le Monde,* May 7, 1969, p. 4.

A professor in the National School of Statistics and Economic Administration, he has served in the economic and financial service of the treasury department, as secretary-general of the commission for the economic budgets and accounts of the nation, and as technical adviser in the estimates department in the economy and finance ministry. Rocard seeks to join technocracy and socialism, arguing that socialism without liberty is but a Soviet travesty. Aware that the old Left is dying, Rocard is a representative of the "new Left" who has his eye to French youth and the future, for he knows that a much younger electorate will begin to emerge in France by 1975.

Louis Ducatel, sixty-seven-year-old engineer and industrialist who comes from Frevent in the Pas-de-Calais, served twenty years in the Paris municipal council. He joined the Rally of the Republican Left in 1957, belonging later to the Republican Center and serving as its vice-president. In 1967 he founded the Association for the Defense of Private Enterprise.

Alain Krivine, liberal arts student, is twenty-seven years old and a candidate for the *agrégation* in history. A member at the age of seventeen of the Communist Youth, he resigned from the Communist party in 1966 and founded the Revolutionary Communist Youth (JCR), an organization which was dissolved in June 1968 by the regime. At the time of the presidential race Krivine was a member of the French army, serving in the 150th Infantry Regiment stationed in Verdun. Trotskyite Krivine ran as a candidate of the Communist League. Revolutionary violence is, he says, the only way of establishing socialism in France; however, he also assures his listeners that "The blood-bath is not obligatory." [13]

THE CAMPAIGN

Various questions relative to the future of the presidential office remained unclarified during the presidential campaign. First, it was apparent that a Gaullist president could not under any circumstances claim all of the powers held previously by General de Gaulle; however, it also was recognized that the new Presi-

[13] *L'Express,* 934 (June 2–8, 1969), 64.

dent—Gaullist or non-Gaullist—would have to exercise responsibility in policy determination, for he is elected by universal suffrage and expected to use this function. Consequently people going to the polls found it difficult to know in advance how much power was to be transferred from the Élysée Palace to the Matignon. Second, if a Left candidate were elected president, he would be confronted with the difficult task of representing a majority different from the one that dominated the National Assembly. He would dissolve the National Assembly and hope for the return of a majority consistent with the one that elected him. Would he be capable of getting that majority? Third, if a centrist president were elected, would he continue to depend for his support on the aid of Center and Left electors, or would he subsequently repudiate the Left that had been instrumental in bringing him to office and rely primarily on the support of centrists and some Gaullists (Poher's aphorism, "I will be the President of all the French" was designed for the campaign and not the realities of French politics, and nobody knew that better than Poher)? Finally, would the results of the presidential election plunge the country into a new crisis and threaten a return to chronic political instability?

The presidential campaign centered almost exclusively on two figures—Gaullist Georges Pompidou and centrist Alain Poher. The other five candidates were given virtually no chance of winning the office. Georges Pompidou conducted a whirlwind *campaign Américaine* under the direction of Olivier Guichard which took him thousands of miles in several weeks.[14] Poher, who traveled little prior to the first ballot, spending most of his time in the capital periodically releasing statements from the Élysée Palace, took to the countryside after the first ballot and toured the nation by jet. Pompidou was backed in his campaign by an elaborate party machine, while Poher had at his disposal virtually none.

During the campaign Pompidou sought to create before the country an image of confidence, preciseness, and intellect, distinguishing all the while between himself and de Gaulle. In

---

[14] For description of Pompidou's "brain trust" see *Le nouvel observateur,* 238 (June 3–8, 1969), 11.

fact, he repeatedly assured the populace that he would not govern as had de Gaulle, that his cabinet would include more political figures and fewer technocrats, that the National Assembly will be consulted and restored to a position of respect, and that referenda will not be held for a long time to come. At the same time, he retained aspects of Gaullism which had not been rejected by the populace, assuring it that France will not lose under him its national prestige and independence of other nations, particularly the United States and the USSR.[15]

Pompidou's strategy was to retain his Gaullist clientele while capturing a portion of the centrist electorate. The winner, said Pompidou, had to be a national candidate, or other than one elected with Communist votes. Centrist Jacques Médecin, deputy mayor of Nice, who supported Pompidou, announced that he could not uphold Poher, "A candidate in need of 50 percent Communist votes." Joseph Fontanet, long associated with centrism, supported Pompidou on the ground that only he could produce a stable majority. Fontanet argued that the socialists no longer would be willing to play the centrist game once Poher dissolved the National Assembly.[16] Centrist Alain Duhamel also withheld support from Poher.

Giscard d'Estaing (who had failed to endorse the referendum of April 27) supported Pompidou's candidacy conditionally, as an ally of *mais oui,* receiving from Pompidou guarantees that he will "continue working to build Europe," that "it is desirable that Europe should be enlarged," that he will "support the free dissemination of information" on the national radio-TV network (ORTF), and that he will encourage "cooperation between the executive and the legislature in a spirit of open-mindedness, regarding both men and issues." [17]

Poher, a relatively unknown figure until he became interim

---

[15] See *Le Monde,* May 1, 1969, p. 1, for Pompidou's definition of the themes of his campaign.

[16] *L'Express,* 934 (June 2–8, 1969), 58. *Le Monde,* May 18–19, 1969, p. 1. During the campaign Poher promised that he would "do all in order to avoid a dissolution."

[17] See *Le Monde,* April 16, 1969, p. 11, for text of d'Estaing's statement of why he refused to support the referendum. See *Le Monde,* May 3, 1969, p. 2, for text of d'Estaing's agreement with Pompidou.

president of the republic, presented himself early in May as the candidate capable of defeating Pompidou. Until then few Frenchmen knew that there was a Poher or that he presided over the Senate. During the campaign President Poher made the most of his new position, giving himself a substantial part of the limelight and attaining a prominence that he had not had previously. Instead of resigning from the interim post while campaigning, Poher chose to remain instead in the Élysée. No constitutional requirement prevented him from playing the game this way. Although his ties with the Center were well known, Poher rejected as a candidate any particular party affiliation.

Poher's strategy was: (1) to capture the centrist vote; (2) to perform respectably and prevent Pompidou from winning on the first ballot and then defeat him on the second ballot with the aid of the Center and of Mollet, Defferre, Mendès-France, and other figures and parties of the Left; (3) to get the support of the Communist party on the second ballot, for it was impossible for Poher to win the presidency without a good number of its votes; (4) to convince a large part of the electorate that he would become after his election other than a captive of the Left, and that he would be able to find a supporting majority that would not be Gaullist or "Popular Front." Edgard Pisani, a former minister of Pompidou who supported Poher, argued that Poher would be able to find a "real majority" and that it would be sustained by the Socialist party's willingness to continue playing the centrist game. However, some Gaullist deputies accused Poher of engaging simultaneously in the search for both a "third force" and Communist votes, strengthening the fear among some electors, particularly centrists, that his victory would lead to further political instability.[18] Pompidou, who rode this point hard, delighted in telling the country that a Poher victory could not fail to herald a return to the instability of the Fourth Republic.[19]

Poher sought in his campaign to reject any affiliation whatsoever with de Gaulle's conceptions of presidential leadership

---

[18] *L'Express,* 934 (June 2–8, 1969), 60.

[19] *L'Express,* 934 (June 2–8, 1969), 60. Pompidou stated, "M. Poher does not know where he is going, with whom he will govern, and on which majority he will be upheld."

—"The State belongs to no one. It cannot become the property of a party or a clan." At the same time Poher did not seek to devaluate the presidency, insisting that the president should be the animator of the executive.[20] The president must take precedence over the premier, for he is elected by universal suffrage and responsible to the people. Nevertheless, there should not be a presidential "reserved sector," for a government's activities must cover the entirety of national affairs. In the modern state with its many complex problems, the executive power should be distributed and the premier should not be weak. Poher explained that de Gaulle had taken advantage of the "reserved sector" and functioned too often in isolation. Finally, unlike de Gaulle, Poher maintained throughout his campaign support for a federated Europe and ties with NATO—and unlike de Gaulle, who had condemned political parties and kept his distance from them, Poher accepted political parties while claiming no particular affiliation with any one of them.

Gaston Defferre and Jacques Duclos competed in the campaign both for the presidency and primacy on the Left. SFIO candidate Defferre was supported by Mendès-France (his future premier) who sought to regain his PSU adherents of 1968 and other elements of the Left. If Defferre failed to place first or second on the first ballot, he and Mendès-France agreed to support Poher on the second ballot. Defferre was received in silence, however, by Mitterand and—although nominated by the SFIO—with reservations by Mollet and many members of that party. In fact, Mollet let it be known in private that he did not vote on the first ballot for Defferre.[21] Duclos, with an extraordinary party organization behind him, sought to recover for the Communist party many of the electors lost to it in 1968 and to thrust the party forward to the status of the most important component of the Left. Early in the campaign it was thought that the Communist party would support Poher on the second ballot (if Duclos failed to place first or second on the first ballot), but that expectation exploded when the Communist party stated that there is little difference between Poher and Pompidou and recommended abstention on the second ballot.

[20] *Le Monde*, April 15, 1969, p. 1. Poher: "We must organize a regime of a truly presidential type."

[21] *L'Express*, 934 (June 2–8, 1969), 61.

Michel Rocard was in the race to "shape up" for the future and to remind people that there is a "New Left" and a technocratic socialism which is an alternative to capitalism. Krivine and Ducatel were in the contest to spread their "message," one Trotskyism, the other conservative economics.

RESULTS OF THE FIRST BALLOT

Participation in voting was high in the metropole, with only 21.8 percent abstentions and 1.28 percent blank and null ballots (Table P–1). Voting in metropolitan France was as follows: Pompidou 43.95 percent, Poher 23.42 percent, Duclos 21.52 percent, Defferre 5.07 percent, Rocard 3.66 percent, Ducatel 1.28 percent, Krivine 1.06 percent.[22] Pompidou's vote exceeded that received by de Gaulle in the first ballot of the presidential election of 1965 and was slightly superior to the total Gaullist vote on the first ballot in the legislative elections of 1968. With the exception of the Seine-Saint-Denis (where Duclos led the voting), Pompidou headed the list in all of the departments of France. Pompidou ran first in the Gaullist bastions—in Alsace, Moselle, Morbihan, Finistère, Ille-et-Vilaine, Maine-et-Loire, Vendée, in the Manche and Mayenne, in the south of the Massif Central (Cantal, Lozère, Haute-Loire, Aveyron) and in Corsica and the Basses-Pyrénées. Sometimes in these departments Pompidou exceeded de Gaulle's vote in 1965 (Lot, Savoie, Puy-de-Dôme, Charante, Mayenne); in others Pompidou ran somewhat behind the General's previous performance (Meuse, Vosges, Orne, Moselle). In Paris Pompidou exceeded de Gaulle's performance in the presidential election of 1965, obtaining 45.20 percent of the vote.

Poher failed to lead the voting in any large department or great city. Nevertheless, his presence on the first ballot deprived Pompidou of a victory. The only large departments that supported Poher were the Gironnde and the Alpes-Maritimes. Four departments gave him in excess of 30 percent of the vote. In Paris Poher received 23.60 percent of the vote. His home

[22] For complete coverage of first ballot voting in metropolitan France, see *Le Monde,* June 3, 1969. For commentaries by Raymond Barrillon and Pierre Viansson-Ponté, see pp. 1, 2, 5. Figures in this section are relative to the vote cast and not to the registered vote.

town of Ablon, where Poher serves as mayor, failed to give him a majority.

Jacques Duclos regained much of the vote lost by the Communist party in the legislative elections of 1967 and 1968. Duclos exceeded Poher's vote in thirty-two departments (among them the Bouches-du-Rhône, Pas-de-Calais, Nord, Somme,

Table P–1 The results of the presidential elections of June 1 and 15, 1969 in metropolitan France

	June 15, 1969			June 1, 1969		
Registered voters	28,747,988			28,775,876		
Voters	19,851,728			22,500,644		
Abstentions	8,896,260 (30.94%)			6,275,232 (21.8%)		
Blank or null ballots	1,294,629 (4.5%)			289,922 (1%)		
Votes cast	18,557,099 (64.55%)			22,210,711 (77.18%)		
	Votes Received	Percent of Votes Cast	Percent of Registered Voters	Votes Received	Percent of Votes Cast	Percent of Registered Voters
Pompidou	10,686,498	57.58	37.17	9,763,428	43.95	33.92
Poher	7,870,601	42.41	27.37	5,202,271	23.42	18.07
Duclos				4,781,838	21.52	16.61
Defferre				1,128,049	5.07	3.92
Rocard				814,053	3.66	2.82
Ducatel				284,820	1.28	0.98
Krivine				236,263	1.06	0.82

Source: Reproduced in *Le Monde,* June 17, 1969, p. 1.

Côtes-du-Nord, Dordogne, Marne, Oise, Cher, Seine-Maritime, Puy-de-Dôme). Even in those departments won by Poher, Duclos sometimes was able to exceed Poher's vote in the large cities. Duclos' strength was concentrated in the departments of the Centre (Allier, Haute-Vienne, Creuse, Corrèze) and in the Bouches-du-Rhône and Gard. In Marseilles Duclos defeated both Poher and mayor Gaston Defferre. Duclos also ran ahead of Defferre in Grenoble, Mendès-France's home town, where the latter campaigned for Defferre. Duclos received 18.6 percent of the vote in Paris.

Gaston Defferre ran a disastrous campaign, failing to surpass the vote given to Michel Rocard in the Loire, Côtes-du-Nord, and the Rhône. Defferre received only 6 percent of the vote in Paris, running not too far ahead of Rocard's 4.3 percent. Krivine and Ducatel, who hardly were in the race, obtained in Paris 1.5 percent and .8 percent of the vote.

THE SECOND BALLOT

Pompidou and Poher faced each other on the second ballot. Pompidou won the presidency with 57.58 percent of the votes cast in metropolitan France and 37.17 percent of the registered vote.[23] Poher received 42.41 percent of the votes cast and 27.37 percent of the registered vote. Abstentions were 30.94 percent and blank and null ballots 4.5 percent. Abstentions reached 34.69 percent in Paris (higher than the national average but lower than those recorded in the legislative elections of 1962). If the blank and null ballots are added to the abstentions, the percentage is without precedent. Approximately two million voters refused to choose between Pompidou and Poher. The blank and null ballots established a national record. The highest percentage attained previously was 4.06 percent in the referendum of April 1962, which ratified the agreements of Evian on Algeria. Normally, blank and null ballots vary between 1 percent and 2.5 percent of the registered voters.

Pompidou received a higher percentage of the vote than de Gaulle had received on the second ballot in the presidential elections of 1965; nevertheless, because of abstentions and blank and null ballots Pompidou received two million votes fewer than the General had received in 1965. Sixteen departments gave Pompidou absolute majorities on the second ballot. He earned his highest percentage in his native Cantal, 82.92 percent. In twenty departments Pompidou returned in excess of 60 percent

[23] For complete coverage of second ballot voting in metropolitan France, see *Le Monde*, June 17, 1969. See pp. 1, 3, for comments by Pierre Viansson-Ponté. Figures in this section are relative to the vote cast and not to the registered vote.

of the vote (including the Corrèze, Aveyron, Puy-de-Dôme, Haute-Loire). Forty-five departments gave him a percentage of the vote superior to his national average. Where Pompidou did poorly, it was in such places as the Bouches-du-Rhône, the Alpes-Maritimes, the Haute-Garonne, and the Communist stronghold of Seine-Saint-Denis (where abstentionism attained 49.68 percent).

Poher picked up between the two ballots approximately 2.6 million votes and almost twenty percentage points. Observers noted that this increase was not the result alone of the support of people who had voted for Defferre, Krivine and Rocard on the first ballot. *Le Monde* states that Poher's surge on the second ballot did not derive either from support received from old areas of the former MRP, where Jean Lecanuet obtained some of his best results in the presidential election of 1965. *Le Monde* estimates that the Communist party's demand for abstention was rejected by approximately one fourth of the Communist electorate and that perhaps 1,200,000 of its voters cast for Poher. It also has been noted that the *gauchisation* of Poher's campaign between the first and second ballots probably did not succeed in driving a great number of moderate first ballot Poher voters toward Pompidou, the percentage being estimated as perhaps seven percent.[24]

After his election Pompidou named Jacques Chaban-Delmas premier. The new president of the council of ministers, who succeeded Couve de Murville, is a former inspector of finance, a member of Free France during World War II, general of a brigade at the age of twenty-nine, deputy from the Gironnde, mayor of Bordeaux, head of the parliamentary group of the late Rally of the French people (RPF) and until June 1969 President of the National Assembly. Chaban-Delmas served under the Fourth Republic as a minister of defense, achieving some notoriety as a result of his involvement in plots against it. Pierre Viansson-Ponté describes the handsome and *sportif*

---

[24] See Roger Priouret, "Derriere la façade," *L'Express,* 936 (June 16–22, 1969), 97; Jean-Jacques Servan‑Schreiber, "L'ère nouvelle," *L'Express,* 936 (June 16–22, 1969), 49; Jacques Ozouf, "La second tour. De l'immobilisme à l'immobilier," *Le nouvel observateur,* 240 (June 17–22, 1969), 4–5.

premier as the man who always is on an elevator—with his eyes skyward.[25] Chaban-Delmas' cabinet consists of Gaullists, pro-Gaullist centrist elements, and Independent Republican Giscard d'Estaing who was rewarded with the ministry of finance (after it was first declined by Antoine Pinay).

CONCLUSION

The election of Georges Pompidou verified—at least for the time being—that Gaullism had survived the departure of de Gaulle and that the system bequeathed by de Gaulle to the Fifth Republic had outlasted him. Pompidou's election also suggested that the system is destined subsequently for some important transformations, for a Gaullism without de Gaulle is bound to differ from a Gaullism with de Gaulle. Second, the presidential election demonstrated the devastation of the old non-Communist Left. Defferre and Mendès-France suffered crushing defeats, Mollet slipped to the point where he has become peripheral, and Mitterand and his Convention of Republican Institutions are immersed in feebleness. On the other hand, Michel Rocard, secretary-general and representative of the "New Left" made an unexpectedly strong showing in the presidential race, suggesting that his force is not to be disregarded in the France of the future. Will the "New Left" acquire additional strength and maturity? Third, the Center, still weak in 1969, appeared to be stronger than it was in 1965 when it presented Jean Lecanuet as its candidate. Will the Center gain additional strength in future years, or was 1969 but the time for a momentary rally by a force destined to dwindle further in French life? Fourth, in defeating Poher the populace rejected a possible return to "third force" coalitions and the instability they threaten to produce. Fifth, the Communist party regained on the first ballot a considerable number of votes lost by it in previous elections. With the Communist Left remaining firm, the old Left crushed, and the Center always ready to return to its continuing condition of decay, will the only real political competition in the France of the

---

[25] Pierre Viansson-Ponté, *Les gaullistes: Rituel et annuaire* (Paris: Éditions du Seuil, 1963), pp. 87–92. See for portrait of Chaban-Delmas.

future be between Communists and Gaullists (as the Gaullists have insisted for years)? Sixth, the Communist party's recommendation for abstention on the second ballot assured the election of Pompidou. That abstention did not signal for the party isolation or a return to the wilderness in which it lived for so many years prior to 1962. Duclos' performance on the first ballot demonstrated the durability of his party. The Communist Left came out of the presidential contest very much alive, whereas the classical non-Communist Left came away in full retreat. Now perhaps the party can devote itself more effectively to attempts to establish its leadership over the Left? Seventh, although Georges Pompidou was elected on the second ballot by 57.58 percent of the votes cast, he is—as was Charles de Gaulle after the presidential election of 1965—a minority president. Pompidou was elected with the support only of 37.17 percent of the registered voters. Will he in subsequent years succeed in becoming a majority president? Finally, Gaullism remains on, but so do so many of the social and economic problems which have plagued the Gaullist regime for years. If these problems were not solved by de Gaulle, there is some question as to whether they will be remedied by Gaullists without de Gaulle. June 1969 marked yet another phase in the continuing crisis of Gaullism; however, that crisis no longer involves General de Gaulle.

BIBLIOGRAPHY

The best source of daily information on French politics and government is *Le Monde,* the great newspaper which contains information normally not available in other publications, and which serves as an example of the very best in reporting. *Le Monde* also publishes a weekly issue (*Sélection hebdomadaire*); an English-language edition has just been issued. *Le Canard enchaîné* is a weekly newspaper that prides itself on its great wit (justly so) and extraordinary breadth of coverage. The daily *Le Figaro* periodically contains articles by Raymond Aron, university professor and author of numerous important studies. *L'Express* and *Le nouvel observateur* are weekly news magazines. *L'Express* once reflected the views of Pierre Mendès-France, and during the Algerian war the publication devoted many editorials to condemnation of the conflict. *L'Express* subsequently underwent transformation, adopting a new look and becoming a periodical of mass consumption. Now it is without partisan political orientation, and its circulation is great. *Le nouvel observateur* is the former *France-Observateur,* the organ of expression of the classic Left. Although in recent years it has diminished in quality, *Le nouvel observateur* remains a "must" for those interested in tracking the views and innumerable doctrinal currents of the Left. *Sondages* is published quarterly by the French Institute of Public Opinion and is of value to those interested in keeping pace with the institute's public opinion inquires (issues cover, for example, the peasantry, politics and religion, legislative and presidential elections). The *Journal officiel de la République* comprises parliamentary debates, laws, decrees, and so forth. Among the professional reviews, the *Revue française de science politique, Revue française de sociologie, Revue de droit publique et des sciences, Politique étrangère, Droit social,* and the *Revue administrative* contain specialized articles which are helpful and illuminating. Attention is called to that part of the *Revue française de science politique* entitled *Les forces politiques en France,* which is invaluable for readers who wish to keep abreast of new trends and events (and which may be used profitably in conjunction with *L'Année politique, économique, sociale, et diplomatique en France* [*Presses universitaires de France*], an annual account of political, social, diplomatic, and economic phenomena). Two journals of political and social criticism are of special importance—the Catholic *Esprit,* and *Les temps modernes* (issues of the latter deal periodically with single themes of great relevance).

Chapter One

Alain. *Le citoyen contre les pouvoirs.* Paris: Éditions du Sagittaire, 1925.

Bauchet, Pierre. *Economic Planning: The French Experience,* translated by Daphne Woodward. New York: Praeger, 1964.

Bosworth, William. *Catholicism and Crisis in Modern France; French Catholic Groups at the Threshold of the Fifth Republic.* Princeton, N.J.: Princeton University Press, 1962.

Brogan, Denis W. *France under the Republic.* New York: Harper & Row, 1940.

———. *The French Nation: From Napoleon to Pétain, 1814–1940.* New York: Harper & Row, 1948.

Dupeux, Georges. *La société française 1789–1960.* Paris: Colin, 1964.

Duverger, Maurice, *La cinquième République.* 3d ed. Paris: Presses Universitaires de France, 1963.

Earle, Edward M. (ed.). *Modern France.* Princeton, N.J.: Princeton University Press, 1951.

Fauvet, Jacques. *La France déchirée.* Paris: Arthème Fayard, 1957.

————. *La IVᵉ République.* Paris: Arthème Fayard, 1959.

Fauvet, Jacques, and Henri Mendras. *Les paysans et la politique.* Paris: Colin, 1958.

Gervais, Michel, Claude Servolin, and Jean Weil. *Une France sans paysans.* Paris: Seuil, 1965.

Goguel, François and Alfred Grosser. *La politique en France.* Paris: Colin, 1964.

Hoffmann, Stanley, *et al. In Search of France.* New York: Harper & Row, 1965.

Jeanneney, Jean-Marcel. *Économie politique.* Paris: Presses Universitaires, 1962.

Leites, Nathan. *Images of Power in French Politics.* 2 vols. Santa Monica, Calif.: The Rand Corporation, 1962.

Luethy, Herbert. *France against Herself.* New York: Praeger, 1955.

Mendès-France, Pierre. *A Modern French Republic,* trans. by Anne Carter. New York: Hill & Wang, 1963.

Philip, André. *Histoire des faits économiques et sociaux.* 2 vols. Paris: Éditions Montaigne, 1963.

Phlipponneau, Michel. *La Gauche et les régions.* Paris: Calmann-Lévy, 1967.

Priouret, Roger. *La République des députés.* Paris: Bernard Grasset, 1959.

Thomson, David. *Democracy in France since 1870.* 4th ed. New York: Oxford, 1964.

Viansson-Ponté, Pierre. *Risques et chances de la Vᵉ République.* Paris: Plon, 1959.

Werth, Alexander. *France, 1940–55.* New York: Holt, Rinehart and Winston, Inc., 1956.

————. *The Twilight of France.* New York: Harper & Row, 1942.

Williams, Philip M. *Crisis and Compromise: Politics in the Fourth Republic.* London: Longmans, 1964.

————, and Martin Harrison. *De Gaulle's Republic,* 2d ed. London: Longmans, 1962.

Wright, Gordon. *Rural Revolution in France: The Peasantry in the Twentieth Century.* Stanford, Calif.: Stanford University Press, 1964.

Chapter Two

Amado, G. *Les enfants difficiles: Observations et réadaptation.* Paris: Presses Universitaires, 1955.

Bastide, R. *Sociologie et psychanalyse.* Paris: Presses Universitaires, 1950.

Château, J. *L'enfant et ses conquêtes.* Paris: Vrin, 1960.

Chombart de Lauwe, M.J. *Psychopathologie sociale de l'enfant inadapté.* Paris: Éditions du CNRS, 1959.

Chombart de Lauwe, P.H. *La maladie mentale comme phénomène social* in Institut national d'hygiène, *Études de socio-psychiatrie,* Monograph 7. Paris: 1955.

————. *La vie quotidienne des familles ouvrières.* Paris: Éditions du CNRS, 1956.

Clausse, A. *Philosophie de l'étude du milieu.* Paris: Éditions du Scarabée, 1961.

Duchac, R. *Sociologie et psychologie.* Paris: Presses Universitaires, 1963.

Duquesne, Jacques. *Les 16–24 ans.* Paris: Le Centurion, 1963.

Durkheim, Émile. *Éducation et sociologie,* 4th ed. Paris: Alcan, 1938.

————. *Les formes élémentaires de la vie religieuse.* Paris: Alcan, 1912.

Fau, R. *Les groupes d'enfants et d'adolescents.* Paris: Presses Universitaires, 1952.

————. *Le travail en miettes.* Paris: Gallimard, 1956.

Fraser, W. R. *Education and Society in Modern France.* London: Routledge, 1963.

Friedmann, G. *Où va le travail humain?* Paris: Gallimard, 1956.

Halbwachs, M. *Les cadres sociaux de la mémoire.* Paris: Alcan, 1925.

————. *La classe ouvrière et les niveaux de vie.* Paris: Alcan, 1913.

Halls, W. D. *Society, Schools and Progress in France.* Oxford: Pergamon Press, 1965.

Institut national d'études démographiques, *Le niveau intellectuel des infants d'âge scolaire,* Vol. II (*Travaux et documents,* No. 23). Paris: 1954.

Kandel, I. L. *The Reform of Secondary Education in France.* New York: Columbia University Press, 1924.

Leroi-Gourhan, A. *L'homme et la matière.* Paris: Michel, 1945.

Mauss, M. *Sociologie et anthropologie.* Paris: Presses Universitaires, 1960.

Metraux, Rhoda, and Margaret Mead. *Themes in French Culture:*

A Preface to a Study of the French Community. Stanford, Calif.: Stanford University Press, 1954.

Moscovici, S. *La psychanalyse: Son image et son public*. Paris: Presses Universitaires, 1961.

Piobetta, J. B. *Les institutions universitaires en France*. Paris: Presses Universitaires, 1961.

Porot, M. *L'enfant et les relations familiales*. Paris: Presses Universitaires, 1959.

Stoetzel, J. *La psychologie sociale*. Paris: Flammarion, 1963.

Wylie, Lawrence. *Village in the Vaucluse*, revised ed. New York: Harper & Row, 1964.

————. (ed.). *Chanzeaux: A Village in Anjou*. Cambridge, Mass.: Harvard University Press, 1966.

Chapter Three

Aron, Raymond. *Immuable et changeante*. Paris: Calmann-Lévy, 1959.

Blum, Léon. *For All Mankind*. New York: Viking, 1946.

————. *L'oeuvre de Léon Blum*. 3 vols. Paris: A. Michel, 1954, 1955, 1958.

Bodley, J. E. C. *The Church in France*. New York: Crowell-Collier-Macmillan, 1906.

Bruclain, Claude. *Le socialisme et l'Europe*. Paris: Seuil (Collection Jean Moulin), 1965.

Deutsch, Emeric, Denis Lindon, and Pierre Weil. *Les familles politiques*. Paris: Les éditions de minuit, 1966.

Einaudi, M., and F. Goguel. *Christian Democracy in Italy and France*. South Bend, Ind.: University of Notre Dame Press, 1952.

Fauvet, Jacques, and Alain Duhamel. *Histoire du parti communiste français*. 2 vols. Paris: Arthème Fayard, 1964, 1965.

Fougeyrollas, Pierre. *La conscience politique dans la France contemporaine: Essai*. Paris: Éditions Denoël, 1963.

Halévy, Élie. *Histoire du socialisme européen*. Paris: Gallimard, 1948.

Kohn, Hans. *Making of the Modern French Mind*. Princeton, N.J.: Van Nostrand, 1955.

Martin, Kingsley. *French Liberal Thought in the Eighteenth Century*. London: Benn, 1929.

Mayer, J. P. *Political Thought in France from the Revolution to the Fourth Republic*, revised ed. London: Faber, 1949.

Philip, André. *La démocratie industrielle*. Paris. Presses Universitaires, 1955.

————. *Pour un socialisme humaniste*. Paris: Plon, 1960.

Pierce, Roy. *Contemporary French Political Thought*. New York: Oxford, 1966.

Rémond, René. *La droite en France de 1815 à nos jours: Continuité et diversité d'une tradition politique*. Paris: Aubier, 1954.

Scott, J. A. *Republican Ideas and the Liberal Tradition in France, 1870–1914*. New York: Columbia University Press, 1951.

Sérant, Paul. *Où va la droite?* Paris: Plon, 1958.

Soltau, Roger. *French Political Thought in the Nineteenth Century*. New Haven, Conn.: Yale University Press, 1931.

Suffert, Georges. *Les Catholiques et la gauche*. Paris: F. Maspero, 1960.

Viansson-Ponté, Pierre. *Les Gaullistes*. Paris: Seuil, 1963.

Chapter Four

Anderson, Robert T., and Barbara Gallatin Anderson. *Bus Stop for Paris: The Transformation of a French Village*. New York: Doubleday, 1965.

Chapman, Brian. *Introduction to French Local Government*. London: G. Allen, 1953.

————. *The Prefects and Provincial France*. London: G. Allen, 1955.

Crozier, Michel. *The Bureaucratic Phenomenon*. Chicago: University of Chicago Press, 1964.

Goguel, François and Alfred Grosser. *La politique en France*. Paris: Colin, 1964.

Gournay, Bernard. *Introduction à la science administrative*. Paris: Colin, 1966.

Kesselman, Mark. *The Ambiguous Consensus: A Study of Local Government in France*. New York: Knopf, 1967.

Lanversin, Jacques de. *L'aménagement du territoire*. Paris: Librairies Techniques, 1965.

Lavau, Georges. *La région et la réforme administrative*. Paris: Entretiens du Samedi, 1964.

Marie, Christiane. *L'évolution du comportement politique dans une ville en expansion: Grenoble, 1871–1965*. Paris: Colin, 1966.

Phlipponneau, Michel. *La Gauche et les régions*. Paris: Calmann-Lévy, 1967.

Ridley, Fred, and Jean Blondel. *Public Administration in France*. New York: Barnes & Noble, 1965.

Wylie, Lawrence. *Village in the Vaucluse*, revised ed. New York: Harper & Row, 1964.

———— (ed.). *Chanzeau: A Village in Anjou*. Cambridge, Mass.: Harvard University Press, 1966.

Chapter Five

Bloch-Morhange, J. *Les politiciens*. Paris: Arthème Fayard, 1961.

Bromberger, Merry. *Le destin secret de Georges Pompidou*. Paris: Arthème Fayard, 1965.

Buron, Robert. *Le plus beau des métiers*. Paris: Plon, 1963.

Charlot, Jean. *L'UNR: Étude du pouvoir au sein d'un parti politique*. Paris: Colin, 1967.

Club Jean Moulin. *Un parti pour la gauche*. Paris: Seuil, 1965.

Debré, Michel. *Au service de la nation: Essai d'un programme politique*. Paris: Stock, 1963.

Depreux, Édouard. *Renouvellement du socialisme*. Paris: Calmann-Lévy, 1960.

De Tarr, Francis. *The French Radical Party from Herriot to Mendès-France*. New York: Oxford, 1961.

Duverger, Maurice. *Les partis politiques et classes sociales en France*. Paris: Colin, 1955.

Einaudi, M., J. M. Domenach, and A. Garosci. *Communism in Western Europe*. Ithaca, N.Y.: Cornell University Press, 1951.

Fauvet, Jacques and Alain Duhamel. *Histoire du parti communiste français,* 2 vols. Paris: Arthème Fayard, 1964, 1965.

Fauvet, Jacques and Henri Mendras. *Les paysans et la politique*. Paris: Colin, 1958.

La Nef. Face à face Edgar Faure, François Mitterand. Paris: Tallandier, March–May 1967, No. 30.

Malterre, Jacques, and Paul Benoist. *Les partis politiques français*. Paris: Bibliothèque de l'Homme d'action, 1956.

Manceron, Claude. *Cent mille voix par jour pour Mitterand*. Paris: Robert Laffont, 1966.

Maurice, Gaston. *Le parti radicale*. Paris: Marcel Rivière, 1928.

Milhaud, Albert. *Histoire du radicalisme*. Paris: Société d'Éditions, 1951.

Mitterand, François. *Le coup d'état permanent*. Paris: Plon, 1964.

Mollet, Guy. *13 mai 1958–12 mai 1962*. Paris: Plon, 1962.

Nicolet, Claude. *Le radicalisme*. Paris: Presses Universitaires, 1956.

Philip, André. *Les socialistes*. Paris: Seuil, 1967.

Rossi, A. *A Communist Party in Action*. New Haven, Conn.: Yale University Press, 1949.

Suffert, Georges. *De Defferre à Mitterand: La campagne présidentelle*. Paris: Seuil, 1966.

Uri, Pierre. *Pour gouverner.* Paris: Robert Laffont, 1967.

Viansson-Ponté, Pierre. *Bilan de la Vᵉ République: Les politiques.* Paris: Calmann-Lévy, 1967.

Chapter Six

Campbell, Peter. *French Electoral Systems and Elections Since 1789,* 2d ed. London: Faber, 1965.

Charnay, Jean-Paul. *Le suffrage politique en France.* Paris: Mouton, 1965.

Deutsch, Emeric, Denis Lindon, and Pierre Weil. *Les familles politiques.* Paris: Les éditions de minuit, 1966.

Duverger, Maurice. *The French Political System.* Chicago: University of Chicago Press, 1958.

Goguel, François. *France under the Fourth Republic.* Ithaca, N.Y.: Cornell University Press, 1952.

————, *et al. Le référendum du 8 avril 1962.* Paris: Colin, 1963.

————. *Le référendum du 8 janvier 1961.* Paris: Colin, 1962.

————. *Le référendum d'octobre et les élections de novembre 1962.* Paris: Colin, 1962.

Meynaud, Jean, and Alain Lancelot. *La participation des français à la politique.* Paris: Presses Universitaires, 1965.

Touchard, Jean, *et al. L'Établissement de la cinquième république: Le référendum du septembre et les élections de novembre 1958.* Paris: Colin, 1960.

Vedel, Georges, *et al. La dépolitisation: Mythe ou réalité?* Paris: Colin, 1962.

Chapter Seven

Adam, Gerard. *La C.F.T.C. 1940–1958.* Paris: Colin, 1964.

Clark, James M. *Teachers and Politics in France: A Pressure Group Study of the Fédération de l'Éducation nationale.* Syracuse, N.Y.: Syracuse University Press, 1967.

Ehrmann, Henry W. *French Labor from Popular Front to Liberation.* New York: Oxford, 1947.

————. *Organized Business in France.* Princeton, N.J.: Princeton University Press, 1957.

Hamon, Léo. *Les nouveaux comportements politiques de la classe ouvrière.* Paris: Presses Universitaires, 1962.

Kayser, Jacques. *Le quotidien français.* Paris: Colin, 1963.

Lavau, Georges. "Political Pressures by Interest Groups in France," in *Interest Groups on Four Continents,* Henry W. Ehrmann (ed.). Pittsburgh: University of Pittsburgh Press, 1958, pp. 60–95.

Le Bourre, Raymond. *Le syndicalisme français dans las Ve République*. Paris: Calmann-Lévy, 1959.

Lorwin, Val. *The French Labor Movement*. Cambridge: Harvard University Press, 1954.

Mallet, Serge. *La nouvelle classe ouvrière*. Paris: Seuil, 1963.

———. *Les paysans contre le passé*. Paris: Seuil, 1962.

Meynaud, Jean. *Les groupes de pression*. Paris: Colin, 1958.

———. *Nouvelles études sur les groupes de pression en France*. Paris: Colin, 1962.

———, and Alain Lancelot. *Les attitudes politiques*. Paris: Presses Universitaires, 1964.

Rémond, Réne. *Les Catholiques, le communisme et les crises, 1929–1959*. Paris: Colin, 1960.

Reynaud, Jean-Daniel. *Les syndicats en France*. Paris: Colin, 1963.

Tavernier, Yves. *La F.N.S.E.A.* Paris: Fondation nationale des sciences politiques, 1965.

Chapter Eight

Club Jean Moulin. *L'état et le citoyen*. Paris: Seuil, 1961.

Cotteret, Jean-Marie. *Le pouvoir législatif en France*. Paris: Pichon and Durand-Auzias, 1962.

Duverger, Maurice. *La cinquième République*. Paris: Presses Universitaires, 1959.

———. *Institutions politiques*. Paris: Presses Universitaires, 1965.

Gooch, R. K. *The French Parliamentary Committee System*. New York: Appleton-Century-Crofts, 1935.

———. *Parliamentary Government in France: Revolutionary Origins, 1789–1791*. Ithaca, N.Y.: Cornell University Press, 1960.

Guichard-Ayoub, Élaine, Charles Roig, and Jean Grange. *Études sur le Parlement de la Ve République*. Paris: Presses Universitaires, 1965.

Hauriou, André. *Droit constitutionel et institutions politiques*. Paris: Éditions Montchrestien, 1966.

Lidderdale, D. W. S. *The Parliament of France*. New York: Praeger, 1952.

Mavrinac. A. *Organization and Procedure of the National Assembly of the Fifth French Republic*. London: Hansard Society, 1960.

Prélot, Marcel. *Le parlementarisme peut-il être limité sans être annihilé?* Paris: Entretiens du samedi, 1965.

Priouret, Roger. *La République des députés*. Paris: Barnard Grasset, 1959.

Rémond, René. *La vie politique en France*. Paris: Colin, 1965.

Vedel, Georges, and François Goguel. *Les institutions politiques de la France*. Paris: Entretiens du samedi, 1964.

Chapter Nine

Aron, Robert. *An Explanation of de Gaulle*, trans. by Marianne Sinclair. New York: Harper & Row, 1966.

Barker, Ernest. *The Development of Public Services in Western Europe, 1660–1930*. New York: Oxford, 1944.

Catherine, Robert. *Le fonctionnaire français*. Paris: Michel, 1961.

de Gaulle, Charles. *The Call to Honour, 1940–1942*. New York: Viking, 1955.

———. *Unity, 1942–1944*. New York: Simon & Schuster, 1959.

———. *Salvation, 1944–1946*. New York: Simon & Schuster, 1960. 1960.

Department of Political Science, University of California, Berkeley. *The Fifth Republic*. Berkeley: University of California Press, 1961.

Fauvet, Jacques. *La IVᵉ République*. Paris: Arthème Fayard, 1959.

Fisher, H. A. L. *Bonapartism*. New York: Oxford, 1908.

French Embassy (Press and Information Division), *Major Addresses, Statements and Press Conferences of General Charles de Gaulle, May 19, 1958–January 31, 1964*. New York: Ardlee Service, 1964.

Funk, Arthur. *Charles de Gaulle: The Crucial Years, 1943–1944*. Norman, Okla.: University of Oklahoma Press, 1959.

Furniss, Edgar S., Jr. *De Gaulle and the French Army: A Crisis in Civil-Military Relations*. New York: Twentieth Century, 1964.

———. *France, Troubled Ally: de Gaulle's Heritage and Prospects*. New York: Harper & Row, 1960.

Macridis, Roy. *De Gaulle: Implacable Ally*. New York: Harper & Row, 1966.

———, and Bernard Brown. *De Gaulle's Republic: Quest for Unity*. Homewood, Ill.: Dorsey Press, 1960.

Monteil, U. *Les Officiers*. Paris: Seuil, 1958.

Robson, W. A. *The Civil Service in Britain and France*. London: Hogarth, 1956.

Sirius. *Le suicide de la IVᵉ Republique*. Paris: Les Éditions du Cerf, 1958.

Tesson, Philippe. *De Gaulle Iᵉʳ*. Paris: Éditions A. Michel, 1965.

Thomson, David. *Two Frenchmen: Pierre Laval and Charles de Gaulle*. London: Cresset Press, Ltd., 1951.

Werth, Alexander. *De Gaulle: A Political Biography*. New York: Simon & Schuster, 1966.

Chtapter Ten

Amos, Maurice S., and F. P. Walton. *Introduction to French Law*. New York: Oxford, 1935.

David, René, and Henry P. de Vries. *The French Legal System*. New York: Oceana, 1958.

Ensor, R. C. K. *Courts and Judges in France, Germany and England*. New York: Oxford, 1933.

Hamson, Charles J. *Executive Discretion and Judicial Control: An Aspect of the French Conseil d'État*. London: Stevens & sons, 1960.

Ridley, F., and J. Blondel. *Public Administration in France*. New York: Barnes & Noble, 1965.

Weil, Prosper. *Le droit administratif*. Paris: Presses Universitaires, 1966.

Chapter Eleven

Ambler, John S. *The French Army in Politics: 1945–1962*. Columbus, Ohio: Ohio State University Press, 1966.

Andrews, William. *French Politics and Algeria*. Des Moines, Iowa: Meredith Publishing Company, 1962.

Beloff, Nora. *The General Says "No."* Baltimore: Penguin Books, 1964.

Cady, John F. *The Roots of French Imperialism in Eastern Asia*. Ithaca, N.Y.: Cornell University Press, 1956.

Delavignette, Robert. *Freedom and Authority in French West Africa*. New York: Oxford, 1950.

Deutsch, Karl W., *et al. France, Germany and the Western Alliance: A Study of Elite Attitudes on European Integration*. New York: Scribner, 1967.

Girardet, Raoul. *La crise militaire française, 1945–1962*. Paris: Colin, 1964.

Gonidec, P. F. *L'évolution des territoires d'outre mer depuis 1946*. Paris: Pichon, 1958.

Hammer, Ellen. *The Struggle for Indo-China*. Stanford, Calif.: Stanford University Press, 1954.

Kelly, George Armstrong. *Lost Soldiers: The French Army and Empire in Crisis, 1947–1962*. Cambridge, Mass.: M.I.T. Press, 1964.

La Gorce, Paul-Marie de. *La République et son armée.* Paris: Arthème Fayard, 1963.

Massip, Roger. *De Gaulle et l'Europe.* Paris: Flammarion, 1963.

Meisel, James H. *The Fall of the Republic.* Ann Arbor, Mich.: University of Michigan Press, 1962.

Nobecourt, Jacques, and Jean Planchais. *Une histoire politique de l'armée,* 2 vols. Paris: Seuil, 1967.

Priestley, Herbert I. *France Overseas: A Study of Modern Imperialism.* New York: Appleton-Century-Crofts, 1938.

Reynaud, Paul. *La politique étrangère du Gaullisme.* Paris: René Juillard, 1964.

Schneider, Bertrand. *La Ve République et l'Algérie.* Paris: Éditions Témoignage Chrétien, 1959.

Appendixes

APPENDIX A
THE FRENCH CONSTITUTION

**Adopted by the referendum
of September 28, 1958
Promulgated October 4, 1958
Amended in 1960, 1962,
and 1963**

PREAMBLE

The French people hereby solemnly proclaims its attachment
to the Rights of Man and to the principles of national sovereignty
as defined by the Declaration of 1789, confirmed and comple-
mented by the Preamble of the Constitution of 1946.

By virtue of these principles and that of the free determination of peoples, the Republic hereby offers to the overseas territories that express the desire to adhere to them, new institutions
based on the common ideal of liberty, equality, and fraternity
and conceived with a view to their democratic evolution.

Article I

The Republic and the peoples of the overseas territories who,
by an act of free determination, adopt the present Constitution
thereby institute a Community.

The Community shall be based on the equality and the
solidarity of the peoples composing it.

TITLE I ON SOVEREIGNTY

Article 2

France shall be a republic, indivisible, secular, democratic, and social. It shall ensure the equality of all citizens before the law, without distinction of origin, race or religion. It shall respect all beliefs.

The national emblem shall be the tricolor flag, blue, white, and red.

The national anthem shall be the "Marseillaise."

The motto of the Republic shall be "Liberty, Equality, Fraternity."

Its principle shall be government of the people, by the people, and for the people.

Article 3

National sovereignty belongs to the people, which shall exercise this sovereignty through its representatives and through the referendum.

No section of the people, nor any individual, may attribute to themselves or himself the exercise thereof.

Suffrage may be direct or indirect under the conditions stipulated by the Constitution. It shall always be universal, equal and secret.

All French citizens of both sexes who have reached their majority and who enjoy civil and political rights may vote under the conditions to be determined by law.

Article 4

Political parties and groups may compete for votes. They may form and carry on their activities freely. They must respect the principles of national sovereignty and of democracy.

TITLE II THE PRESIDENT OF THE REPUBLIC

Article 5

The President of the Republic shall see that the Constitution is respected. He shall ensure, by his arbitration, the regular functioning of the public powers, as well as the continuity of the state.

He shall be the guarantor of national independence, of the integrity of the territory, and of respect for Community agreements and for treaties.

Article 6

The President of the Republic shall be elected for seven years by universal direct suffrage.

The procedures of implementation of the present article shall be determined by an organic law.

Article 7

The President of the Republic shall be elected by an absolute majority of the votes cast. If a majority is not obtained at the first ballot, a second ballot shall take place on the second Sunday following the first ballot. Only the two candidates who receive the greatest number of votes at the first ballot, excluding those who did better but who withdrew, may present themselves at the second ballot.

The Government shall be responsible for organizing the election.

The election of the new President of the Republic shall take place at least twenty days and not more than thirty-five days before the expiration of the powers of the current President.

In the case of vacancy of the Presidential office for any reason whatsoever, or if the President is declared incapable of exercising his functions by the Constitutional Council, the question being referred to the latter by the Government and the decision being taken by an absolute majority of the members of the Council, the functions of the President, with the exception of those listed in Articles 11 and 12, shall be temporarily exercised by the President of the Senate, or, if the latter is in turn incapable, by the Government.

In case of vacancy or when the Constitutional Council declares the President permanently incapable of exercising his functions, the ballot for the election of the new President shall take place, except in case of *force majeure* officially noted by the Constitutional Council, at least twenty days and not more than thirty-five days after the beginning of the vacancy or the declaration of the permanent character of the incapability.

In case of vacancy of the Presidency of the Republic or

during the time between the declaration of the incapability of the President of the Republic and the election of his successor, Articles 49, 50 and 89 may not be invoked.

Article 8

The President of the Republic shall appoint the Premier. He shall terminate the functions of the Premier when the latter presents the resignation of the government.

At the proposal of the Premier, he shall appoint the other members of the Government and shall terminate their functions.

Article 9

The President of the Republic shall preside over the Council of Ministers.

Article 10

The President of the Republic shall promulgate the laws within fifteen days following the transmission to the government of the finally adopted law.

He may, before the expiration of this time limit, ask Parliament for a reconsideration of the law or of certain of its articles. This reconsideration may not be refused.

Article 11

The President of the Republic, on the proposal of the government during [parliamentary] sessions, or on joint motion of the two assemblies, published in the *Journal Officiel,* may submit to a referendum any bill dealing with the organization of the public powers, entailing approval of a Community agreement, or providing for authorization to ratify a treaty that, without being contrary to the Constitution, might affect the functioning of the institutions.

When the referendum decides in favor of the bill, the President of the Republic shall promulgate it within the time limit stipulated in the preceding article.

Article 12

The President of the Republic may, after consultation with the Premier and the presidents of the assemblies, declare the dissolution of the National Assembly.

General elections shall take place twenty days at the least and forty days at the most after the dissolution.

The National Assembly shall convene by right on the second Thursday following its election. If this meeting takes place between the periods provided for ordinary sessions, a session shall, by right, be opened for a fifteen-day period.

There may be no further dissolution within a year following these elections.

Article 13

The President of the Republic shall sign the ordinances and decrees decided upon in the Council of Ministers.

He shall make appointments to the civil and military posts of the state.

Councillors of State, the Grand Chancellor of the Legion of Honor, ambassadors and envoys extraordinary, master councillors of the Audit Office, prefects, representatives of the government in the overseas territories, general officers, rectors of academies [regional divisions of the public educational system], and directors of central administrations shall be appointed in meetings of the Council of Ministers.

An organic law shall determine the other posts to be filled in meetings of the Council of Ministers, as well as the conditions under which the power of the President of the Republic to make appointments to office may be delegated by him to be exercised in his name.

Article 14

The President of the Republic shall accredit ambassadors and envoys extraordinary to foreign powers; foreign ambassadors and envoys extraordinary shall be accredited to him.

Article 15

The President of the Republic shall be commander of the armed forces. He shall preside over the higher councils and committees of national defense.

Article 16

When the institutions of the Republic, the independence of the nation, the integrity of its territory or the fulfillment of its international commitments are threatened in a grave and immediate manner and when the regular functioning of the constitutional governmental authorities is interrupted, the President of the Republic shall take the measures commanded by these circumstances, after official consultation with the Premier, the Presidents of the assemblies and the Constitutional Council.

He shall inform the nation of these measures in a message.

These measures must be prompted by the desire to ensure to the constitutional governmental authorities, in the shortest possible time, the means of fulfilling their assigned functions. The Constitutional Council shall be consulted with regard to such measures.

Parliament shall meet by right.

The National Assembly may not be dissolved during the exercise of emergency powers [by the President].

Article 17

The President of the Republic shall have the right of pardon.

Article 18

The President of the Republic shall communicate with the two assemblies of Parliament by means of messages, which he shall cause to be read, and which shall not be followed by any debate.

Between sessions, Parliament shall be convened especially for this purpose.

Article 19

The acts of the President of the Republic, other than those provided for under Articles 8 (first paragraph), 11, 12, 16, 18, 54, 56, and 61, shall be countersigned by the Premier and, should circumstances so require, by the appropriate ministers.

TITLE III   THE GOVERNMENT

Article 20

The government shall determine and conduct the policy of the nation.

It shall have at its disposal the administration and the armed forces.

It shall be responsible to the parliament under the conditions and according to the procedures stipulated in Articles 49 and 50.

Article 21

The Premier shall direct the operation of the government. He shall be responsible for national defense. He shall ensure the execution of the laws. Subject to the provisions of Article 13, he shall have regulatory powers and shall make appointments to civil and military posts.

He may delegate certain of his powers to the ministers.

He shall replace, should the occasion arise, the President of the Republic as the chairman of the councils and committees provided for under Article 15.

He may, in exceptional instances, replace him as the chairman of a meeting of the Council of Ministers by virtue of an explicit delegation and for a specific agenda.

Article 22

The acts of the Premier shall be countersigned, when circumstances so require, by the ministers responsible for their execution.

Article 23

The functions of members of the government shall be incompatible with the exercise of any parliamentary mandate, with the holding of any office, at the national level in business, professional or labor organizations, and with any public employment or professional activity.

An organic law shall determine the conditions under which the holders of such mandates, functions or employments shall be replaced.

The replacement of the members of parliament shall take place in accordance with the provisions of Article 25.

TITLE IV   THE PARLIAMENT

Article 24

The parliament shall comprise the National Assembly and the Senate.

The deputies to the National Assembly shall be elected by direct suffrage.

The Senate shall be elected by indirect suffrage. It shall ensure the representation of the territorial units of the Republic. Frenchmen living outside France shall be represented in the Senate.

Article 25

An organic law shall determine the term for which each assembly is elected, the number of its members, their emoluments, the conditions of eligibility and the system of ineligibilities and incompatibilities.

It shall likewise determine the conditions under which, in the case of a vacancy in either assembly, persons shall be elected to replace the deputy or senator whose seat has been vacated until the holding of new complete or partial elections to the assembly concerned.

Article 26

No member of Parliament may be prosecuted, sought, arrested, detained or tried as a result of the opinions or votes expressed by him in the exercise of his functions.

No member of Parliament may, during Parliamentary sessions, be prosecuted or arrested for criminal or minor offenses without the authorization of the assembly of which he is a member except in the case of *flagrante delicto*.

When Parliament is not in session, no member of Parliament may be arrested without the authorization of the Secretariat of the assembly of which he is a member, except in the case of *flagrante delicto*, of authorized prosecution or of final conviction.

The detention or prosecution of a member of Parliament shall be suspended if the assembly of which he is a member so demands.

Article 27

All binding instructions [upon members of Parliament] shall be null and void.

The right to vote of the members of Parliament shall be personal.

An organic law may, under exceptional circumstances,

authorize the delegation of a vote. In this case, no member may be delegated more than one vote.

Article 28

Parliament shall convene by right in two ordinary sessions a year. The first session shall begin on October 2d and last eighty days.

The second session shall begin on April 2d and may not last longer than ninety days.

If October 2d or April 2d is a public holiday, the opening of the session shall take place on the first weekday following.

Article 29

Parliament shall convene in extraordinary session at the request of the Premier, or of the majority of the members comprising the National Assembly, to consider a specific agenda.

When an extraordinary session is held at the request of the members of the National Assembly, the closure decree shall take effect as soon as the Parliament has exhausted the agenda for which it was called, and at the latest twelve days from the date of its meeting.

Only the Premier may ask for a new session before the end of the month following the closure decree.

Article 30

Apart from cases in which Parliament meets by right, extraordinary sessions shall be opened and closed by decree of the President of the Republic.

Article 31

Members of the Government have access to both assemblies. They are heard when they so request.

They may be assisted by Government commissioners.

Article 32

The President of the National Assembly is elected for the life of each Parliament. The President of the Senate is elected after each partial renewal.

Article 33

The sittings of both assemblies are public. A full report of debates is published in the *Journal Officiel.*

Each assembly may meet in secret session at the request of the Prime Minister or of one-tenth of its members.

TITLE V ON RELATIONS BETWEEN PARLIAMENT AND THE GOVERNMENT

Article 34

All laws shall be passed by Parliament.

Laws shall establish the rules concerning:

—civil rights and the fundamental guarantees granted to the citizens for the exercise of their public liberties; the obligations imposed by the national defense upon the persons and property of citizens;

—nationality, status and legal capacity of persons, marriage contracts, inheritance and gifts;

—determination of crimes and misdemeanors as well as the penalties imposed therefore; criminal procedure; amnesty; the creation of new juridical systems and the status of magistrates;

—the basis, the rate and the methods of collecting taxes of all types; the issuance of currency.

Laws shall likewise determine the rules concerning:

—the electoral system of the Parliamentary assemblies and the local assemblies;

—the establishment of categories of public institutions;

—the fundamental guarantees granted to civil and military personnel employed by the State;

—the nationalization of enterprises and the transfer of the property of enterprises from the public to the private sector.

Law shall determine the fundamental principles of:

—the general organization of national defense;

—the free administration of local communities, the extent of their jurisdiction and their resources;

—education;

—property rights, civil and commercial obligations;

—legislation pertaining to employment, unions and social security.

The financial laws shall determine the financial resources and obligations of the State under the conditions and with the reservations to be provided for by an organic law.

—Laws pertaining to national planning shall determine the objectives of the economic and social action of the State.

The provisions of the present article may be developed in detail and amplified by an organic law.

Article 35

Parliament shall authorize the declaration of war.

Article 36

Martial law shall be decreed in a meeting of the Council of Ministers. Its prorogation beyond twelve days may be authorized only by parliament.

Article 37

Matters other than those that fall within the domain of law shall be of a regulatory character.

Legislative texts concerning these matters may be modified by decrees issued after consultation with the Council of State. Those legislative texts which shall be passed after the entry into force of the present Constitution shall be modified by decree, only if the Constitutional Council has stated that they have a regulatory character as defined in the preceding paragraph.

Article 38

The government may, in order to carry out its program, ask parliament for authorization to take through ordinances, during a limited period, measures that are normally within the domain of law.

The ordinances shall be enacted in meetings of the Council of Ministers after consultation with the Council of State. They shall come into force upon their publication, but shall become null and void if the bill for their ratification is not submitted to parliament before the date set by the enabling act.

At the expiration of the time limit referred to in the first paragraph of the present article, the ordinances may be modified only by law in those matters which are within legislative domain.

Article 39

The Premier and the members of parliament alike shall have the right to initiate legislation.

Government bills shall be discussed in the Council of Ministers after consultation with the Council of State and shall be filed with the secretariat of one of the two assemblies. Finance bills shall be submitted first to the National Assembly.

Article 40

The bills and amendments introduced by the members of parliament shall be inadmissible when their adoption would have as a consequence either a diminution of public financial resources, or the creation or increase of public expenditures.

Article 41

If it appears in the course of the legislative procedure that a Parliamentary bill or an amendment is not within the domain of law or is contrary to a delegation [of authority] granted by virtue of Article 38, the Government may declare its inadmissibility.

In case of disagreement between the Government and the President of the assembly concerned, the Constitutional Council, upon the request of either party, shall rule within a time limit of eight days.

Article 42

The discussion of Government bills shall pertain, in the first assembly to which they have been referred, to the text presented by the Government.

An assembly, given a text passed by the other assembly, shall deliberate on the text that is transmitted to it.

Article 43

Government and parliamentary bills shall, at the request of the Government or of the assembly concerned, be sent for study to committees especially designated for this purpose.

Government and parliamentary bills for which such a request has not been made shall be sent to one of the permanent committees, the number of which shall be limited to six in each assembly.

Article 44

Members of Parliament and of the Government shall have the right of amendment.

After the opening of the debate, the Government may oppose the examination of any amendment which has not previously been submitted to committee.

If the Government so requests, the assembly concerned shall decide, by a single vote, on all or part of the text under discussion, retaining only the amendments proposed or accepted by the Government.

Article 45

Every Government or private member's bill is discussed successively in the two assemblies with a view to agreement on identical versions.

When, as a result of disagreement between the two assemblies, a bill has not been passed after two readings in each assembly, or, if the Government has declared the bill urgent, after a single reading by each assembly, the Prime Minister is entitled to have the bill sent to a joint Committee composed of equal numbers from the two assemblies, with the task of finding agreed versions of the provisions in dispute.

The version prepared by the joint committee may be submitted by the Government to the two assemblies for their approval. No amendment may be accepted without the agreement of the Government.

If the joint committee does not produce an agreed version, or if the version agreed is not approved as provided for in the preceding paragraph, the Government may ask the National Assembly, after one more reading by the National Assembly and by the Senate, to decide the matter. In this case, the National Assembly may adopt either the version prepared by the joint committee or the last version passed by itself, modified, if necessary, by one or any of the amendments passed by the Senate.

Article 46

The laws that the Constitution characterizes as organic laws are passed and amended under the following conditions.

The Government or parliamentary bill may be considered and voted on by the first assembly to which it is referred only at the expiration of a period of fifteen days after its introduction.

The procedure described in Article 45 applies. However, in the absence of agreement between the two assemblies, the text may be adopted by the National Assembly at final reading only by an absolute majority of its members.

The organic laws concerning the Senate must be passed in the same terms by the two assemblies.

The organic laws may be promulgated only after certification by the Constitutional Council of their conformity with the Constitution.

Article 47

The Parliament shall pass finance bills under the conditions to be stipulated by an organic law.

Should the National Assembly fail to reach a decision on first reading within a time limit of forty days after a bill has been filed, the government shall refer it to the Senate, which must rule within a time limit of fifteen days. The procedure set forth in Article 45 shall then be followed.

Should Parliament fail to reach a decision within a time limit of seventy days, the provisions of the bill may be enforced by ordinance.

Should the finance bill establishing the resources and expenditures of a fiscal year not be filed in time for it to be promulgated before the beginning of that fiscal year, the government shall urgently request Parliament for the authorization to collect the taxes and shall make available by decree the funds needed to meet the government commitments already voted.

The time limits stipulated in the present article shall be suspended when the Parliament is not in session.

The Audit Office shall assist parliament and the government in supervising the implementation of the finance laws.

Article 48

The discussion of the bills filed or agreed upon by the government shall have priority on the agenda of the assemblies in the order determined by the government.

One meeting a week shall be reserved, by priority, for questions asked by members of Parliament and for answers by the government.

Article 49

The Premier, after deliberation by the Council of Ministers, shall make the government responsible, before the National Assembly, for its program or, should the occasion arise, for a declaration of general policy.

When the National Assembly adopts a motion of censure, the responsibility of the government shall thereby be questioned. Such a motion is admissible only if it is signed by at least one-tenth of the members of the National Assembly. The vote may not take place before forty-eight hours after the motion has been filed. Only the votes that are favorable to a motion of censure shall be counted; the motion of censure may be adopted only by a majority of the members comprising the assembly. Should the motion of censure be rejected, its signers may not introduce another motion of censure during the same session, except in the case provided for in the paragraph below.

The Premier may, after deliberation by the Council of Ministers, make the government responsible before the National Assembly for the adoption of a given text. In this case, this text shall be considered as adopted, unless a motion of censure, filed during the twenty-four hours that follow, is carried under the conditions provided for in the preceding paragraph.

The Premier shall have the right to request the Senate for approval of a declaration of general policy.

Article 50

When the National Assembly adopts a motion of censure, or when it disapproves the program or a declaration of general policy of the government, the Premier must hand the resignation of the government to the President of the Republic.

Article 51

The closure of ordinary or extraordinary sessions shall by right be delayed, should the occasion arise, in order to permit the application of the provisions of Article 49.

TITLE VI   ON TREATIES
AND INTERNATIONAL AGREEMENTS

Article 52

The President of the Republic shall negotiate and ratify treaties.

He shall be informed of all negotiations leading to the conclusion of an international agreement not subject to ratification.

Article 53

Peace treaties, commercial treaties, treaties or agreements relative to international organizations, those that imply a commitment for the finances of the State, those that modify provisions of a legislative nature, those relative to the status of persons, those that call for the cession, exchange, or addition of territory may be ratified or approved only by a law.

They shall go into effect only after having been ratified or approved.

No cession, no exchange, no addition of territory shall be valid without the consent of the populations concerned.

Article 54

If the Constitutional Council, the matter having been referred to it by the President of the Republic, by the Premier, or by the President of one or the other assembly, shall declare that an international commitment contains a clause contrary to the Constitution, the authorization to ratify or approve this commitment may be given only after amendment of the Constitution.

Article 55

Treaties or agreements duly ratified or approved shall, upon their publication, have an authority superior to that of laws, subject, for each agreement or treaty, to its application by the other party.

TITLE VII   THE CONSTITUTIONAL COUNCIL

Article 56

The Constitutional Council shall consist of nine members, whose term of office shall last nine years and shall not be renewable. One third of the membership of the Constitutional Council shall be renewed every three years. Three of its members shall be appointed by the President of the Republic, three by the President of the National Assembly, three by the President of the Senate.

In addition to the nine members provided for above, former Presidents of the Republic shall be members ex officio for life of the Constitutional Council.

The President shall be appointed by the President of the Republic. He shall have the casting vote in case of a tie.

Article 57

The office of member of the Constitutional Council shall be incompatible with that of minister or member of Parliament. Other incompatibilities shall be determined by an organic law.

Article 58

The Constitutional Council shall ensure the regularity of the election of the President of the Republic.

It shall examine complaints and shall announce the results of the vote.

Article 59

The Constitutional Council shall rule, in the case of disagreement, on the regularity of the elections of deputies and senators.

Article 60

The Constitutional Council shall ensure the regularity of referendum procedures and shall announce the results thereof.

Article 61

Organic laws, before their promulgation, and standing orders of the Parliamentary assemblies, before they come into application, must be submitted to the Constitutional Council, which shall rule on their constitutionality.

Article 62

A provision declared unconstitutional may not be promulgated or implemented.

The decisions of the Constitutional Council may not be appealed to any jurisdiction whatsoever. They must be recognized by the public powers and by all administrative and juridical authorities.

Article 63

An organic law shall determine the rules of organization and functioning of the Constitutional Council, the procedure to be followed before it, and in particular the periods of time allowed for laying disputes before it.

TITLE VIII   ON JUDICIAL AUTHORITY

Article 64

The President of the Republic shall be the guarantor of the independence of the judicial authority.

He shall be assisted by the High Council of the Judiciary.

An organic law shall determine the status of magistrates.

Magistrates may not be removed from office.

Article 65

The High Council of the Judiciary shall be presided over by the President of the Republic. The Minister of Justice shall be its vice-president ex officio. He may preside in place of the President of the Republic.

The High Council shall, in addition, include nine members appointed by the President of the Republic in conformity with the conditions to be determined by an organic law.

The High Council of the Judiciary shall present nominations for judges of the Court of Cassation [supreme court of appeal] and for first presidents of courts of appeal. It shall give its opinion under the conditions to be determined by an organic law on proposals of the Minister of Justice relative to the nomination of the other judges. It shall be consulted on questions of pardon under conditions to be determined by an organic law.

The High Council of the Judiciary shall act as a disciplinary council for judges. In such cases, it shall be presided over by the First President of the Court of Cassation.

Article 66

No one may be arbitrarily detained.

The judicial authority, guardian of individual liberty, shall ensure the respect of this principle under the conditions stipulated by law.

TITLE IX   THE HIGH COURT OF JUSTICE

Article 67

A High Court of Justice shall be instituted.

It shall be composed of members [of Parliament] elected, in equal number, by the National Assembly and the Senate after each general or partial election to these assemblies. It shall elect its President from among its members.

An organic law shall determine the composition of the High Court, its rules, and also the procedure to be followed before it.

Article 68

The President of the Republic shall not be held accountable for actions performed in the exercise of his office except in the case of high treason. He may be indicted only by the two assemblies ruling by identical vote in open balloting and by an absolute majority of the members of said assemblies. He shall be tried by the High Court of Justice.

The members of the Government shall be criminally liable for actions performed in the exercise of their office and deemed to be crimes or misdemeanors at the time they were committed. The procedure defined above shall be applied to them, as well as to their accomplices, in case of a conspiracy against the security of the State. In the cases provided for by the present paragraph, the High Court shall be bound by the definition of crimes and misdemeanors, as well as by the determination of penalties, as they are established by the criminal laws in force when the acts are committed.

TITLE X   THE ECONOMIC AND SOCIAL COUNCIL

Article 69

The Economic and Social Council, when called upon by the Government, gives its opinion on Government bills, ordinances, or decrees, as well as on parliamentary bills submitted to it.

A member of the Economic and Social Council may be designated by it to present before the parliamentary assemblies the opinion of the Council on the Government or parliamentary bills which are submitted to it.

Article 70

The Economic and Social Council may also be consulted by the Government on any economic or social problem concerning the Republic or the Community. Any plan or Government bill concerning a program of an economic or social character is submitted to it for its opinion.

Article 71

The composition of the Economic and Social Council and its rules of procedure are specified by an organic law.

TITLE XI   ON TERRITORIAL UNITS

Article 72

The territorial entities of the Republic are the *communes,* the *départements,* and the Overseas Territories. Any other territorial entity is created by law.

These entities are freely administered by elected councils in conditions laid down by law.

In the *départements* and territories, the Government delegate is responsible for the interests of the nation, supervises the administration and ensures the observance of the law.

Article 73

The status as defined by law and the administrative organization of the Overseas *départements* may be modified by measures intended to adapt them to local conditions.

Article 74

The Overseas Territories of the Republic have a special organization which takes account of the interests of each within the framework of the general interests of the Republic. This organization is laid down and modified by law, after consultation with the Territorial Assembly of the Territory concerned.

Article 75

Citizens of the Republic who do not enjoy ordinary civil status, the only status to which Article 34 may be construed as referring, keep their personal status so long as they have not renounced it.

Article 76

Overseas Territories may keep their status within the Republic. If they express the desire to do so, by a decision of their Territorial Assembly, within the period fixed by Article 91, para. 1, they become either Overseas *départements* or, grouped together or separately, member States of the Community.

TITLE XII   ON THE COMMUNITY

Article 77

In the Community instituted by the present Constitution, the States shall enjoy autonomy; they shall administer themselves and manage their own affairs democratically and freely.

There shall be only one citizenship in the Community.

All citizens shall be equal before the law, whatever their origin, their race, and their religion. They shall have the same duties.

Article 78

The Community's jurisdiction shall extend over foreign policy, defense, currency, common economic and financial policy, as well as over policy on strategic raw materials.

It shall include, in addition, except in the case of specific agreements, the supervision of the tribunals, higher education, the general organization of external transportation and transportation within the Community, as well as of telecommunications.

Special agreements may create other common jurisdictions or regulate any transfer of jurisdiction from the Community to one of its members.

Article 79

The member States shall benefit from the provisions of Article 77 as soon as they have exercised the choice provided for in Article 76.

Until the measures required for implementation of the present title go into force, matters within the common jurisdiction shall be regulated by the Republic.

Article 80

The President of the Republic shall preside over and represent the Community.

The institutional organs of the Community shall be an Executive Council, a Senate and a Court of Arbitration.

Article 81

The member States of the Community shall participate in the election of the President according to the conditions stipulated in Article 6.

The President of the Republic, in his capacity as President of the Community, shall be represented in each State of the Community.

Article 82

The Executive Council of the Community shall be presided over by the President of the Community. It shall consist of the Premier of the Republic, the heads of government of each of the member states of the Community, and of the ministers responsible for the common affairs of the Community.

The Executive Council shall organize the cooperation of members of the Community at government and administrative levels.

The organization and procedure of the Executive Council shall be determined by an organic law.

Article 83

The Senate of the Community is composed of delegates chosen from among their own number by the Parliament of the Republic and the legislative assemblies of the other members. The number of delegates from each State is fixed in a manner which takes account of its population and of the responsibilities which it assumes within the Community.

It holds two sessions a year, which are opened and closed by the President of the Community and may not last longer than one month each.

At the request of the President, it discusses common economic and financial policy, before the Parliament of the Republic and, in appropriate circumstances, the legislative assemblies of other members of the Community pass laws in this field.

The Senate of the Community considers the acts, international agreements, and treaties referred to in Articles 35 and 53, where these involve obligations for the Community.

It takes binding decisions in the fields in which power has been delegated to it by the legislative assemblies of members of the Community. The decisions are promulgated in the States concerned in the same ways as the laws of the territories.

An organic law determines its composition and the rules under which it functions.

Article 84

A Court of Arbitration of the Community shall rule on litigations occurring among members of the Community.

Its composition and its jurisdiction shall be predetermined by an organic law.

Article 85

By derogation from the procedure provided for in Article 89, the provisions of the present title that concern the functioning of the common institutions shall be amendable by identical laws passed by the Parliament of the Republic and by the Senate of the Community.

The provisions of the present title may also be amended by agreements concluded between all the States of the Community; the new provisions shall be put into force under the conditions required by the Constitution of each State.

Article 86

A change of status of a member State of the Community may be requested, either by the Republic, or by a resolution of the legislative assembly of the State concerned confirmed by a local referendum, the organization and supervision of which shall be ensured by the institutions of the Community. The procedures governing this change shall be determined by an agreement approved by the Parliament of the Republic and the legislative assembly concerned.

Under the same conditions, a member State of the Community may become independent. It shall thereby cease to belong to the Community.

A member State of the Community may also, by means of agreements, become independent without thereby ceasing to belong to the Community.

An independent State not a member of the Community may, by means of agreements, join the Community without ceasing to be independent.

The position of these States within the Community shall be determined by agreements concluded to this end, in particular the agreements mentioned in the preceding paragraphs as well as, should the occasion arise, the agreements provided for in the second paragraph of Article 85.

Article 87
The particular agreements made for the implementation of the present title shall be approved by the parliament of the Republic and the legislative assembly concerned.

TITLE XIII   ON AGREEMENT OF ASSOCIATION

Article 88
The Republic or the Community may conclude agreements with States desiring to form an association with either, in order to develop their civilizations.

Article 89
The right to propose amendments to the Constitution belongs concurrently to the President of the Republic, on the proposal of the Prime Minister, and to members of Parliament.

The amending project or proposal must be passed by the two assemblies in the identical terms. The amendment becomes effective when it has been approved by referendum.

However, the amending project is not submitted to a referendum when the President of the Republic decides to submit it to Parliament, meeting as Congress; in this case the amendment is accepted only if it obtains a majority of three-fifths of the votes cast. The Bureau of the Congress is that of the National Assembly.

The amendment procedure may not be initiated or pursued when the integrity of the territory is under attack.

The Republican form of government is not subject to revision.

TITLE XIV   TEMPORARY PROVISIONS

Article 90

The ordinary session of Parliament is suspended. The mandate of the members of the present National Assembly shall expire on the day that the Assembly elected under the present Constitution convenes.

Until this meeting, the Government alone shall have the authority to convene Parliament.

The mandate of the members of the Assembly of the French Union shall expire at the same time as the mandate of the members of the present National Assembly.

Article 91

The institutions of the Republic, provided for by the present Constitution, shall be established within four months counting from the time of its promulgation.

This period shall be extended to six months for the institutions of the Community.

The powers of the President of the Republic now in office shall expire only when the results of the election provided for in Articles 6 and 7 of the present Constitution are proclaimed.

The member states of the Community shall participate in this first election under the conditions derived from their status at the date of the promulgation of the Constitution.

The established authorities shall continue in the exercise of their functions in these states, according to the laws and regulations applicable when the Constitution goes into force, until the establishment of the authorities provided for by their new regimes.

Until its definitive constitution, the Senate shall consist of the present members of the Council of the Republic. The organic laws that shall determine the definitive constitution of the Senate must be passed before July 31, 1959.

The powers conferred on the Constitutional Council by Articles 58 and 59 of the Constitution shall be exercised, until the establishment of this Council, by a committee composed of the Vice-president of the Council of State, as Chairman, the First President of the Court of Cassation, and the First President of the Audit Office.

The peoples of the member states of the Community shall continue to be represented in Parliament until the entry into force of the measures necessary to the implementation of Title XII.

Article 92

The legislative measures necessary to the establishment of the institutions and, until they are established, to the functioning of the public powers, shall be taken in meetings of the Council of Ministers, after consultation with the Council of State, in the form of ordinances having the force of law.

During the time limit set in the first paragraph of Article 91, the government shall be authorized to determine, by ordinances having the force of law and passed in the same way, the system of elections to the assemblies provided for by the Constitution.

During the same period and under the same conditions, the government may also adopt measures, in all domains, which it may deem necessary to the life of the nation, the protection of citizens or the safeguarding of liberties.

APPENDIX B
ELECTORAL
MAPS

Legislative Elections, 1958, First Ballot, Metropolitan Returns

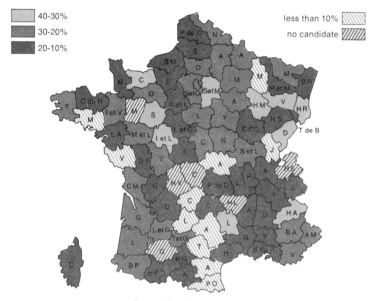

Legend:
- 40-30%
- 30-20%
- 20-10%
- less than 10%
- no candidate

A–1   The Gaullist vote

Source: Le Monde, March 7, 1967, p. 3.

Legislative Elections, 1958, First Ballot, Metropolitan Returns

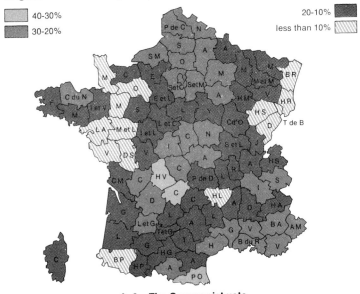

A–2   The Communist vote

Source: Le Monde, March 7, 1967, p. 3.

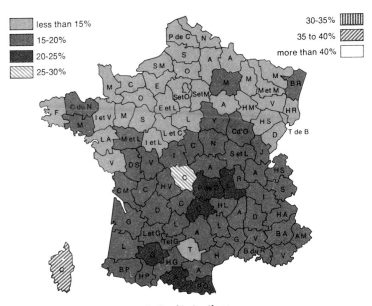

A–3   Abstentions

Source: Le Monde, March 7, 1967, p. 3.

Legislative Elections, 1962, First Ballot, Metropolitan Returns

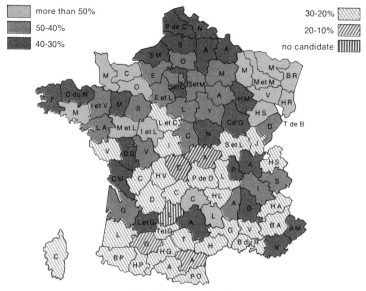

A–4   The Gaullist vote

Source: *Le Monde,* March 7, 1967, p. 3.

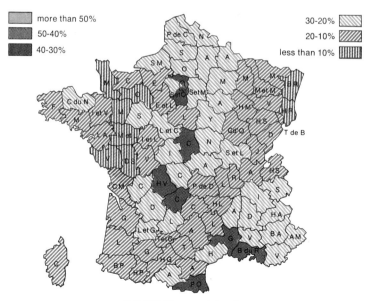

A-5 The Communist vote

Source: *Le Monde,* March 7, 1967, p. 3.

Legislative Elections, 1962, First Ballot, Metropolitan Returns

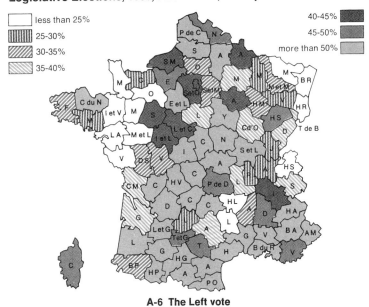

A-6 The Left vote

Source: Le Monde, December 7, 1965, p. 3.

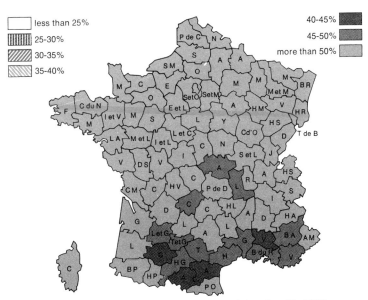

A-7 The "Yes" vote in the referendum of October 28, 1962

Source: Le Monde, December 7, 1965, p. 3.

Legislative Elections, 1962, First Ballot, Metropolitan Returns

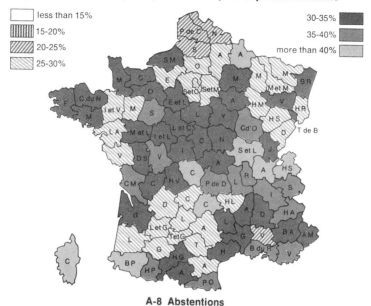

less than 15%

15-20%

20-25%

25-30%

30-35%

35-40%

more than 40%

A-8 Abstentions

Source: Le Monde, March 7, 1967, p. 3.

Legislative Elections, 1967, First Ballot, Metropolitan Returns

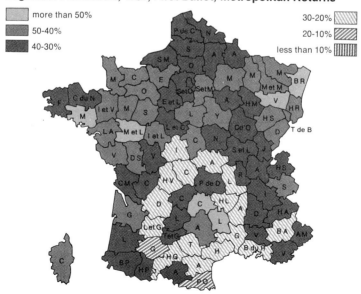

more than 50%

50-40%

40-30%

30-20%

20-10%

less than 10%

A-9 The Gaullist vote

Source: Le Monde, March 7, 1967, p. 3.

Legislative Elections, 1967, First Ballot, Metropolitan Returns

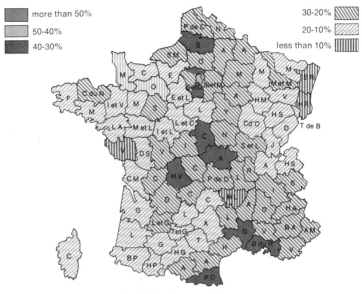

- more than 50%
- 50-40%
- 40-30%
- 30-20%
- 20-10%
- less than 10%

A-10 The Communist vote

Source: *Le Monde*, March 7, 1967, p. 3.

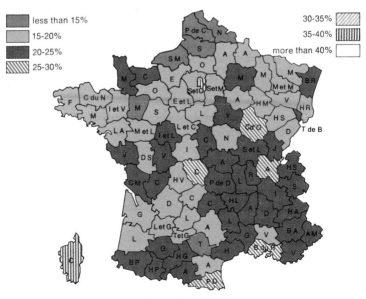

- less than 15%
- 15-20%
- 20-25%
- 25-30%
- 30-35%
- 35-40%
- more than 40%

A-11 Abstentions

Source: *Le Monde*, March 7, 1967, p. 3.

Legislative Elections, 1967, First Ballot, Metropolitan Returns

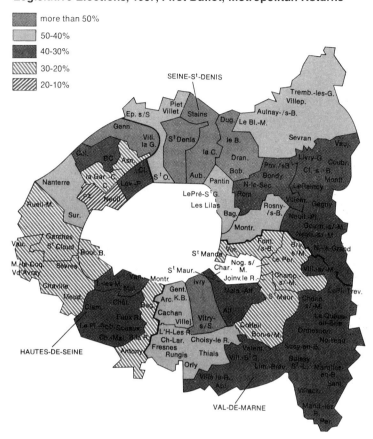

Legend:
- more than 50%
- 50-40%
- 40-30%
- 30-20%
- 20-10%

SEINE-St-DENIS

Tremb.-les-G.
Villep.
Ep. s/S
Piet
Villet
Stains
Aulnay-/s-B.
Genn.
Dug.
Le Bl.-M.
Vill.
la G.
S^{t}Denis
le B.
Sevran
Vauj.
C.)i.
BC
Asn.
la C.
Dran.
Livry-G.
Coubr.
Cl.
Ci.
Bob.
Pav./sB
Cf. s. B.
Montf.
Nanterre
la Gar.
C.
Lev.-R.
S^t O.
Aub.
Pantin
Bondy
LeRaincy
Gagny
Rueil-M.
P.
Neuil.
N-le-Sec.
Rom.
Villem.
Sur.
LePré-S^{t}G.
Les Lilas
Bag.
Rosny-
/s-B.
Neuil-Pl.
Gourn.-s/-M.
Neuil.-s/-M.
Montr.
Vau.
Garches
St Cloud
Bool. B.
Font
s-B
Br.
B./M.
N-le-Grand
M. la Coq.
Sèvres
St Mande
Vin.
Le Per.
Vill.-s/-M.
Vd/Avray
Chav.
St Maur.
Nog. s/
Char.
M.
Champ.
s/-M
Graville
Montr.
Gent.
ivry
Joinv.le R.
St Maur
LePl. Trev.
Meud.
Chât.
Mais.-Alf.
Chenn.
s/-M.
Clam.
Arc.
K.B.
Alf.
Le Quèue
Faux R.
Cachan
Villej
Vitry-
s/S
Créteil
Ormesson
La Pl.-Rob-Sceaux
Villej
Ch-Mai.
B^le R.
L'H-Les R.
Bon.-s/-M.
Noiseau
HAUTES-DE-SEINE
Antony
Ch-Lar.
Choisy-le R.
Valent.
Sucy-en-B.
Boissy
Fresnes
Rungis
Thiais
gif.-s/-L.
Mand.les
R.
Per.
Orly
Lim.-Brév.
B^y-L.
Marolles-
en-B.
Ville-le-R.
Sant
Ablis
Villecr.
VAL-DE-MARNE
Mand.-les
R.
Per.

A-12 The Communist vote in the Paris suburbs

Source: Le Monde, March 8, 1967, p. 3.

Legislative Elections, 1967, Seats Won By Party, Metropolitan Returns

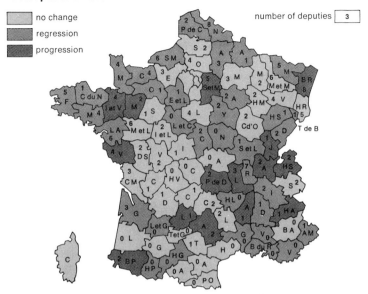

A-13 The Union of Democrats for the Fifth Republic, the Independent Republicans, pro-Gaullist Democratic Center, and pro-Gaullist Affiliates

Source: Le Monde, March 14, 1967, p. 3.

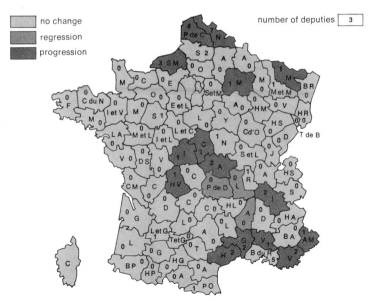

A-14 The Communist party

Source: Le Monde, March 14, 1967, p. 3.

Legislative Elections, 1967, Seats Won By Party, Metropolitan Returns

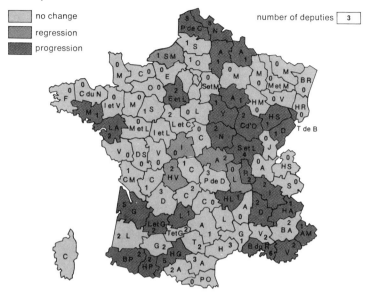

A-15 The Federation of the Left

Source: Le Monde, March 14, 1967, p. 3.

Legislative Elections, 1968, First Ballot, Metropolitan Returns

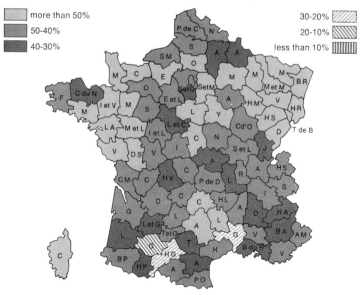

A-16 The Gaullist vote

Source: Le Monde, June 25, 1968, p. 2

Legislative Elections, 1968, First Ballot, Metropolitan Returns

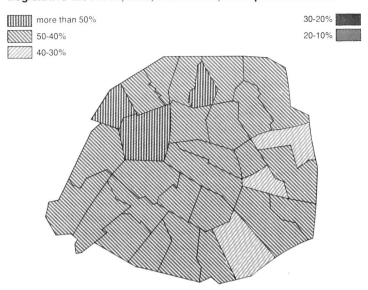

Pattern	Range	Pattern	Range
more than 50%		30-20%	
50-40%		20-10%	
40-30%			

A-17 The Gaullist vote in Paris

Source: Le Monde, June 25, 1968, p. 6.

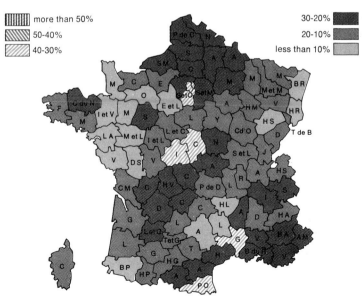

Pattern	Range	Pattern	Range
more than 50%		30-20%	
50-40%		20-10%	
40-30%		less than 10%	

A-18 The Communist vote

Source: Le Monde, June 25, 1968, p. 2.

Legislative Elections, 1968, First Ballot, Metropolitan Returns

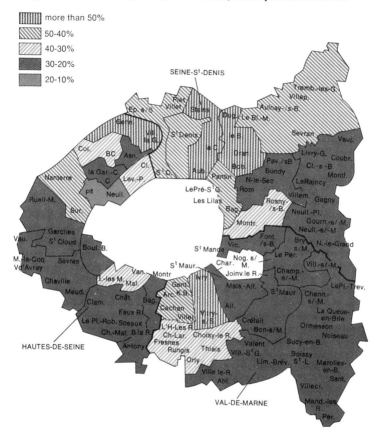

Legend:
- more than 50%
- 50-40%
- 40-30%
- 30-20%
- 20-10%

SEINE-St-DENIS

Tremb.-les-G.
Villep.
Aulnay-/-s-B.
Ep.-e-/-S.
Piet.
Villet.
Sevran
Vauj.
Gem.
Vdl.
la G.
St Denis
Dug.
Le Bl.-M.
Col.
e C.
Livry-G. Coubr.
BC
Asn.
Dran
Cl.-s-B.
Nanterre
Cf.
Bob.
Pav./sB
Montf.
la Gar.-C.
S.-O.
Bondy
LeRaincy
C
Lev.-P.
Aub.
N-le-Sec
Pantin
P.
Neuil.
Villem.
Ruell-M.
LePré-S^t-G.
Rom.
Rosny-
Gagny
Bl.
Les Lilas
Bag.
/s-B.
Neuil.-Pl.
Sut.
Montr.
Gourn.-s/-M.
Vau.
Garches
St Cloud
Font.
Neuil.-s/-M
M.-la-Coq.
Boul.-B.
/s-B.
Bry
N-le-Grand
Vd'Avray
Sevres
St Mande
Vin.
Le Per.
Nog. s/
Chaville
Van.
Montr
Char. M.
Vill.-s/-M.
Meud.
I.-les M.
Mal.
St Maur.
Joinv.le R.
LePl.-Trev.
Mais.-Alf.
Champ.-
Clam.
Chât.
Bag.
Gent.
Nty
s/-M.
Chenn.-
Meud.
Arc.-K.B.
St Maur
s/-M.
Faux R.
Cachan
Alf.
La Queue-
Le Pl.-Rob. Sceaux
Villej.
Vitry
en-Brie
Ch.-Mat. B.la R.
L'H-Les R.
-s-S.
Créteil
Ormesson
Noiseau
HAUTES-DE-SEINE
Antony
Ch.-Lar.
Choisy-le R.
Bon-s/M.
Sucy-en-B.
Fresnes
Thiais
Valent.
Rungis
Vili.-S^t-G.
Boissy
Orly
Lim.-Brév.
S^t-L.
Marolles-
en-B.
Ville le-R.
Abl.
Sant.
Villecr.
Mand.-les-
R.-
VAL-DE-MARNE
Per.

A-19 The Communist vote in the Paris suburbs

Source: Le Monde, June 25, 1968, p. 9.

Legislative Elections, 1968, First Ballot, Metropolitan Returns

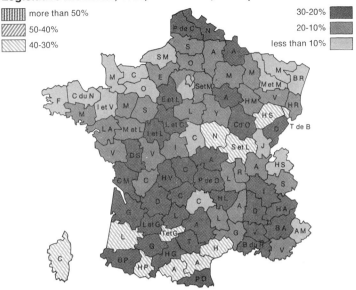

A-20 The Federation of the Left

Source: Le Monde, June 25, 1968, p. 2.

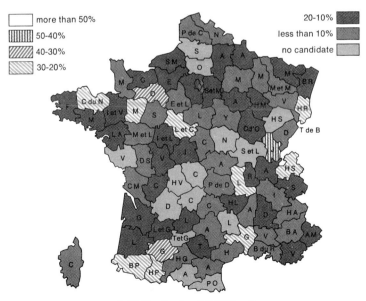

A-21 The Center (CPDM) vote

Source: Le Monde, June 25, 1968, p. 2.

Legislative Elections, 1968, Second Ballot, Metropolitan Returns

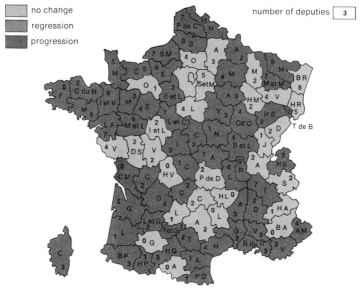

A-22 The Gaullist vote

Source: Le Monde, July 2, 1968, p. 3.

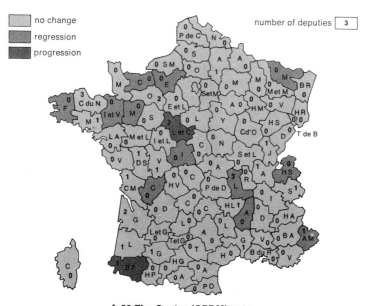

A-23 The Center (CPDM) vote

Source: Le Monde, July 2, 1968, p. 3.

Legislative Elections, 1968, Second Ballot, Metropolitan Returns

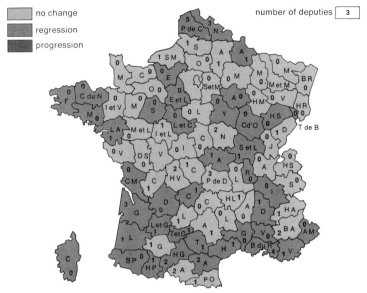

no change
regression
progression

number of deputies [3]

A-24 The Federation of the Left

Source: Le Monde, July 2, 1968, p. 3.

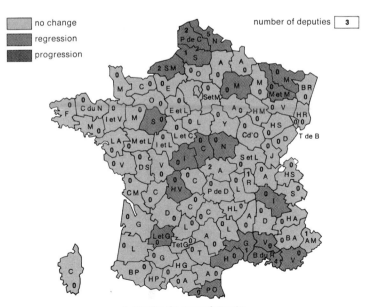

no change
regression
progression

number of deputies [3]

A-25 The Communist vote

Source: Le Monde, July 2, 1968, p. 3.

Legislative Elections, 1968, Second Ballot, Metropolitan Returns

deputy, Gaullist

deputy, C.P.D.M.

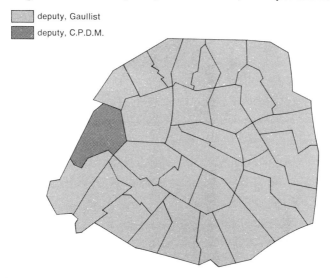

A-26 Distribution of seats in Paris

Source: Le Monde, July 2, 1968, p. 7.

Presidential Election, 1965, First Ballot, Metropolitan Returns

less than 25%

25-30%

30-35%

35-40%

40-45%

45-50%

more than 50%

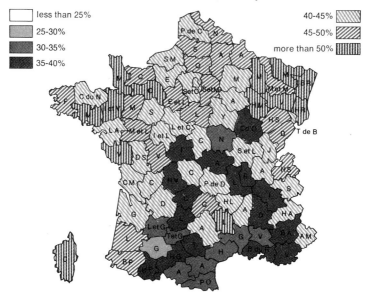

A-27 The de Gaulle vote

Source: Le Monde, December 7, 1965, p. 3.

Presidential Election, 1965, First Ballot, Metropolitan Returns

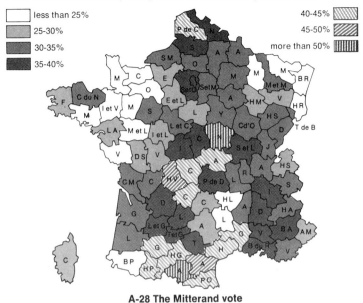

A-28 The Mitterand vote

Source: Le Monde, December 7, 1965, p. 3.

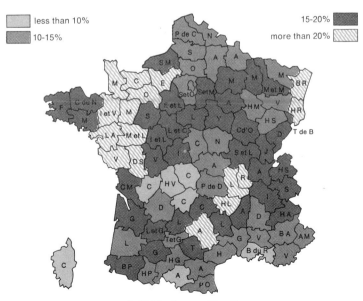

A-29 The Lecanuet vote

Source: Le Monde, Sélection hebdomadaire, December 16–22, 1965, p. 3.

Presidential Election, 1965, First Ballot, Metropolitan Returns

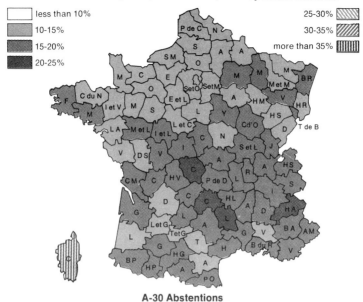

Legend:
- less than 10%
- 10-15%
- 15-20%
- 20-25%
- 25-30%
- 30-35%
- more than 35%

A-30 Abstentions

Source: Le Monde, December 9, 1965, p. 2.

Presidential Elections, 1965, Second Ballot, Metropolitan Returns

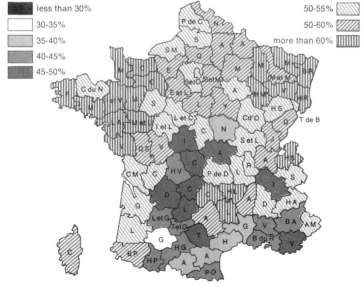

Legend:
- less than 30%
- 30-35%
- 35-40%
- 40-45%
- 45-50%
- 50-55%
- 50-60%
- more than 60%

A-31 The de Gaulle vote

Source: Le Monde, Sélection hebdomadaire, December 16–22, 1965, p. 3.

Presidential Election, 1965, Second Ballot, Metropolitan Returns

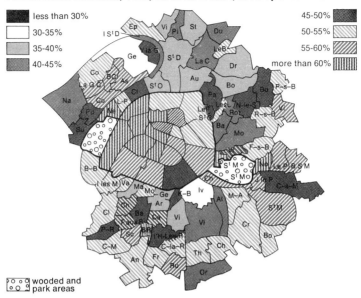

A-32 The de Gaulle vote in Paris and its suburbs

Source: Le Monde, December 21, 1965, p. 3.

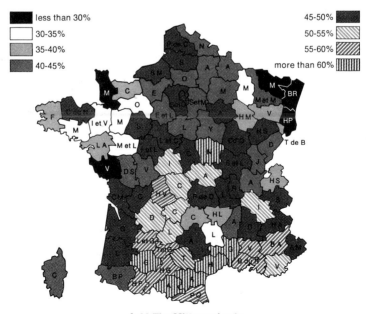

A-33 The Mitterand vote

Source: Le Monde, Sélection hebdomadaire, December 16–22, 1965, p. 3.

Presidential Election, 1965, Second Ballot, Metropolitan Returns

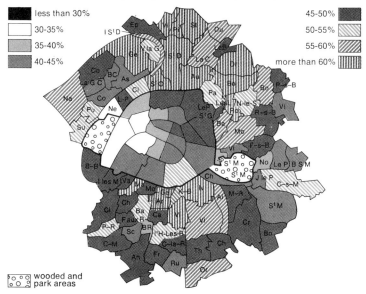

less than 30%

30-35%

35-40%

40-45%

45-50%

50-55%

55-60%

more than 60%

wooded and park areas

A-34 The Mitterand vote in Paris and its suburbs

Source: Le Monde, December 21, 1965, p. 3.

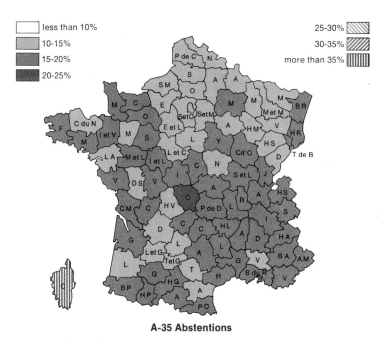

less than 10%

10-15%

15-20%

20-25%

25-30%

30-35%

more than 35%

A-35 Abstentions

Source: Le Monde, Sélection hebdomadaire, December 16–22, 1965, p. 3.

Presidential Election, 1965, Second Ballot, Metropolitan Returns

The France that rejected de Gaulle:-

Departments voting *no* Oct. 1962

Departments putting Mitterand ahead 5. Dec. 1965

Departments putting Mitterand ahead 19. Dec. 1965

The France that accepted de Gaulle reluctantly:-

Departments giving him less than 43.7% 5. Dec. 1965

Departments giving him less than 54.5% 19. Dec. 1965

The France that remained loyal to de Gaulle:-

Departments giving him more than his national share of the votes in both rounds

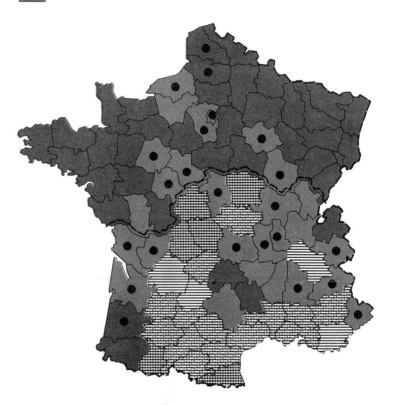

A-36 The France of de Gaulle, 1962 and 1965

Source: The Manchester Guardian Weekly, December 30, 1965, p. 4.

Presidential Election, 1969, Second Ballot, Metropolitan Returns

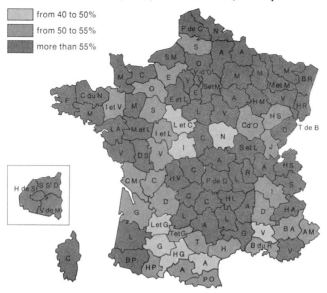

from 40 to 50%

from 50 to 55%

more than 55%

A-37 The Pompidou vote

Source: Le Monde, June 17, 1969, p. 4. Percentages relative to the vote cast.

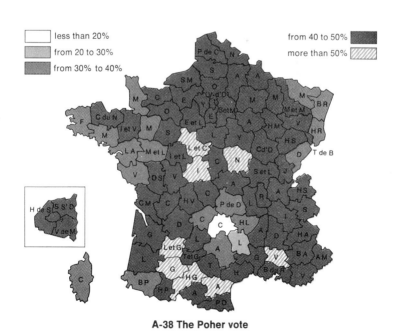

less than 20%

from 20 to 30%

from 30% to 40%

from 40 to 50%

more than 50%

A-38 The Poher vote

Source: Le Monde, June 17, 1969, p. 4. Percentages relative to the vote cast.

INDEX

29-300